BASC™-2
Intervention Guide

Kimberly J. Vannest, PhD

Cecil R. Reynolds, PhD

Randy W. Kamphaus, PhD

PEARSON

BASC–2 Intervention Guide

Printed in the United States of America
Published by Pearson
P.O. Box 1416
Minneapolis, MN 55440
800.627.7271
www.PearsonAssessments.com

ISBN-10: 0-9790658-2-8

A 0 9 8 7 6 5 4 3 2 1

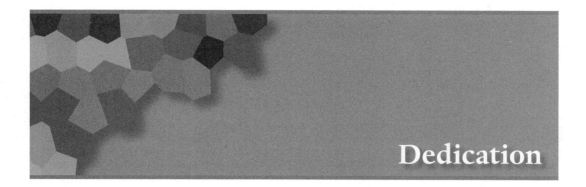

Dedication

This book is dedicated to three inspirational and dedicated teachers, my brother Kevin and parents Karen and Frank (14, 30, and 39 years in the classroom, respectively). KV

To Henry J. L. Brathwaite V.
Thanks for adding another measure of inspiration. RWK

To Daphne D. Reynolds for her love, lessons in life, and model of service. CRR

About the Authors

Kimberly J. Vannest, PhD, is Assistant Professor of Educational Psychology, a Regents Fellow, and Center for Teaching Excellence Teaching Scholar at Texas A&M University. She has received the Montague-Center for Teaching Excellence Scholar Award and the Outstanding New Faculty Award from the College of Education and Human Development Advisory Committee. She is an active reviewer and editorial board member of journals in the fields of behavior disorders, assessment, special education, and policy. Her service contributions to the field include participation in the Council for Exceptional Children, the American Educational Research Association, and the Midwest Symposium for Leadership in Behavior Disorders. Her areas of scholarship include more than 30 peer-reviewed journal articles on effective academic and behavior interventions for students with emotional and behavioral disabilities and data-driven decision making. She also brings nearly 20 years of experience teaching students and teachers. She began as a secondary business and vocational education teacher, and went on to develop expertise and receive credentials and recognition for her work in special education high school classes in Southern California. She also taught middle school in Missouri, worked on K–12 school reform for the Louisiana governor's office, and has trained teachers in academic and behavioral methods throughout the United States for over 15 years.

Cecil R. Reynolds, PhD, is Emeritus Professor of Educational Psychology, Professor of Neuroscience, and Distinguished Research Scholar at Texas A&M University. Well known for his work in psychological testing and assessment, he is author or editor of more than 45 books, including *The Handbook of School Psychology*, the *Encyclopedia of Special Education*, and the two-volume *Handbook of Psychological and Educational Assessment of Children*. He also authored or co-authored more than a dozen tests including the *BASC–2 Behavioral and Emotional Screening System* (BASC–2 BESS), *Behavioral Assessment System for Children, Second Edition* (BASC–2), the *Revised Children's Manifest Anxiety Scale, Second Edition,* the *Reynolds Intellectual Assessment Scales*™, and has published more than 300 scholarly works. Dr. Reynolds has received a number of national awards for his work, including the Lightner Witmer Award from the American Psychological Association (APA) and Early Career Awards from two APA divisions (15, Educational Psychology, and 5, Measurement and Statistics). He is a recipient of the APA Division 16 Senior Scientist Award, the National Academy of Neuropsychology's Distinguished Clinical Neuropsychologist Award, and several other national awards for his research on testing and assessment. Dr. Reynolds is the former editor-in-chief of *Archives of Clinical Neuropsychology* and has served as associate editor of the *Journal of School Psychology*. He is editor-in-chief of *Applied Neuropsychology* and a member of the editorial boards of 13 journals. Active in professional affairs, he has served as president of the National Academy of Neuropsychology, a member of APA's Committee on Psychological Testing and Assessment, president of three APA divisions (5, 16, and 40), and on the executive committee of the National Association of School Psychologists.

Randy W. Kamphaus, PhD, is Dean of the College of Education and Distinguished Research Professor at Georgia State University. He has received the Russell H. Yeany Jr. Research Award from the College of Education at the University of Georgia, and has twice received college-wide teaching awards. A focus on issues related to clinical assessment has led Dr. Kamphaus to pursue research in classification methods, differential diagnosis, test development, and learning disability and attention-deficit/hyperactivity disorder (ADHD) assessment. Dr. Kamphaus, who co-authored the BASC–2 BESS and the widely used BASC–2, has served as principal investigator, co-investigator, and consultant on federally funded research projects dealing with mental health screening, early intervention and prevention, child classification methods, prevalence of ADHD and conduct disorder in Latin America, and aggression reduction in schools. As a licensed psychologist and a Fellow of the American Psychological Association (APA), he has contributed extensively to his profession and served as president of APA's Division of School Psychology and as a member of the APA Council of Representatives. Dr. Kamphaus also has authored or co-authored 12 books, including *Clinical Assessment of Child and Adolescent Intelligence* and *Clinical Assessment of Child and Adolescent Personality and Behavior* (with Dr. Paul Frick), five psychological tests, and more than 80 scientific journal articles and book chapters. He also participates in scholarship in the field through work as editor of *School Psychology Quarterly* and ad hoc reviewer for several journals. Dr. Kamphaus is a frequent guest lecturer and speaker.

Acknowledgments

There are many individuals who have contributed to the completion of this book and to whom I am inspired or grateful or both.

Particularly important are Judy Harrison and Rob Altmann for their tireless faith and commitment to the project. Your work is outstanding, and your contributions are amazing.

My co-authors, Cecil Reynolds and Randy Kamphaus, whose scholarship and encouragement are prized beyond words—I would not have this privilege without you both. Your influence on the field, and your dedication to children and the people who serve them humbles me beyond measure.

I would also like to acknowledge the support of a steadfast mentor, Richard Parker, and a remarkable former student, Tara Hanway-Kalis; both are inspirations to me. Thanks are also due the many, many helping moments of Leanne Brown, Lunda Ramsey, Ben Mason, and Denise Soares.

Acknowledgment is due to Mike Buckley for his support and patience throughout this process, and to Jack for the moments when a hand-drawn cardboard laptop would balance on your lap while you kept me company "working," for all the nights you asked me to write next to you until you fell asleep, and, finally, for the day you typed pages of Xs in rows and printed the pages to go in red folders for a "documentary." Someday, I'll tell you about deleting my chapter files.

I hope this book helps create a world where all children get what they need for emotional and behavioral health.

Kimber Vannest
Texas A&M University
September 2008

As always, but never enough, my appreciation and admiration to Julia, the best partner one could have in life, and a pretty terrific interventionist in her ongoing therapy practice. Her support and her lessons in loving and life continue to inspire me.

Cecil R. Reynolds
Texas A&M University
September 2008

I am grateful for the dedication and talent of my co-authors, Drs. Kimber Vannest and Cecil R. Reynolds, and Rob Altmann of Pearson. My additional mentors, colleagues, and students have contributed to this work in both direct and indirect ways. For these contributions, I am equally thankful.

Randy W. Kamphaus
Georgia State University
September 2008

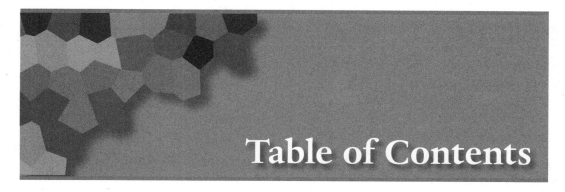

Table of Contents

List of Figures

List of Tables

Chapter 1

Introduction

While scientific methods for diagnosing emotional and behavioral problems in children have made tremendous strides in recent years, intervention science has not kept pace. Many psychologists, teachers, and other professionals in the schools have access to tools that provide reliable and valid data for identifying the nature of a child's problems, but lack access to clear guidelines for taking the next step: designing and implementing research-supported interventions that will effectively reduce a child's problem behavior and increase his or her healthy or positive behavior.

As a component of the *Behavior Assessment System for Children,* Second Edition (BASC™–2), product family, the BASC–2 Intervention Guide addresses this need for a comprehensive source book of effective interventions that are appropriately matched to the specific problem a child is expressing. The BASC–2 Intervention Guide is carefully grounded in intervention science and translates this science into everyday applications that are appropriate and effective for school applications and for consulting with parents. As such, this intervention guide fills a critical void in current professional resources by providing information both about what to do and how to do it when remediating emotional and behavioral problems.

This chapter provides a comprehensive overview of the BASC–2 Intervention Guide features, including a listing of its primary features, a summary of each of its components, its relationship to the BASC–2 family of assessment tools, a summary of its development, and a general summary regarding its use.

Features

The BASC–2 Intervention Guide provides effective interventions for remediating emotional and behavioral problems experienced by children and adolescents from preschool age through high school. While designed for use with the BASC–2 family of assessment tools, the information contained in this guide will prove helpful regardless of the assessment or screening tools used to identify risk and emotional and behavioral problems, and should be of interest to any professional charged with helping to remediate such problems or who is being trained for such work. These professionals include, for example, school psychologists, clinical child and adolescent psychologists, clinical psychologists, pediatric psychologists, school counselors, clinical social workers, behavioral specialists, educational diagnosticians, directors of special education, psychiatrists, and most pediatricians, especially developmental pediatricians. The applicability of this guide goes beyond just those professionals who are trained and qualified to make an educational classification decision or diagnosis. It can also be helpful to a variety of other school professionals (e.g., teachers) who are often involved in interventions. The interventions included in this guide were identified and selected through a rigorous process, with particular emphasis placed on demonstrated evidence of their effectiveness in the research literature and their practical applicability in a school setting. However, the interventions are also relevant to clinicians working outside school settings. Given the central role that school plays in a child's life, interventions that take place or are evaluated strictly outside of the school setting would be very limited in scope, and probably would prove limited in their utility or benefits to the child and to the family. The interventions provided in this guide have been shown through empirical research studies to be effective (or, at a minimum, to have preliminary empirical support sufficient to indicate considerable promise in the treatment or management of behavioral and emotional disorders in this population) for children with a wide range of behavioral or emotional problems, including aggression, hyperactivity, attentional difficulties, pervasive developmental disorders, severe emotional disturbances, and even social maladjustment and conduct disorders, among others. Note that interventions for certain problems, such as substance abuse, eating disorders, sexual disorders, and gang affiliation, were intentionally omitted from this intervention guide because their remediation requires considerable cooperation with and assistance from professionals outside the school setting (e.g., medical or criminal justice personnel and agencies).

The BASC–2 Intervention Guide offers a number of features for efficiently implementing effective behavioral and emotional interventions for children, including:

- Comprehensive coverage of a wide range of emotional and behavioral problems, including aggression, conduct problems, hyperactivity, attention problems, academic problems, anxiety, depression, and somatization, and problems with functional communication, adaptability, and social skills

- Descriptive overviews of the characteristics and conditions of, as well as presentations of, the theoretical framework for each behavioral or emotional problem, providing the grounding necessary for clinicians and practitioners to select appropriate interventions

- An easy-to-follow presentation of the critical components that aid in the successful implementation of each intervention, such as essential elements and key procedural steps

- Summaries of empirical research studies that support the use of each intervention

- Considerations for the implementation of the interventions, including, among others, issues related to teaching, age or developmental level, and cultural or language differences

- A direct link between the interventions presented in the guide and the scales found on the BASC–2 Teacher Rating Scales (TRS), Parent Rating Scales (PRS), and Self-Report of Personality (SRP), making the interventions easy for BASC–2 users to implement

- Information included in the BASC–2 ASSIST™ and ASSIST Plus reports that provides suggestions for interventions based on the scores obtained on the BASC–2 rating scale forms

- The BASC–2 Parent Tip Sheets, which allow parents to participate effectively in the remediation of their child's emotional and behavioral problems

- The BASC–2 Intervention Guide Documentation Checklist, which helps the professional successfully document the steps taken during the intervention program and their outcomes, helping to facilitate discussions in meetings with a child's parents, teachers, and school administrative personnel

- The BASC–2 Classroom Intervention Guide, designed for general- and special-education teachers, which includes general classroom management strategies as well as individual and small-group interventions for dealing with students experiencing emotional and behavioral problems

Each chapter in this intervention guide provides intervention strategies that have been successful in remediating the specific behavioral or emotional problem presented in the chapter (e.g., aggression, anxiety, etc.). For each problem, a description of its characteristics and conditions is provided, along with sample items from its corresponding BASC–2 scale(s). A brief discussion of the theoretical framework that underlies the cause(s) of the problem is also given, providing the foundation for the various intervention approaches that are discussed.

The number of interventions presented in each chapter varies and is determined by the number of interventions that have been shown to be effective in published research studies. Table 1.1 lists the types of interventions discussed in each chapter. As shown in the table, some interventions are unique to a specific problem, while others are repeated across problem behaviors with appropriate modifications.

For each intervention presented in this guide, an overview of the intervention is provided, along with one or more brief examples or case studies that illustrate how the intervention strategy might be used to remediate a particular behavior problem. Also included is a listing of the key elements associated with each intervention strategy, and when necessary, a discussion of implementation is provided.

Perhaps the most critical element of each intervention strategy is the list of procedural steps for implementation. These procedural steps provide a clear, concise set of instructions for implementing the intervention and should provide practitioners with sufficient detail to apply the intervention successfully. Conceptually, these steps draw from the collection of intervention strategies reported in the research literature, but their presentation is based largely on our collective knowledge and experience implementing successful interventions with children with a broad range of emotional and behavioral problems. We created these procedural steps to represent a "master list" of best practices for implementing these interventions.

Each chapter also provides the research-based evidence that supports the procedures and the use of each intervention in the remediation of the behavioral or emotional problem presented. As the body of evidence supporting the use of these interventions is typically quite vast, these sections are provided as an overview of the research examining the effectiveness of the intervention strategy and, therefore, present summaries of selected studies and their findings.

Finally, special considerations for the implementation of the interventions are also discussed, including factors related to the child's age and developmental level, the family's cultural and language background, and the context of the intervention (e.g., clinical versus classroom-based approaches, group versus individual intervention). By taking such factors into consideration when selecting interventions, practitioners will be able to make recommendations with confidence.

Table 1.1 Intervention Types by Chapter

Chapter Title	Interventions
Interventions for Aggression	**Problem-Solving Training**
	Cognitive Restructuring
	Verbal Mediation
	Social Skills Training
	Peer-Mediated Conflict Resolution and Negotiation
	Replacement Behavior Training
Interventions for Conduct Problems	Token Economy Systems
	Interdependent Group-Oriented Contingency Management
	Anger Management Skills Training
	Problem-Solving Training
	Social Skills Training
	Moral Motivation Training
	Parent Training
	Multimodal Interventions
	Multisystemic Therapy

Continued on next page

Interventions for Hyperactivity	Functional Assessment
	Contingency Management
	Parent Training
	Self-Management of Hyperactivity
	Task Modification
	Multimodal Interventions
Interventions for Attention Problems	Contingency Management
	Daily Behavior Report Cards
	Modified Task-Presentation Strategies
	Self-Management of Attention
	Classwide Peer Tutoring
	Computer-Assisted Instruction
	Multimodal Interventions
Interventions for Academic Problems	Advance Organizers **Presentation Strategies** Task-Selection Strategies
	Peer Tutoring Classwide Peer Tutoring
	Cognitive Organizers Mnemonics Self-Monitoring Self-Instruction Reprocessing Strategies
Interventions for Anxiety	Exposure-Based Techniques
	Contingency Management
	Modeling
	Family Therapy
	Integrated Cognitive–Behavioral Therapy

Continued on next page

Interventions for Depression	Cognitive–Behavioral Therapy Psychoeducation Problem-Solving Skills Training Cognitive Restructuring Pleasant-Activity Planning Relaxation Training Self-Management Training Family Involvement
	Interpersonal Therapy (or Psychotherapy) for Adolescents
Interventions for Somatization	**Behavioral Interventions**
	Multimodal Cognitive–Behavioral Therapy
Interventions for Problems With Adaptability	**Functional Behavioral Assessment**
	Precorrection
	Procedural Prompts and Behavioral Momentum
	Self-Management Training
	Cognitive Behavior Management
Interventions to Enhance Functional Communication	**Functional Communication Training**
	Picture Exchange Communication System
	Video Modeling
	Milieu Teaching
	Pivotal Response Training
Interventions to Enhance Social Skills	**Social Skills Training**

Note. Interventions in bold are included in the standard and progress monitor reports included in the BASC–2 ASSIST and ASSIST Plus software programs.

Supplemental Components

Several supplemental components—the BASC–2 Parent Tip Sheets, BASC–2 Intervention Guide Documentation Checklist, and BASC–2 Classroom Intervention Guide—have been developed as part of the BASC–2 Intervention Guide system. These components can be used in conjunction with this intervention guide to facilitate and enhance the implementation of the intervention strategies described in this guide, and to increase the likelihood of obtaining high levels of treatment fidelity. Each of these components is described below.

BASC–2 Parent Tip Sheets

The BASC–2 Parent Tip Sheets (one for each content chapter in this guide) were developed to further the involvement of parents in the intervention process. The tip sheets are designed for use by parents, caregivers, or persons filling a similar role and are most effective when used with guidance from a school psychologist or other professional responsible for implementing the interventions. The authors' collective clinical experience working with families suggests that parents will appreciate the availability of these tip sheets and that their use will enhance rapport between parents and clinicians. As a result, parents may feel more valued and more included in the treatment process.

Each tip sheet corresponds to a particular chapter in this guide and provides a brief background about the nature and the causes of the specified problem behavior as well as some suggestions for how parents can work best with their child to help increase the chances for successful intervention. Each tip sheet also provides three or four intervention strategies for each behavioral or emotional problem, which correspond to at least a subset of the strategies found in this guide. In addition, the tip sheets include a chart for tracking the use of selected interventions and the child's progress in reducing the incidence of problem behavior and increasing positive alternative behavior. Finally, each tip sheet lists several useful websites where parents with Internet access can find additional resources related to their child's specific behavior problems.

BASC–2 Intervention Guide Documentation Checklist

In today's educational climate, documentation of the services provided to a student is becoming increasingly important for reasons that range from ensuring that a child does not fall through the cracks of a large system to documenting that a school has done all it can for a child in the event of an educational or legal hearing or proceeding. The BASC–2 Intervention Guide Documentation Checklist is designed to facilitate the recording of the steps that have been taken to remediate or manage a child's behavioral or emotional problems. It provides a simple and efficient way of recording the steps that have been taken with the child, using a variety of check-box and fill-in-the-blank items. In addition to recording the steps that have been taken with the child, the checklist includes a section that allows the user to record the fidelity of the intervention approaches that have been used, a factor that is critical to the success of any intervention program.

BASC–2 Classroom Intervention Guide

Children often express manifestations of their emotional and behavioral problems in the classroom, and teachers are in a unique position to provide immediate help to correct problem behaviors. The BASC–2 Classroom Intervention Guide is designed to include teachers in the intervention process and harness this direct involvement in the remediation of problem behaviors. While some teachers are very effective in managing classroom misbehavior and helping children deal with their emotional and behavioral problems, many teachers would benefit from learning additional strategies. The classroom guide is designed to provide both general-education and special-education teachers with the tools they need to deal effectively with emotional and behavioral problems experienced by their students (in the case of specific students) and serves as an educational tool for teachers so they are better equipped to respond more independently in future cases.

The classroom guide consists of two workbooks that are categorized into two general types of behavioral or emotional problems: externalizing and school problems, and internalizing and adaptive skill problems. In addition to classroom management strategies, these workbooks contain interventions for a variety of emotional and behavioral problems that can be used in any general- or special-education classroom setting, day treatment facility, or after-school program. As with the BASC–2 Parent Tip Sheets, school psychologists or other professionals that are working with teachers can use these workbooks as a tool for establishing a communication channel and engaging teachers to be a part of the solution for remediating a child's emotional and behavioral problems.

Relationship to Other BASC–2 Components

While the BASC–2 Intervention Guide can be used independently, it is also a part of a comprehensive system for screening, assessing, and remediating a child's emotional and behavioral problems. The components of this system are presented in Table 1.2, and are discussed on next page.

Table 1.2 Components of the BASC–2 Intervention Decision-Making System

Function	Component
Screening	*BASC–2 Behavioral and Emotional Screening System* (BESS)
Comprehensive Assessment	*Behavior Assessment System for Children,* Second Edition (BASC–2) *Parenting Relationship Questionnaire* (PRQ™)
Intervention	BASC–2 Intervention Guide BASC–2 Parent Tip Sheets BASC–2 Classroom Intervention Guide BASC–2 Intervention Guide Documentation Checklist
Monitoring Progress	*BASC–2 Progress Monitor*

BASC–2 Behavioral and Emotional Screening System

The *BASC–2 Behavioral and Emotional Screening System* (BESS) is designed to identify behavioral and emotional strengths and weaknesses in children and adolescents from preschool age through high school. It consists of brief screening measures that can be completed by teachers, parents, and students. A total score, which is a reliable and accurate predictor of a wide range of behavioral problems, is provided for each form. In addition to individual results, the computer scoring software can provide group-level reporting options that are useful for monitoring the behavioral and emotional status of children in a variety of groups, such as classrooms, grades, schools, districts, or communities. This tool can be the first step in identifying possible emotional and behavioral problems that may require intervention.

Behavior Assessment System for Children, Second Edition

The *Behavior Assessment System for Children,* Second Edition (BASC–2), is a multimethod, multidimensional system used to evaluate the behavior and self-perceptions of children and young adults ages 2 through 21 years. The BASC–2 was designed to facilitate the differential clinical diagnosis and educational classification of a variety of emotional and behavioral disorders of children and to aid in the design of treatment plans. When used individually, the BASC–2 components are reliable and psychometrically sophisticated instruments that provide an array of beneficial data, providing the clinician with a coordinated set of tools for evaluation, diagnosis, and treatment planning. The BASC–2 is considered the primary tool for identifying emotional and behavioral problems in need of intervention.

Parenting Relationship Questionnaire

The *Parenting Relationship Questionnaire* (PRQ) is a self-report measure completed by one or both parents (or caregivers) and is designed to capture a parent's perspective of the parent–child relationship (or the perspective of a person serving in a similar role). It assesses traditional parent–child dimensions such as attachment and involvement and also provides information on parenting style, parenting confidence, stress, and satisfaction with the child's school. The questionnaire can be used in clinical, pediatric, counseling, school, and other settings where there is a need to understand the nature of the parent–child relationship. A parent's relationship with his or her child has been shown to be related to a number of factors influencing the healthy social and emotional development of a child, including academic performance, language development, self-esteem, and social competence. In addition, the successful implementation of interventions for emotional and behavioral problems is often strongly influenced by the parent–child relationship. For example, problems with parent-child communication could be identified and considered as a component in the implementation of interventions for emotional and behavioral problems.

BASC–2 Progress Monitor

The *BASC–2 Progress Monitor* is designed to track the behavioral and emotional functioning of children involved in a program to remediate their emotional and behavioral problems. It consists of brief (15- to 20-item) teacher, parent, and student forms across four content areas: externalizing and school problems, internalizing problems, social withdrawal, and adaptive skills. A total score is provided for each form, and the scoring and reporting software can be used to track a child's behavioral and emotional functioning over time and to compare scores across raters. These forms can be used to establish the effectiveness of intervention strategies.

Development

The interventions presented in this guide were selected based on published research demonstrating their effectiveness for use in remediating emotional and behavioral problems experienced by children. There is a large amount of variability in the methodologies used across these research studies, ranging from single-case studies to comprehensive meta-analyses. As a result, the criteria for evaluating the effectiveness of an intervention had to accommodate this variability. Standard criteria such as effect size, statistical significance, and clinical significance were considered. In addition, we also evaluated the merits of each study (e.g., quality of research design, apparent quality of treatment fidelity) based on our clinical and research experiences, and only included those studies that appeared to meet at least minimal requirements.

Selecting BASC–2 Scales to Include

Before literature reviews were conducted, the scales included on the BASC–2 teacher, parent, and student rating scales were reviewed to determine which emotional and behavioral problems would be included in this guide. Emphasis was placed on maximizing the coverage of BASC–2 scales and determining which emotional and behavioral problems had enough available evidence for the effectiveness of the interventions offered herein. The decision to include many of the scales was fairly straightforward (e.g., Aggression, Hyperactivity, Anxiety). Some scales were combined because of their similarity to other scales within and across BASC–2 forms and their treatment in the research literature. For example, the Learning Problems, Study Skills, Attitude to Teachers, and Attitude to School scales were combined into a single Academic Problems chapter. This process resulted in only a few BASC–2 scales being omitted from this guide. For example, Atypicality, although an important dimension to assess, does not have a large research base demonstrating effective remediation strategies, except for specific disorders (such as childhood schizophrenia) that may cause elevations on this scale. More commonly, elevated Atypicality scores may be indicators of other problems that usually require additional follow-up. Table 1.3 shows the BASC–2 scales that are included in this intervention guide.

Table 1.3 List of BASC–2 TRS, PRS, and SRP Scales Included in Intervention Chapters

Scale	BASC–2 Form	Intervention Chapter
Adaptability	TRS, PRS	Adaptability
Aggression	TRS, PRS	Aggression
Anxiety	TRS, PRS, SRP	Anxiety
Attention Problems	TRS, PRS, SRP	Attention Problems
Attitude to School	SRP	Academic Problems
Attitude to Teachers	SRP	Academic Problems
Conduct Problems	TRS, PRS	Conduct Problems
Depression	TRS, PRS, SRP	Depression
Functional Communication	TRS, PRS	Functional Communication
Hyperactivity	TRS, PRS, SRP	Hyperactivity
Interpersonal Relations	SRP	Social Skills
Learning Problems	TRS	Academic Problems
Social Skills	TRS, PRS	Social Skills
Somatization	TRS, PRS, SRP	Somatization

Continued on next page

Study Skills	TRS	Academic Problems
Withdrawal	TRS, PRS	Anxiety

Note. TRS=Teacher Rating Scales, PRS=Parent Rating Scales, and SRP=Self-Report of Personality.

Selecting Intervention Studies

For each problem area, a comprehensive literature review was conducted using electronic databases in psychology and education. Keywords for each subscale and for items within the scale (e.g., aggression, depression, lying) were used alone and in combination with keywords such as "treatment," "evidence-based practice," and "interventions." Abstracts were initially reviewed for the following criteria: evidence of treatment effect, age of study participants (2 to 21 years), and evidence of treatment fidelity. Studies that met at least some of these criteria were retained for further evaluation. For each retained research study or meta-analysis, reference lists were checked and additional research was included for review using the aforementioned criteria. A hand search was also conducted of the tables of contents of books and leading journals to cross-reference against all studies that had met our criteria for inclusion. This triangulation of three search methods provided a thorough view of the professional literature for each scale topic and included reviews of more than 1,000 studies.

Intervention methods provided in this guide were chosen because of the strength of the evidence for their effectiveness found in published research literature based on standards established by professional organizations, including the Council for Exceptional Children (CEC), the American Psychological Association (APA), the American Educational Research Association (AERA), and the National Association of School Psychologists (NASP). The annotated studies presented are representative of what works (i.e., not all of the studies on intervention for aggression are included but all were used to create the procedures and to determine the effects of intervention). The procedural steps were determined by listing the articulated procedures from the study, typically found in the research methodology procedure section. These lists were compared across studies to identify common and uncommon steps, primary or critical components, and secondary or irrelevant components. This resulted in the creation of one common or master set of procedures that appeared to be relevant for use in the field rather than just as research protocol. The procedural steps were reviewed by ad hoc consultation with school psychologists, counselors, and teachers where applicable. These procedural steps and the research studies, summarized in the Evidence for Use sections of this guide, provide *general* support for the use of the intervention methodologies as well as preliminary (albeit strong) evidence for the validity of the procedural steps as they are presented in this guide. As the interventions articulated in this guide are used in field settings across ages and types of student problems, it is anticipated that additional research will be conducted to further substantiate the strength of their effectiveness.

It is helpful to note that several intervention methods (e.g., contingency management) appear as effective practice for more than one type of problem behavior. Each method is presented along with a review of the literature that supports its use for a specific behavior and with the steps and examples for use. For example, the procedural steps for contingency management may differ slightly depending on which condition is being treated.

Creating the BASC–2 Parent Tip Sheets

The BASC–2 Parent Tip Sheets were developed from the intervention strategies presented in this guide. Primary consideration was given to presenting information in a simple and engaging way. Readability of the text was paramount. Traditional readability metrics such as the Flesch Reading Ease Score and the Flesch-Kincaid Reading Index were used to evaluate the text written for the tip sheets. Whenever possible, sentences were rewritten to lower the readability level (as indicated by the readability metrics) while retaining the intended structure and tone of the text. For example, some of the terminology describing the interventions was changed from how it was presented in the research literature to make it more meaningful to parents. For the Anxiety tip sheet, the phrase "contingency management" was replaced with "rewarding brave behavior." Care also was taken to avoid simplifying the text too much, in order to maintain the utility of the document for all persons using the tip sheets. Upon completion of the tip sheets, each was subjected to a final readability analysis, resulting in an average Flesch-Kincaid Grade Level score of 7.7 (range of 6.9 to 8.7), indicating about a seventh-grade reading level.

Using the Interventions

Effective development, adoption, and sustainability of an intervention is based in part on choosing an intervention that is appropriate given the child's strengths and weaknesses and the strengths and weaknesses of the setting in which the intervention will be implemented. This process is aided by an understanding of the background of the child, his or her family, and the interventions that have been implemented or attempted previously. The BASC–2 Intervention Guide is not a cookbook with a recipe for treating a particular problem behavior. Rather, it is a planning guide for the informed selection, implementation, and evaluation of efficient and effective treatment practices in schools, clinics, and homes. It provides step-by-step procedures for implementation once an appropriate intervention has been selected.

Children with emotional and behavioral disorders are frequently characterized by comorbidity of problems. As such, the simultaneous presentation of multiple symptoms necessitates prioritizing problems prior to addressing them. Some interventions may result in improvement to co-occurring behavior problems, but it is also fairly common to see one behavior improve while another gets worse or to see an alternate behavior emerge. To assist practitioners in determining an appropriate sequence of interventions in such cases, some thoughts on data-driven decision making are provided here.

The prioritization of problem behaviors (i.e., which to address, and which to address first) is often a complicated one. Certainly behaviors that indicate a threat to self or others or that result in property damage require some immediate resolution (e.g., aggression, conduct problems). Next to be addressed would be those problems that interfere with daily life or pose a threat to long-term adjustment and wellness (e.g., attention, learning, hyperactivity, depression, and communication problems). Finally, consideration should be given to problems that may lead to stigmatization or struggles at school and in the community and that may create obstacles to becoming a more fully functioning individual (e.g., somatization, anxiety, social skills problems). These are not rules for triage but examples of how some conditions might be addressed in the context of the bigger picture. Consider also the relationship between the problems or risk. Is the child's depression caused by his or her learning problems or are the learning problems caused by the depression? If so, addressing one may eradicate the other. The severity of the problems should also be taken into consideration, and the most severe problems should be addressed first. Is the conduct problem a risk but the social skills so significant that the social skills require immediacy in treatment?

Using the BASC–2 ASSIST and ASSIST Plus Reports

A program upgrade for BASC–2 ASSIST and ASSIST Plus scoring software is available that will generate an intervention guide narrative for Teacher Rating Scales, Parent Rating Scales, and Self-Report of Personality reports. This narrative includes information about the specific emotional and behavioral problems a child may be having, based on the ratings of items on the TRS, PRS, or SRP forms. It also includes a summary of up to two interventions for each identified problem area (Table 1.1 indicates which interventions will appear in an ASSIST report) and a classification of BASC–2 subscale scores into primary (i.e., clinically significant) and secondary (i.e., at risk) intervention areas. For each intervention, a brief summary is provided, along with an example that demonstrates appropriate use of the intervention. Procedural steps for implementing the intervention are also provided, along with considerations for implementing the intervention and a list of research studies that report on the effectiveness of the intervention technique. Due to space considerations in the reports, the narratives generated are restricted to a maximum of three BASC–2 intervention areas. Problem areas beyond the top three presented, as well as additional intervention techniques not included in the narrative, can be found in this guide.

The interventions listed in the ASSIST and ASSIST Plus reports are based on the child's T scores. In the event of a tie between scales, scales are prioritized with respect to the impact of problems on the child, others, or academic performance. Scales associated with the Aggression, Conduct Problems, Depression, Anxiety, Hyperactivity, Attention Problems, and Academic Problems intervention areas are given priority over scales associated with other intervention areas. For example, consider a child who has a total of four TRS scales with a T score of 75: Aggression, Conduct Problems, Depression, and Somatization.

Given the limit of reporting up to three significant scale elevations and the specified scale hierarchy, the software would generate interventions for Aggression, Conduct Problems, and Depression but would not list Somatization interventions (because Somatization has a lower priority ranking than the other scales). However, the software report would still identify Somatization as a problem area and would refer the user to the intervention guide for information on specific intervention methods. (Additional information about these reports can be found in the Help section of the BASC–2 ASSIST or ASSIST Plus software.)

Using the BASC–2 Parent Tip Sheets

Although the BASC–2 Parent Tip Sheets have been designed to be easily understood by parents, it is important to let parents know how to use them. For example, each tip sheet contains three or four suggested intervention approaches. In many cases, it would be appropriate to indicate which intervention the parent should try first. This can be done by putting a star or a number next to the desired or prioritized intervention. Each tip sheet includes a guide for tracking progress and for documenting how often the parent works with his or her child. Some parents are unfamiliar with progress monitoring and may need some initial guidance so they are not intimidated by the process. Also, it can be helpful to identify when the tip sheets' progress monitoring form should be returned and when they will be reviewed with the parents. Steps like these can help maximize parental involvement in the intervention process.

Monitoring Progress

A key component to the successful implementation of an intervention is determining its impact on a child's behavioral and emotional functioning. Interventions that improve a child's functioning are generally continued or systematically faded, while interventions that do not improve a child's functioning are modified or perhaps discontinued. There are a number of ways to assess the impact of an intervention, which all depend on the content of the intervention and the method of inquiry. Commonly used informal methods of monitoring progress in school and clinical settings (such as unstructured interviews or scheduled discussions) leave the degree of communication and the sensitivity of the measurement almost to chance. This informal approach is inadequate. For example, some questions, such as "how is it going" or "have things improved," provide little information for data-driven decision making and are unreliable methods of documenting results. The purposes for gathering the information (e.g., for use in prereferral, clinical diagnosis, determining response to intervention, litigation documentation, monitoring progress on goals and objectives) and the behavior or condition being monitored may determine the number and types of monitoring procedures. Improving specific behaviors (e.g., staying seated in class, making eye contact) often requires frequent evaluation of the behaviors' effects. The BASC–2 Parent Tip Sheets provide a form for progress monitoring at home. The BASC–2 Intervention Guide Documentation Checklist provides a method for articulating the level of intervention that occurred and the degree to which it was successful. Other informal methods, such as a home–school note or a daily behavior report card (DBRC), provide useful feedback to parents and professionals for assessing the effects of an intervention as well. Such approaches require relatively little effort, can be repeated frequently, and are well suited for answering questions for a specific period of time (e.g., math class performance, daily changes in aggression). However, these approaches are not as helpful for evaluating behavioral and emotional functioning at a broader level or for determining if a child's functioning is still at an elevated or clinical level with respect to a normative population.

Another approach to evaluating the effectiveness of an intervention program is to use direct observation techniques (e.g., the BASC–2 Student Observation System and the BASC–2 Portable Observation Program). In general, these techniques require a person to observe a child's behavior in a classroom or other setting for a specified time period (e.g., 30 minutes). At their most basic level, direct observation techniques utilize ratings that are categorized into a dichotomy (e.g., on-task and off-task behaviors), while more robust techniques capture ratings across a variety of behaviors, reporting on metrics such as the total number of positive and negative behaviors, in terms of both counts and percentages. These observational approaches require more time and effort than do informal checklists, and, as a result, may not be used as frequently. However, they often provide a broader view of a child's behavioral and emotional functioning, which can be important for gaining a broader perspective of the effects of an intervention program.

A third approach to evaluating the effectiveness of an intervention program is to use a standardized behavior rating tool like the *BASC–2 Progress Monitor* forms. Behavior rating forms are commonplace in school and clinical settings and are considered very efficient ways to capture information about a child's level of behavioral and emotional functioning. Although they are probably not appropriate for use on a daily basis, these forms can be used every few weeks, and provide an indication of both the degree of individual change (via changes in scale scores) and the current level of functioning (via comparisons to normative populations).

Over longer periods of time, a BASC–2 TRS, PRS, or SRP might prove useful if the child develops other problems while one problem is being addressed. A comprehensive rating scale like the TRS, PRS, and SRP can help monitor these trends in behavior and provide an early indication of newly forming problems. The BASC–2 ASSIST and ASSIST Plus software also contain features that allow the user to monitor changes in a child's behavior over time when using the Progress Report and the Multirater Report. These changes can be evaluated both graphically and statistically.

When choosing the method and frequency of evaluation, one must always carefully consider the link between the intervention method and the rating approach. Does the content of the intervention program align with the behaviors or emotions that are evaluated by the rating method? For example, an intervention method aimed at improving a child's attention level will probably focus on behaviors associated with staying on task and listening in class. Concerning rating frequency, is it reasonable to believe that the intervention will lead to changes in behavior or emotions in the designated amount of time between the intervention and the rating? For example, reducing a child's depression or anxiety level to a normal range is something that is probably best measured in weeks or months, not days. Failure to consider this link may lead to inaccurate conclusions about the effectiveness of an intervention program.

Summary

In the chapters that follow, we present evidence-based interventions to be considered when developing a treatment plan for children or adolescents who have or are at risk for developing specific emotional and behavioral disorders. The interventions presented differ in their application of one or more behavioral, cognitive–behavioral, or social-learning theories, but they are all shaped by the fundamental goals of treatment: prevention, management, and remediation of problem behaviors.

It is important to remember that for each individual the factors to consider will be as varied as the causes and consequences of his or her disorder. Professionals are encouraged to pay close attention to the considerations for use of each intervention to determine which will be most effective for achieving expected treatment outcomes. Additionally, an effective intervention strategy should consider the trajectory of a particular disorder's development, and the methods and strategies selected should specifically address a child's location in that trajectory. In addition, it is essential that the interventions that are determined to be most effective for prevention and remediation of the problem behavior be incorporated into the treatment plan.

Overall, treatment typically involves the remediation of more than one behavioral or emotional problem. Multiple problems (e.g., learning failure, attention deficits) interrelate in both direct and indirect ways. A treatment strategy can be seen as a system of intervention processes that is dependent on multiple variables working in concert. The goal of effective treatment should be the orchestration of these concurrent processes to maximize treatment success and to provide the greatest benefit to the child.

References

Kamphaus, R. W., & Reynolds, C.R. (2006). *Parenting Relationship Questionnaire.* Minneapolis, MN: NCS Pearson.

Kamphaus, R. W., & Reynolds, C. R. (2007). *BASC–2 Behavioral and Emotional Screening System.* Minneapolis, MN: NCS Pearson.

Reynolds, C. R., & Kamphaus, R. W. (2002). *The clinician's guide to the Behavioral Assessment System for Children* (BASC). New York: Guilford.

Reynolds, C. R., & Kamphaus, R. W. (2004). *Behavior Assessment System for Children* (2nd ed.; BASC–2). Circle Pines, MN: American Guidance Service.

Reynolds, C. R., & Kamphaus, R. W. (in press). *BASC–2 Progress Monitor.* Minneapolis, MN: NCS Pearson.

Vannest, K., Reynolds, C. R., & Kamphaus, R. W. (2008). BASC–2 Intervention Guide Documentation Checklist. Minneapolis, MN: NCS Pearson.

Vannest, K., Reynolds, C. R., & Kamphaus, R. W. (in press). BASC–2 Classroom Intervention Guide. Minneapolis, MN: NCS Pearson.

Chapter 2

Interventions for Aggression

This chapter focuses on interventions for children and adolescents identified as having problems with aggression. The discussion of these methods is presented in three sections. The first section in this chapter discusses the characteristics and conditions of aggression and provides sample items from the BASC–2 Aggression scale. While describing the construct for aggressive behavior, this initial section also delineates the differences in at-risk and clinical significance indicators on the Aggression scale. The second section describes the theoretical framework for understanding aggressive behaviors and the selection of interventions presented in this chapter. In the third section, interventions that have evidence or show promise for reducing aggressive behavior in school settings are described. The presentation of each provides an overview of the intervention and is divided into three subsections: Implementation, Evidence for Use, and Considerations. The chapter's three main sections provide the foundation on which additional BASC–2 intervention components are built, including both classroom-based and home-based strategies.

Characteristics and Conditions of Aggression

Aggression is characterized by hostile or destructive behaviors. The research literature commonly refers to two categories of aggression that differ in their goals: object-oriented and person-oriented. The goal of object-oriented aggression (sometimes called instrumental aggression) is to obtain an object that is desired or to escape an aversive situation. For example, a child may hit another child to get a toy that he or she wants or shove away a parent to avoid being given a bath. This type of aggression is found mainly in young children or individuals who lack verbal communication skills. Older children, however, tend to exhibit person-oriented aggression, the goal of which is to obtain control, gain access to people or things, or escape from individuals; behavioral motivation may include dominance and revenge. This category of aggression includes forms of direct and indirect aggression (i.e., victim present or not, respectively) and relational aggression (i.e., the use of peer relationships) to inflict harm to others (Reynolds & Fletcher-Janzen, 2007). For example, a child may hit another child as retribution for being embarrassed earlier in the day (direct physical aggression), spread rumors about another child (indirect aggression), or restrict friendships among peers to isolate others (relational aggression).

While the previous examples describe physical and relational aggression, a child may also be considered aggressive because of certain verbalizations. The BASC–2 captures both verbal and physical aggression. Verbal aggression is characterized by behaviors such as arguing, name-calling, or vocalizing threats. Physical aggression is characterized by behaviors that involve damage to property, self, or others. The items on the BASC–2 Aggression scale give greater weight to verbal aggression because it is the more common expression of aggression. Sample BASC–2 items from the Aggression scale include: "Annoys others on purpose," "Hits other children," and "Bullies others" (Reynolds & Kamphaus, 2004).

Children and adolescents who exhibit aggressive behaviors may have inadequacies in problem solving and deficiencies in the specific areas of identifying alternatives, considering consequences, and determining causalities. They may also engage in means–ends thinking and have difficulty understanding other perspectives.

Theoretical Framework for Approaching Aggressive Behaviors

Although there are many theories on the causes of aggression, most approaches fit within one or more of five models: psychodynamic, drive theory, etiological/biological, social learning theory, and cognitive–behavioral perspectives. However, not all of these theories provide the support necessary to form the foundations for effective intervention strategies and the remediation of aggressive behaviors. The psychodynamic and drive theory models have limited utility and weak or unsupportable hypotheses. The biological attributions of aggression, although supportable, are insufficient as a sole basis from which to intervene because extraneous factors may interfere with the intervention's selection, delivery, and sustainability. In contrast, the social learning and cognitive–behavioral theories provide strong evidence for the origins of aggression as a learned behavior and also offer a starting place for intervention utility; therefore, the interventions presented in this chapter fit primarily within a social learning or cognitive–behavioral construct.

Interventions

A variety of interventions have been shown to reduce or have shown promise for reducing aggressive behavior in school settings. The interventions presented below have been considered effective, as evidenced by peer-reviewed research and/or espoused by professional organizations. (For more on determination of evidence, see chapter 1, page 12.) These interventions have been classified based on their critical characteristics (referred to as "elements"), resulting in the following groupings:

    I. Problem-Solving Training

   II. Cognitive Restructuring

  III. Verbal Mediation

IV. Social Skills Training

V. Peer-Mediated Conflict Resolution and Negotiation

VI. Replacement Behavior Training

I. Problem-Solving Training

Problem solving is the application of a set of skills to address situations that may be resolved in different ways. Training in problem solving teaches students a sequential and deliberate process for handling potentially negative situations that arise in social interactions (Polsgrove & Smith, 2004). Problem solving is taught through modeling, direct instruction, and guided practice.

For example, a junior-high school student, while seeking help from a classmate on an assignment, may respond to a teacher's request to stay on task with profanity or other verbally aggressive outbursts. Alternatively, a student using a problem-solving approach to responding to a teacher's request would identify different ways to acknowledge the teacher while requesting help from classmates. He or she might explain the situation instead of becoming verbally aggressive.

Implementation

Problem-solving approaches rely on the development of skills that can be internalized and transferred to a variety of problems and settings. The basic elements of problem-solving approaches include the following:

1. Problem recognition

2. Problem definition and goal setting

3. Generation of possible solutions

4. Evaluation of solutions

5. Plan design and implementation

6. Plan evaluation

Prior to developing a problem-solving strategy, an evaluation of a child's current problem-solving skill level is necessary to develop an effective intervention. Children can differ widely in their ability to understand and implement each of the basic elements. For example, a child may be able to recognize when a problem exists but may have trouble defining it. In such cases, the initial problem-solving approach should focus on the problem-definition and goal-setting element. The best strategy for assessing the child's current level of problem-solving functioning is to provide a scenario and a list of each of the steps in the problem-solving sequence and to ask the child to identify each step using the scenario. Alternatively, you could ask the student to retell the problem in the scenario as he or she sees it. This method of skill assessment is helpful in identifying possible issues with the student's problem-solving abilities. For instance, if the student responds incorrectly, by inaccurately identifying the problem or articulating nonsensical or unrelated reasons for the actual problem behavior, this may indicate weaknesses in problem identification; other answers might properly identify the problem but demonstrate an inability to generate alternative responses. Thus, walking through the steps of problem assessment with one or more examples should provide a thorough screening of a child's current functioning level.

Teaching problem-solving skills to children with aggression problems may be best achieved using real or invented examples from school, provided they are relevant. Skits or role-plays involving a teacher with one or more students can be used for demonstration, although written examples or videos may also be appropriate. Such examples should provide background information about the situation, model the behaviors to be learned, and guide students through a problem scenario they are asked to solve. Upon completion of the examples, children can be asked to answer questions about the scenarios or to review the main points of each example. Children can provide answers in a variety of ways, including on a chalk or white board, a worksheet, large index cards, or a flip chart. When children provide answers, it is important they are recognized for their contributions each step of the way. Initially a teacher should encourage all efforts (correct answers can be emphasized later). This support for participation will allow the adult to assess where children are in their problem-solving skills.

The best example scenarios are ones that the child has seen or experienced that can be carried through each step of problem solving. Although the child may not initially be able to work through all of the steps, he or she will become more proficient with each step as more examples are given. After learning the problem-solving elements through teacher-generated examples, the approach can be reinforced by asking the child to generate his or her own problem scenarios. The procedural steps for incorporating problem-solving training into the treatment of an individual child with aggression are listed in Figure 2.1.

Figure 2.1 Procedural steps for the application of problem-solving training

1. Provide a list of steps for problem solving.

2. Demonstrate or present a problem scenario. Have the children role-play a real or contrived example and then respond with the subsequent steps. Alternatively, a teacher may role-play an example and have the children respond.

3. Identify the problem in the scenario. Prompt as necessary to encourage the children to include all emotional, social, and environmental features of the situation.

Continued on next page

4. Ask questions to determine the goals of the problem behavior. Common questions may include:

    a. What is the person featured in the example hoping to get out of the situation?

    b. What is(are) the other person(s) hoping to get out of the social exchange?

5. List a number of alternative solutions.

    a. Think of at least three different ways to handle the given situation.

    b. Include all ideas that the children think of, regardless of how realistic.

    c. Be sure to include at least one solution that represents a "desired" response (i.e., one that most people would consider appropriate) to demonstrate how the person featured can get what he or she needs without using aggression.

6. Evaluate the list by asking questions such as:

    a. Which potential solutions will get the person in the example what he or she needs?

    b. Which solutions will probably work? Which solutions probably will not work?

    c. What are the costs and benefits of each solution?

7. Choose the best solution.

8. Design a plan to achieve the solution. Ask questions such as:

    a. Do you think the person in the example will get what he/she needs with this solution? Why or why not?

    b. Do you believe the person featured can perform the new behavior? Why or why not?

9. Practice the plan. The teacher (or a peer) may need to model or role-play the plan before the child can practice it.

10. Implement the plan. The teacher may test the child by engaging in the problem behavior to assess the child's ability to respond in accordance with the plan.

11. Create a reinforcement and evaluation plan. The child should report back on using the plan, and reinforcement and feedback should be provided when the child reports engaging in the newly learned behaviors. Reinforcement and corrective feedback should occur at a 1:1 ratio for any new behavior. A 1:1 ratio occurs when praise, support, or reinforcement occurs relative to each instance of a new behavior, in this case, the child's reported use of part or all of the steps for problem-solving in dealing with a specific conflict.

Evidence for Use

Problem-solving training can effectively prevent or decrease aggressive and other problem behaviors (Conduct Problems Prevention Research Group, 1999; Duanic, Smith, Brank, & Penfield, 2006; Kazdin, Siegel, & Bass, 1992; Lochman, Burch, Curry, & Lampron, 1984; Sukhodolsky, Golub, Stone, & Orban, 2005). Problem-solving training can also effectively increase self-reliant thinking patterns and decrease impulsiveness that is associated with aggressive behavior (Goldstein, Glick, & Gibbs, 1998; Henggeler, Schoenwald, Borduin, Rowland, & Cunningham, 1998; Jackson, Jackson, & Bennet, 1998).

The following studies summarize some of the key research findings associated with problem-solving techniques and aggression.

Conduct Problems Prevention Research Group. (1999). Initial impact of the Fast Track prevention trial for conduct problems: II. Classroom effects. *Journal of Consulting and Clinical Psychology, 67*(5), 648–657.

This study of the effectiveness of the PATHS® (Promoting Alternative THinking Strategies) component of the Fast Track prevention model compared 198 intervention and 180 nonintervention classrooms in four U.S. neighborhoods that experienced higher-than-average crime levels. The intervention consisted of a 57-item social-competence curriculum implemented by Grade 1 teachers that focused on self-control, emotional awareness, peer relations, and problem solving. Results indicated that PATHS can positively impact aggression and peer relations. This study is significant for its use of the classroom, rather than the student, as the unit of analysis.

Daunic, A. P., Smith, S. W., Brank, E. M., & Penfield, R. D. (2006). Classroom-based cognitive–behavioral intervention to prevent aggression: Efficacy and social validity. *Journal of School Psychology, 44*(2), 123–139.

This study investigated the efficacy of a newly developed cognitive–behavioral social problem-solving curriculum, Tools for Getting Along: Teaching Students to Problem Solve. The curriculum, implemented by classroom teachers in Grades 4 and 5, produced positive outcomes in 165 target students at risk for disruptive and/or aggressive behavior, including increased problem-solving knowledge and improved teacher ratings of reactive and proactive aggression. Improvements were maintained over several months.

Kazdin, A. E., Siegel, T. C., & Bass, D. (1992). Cognitive problem-solving skills training and parent management training in the treatment of antisocial behavior in children. *Journal of Consulting and Clinical Psychology, 60*(5), 733–747.

A randomized study of 97 children ages 7 to 13 years evaluated problem-solving skills training (PSST) and parent management training (PMT) (each separately and combined) to determine which combination was more effective. Although

PSST, PMT, and PSST + PMT each improved children's functioning, the combined treatment produced more marked, pervasive, and durable changes in children's functioning and greater changes in parental functioning posttreatment and at one-year follow-up. A larger proportion of children receiving combination treatment reached normal levels of functioning.

Lochman, J. E., Burch, P. R., Curry, J. F., & Lampron, L. B. (1984). Treatment and generalization effects of cognitive–behavioral and goal-setting interventions with aggressive boys. *Journal of Consulting and Clinical Psychology, 52*(5), 915–916.

The purpose of this study was to examine the efficacy of treatment programs that include social problem-solving and goal-setting components, alone or in combination. The comparison involved 76 boys ages 9 to 12 years who were identified as aggressive. They were randomly assigned to one of four treatment conditions: anger-coping, goal-setting, anger-coping plus goal-setting, and a no-treatment condition. Conditions with anger-coping interventions consisted of 12 weekly sessions focused on improving social problem-solving skills. The 8-week goal-setting component consisted of weekly goal setting with daily monitoring by teachers and contingent reinforcement. At one-month follow-up, the students in groups containing anger-coping components (i.e., focused on social problem-solving) showed less aggressive behavior and a tendency toward improved self-esteem both at school and home. However, teacher and peer perceptions of the boys' behavior did not change significantly, indicating either a steadfast perception of the boys' reputations or a limit to the treatment effects.

Sukhodolsky, D. G., Golub, A., Stone, E. C., & Orban, L. (2005). Dismantling anger control training for children: A randomized pilot study of social problem-solving versus social skills training components. *Behavior Therapy, 36*(1), 15–23.

This randomized pilot study compared two modules of anger control training in 26 boys (mean age, 9.6 years) with excessive anger, aggression, and disruptive behavior. Results showed social problem solving and social skills training to be equally effective in reducing aggression, conduct problems, and frequency of anger expression. Likewise, improvements were similar for relationships with parents and responses to peer provocation. However, social problem solving was more effective in reducing hostile attribution bias, whereas social skills training was more effective in improving anger control skills.

Considerations

For Teaching

When teaching problem-solving skills, instructors should be sure to allow time for modeling and guided practice. These steps are frequently skipped when teaching time gets compressed, but modeling and guided practice are critical for teaching problem-solving skills, as they are not learned from worksheets or in discussions. They must be practiced. Students learn problem solving most effectively by doing, primarily through role-play and practice situations. Teacher behavior may affect student outcomes (Frey, Hirschstein, & Guzzo, 2000). As such, supportive practices are critical, and teachers who involve students in identifying problems and constructing solutions will see better results.

For Culture and Language Differences

Practitioners should remember to choose language carefully when role-playing. In general, the use of the word "need" should be avoided except when truly meant as a need. Also, when working with students whose primary language and culture differ from yours, be sensitive in encouraging and affirming student responses to identifying problems and creating alternative solutions to them. Identifying feelings or problems in others, or taking the perspective of others, may be a new experience or task demand for some students. Language that identifies feelings will vary for different cultures, not only in terms of translation but also in terms of existence. Some languages do not have a vocabulary for emotions or feelings. In some cases, these differences may require additional teaching.

For Age and Developmental Level

Students who are younger, developmentally delayed, or who lack communicative skills will have additional difficulties in creating language to explain the actions of others; therefore, symbols or puppets might be an alternative for instructional or communicational needs. In addition, fixed choices, such as "Which is the problem: x or y?," can help bridge this functional gap. Younger students will need both stories and examples that are well matched to their age and developmental level. For example, early childhood participants will respond more readily to stories about toys and tangibles around them, while high school-aged children will identify with emotions and problems associated with adolescence.

For Safety

When working with physical aggression, role-playing should be used with caution. Adults should know the personal and social histories of each individual with whom they are working. For example, two adolescents who have a long standing turf war as gang members would not make good independent role-play partners reenacting a problem-solving scenario about avoiding a fight. Also, students should not be coerced into participation. Successful intervention for aggression using problem-solving techniques requires a degree of willing participation from those being treated.

II. Cognitive Restructuring

Cognitive restructuring (also referred to in the research literature as Rational Emotive Therapy [Ellis, 1962], social-judgment training, and attribution training [Harris, Wong, & Keogh, 1985; Michenbaum, 1977]) is a strategy in which individuals learn to identify irrational or inaccurate beliefs, along with the events that lead to these beliefs. Such beliefs often result in destructive emotions and subsequent maladaptive behaviors (e.g., aggression). For example, a student may irrationally identify a neutral look or comment from another person as aggressive or negative and respond aggressively. Or, a student may associate a teacher's request to come to the front of the classroom with being in trouble and, therefore, behave aggressively to avoid the negatively perceived encounter.

Since cognitive restructuring addresses the causal perceptions of success and failure—locus of control, stability, and controllability (Weiner, 1985)—the key to its use is modifying the beliefs that cause or lead up to the aggressive behavior; this modification of beliefs results in newly formed attributions. Through cognitive restructuring, students replace cognitive distortions that are disruptive and self-defeating by identifying irrational beliefs; understanding self-condemnation, frustration intolerance, and blame and criticism of others; and learning to develop a system for disputing these beliefs (Ellis, 1986; Walen, DiGiuseppe, & Wessler, 1980; Wessler & Wessler, 1980; Young, 1977). As such, existing beliefs are replaced with more constructive ones that lead to more positive emotions and appropriate behaviors. Thus, the beliefs are the target of the intervention, and solutions are generated that can be applied and generalized during subsequent opportunities.

Implementation

Cognitive restructuring centers on the child recognizing appropriate alternative explanations for behavior, identifying irrational and inaccurate beliefs about behaviors, and replacing these irrational beliefs with more rational ones. The basic elements of a cognitive restructuring approach include the following:

1. Recognition of emotional or behavioral signals (or antecedents) that suggest a problem

2. Identification of beliefs that are responsible for the association between the emotional or behavioral signal and the irrational behavior

3. Disputation of the irrational or inaccurate belief

4. Generation of a more rational belief

5. Development of a plan to internalize the rational belief

An outline of the procedures for implementing cognitive restructuring is presented in Figure 2.2. When using this intervention strategy with children, it can be helpful to use invented practice examples from stories, worksheets, or videos to develop skills for identifying irrational or mistaken attributions. With time and practice, the child will be able to generate his or her own examples that have occurred in the past and will eventually be able to relate examples from current experiences he or she is facing. Also, after achieving competence with the strategy, it can also be used as an "on the fly" intervention, with an adult quickly prompting a child to identify the "irrational" belief(s) that are supporting a current behavior.

It is important to understand that the child is the change agent in this intervention, while the person working with the child functions as a facilitator by assisting with the recognition, replacement, and verbalization of irrational beliefs. When modeling the procedures for the child, it is important to help the child develop more rational attributions so that he or she can gain more self-control over the replacement process. Both individual and group training can be equally effective techniques when implementing this intervention. Additionally, just-in-time services can be provided for children who have learned how to recognize signals and identify underlying beliefs. This assistance is gradually faded so that children learn to progress independently through all steps and report back on their experiences.

Figure 2.2 Procedural steps for the application of cognitive restructuring

1. Ask the student to describe a problem they are experiencing (where aggression is involved). Ask also for any physical and emotional feelings before, during, and after the event.

2. Ask the student to identify "why" the incident happened, from both his or her own perspective and the perspective of any others involved.

3. Confront irrational or inaccurate beliefs by contrasting them with different perspectives or by drawing them to ridiculous conclusions. For example, a counselor might say, "So, when Principal Ramsey calls me to the office, it means he is going to yell at me?"

4. Create or determine a more likely or equally plausible (rational) replacement thought or belief with the student. For example, when a teacher calls my name, it may be to ask me to do something, not because I'm in trouble.

5. Practice applying the new thought or belief to different situations by role-playing with the student.

6. Ask the student to keep a log or journal of when the replacement thought or belief is used in different environments.

7. Generalize and reinforce the use of the rational thoughts in different situations.

Evidence for Use

Cognitive restructuring has been found to be effective at reducing aggression (Hudley & Friday, 1996; Hudley & Graham, 1993; Pecukonis, 1990). The majority of research has determined that aggression is the result of applying inflexible, impulsive, and negative attributions (or hostile intent) to misperceived ambiguous events, resulting in cognitive distortions and a corresponding belief that aggression is considered an appropriate response to the situation (Dodge & Coie, 1987; Hudley & Friday, 1996; Hudley & Graham, 1993; Goldstein, 1995). Cognitive restructuring has been found to remediate these cognitive distortions and has resulted in a reduction of aggressive behaviors (Guerra & Slaby, 1990; Hudley & Friday, 1996; Hudley & Graham, 1993).

The following studies summarize some of the key research findings associated with cognitive restructuring techniques and aggression.

Guerra, N. G., & Slaby, R. G. (1990). Cognitive mediators of aggression in adolescent offenders: 2 Intervention. *Developmental Psychology, 26*(2), 269–277.

To determine whether cognitive mediation training could alter the social-cognitive basis for aggressive behavior, this study divided 120 juveniles incarcerated for aggressive offenses into a cognitive mediation training group, an attention control group, or a no-treatment group. In contrast to the control group, the subjects given short-term cognitive mediation training increased their skills in solving social problems, reduced their endorsement of beliefs supporting aggression, and reduced their subsequent aggressive, impulsive, and inflexible behavior. Recidivism appeared less likely in the cognitive mediation training group, although differences between groups were not significant.

Hudley, C., & Graham, S. (1993). An attributional intervention to reduce peer-directed aggression among African-American boys. *Child Development, 64*(1), 124–138.

An attributional intervention program was developed to study peer-directed aggression in African-American boys. Approximately 100 aggressive and nonaggressive boys between the ages of 10 and 12 years were randomly assigned to the attributional intervention, attention training, or no-treatment conditions. Pretesting and posttesting assessed the boys' judgment of intent, feelings of anger, and aggressive behavior in response to hypothetical and actual peer provocation. Teacher ratings and disciplinary referrals were additional sources of data. Results showed that aggressive children's tendencies toward biased attributions are amenable to retraining and that such retraining can significantly reduce aggressive behavior.

Considerations

For Teaching

Cognitive restructuring requires the willing participation of the child in addition to cognitive and verbal abilities. Additionally, the adult teaching cognitive restructuring will need to be skilled in identifying distortion in a child's thinking. Keep in mind that the cognitions of children and youth—their perspectives on what is real and what is a significant problem—are largely determined by their experience and age. This restructuring is intended to, for example, assist a child in understanding that not sitting by a friend at lunch might be the result of some external factor, such as the lunch line moving faster on one side of the cafeteria, as opposed to a distorted cognition, such as the friend disliking the child.

For Culture and Language

In addition, there is considerable potential for familial, cultural, or economic values to influence a child's belief system about what is reality and what is a cognitive distortion. Often, a mismatch exists between a dominant culture and a minority one, or the culture of a school conflicts with that of the family. Sensitivity to norms and assumptions should be a part of the cognitive restructuring approach. Parental perceptions of world events and cultural habits will have a tremendous impact on the perspectives of youth. For example, an immigrant from a country in which police are known to come in the middle of the night and remove people from their homes will transmit different beliefs and expectations to their children. Likewise, a family who has experienced parental incarceration for drug use or illegal activity may transmit values that are different from those expected by a teacher.

For Age and Developmental Level

In some studies, children have identified patterns of typical playground behavior that are expected from their friends and have demonstrated different opinions than the adults about classifications of appropriate behaviors and priorities. This variance underscores the need to allow children full expression of their beliefs about the problems they are having.

Additionally, both the linguistic and emotional development of the child should be considered when identifying areas to change. For instance, at some ages or stages, children may truly believe that they are not responsible for their problems. At other stages, they may assume all the responsibility when doing so is not appropriate. Another example is related to prediction: young children, perhaps up to age 8, will have tremendous difficulty with prediction and might be unable to anticipate what might happen next or where a scenario is headed.

III. Verbal Mediation

Verbal mediation refers to the use of language to promote a positive influence on a person's cognitions and behavior. More specifically, verbal mediation refers to the use of private speech (i.e., not heard by others) for the purpose of self-regulation of behavior. While language traditionally is considered to be a tool used to communicate with others, it can also be used to communicate with oneself, as a way to self-regulate behavior (Berk, 1992; Skinner, 1953; Vygotsky 1930, 1978; Vygotsky, 1934, 1987).

For example, a kindergarten student might softly repeat the directions his mother gave him to refrain from biting his little brother, saying, "I will not bite Tommy, I will not bite Tommy." Or, an eighth grader might move his lips silently while repeating a phrase in his head, encouraging himself not to get frustrated or angry in the face of adversity. Or, a high school girl may silently repeat a mantra not to get angry when cut off in traffic by another driver. In each case, the self-talk is used to mediate the actual behavior.

Verbal mediation has been referred to as a core component in cognitive modeling (Bandura, 1986) and self-instruction training (Hinshaw & Erhardt, 1991; Kaplan & Carter, 1995; Meichenbaum, 1985) and has led to self-monitoring and self-regulation strategies. Verbal mediation is also used in short-term memory, for example, when rehearsing phonological information in the articulation loop of working memory (Baddeley & Hitch, 1974).

Implementation

The goal of verbal mediation is for children to internalize verbal directions, procedures, or rules that control their behavior so that self-regulation occurs. The basic elements of the verbal mediation strategy include the following:

1. Implementation of cognitive models (i.e., teacher says, teacher does)

2. Implementation of overt external guidance (i.e., teacher says, child does)

3. Implementation of overt self-guidance (i.e., child says, child does)

4. Implementation of faded overt self-guidance (i.e., child whispers, child does)

5. Implementation of covert self-instruction (i.e., child thinks, child does)

An outline of the procedures for implementing verbal mediation is presented in Figure 2.3. Teaching verbal mediation involves identifying the current self-talk that occurs prior to incidents of aggression and replacing maladaptive self-speech with a new script. Alternatively, if no self-talk occurs prior to incidents of aggression, then a new script is created to self-regulate aggression. Depending on the age and developmental level of the child, the script may be as simple as "I will not hit on the playground," or as complex as several sentences describing the antecedent or setting of the event, the plan for action, and the desired outcome. For example, a high school student who regularly gets provoked during lunch by another student might create and internalize a script such as: "When I see Joe, he will try to bait me into fighting with him. When I see Joe, I will walk in the other direction and smile. I will beat Joe by smiling. I will have a good day and Joe will not."

Evidence for Use

Verbal mediation is effective at reducing aggression in normally developing and developmentally disabled youth and adults (Camp, Blom, Hebert, & van Doorninck, 1977; Chapman, Shedlack, & France, 2006; Dangel, Deschner, & Rasp, 1989; Seay, Fee, Holloway, & Giesen, 2003). Camp (1977) and Camp et al. (1977) found that boys ages 5 to 8 years who exhibited aggressive behavior had developed fewer verbal mediation skills than their nonaggressive peers. After implementing a program to teach verbal mediation skills, the experimental group improved in the areas of verbal mediation and prosocial behavior. Chapman et al. (2006) found verbal mediation effective in adults with developmental disabilities when implemented in the form of self-instructional techniques. Verbal mediation has been effectively combined with other cognitive and behavioral techniques (e.g., problem solving, reinforcement, and relaxation training) to decrease aggression (Dangel et al., 1989; Seay et al., 2003).

The following studies summarize some of the key research findings associated with verbal mediation techniques and aggression.

Camp, B. W. (1977). Verbal mediation in young aggressive boys. *Journal of Abnormal Psychology, 86*(2), 145–153.

Based on the hypothesis that aggressive boys may have an ineffective linguistic control system, aggressive ($n = 49$) and non-aggressive ($n = 46$) first- and second-grade boys were given tests of verbal ability, self-guiding speech, nonverbal intelligence, reading achievement, impulsivity, ability to inhibit responses, and response modulation after overt and covert commands. Discriminant function analysis showed 88% of cases to be classified correctly. Variables with high scores that contributed to the aggressive classification were vocabulary, immature and irrelevant private speech, fast reaction times, baseline speed of finger tapping, inhibition errors, and speed of responding during covert commands for slowing. These results offered proof that self-speech could be a promising intervention.

Camp, B. W., Blom, G. E., Hebert, F., & van Doorninck, W. J. (1977). "Think aloud": A program for developing self-control in young aggressive boys. *Journal of Abnormal Child Psychology, 5*(2), 157–169.

This study tested whether "Think Aloud," a program to foster verbal mediation skills, would improve test performance and teacher ratings of classroom behavior in hyperaggressive boys. The trained group consisted of 12 second-grade boys who participated in 30-minute individual sessions daily for 6 weeks. The trained group and an aggressive control group had similar preintervention cognitive test scores. However, the postintervention cognitive scores of the trained group showed significant improvement, with a pattern resembling that of the normal control group rather than the aggressive control group. Both the trained and untrained groups received improved teacher ratings of aggression; however, teachers found improvement in a significantly larger number of prosocial factors in the trained group.

Dangel, R. F., Deschner, J. P., & Rasp, R. R. (1989). Anger control training for adolescents in residential treatment. *Behavior Modification, 13*(4), 447–458.

This study evaluated the effects of anger control training in 12 adolescents residing at a treatment center who had a history of aggression. A multiple baseline design was partially controlled for the effect of the residential treatment program. Anger control training, conducted in six 1-hour sessions over 5 weeks, included thought stopping, relaxation training, and problem-solving self-talk. Houseparents logged incidents of verbal and physical aggression, which had good interobserver reliability. Of the 10 adolescents who completed the study, 9 reduced their rates of aggression according to both observational data and teacher reports; one adolescent's aggression briefly increased but then decreased.

Seay, H. A., Fee, V. E., Holloway, K. S., & Giesen, J. M. (2003). A multicomponent treatment package to increase anger control in teacher-referred boys. *Child and Family Behavior Therapy, 25*(1), 1–18.

Multiple anger control techniques were combined in this study of 16 boys ages 7 to 10 years identified by teachers as having anger problems. The intervention included modeling, rehearsal with self-talk problem solving, daily report cards, and a praise phase, administered in two sessions per week for 3 weeks. Compared to controls, the boys who received training had significantly higher scores on the Aggression Control factor of the Olweus Aggression Inventory and the Compliment observation category at posttesting. Scores were significantly higher for controls than for treated boys on the Dislike Factor of the Peer Status Rating Scale-Child Report Form and the Threat observation category.

Considerations

For Teaching

Students will need opportunities to practice, and training and rehearsal would ideally be paired with a reinforcer, at least initially, until contingency reinforcers occur naturally. The skill sets associated with verbal mediation can be rehearsed with a variety of topics, not just aggression. The development of self-talk and the awareness of self-talk in general will improve a student's ability to create and use verbal scripting for aggression issues that are more difficult to address. Teacher modeling is helpful for this. Teachers can overtly engage in self-talk throughout the day to help students become more aware of how it can be applied when on his or her own. Students can also engage in revising internal speech by having "sessions" where they engage in an activity, talking out loud to themselves about each action.

For Age and Developmental Level

In using verbal mediation as an intervention for aggression, it is important to consider the verbal and cognitive abilities of the student. If the student's language abilities are limited, this intervention will be less functionally useful. However, if speech exists, students of all ages can benefit from this strategy. The naturally occurring nature of the self-speech makes it ideal as an intervention across the age spectrum because, although the complexity of the speech will certainly differ across ages, the mediating factors of the self-speech should not.

IV. Social Skills Training

Social skills generally refer to skills that enable effective functioning when interacting with others. Social skills have been defined by Gresham (1986) as having dimensions of peer acceptance, behavioral skills, and social validity. Social skills training or similar intervention programs generally present a child with a series of lessons, each targeting a specific social skill, so that the child can apply newly learned skills when opportunities arise.

For example, a first-grade student may grab objects from playmates rather than making requests or waiting his or her turn, a behavior that may be perceived as aggressive. Such behavior may be remediated through social skills training that focuses on developing skills associated with making requests and sharing. Or, a freshman in high school who frequently interrupts the conversations of others may experience social rejection and isolation that may result in aggressive or retaliatory responses toward those responsible for his dejected feelings. Such a student would benefit from learning specific conversation skills such as joining a conversation, taking turns in conversations, and/or active listening. In both scenarios, the skills learned in the lessons are expected to be practiced and applied or transferred to the next occurrence of an appropriate situation.

Oftentimes, aggressive behaviors in children are linked to the absence of particular social skills. This lack of social skills indicates a deficiency in the child's social competency.

While social skills and social competency may seem synonymous, they are not. Social competency is a construct that includes social skills as well as other important factors, such as positive relationships with others, accurate and age-appropriate social cognition, absence of maladaptive behaviors, and effective social behaviors (Vaughn & Hogan, 1990). Social competency, therefore, is necessary for successful treatment and remediation of aggressive behaviors.

Social competency is made up of discrete skills that must be taught in isolation but integrated seamlessly into the individual's life and actions. Typically, when a child lacks social competency his or her behavioral deficiency is addressed through a program of training based on a series of related skills. For example, it is insufficient to teach a child to "be nice," "behave," or "play fair" because the skill sets that make up "nice" and "fair," such as taking turns and sharing, have to be taught individually and then incorporated into the child's general behavior.

Implementation

Social skills training is used to develop skills that will enable children to engage in appropriate interactions with others. The major elements associated with many social skills training programs include the following:

1. Determination of social skill deficits

2. Demonstration of appropriate social skills via explanations and explicit modeling

3. Application of learned social skills in contrived scenarios

4. Administration of feedback and reinforcement for appropriate responses

5. Application of learned social skills in an actual situation

Social skills training is grounded in a behaviorist framework, placing a strong emphasis on behavior replacement training and differential reinforcement to distinguish inappropriate behavior from behaviors that exhibit strong social validity. These training programs often require a child to generate multiple strategies for engaging in appropriate social behavior. These strategies may include expressing empathy, becoming aware of the consequences of one's own and others' behavior, and identifying appropriate paths to reach desired goals.

There are many social skills improvement programs that have been developed, such as Skillstreaming (Goldstein, 1988), ACCEPTS (Walker et al., 1983), Teaching Social Skills (Rutherford, Chipman, DiGangi, & Anderson, 1992), and Connection (Johnson, Bullis, Mann, Benz, & Hollenbeck, 1999). (For others, see Alberg et al., 1994.) However, the basic procedural steps for applying social skills training to reduce aggressive behaviors can be implemented without the use of such formalized programs (see Figure 2.4).

Figure 2.4 Procedural steps for the application of social skills training

1. When implementing interventions in small groups, group children according to similar levels of social skills deficits.

2. Establish performance goals that are easy for children to achieve.

3. Set well-defined, clear boundaries for each goal by establishing consequences for aggressive behavior that exceeds the boundaries. Post the boundaries in a highly visible area.

4. Determine common social skills or social competency deficits (e.g., turn taking, being assertive, waiting patiently, responding politely to negative feedback) that may be responsible for triggering the child's aggressive actions and prioritize them for intervention.

5. Focus on teaching only one skill per session.

6. Facilitate the retention of learned behaviors by reviewing skills that were taught during previous intervention sessions.

7. When presenting the steps associated with the social skill being taught:

    a. Use visual representations of each step.

    b. Require steps to be written on note cards or paper.

    c. Require children to recite the steps verbally.

    d. Model the correct behavior associated with each step.

8. Engage children in a discussion (e.g., brainstorming) centered on recent events that required the use of the skill.

9. Encourage children to role-play the skill while others coach them.

10. Reinforce generalization of the skill by having the children record in a journal their experiences using the skill each day.

11. Distribute copies of the skill steps to the children's teachers and parents, and ask them to monitor and reinforce the appropriate use of the skill.

12. Maintain skill acquisition by holding periodic refresher sessions.

Evidence for Use

Social skills training has demonstrated success in treating a number of maladaptive behaviors, including physical and verbal aggression. Two factors that promote its success are programming for maintenance and generalization and the availability of natural reinforcers. As previously mentioned, social skills, as discrete behaviors, must be taught so as to allow children to generalize them, and they must have enough exemplars to be adaptable to a variety of appropriate situations. Therefore, particular attention must be paid to context. For example, the skills associated with handshaking as part of a greeting could be generalized for use in formal situations, such as job interviews, or meeting adults in social settings. However, such skills would not be as relevant for two fourth graders greeting each other on a playground. Similarly, teaching a child how to request a turn to speak to an adult respectfully, without interrupting, is an appropriate and expected skill for settings such as a restaurant or classroom but would not transfer to a pickup basketball game in a park.

The following studies summarize some of the key research findings associated with social skills training techniques and aggression.

Kavale, K. A., Mathur, S. R., Forness, S. R., Rutherford, R. B., & Quinn, M. M. (1997). Effectiveness of social skills training for students with behavior disorders: A meta-analysis. In T. E. Scruggs & M. A. Mastropieri (Eds.), *Advances in learning and behavioral disabilities* (Vol. 11, pp. 1–26). Greenwich, CT: JAI.

Although social skills training for children with emotional or behavioral problems is popular, this meta-analysis of group and single-subject research demonstrated small to moderate effects. For group designs, the synthesized data showed a small (0.199) training effect. It was determined that only about 58% of students would benefit from social skills training, and the gain would be a modest eight percentile ranks. For single-subject designs, the percentage of overlapping data was 62%, which indicated a modest effect.

Mathur, S. R., Kavale, K. A., Quinn, M. M., Forness, S. R., & Rutherford, R. B. (1998). Social skills interventions with students with emotional and behavioral problems: A quantitative synthesis of single-subject research. *Behavioral Disorders, 23*(3), 193–201.

A meta-analysis of single-subject design methodology included 64 studies that investigated the efficacy of social skills instruction. The studies included 283 participants with an average age of about 10 years and an average IQ of 87; 72% were boys. Evaluation of the proportion of nonoverlapping data between baseline and treatment showed the effects of instruction to be modest, with 62% of data not overlapping.

Quinn, M. M., Kavale, K. A., Mathur, S. R., Rutherford, R. B., & Forness, S. R. (1999). A meta-analysis of social skills interventions for students with emotional or behavioral disorders. *Journal of Emotional and Behavioral Disorders, 7*(1), 54–64.

A meta-analysis of 35 studies of social skill interventions in students with emotional or behavioral disorders resulted in a pooled mean effect size of 0.199. This indicated that the expected gain from training was a modest eight percentile ranks for the average student. Interventions that focused on teaching and measuring specific social skills, such as cooperation or social problem solving, had slightly larger effect sizes than those from more global interventions.

Schneider, B. H. (1991). A comparison of skill-building and desensitization strategies for intervention with aggressive children. *Aggressive Behavior, 17*(6), 301–311.

In this study, 41 institutionalized aggressive children ages 7 to 13 years were randomly assigned to treatment that included cognitive–behavioral skill building or desensitization/imagery techniques. Role-play assessment showed that the skill-building group mastered 84% of their training objectives. Analysis of behavioral observations on the playground showed significant reduction in aggression and significant increase in cooperative play for both groups. When difference scores were analyzed, reduction in aggression was significantly greater in the skill-building group, but gains in cooperative play were similar between groups.

Sukhodolsky, D. G., Golub, A., Stone, E. C., & Orban, L. (2005). Dismantling anger control training for children: A randomized pilot study of social problem-solving versus social skills training components. *Behavior Therapy, 36*(1), 15–23.

This study (also annotated in the problem-solving intervention previously presented) compared two methods of anger control training in 26 boys (mean age of about 10 years) with excessive anger, aggression, and disruptive behavior. One group received treatment that targeted social problem-solving skills, while the other group received treatment that focused on social skills training. Both methods were shown to be equally effective in reducing aggression and improving relationships with parents. Social skills training was shown to be more effective in improving anger control skills, while problem solving was more effective in reducing hostile attributional bias.

Considerations

For Teaching

Instructors should allow time for modeling and guided practice when planning to implement social skills training. Students need to learn by doing, primarily through role-play and frequent practice situations. Teacher behavior may affect student outcomes (Frey, Hirschstein, & Guzzo, 2000), so social skills modeling throughout a school day will serve to strengthen students' skills. Supportive, nurturing practices are also critical for successful outcomes of social skills training, as are teachers who present opportunities for students to use social skills. For example, instruction in how to hang out after school may not show up on a teacher's top 10 list of important lessons, but it is important for the student struggling with social skills and, therefore, should be identified as such. Additionally, generic application of social skills training to groups of students prevents individual students from being stigmatized and reduces violence and aggression across the population. Individual targeting and lengthening of treatment will increase results for individuals.

For Age and Developmental Level

Many students' social skills are limited by lack of experience or age-appropriate training. For children with autism or other developmental disabilities, social skills are affected by more profound circumstances. While reinforcers that trigger aggression often become evident during typical interventions, they may not apply to treatments for some children. A child with disabilities or social skills that differ drastically from those of his or her peers may not experience the benefits of treatment (e.g., an increase in friends, greater social understanding). Therefore, social skills training, although necessary in its own right, may not be the most effective intervention for aggression in every case.

V. Peer-Mediated Conflict Resolution and Negotiation

Peer-mediated conflict resolution and negotiation is a schoolwide program of training that uses students as arbitrators who negotiate and resolve conflict among peers. A small group of students, representing a cross section of the student population, undergoes training and members then serve as peer mediators. Students or adults may refer cases for peer-mediated conflict resolution and negotiation, and participation in the program is voluntary.

For example, two girls have a disagreement over who was invited to a party. This disagreement results in repeated fighting and begins to involve larger circles of girls. A teacher completes a referral and sends the girls to peer-mediated conflict resolution and negotiation. Trained peer mediators meet with the girls, help resolve the conflict, and make follow-up contact.

Implementation

The goal of peer-mediated conflict resolution and negotiation is to empower students to handle conflicts and misunderstandings. When peers mediate, school contexts and youth perspectives are naturally incorporated into negotiations. Peers may have unique vantage points from which to address the issues that arise for kids in schools. The basic elements of a peer-mediated conflict resolution and negotiation approach include the following:

1. Selection and training of students for conflict resolution training

2. Raising awareness of the program among students and school staff members

3. Facilitation and support of referrals by teachers or students to peer mediators

4. Supervision of peer mediators by school staff members

An outline of the procedures for implementing peer-mediated conflict resolution is presented in Figure 2.5. A peer-mediated program can have a powerful impact on a school campus when adequate time and care are involved in its initiation; therefore, these programs require a heavier time investment on the front end (i.e., during the organizational planning stages). Peer mediation is only as good as the training, support, and supervision provided by the adult coach, and this intervention should be integrated into the school climate to be effective.

Figure 2.5 Procedural steps for the application of peer-mediated conflict resolution and negotiation

1. Acquire program approval from building-level administration.

2. Identify adult leaders who demonstrate a strong commitment to managing and monitoring the program.

3. Create a committee (e.g., faculty, administration, and parents) that will make decisions about curriculum delivery and the selection of peer mediators.

4. Select a small group of students who will commit to serve as peer mediators; the group should represent the student population with respect to age, grade, race/ethnicity, socioeconomic level, language, and other relevant characteristics.

5. Train all program members in mediation processes, which include active listening, communication, problem solving, negotiation, conflict resolution, and social skills. Basic steps include teaching mediation and negotiation through role-playing. Training ranges from 2-day intensive workshops (see The National Association for Mediation in Education) to 20 hours of training delivered in 30-minute sessions (see Johnson & Johnson, 1991).

6. Establish logistical procedures for the program, including the referral process, availability of and access to peer mediators, and any other necessary requirements for your campus.

7. Announce the program schoolwide and explain the process for referrals and handling conflict. This can be done in an assembly or as a general announcement. Students and teachers who will participate in the program need to understand how the process will work.

8. Utilize frequent check-ins with those involved in the process and data collection to determine program effectiveness and further training needs.

Evidence for Use

Peer-mediated conflict resolution and negotiation appears to be an effective strategy for resolving disputes between students. In their studies of schoolwide peer mediation, Daunic, Smith, Robinson, Miller, and Landry (2000) and Smith et al. (2002) report that 95% of referred conflicts reached agreement through avoidance or ending the offending behavior. Further, disciplinary incidents declined at two of three middle schools where the programs were implemented, and high levels of satisfaction were reported with the processes and results. Johnson et al. (1995) found after teaching conflict resolution skills that 40% of conflicts were resolved through negotiation. Stevahn et al. (2002) found increased academic success in first through ninth grade students when conflict resolution was integrated into the social studies curriculum.

The following studies summarize some of the key research findings associated with peer-mediated conflict resolution and negotiation and aggression.

Johnson, D. W., Cotten, B., Johnson, R., Harris, D., Mitchell, J., & Louison, S. (1996). Effectiveness of conflict managers in an inner-city elementary school. *Journal of Educational Research, 89*(5), 280–285.

In this study of an underperforming inner-city elementary school, 47 boys and girls in Grades 3 and 4 volunteered to participate in a peer mediation program and received one and a half days of training in communication, assertiveness, and mediation skills. They mediated conflicts in pairs and completed a mediation report form that provided data on types of conflict, resolution strategies, agreements resulting from mediation, and sex of the disputants. Over the school year, the pairs mediated 343 conflicts and were successful 98% of the time. Most conflicts (87%) arose from relationship issues that led to physical or verbal aggression. Physical or verbal force was the strategy most commonly (91%) used to resolve conflict, and agreement to avoid each other was the most common (84%) solution.

Johnson, D. W., Johnson, R., Dudley, B., Ward, M., & Magnuson, D. (1995). The impact of peer mediation training on the management of school and home conflicts. *American Educational Research Journal, 32*(4), 829–844.

This study examined conflict types and resolution strategies used at school and at home in a sample of students from a suburban Midwestern elementary school. A group of 144 students received nine hours of peer mediation training; 83 students served as controls. Data were obtained from conflict report forms that teachers asked students to complete about any conflicts they experienced at school or home. Of the 783 conflicts reported, 209 occurred at school and 574 at home. The majority of conflicts (74%) arose over preferences and possession/access, although these types were more frequent at school than at home. Compared to the control group, trained students were more likely to use negotiation instead of force as a strategy and to achieve integrative agreement.

Lindsay, P. (1998). Conflict resolution and peer mediation in public schools: What works? *Mediation Quarterly, 16*(1), 85–99.

The author evaluated the effectiveness of conflict resolution and peer mediation programs in 14 elementary, middle, and high schools. Data from these schools were compared to a control sample of three schools that did not offer similar programs. Interviews and surveys of teachers and other school personnel provided both qualitative and quantitative data. Perception of the effect of these programs on discipline and curriculum was generally positive. Of questionnaire respondents, 38% believed fighting at their school decreased and 53% believed their school was safer. Respondents also perceived a positive effect on school culture in terms of students taking responsibility for their actions. The two problems in teaching conflict resolution that were mentioned most often concerned time constraints and influence of family and society.

Smith, S. W., Daunic, A. P., Miller, M. D., & Robinson, T. R. (2002). Conflict resolution and peer mediation in middle schools: Extending the process and outcome knowledge base. *The Journal of Social Psychology, 142*(5), 567–586.

This 4-year study in three middle schools consisted of a schoolwide conflict resolution curriculum and peer mediation training of 25 to 30 students per school. To evaluate the curriculum and peer mediation approach, the authors gathered school climate ratings from teachers and students, tracked disciplinary incidents, collected mediation data, and compared mediators with a matched sample to measure attitudinal change. Results showed no evidence of schoolwide change in student attitudes or teacher views of school climate. However, a promising downward trend in disciplinary incidents was noted at two of the three schools, and both trained mediators and those who had been referred for mediation were highly satisfied with the mediation process.

Stevahn, L., Johnson, D. W., Johnson, R. T., & Schultz, R. (2002). Effects of conflict resolution training integrated into a high school social studies curriculum. *Journal of Social Psychology, 142*(3), 305–331.

In this study, two of four social studies classes from a California high school received conflict resolution and peer mediation training as part of their class curriculum over a 5-week period. The other two classes served as controls. Results showed training to be effective in reducing conflict and promoting academic achievement. Compared to controls, trained students were more successful in learning integrative negotiation and peer mediation procedures, applying these procedures, choosing an integrative approach to negotiation over a distributive one, and developing positive attitudes toward conflict. In addition, they showed greater long-term retention of academic learning and greater transfer of learning from social studies to language arts.

Considerations

For Teaching

Teachers are most supportive when they are involved and informed of the process of peer mediation. This intervention is largely dependent on the support of building-level administration and faculty to refer and support the peer mediators. Teams of individuals who sponsor and advise these peer mediators and the process will assist in the successful maintenance of the program. Be aware that some children may be resistant to participating and helping resolve conflict due to their participation in a student group (e.g., a gang). Such groups can cause problems that will require intervention beyond peer mediation.

For Culture and Language Differences

Social acceptability may be limited for some students based on their need for social independence. Recognize that cultural differences influence how groups identify, perceive, and manage conflict. What is conflict for one may not be conflict for another, and identifying cultural expectations for conflict resolution is helpful and easily handled in this peer format.

For Age and Developmental Level

Peer mediation has been typically used at the middle and high school levels; in some cases, it may be appropriate for upper elementary students. Children who are very young may not benefit from the approach, as they are not developmentally ready to understand conflict from another person's point of view.

VI. Replacement Behavior Training

Replacement behavior training focuses on teaching new skills and behaviors that can be used to replace undesirable behaviors. Replacement behaviors are taught and reinforced to promote their adoption, maintenance, and generalization. When dealing with aggression, the aggressive behavior (e.g., hitting or name calling) is replaced with an alternative behavior that fulfills the same need for the individual. The replacement behavior is thought to be functionally equivalent to the initial behavior because it serves a similar purpose and allows the individual access to the same or greater contingencies of reinforcement.

For example, an elementary school student who frequently hits other students to gain attention from peers would be taught new verbal skills that would be used to replace the aggressive behavior. Use of these new verbal skills would enable the student to receive attention from the teacher and classmates without having to hit others. Or, a high school student may verbally assault teachers and peers when frustrated, resulting in an escape from the task or situation that is causing the frustration. This student would be taught an appropriate method of escaping the situation, such as asking to be excused or verbalizing frustration, along with a replacement strategy for tolerating the frustration. Reinforcement would take the form of allowing the escape when appropriately sought.

Reinforcement is central to teaching replacement behaviors. Initially, replacement behaviors are reinforced at a 1:1 ratio of reinforcement for each occurrence of the new behavior. This reinforcement schedule should be faded slowly over time (e.g., to a 1:2 and then a 1:4 ratio) while watching for natural contingencies of reinforcement (e.g., teacher praise, new friends, better grades). If natural contingencies do not occur, artificial reinforcers should be maintained. Another key component in replacement behavior techniques is the identification of antecedents to the problem behavior. Similar to the process in other intervention techniques like frustration management training, relaxation training, and assertiveness training (Colter & Guerra, 1976; Wilkinson & Canter, 1982; Wolpe & Lazurus, 1966), identifying antecedents can help students recognize when a situation is primed for engaging in an undesirable behavior. This recognition can serve as a prompt or stimulus for the student to use the newly learned behavior that is more appropriate for the situation.

Implementation

The goal of implementing replacement behavior training is to reduce aggressive behavior by teaching and reinforcing (immediate reinforcement with gradual fading) an alternate behavior that serves the same function (i.e., meets the same need) as the aggressive behavior. The basic elements of replacement behavior training techniques include the following:

1. Administration of a functional behavioral assessment (FBA)

   a. Creation of an operational definition of the aggressive behavior

   b. Identification of the settings, antecedents, and consequences contributing to or resulting from the aggressive behavior

   c. Identification of the behavior's function (e.g., to escape or avoid, tangible reward, stimulation)

   d. Selection of a replacement behavior that will serve the same function

   e. Selection of the potential reinforcers

2. Evaluation of FBA data and implementation plan, and revision as necessary

An outline of the procedures for implementing replacement behavior training is presented in Figure 2.6. To some degree, replacement behavior training has its roots in basic applied behavior analysis and as such is successful largely based on the ability to identify contingencies in the environment that trigger and support the aggressive behavior. Individuals with applied behavior analysis training may be able to do this more efficiently than teacher teams; however, the skill set is not especially complex. Identifying the setting events and the antecedents to the behavior will inform the function of the behavior (i.e., escaping a person or task versus access to a tangible or social reinforcer). Likewise, identifying the consequences (e.g., class laughter and attention for talking back to the teacher, lack of consequences for failure to do homework or class assignments) that maintain the behavior will typically be helpful for managing the aggression.

Teacher behavior and task demands are frequently found to be antecedents for certain types of maladaptive behaviors. However, eliminating task demands is not the preferred choice to manage aggression for escape. Instead, finding ways to minimize the frustration of the task demand is the critical change needed (e.g., providing choices or quick access to help). Finally, matching the effort coefficient in the replacement behavior is paramount. For example, a student who aggresses by throwing a pencil to get immediate teacher attention and assistance or to avoid an aversive task will not find writing an essay on why he needs help or filling out a problem-solving worksheet to be a functionally equivalent behavioral replacement. Both these behaviors require much more effort. Likewise, raising a hand and waiting 10 minutes for help is less efficient for the student than throwing the pencil and receiving immediate assistance.

Figure 2.6 Procedural steps for the application of replacement behavior training

1. Conduct a functional behavioral assessment using a team approach when appropriate (i.e., obtain input from parents, teachers, authority figures, administrators, and any other key stakeholders) to determine the function of the aggressive behavior.

2. Review the problem behavior with the child (when appropriate) to reach an agreement on the nature of it.

3. Identify and teach the child several replacement behaviors that will be suitable for eliminating the aggressive behavior and the reinforcers to support them. These behaviors may include:

    a. functional communication, such as pictorial representations or sign language

    b. effective social skills (e.g., clarifying another person's complaints or anger, expressing anger)

4. Work with the child to determine the appropriate use of the replacement behavior and the antecedents that may prompt it; this may include developing temporary prompts from teachers or others that can be used to help the child identify when to use a replacement behavior.

5. Model the replacement behavior (and antecedent, if one is used) for the child.

6. Allow the child to demonstrate understanding of and ability to perform the new behavior.

7. Let all adults who may be working with the child know what the appropriate replacement behaviors are so behaviors can be monitored and generalized across settings (e.g., home, extracurricular activities, cafeteria, library, and community).

8. Gradually fade prompts being given by teachers or others.

9. Reinforce new behaviors using a 1:1 ratio initially, and then gradually fade the reinforcement.

Evidence for Use

Replacement behavior training has been demonstrated to be an effective intervention for remediating aggressive behavior. Differential reinforcement (i.e., reinforcing the use of the replacement behavior) and noncontingent reinforcers (i.e., providing reinforcement if the undesirable behavior does not occur, even if the replacement behaviors are not seen) have been found to be very effective for decreasing aggressive acts, including self-injury, with a variety of individuals (Fischer, Iwata, & Mazalesk, 1997; Friman, Barnard, Altman, & Wolf, 1986; Hegel & Ferguson, 2000; Lerman, Kelley, Vorndran, Kuhn, & Larue, 2002; Repp & Deitz, 1974).

The following studies summarize some of the key research findings associated with replacement behavior training and aggression.

Fischer, S. M., Iwata, B. A., & Mazalesk, J. L. (1997). Noncontingent delivery of arbitrary reinforcers as treatment for self-injurious behavior. *Journal of Applied Behavior Analysis, 30*(2), 239–249.

This study examined the effects of noncontingent reinforcement (NCR) in reducing the frequency of self-injurious behavior (SIB) in individuals with developmental disabilities. A functional analysis was done to determine which reinforcers could serve as arbitrary or direct reinforcers. These two types of reinforcers were then presented either contingently or noncontingently. The results of this study demonstrated that noncontingent delivery of the arbitrary reinforcers was effective in reducing incidences of SIB. The authors conclude that arbitrary noncontingent reinforcers can be useful when reinforcers cannot be identified, as might be the case for behavior that is maintained by automatic reinforcement (i.e., situations in which behavior is maintained by operant mechanisms independent of the social environment).

Friman, P. C., Barnard, J. D., Altman, K., & Wolf, M. W. (1986). Parent and teacher use of DRO and DRI to reduce aggressive behavior. *Analysis and Intervention in Developmental Disabilities, 6*(4), 319–330.

This study examined the effects of using DRO (differential reinforcement of other behavior) and DRI (differential reinforcement of incompatible behavior) to decrease aggressive pinching in a child with severe mental retardation. In the DRO condition, a reinforcer was given for each interval in which no pinching occurred. This reinforcement decreased pinching from 50% of the intervals to near zero. The DRI condition involved reinforcement with food and drink at mealtime whenever the subject's hands were in a position that was incompatible with pinching. Use of DRI also reduced instances of pinching to near zero. This study demonstrated that use of reinforcement-based behavioral procedures can decrease aggressive behavior in both a home and school setting.

Lerman, D. C., Kelley, M. E., Vorndran, C. M., Kuhn, S. A., & Larue, R. H. (2002). Reinforcement magnitude and responding during treatment with differential reinforcement. *Journal of Applied Behavior Analysis, 35*(1), 29–48.

The two experiments described here were part of a preliminary evaluation of whether the magnitude of reinforcement alters response to treatment with differential reinforcement of alternative behavior (DRA). The first experiment evaluated the effects of two reinforcement magnitudes (e.g., being allowed to play with an object for 20 seconds vs. 60 seconds) on resistance to extinction by reinforcing and extinguishing communication responses after the responses had been acquired in treatment. In the second experiment, the effects of reinforcement magnitude on characteristics of responding were evaluated during the maintenance of communication responses. Results in the three patients studied indicated that reinforcement magnitude provided some resistance to extinction.

Repp, A. C., & Deitz, S. M. (1974). Reducing aggressive and self-injurious behavior of institutionalized retarded children through reinforcement of other behaviors. *Journal of Applied Behavior Analysis, 7*(2), 313–325.

This study sought to determine whether combining the DRO (differential reinforcement of other behavior) procedure with other techniques would make it more successful in reducing aggressive and self-injurious behaviors in children with mental retardation. In the 4 children studied, the DRO procedure was combined with either mild verbal punishment, a brief timeout, instructions, or response cost, resulting in a reduction in aggressive responses.

Considerations

For Teaching

In using replacement behavior training as an intervention for aggression, it is important to consider the function of the maladaptive behavior, the effort that will be expended in learning and using a new behavior, and the ability of the new behavior to provide the same benefit as the maladaptive behavior provided. In addition, when using this intervention the teacher must recognize that, by definition, a reinforcer is something reinforcing to that specific child. Therefore, the person distributing the reinforcer should be aware of reinforcement saturation. For example, a student who has 10 chocolate bars in her lunch may not be motivated by a small treat from the teacher. Likewise, peer attention will only be effective as a motivator while one has control over it. The strength of the reinforcer should also be considered. A student who ditches class to spend time with a boyfriend may not be interested in a candy bar for staying in class.

For Age and Developmental Level

Inadequate functional language and communication abilities are often precursors to aggressive behaviors. Language abilities should be assessed and, when determined to be a contributing factor in the aggressive behavior, communication skills (verbal or pictorial) should be a primary replacement.

Summary

This chapter presented a review of the characteristics of and conditions for problems related to aggressive behavior, along with a summary of interventions that have been shown to be effective in remediation of such problems. These interventions included problem-solving training, cognitive restructuring, verbal mediation, social skills training, peer-mediated conflict resolution and negotiation, and replacement behavior training. While each intervention presented differs in its application of one or more behavioral, cognitive–behavioral, or social learning theories, all are shaped by the fundamental goals of treatment: prevention and remediation of problem behaviors. The information presented in this chapter forms the basis of the supplemental classroom- and home-based materials that correspond to this book.

References

Alberg, J., Petry, C. A, Eller, S., Warger, C. L., Cook, B., & Cross, D. (1994). *The social skills planning guide*. Longmont, CO: Sopris West.

Baddeley, A. D., & Hitch, G. J. (1974). Working memory. In G.A. Bower (Ed.), *Recent advances in learning and motivation*, (Vol. 8, pp. 47–89). New York: Academic Press.

Bandura, A. (1986). *Social foundations of thought and action: A social cognitive theory*. Englewood Cliffs, NJ: Prentice Hall.

Berk, L. (1992). Children's private speech: An overview of theory and the status of research. In R. M. Diaz & L. E. Berk (Eds.), *Private speech: From social interaction to self-regulation* (pp. 17–53). Hillsdale, NJ: Erlbaum.

Camp, B. W. (1977). Verbal mediation in young aggressive boys. *Journal of Abnormal Psychology, 86*(2), 145–153.

Camp, B. W., Blom, G. E., Hebert, F., & van Doorninck, W. J. (1977). "Think aloud": A program for developing self-control in young aggressive boys. *Journal of Abnormal Child Psychology, 5*(2), 157–169.

Chapman, R. A., Shedlack, K. J., & France, J. (2006). Stop-think-relax: An adapted self-control training strategy for individuals with mental retardation and coexisting psychiatric illness. *Cognitive and Behavioral Practice, 13*(3), 205–214.

Colter, S. B., & Guerra, J. J. (1976). *Assertion training: A humanistic-behavioral guide to self-dignity*. Champaign, IL: Research Press.

Conduct Problems Prevention Research Group (1999). Initial impact of the Fast Track prevention trial for conduct problems: II. Classroom effects. *Journal of Consulting and Clinical Psychology, 67*(5), 648–657.

Dangel, R. F., Deschner, J. P., & Rasp, R. R. (1989). Anger control training for adolescents in residential treatment. *Behavior Modification, 13*(4), 447–458.

Daunic, A. P., Smith, S. W., Brank, E. M., & Penfield, R. D. (2006). Classroom-based cognitive–behavioral intervention to prevent aggression: Efficacy and social validity. *Journal of School Psychology, 44*(2), 123–139.

Daunic, A. P., Smith, S. W., Robinson, T. R., Miller, M. D., & Landry, K. L. (2000). School-wide conflict resolution and peer mediation programs: Experiences in three middle schools. *Intervention in School and Clinic, 36*(2), 94–100.

Dodge, K. A., & Coie, J. D. (1987). Social-information-processing factors in reactive and proactive aggression in children's peer groups. *Journal of Personality and Social Psychology, 53*(6), 1146–1158.

Ellis, A. (1962). *Reason and emotion in psychotherapy*. New York: Lyle Stuart.

Ellis, A. (1986). An emotional control card for inappropriate and appropriate emotions in using rational-emotive imagery. *Journal of Counseling and Development, 65*(4), 205–206.

Fischer, S. M., Iwata, B. A., & Mazalesk, J. L. (1997). Noncontingent delivery of arbitrary reinforcers as treatment for self-injurious behavior. *Journal of Applied Behavior Analysis, 30*(2), 239–249.

Frey, K. S., Hirschstein, M. K., & Guzzo, B. (2000). Second step: Preventing aggression by promoting social competence. *Journal of Emotional and Behavioral Disorders, 8*(2), 102–112.

Friman, P. C., Barnard, J. D., Altman, K., & Wolf, M. W. (1986). Parent and teacher use of DRO and DRI to reduce aggressive behavior. *Analysis and Intervention in Developmental Disabilities, 6*(4), 319–330.

Goldstein, A. P. (1988). *The prepare curriculum: Teaching prosocial competencies.* Champaign, IL: Research Press.

Goldstein, A. P., Glick B., & Gibbs, J. C. (1998). *Aggression replacement training: A comprehensive intervention for aggressive youth* (Rev. ed.). Champaign, IL: Research Press.

Goldstein, S. (1995). *Understanding and managing children's classroom behavior.* New York: John Wiley & Sons.

Gresham, F. M. (1986). Conceptual and definitional issues in the assessment of children's social skills: Implications for classification and training. Social Skills Training [Special issue]. *Journal of Clinical Child Psychology, 15*(1), 3–15.

Guerra, N. G., & Slaby, R. G. (1990). Cognitive mediators of aggression in adolescent offenders: 2. Intervention. *Developmental Psychology, 26*(2), 269–277.

Harris, K. R., Wong, B. L., & Keosh, B. K. (Eds.). (1985). Cognitive-behavior modification with children: A critical review of the state of the art. (Special issue). Journal of Abnormal Child Psychology, 13(3), 329–476.

Hegel, M. T., & Ferguson, R. J. (2000). Differential reinforcement of other behavior to reduce aggressive behavior following traumatic brain injury. *Behavior Modification, 24*(1), 94–101.

Henggeler, S. W., Schoenwald, S. K., Borduin, C. M., Rowland, M. D., & Cunningham, P. B. (1998). *Multisystemic treatment of antisocial behavior in children and adolescents.* New York: Guilford.

Hinshaw, S. P., & Erhardt, D. (1991). Attention deficit-hyperactivity disorder. In P. C. Kendall (Ed.), *Child and adolescent therapy: Cognitive-behavioral procedures* (pp. 98–128). New York: Guilford.

Hudley, C., & Friday, J. (1996). Attributional bias and reactive aggression. *American Journal of Preventive Medicine, 12*(Suppl. 1), 75–81.

Hudley, C., & Graham, S. (1993). An attributional intervention to reduce peer-directed aggression among African-American boys. *Child Development, 64*(1), 124–138.

Jackson, D. A., Jackson, N. F., & Bennett, M. L. (1998). *Teaching social competence to youth and adults with developmental disabilities: A comprehensive program.* Austin, TX: ProEd.

Johnson, D. W., Cotten, B., Johnson, R., Harris, D., Mitchell, J., & Louison, S. (1996). Effectiveness of conflict managers in an inner-city elementary school. *Journal of Educational Research, 89*(5), 280–285.

Johnson, D. W., & Johnson, R. (1991). *Teaching students to be peacemakers.* Edina, MN: Interaction Book Company.

Johnson, D. W., Johnson, R., Dudley, B., Ward, M., & Magnuson, D. (1995). The impact of peer mediation training on the management of school and home conflicts. *American Educational Research Journal, 32*(4), 829–844.

Johnson, M., Bullis, M., Mann, S., Benz, M., & Hollenbeck, K. (1999). *The CONNECTIONS curriculum.* Eugene: Institute on Violence and Destructive Behavior, College of Education, University of Oregon.

Kaplan, J., & Carter, J. (1995). Beyond behavior modification: A cognitive–behavioral approach to behavior management in the school (3rd ed.). Austin, TX: Pro-Ed.

Kavale, K. A., Mathur, S. R., Forness, S. R., Rutherford, R. B., & Quinn, M. M. (1997). Effectiveness of social skills training for students with behavior disorders: A meta-analysis. In T. E. Scruggs & M. A. Mastropieri (Eds.), *Advances in learning and behavioral disabilities* (Vol. 11, pp. 1–26). Greenwich, CT: JAI.

Kazdin, A. E., Siegel, T. C., & Bass, D. (1992). Cognitive problem-solving skills training and parent management training in the treatment of antisocial behavior in children. *Journal of Consulting and Clinical Psychology, 60*(5), 733–747.

Lerman, D. C., Kelley, M. E., Vorndran, C. M., Kuhn, S. A., & Larue, R. H. (2002). Reinforcement magnitude and responding during treatment with differential reinforcement. *Journal of Applied Behavior Analysis, 35*(1), 29–48.

Lindsay, P. (1998). Conflict resolution and peer mediation in public schools: What works? *Mediation Quarterly, 16*(1), 85–99.

Lochman, J. E., Burch, P. R., Curry, J. F., & Lampron, L. B. (1984). Treatment and generalization effects of cognitive–behavioral and goal-setting interventions with aggressive boys. *Journal of Consulting and Clinical Psychology, 52*(5), 915–916.

Mathur, S. R., Kavale, K. A., Quinn, M. M., Forness, S. R., & Rutherford, R. B. (1998). Social skills interventions with students with emotional and behavioral problems: A quantitative synthesis of single-subject research. *Behavioral Disorders, 23*(3), 193–201.

Meichenbaum, D. (1977). *Cognitive–behavior modification: An integrative approach.* New York: Plenum Press.

Meichenbaum, D. (1985). *Stress inoculation training.* New York: Pergamon.

Pecukonis, E. V. (1990). A cognitive/affective empathy training program as a function of ego development in aggressive adolescent females. *Adolescence, 25*(97), 59–76.

Polsgrove, L., & Smith, S. (2004). Informed practice in teaching students self-control. In R. Rutherford, Jr., M. Quinn, & S. Mathur (Eds.), *Handbook of Research in Emotional and Behavioral Disorders* (pp. 399–425). New York: Guilford.

Quinn, M. M., Kavale, K. A., Mathur, S. R., Rutherford, R. B., & Forness, S. R. (1999). A meta-analysis of social skills interventions for students with emotional or behavioral disorders. *Journal of Emotional and Behavioral Disorders, 7*(1), 54–64.

Repp, A. C., & Deitz, S. M. (1974). Reducing aggressive and self-injurious behavior of institutionalized retarded children through reinforcement of other behaviors. *Journal of Applied Behavior Analysis, 7*(2), 313–325.

Reynolds, C. R. & Fletcher-Janzen, E. (Eds.). (2007). Encyclopedia of special education: A reference for the education of children, adolescents, and adults with disabilities and other exceptional individuals (3rd ed., Vol. 1). New York: John Wiley & Sons.

Reynolds, C. R., & Kamphaus, R. W. (2004). *Behavior Assessment System for Children* (2nd ed.). Circle Pines, MN: AGS Publishing.

Rutherford, R., Chipman, J., DiGangi, S., & Anderson, C. (1992). *Teaching social skills: A practical instructional approach.* Reston, VA: Exceptional Innovations.

Schneider, B. H. (1991). A comparison of skill-building and desensitization strategies for intervention with aggressive children. *Aggressive Behavior, 17*(6), 301–311.

Seay, H. A., Fee, V. E., Holloway, K. S., & Giesen, J. M. (2003). A multicomponent treatment package to increase anger control in teacher-referred boys. *Child and Family Behavior Therapy, 25*(1), 1–18.

Skinner, B. F. (1953). *Science and Human Behavior.* New York: Macmillan.

Smith, S. W., Daunic, A. P., Miller, M. D. & Robinson, T. R. (2002). Conflict resolution and peer mediation in middle schools: Extending the process and outcome knowledge base. *Journal of Social Psychology, 142*(5), 567–586.

Stevahn, L., Johnson, D. W., Johnson, R. T., & Schultz, R. (2002). Effects of conflict resolution training integrated into a high school social studies curriculum. *Journal of Social Psychology, 142*(3), 305–331.

Sukhodolsky, D. G., Golub, A., Stone, E. C., & Orban, L. (2005). Dismantling anger control training for children: A randomized pilot study of social problem-solving versus social skills training components. *Behavior Therapy, 36*(1), 15–23.

Vaughn, S., & Hogan, A. (1990). Social competence and learning disabilities: A prospective study. In H. L. Swanson & B. Keogh (Eds.), *Learning disabilities: Theoretical and research issues* (pp. 175–191). Hillsdale, NJ: Erlbaum.

Vygotsky, L. S. (1978). *Mind in society: The development of higher mental processes* (M. Cole, V. John-Steiner, S. Scribner, & E. Souberman, Eds. & Trans.). Cambridge, MA: Harvard University Press. (Original work published 1930, 1933, & 1935)

Vygotsky, L. S. (1987). Thinking and speech. In R. W. Rieber & A. S. Carton (Eds.), *The collected works of L. S. Vygotsky: Vol. 1* (pp. 37–285). New York: Plenum Press. (Original work published 1934)

Walen, S. R., DiGiuseppe, R., & Wessler, R. (1980). *A practitioner's guide to rational-emotive therapy* (1st ed.). New York: Oxford University Press.

Walker, H. M., McConnell, S., Holmes, D., Todis, B., Walker, J., & Golden, N. (1983). The Walker social skills curriculum: The ACCEPTS program. Austin, TX: Pro-Ed.

Weiner, B. (1985). An attributional theory of achievement motivation and emotion. *Psychological Review, 92*(4), 548–573.

Wessler, R. A., & Wessler, R. L. (1980). *The principles and practice of rational-emotive therapy* (1st ed.). San Francisco: Proquest Info & Learning.

Wilkinson, J., & Canter, S. (1982). *Social skills training manual: Assessment, program design, and management of training.* New York: Wiley.

Wolpe, J., & Lazarus, A. (1966). *Behavior therapy techniques: A guide to the treatment of neuroses.* New York: Pergamon Press.

Young, H. S. (1977). Counseling strategies with working class adolescents. In J. L. Wolfe & E. Brand (Eds.), *Twenty years of rational therapy: Proceedings of the first national conference on rational psychotherapy.* New York: Institute for Rational Living.

Chapter 3

Interventions for Conduct Problems

This chapter, which focuses on interventions for children and adolescents identified as at risk for or expressing conduct problems, has three major sections. First, the characteristics and conditions for the socially deviant and disruptive behaviors that are most commonly referred to as conduct disorder (Reynolds & Kamphaus, 2004) are briefly presented, along with sample items from the BASC–2 Conduct Problems scale. Second, the theoretical framework for approaching conduct problems interventions is described. Third, interventions that have evidence or show promise for remediating conduct problems (including those that are multimodal and multisystemic) are described. Each presentation provides an overview of the intervention method and is divided into three subsections: Implementation, Evidence for Use, and Considerations. The chapter's three main sections provide the foundation on which additional BASC–2 intervention components are built, including both classroom-based and home-based strategies.

Characteristics and Conditions of Conduct Problems

Conduct disorder, as named in the *Diagnostic and Statistical Manual of Mental Disorders, Fourth Edition, Text Revision* (*DSM–IV®–TR*; American Psychiatric Association, 2000), is a childhood behavior disorder characterized by aggressive and destructive activities that interfere with successful life functioning. Children and adolescents with conduct disorder usually exhibit a repetitive and persistent pattern of behaviors that violate societal norms and the rights of other people. With rates of occurrence estimated at 9% for males and 2% for females, conduct disorder is one of the most prevalent categories of mental health problems of children in the United States (Thackery, 2003). The *DSM–IV–TR* assigns behaviors associated with conduct disorder to one of four categories: aggressive conduct, nonaggressive conduct, deceitfulness and theft, and rule violations. Aggressive conduct includes overt antisocial behaviors such as tantrums, destruction of property, fighting, assaulting or causing physical harm to others, bullying, using weapons, threatening or intimidating others, stealing with victim confrontation, sexual misconduct, setting fires with the intent of destroying property, and cruelty to people and/or animals. Nonaggressive conduct includes overt antisocial behaviors such as seeking revenge, substance abuse, and classroom disruption. Deceitfulness and theft include behaviors such as lying to attain tangibles or intangibles, stealing without victim confrontation, and lying to avoid responsibility or to escape consequences. Rule violations include breaking or disregarding rules established by the law, institutions (e.g., schools), and parents or guardians, including disobedience, breaking and entering without victim confrontation, school truancy, and running away. The BASC–2 Conduct Problems scale includes a selection of items that measure aspects from each of the four categories. Sample items include: "Breaks the rules," "Steals," and "Uses others' things without permission" (Reynolds & Kamphaus, 2004).

Dealing with children and adolescents with conduct problems can be extremely challenging and frustrating for professionals and caregivers. There is enormous resistance to change, in part due to the intrinsically rewarding nature of these behaviors for the individuals (Frick, 2006; Tarolla, Wagner, Rabinowitz, & Tubman, 2002). These change-resistant and stable behaviors are symptoms of a chronic disability that often manifests problems into adulthood (Borduin & Schaeffer, 1998; Kazdin, Siegel, & Bass, 1992; Tarolla et al., 2002), and the behavioral trajectory of this population can lead to incarceration at a high cost to society (Hemphill, Toumbourou, Herrenkohl, McMorris, & Catalano, 2006; Mpofu & Crystal, 2001; Tarolla et al., 2002). Therefore, prevention for children at risk and treatment for those already identified as having conduct problems are critical in interrupting the progression of the disorder and thus preventing serious long-term consequences. Longitudinal research has established risk factors for students in the early stages of the behavioral trajectory of conduct problems, and strong evidence exists for a wide range of effective prevention and intervention programs (Brestan & Eyberg, 1998; Frick, 2006; Tarolla et al., 2002; Wilson, Gottfredson, & Najaka, 2001).

Theoretical Framework for Approaching Conduct Problems

Most theoretical approaches for remediating conduct problems involve behavioral, cognitive–behavioral, or social learning theories. For example, children and adolescents with conduct problems often have deficits in social information processing; therefore, cognitive–behavioral theory is applicable (Frick, 2000; Lipsey & Wilson, 1998). It is also well established that children whose parents lack effective parenting skills are at a greater risk for developing conduct problems; therefore, some strategies originate in social learning theory (Patterson, Chamberlain, & Reid, 1982; Patterson, Reid, & Dishion, 1992; Woolgar & Scott, 2005). In addition, a large quantity of empirical evidence indicates support for the treatment of conduct problems using multimodal or multisystemic approaches that combine theoretical perspectives (Frick, 2000; Kazdin et al., 1992; Lochman & Wells, 2004; Woolgar & Scott, 2005). These approaches combine behavioral, cognitive–behavioral, and/or social learning (including family-based theory) perspectives, and do not exclude a biological orientation.

Effective intervention for conduct problems is as much about timing in the development of the disorder as it is about the use of specific theoretical approaches. The systematic development of conduct disorder is such that early intervention is the most critical component for children or adolescents identified as at risk. Therefore, methods and strategies in this chapter have been specifically selected to address the development of conduct problems through early prevention and intervention.

Interventions

Interventions in this chapter include prevention as well as remediation efforts. When choosing interventions, practitioners are encouraged to pay close attention to the considerations for use of each intervention, to be cognizant of timing in the developmental trajectory of the disorder, and to recognize which interventions are most effective for prevention and which are most effective for remediation.

The intervention strategies for preventing and/or remediating conduct problems have been classified into nine categories. Note that the multimodal and multisystemic interventions are combinations of various intervention strategies. The categories of interventions discussed in this chapter are the following:

   I. Token Economy Systems

  II. Interdependent Group-Oriented Contingency Management

 III. Anger Management Skills Training

 IV. Problem-Solving Training

  V. Social Skills Training

 VI. Moral Motivation Training

VII. Parent Training

VIII. Multimodal Interventions

 IX. Multisystemic Therapy

Multisystemic therapy (MST) is typically implemented by highly trained professionals and is often used by community mental health and child protection agencies. Therefore, implementation may be difficult in some educational environments (Borduin et al., 1995; Henggeler, Melton, & Smith, 1992; Tarolla et al., 2002). However, multisystemic therapy is covered here due to its demonstrated effectiveness in remediating severe conduct problems in children and adolescents (Frick, 2000; Henggeler, Cunningham, Pickrel, Schoenwald, & Brondino, 1996; Tarolla et al., 2002).

I. Token Economy Systems

A token economy system is a behavioral technique that allows children to earn points or tokens that can later be exchanged for positive reinforcers. Token economy systems are based on operant learning theory (Skinner, 1931) and combine differential reinforcement with a response-cost technique, providing a concrete visual representation of teacher approval (Alberto & Troutman, 2003; Bushell, 1973). Along with earning tokens for demonstration of the desired behavior or set of behaviors, a child can also have tokens removed for inappropriate behavior. This removal is called "response cost." Response cost is considered punishment if it results in a subsequent reduction in the targeted problem behavior.

Token distribution and removal is done on a specific ratio, much like a banking system. A child earns tokens by engaging in certain behaviors, and tokens are spent by exchanging them for tangible or intangible reinforcers. The tokens take on the reinforcing quality of the item for which they can be exchanged, providing immediate or delayed self-reinforcement for the individual. Fees or fines occur when a child engages in inappropriate or undesirable behavior, resulting in removal of the token(s). The cost of these undesirable behaviors should be explained prior to engaging in the token economy.

For example, a teacher places a marble in a jar each time a student with conduct problems follows specific classroom rules during a class period. At the end of each day, the child may choose to trade the marbles for a reinforcer (e.g., extra computer time, a no-homework pass, a keychain) or save the marbles to purchase a larger reinforcer (e.g., a free class period or a snack pass). If the child doesn't follow the classroom rules, he or she loses a marble.

Implementation

The goal of implementing a token economy system is to increase on-task behavior and reduce antisocial and disruptive behavior by systematically reinforcing appropriate behavior and punishing problem behavior. The basic elements of a token economy system include the following:

1. Creation of a visual chart of behaviors that will earn tokens, with values assigned for each behavior

2. Specification of when the child will receive the earned tokens

3. Determination of tokens, either concrete or written (e.g., bingo chips, paper tickets, or a point sheet)

4. Creation of a visual chart of reinforcers, the quantity of tokens needed to purchase each reinforcer, and the schedule for access to the reinforcers

5. Access to the reinforcers (tangible, nontangible, or activity) when criteria for obtaining them are met

First, the key stakeholders determine and describe the targeted (problem) behavior in concrete, observable terms. Next, the method by which points will be earned and lost is established, the facilitator provides visual representation of the behavior and the amount of points to be earned or lost, and the facilitator demonstrates the procedures by modeling and role-playing with the children. Then, the facilitator awards or removes points throughout the day. Finally, at a predetermined time (e.g., once a day or twice a week), the children are allowed to exchange the tokens or points for reinforcers (see Figure 3.1).

Figure 3.1 Procedural steps for the application of a token economy system

1. Describe the targeted (problem) behavior and replacement (appropriate) behavior in concrete and observable terms.

2. Determine the list of reinforcers to use, and post them in a highly visible location.

3. Create a visual aid or chart that represents the behaviors that result in earning reinforcers and those that result in loss.

4. Determine the method for removing reinforcers, and list the procedure. Considerations might include whether students return items that were earned (and how they do so) or pay a fine for items that cannot be returned (e.g., food snacks).

5. Explain the system to the children using visual representation (e.g., a poster).

6. Model the behaviors that will earn or cost the children tokens or points.

7. Have the children practice the targeted behavior followed by acceptable replacement behaviors; behaviors related to returning items that were earned can also be practiced.

8. Provide a visual cue to the children to keep track of points lost; cues can be tangible tokens or other visual cues (e.g., a daily point sheet, group points tallied on a white board or a chart).

9. Add points or tokens when the replacement behavior occurs.

10. Remove points or tokens when the targeted behavior occurs.

11. Provide a predetermined time to exchange the tokens or points for reinforcers.

12. Fade out the response-cost intervention with the extinction of the targeted behavior.

Evidence for Use

Freeman (2004) labels token economy systems as a tried-and-true intervention for conduct disorders. McCurdy, Mannella, and Eldridge (2003) found a 55% decrease in office referrals for fighting and a 46% overall decrease in referrals when a schoolwide token economy system was implemented (in conjunction with schoolwide positive behavior support). Burchard and Barrera (1972) compared the use of two punishment techniques: time out and cost response (as in loss of tokens or reinforcers in the token economy system). They found that both techniques were effective at decreasing antisocial behavior in a group of adolescents who were mildly mentally retarded and exhibited a great deal of antisocial behavior, including stealing, fighting, swearing, and bullying. Bry and George (1979) implemented a token economy system with 20 seventh-grade students exhibiting low academic motivation, numerous disciplinary office referrals, and family problems, and then compared their behavioral progress to a control group. The researchers found a decrease in tardiness and absenteeism as well as an increase in grade point average.

The following studies summarize some of the key research findings associated with the use of token economy systems in children and adolescents with conduct problems.

Baer, A. M., Rowbury, T., & Baer, D. M. (1973). The development of instructional control over classroom activities of deviant preschool children. *Journal of Applied Behavior Analysis, 6*(2), 289–298.

This study of 3 extremely noncompliant preschool-age children investigated differential reinforcement as a technique for establishing instructional control. For all 3 children, compliance at least doubled from baseline when access to free playtime, materials, and a snack—mediated by a token economy system—was made contingent on following the teacher's instructions to complete a specific academic task. For 2 of the children, who did not respond sufficiently to differential reinforcement alone, a timeout contingency was added, increasing compliance to nearly 100%.

Bry, B. H., & George, F. E. (1979). Evaluating and improving prevention programs: A strategy from drug abuse. *Evaluation and Program Planning, 2*(2), 127–136.

This report documents a methodology for evaluating and improving prevention programs, using the Early Secondary Prevention Program in Monmouth County, New Jersey, as an example. This drug abuse prevention program was simultaneously implemented at two middle schools. The program involved biweekly meetings with students, and appropriate behavior was rewarded through the use of a token economy system. Results were measured by student attendance, promptness, and achievement, as well as teacher ratings. At the end of the first year, statistically significant positive program effects were found at one school. Process improvements implemented at the second school improved the next year's results.

Burchard, J. D., & Barrera, F. (1972). An analysis of timeout and response cost in a programmed environment. *Journal of Applied Behavior Analysis, 5*(3), 271–282.

Eleven boys (6 of whom completed the study) in an institute for children with mild mental retardation were observed during differing periods of timeout and response cost to see which was most effective in lowering the rates of problem behavior. The timeouts and response costs used were 5 tokens, 30 tokens, 5 minutes, and 30 minutes. As anticipated, the higher-cost reinforcements were more effective than the lower-cost ones, which actually increased the occurrences of problem behavior.

There was very little difference in the effectiveness of the 30-minute timeout and the 30-token response cost; both were equally effective. However, because of the amount of time wasted in multiple extended timeouts, response cost may be more desirable.

Field, C. E., Nash, H. M., Handwerk, M. L., & Friman, P. C. (2004). A modification of the token economy for nonresponsive youth in family-style residential care. *Behavior Modification, 28*(3), 438–457.

Although research confirms successful use of token economy systems for motivating behavioral change in individuals at residential treatment facilities, some children do not respond to such systems. In this study, investigators selected 3 such nonresponders and modified (increased) the frequency and immediacy of their access to the rewards earned with tokens. A treatment-withdrawal experimental design determined that the number of intense behavioral episodes each child exhibited decreased substantially as the rewards earned increased, providing evidence that modified token economies (those with an increased frequency and immediacy of rewards) can be used successfully even with children who were nonresponsive to traditional token economies.

McCurdy, B. L., Mannella, M. C., & Eldridge, N. (2003). Positive behavior support in urban schools: Can we prevent the escalation of antisocial behavior? *Journal of Positive Behavior Interventions, 5*(3), 158–170.

This 2-year case study of positive behavior support, the Key-to-Success project, was implemented in a culturally diverse urban elementary school with increasing student behavior problems. Working with behavioral consultants, the school leadership team developed a positive approach to reduce disruptive behavior schoolwide and prevent future escalation of antisocial behaviors, including fighting. This approach included a token economy system in which students who followed the schoolwide rules were provided with "keys" that could be exchanged weekly for rewards. After 2 years, the number of office discipline referrals (ODRs) per student decreased 46%. Fighting ODRs, among the most serious offenses, decreased 55%.

O'Leary, K. D., & Becker, W. C. (1967). Behavior modification of an adjustment class: A token reinforcement program. *Exceptional Children, 33*(9), 637–642.

In this study, 8 particularly disruptive students were observed first in a base trial and then while participating in a token reinforcement program to determine whether the program could reduce inappropriate behavior. Initially, the students were individually rated each day based on their adherence to class rules. The students who rated high enough could select a small reward at the end of the day. Later, ratings accumulated for 2, 3, or 4 days before reinforcement was offered to discover if the delayed gratification produced the same effect. For all 8 students, disruptive behavior markedly decreased (from 76% to 10%) over the course of the study, continuing even when gratification was delayed.

Considerations

For Teaching

When utilizing a token economy system, teachers should avoid using tokens as bribery, randomly offering tokens for jobs, or using threatening comments (Goldstein, 1995). The difference between bribery and appropriate use of reinforcement can be subtle and is often determined by the situation in which the reinforcer is offered. For example, consider a child who begins to whine and refuses to engage in work that is requested by the teacher. As the child begins to stamp his feet and becomes louder and louder, the teacher responds by telling the child to go back to his seat and sit down. The child responds to this latest request from the teacher by stating his disdain for math even more loudly. In an effort to end the child's tantrum, the teacher responds by telling the child he can go to recess early if he stops. In this case, the token (i.e., recess) serves as a bribe rather than an appropriate reinforcement. Tokens should be clearly articulated up front and used consistently to reinforce appropriate behavior, not as bribes to end inappropriate behavior while it is occurring. In the example, a more efficient response by the teacher might have been to calmly use a reminder about earning tokens at the beginning of the lesson to prevent the child from engaging in the tantrum. Then, if the child began to act up, the teacher could calmly redirect his attention while ignoring the initial behavioral response.

For Age and Developmental Level

Access to re-earning lost tokens should always be clear to all students. Younger children may engage in very inappropriate behavior when things are taken away, so caution should be used as to what age or developmental level is appropriate for using token economies. Another general consideration for teachers or implementers is the quality of the reinforcer. Reinforcers must be sufficient to compete with naturally occurring reinforcement from problem behaviors, and access to other reinforcers should be limited as much as possible. Moreover, it is important that the reinforcement schedule be appropriately distributed so that enough tokens can be earned to outweigh the loss of tokens in order to avoid student apathy. Satiation can occur with reinforcers, so modifications or routine changes can maintain student interest. The reinforcers, as well as the program, should be frequently evaluated for effectiveness and modified as needed. Keep in mind that positive strategies are generally more effective and should be attempted before response-cost strategies.

For Culture and Language Differences

Although there has been recent interest in studies examining the role of culture in the success of individual- and group-level reinforcers, no definitive patterns of their use has emerged. In fact, most children successfully learn differences between school and home expectations and respond remarkably well to the transitions. It is important to note that language and culture factors may necessitate additional training, such as providing more examples and nonexamples, so that the token system is clearly understood. Families may also require additional information about earning or losing points to prevent miscommunication and inconsistent reinforcement schedules. In some families, the behavior of children may be influenced, in part, by cultural perspectives regarding family identity, pride, and respect, and these factors should be considered when presenting and explaining token systems.

II. Interdependent Group-Oriented Contingency Management

Interdependent group-oriented contingency management interventions are group management systems that reinforce the cumulative behavior of a group as a whole. Unlike token economy systems (Intervention I), interdependent group-oriented contingency management interventions focus on group performance (Bandura, 1969) rather than individual performance. In other words, the target behaviors or responses are the same for each individual in the group. Response contingencies, or expected behaviors for reinforcement, are concurrently in effect for each group member (Alberto & Troutman, 2003).

For example, several students in a fourth-grade classroom are ignoring directions, stealing from other students, and exhibiting aggressive behaviors. The teacher splits the class into two teams and institutes the management plan. The teams are given points for following directions and practicing defined prosocial behaviors, and points are deducted for engaging in inappropriate behaviors.

Implementation

The goal of implementing interdependent group-oriented contingency management is to decrease classroom disruption and antisocial behavior and to increase appropriate and on-task behavior by systematically reinforcing appropriate behavior at a group level. Prevention of future conduct problems and intervention at early stages of conduct problems are the primary targets of this intervention. The basic elements of interdependent group-oriented contingency management include the following:

1. Creation of a visual chart of behaviors that will earn points and rule violations that will cause loss of points

2. Division of children into teams

3. Creation of a scoreboard (placed in a highly visible area) that will be used to tally points per team

4. Determination of reinforcers

5. Access to the reinforcers for the team with the most points at the end of the predetermined interval

The following process should be employed prior to implementation of interdependent group-oriented contingency management. First, determine the target behavior (based on assessment) that can best be addressed by means of a group intervention. Second, establish goals and objectives for the students and key stakeholders. Third, determine specific techniques to be used. Fourth, create a strategy for reinstating the contingency plan on an intermittent schedule to maintain behavioral progress. Fifth, implement the program (see Figure 3.2).

Figure 3.2 Procedural steps for the application of interdependent group-oriented contingency management

1. Divide the class or group into teams.

2. Model the appropriate behaviors and instruct students to role-play them.

3. Determine the reinforcer for the day and/or week.

4. Visually represent points earned or lost by using tally marks. The game is played in innings or at intervals throughout the school day.

5. Reinforce the winning team daily and/or weekly. Reinforcers can include activity, social, edible, or tangible rewards.

Evidence for Use

A great deal of empirical evidence has established the efficacy of interdependent group-oriented contingency management, based on the "good behavior game" established by Barrish, Saunders, and Wolf in 1969 (Embry, 2002; Tingstrom, Sterling-Turner, & Wilczynski, 2006). Several studies using interdependent group-oriented contingency management have reported an 80% to 99% decrease in disruptive behavior in elementary classrooms (Barrish et al., 1969; Bostow & Geiger, 1976; Grandy, Madsen, & De Mersseman, 1973; Medland & Stachnik, 1972). Efficacy has also been established for students with varying disabilities across grades and settings (Darveaux, 1984; Phillips & Christie, 1986; Salend, Reynolds, & Coyle, 1989).

The following studies summarize some of the key research findings associated with the use of interdependent group-oriented contingency management in children and adolescents with conduct problems.

Barrish, H. H., Saunders, M., & Wolf, M. M. (1969). Good behavior game: Effects of individual contingencies for group consequences on disruptive behavior in a classroom. *Journal of Applied Behavior Analysis, 2*(2), 119–124.

This study, conducted in a fourth-grade classroom of 24 students, investigated a technique designed to reduce disruptive behavior using a game involving privileges. The students were divided into two teams. During the game, when a student broke one of the rules for out-of-seat or talking-out behavior, that student's team received a mark on the chalkboard that contributed to the team losing privileges (e.g., extra recess, first to go to lunch). Incidence of out-of-seat behavior decreased from 82% to 9% when the game was being played, and talking-out behavior decreased from 96% to 19%.

Bostow, D., & Geiger, O. G. (1976). Good behavior game: A replication and systematic analysis with a second grade class. *School Applications of Learning Theory, 8*(2), 18–25.

For this study, good behavior was made into a game in a second-grade classroom. The teacher in the observed classroom divided the students into two teams, assigning negative points whenever a student broke one of the five classroom rules. The winning team at the end of each session (60 minutes) went through the lunch line first, and each team member received a cookie. When the game was implemented, inappropriate behavior decreased significantly (from an average of 34.2 rule-breaking behaviors per session to 6.3 per session), and it increased when the game was discontinued. In addition, the study found that students enjoyed the game and complained when the trial came to an end.

Grandy, G. S., Madsen, C. H., & De Mersseman, L. M. (1973). The effects of individual and interdependent contingencies on inappropriate classroom behavior. *Psychology in the Schools, 10,* 488–493.

This study investigated which contingency—individual or group—was more effective in decreasing students' inappropriate behavior. After documenting baseline student behavior in a classroom for 15 days, students were given individual incentives: each student who did not leave his or her seat or speak out of turn was given 30 minutes of free time. Then, researchers tested a group contingency: if five or fewer total rule violations were observed, the entire class was rewarded with free time. The study found that both contingencies were extremely effective in decreasing students' inappropriate behavior; however, the majority of students preferred the individual contingency.

Harris, V. W., & Sherman, J. A. (1973). Use and analysis of the "good behavior game" to reduce disruptive classroom behavior. *Journal of Applied Behavior Analysis, 6*(3), 405–417.

In this replication of the good behavior game in a fifth- and a sixth-grade classroom, the technique was again found effective in significantly reducing disruptive talking and out-of-seat behavior. Several manipulations of the game in the sixth-grade classroom determined that the following components influenced its effectiveness: division of the class into teams, positive consequences for a team winning the game, and criteria set for winning (i.e., number of points needed to achieve the reward). Whether or not students received direct feedback (i.e., marks on the blackboard) did not seem to affect disruptive behavior. Despite a marked reduction in disruptive behavior, little or no improvement occurred in academic performance.

Medland, M. B., & Stachnik, T. J. (1972). Good-behavior game: A replication and systematic analysis. *Journal of Applied Behavior Analysis, 5*(1), 45–51.

A reading class of 28 fifth-grade students, divided into two groups of 14 students each, participated in this study of the good behavior game. Game components included presenting the classroom rules, providing response feedback (red and green lights for bad and good behavior), and implementing group contingencies (extra recess and extra free time) if criteria were met. The game effectively reduced talking out, disruptive behaviors, and out-of-seat behaviors. Rates for these behaviors dropped from their baseline measure in both groups, by almost 99% and 97%, respectively.

Salend, S. J., Reynolds, C. J., & Coyle, E. M. (1989). Individualizing the good behavior game across type and frequency of behavior with emotionally disturbed adolescents. *Behavior Modification, 13*(1), 108–126.

This study individualized the good behavior game to address various types and frequencies of behavior exhibited by three classes of students with severe behavioral disturbance. The students were divided into groups based on the inappropriate behavior they most frequently performed. These behaviors included inappropriate verbalizations, touching, negative comments, cursing, and drumming/tapping. Data showed the individualized technique was effective in reducing these behaviors and was well received by both teachers and students.

Considerations

For Teaching

A study completed by Harris and Sherman (1973) found that interdependent group-oriented contingency management did not significantly impact academic progress, so consideration should be given to effective instructional techniques to be used in conjunction with the intervention. Johnson, Turner, and Konarski (1978) found that the positive effects of the intervention began to diminish after 2 months. To help prevent this from happening, refresher sessions can be used intermittently after conclusion of the initial intervention.

For Age and Developmental Level

Younger children will require steadier, more prolonged use of the intervention in order to generalize the skills to other contexts. Reinforcers and contingencies should be age-appropriate and based on the developmental level of the students. Reinforcer selection can be done in several different ways: 1) groups can vote on reinforcers from a reinforcer menu, 2) groups can spin the reinforcer wheel, or 3) the teacher can use mystery motivators (Sheridan, 1995). Note that younger children will be more likely to make selections from a list, whereas older children might respond better to creating a list as a group and then making individual decisions.

For Culture and Language Differences

Peer pressure, peer competition, and peer recognition are factors to consider when using interdependent group-oriented contingency management (Embry & Straatemeier, 2001). While these factors can be motivating, they may not be as effective for cultures where competition is less important or even discouraged. Rotating group membership is one way to negate some of this effect. By frequently changing membership in teams, the stigmatizing effect for less competitive individuals can be reduced or removed. An additional method for lessening this effect would be the distribution of points for appropriate team-oriented group behavior (e.g., cooperation, mutual respect).

III. Anger Management Skills Training

Children and adolescents identified as having conduct problems frequently do not use appropriate anger management techniques. Anger management skills training is a cognitive–behavioral, skill-building approach to reducing socially inappropriate responses to anger. Prosocial techniques for coping with feelings of anger are taught in 30-minute sessions conducted weekly over 10 weeks.

For example, a 17-year-old male becomes physically and verbally aggressive whenever another boy speaks to his girlfriend. Through anger management skills training, he is taught to identify the cause of his anger and his physiological reactions, and he learns to walk away from the situation as an anger management technique.

Implementation

The goal of anger management skills training is to decrease the incidence of physical aggression, verbal aggression, and revenge-seeking behaviors by teaching children to recognize the triggers of their anger and to use alternative coping techniques. The basic elements of anger management skills training include the following:

1. Recognition of events or triggers that cause anger, including thinking patterns

2. Recognition of physiological reactions to anger

3. Selection of an anger management technique that the person is willing to try

4. Evaluation of the effectiveness and appropriate use of the technique

5. Modification of the technique as needed

Begin anger management skills training by explaining the reasons physical and verbal aggression are ineffective methods of anger management. These reasons include social consequences (e.g., losing friendships), legal ramifications, and moral considerations. Next, explain the physiological features, or cues, of anger arousal. Then, introduce effective prosocial anger management techniques, allowing the children or adolescents to choose the method(s) they find most comfortable. Instruct the children or adolescents to keep a journal of anger-provoking incidents experienced throughout the day. Also, set up safe situations for them to practice the anger management technique and learn how to transfer the new skill(s) to everyday situations. Finally, at the end of the training, socially reinforce participation and completion with a ceremony (see Figure 3.3).

Figure 3.3 Procedural steps for the application of anger management skills training

1. Begin by introducing the components of anger, such as anger triggers and physiological signs of anger arousal (cues).

2. Ask the children to name things that make them angry (triggers), and create a list on a white board, overhead projector, or poster.

3. Discuss the physiological reactions (cues) to anger experienced by each child.

4. Have facilitators model the triggers and ask the children to identify the cues to anger arousal.

5. Explain that prosocial anger management methods are those that do not result in verbal or physical aggression or negative consequences for actions.

6. Introduce prosocial anger management techniques such as relaxation (e.g., counting or deep breathing), assertiveness skills, anticipation (e.g., recognizing physical signs of anger), self-instruction (e.g., substituting appropriate self-talk for anger-arousing thoughts), self-evaluation, and problem solving.

7. Give students visual cues, such as note cards with pictures or text, explaining the method to use if necessary.

8. Allow the children to role-play the triggers and cues.

9. Instruct the children to keep a log of incidents throughout the day that make them feel angry. Begin subsequent sessions by discussing these logs.

10. Practice the skill(s) to use in real-life situations by setting up an unexpected event for one or a few students. Tell the student that another person (e.g., parent, teacher, or friend) will try to make him or her angry so that he or she can practice the newly learned skills. (It is critical to provide a warning to the student about the unexpected event.) After the event occurs, have the student report on these occurrences and explain what prosocial methods were used successfully and to what degree.

11. Reinforce participation and completion of the course in a social situation (e.g., an awards ceremony).

Evidence for Use

Nugent, Champlin, and Wiinimaki (1997) report that using anger management skills training reduced aggressive behavior in adolescents identified as delinquent and placed in group-home settings. Kellner and Bry (1999) also found small improvement in the aggression of 7 boys in a day school when anger management techniques were implemented.

The following studies summarize some of the key research findings associated with the use of anger management skills training in children and adolescents with conduct problems.

Dykeman, B. F. (1995). The social cognitive treatment of anger and aggression in four adolescents with conduct disorder. *Journal of Instructional Psychology, 22*(2), 194–200.

This study looked at the effectiveness of social cognitive treatment in reducing anger and aggressive behavior. Four adolescents with childhood-onset conduct disorder participated in 24 sessions of social cognitive intervention. Each adolescent was paired with another adolescent and met with a therapist in Pair Therapy for 24 one-hour sessions over 12 weeks. All 4 students received fewer disciplinary referrals involving aggression during a 4-week period after treatment as compared to the 4-week period just prior to treatment.

Feindler, E. L., Marriott, S. A., & Iwata, M. (1984). Group anger control training for junior high school delinquents. *Cognitive Therapy and Research, 8*(3), 299–311.

Thirty-six junior high students attending a specialized program for disruptive students were selected for a group anger control training program based on their high rates of classroom and/or community disruption. The training program was conducted in 10 biweekly 50-minute sessions and included teaching of skills such as self-monitoring, self-evaluation, "thinking ahead," and relaxation. The data provide modest support for the efficacy of anger control training in reducing incidences of aggressive behaviors. Results also indicate that anger control training has its greatest impact on low-frequency, high-severity, aggressive behaviors.

Kellner, M. H., & Bry, B. H. (1999). The effects of anger management groups in a day school for emotionally disturbed adolescents. *Adolescence, 34*(136), 645–651.

This study examined the effects of an anger management program on the aggressive behavior of 7 students attending a day school for adolescents with emotional disturbance. The program included psychoeducation, anger discrimination training, logging incidents of anger, and training in prosocial responses to anger. Prior to participation in the program, the students' mean score on the Conduct subscale of a behavior rating scale completed by teachers was 92.57; after participation, their mean score was 80.28. Individually, each student's score either improved or stayed the same; overall, the students' improvement was statistically significant.

McCarthy-Tucker, S., Gold, A., & Garcia, E. (1999). Effects of anger management training on aggressive behavior in adolescent boys. *Journal of Offender Rehabilitation, 29*(3/4), 129–141.

This study investigated the impact of anger management training on the aggressive behavior of 8 adolescent males living in a residential treatment facility. The subjects attended 12 one-hour group sessions biweekly with lessons that included concepts such as assertiveness, communication, and relaxation, and completed homework that involved journaling about anger-producing situations, observing anger cues, and practicing skills learned during group sessions. Results indicated that the anger management training was effective in reducing aggressive behavior, evidenced by observations, interviews, and responses to items on both the Novaco Provocation Inventory and the State-Trait Anger Expression Inventory.

Nugent, W. R., Champlin, D., & Wiinimaki, L. (1997). The effects of anger control training on adolescent antisocial behavior. *Research on Social Work Practice, 7*(4), 446–462.

This study describes the effects of an anger control training (ACT) program instituted in a group home for adolescents in state custody for unruly and delinquent behavior. Comparisons were made between changes in antisocial behavior by adolescents who completed ACT and changes shown by comparable adolescents in state custody and comparable adolescents in group homes. Results indicated that adolescents who received ACT showed greater improvement in reducing antisocial behavior than those in either comparison group. In addition, the longer the period in the ACT program, the more significant the effect on reducing the aggressive behaviors.

Considerations

For Teaching

Socially acceptable anger management techniques are rarely reinforced within the peer groups of children and adolescents, and home and community environments sometimes are not conducive to their use either; therefore, multimodal or multisystemic therapy is often necessary to maintain the skills learned in anger management programs. Exercise caution when using anger management programs in groups of students with conduct problems, because this can lead to discovery of new deviant peer groups. Anger management techniques are often better taught in heterogeneous groups or on an individual basis.

For example, 6 boys with conduct problems are brought together for afterschool treatment groups. While group sessions go well, the students hear new ideas from one another about ways to be deviant. After the group session, the boys wait for rides, walk home, or are potentially unsupervised in unstructured settings. This opportunity can lead to new partnerships in deviant behavior or engaging in conduct problems.

For Culture and Language Differences

Anger, aggression, and conduct problems may be modeled and reinforced at home as a part of gender roles that are influenced by cultural beliefs (e.g., a dominant and aggressive patriarch or matriarch). Unfortunately, behaviors that are used to manage other family members can spill over into the school setting (e.g., intimidating a teacher who referred a student for a behavioral problem, being unwilling to seek help or work with others who are trying to help). Intervention can be difficult in such situations. But intervention is still advised and certainly warranted, if for no other reason than to indicate that the school environment has a culture that maintains certain expectations of its students and its students' parents.

IV. Problem-Solving Training

Children and adolescents with conduct problems often misperceive social information, such as environmental cues and neutral actions of others. As a result, they attribute unintended aggression to these cues and actions and respond aggressively and inappropriately. Problem-solving training is a cognitive–behavioral technique that teaches children and adolescents to alter these cognitive distortions and think before they act. Professionals teach students to follow specific steps for problem solving, leading to more appropriate responses to problems.

For example, in a mixed-grade high school, an emotional–behavioral disability teacher asked a student to decorate and write his own thank you cards to his classmates as part of a language arts lesson and to develop social skills. Mike, a student in the class, received his card and immediately tore it up, turned over a desk, and sulked in the back of the classroom. After de-escalating the situation, the teacher asked Mike why he did that. Mike was only able to articulate how much he hated his peers. The teacher retrieved the card and reviewed it with Mike. Mike indicated that he thought the drawings in the card made fun of him, and he didn't understand that the drawings and words were simply ways of showing thanks or appreciation. In situations such as this, problem-solving approaches can be used both to identify the misperception and to determine a more appropriate response.

Implementation

The goal of problem-solving training is to identify and reduce cognitive distortions, noncompliance, and aggression, and to increase the use of active listening skills and effective communication skills by learning basic problem-solving skills and applying them in appropriate situations. The basic elements of problem-solving training include the following:

1. Recognition that a problem exists

2. Identification of the problem

3. Generation of causes and possible solutions—paying close attention to possible bias or misinterpretations

4. Determination of consequences, both positive and negative, for each of the possible solutions

5. Selection and implementation of the best solution

6. Evaluation of the success of the solution, and determination of places for improvement

Professionals teach problem-solving skills by helping children or adolescents to appropriately analyze social situations using a two-stage process. First, children are taught to stop and think about the situation that is occurring before acting and to consider their own feelings and the feelings of others. Second, children are taught to consider others' perspectives and determine several possible solutions that will result in a positive resolution for all involved (see Figure 3.4).

Figure 3.4 Procedural steps for the application of problem-solving training

1. Use an example to identify and discuss a behavioral incident. This example may include a direct observation, reading a written scenario that describes an incident, or viewing a video demonstration. Ask questions that lead the student to identify cues as if making predictions in a story, such as overt feelings, facial representations, and potential feelings. If using a video, pausing and rewinding with cues like, "Did you see...?" can be helpful. As a replacement for verbal cuing, provide questions ahead of time for students to respond to during a role-play or video.

2. Assist the child in defining social cues received and delivered through body language, tone of voice, and posture, and identify any cognitive distortions. Immediately correct each miscue, and use peer discussion when appropriate to determine the most likely feelings or attributions of behavior.

3. Generate alternative solutions to the social problem presented in the example, listing them on a white board, overhead projector, or poster.

4. Brainstorm the likely consequences (positive and negative) of each solution, and verbally or visually represent them. Students can write these down first, and the responses can be collected and shared with the group by a teacher writing them on the classroom board (to allow anonymity in answering). If anonymity of responses is not important, then the teacher can ask students to provide descriptions in their own words and can do something simple like a red check or green star using markers on a white board to reflect the positive and negative consequences.

5. Determine the best solution through discussion and feedback.

Continued on next page

---

6. Implement the choices and practice them.

7. Assign homework that asks the student to practice the behaviors in real situations and to write them down in a notebook (recording the type of incident, the solutions tried, and the outcome).

8. Review the notebook with the child at the next session, and evaluate the implementation.

Evidence for Use

Kazdin, Esveldt-Dawson, French, and Unis (1987) found that problem-solving training reduced overall behavioral problems at home and school, and decreased the use of aggression in students with conduct problems. Gottfredson and Wilson (2003) found that programs that used cognitive–behavioral strategies, such as problem solving, had a larger average effect when serving high-risk youths as compared to programs serving entire school populations.

The following studies summarize some of the key research findings associated with the use of problem-solving training in children and adolescents with conduct problems.

Azrin, N. H., Donohue, B., Teichner, G. A., Crum, T., Howell, J., & DeCato, L. A. (2001). A controlled evaluation and description of individual-cognitive problem solving and family-behavior therapies in dually-diagnosed conduct-disordered and substance-dependent youth. *Journal of Child & Adolescent Substance Abuse, 11*(1), 1–43.

This study was one of the first to analyze adolescents with both conduct disorders and substance dependency. The adolescents were randomly assigned to either family-based therapy or independent cognitive problem-solving therapy, and results were monitored pretreatment, posttreatment, and at a 6-month follow-up. The study's results showed little difference between the two groups, with both groups demonstrating a significant decrease in illicit drug use, as well as improvement in school performance, family relationships, mood, and overall satisfaction of both the youths and their parents.

Dishion, T. J., & Andrews, D. W. (1995). Preventing escalation in problem behaviors with high-risk young adolescents: Immediate and 1-year outcomes. *Journal of Consulting and Clinical Psychology, 63*(4), 538–548.

This study examined the effects of parent-focused, child-focused, and materials-only interventions for reducing problem behaviors in high-risk youth. The study included 158 families with children between the ages of 10 and 14. Results showed that problem-solving skills increased and parent–child coercive interactions decreased significantly following both the parent-focused and teen-focused interventions, compared to subjects in the materials-only or the control group. This study also demonstrated that interventions grouping high-risk adolescents together on a regular basis led to escalations in tobacco use and problem behavior at school, suggesting the need to re-evaluate strategies that aggregate high-risk adolescents into group intervention programs.

Fraser, M. W., Galinsky, M. J., Smokowski, P. R., Day, S. H., Terzian, M. A., Rose, R. A., et al. (2005). Social information-processing skills training to promote social competence and prevent aggressive behavior in the third grade. *Journal of Consulting and Clinical Psychology, 73*(6), 1045–1055.

This study of three successive classes of third graders ($N = 548$) evaluated a school-based prevention program, Making Choices: Social Problem Solving Skills for Children (MC), which was designed to promote social competence and reduce aggression by strengthening skills in processing social information, solving social problems, and regulating emotions. The first class received the standard health curriculum; the second class, the MC program; and the third class, the MC program augmented with teacher and parent activities (MC Plus). The results showed that, compared with the standard curriculum class, students in both intervention groups demonstrated increases in social competence and decreases in social and physical aggression.

Gottfredson, D. C., & Wilson, D. B. (2003). Characteristics of effective school-based substance abuse prevention. *Prevention Science, 4*(1), 27–38.

This meta-analysis of 136 contrasts from 94 previous studies sought to determine which characteristics of school-based drug prevention programs made them most effective. It was found that interventions are moderately more effective when they target high-risk youth alone (rather than a universal intervention) when students are in their middle school years, although neither of these findings was statistically significant. Peers as leaders were found to be highly effective, although if they taught alongside teachers, this effect disappeared. Duration of the program did not seem to matter, probably because prolonging a fairly ineffective program does not help. Further research goals are discussed.

Kazdin, A. E., Esveldt-Dawson, K., French, N. H., & Unis, A. S. (1987). Problem-solving skills training and relationship therapy in the treatment of antisocial child behavior. *Journal of Consulting and Clinical Psychology, 55*(1), 76–85.

In this treatment comparison, 56 children between the ages of 7 and 13 who were hospitalized for antisocial behavior were randomly assigned to receive problem-solving skills training (PSST), nondirective relationship therapy (RT), or treatment contact only. Those receiving PSST showed significantly greater decreases in aggressive behaviors and overall behavior problems than those receiving RT or treatment contact. The between-group differences and within-group changes of PSST persisted up to a year after treatment. When normative data were used to evaluate the clinical impact of treatment, significantly more children in the PSST group than in the other groups fell within the normative range for prosocial behavior.

Kazdin, A. E., Siegel, T. C., & Bass, D. (1992). Cognitive problem-solving skills training and parent management training in the treatment of antisocial behavior in children. *Journal of Consulting and Clinical Psychology, 60*(5), 733–747.

A randomized study evaluated problem-solving skills training (PSST) and parent management training (PMT)—each separately and both combined—to determine which training was more effective in 97 children aged 7 to 13 years. Although PSST, PMT, and PSST+PMT each improved children's functioning, the combined treatment produced more marked, pervasive, and durable changes in children's functioning and greater changes in parental functioning posttreatment and at a 1-year follow-up. A larger proportion of children receiving combination treatment reached normal levels of functioning.

Considerations

For Teaching

Problem solving can be readily incorporated into a variety of academic lessons in the classroom. At the most basic level, the ability to recognize choices or options for reaching a solution is parallel to seeing a variety of viewpoints or multiple solutions to a problem. The more frequently problem solving is practiced across different scenarios, the more likely it will generalize and transfer to other settings. Ideally, both generalization and transfer are programmed into the scheduling and curriculum for frequent opportunities to improve skill fluency.

For Culture and Language Differences

Problem solving can be different across cultures because of how problems are identified. Some cultures do not assign ownership for problems. Events are seen as random occurrences and not as the results of human actions. For example, a description used to indicate a broken glass might be "the glass broke" rather than "he broke the glass." Another example would be the relationship of future events to the spiritual or divine. Expressions like "Insha'Alla" (meaning, "if God wills it") may reflect a perceived lack of control or self-determination that deems the need for certain safety precautions, medicines, or other preventative measures unnecessary because problems that occur are viewed as manifestations of supernatural or divine control.

V. Social Skills Training

Social skills training is a cognitive–behavioral approach that involves teaching the prosocial skills concepts needed for children and adolescents to function successfully in their environments. Social skills training is necessary for students with deficits in social competency, which are commonly found among those with conduct problems. Social competency includes the absence of maladaptive behaviors, positive relationships with others, accurate and age-appropriate social cognition, and effective social behaviors needed for students to be accepted by appropriate peers (Bierman, Miller, & Stabb, 1987). It is important to note that peer rejection is often considered a precursor to the development of conduct problems.

For example, when Johnny, an 8-year-old with conduct problems, is redirected by his teacher for talking in class, he turns and hits Suzy. He was talking to Suzy and blames her for getting him in trouble. In this case, it would be appropriate to teach Johnny the social skill of dealing with an accusation.

Implementation

The goal of social skills training is to prevent and remediate components of conduct problems for at-risk children and adolescents by teaching them prosocial skills that can be used as an alternative to maladaptive behaviors. The basic elements of social skills training include the following:

1. Identify social skills deficits

2. Teach appropriate replacement social skills

3. Practice use of social skills in contrived settings (e.g., role-play)

4. Use corrective feedback and reinforcers for demonstrations of new behavior

5. Practice social skills in naturalistic settings with reinforcers and feedback to the extent possible

Students with childhood-onset conduct problems exhibit a lack of competency in specific social skills. This lack of competency directly relates to antisocial behaviors and results in an increased risk of continuing on the conduct problems trajectory. This situation can be remediated with direct social skills instruction. Social skills are taught through a process that involves visually representing and modeling the skill, role-playing and practicing the skill, and then transferring and maintaining the skill in the natural social environment of the child (see Figure 3.5).

Evidence for Use

Social skills training is effective in preventing children with early-onset conduct problems from continuing a trajectory leading to increased antisocial and delinquent behavior (Bierman et al., 1987; Webster-Stratton, Reid, & Hammond, 2001).

The following studies summarize some of the key research findings associated with the use of problem-solving training in children and adolescents with conduct problems.

Figure 3.5 Procedural steps for the application of social skills training

1. Determine group membership based on common social skills deficits.

2. Establish group norms and post them in a highly visible area.

3. Set well-defined boundaries by establishing the consequences for engaging in antisocial behavior during group sessions, and post the consequences in a highly visible area.

4. Teach one social skill per session. At the beginning of each subsequent session, review the skill taught during the previous session.

5. Visually represent the steps involved in demonstrating the social skill.

6. Ask the children to write the steps on note cards or paper.

7. Have the children verbally recite the steps.

8. Model the steps to achieve the skill.

9. Brainstorm a recent event that required the use of the skill.

10. Ask two children to role-play the skill while the others coach them.

11. Have the children journal about experiences with the skill outside of the sessions, providing generalization of the skill.

12. Send a written copy of the skill steps to the children's teachers and parents, asking them to practice and reinforce the appropriate use of the skill.

13. Maintain skill acquisition by holding periodic refresher sessions.

Bierman, K. L., Miller, C. L., & Stabb, S. D. (1987). Improving the social behavior and peer acceptance of rejected boys: Effects of social skill training with instructions and prohibitions. *Journal of Consulting and Clinical Psychology, 55*(2), 194–200.

This study compared the effects of instruction in social skills versus prohibitions for negative social behavior. Subjects included 32 second- and third-grade boys with highly negative social behavior who had been rejected by their peers. The students were randomly assigned to receive instruction in social skills (e.g., sharing, helping, cooperating); prohibitions and response cost for negative behavior; a combination of instructions and prohibitions; or no treatment. Prohibitions with response cost for negative behavior reduced negative behaviors immediately and at a 6-week follow-up but increased positive responses from peers only temporarily. Social skills instruction and rewards for specific positive behaviors resulted in less immediate but more stable improvements.

Kamps, D. M., Tankersley, M., & Ellis, C. (2000). Social skills interventions for young at-risk students: A 2-year follow-up study. *Behavioral Disorders, 25*(4), 310–324.

This study of children in Head Start through first grade who were identified as at risk for behavioral problems assessed the effects of a social skills training intervention program. The program consisted of social skill lessons from an established curriculum one to three times per week, plus reinforcement, peer tutoring, and parent support. The results showed that students who received the intervention displayed more positive peer interaction and fewer instances of problem behaviors than those in the control group. In addition, positive teacher reinforcement further improved student behavior.

Webster-Stratton, C., & Hammond, M. (1997). Treating children with early-onset conduct problems: A comparison of child and parent training interventions. *Journal of Consulting and Clinical Psychology, 65*(1), 93–109.

This study of 97 families sought to determine whether child training or parent training is more effective in treating early-onset conduct problems. Each family received one or both of these interventions or no treatment. Interventions that involved child training were superior to those that involved parent training for improving problem-solving and conflict-management skills. Interventions that involved parent training were superior in terms of child behavior improvements (as reported by parents), parent behaviors, and participant satisfaction. At a 1-year follow-up, all significant results of treatment were maintained and a positive delayed effect of combination therapy on deviance at home was noted.

Webster-Stratton, C., Reid, J., & Hammond, M. (2001). Social skills and problem-solving training for children with early-onset conduct problems: Who benefits? *Journal of Child Psychology and Psychiatry, 42*(7), 943–952.

In this study, the investigators examined their social skills, problem-solving, and anger-management curriculum (Incredible Years: Dinosaur Curriculum) for long-term effectiveness and ability to generalize across settings. Children with early-onset conduct problems from 99 families were randomly assigned to receive this curriculum or to be in a control group. Compared with controls, the children who underwent intervention had statistically and clinically greater improvement in conduct and in cognitive social problem-solving strategies. These results occurred in both home and school settings and were sustained at 1 year. The presence of attention-deficit/hyperactivity disorder or family stress did not affect a child's ability to benefit from treatment, but negative parenting did emerge as a risk factor.

Considerations

For Teaching

Deficits can occur in a variety of commonly used social skills that are seen as standards in the classroom. Social skills that can be targeted for development during daily instruction include preparing for a stressful conversation, expressing a complaint to others, dealing with group pressure, responding to the anger of others, avoiding fights with peers, dealing with an accusation from adults or peers, responding to the feelings of others, expressing affection, helping others, and dealing with failure. Many of these social skills lessons can be incorporated into regular curriculum through readings for literature or social studies, assigned topics for language arts or story writing, or even problems for mathematics where a narrative or paragraph is used.

For Culture and Language Differences

Social skills training, although effective in small groups, might be more effective in one-on-one settings with children from cultures where public discussion of individual challenges, emotions, and choice-making is perceived as inappropriate, or where social skills expectations differ based on gender or age group. Some children may not be expected to be assertive, discuss feelings, or respond to stress or anger. Even helpfulness may be interpreted as subservience, weakness, or a lack of such culturally esteemed qualities as independence or strength.

VI. Moral Motivation Training

Moral motivation training is a group-oriented cognitive intervention designed to accelerate the development of moral reasoning (Arbuthnot & Gordon, 1986). Moral motivation training can decrease antisocial behavior by increasing the level of moral functioning of children and adolescents with inadequate moral reasoning skills through role-playing and group discussions of a variety of moral dilemmas. The ultimate intent of the role-playing and group discussions is to reach a consensus among the members of the group, reflecting moral maturity (Palmer, 2005).

For example, with a group of students, the facilitator reads a scenario in which a parent is ill and the family can't afford medicine. The students are asked to determine if it would be appropriate for a child to steal the needed medicine for the parent. Adding information to the scenario, such as the parent will die without the medicine or the owner of the pharmacy is on the verge of bankruptcy, increases the difficulty of the decision and increases opportunities for debate amongst the students. The focus of the exercise is less on resolving the dilemma and more on the reasoning processes used to achieve an answer.

Moral motivation training is expected to help children progress to more advanced levels of moral development as defined by Kohlberg (1969) and originally described in the work of Piaget (1932). Kohlberg delineated three levels of moral development: preconventional, conventional, and postconventional. At the preconventional level, an individual's moral judgment is concrete and self-centered. At the conventional level, moral judgments are based on relationships with others, and at the postconventional level, moral judgments are based on societal needs.

Implementation

The goal of moral motivation training is to decrease antisocial behavior, including truancy, absenteeism, and behavioral infractions, through development of moral reasoning skills. The basic elements of moral motivation training include the following:

1. Determination of the discussion group members and the moral developmental stage of each individual

2. Introduction of active listening skills to the group members to encourage the group process

3. Presentation of moral dilemmas, often created by selfish behavior, during group discussion

4. Identification of possible solutions to the dilemma

5. Presentation of probing questions to advance the moral developmental stage of the group members

Moral motivation training uses the cognitive skills of listening and discussion to develop internalized rules for and conceptual understanding of ethics or an awareness of social justice, right and wrong, and relative right and wrong. Procedurally, this can be done in small- to medium-size groups as long as there is room for discussion and participation by all members. One-on-one discussions may also be used but may generate less discussion. When a child/adult dyad is used, the level of discussion may be less effective because the child may feel compelled to present the ideas that he or she believes the adult wants to hear (see Figure 3.6).

Figure 3.6 Procedural steps for the application of moral motivation training

1. Assess a child's current level of moral reasoning by asking brief, informal questions that present common moral dilemmas.

2. Read a moral decision-making scenario to the group, and request a decision for the presented problem.

3. Challenge the group's decision by encouraging group members at higher moral reasoning levels to debate the decision.

4. Add more details to the scenario, making the decision more difficult.

5. Continue this process, having group members functioning at the more advanced moral levels challenge the moral reasoning of those at lower levels. Also have students challenge each other by articulating decisions considered further up in the hierarchy of moral levels.

Evidence for Use

Several studies have established a direct correlation between reaching higher moral reasoning developmental stages and decreasing maladaptive behaviors associated with conduct disorder, such as aggression, cheating, and feelings of guilt. Forney, Forney, and Crutsinger (2005) found that a developmental shift in moral reasoning, from preconventional to conventional, led to decreases of intention to participate in delinquent behavior (i.e., stealing). In addition, higher levels of prosocial behaviors have been documented with higher levels of moral reasoning, including honesty, honoring contracts, and generosity (Blasi, 1980; Jennings, Kilkenny, & Kohlberg, 1983; Jurkovic, 1980; Kohlberg, 1969, 1975). Moreover, children with antisocial problems may exhibit prolonged immaturity in the area of socio-moral judgment (Gibbs, 2003), making them potential candidates for moral motivation training. However, Bear and Richards (1981) found that an increase in an individual's moral developmental stage resulted in only a small decrease in behavioral difficulties in these children (Arbuthnot & Gordon, 1986; Zimmerman, 1983). Yet Goldstein (1988) contends that when used after the successful acquisition of prosocial skills, moral motivation training will decrease antisocial behavior in youth with conduct disorders.

The following studies summarize some of the key research findings associated with the use of moral motivation training in children and adolescents with conduct problems.

Arbuthnot, J., & Gordon, D. A. (1986). Behavioral and cognitive effects of a moral reasoning development intervention for high-risk behavior-disordered adolescents. *Journal of Consulting and Clinical Psychology, 54*(2), 208–216.

This study investigated whether adolescents at risk for juvenile delinquency would benefit from an intervention designed to accelerate moral reasoning development. The 48 participants, who ranged in age from 13 to 17, attended between 16 and 20 weekly moral-dilemma discussion sessions, each approximately 45 minutes in length. The sessions involved presenting an example of a moral dilemma and talking through it while the facilitator prompted the students with probing questions. Results showed advances in moral reasoning and significant reduction in school office referrals and other problem behaviors. A subgroup of 22 students provided 1-year follow-up data, which showed continued behavior improvement and progress in socio-moral reasoning.

Bear, G. G., & Richards, H. C. (1981). Moral reasoning and conduct problems in the classroom. *Journal of Educational Psychology, 73*(5), 664–670.

This study examined how the levels of moral reasoning of 60 sixth graders, based on Kohlberg's Moral Judgment Interview, affected their rate of conduct problems in the classroom. As predicted, it was determined that higher levels of moral reasoning correlated with a consistently low rate of conduct problems.

Among children with lower levels of moral reasoning, there was a great degree of variance. However, moral reasoning accounted for only about 10% of the variance in conduct; academic performance, sex, and social status also accounted for some of it. Therefore, training in moral reasoning, while a worthwhile goal in itself, should be accompanied by behavioral intervention when more immediate or drastic changes in conduct are desired.

Blatt, M. M., & Kohlberg, L. (1975). The effects of classroom moral discussion upon children's level of moral judgment. *Journal of Moral Education, 4*(2), 129–161.

This study reported on the effects of moral education in schools, using Kohlberg's index of moral thinking. In the first stage of the experiment, one Jewish Sunday School classroom was studied; in the second stage, four public school classrooms plus several control groups were studied. All participants were first given a pretest addressing moral dilemmas. The experimental group discussed moral problems for 12 hours over the course of 12 weeks. These discussions challenged students to think at a higher stage of moral thinking. Posttesting as well as 1-year follow-up testing showed that the experimental group moved toward a higher level of moral thinking than the control groups.

Forney, W. S., Forney, J. C., & Crutsinger, C. (2005). Developmental stages of age and moral reasoning as predictors of juvenile delinquents' behavioral intention to steal clothing. *Family and Consumer Sciences Research Journal, 34*(2), 110–126.

One hundred juvenile delinquents aged 11 to 17 who were first-time shoplifting offenders were the subject of this study, which analyzed whether the collective factors of age group and levels of moral reasoning were a predictor of an intention to steal. The preteen and teen delinquents were given questionnaires that listed common reasons people steal and were told to rate them according to how they felt about the reasons and whether or not each was an acceptable reason to steal. Preteens were more likely than teens to have a positive attitude toward preconventional dimensions of moral reasoning (e.g., need, risk) while teens were more likely to identify with conventional dimensions of moral reasoning (e.g., peers) for stealing. In addition, preteens were less likely than teens to consider the risks involved before stealing. The findings suggest that a developmental shift to a higher level of moral reasoning led to a decrease in intention to steal; furthermore, it seemed that age group was less of an indicator of behavioral intent than was level of moral reasoning.

Niles, W. J. (1986). Effects of a moral development discussion group on delinquent and predelinquent boys. *Journal of Counseling Psychology, 33*(1), 45–51.

This study assessed the effects of using moral discussion groups (MDGs; Blatt & Kohlberg, 1975) to improve moral reasoning skills (and, as a result, classroom behavior) in 59 delinquent or predelinquent adolescents. Results indicated that MDGs were effective in helping students advance from one level of moral reasoning to another, when compared to a control group. However, this study also showed that these advances in moral reasoning did not lead to any improvements in classroom behavior.

Considerations

For Teaching

If used in a classroom setting, moral motivation training may best be done in civics, social studies, or liberal studies classes. If moral motivation training is used, groups should ideally include only one or two individuals identified as having conduct problems or being at risk for developing conduct problems. In addition, group membership should include youths assessed at different levels of moral reasoning in order to challenge individuals to think and rethink scenarios.

For Age and Developmental Level

Young and very young children are unlikely candidates for moral motivation training due to the cognitive and language demands of the intervention. Preteens and teens, however, are ideal candidates for the discussion because their age groups are more experienced with moral dilemmas and more likely to be familiar with social rules and norms.

For Culture and Language Differences

The studies that provide the evidence for using this intervention method are somewhat dated and Eurocentric in nature. Although this does not invalidate the findings, it does mean that the user should consider how culture might influence the developmental stages of ethical or moral reasoning. In some cultures, definitions of the self or of relationships may or may not hold as much influence for determining behavioral and cultural norms. Expectations or belief in a greater good may also vary across cultures, with some adopting higher principles earlier.

VII. Parent Training

Parent training is a parent-focused, psychoeducational (or social learning) intervention that facilitates appropriate interactions between children and parents, leading to an increase in positive interactions and a decrease in coercive interactions (Dean, Myors, & Evans, 2003; Dishion & Andrews, 1995). Parent training teaches specific parenting skills and effective child management techniques by focusing on the thought processes and behaviors of the parent. This type of instruction assists parents in avoiding the use of coercive disciplinary procedures to obtain behavioral compliance. Such disciplinary procedures often result in children mimicking coercive communication patterns and becoming resistant to learning functional social skills (Martinez & Forgatch, 2001). Bor and Sanders (2004) identified parental coercive behaviors as hitting, scolding, and shouting. Children's coercive behavior frequently reflects actions modeled by a parent and is often exhibited as yelling, hitting, and throwing objects while refusing to comply with a request.

The combination of parental coercive behavior and child coercive behavior results in a negative cycle that begins with a directive given by the parent. In one scenario, the child's negative behavior is negatively reinforced (e.g., after the child gives a coercive response such as whining, the parent does not persist with the directive and the child does not comply). In a second scenario, the parent's negative behavior is negatively reinforced (e.g., the child's coercive behavior stops when the parent uses continual and escalating coercive behaviors, such as shouting).

For example, Katy, a 5-year-old who is exhibiting conduct problems, is often deceitful and violates the rights of others by bullying or destroying property. When Katy wants the toy another child is playing with, she aggressively demands that the child give her the toy. If this doesn't get the result she wants, she screams and becomes more violent. If an adult intervenes, Katy immediately acts innocent, blaming the other child for the confrontation. In parent training, Katy's parents are taught to recognize this coercive cycle and to reinforce Katy when she verbally asks for what she wants and/or states her feelings verbally. Her parents are also taught to discipline Katy for her inappropriate behaviors with natural consequences, such as not being allowed to play with a child whom she has bullied for a specific period of time or taking away the object Katy was trying to acquire.

Implementation

The goal of parent training is to decrease antisocial behavior and prevent conduct problems in at-risk populations by increasing the use of effective parenting skills and positive disciplinary techniques. The basic elements of parent training include the following:

1. Teaching or coaching parents to understand coercive parent–child interactions and their cycle

2. Teaching appropriate skill sets through modeling, including:

    a. Effective reinforcement strategies and different types of reinforcers (e.g., verbal praise, social reinforcers, tangible reinforcers, and activity reinforcers)

    b. Observation skills

    c. Play skills

    d. Response-cost techniques

    e. Timeout procedures

f. Punishment and extinction

g. Relationship enhancement skills (e.g., partner support, communication, and problem solving)

h. Self-regulation/monitoring skills

i. Token economy and reward charts

j. Contingency contracts

k. Mood management

l. Self-determination

m. Relaxation techniques

n. Stress reduction techniques

o. Anger management techniques

p. Self-monitoring and self-reward

Implementation of parent training begins by first conducting an intake assessment with the family. This assessment includes an evaluation of the family climate to determine the needs of the family and any barriers to success, including cultural–parental expectations (Forehand & Kotchick, 2002). Based on the intake assessment, skill deficits are identified. Then, goals and objectives are formulated that can be achieved by implementing family and parent management techniques. The targets of the intervention are the child's coercive behaviors as well as the actions of the parent(s) that appear to reinforce these behaviors. Additionally, this initial assessment provides a broad overview of the goals of the intervention, the relevance to the family of the information to be presented, and the responsibilities of the parents in the process (e.g., follow-through and attendance).

Next, the logistics of the intervention's implementation are determined. These logistics include making decisions about the format of the training (e.g., individual, group, or group with individual consultation sessions), the location of the intervention (e.g., at the home, at a community agency, or in the school), and the time of the intervention (e.g., convenience for parents should be considered when using a group format).

Begin the intervention by teaching parents to use effective discipline techniques such as differential reinforcement and timeout procedures (see Figure 3.7). Throughout the process, assist parents in choosing the specific parenting and child management techniques, based on effective child-rearing practices, that they wish to implement. At the end of each session, hold a family meeting to practice parenting and communication skills through modeling and role-play. Video vignettes can be used during the family meeting for behavioral modeling and discussion prompts (Spaccarelli, Cotler, & Penman, 1992; Webster-Stratton, 1984, 1994). Both parent training and the parent's application of the training should be monitored to determine the effects of one or more of the training topics. Some parents may respond well and need only one or two trainings on topics, while other families may benefit from ongoing parenting training, such as semester- or year-long evening courses on campus. After training sessions are completed, refresher sessions or periodic individual sessions may be needed to review and maintain the skills learned. In many cases, parents will receive training in three or four topics over several sessions. For a family struggling with a child with conduct disorder, one-time sessions would be inadequate, but lengthy, repeat visits may be impracticable.

Figure 3.7 Procedural steps for the application of parent training

1. Find a mutually satisfactory time for meeting, and determine the appropriate number of trainings that might be needed. Consider creating a partnership contract to agree to the number of sessions and the number of techniques that will be taught.

2. Begin each session by reviewing the effective parenting technique discussed in the previous session, reviewing the homework assignment, and answering specific parental questions.

3. Teach a specific parenting technique, using descriptions and examples to demonstrate relevance to the individual.

4. Verbally describe the technique.

5. Discuss parental concerns about using the technique, and provide evidence of its effectiveness so that families know what to expect.

6. Give specific verbal examples.

7. Model the technique.

8. Ask the parents for an example of a time when the technique could have been effective, and role-play the technique using the given example. If conducting training in after-school or parent groups, be sure to do role-play examples with several parents so everyone who attends is involved and contributes.

9. For individual family sessions in the home rather than large parent groups at school, bring the child into the session and briefly explain the technique to him or her. Have the parents role-play the technique with the child. Provide feedback after the performance, highlighting positive statements regarding the parents' implementation.

10. Encourage independent implementation by requesting the use of the technique a specific number of times by the next session. Additionally, request that the parents document the effects, including any problems encountered, and note any questions they have.

Evidence for Use

Parent-training techniques have been empirically found to be some of the most effective techniques for preventing and reducing conduct problems, increasing positive parent–child interactions, reducing aggression, and facilitating beneficial parent and child behavioral changes in the home (Biglan & Taylor, 1998; Brestan & Eyberg, 1998; Forehand & Kotchick, 2002; Webster-Stratton, 1993; Webster-Stratton & Hammond, 1997). Decreases in negative parent–child interactions (e.g., critical parental statements) and improved child behavior (i.e., decreased problem behaviors and increased prosocial behaviors) reinforce the beneficial aspect that parent-training programs have for at-risk children and their families (Reid, Webster-Stratton, & Baydar, 2004; Webster-Stratton, 1998). In three studies comparing parent-focused and child-focused interventions with high-risk children or adolescents and youth with conduct problems, parent-focused interventions were found to be more or equally effective in reducing child behavior problems (Dishion & Andrews, 1995; Kazdin et al., 1992; Webster-Stratton & Hammond, 1997).

The following studies summarize some of the key research findings associated with parent training and conduct problems.

Dadds, M. R., & McHugh, T. A. (1992). Social support and treatment outcome in behavioral family therapy for child conduct problems. *Journal of Consulting and Clinical Child Psychology, 60*(2), 252–259.

This study examined the effects of child management training (CMT) with and without adjunctive ally support training (AST). Participants were 22 disadvantaged single parents of children with conduct problems. Half of the participants selected allies, who were then given introductory training in supporting the single parents. The other half did not receive formal support. Pretreatment, posttreatment, and 6-month follow-up levels of parent behavior, child deviance, social support, and parental depression were evaluated in both groups. Results demonstrated that the formal adjunctive ally support did not make a significant difference; however, social support from friends was shown to be critical to the long-term success of the training.

Dean, C., Myors, K., & Evans, E. (2003). Community-wide implementation of a parenting program: The South East Sydney Positive Parenting Project. *Australian e-Journal for the Advancement of Mental Health, 2*(3). Retrieved June 4, 2006, from http://www.auseinet.com/journal/vol2iss3/dean.pdf

Detailing the implementation of a community-wide parenting program in South East Sydney (the Positive Parenting Project), this paper documents that an evidence-based program formerly utilized only in small, controlled settings can be successful as a broader, community-based program. Public health services and various government and community agencies, such as preschools and churches, collaborated to offer this program at a low cost to parents. Evaluations after the program's completion and at 6- and 12-month follow-up dates revealed that improvements were sustained in parental mental health and in reduced disruptive child behavior, dysfunctional parenting, and conflict between parents.

Dishion, T. J., & Andrews, D. W. (1995). Preventing escalation in problem behaviors with high-risk young adolescents: Immediate and 1-year outcomes. *Journal of Consulting and Clinical Psychology, 63*(4), 538–548.

This study examined the effects of parent-focused, child-focused, and materials-only interventions for reducing problem behaviors in high-risk youth. The study included 158 families with children between the ages of 10 and 14. Results showed that problem-solving skills increased and parent–child coercive interactions decreased significantly following both the parent-focused and teen-focused interventions, compared to subjects in the materials-only group or the control group. This study also demonstrated that interventions grouping high-risk adolescents together on a regular basis led to escalations in tobacco use and problem behavior at school, suggesting the need to re-evaluate strategies that aggregate high-risk adolescents into group intervention programs.

Kazdin, A. E., Siegel, T. C., & Bass, D. (1992). Cognitive problem-solving skills training and parent management training in the treatment of antisocial behavior in children. *Journal of Consulting and Clinical Psychology, 60*(5), 733–747.

A randomized study evaluated problem-solving skills training (PSST) and parent management training (PMT)—each separately and both combined—to determine which training was more effective in 97 children aged 7 to 13 years. Although PSST, PMT, and PSST+PMT each improved children's functioning, the combined treatment produced more marked, pervasive, and durable changes in children's functioning and greater changes in parental functioning posttreatment and at a 1-year follow-up. A larger proportion of children receiving combination treatment reached normal levels of functioning.

Reid, M. J., Webster-Stratton, C., & Baydar, N. (2004). Halting the development of conduct problems in Head Start children: The effects of parent training. *Journal of Clinical Child and Adolescent Psychology, 33*(2), 279–291.

For this study, nine Head Start centers were randomly assigned to implement the Incredible Years Parent Training Program or to serve as the control group. Before intervention, all 882 participants were observed at home to determine baseline. Children were considered based on their rate of problem behavior, and mothers were considered if they made 10 or more critical statements to their children within the 30-minute observation. Results were tracked based on problem levels at baseline, whether the mothers attended training, and whether they improved. It was found that without parent training, children showed rapid increases in problem behavior. However, about two-thirds of the mothers made an effort to attend training, and for those who showed improvement (at least a 30% decrease in criticisms), child conduct problems decreased and prosocial behaviors increased, pointing to the validity of parent training programs as a method for improving the behavior of young children.

Webster-Stratton, C. (1998). Preventing conduct problems in Head Start children: Strengthening parenting competencies. *Journal of Consulting and Clinical Psychology, 66*(5), 715–730.

Nine urban Head Start centers were chosen for this study and were randomly assigned to either the intervention or control group. In all, 542 families, with an average income of $10,000 and many other factors that put children at risk for conduct problems, participated in the study. In the centers chosen for the intervention group, 75% of families chose to participate in the 8-week PARTNERS parent training. At postassessment, 65% of participant mothers who were considered high risk at preassessment showed at least a 30% reduction in critical statements, compared to only 52% in the control group. Significant improvements in children's behavior in the intervention group were also noted. Some improvements were maintained at 1-year follow-up, although some of the differences between groups were no longer clinically significant.

Webster-Stratton, C., & Hammond, M. (1997). Treating children with early-onset conduct problems: A comparison of child and parent training interventions. *Journal of Consulting and Clinical Psychology, 65*(1), 93–109.

This study of 97 families sought to determine whether child training or parent training is more effective in treating early-onset conduct problems. Each family received one or both of these interventions or no treatment. Interventions that involved child training were superior to those that involved parent training for improving problem-solving and conflict-management skills. Interventions that involved parent training were superior in terms of child behavior improvements (as reported by parents), parent behaviors, and consumer satisfaction. At a 1-year follow-up, all significant results of treatment were maintained and a positive "delayed effect" of combination therapy on deviance at home was noted.

Considerations

For Teaching

Behavioral parent training is effective as a preventative measure and as an intervention (Taylor, Eddy, & Biglan, 1999), and in both uses, certain factors should be considered when implementing them. First, it may be best to limit training groups to no more than 16 participants or eight families. Parents will benefit most by spending approximately 45 hours in training (Patterson & Narrett, 1990). Also, it is critical to establish maintenance procedures after the intervention has ended, because behavioral difficulties often resurface. There may be certain barriers to achieving success with behavioral parent training, including family stressors, a lack of parent compliance with expectations of therapy, the necessity for treatment flexibility due to heterogeneous family characteristics, and therapist feelings of hopelessness and ineffectiveness.

For Age and Developmental Level

Behavioral parent training is most effective when the children are between 5 and 10 years old (Patterson & Narrett, 1990). Parent training is certainly appropriate for children at the pre-K level, but conduct problems are unlikely to appear at very early ages. Additionally, there would be less learned behavior to address and parent–child relationship history to consider for students who are younger.

For Culture and Language Differences

Some research suggests therapists can be insensitive to cultural differences in parenting attitudes and parental expectations of child behavior and the intervention process (Forehand & Kotchick, 2002). Parents might bring preconceived notions about therapy that are not cognitive–behavioral in nature. Moreover, many parents have strong beliefs about child-rearing practices, and overcoming resistance for successful implementation may prove difficult (Kazdin, 2005). Because of these and other barriers, additional techniques to encourage parent participation are often necessary. Parents may also need specific assistance with implementing interventions in the home, and at times, parental issues may emerge that require alternate treatment methods or referrals to different agencies. While some of these issues are not specific to culture or language, they would certainly be influenced by differences.

VIII. Multimodal Interventions

Multimodal interventions consist of a combination of two or more affective, social, behavioral, and cognitive components (Webster-Stratton & Hammond, 1997). In general, most multimodal interventions for conduct problems combine child treatment with parent training to create a more efficacious intervention. However, efficacy exists for combining different intervention approaches with the child only. For instance, Goldstein (1988) lists a great deal of empirical research pointing to the combined use of social skills training, problem-solving training, and moral motivation training.

As an example of a multimodal intervention for child treatment combined with parent training, Johnny, a 15-year-old with conduct problems, is failing all of his classes, is absent from school a majority of the time, and has been arrested for shoplifting. Johnny is caught stealing from a classmate and becomes aggressive with the teacher when confronted. When Johnny's mother arrives at school, the teacher notices that the mother uses harsh language and threatens to take away all of his privileges for a year. When Johnny raises his voice, his mother begins to withdraw the threats of punishment to avoid embarrassment in front of the teacher. Johnny is exhibiting behavior that suggests he has deficits in problem solving and social skills; therefore, both problem-solving and social skills training should be prescribed. Additionally, parent training should be provided to assist Johnny's mother in using more effective parenting skills.

Implementation

The goal of multimodal interventions is to decrease antisocial and delinquent behavior by implementing two or more different types of intervention approaches. The basic elements of multimodal interventions include the following:

1. Provide multiple treatments with appropriate personnel simultaneously or in sequence, including:

    a. Parent training

    b. Problem-solving skills training

    c. Social skills training

    d. Anger management skills training

    e. Moral motivation training

    f. Proactive classroom management

    g. Cooperative learning

2. Determine the responsible parties for implementing and monitoring treatments

Five procedural steps are established for implementing multimodal interventions (see Figure 3.8). First, determine the exact interventions within the multimodal framework based on assessment results indicating the causal factors associated with the conduct problems. Second, determine the length of treatment based on the severity of the causal factors. (With multimodal interventions, treatment may be provided for longer periods of time than with single interventions.) Third, based on the prescribed intervention, identify the specific members of the team who will provide services (e.g., psychologist, social worker, case worker). Fourth, implement the interventions simultaneously. Fifth, transfer the learned behaviors and techniques to the natural environment.

> ## Figure 3.8 Procedural steps for the application of multimodal interventions
>
> 1. Determine the intervention approaches to be used.
>
> 2. Determine the length of treatment.
>
> 3. Determine the person most qualified to implement the interventions (this may be an individual or team of professionals).
>
> 4. Implement the interventions simultaneously, as described in the procedural steps for each intervention.
>
> 5. Generalize treatment effects to natural environments.

Evidence for Use

Webster-Stratton and colleagues have used multimodal treatments and found that conduct problems did not recur with at-risk populations (Reid et al., 2004; Webster-Stratton, 1998; Webster-Stratton & Hammond, 1997; Webster-Stratton et al., 2001). In addition, Dishion and Andrews (1995) found multimodal treatment that includes child and parent treatment to be effective at treating adolescent conduct problems. Although problem solving is effective in reducing the incidence of conduct disorder in children and adolescents, it is better used as a part of multimodal or multisystemic training (Taylor et al., 1999).

The following studies summarize some of the key research findings associated with the use of multimodal interventions in children and adolescents with conduct problems.

Conduct Problems Prevention Research Group. (1999). Initial impact of the Fast Track prevention trial for conduct problems: I. The high-risk sample. *Journal of Consulting and Clinical Psychology, 67*(5), 631–647.

This article examines implementation of Fast Track, a long-term, multicomponent, multisite program designed to prevent antisocial behavior in high-risk children. Participants included 891 behaviorally disruptive kindergarteners and their parents, divided into intervention and control groups. Intervention consisted of the PATHS® (Promoting Alternative THinking Strategies) curriculum plus social skills training, academic tutoring, parent training, and home visiting. At the end of Grade 1, children in the intervention group showed significantly more progress than those in the control group in acquiring emotional and social coping skills, which were accompanied by more positive peer relations. Compared with control parents, those in the intervention group showed more warmth and positive involvement, more appropriate and consistent discipline, more positive school involvement, and less harsh discipline.

Kazdin, A. E., Siegel, T. C., & Bass, D. (1992). Cognitive problem-solving skills training and parent management training in the treatment of antisocial behavior in children. *Journal of Consulting and Clinical Psychology, 60*(5), 733–747.

A randomized study evaluated problem-solving skills training (PSST) and parent management training (PMT)—each separately and both combined—to determine which training was more effective in 97 children aged 7 to 13 years. Although PSST, PMT, and PSST+PMT each improved children's functioning, the combined treatment produced more marked, pervasive, and durable changes in children's functioning and greater changes in parental functioning posttreatment and at a 1-year follow-up. A larger proportion of children receiving combination treatment reached normal levels of functioning.

Leeman, L. W., Gibbs, J. C., & Fuller, D. (1993). Evaluation of a multi-component group treatment program for juvenile delinquents. *Aggressive Behavior, 19,* 281–292.

Equipping Youth to Help One Another (EQUIP), which incorporates social skills training, anger management, and moral education into a peer group format, was evaluated in this study of 57 adolescents in a medium-security correctional facility. Compared with two control groups, the EQUIP group showed substantial gains in social skills and behavior. Institutional conduct gains were highly significant in terms of self-reported misconduct, staff-filed incident reports, and unexcused absences from school. The program's impact was sustained over time, as evidenced by a recidivism rate half that of controls at 6 months and one-third at 1 year.

O'Donnell, J., Hawkins, J. D., Catalano, R. F., Abbott, R. D., & Day, L. E. (1995). Preventing school failure, drug use, and delinquency among low-income children: Long-term intervention in elementary schools. *American Journal of Orthopsychiatry, 65*(1), 87–100.

This article reports on the cumulative effects of the Seattle Social Development Project, a 6-year, elementary school program of classroom, child, and parent interventions designed to reduce the risk of school failure, drug use, and delinquency in low-income children. At the end of sixth grade, girls in the intervention group perceived more opportunities and reinforcements for involvement in the classroom and expressed stronger bonding to school than girls in the control group; they were also less likely to start using tobacco (significant difference), alcohol, or marijuana. Boys in the intervention group improved in social competencies and academic skills and efforts. In addition, they tended to become delinquent at lower rates than controls but had similar rates of drug initiation.

Reid, M. J., Webster-Stratton, C., & Baydar, N. (2004). Halting the development of conduct problems in Head Start children: The effects of parent training. *Journal of Clinical Child and Adolescent Psychology, 33*(2), 279–291.

For this study, nine Head Start centers were randomly assigned to either implement the Incredible Years Parent Training Program or to serve as the control group. Before intervention, all 882 participants were observed at home to determine baseline. Children were considered based on their rate of problem behavior, and mothers were considered if they made 10 or more critical statements to their children within the 30-minute observation. Results were tracked based on problem levels at baseline, whether the mothers attended training, and whether they improved. It was found that without parent training, children showed rapid increases in problem behavior. However, about two-thirds of the mothers made an effort to attend training, and for those who showed improvement (at least a 30% decrease in criticisms), child conduct problems decreased and prosocial behaviors increased, pointing to the validity of parent training programs as a method for improving the behavior of young children.

Webster-Stratton, C. (1998). Preventing conduct problems in Head Start children: Strengthening parenting competencies. *Journal of Consulting and Clinical Psychology, 66*(5), 715–730.

Nine urban Head Start centers were chosen for this study and were randomly assigned to either the intervention or control group. In all, 542 families, with an average income of $10,000 and many other factors that put children at risk for conduct problems, participated in the study. In the centers chosen for the intervention group, 75% of families chose to participate in the 8-week PARTNERS parent training. At postassessment, 65% of participant mothers who were considered high risk at preassessment showed at least a 30% reduction in critical statements, compared to only 52% in the control group. Significant improvements in children's behavior in the intervention group were also noted. Some improvements were maintained at 1-year follow-up, although some of the differences between groups were no longer clinically significant.

Webster-Stratton, C., & Hammond, M. (1997). Treating children with early-onset conduct problems: A comparison of child and parent training interventions. *Journal of Consulting and Clinical Psychology, 65*(1), 93–109.

This study of 97 families sought to determine whether child training or parent training is more effective in treating early-onset conduct problems. Each family received one or both of these interventions or no treatment. Interventions that involved child training were superior to those that involved parent training for improving problem-solving and conflict-management skills. Interventions that involved parent training were superior in terms of child behavior improvements (as reported by parents), parent behaviors, and consumer satisfaction. At a 1-year follow-up, all significant results of treatment were maintained and a positive "delayed effect" of combination therapy on deviance at home was noted.

Webster-Stratton, C., Reid, J., & Hammond, M. (2001). Social skills and problem-solving training for children with early-onset conduct problems: Who benefits? *Journal of Child Psychology and Psychiatry, 42*(7), 943–952.

In this study, the investigators examined their social skills, problem-solving, and anger management curriculum (Incredible Years: Dinosaur Curriculum) for long-term effectiveness and generalizability across settings. Children with early-onset conduct problems from 99 families were randomly assigned to receive this curriculum or to a control group. Compared with controls, the children who underwent intervention had statistically and clinically greater improvement in conduct problems and in cognitive social problem-solving strategies. These results occurred in both home and school settings and were sustained at 1 year. The presence of attention-deficit/hyperactivity disorder or family stress did not affect a child's ability to benefit from treatment, but negative parenting did emerge as a risk factor.

Considerations

For Teaching

Multimodal interventions will involve the coordination of multiple professionals, in and out of the school environment, which may or may not include the classroom teacher. Therefore, collaborative relationships, teaming, and shared goals will be critical components for successful implementation, progress monitoring, and information sharing across treatment providers.

For Families

Multimodal interventions are prescribed for children with serious conduct problems or early-onset conduct problems in which family factors have been determined to be contributors to the problem. Thus, professionals must ensure that families understand the commitment required and that expectations are specifically stated between the clinician and the family. However, family participation is often difficult to obtain, so opportunities for encouragement should be maximized when possible.

For Age and Developmental Level

Developmental changes in children will co-occur with sequential treatments; thus trainings about childhood stages may need to be revisited if the family of a 5-year-old continues to receive treatment for several years. Techniques that were appropriate at age 5 may need modification as the child gets older.

For Culture and Language Differences

Parent buy-in and consent for a multimodal intervention might be confounded by unknown or less-than-understood differences about cultural perceptions of individual treatments and combinations of treatments.

IX. Multisystemic Therapy

Multisystemic therapy is a short-term, home-based, family-focused intervention used with children and adolescents with severe conduct problems (Henggeler, Schoenwald, Borduin, Rowland, & Cunningham, 1998). This therapy is characterized as an action-oriented, intensive, in-home treatment provided by qualified mental health providers that addresses behavior across all areas of adolescent functioning, generally lasting for 3 or 4 months (Henggeler et al. 2006; Thomas, 2006). Parent training and adolescent coping skills training are used with the adolescent, family, school, and peer group, simultaneously providing a combination of all effective treatments in multiple environments, based on the family systems approach.

For example, Randy, an 18-year-old, is currently taking medication for attention-deficit/hyperactivity disorder (ADHD). He has been arrested multiple times for felony activities, is at risk for out-of-home placement, and has earned only enough credits in high school to be considered a first-semester sophomore. He is a member of a gang and has been suspended from school 10 out of the last 20 days. He lives with his mother, who is unemployed, bipolar, and an alcoholic; his 16-year-old sister, who has been diagnosed with anxiety and depression; and his sister's 2-year-old son. To address these factors, the multisystemic therapy team would devise a treatment plan to address all issues within Randy's home, school, and social environments and would include team members from the school, community, mental health agency, and juvenile justice system.

Implementation

The goal of multisystemic therapy is to reduce delinquent, criminal, and/or antisocial and aggressive behavior, and to increase family cohesion while empowering families to solve future problems. The basic elements of multisystemic therapy include the following:

1. Selection of highly trained professionals with small caseloads

2. Coordination of services with multiple community and school agencies

3. Implementation of problem-solving training

4. Completion of a strengths-based assessment to determine the behavioral problems and reinforcers within all environments

5. Individual and comprehensive case conceptualization

6. Formation of a treatment plan, integrating action-oriented interventions, family strengths and responsibilities, and services into all environments

---

7. Accountability of treatment teams

8. Implementation of behavioral and cognitive–behavioral interventions

9. Case management

Before multisystemic therapy is implemented, treatment teams of highly trained therapists and supervisors must be established. These teams will frequently meet together and with other agencies to review treatment progress, plan interventions, and continue training (see Figure 3.9). The next step is to conduct an assessment and write an individualized treatment plan based on identified family and youth strengths, including interventions to be provided in multiple environments (e.g., home, school). Specific interventions to be implemented are chosen based on individual needs and consideration of the interacting effects created between the child and the different environments. The treatment plan should be reviewed often and modified as needed. Finally, the team implements the plan with multiple weekly sessions. Therapy is intensive (services are provided to youth and families as needed, 24 hours a day, 7 days a week), but it is short-term and ends when goals have been achieved.

Figure 3.9 Procedural steps for the application of multisystemic therapy

1. Create multisystemic therapy teams with a team supervisor who oversees the MST therapist and observes therapy in the child or adolescent's home.

2. Provide extensive training for MST therapists by a multisystemic therapy consultant before beginning the intervention and then periodically (e.g., once a month).

3. Hold weekly MST team meetings for peer and supervisory consultation.

4. Consult and meet regularly with individuals from other agencies who are providing services to the child or adolescent (e.g., teachers, school administrators, probation officers, child protective service case managers, and mental health case workers).

5. Provide adolescents with the ability to contact their MST therapists around the clock, and prepare the therapists to provide services by making home visits.

Continued on next page

6. Write and implement a highly individualized treatment plan that addresses all domains of adolescent or child functioning. Such plans may include:

    a. Teaching cognitive–behavioral skills to youth, addressing issues such as problem-solving or anger management deficits

    b. Teaching effective discipline skills to parents, such as differential reinforcement, response-cost techniques, and contracting skills

    c. Teaching observational skills for parents to use in monitoring peer group relations, such as association with deviant peers and school truancy issues

    d. Assisting families in parent–school relationships by participating in parent–teacher meetings and special-education meetings, assisting with homework completion, and handling school disciplinary referrals

    e. Teaching family management strategies, such as scheduling and family member responsibilities (e.g., chore lists)

7. Evaluate outcomes continuously and modify the treatment plan as needed, with assistance from peer and supervisory consultants.

8. Assure treatment generalization by assigning homework to be completed by the entire family based on the interventions being used, and provide feedback on completion and success at every session.

9. Provide a referral for less-intensive treatment following completion of multisystemic therapy.

Evidence for Use

Multiple studies have found that multisystemic therapy decreases the rate at which youth are re-arrested (Henggeler et al., 1996). Henggeler et al. (1998) found a decrease in antisocial behavior and an increase in family cohesion.

The following studies summarize key research findings associated with multisystemic therapy and conduct problems.

Borduin, C. M., Mann, B. J., Cone, L. T., Henggeler, S. W., Fucci, B. R., Blaske, D. M., et al. (1995). Multisystemic treatment of serious juvenile offenders: Long-term prevention of criminality and violence. *Journal of Consulting and Clinical Psychology, 63*(4), 569–578.

This study compared multisystemic therapy (MST), which focuses on the family, school, neighborhood, and other systems that affect adolescent behavior, with individual therapy. Participants were 140 families with a 12- to 17-year-old adolescent who had at least two arrests. Based on posttreatment evaluation and follow-up data gathered for 4 years after the treatment was completed, the results showed that adolescents receiving MST had significantly fewer behavioral problems and a lower probability of subsequent arrest, as well as more family cohesion and adaptability, than did those who received individual therapy.

Henggeler, S. W., Melton, G. B., Brondino, M. J., Scherer, D. G., & Hanley, J. H. (1997). Multisystemic therapy with violent and chronic juvenile offenders and their families: The role of treatment fidelity in successful dissemination. *Journal of Consulting and Clinical Psychology, 65*(5), 821–833.

This study sought to determine whether multisystemic therapy (MST) could have the same positive results as previously documented when conducted as normal clinical training without the oversight of an MST expert. After 155 adolescents participated in the therapy, it was discovered that MST did reduce the percentage of re-arrests and days incarcerated but not by as significant a percentage as previous data had shown, revealing the importance of treatment fidelity. The authors concluded that the costs of training facilitators properly to ensure strong adherence to therapy protocol outweigh the potential costs of ineffective therapy.

Henggeler, S. W., Melton, G. B., & Smith, L. A. (1992). Family preservation using multisystemic therapy: An effective alternative to incarcerating serious juvenile offenders. *Journal of Consulting and Clinical Psychology, 60*(6), 953–961.

In comparing multisystemic therapy (MST) to the traditional therapy offered by South Carolina's Department of Youth Services, this study found that 84 serious juvenile offenders responded better to MST than to traditional therapy. Pretreatment, posttreatment, and follow-up assessments showed that youths who underwent MST had fewer arrests and offenses, shorter incarcerations, and improved family relations. These results appeared to be consistent regardless of divergent backgrounds, strengths, and weaknesses.

Rowland, M. D., Halliday-Boykins, C. A., Henggeler, S. W., Cunningham, P. B., Lee, T. G., Kruesi, M. J. P., et al. (2005). A randomized trial of multisystemic therapy with Hawaii's Felix Class youths. *Journal of Emotional and Behavioral Disorders, 13*(1), 13–23.

In this study, youths with serious mental health disorders were randomly placed into either multisystemic therapy (MST) or the traditional therapy provided by the Hawaii Continuum of Care. Those who underwent MST experienced a significant decrease in self-reported minor criminal activity and a smaller decrease in arrests per month. Caregivers of those who underwent MST reported greater satisfaction with social support than did those of youths who underwent traditional therapy. Additionally, youths receiving MST spent more days per month in general education settings and fewer days in out-of-home placement than those who received traditional therapy.

Timmons-Mitchell, J., Bender, M. B., Kishna, M. A., & Mitchell, C. C. (2006). An independent effectiveness trial of multisystemic therapy with juvenile justice youth. *Journal of Clinical Child and Adolescent Psychology, 35*(2), 227–236.

This randomized clinical study, the first to assess the effectiveness of multisystematic therapy (MST) in the United States without oversight of the model developers, sought to determine the effectiveness of MST on a broader basis among juvenile offenders. Pre- and posttreatment data showed that youths in traditional therapy were 3.2 times more likely to be re-arrested than youths who underwent MST. This community-based, independent study revealed substantial increases in the youths' ability to function in the home, at school, and in the community, indicating that the primary goals of MST can be met without the management of the model's developers.

Considerations

For Teaching

Multisystemic therapy is unlikely to occur in the classroom but may involve a teacher for data collection or interviews to determine needs. Academic deficits should not be overlooked, however, because severe conduct disorders would probably interfere with school attendance and participation.

For Families

Multisystemic therapy is appropriate for severe conduct disorders. However, it requires a great deal of in-home intervention, with sessions provided on a daily to weekly basis (Thomas, 2006). There also may be a number of obstacles to overcome when implementing multisystemic therapy. For example, defensive family patterns can significantly interfere with problem-solving and communication skills training (Margolin, Burman, & John, 1989). To address this problem, the therapist must understand the function of the behavior and how it is maintained by the family system. It is important that the therapist does not make value judgments about the behavior as moral or immoral. In addition, for multisystemic therapy to be optimized, Robbins et al. (2006) found that alliances must be established between the therapist and the adolescent as well as between the therapist and the mother.

Summary

This chapter presented a review of the characteristics of and conditions for conduct problems, along with a summary of interventions that have been shown to be effective in remediation of conduct problems. These interventions included token economy systems, interdependent group-oriented contingency management, anger management skills training, problem-solving training, social skills training, moral motivation training, parent training, multimodal interventions, and multisystemic therapy. While each intervention presented differs in its application of one or more behavioral, cognitive–behavioral, or social learning theories, all are shaped by the fundamental goals of treatment: prevention and remediation of problem behaviors. The information presented in this chapter forms the basis of the supplemental classroom- and home-based materials that correspond to this book.

References

Alberto, P. A., & Troutman, A. C. (2003). *Applied behavior analysis for teachers* (6th ed.). Upper Saddle River, NJ: Prentice Hall.

American Psychiatric Association. (2000). *Diagnostic and statistical manual of mental disorders* (4th ed., text revision). Washington, DC: Author.

Arbuthnot, J., & Gordon, D. A. (1986). Behavioral and cognitive effects of a moral reasoning development intervention for high-risk behavior-disordered adolescents. *Journal of Consulting and Clinical Psychology, 54*(2), 208–216.

Azrin, N. H., Donohue, B., Teichner, G. A., Crum, T., Howell, J., & DeCato, L. A. (2001). A controlled evaluation and description of individual-cognitive problem solving and family-behavior therapies in dually-diagnosed conduct-disordered and substance-dependent youth. *Journal of Child & Adolescent Substance Abuse, 11*(1), 1–43.

Baer, A. M., Rowbury, T., & Baer, D. M. (1973). The development of instructional control over classroom activities of deviant preschool children. *Journal of Applied Behavior Analysis, 6*(2), 289–298.

Bandura, A. (1969). *Principles of behavior modification.* New York: Holt, Rinehart, & Winston.

Barrish, H. H., Saunders, M., & Wolf, M. M. (1969). Good behavior game: Effects of individual contingencies for group consequences on disruptive behavior in a classroom. *Journal of Applied Behavior Analysis, 2*(2), 119–124.

Bear, G. G., & Richards, H. C. (1981). Moral reasoning and conduct problems in the classroom. *Journal of Educational Psychology, 73*(5), 644–670.

Bierman, K. L., Miller, C. L., & Stabb, S. D. (1987). Improving the social behavior and peer acceptance of rejected boys: Effects of social skill training with instructions and prohibitions. *Journal of Consulting and Clinical Psychology, 55*(2), 194–200.

Biglan, A., & Taylor, T. K. (1998). Behavioral family interventions for improving child-rearing: A review of the literature for clinicians and policy makers. *Clinical Child and Family Psychology Review, 1*(1), 41–60.

Blasi, A. (1980). Bridging moral cognition and moral action: A critical review of the literature. *Psychological Bulletin, 88*(1), 1–45.

Blatt, M. M., & Kohlberg, L. (1975). The effects of classroom moral discussion upon children's level of moral judgment. *Journal of Moral Education, 4*(2), 129–161.

Bor, W., & Sanders, M. R. (2004). Correlates of self-reported coercive parenting of preschool-aged children at high risk for the development of conduct problems. *Australian and New Zealand Journal of Psychiatry, 38*(9), 738–745.

Borduin, C. M., Mann, B. J., Cone, L. T., Henggeler, S. W., Fucci, B. R., Blaske, D. M., et al. (1995). Multisystemic treatment of serious juvenile offenders: Long-term prevention of criminality and violence. *Journal of Consulting and Clinical Psychology, 63*(4), 569–578.

Borduin, C. M., & Schaeffer, C. M. (1998). Violent offending in adolescence: Epidemiology, correlates, outcomes, and treatment. In T. P. Gullotta, G. R. Adams, & R. Montemayor (Eds.), *Delinquent violent youth: Theory and interventions* (pp. 144–174). Newbury Park, CA: Sage.

Bostow, D., & Geiger, O. G. (1976). Good behavior game: A replication and systematic analysis with a second grade class. *School Applications of Learning Theory, 8*(2), 18–25.

Brestan, E. V., & Eyberg, S. M. (1998). Effective psychosocial treatments of conduct-disordered children and adolescents: 29 years, 82 studies and 5,272 kids. *Journal of Clinical Child Psychology, 27*(2), 180–189.

Bry, B. H., & George, F. E. (1979). Evaluating and improving prevention programs: A strategy from drug abuse. *Evaluation and Program Planning, 2*(2), 127–136.

Burchard, J. D., & Barrera, F. (1972). An analysis of timeout and response cost in a programmed environment. *Journal of Applied Behavior Analysis, 5*(3), 271–282.

Bushell, D. (1973). *Classroom behavior: A little book for teachers.* Englewood Cliffs, NJ: Prentice Hall.

Conduct Problems Prevention Research Group. (1999). Initial impact of the Fast Track prevention trial for conduct problems: I. The high-risk sample. *Journal of Consulting and Clinical Psychology, 67*(5), 631–647.

Dadds, M. R., & McHugh, T. A. (1992). Social support and treatment outcome in behavioral family therapy for child conduct problems. *Journal of Consulting and Clinical Psychology, 60*(2), 252–259.

Darveaux, D. X. (1984). The good behavior game plus merit: Controlling disruptive behavior and improving student motivation. *School Psychology Review, 13*(4), 510–514.

Dean, C., Myors, K., & Evans, E. (2003). Community-wide implementation of a parenting program: The South East Sydney Positive Parenting Project. *Australian e-Journal for the Advancement of Mental Health, 2*(3). Retrieved June 4, 2006, from http://www.auseinet. com/journal/vol2iss3/dean.pdf

Dishion, T. J., & Andrews, D. W. (1995). Preventing escalation in problem behaviors with high-risk young adolescents: Immediate and 1-year outcomes. *Journal of Consulting and Clinical Psychology, 63*(4), 538–548.

Dykeman, B. F. (1995). The social cognitive treatment of anger and aggression in four adolescents with conduct disorder. *Journal of Instructional Psychology, 22*(2), 194–200.

Embry, D. D. (2002). The good behavior game: A best practice candidate as a universal behavioral vaccine. *Clinical Child and Family Psychology Review, 5*(4), 273–297.

Embry, D. D., & Straatemeier, G. (2001). *The PAX acts game manual: How to apply the good behavior game.* Tucson, AZ: PAXIS Institute.

Feindler, E. L., Marriott, S. A., & Iwata, M. (1984). Group anger control training for junior high school delinquents. *Cognitive Therapy and Research, 8*(3), 299–311.

Field, C. E., Nash, H. M., Handwerk, M. L., & Friman, P. C. (2004). A modification of the token economy for nonresponsive youth in family-style residential care. *Behavior Modification, 28*(3), 438–457.

Forehand, R., & Kotchick, B. A. (2002). Behavioral parent training: Current challenges and potential solutions. *Journal of Child and Family Studies, 11*(4), 377–384.

Forney, W. S., Forney, J. C., & Crutsinger, C. (2005). Developmental stages of age and moral reasoning as predictors of juvenile delinquents' behavioral intention to steal clothing. *Family and Consumer Sciences Research Journal, 34*(2), 110–126.

Fraser, M. W., Galinsky, M. J., Smokowski, P. R., Day, S. H., Terzian, M. A., Rose, R. A., et al. (2005). Social information-processing skills training to promote social competence and prevent aggressive behavior in the third grade. *Journal of Consulting and Clinical Psychology, 73*(6), 1045–1055.

Freeman, K. A. (2004). Introduction to special issue on adolescent conduct problems. *Behavior Modification, 28*(3), 323–330.

Frick, P. J. (2000). A comprehensive and individualized treatment approach for children and adolescents with conduct disorders. *Cognitive and Behavioral Practice, 7*(1), 30–37.

Frick, P. J. (2006). Developmental pathways to conduct disorder. *Child and Adolescent Psychiatric Clinics of North America, 15*(2), 311–331.

Gibbs, J. C. (2003). Equipping youth with mature moral judgment. *Reclaiming Children and Youth, 12*(3), 148–153.

Goldstein, A. P. (1988). *The PREPARE curriculum: Teaching prosocial competencies.* Champaign, IL: Research Press.

Goldstein, S. (1995). *Understanding and managing children's classroom behavior.* New York: Wiley & Sons.

Gottfredson, D. C., & Wilson, D. B. (2003). Characteristics of effective school-based substance abuse prevention. *Prevention Science, 4*(1), 27–38.

Grandy, G. S., Madsen, C. H., & De Mersseman, L. M. (1973). The effects of individual and interdependent contingencies on inappropriate classroom behavior. *Psychology in the Schools, 10,* 488–493.

Harris, V. W., & Sherman, J. A. (1973). Use and analysis of the "good behavior game" to reduce disruptive classroom behavior. *Journal of Applied Behavior Analysis, 6*(3), 405–417.

Hemphill, S. A., Toumbourou, J. W., Herrenkohl, T. I., McMorris, B. J., & Catalano, R. F. (2006). The effect of school suspensions and arrests on subsequent adolescent antisocial behavior in Australia and the United States. *Journal of Adolescent Health, 39*(5), 736–744.

Henggeler, S. W., Cunningham, P. B., Pickrel, S. G., Schoenwald, S. K., & Brondino, M. J. (1996). Multisystemic therapy: An effective violence prevention approach for serious juvenile offenders. *Journal of Adolescence, 19,* 47–61.

Henggeler, S. W., Halliday-Boykins, C. A., Cunningham, P. B., Randall, J., Shapiro, S. B., & Chapman, J. E. (2006). Juvenile drug court: Enhancing outcomes by integrating evidence-based treatments. *Journal of Consulting and Clinical Psychology, 74*(1), 42–54.

Henggeler, S. W., Melton, G. B., Brondino, M. J., Scherer, D. G., & Hanley, J. H. (1997). Multisystemic therapy with violent and chronic juvenile offenders and their families: The role of treatment fidelity in successful dissemination. *Journal of Consulting and Clinical Psychology, 65*(5), 821–833.

Henggeler, S. W., Melton, G. B., & Smith, L. A. (1992). Family preservation using multisystemic therapy: An effective alternative to incarcerating serious juvenile offenders. *Journal of Consulting and Clinical Psychology, 60*(6), 953–961.

Henggeler, S. W., Schoenwald, S. K., Borduin, C. M., Rowland, M. D., & Cunningham, P. B. (1998). *Multisystemic treatment of antisocial behavior in children and adolescents.* New York: Guilford Press.

Jennings, W., Kilkenny, R., & Kohlberg, L. (1983). Moral development theory and practice for youthful and adult offenders. In W. Laufer & J. Day (Eds.), *Personality theory, moral development, and criminal behavior* (pp. 281–355). Lexington, MA: Lexington Books.

Johnson, M. R., Turner, P. F., & Konarski, E. A. (1978). The good behavior game: A systematic replication in two unruly transitional classrooms. *Education and Treatment of Children, 1*(3), 25–33.

Jurkovic, G. J. (1980). The juvenile delinquent as a moral philosopher: A structural-developmental perspective. *Psychological Bulletin, 88,* 709–772.

Kamps, D. M., Tankersley, M., & Ellis, C. (2000). Social skills interventions for young at-risk students: A 2-year follow-up study. *Behavioral Disorders, 25*(4), 310–324.

Kazdin, A. E. (2005). *Parent management training: Treatment for oppositional, aggressive, and antisocial behavior in children and adolescents.* New York: Oxford University Press.

Kazdin, A. E., Esveldt-Dawson, K., French, N. H., & Unis, A. S. (1987). Problem-solving skills training and relationship therapy in the treatment of antisocial child behavior. *Journal of Consulting and Clinical Psychology, 55*(1), 76–85.

Kazdin, A. E., Siegel, T. C., & Bass, D. (1992). Cognitive problem-solving skills training and parent management training in the treatment of antisocial behavior in children. *Journal of Consulting and Clinical Psychology, 60*(5), 733–747.

Kellner, M. H., & Bry, B. H. (1999). The effects of anger management groups in a day school for emotionally disturbed adolescents. *Adolescence, 34*(136), 645–651.

Kohlberg, L. (1969). Stage and sequence: The cognitive-developmental approach to socialization. In D. A. Goslin (Ed.), *Handbook of socialization theory and research* (pp. 347–480). Chicago: Rand McNally.

Kohlberg, L. (1975). The cognitive-developmental approach to moral education. *Phi Delta Kappan, 56,* 670–677.

Leeman, L. W., Gibbs, J. C., & Fuller, D. (1993). Evaluation of a multi-component group treatment program for juvenile delinquents. *Aggressive Behavior, 19,* 281–292.

Lipsey, M. W., & Wilson, D. B. (1998). Effective intervention for serious juvenile offenders: A synthesis of research. In R. Loeber & D. P. Farrington (Eds.), *Serious and violent juvenile offenders: Risk factors and successful interventions* (pp. 313–345). London: Sage.

Lochman, J. E., & Wells, K. C. (2004). The Coping Power Program for preadolescent aggressive boys and their parents: Outcome effects at the 1-year follow-up. *Journal of Consulting and Clinical Psychology, 72*(4), 571–578.

Margolin, G., Burman, B., & John, R. S. (1989). Home observations of married couples reenacting naturalistic conflicts. *Behavioral Assessment, 11,* 101–118.

Martinez, C. R., & Forgatch, M. S. (2001). Preventing problems with boys' noncompliance: Effects of a parent training intervention for divorcing mothers. *Journal of Consulting and Clinical Psychology, 69*(3), 416–428.

McCarthy-Tucker, S., Gold, A., & Garcia, E. (1999). Effects of anger management training on aggressive behavior in adolescent boys. *Journal of Offender Rehabilitation, 29*(3/4), 129–141.

McCurdy, B. L., Mannella, M. C., & Eldridge, N. (2003). Positive behavior support in urban schools: Can we prevent the escalation of antisocial behavior? *Journal of Positive Behavior Interventions, 5*(3), 158–170.

Medland, M. B., & Stachnik, T. J. (1972). Good-behavior game: A replication and systematic analysis. *Journal of Applied Behavior Analysis, 5*(1), 45–51.

Mpofu, E., & Crystal, R., (2001). Conduct disorder in children: Challenges and prospective cognitive–behavioural treatments. *Counselling Psychology Quarterly, 14*(1), 21–32.

Niles, W. J. (1986). Effects of a moral development discussion group on delinquent and predelinquent boys. *Journal of Counseling Psychology, 33*(1), 45–51.

Nugent, W. R., Champlin, D., & Wiinimaki, L. (1997). The effects of anger control training on adolescent antisocial behavior. *Research on Social Work Practice, 7*(4), 446–462.

O'Donnell, J., Hawkins, J. D., Catalano, R. F., Abbott, R. D., & Day, L. E. (1995). Preventing school failure, drug use, and delinquency among low-income children: Long-term intervention in elementary schools. *American Journal of Orthopsychiatry, 65*(1), 87–100.

O'Leary, K. D., & Becker, W. C. (1967). Behavior modification of an adjustment class: A token reinforcement program. *Exceptional Children, 33*(9), 637–642.

Palmer, E. J. (2005). The relationship between moral reasoning and aggression, and the implications for practice. *Psychology, Crime & Law, 11*(4), 353–361.

Patterson, G. R., Chamberlain, P., & Reid, J. B. (1982). A comparative evaluation of a parent-training program. *Behavior Therapy, 13*(5), 638–650.

Patterson, G. R., & Narrett, C. M. (1990). The development of a reliable and valid treatment program for aggressive young children. *International Journal of Mental Health, 19*(3), 19–26.

Patterson, G. R., Reid, J. B., & Dishion, T. J. (1992). *Antisocial boys*. Eugene, OR: Castalia.

Phillips, D., & Christie, F. (1986). Behavior management in a secondary school classroom: Playing the game. *Maladjustment and Therapeutic Education, 4*(1), 47–53.

Piaget, J. (1932). *The moral judgment of the child*. New York: Harcourt Brace Jovanovich.

Reid, M. J., Webster-Stratton, C., & Baydar, N. (2004). Halting the development of conduct problems in Head Start children: The effects of parent training. *Journal of Clinical Child and Adolescent Psychology, 33*(2), 279–291.

Reynolds, C. R., & Kamphaus, R. W. (2004). *Behavior Assessment System for Children* (2nd ed.). Circle Pines, MN: AGS Publishing.

Robbins, M. S., Liddle, H. A., Turner, C. W., Dakof, G. A., Alexander, J. F., & Kogan, S. M. (2006). Adolescent and parent therapeutic alliances as predictors of dropout in multidimensional family therapy. *Journal of Family Psychology, 20*(1), 108–116.

Rowland, M. D., Halliday-Boykins, C. A., Henggeler, S. W., Cunningham, P. B., Lee, T. G., Kruesi, M. J. P., et al. (2005). A randomized trial of multisystemic therapy with Hawaii's Felix Class youths. *Journal of Emotional and Behavioral Disorders, 13*(1), 13–23.

Salend, S. J., Reynolds, C. J., & Coyle, E. M. (1989). Individualizing the good behavior game across type and frequency of behavior with emotionally disturbed adolescents. *Behavior Modification, 13*(1), 108–126.

Sheridan, S. M. (1995). *The tough kid social skills book.* Longmont, CO: Sopris West.

Skinner, B. F. (1931). The concept of the reflex in the description of behavior. *Journal of General Psychology, 5,* 427–458.

Spaccarelli, S., Cotler, S., & Penman, D. (1992). Problem-solving skills training as a supplement to behavioral parent training. *Cognitive Therapy and Research, 16*(1), 1–18.

Tarolla, S. M., Wagner, E. F., Rabinowitz, J., & Tubman, J. G. (2002). Understanding and treating juvenile offenders: A review of current knowledge and future directions. *Aggression and Violent Behavior, 7*(2), 125–143.

Taylor, T. K., Eddy, J. M., & Biglan, A. (1999). Interpersonal skills training to reduce aggressive and delinquent behavior: Limited evidence and the need for an evidence-based system of care. *Clinical Child and Family Psychology Review, 2*(3), 169–182.

Thackery, E. (Ed.). (2003). Conduct disorder. In *Gale encyclopedia of mental disorders.* Retrieved October 24, 2006, from http://health.enotes.com/mental-disorders-encyclopedia/conduct-disorder

Thomas, C. R. (2006). Evidence-based practice for conduct disorder symptoms. *Journal of the American Academy of Child and Adolescent Psychiatry, 45*(1), 109–114.

Timmons-Mitchell, J., Bender, M. B., Kishna, M. A., & Mitchell, C. C. (2006). An independent effectiveness trial of multisystemic therapy with juvenile justice youth. *Journal of Clinical Child and Adolescent Psychology, 35*(2), 227–236.

Tingstrom, D. H., Sterling-Turner, H. E., & Wilczynski, S. M. (2006). The good behavior game: 1969–2002. *Behavior Modification, 30*(2), 225–253.

Webster-Stratton, C. (1984). Randomized trial of two parent-training programs for families with conduct-disordered children. *Journal of Consulting and Clinical Psychology, 52*(4), 666–678.

Webster-Stratton, C. (1993). Strategies for helping early school-aged children with oppositional defiant and conduct disorders: The importance of home-school partnerships. *School Psychology Review, 22*(3), 437–457.

Webster-Stratton, C. (1994). Advancing videotape parent training: A comparison study. *Journal of Consulting and Clinical Psychology, 62*(3), 583–593.

Webster-Stratton, C. (1998). Preventing conduct problems in Head Start children: Strengthening parenting competencies. *Journal of Consulting and Clinical Psychology, 66*(5), 715–730.

Webster-Stratton, C., & Hammond, M. (1997). Treating children with early-onset conduct problems: A comparison of child and parent training interventions. *Journal of Consulting and Clinical Psychology, 65*(1), 93–109.

Webster-Stratton, C., Reid, J., & Hammond, M. (2001). Social skills and problem-solving training for children with early-onset conduct problems: Who benefits? *Journal of Child Psychology and Psychiatry, 42*(7), 943–952.

Wilson, D. B., Gottfredson, D. C., & Najaka, S. S. (2001). School-based prevention of problem behaviors: A meta-analysis. *Journal of Quantitative Criminology, 17*(3), 247–272.

Woolgar, M., & Scott, S. (2005). Evidence-based management of conduct disorders. *Current Opinion in Psychiatry, 18*(4), 392–396.

Zimmerman, D. (1983). Moral education. In A. P. Goldstein (Ed.), *Prevention and control of aggression* (pp. 210–240). New York: Pergamon.

Chapter 4

Interventions for Hyperactivity

This chapter presents information for effective interventions for children and adolescents identified with hyperactivity. First, the characteristics and conditions of hyperactivity are briefly discussed, including a description of the construct of hyperactivity and sample items from the BASC–2 Hyperactivity scale. In the second section, the theoretical framework for approaching hyperactivity is described. The third section presents the interventions that have evidence or show promise for management, and in some cases remediation, of hyperactive behaviors in school settings. Each presentation provides an overview of the intervention method and is divided into three subsections: Implementation, Evidence for Use, and Considerations. The last section of this chapter presents a brief summary of the interventions discussed and their content. Together, these four sections provide the foundation on which additional BASC–2 intervention components are built, including both classroom-based and home-based strategies.

Characteristics and Conditions of Hyperactivity

Hyperactivity is defined as overactivity or excessive task-irrelevant physical (i.e., motor) movement (Montague & Warger, 1997). Children and adolescents with hyperactivity often make noises at inappropriate times, leave their assigned seats without permission, and talk during times designated for silence in the classroom (Montague & Warger, 1997). Hyperactivity problems can occur alone or can co-occur with attention problems. Hyperactivity problems are usually exhibited by children in both home and school settings, and can worsen in situations that require sustained mental effort or lack intrinsic appeal (American Psychiatric Association, 2000).

Items from the BASC–2 Hyperactivity scale focus on the hyperactivity and impulsivity aspects of attention-deficit/hyperactivity disorder (ADHD). Items designed to measure hyperactivity include "Fiddles with things while at meals," "Interrupts others when they are speaking," "Is overly active," and "Has poor self-control" (Reynolds & Kamphaus, 2004). Items designed to identify impulsivity include "Acts without thinking" and "Cannot wait to take turn" (Reynolds & Kamphaus, 2004). Impulsive responding is included here because the research literature indicates that, from a psychometric perspective, it is nearly impossible to distinguish impulsive responding apart from the construct of hyperactivity, although the clinical assessment field makes a conceptual distinction between the two constructs.

Theoretical Framework for Approaching Hyperactivity

To date, research suggests there is no single cause of hyperactivity. The belief in a neurological component is strongly held, along with a host of other factors, including environmental agents, food additives, and genetics (National Institute of Mental Health, 2006). First described in 1845 in a children's book with a character dubbed "Fidgety Philip" (Hoffman, 1845), hyperactivity is not a new or under-researched condition. However, a definitive cause or cure is not known. Hyperactivity, like some children's mental health conditions, is subject to misconceptions of causation, such as poor parenting, excess sugar consumption, or lack of discipline. Although approximately 5% of children see improvement with controlled diets, treatment approaches such as those that restrict sugar intake are not considered effective interventions. Cognitive–behavioral and some pharmacological treatments appear to have the greatest efficacy and the greatest breadth of evidence. However, pharmacological interventions are controversial in some spheres.

Interventions

A variety of interventions have been shown to reduce, or have shown promise for reducing, hyperactive behavior. This section provides descriptions of psychologically or behaviorally based interventions that are considered efficacious as evidenced by peer-reviewed research and/or endorsement by professional organizations. The interventions described include the following:

I. Functional Assessment

II. Contingency Management

III. Parent Training

IV. Self-Management

V. Task Modification

VI. Multimodal Interventions

The discussion of multimodal interventions (i.e., interventions implemented in combination) describes research-based combinations of the interventions presented in this chapter. It must be noted that multimodal interventions designed to meet the individual needs of children and adolescents are the most effective school-based interventions for hyperactivity (Abikoff & Hechtman, 1994). In addition, the strongest evidence of effectiveness for interventions to decrease hyperactivity supports the use of psychostimulant medication and/or multimodal interventions with stimulant medication and contingency management (Barkley, 2006; Brown & Sammons, 2002; Crenshaw, Kavale, Forness, & Reeve, 1999; MTA Cooperative Group, 1999; Pelham & Gnagy, 1999; Tamm & Carlson, 2007), although the effects of multimodal interventions may diminish over time (Swanson et al., 2008). Medication interventions are beyond the scope of this intervention guide. However, practitioners frequently choose interventions for children who have been prescribed stimulant medication by a licensed physician; therefore, evidence for the use of behavioral interventions in combination with stimulant medications is presented. Note that the authors of this guide believe the best practice is to implement behavioral interventions first to determine if they are sufficient alone.

I. Functional Assessment

Functional assessment for hyperactivity is an information-gathering process used to determine the function (e.g., attention, escape) of the behavior (e.g., overactivity, inappropriate verbalizations, disruptive behavior) and the circumstances that maintain it (DuPaul & Eckert, 1997). Interventions based on data that are collected during the functional assessment are chosen to modify or eliminate the maintaining circumstances (Gresham, Watson, & Skinner, 2001).

For example, Jacob is an 8-year-old with hyperactivity. Jacob's math teacher, Mrs. Barry, gives the class independent practice time each day. The independent practice is usually a math worksheet with over 30 multiplication problems. Every day, Jacob works on his worksheet for about 5 minutes and then starts meowing like a cat or drumming with his pencils on his desk. His peers laugh and Mrs. Barry sends Jacob out into the hall to finish his work, which he does not complete. An interdisciplinary team completes a functional assessment and determines that the function of the behavior is either to escape from difficult tasks, garner peer attention, or sometimes both. The team determines that Jacob's disruptive behavior is being maintained by the peer attention he receives and his dismissal to the hallway. To remediate Jacob's disruptive behavior, the interdisciplinary team prescribes an evidence-based intervention package that will modify the existing reinforcers and decrease the manifested behaviors.

Implementation

The goal of functional assessment for hyperactivity is to identify the antecedent and consequent events (i.e., events that occur after the behavior) that maintain hyperactive and impulsive behavior, thereby enabling the clinician to develop a plan to modify these events to ultimately reduce the problem behavior. The essential elements of functional assessment include the following:

1. Conducting a functional assessment (including interviews and direct observation)

2. Developing hypotheses for why the behavior occurs

3. Evaluating or testing the hypotheses

4. Selecting an evidence-based intervention strategy

The functional assessment process starts with an interdisciplinary team that gathers descriptive data on the problem behavior through interviews of key stakeholders (e.g., teachers, parents, principal) and direct observation of the child. Next, using the data collected during the assessment, the team develops hypotheses regarding the function of the behavior and the maintaining events. Functions of behavior typically fit into three categories: (1) a way to avoid or escape something (e.g., an academic task), (2) a way to gain access to something (e.g., teacher or peer attention, a toy), or (3) sensory stimulation (e.g., daydreaming) (DuPaul & Ervin, 1996). The team then tests the hypotheses by systematically manipulating the maintaining events to determine accuracy.

After the function of the behavior has been validated, evidence-based interventions are selected and implemented that will best modify or eliminate the maintaining event(s) and decrease the hyperactive behavior. During implementation, interventions are monitored frequently and modified as needed.

For maximum effectiveness, interventions for hyperactivity should be vigilantly and consistently implemented over extended periods of time before fading. Figure 4.1 lists the procedural steps for incorporating functional assessment into the treatment of a child with hyperactivity.

Figure 4.1 Procedural steps for the application of functional assessment

1. Conduct the functional assessment.

   a. Interview relevant stakeholders (e.g., teachers, parents, principal) and observe the child.

   b. Define the problem behavior in observable and measurable terms.

   c. Develop and test hypotheses to determine the function of the behavior.

2. Select and implement an appropriate intervention.

3. Monitor progress and modify the intervention as needed.

Evidence for Use

Functional assessment–based interventions for hyperactivity can reduce disruptive behaviors, such as out-of-seat behavior and inappropriate verbalizations, and can decrease off-task activities (Broussard & Northup, 1995; Ervin, DuPaul, Kern, & Friman, 1998; Umbreit, 1995). The following studies summarize some of the key research findings associated with using functional assessment to determine effective interventions for children and adolescents with hyperactivity.

Broussard, C. D., & Northup, J. (1995). An approach to functional assessment and analysis of disruptive behavior in regular education classrooms. *School Psychology Quarterly, 10*(2), 151–164.

In this study, functional assessments and analyses were conducted on 3 students, aged 6 through 9, in regular education classrooms, who demonstrated frequent disruptive and off-task behaviors. Through classroom observations and interviews of teachers and students, hypotheses were developed regarding reinforcing behaviors that were maintaining the disruptive behaviors. These included teacher attention, peer attention, and escape from difficult academic tasks. These hypotheses were then tested by implementing contingency reversal (i.e., providing reinforcement in the form of attention/escape following positive and appropriate behavior) in order to decrease the amount of disruptive behavior. All 3 students demonstrated marked decreases in disruptive behavior as well as increases in work completion and accuracy.

Ervin, R. A., DuPaul, G. J., Kern, L., & Friman, P. C. (1998). Classroom-based functional and adjunctive assessments: Proactive approaches to intervention selection for adolescents with attention deficit/hyperactivity disorder. *Journal of Applied Behavior Analysis, 31*(1), 65–78.

This study involved conducting functional assessments on 2 students, ages 13 and 14, both of whom were diagnosed with ADHD and oppositional defiant disorder (ODD). Hypotheses were formulated based on interviews with teachers and students as well as direct observations of classroom behavior. The first student showed an increase in off-task behaviors when engaged in long writing tasks. The potential intervention strategies tested included using a computer to write longer assignments and being given extra time to think by allowing the student to brainstorm with a peer prior to journal assignments. Results for the first method showed higher on-task behavior during long writing tasks (about 97% when using a computer vs. 65% when writing by hand). For the second method, on-task behavior increased to about 91% with peer brainstorming vs. 63% without intervention. The second student showed an increase in off-task behaviors following peer attention. Potential intervention strategies tested included self-evaluation procedures for peer-seeking behaviors and reducing social reinforcers from peers by implementing a classwide token system on peer relations. Results for the first intervention showed that self-evaluation led to a decrease in attention-seeking behaviors (about 92% with intervention vs. 63% without). In the second intervention, on-task behaviors were higher when students received consequences for responding to attention-seeking behaviors (about 78% with intervention vs. 58% without). In both cases, interventions derived from functional assessments led to significant decreases in off-task behavior.

Umbreit, J. (1995). Functional assessment and intervention in a regular classroom setting for the disruptive behavior of a student with attention deficit hyperactivity disorder. *Behavioral Disorders, 20*(4), 267–278.

One 8-year-old boy diagnosed with ADHD participated in this study about the effects of functional assessment–based interventions on disruptive behavior during academic instruction. Functional assessment involving interviews and structured observations led the researchers to hypothesize that peer attention and escape from task demands were possibly maintaining the disruptive and inattentive behavior. In the intervention condition, these hypotheses were tested by providing limited access to other children during independent work time as well as allowing the student to request a 1- to 2-minute break from the task. Results showed that disruptive behavior decreased from a baseline of 55% to 95% to virtually 0% with intervention.

Considerations

For Teaching

The research literature indicates that data collection is considered a burden by most teachers. Functional assessments require significant data collection, and teachers may not be trained or experienced in creating forms or using them effectively. Teachers will likely need support in classroom settings. Needs may include training, help supervising students, or assistance in the responsibilities of data collection.

For Culture and Language Differences

The authors of this guide have taken a primarily cognitive–behavioral and biological view of the theoretical basis for understanding hyperactivity. Other cultures may not share this view and may instead believe hyperactivity has a spiritual origin, or may view hyperactivity as a maladaptive trait that should not be addressed. Practitioners should be sensitive to potential explanations by the family.

For Age and Developmental Level

Functional assessments are applicable to any age or developmental level, making this approach a strong intervention method for problem behaviors. Use caution when describing a young child as hyperactive, given that young children are characteristically more active.

II. Contingency Management

In contingency management for hyperactivity, behavioral interventions are used to modify consequent events that are often maintained through the reinforcement of overactive and impulsive behavior (DuPaul & Weyandt, 2006; Frazier & Merrell, 1997). Contingency management programs for hyperactivity include the individual or combined use of behavioral intervention strategies such as token economies, point systems, verbal praise, response cost or timeout (from peers, reinforcers, attention, or privileges), varying amounts and frequency of teacher attention, verbal reprimands, and removal of praise (Chronis, Jones, & Raggi, 2006; Harlacher, Roberts, & Merrell, 2006; Pelham & Gnagy, 1999). Social reinforcement can be incorporated into a contingency management plan through verbal praise and posted records of achievement (Blackman & Silberman, 1980). Response cost may be an effective part of a contingency management plan for children with ADHD (Pfiffner & O'Leary, 1987). The degree of intensity or complexity of a contingency management plan varies based on the individual needs of the child (Daly, Creed, Xanthopoulos, & Brown, 2007; Pelham & Gnagy, 1999).

For example, Clint, a 16-year-old with hyperactivity, talks without permission during Spanish class, taps his pencil on his desk, and gets out of his seat and roams around the room. He and his teacher, Mrs. Gustafson, write a contingency management plan that institutes a point system to address his disruptive behavior. If Clint sits in his seat quietly, he earns points that Mrs. Gustafson records on his point sheet. On Friday, if he has enough points, he is allowed to run errands for the teacher; if he doesn't have enough points, Clint has to sweep the classroom.

Implementation

The goal of contingency management is to decrease activity levels that negatively impact learning by shaping the child's existing behavior and providing opportunities for the new, desired behavior to become internalized. Thus, the target behavior can be behavioral or academic. Specific behavioral objectives for children with hyperactivity may include increasing the duration of productive learning time, decreasing episodes of overactivity, decreasing the frequency of verbal reprimands to correct behavior, or decreasing the number of disruptive, off-task activities. The basic elements of contingency management for hyperactivity include the following:

1. Target behaviors clearly stated in observable terms

2. Pre-established reinforcement and punishment procedures (e.g., methods for earning, losing, and exchanging tokens)

3. Positive reinforcement in appropriate intervals

4. Response-cost contingencies for inappropriate behavior

Begin by defining the behavior in operational terms and determining the baseline rating of hyperactive behavior for the individual child (e.g., how long the child remains seated during lectures or seatwork). Using this baseline data, determine (alone or in conjunction with the child) the behavioral goals and, when applicable, the academic expectations related to those goals. For example, the goal can be based on the frequency of off-task behavior. If the child is out of his or her seat five times every 15 minutes, the goal could be three times every 15 minutes.

Determine the reinforcers to be used by considering the individual likes and dislikes of the child (e.g., if the child likes computer games, computer time can be earned or lost). A survey of the child's preferences is a good way to determine appropriate and meaningful reinforcers.

After selecting the reinforcers, explain the system to the child and make sure he or she understands how to earn and lose points or tokens. Clearly define the behavioral expectations related to the system (i.e., behaviors included and not included). A visual aid used to track behavior will assist the child in understanding which specific behaviors are being targeted. During implementation of the intervention, provide the child with the predetermined reinforcer when he or she meets the preset goals. If goals are not met, the child loses or doesn't earn the reinforcer.

As a modification, use tokens or points that can be cashed in for reinforcers at the end of a specified time period. For example, if the child is on task, he or she earns a token, and if the child is off task, he or she loses a token. Once the child has earned a certain amount of tokens (or at the end of the day or week), he or she chooses an appropriate reinforcer. Token systems are typically more effective once basic behavioral goals have been met, and the tokens can be used to maintain the behavior. The procedural steps for incorporating contingency management into the treatment of a child with hyperactivity are listed in Figure 4.2.

Figure 4.2 Procedural steps for the application of contingency management

1. Define the behavior in operational terms.

2. Determine the behavioral goals.

3. Determine the reinforcers.

4. Explain the system to the child.

5. Implement the chosen reinforcement strategy (e.g., token system).

6. Adjust the reinforcement as needed.

Evidence for Use

Implementation of classroom contingency management interventions has been found to be more effective than typical treatment for ADHD-related behaviors (Pelham, Wheeler, & Chronis, 1998). In addition, token reinforcement for increased task accuracy has been found to decrease hyperactivity and increase academic performance (Ayllon, Layman, & Kandel, 1975). The following studies summarize some of the key research findings associated with contingency management interventions for children and adolescents with hyperactivity.

Ayllon, T., Layman, D., & Kandel, H. J. (1975). A behavioral–educational alternative to drug control of hyperactive children. *Journal of Applied Behavior Analysis, 8*(2), 137–146.

This study measured the hyperactive behavior and academic performance of 3 students (aged 8 to 10 years) diagnosed with and receiving medication for chronic hyperactivity. The participants attended a class for learning disabled students at a private elementary school. Math and reading scores were analyzed, along with behavioral data obtained through direct observation. A token system was used to reward students for correct math and reading responses. Four phases were used in the study: on medication (17 days); off medication (3 days); no medication, reinforcement of math but not reading (6 days); and no medication, reinforcement of math and reading (6 days). Results showed that reinforcement of academic performance had comparable effects to medicine for suppressing hyperactive behavior (combined 20% compared to 24%, respectively) and that reinforcement had a greater positive impact on academic progress than did medication (average of 85% correct for math and reading combined compared to 12%, respectively).

Ayllon, T., & Roberts, M. D. (1974). Eliminating discipline problems by strengthening academic performance. *Journal of Applied Behavior Analysis, 7*(1), 71–76.

This investigation explored the relationship between academic performance and its effect on disruptive behavior, studying 5 fifth-grade boys from an urban public school. Teachers identified these children as the most disruptive of their 38 classmates. Disruptive behavior was defined as out of seat without permission, talking out, and engaging in any motor behavior that interfered with another student's studying. Behavior and academic performance were observed during daily 15-minute reading performance sessions, with data collected on the percentage of disruptive intervals and the percentage of correctly answered questions. A token economy system was employed in which participants earned points for completion and accuracy of academic performance. Results demonstrated that academic performance improved and disruptive behaviors declined with the use of reinforcers. Initial mean baseline disruptive behavior rates ranged from 40% to 50%, dropped to approximately 15% during the first reinforcement phase, jumped to about 40% during second baseline, and dropped to approximately 5% during the second reinforcement phase. Moreover, all but 1 of the participants demonstrated noteworthy academic improvement over the course of the study.

DuPaul, G. J., Guevremont, D. C., & Barkley, R. A. (1992). Behavioral treatment of attention-deficit hyperactivity disorder in the classroom: The use of the Attention Training System. *Behavior Modification, 16*(2), 204–225.

This study examined the effect of an electronic contingency management system, the Attention Training System (ATS), on the on-task behavior of two 6- and

7-year-old boys. The ATS is a device placed on the student's desk that gives a point for each minute of sustained attention and deducts a point when the teacher activates a button that causes a red light to flash. The ATS was presented to the students during academic seatwork periods, and they received a small reinforcer for receiving 70% of the available points. (During baseline conditions, the regular contingency management system in the classroom was still used.) While baseline percentages of on-task behavior were variable and generally low for both boys, introduction of the ATS increased on-task behavior significantly.

Fabiano, G. A., & Pelham, W. E., Jr. (2003). Improving the effectiveness of behavioral classroom interventions for attention-deficit/hyperactivity disorder: A case study. *Journal of Emotional and Behavioral Disorders, 11,* 124–130.

An 8-year-old boy in third grade who had been diagnosed with ADHD was the subject of this case study in which the boy's behavior modification program was assessed and systematically modified to produce a more effective intervention, which was measured as improved student behavior. The participant and a comparison student were observed each school day during two 50-minute periods at 15-second and 6-second intervals. After baseline data (percentage of disruptive intervals and percentage of on-task intervals) were collected, changes were made to the intervention so that reinforcement was given for meeting 75% of behavior goals and immediate feedback was used when disruptive behavior occurred. Additionally, the participant was allowed two reminders for each goal, meaning three violations of a goal needed to occur before he was recorded as failing to meet the goal. Results indicated that behavior improved to a level on par with other classmates, indicating that basing intervention modifications on student observation can be an effective tool in general education classrooms.

McGoey, K. E., & DuPaul, G. J. (2000). Token reinforcement and response cost procedures: Reducing the disruptive behavior of preschool children with attention-deficit/hyperactivity disorder. *School Psychology Quarterly, 15*(3), 330–343.

Four children ages 4 and 5 participated in this study which examined the effects of token reinforcement and response cost procedures on preschool children with ADHD. During the token reinforcement condition, buttons were earned for following classroom rules (e.g., staying on task, listening quietly), with reinforcers given based on the number of buttons earned. In the response-cost condition, each child began with a certain number of buttons and buttons were lost for breaking classroom rules. Both conditions decreased instances of inappropriate behavior markedly. Teachers preferred the response cost procedure because they found it to be a consistent way to correct inappropriate behavior that was easier than "catching a child being good." Teachers opted to continue using the system after completion of the study.

Reitman, D., Hupp, S. D. A., O'Callaghan, P. M., Gulley, V., & Northup, J. (2001). The influence of a token economy and methylphenidate on attentive and disruptive behavior during sports with ADHD-diagnosed children. *Behavior Modification, 25*(2), 305–323.

This study examined the impact of medication and a token economy system on the behavior of 3 children: 2 girls (aged 6 and 7 years) and 1 boy (aged 6 years) attending a summer ADHD treatment program. The children were observed while participating in a kickball game that occurred during a 30-minute recess each day of the 4-week program. Each child received either a dose of medication or a placebo every morning. During each game, data on attentive and disruptive behavior were collected through direct observation and observer ratings. For baseline, no tokens were awarded. During the treatment phase, participants were awarded tokens for attentive behavior, and the tokens could then be exchanged for prizes. Results demonstrated that medication had a positive impact on behavior and that medication combined with the token economy produced the largest improvements in attentive behavior and decreases in disruptive behavior.

Considerations

For Teaching

Teachers are generally adept at procedures that involve classwide prompting or acknowledgement and may need only minimal coaching to be effective with students with hyperactivity. Some issues that typically frustrate teachers include the modification of systems, the immediacy of reinforcer use, the consistency in application, and the setting of goals that will encourage and change student behavior. Teachers must modify the structure of token economy systems when the student loses more points than he or she earns (Abramowitz & O'Leary, 1991), or students will not maintain an interest or be able to access the reinforcer. Reinforcement must be immediate for students with hyperactivity; contingencies that are hours, days, or weeks away are unlikely to be effective. Behavioral interventions for students with hyperactivity require long-term consistency (Pelham & Gnagy, 1999), and once a student engages in appropriate behaviors, fading may occur but monitoring should also occur so that the intervention can be reapplied when necessary. Goal setting or criteria setting for access to reinforcers is as critical as immediate access. If a student is engaging in hyperactive behaviors 90% of the time, a goal of 0% is unrealistic. Goals need to be gradual, and intermediate steps toward reaching a long-term solution are important for reducing hyperactivity. Goals should also be specific when possible, targeting the relevant behaviors that are characteristic of hyperactivity. For example, fidgeting and running around a classroom may have a differential impact on the setting and these behaviors might need to be addressed separately, even if both actions are part of hyperactivity.

For Culture and Language Differences

Home–school communication and the use of contingency management techniques in both settings will improve the application of any intervention. At minimum, attempt to provide communication in the primary language of the parent, and, if necessary, use an adult translator or bilingual staff person to articulate the program of intervention and describe how contingencies could be managed at home.

For Age and Developmental Level

Contingency and reinforcement choices should include the child or adolescent's preferences and should be age and developmentally appropriate.

III. Parent Training

Parent training as an intervention for hyperactivity consists of educating parents about hyperactivity and effective parenting techniques to be used in the home (Daly et al., 2007; Pelham & Gnagy, 1999). In 8 to 12 weekly sessions, parents are taught problem-solving skills, how to give effective commands, how to properly reinforce desired behaviors by establishing clear expectations, how to modify antecedents and consequents of the child's behavior, how to monitor behavior, and how to use positive attention, tangible rewards, response cost, and timeout from positive reinforcers appropriately (Chronis et al., 2001; Chronis, Chacko, Fabiano, Wymbs, & Pelham, 2004; DeNisco, Tiago, & Kravitz, 2005).

For example, Cassidy, a 6-year-old with hyperactivity, becomes easily frustrated with her homework and throws her pencil. Her mother becomes angry, raises her voice, pleads with her to do her work, and ultimately storms out of the room in frustration. If provided with parent training, Cassidy's mother would learn effective techniques, such as response cost and timeout, to encourage Cassidy to complete her homework.

Implementation

The goal of parent training is to teach parents how to understand and improve the behavior of their children. The basic elements of behavioral parent training for hyperactivity include the following:

1. Teaching or coaching parents to understand the biological, behavioral, and cognitive aspects of hyperactivity

2. Teaching appropriate skill sets through modeling, including:

   a. Effective reinforcement strategies and different types of reinforcers (e.g., verbal praise, social activities, toys)

   b. Observation skills

   c. Play skills

d. Response-cost techniques

e. Timeout procedures

f. Self-regulation/monitoring skills

g. Token economy and reward charts

h. Contingency contracts

i. Self-monitoring and self-reward

Parent training begins by first conducting an intake assessment with the family. This assessment includes an evaluation of the family climate to determine the needs of the family and any barriers to success, including cultural–parental expectations (Kotchick & Forehand, 2002). Based on the intake assessment, identify skill deficits and then formulate the goals and objectives that can be achieved by implementing family and parent management techniques. The targets of the intervention are the child's hyperactive behaviors as well as the actions of the parents that appear to reinforce these behaviors. Additionally, this initial assessment provides a broad overview of the goals of the intervention, the relevance of the information to be presented, and the responsibilities of the parents in the process (e.g., follow-through, attendance).

Next, determine the logistics of the intervention's implementation. These logistics include making decisions about the format of the training (e.g., individual, group, group with individual consultation sessions), the location of the intervention (e.g., home, community agency, school), and the time of the intervention (convenience for parents should be considered when using a group format).

Begin the intervention by teaching parents to use effective discipline techniques, such as differential reinforcement and timeout procedures. Throughout the process, assist parents in choosing effective and preferred parenting and child management techniques. At the end of each session, hold a family meeting to practice parenting and communication skills through modeling and role-play. Video vignettes can be used during the family meeting for behavioral modeling and discussion prompts (Spaccarelli, Cotler, & Penman, 1992). Monitor both parent training and the parent's application of the training to determine the effects of one or more of the training topics. Some parents may respond well and need only one or two sessions on a topic, while other families may benefit from ongoing parenting training, such as semester- or year-long evening courses on campus. After training sessions are completed, refresher sessions or periodic individual sessions may be needed to review and maintain the skills learned. In many cases, parents will receive training in three or four topics over several sessions.

The procedural steps presented in Figure 4.3 illustrate how these essential elements are presented in a typical parent training program to remediate symptoms of hyperactivity (Chronis, et al., 2004).

Figure 4.3 Procedural steps for the application of parent training

1. Find a mutually satisfactory time for meeting, and determine the appropriate number of trainings that might be needed. Consider creating a partnership contract to agree on the number of times to meet and the techniques to learn.

2. Begin each session by reviewing the effective parenting technique discussed in the previous session, reviewing the homework assignment, and answering specific parental questions.

3. Teach a specific parenting technique, using language and examples to demonstrate relevance to the parents.

4. Verbally describe the technique.

5. Discuss parental concerns about using the technique, and provide evidence of its effectiveness so that families know what to expect.

6. Give specific verbal examples.

7. Model the technique.

8. Ask the parents for an example of a time when the technique could have been effective, and role-play the technique using the given example. For training in after-school or parent groups, be sure to role-play examples with several parents so everyone who attends is involved and contributes.

9. For individual family sessions in the home rather than large parent groups at school, bring the child into the session and briefly explain the technique to him or her. Have the parents role-play the technique with the child. Provide feedback after the performance, highlighting positive statements regarding the parent's implementation.

10. Encourage independent implementation by requesting the use of the technique a specific number of times before the next session. Additionally, request that the parents document the effects, problems encountered, and any questions they might have.

Evidence for Use

Parent training has been widely shown to decrease behavioral symptoms of ADHD (e.g., inattention, hyperactivity, impulsivity), as evidenced in the research literature (Barkley, 2000; Chronis et al., 2004; Daly et al., 2007; Pelham et al., 1998). Parent training has been found to decrease ADHD symptomatology in the home and school (Bor, Sanders, & Markie-Dadds, 2002; Huang, Chao, Tu, & Yang, 2003; Sonuga-Barke, Daley, Thompson, Laver-Bradbury, & Weeks, 2001). Behavioral manifestations of hyperactivity may also be decreased, including parent–child conflict and disruptive behavior (Bor et al., 2002;

McCleary & Ridley, 1999; Stein, 1999). The use of parent training to decrease hyperactivity leads to increases in compliant behavior and effective parental management style (Pisterman et al., 1989). The following studies summarize some of the key research findings associated with using parent training to address hyperactivity in children and adolescents.

Bor, W., Sanders, M. R., & Markie-Dadds, C. (2002). The effects of the Triple P—Positive Parenting Program on preschool children with co-occurring disruptive behavior and attentional/hyperactive difficulties. *Journal of Abnormal Child Psychology, 30*(6), 571–587.

This study investigated the impact of parent training on children with ADHD and their families using two versions of the Triple P—Positive Parenting Program: the enhanced behavioral family intervention (EBFI) and the standard behavioral family intervention (SBFI). The 87 families that participated were drawn from a pool of 305 families that had previously participated in a study of preschoolers at risk for developing conduct problems and had already been randomly assigned to one of three treatment groups: SBFI (training in 17 child management strategies and planned activities), EBFI (SBFI training plus partner support and coping skills training), or a wait-list control group (WL). Families assigned to EBFI and SBFI received an average of 10–12 parent training sessions lasting 60–90 minutes over the course of 15–17 weeks, with the EBFI families receiving an additional 4 hours of training during two extra sessions. The WL group received no training. Data were collected at preintervention, postintervention, and 1-year follow-up through several means, including a diagnostic interview, taped home observations of parent and child interactions, and nine parent report measures. Results demonstrated that both EBFI and SBFI had positive outcomes for parents and children when compared with the WL group; however, contrary to expectations, the enhanced training did not prove to be a superior intervention on any of the measures utilized by the authors.

Huang, H.-L., Chao, C.-C., Tu, C.-C., & Yang, P.-C. (2003). Behavioral parent training for Taiwanese parents of children with attention-deficit/hyperactivity disorder. *Psychiatry and Clinical Neurosciences, 57*, 275–281.

Twenty-three families participated in this study of the effectiveness of Barkley's parent training program, which bears similarities to the Confucian values dominant in Chinese societies and has proven to be particularly effective in reducing the misbehavior of children with ADHD/ODD. Over the course of nine weekly sessions and one follow-up session (4 weeks later), parents (22 mothers and 1 father) received instruction in the steps of Barkley's training, which involve learning about the causes of misbehavior and concepts of behavior management, how to increase compliance through clear and direct commands and positive consequences, and how to decrease misbehavior through swift and appropriate negative consequences. Data were collected at five points in the study (weeks 1, 4, 6, 7, and 10) using the

Disruptive Behavior Rating Scale–Parent Form (DBRS–PF), Child Attention Profile (CAP), and Home Situations Questionnaire (HSQ). Results showed that the children's behaviors were positively influenced by their parents' participation in Barkley's training program, with mean scores of problem behaviors decreasing across all measures.

McCleary, L., & Ridley, T. (1999). Parenting adolescents with ADHD: Evaluation of a psychoeducation group. *Patient Education and Counseling, 38,* 3–10.

A comprehensive group training and education program for parents whose children were diagnosed with ADHD was the focus of this study, which sought to determine the impact of such group training on parent–child conflict, parenting skills, and child behavior. The parents of 65 adolescents, aged between 12 and 17 years, were divided into groups of 8 to 24 and attended 10 weekly group training sessions. The goals of the parent sessions were to increase understanding of ADHD, help manage their children's problem behaviors, and improve their advocacy skills. Data were collected at pretreatment and posttreatment via a conflict behavior questionnaire and an issues checklist. Results showed that, from preintervention to postintervention, rates of parent–child conflict dropped (from a mean of 10.9 to 8.2), as did number of issues (from a mean of 23.7 to 20.1) and intensity of conflict (from a mean of 2.3 to 2.1). These data suggest that a group parent training approach may be an effective method of helping parents raise children with ADHD.

Pisterman, S., McGrath, P., Firestone, P., Goodman, J. T., Webster, I., & Mallory, R. (1989). Outcome of parent-mediated treatment of preschoolers with attention deficit disorder with hyperactivity. *Journal of Consulting and Clinical Psychology, 57*(5), 628–635.

This study examined the effects of a group parent-training program on compliance in children with ADHD. Baseline behavioral information was collected on 46 preschoolers diagnosed with ADHD through a comprehensive diagnostic interview with the parent who spent the most time with each child, as well as achievement and behavioral assessments administered to each child. Parents were then randomly assigned to one of two groups: immediate treatment (experimental group) or delayed treatment (control group). The training intervention was conducted over 12 weeks, with 10 group sessions and 2 individual sessions, during which the parents received instruction on ADHD, behavior management principles, and realistic expectations. Data were collected via behavior assessments and parent questionnaires at pretreatment, posttreatment, and 3-month follow-up. Results showed that compliance rates rose from about 42% to 58% for the experimental group and rates of noncompliance dropped from about 8% to just 3%, offering support for the efficacy of parent-mediated behavioral treatment of preschoolers with ADHD.

Sonuga-Barke, E. J. S., Daley, D., Thompson, M., Laver-Bradbury, C., & Weeks, A. (2001). Parent-based therapies for preschool attention-deficit/hyperactivity disorder: A randomized, controlled trial with a community sample. *Journal of the American Academy of Child and Adolescent Psychiatry, 40*(4), 402–408.

Parent training (PT) and parent counseling and support (PC&S) were used in this study to determine the impact of parent-based therapies on the behavior of 3-year-olds diagnosed with ADHD. Families assigned to PT participated in eight 1-hour sessions in which the mothers received ADHD education and learned behavioral strategies for increasing attention and reducing difficult behavior. Families assigned to PC&S participated in eight 1-hour sessions in which mothers discussed feelings, issues, and concerns about their children. Regardless of intervention, each child was observed engaging in independent play for 10 minutes at the end of each 1-hour session. Data were collected on ADHD symptoms via observations of the children and clinical interviews with the mothers, as well as on maternal well-being. This information was gathered on the PT and PC&S groups and a waiting-list control group (WLC). Results showed that only the PT group reached a significant level of clinical change (53%, compared with 38% of PC&S and 25% of WLC). Moreover, PT dramatically increased maternal well-being when compared to PC&S and WLC, suggesting the excellent potential of parent training in behavior strategies as an early intervention for children with ADHD.

Stein, D. B. (1999). A medication-free parent management program for children diagnosed as ADHD. *Ethical Human Sciences and Services, 1*(1), 61–79.

Twenty-seven children diagnosed with ADHD–12 boys and 15 girls between the ages of 5 and 11 years–and their parents participated in this investigation of the Caregivers Skills Program (CSP), a parenting program that emphasizes enforcement of consequences for misbehavior and expects children to self-regulate and control behavior without medication and across settings. Parents received training on how to observe, evaluate, and record their children's behavior (data that were collected throughout each phase of the study). After a 4-week baseline phase, a 4-week cognitive treatment phase occurred in which each child learned how to identify problem situations and generate solutions while parents were taught parenting skills such as social reinforcement techniques, activity reinforcement techniques, and timeouts. Next, parents collected behavioral data during a 4-week implementation phase, and follow-up data were collected for a 2-week period occurring 1 year after the last parenting session. Results showed that cognitive training alone did not improve the children's behavior but that the CSP had a significant positive effect on behavior and academic performance (with a 92% improvement rate on the targeted behaviors and 81% of the children improving academically).

Considerations

For Culture and Language Differences

Communication is critical for parent training; thus, using the primary language of the family and understanding the values of the family are essential to building an effective partnership. If beliefs about the condition or the treatment are radically different than those of the school, all key stakeholders would benefit from a discussion about expectations for success in the school setting while maintaining an attitude of tolerance and understanding for the culture of the home.

For Age and Developmental Level

Early intervention is often shown to be effective and is particularly relevant for parent training. Providing training to parents of young children as early as possible can have a positive effect on a child's typical behavior patterns and routines as well as on parenting styles.

IV. Self-Management

Self-management as an intervention for hyperactivity is a process in which children monitor their own activity level, record the results, and compare this level to a predetermined acceptable level of activity (Reid, Trout, & Schartz, 2005). This self-management intervention involves a combination of three behavioral techniques: self-monitoring, self-monitoring plus reinforcement, and self-reinforcement (Mace, Belfiore, & Hutchinson, 2001; Reid et al., 2005). Self-monitoring is the process of observing and recording one's own activity level. A teacher or other professional can add reinforcement to self-monitoring by rewarding the child for exhibiting appropriate activity levels. In self-reinforcement, the child defines his or her own goal for the level of activity and provides a self-reward when the goal is achieved.

For example, Lizzie, a 17-year-old with ADHD, dances and sings when driving with the radio on. On two occasions, Lizzie has run the same stop sign, almost causing an accident. After these two incidents, her mother refused to let her drive to school. As an alternative to removing all of her driving privileges, self-monitoring could be implemented to reduce or eliminate the effect of Lizzie's hyperactive, off-task behavior while driving. Lizzie can be taught to self-monitor her activity level while driving and to reinforce her own appropriate behavior.

Implementation

The goal of self-management is for the child to become aware of his or her own level of activity in order to produce an automatic response without relying on external reinforcement or prompting (Christie, Hiss, & Lozanoff, 1984; Reid et al., 2005). A child's ability to produce this automatic response through internalized controls can decrease his or her situation-specific, inappropriate overactivity. The essential elements of self-management include the following:

1. Child monitoring his or her own activity level

2. Child recording his or her own activity level

3. External reward/reinforcement for appropriate activity level

4. Internal reward (self-reward/self-reinforcement) for appropriate activity level

The procedural steps presented in Figure 4.4 illustrate how these essential elements are incorporated into a self-management program to remediate symptoms of hyperactivity. For example, Todd is challenged by hyperactivity. He fidgets frequently, tapping his pencil on the desk and his feet on the floor. When he hears classmates talking, he jumps into the conversation, regardless of the task he is engaged in. Todd is taught to monitor his fidgeting and impulsive talking by using a watch with a small vibrating alarm set to 1-minute intervals. Todd records on a sticky note on top of his desk if he was hyperactive when the watch vibrated. When he meets his goal, Todd is allowed to lead the class to lunch and sit next to his teacher.

Figure 4.4 Procedural steps for the application of self-management

1. Teach self-monitoring procedures to the child.

   a. Identify the problem behavior and the new behavior to replace it.

   b. Model the replacement behavior, and indicate the level (i.e., the frequency and/or intensity) at which it should occur.

   c. Role-play the expected level and behavior with the child.

   d. Ask the child and the person modeling the behavior (e.g., teacher) to record either a plus (+), indicating appropriate activity level, or a minus (–), indicating overactivity.

   e. Compare both sets of ratings.

   f. Provide reinforcement for accurate child recordings.

   g. Continue this process until the child masters self-recording (i.e., typically with 90% accuracy).

2. Determine if the replacement behavior is happening in the desired setting.

3. As needed, prompt the child to monitor activity (e.g., a beep on a tape recorder).

4. Ask the child to self-record the occurrence of the replacement behavior.

5. Graph the occurrence of the replacement behavior in order to demonstrate success or failure of the targeted behavior and activity level.

6. Provide consistent feedback and appropriate reinforcement.

Evidence for Use

Self-management has been found to decrease levels of overactivity, the amount of misbehavior during independent work periods, inappropriate behavior, and inappropriate vocalizations and verbalizations (Barkley, Copeland, & Sivage, 1980; Christie et al., 1984; Horn, Chatoor & Conners, 1983; Varni & Henker, 1979). The following studies summarize some of the key research findings associated with self-management interventions for children or adolescents with hyperactivity.

Christie, D. J., Hiss, M., & Lozanoff, B. (1984). Modification of inattentive classroom behavior: Hyperactive children's use of self-recording with teacher guidance. *Behavior Modification, 8*(3), 391–406.

Three elementary school-aged boys, none of whom were taking medication, participated in this study of the impact of a self-recording system on classroom behavior. Each participant's typical classroom behavior was videotaped and then used to teach the students how to effectively identify and classify their own behavior. Data were collected daily on percentages of inattentive, inappropriate, and on-task behavior during eight 15-minute observation intervals. The teachers collected baseline data for 1 week, followed by a 2-week treatment phase, during which both the teachers and the participants recorded behavior. One participant and teacher pairing continued to participate in the study after the initial 3-week period, allowing a 1-week reversal phase and a second 2-week treatment phase to be conducted. Results showed self-recording to be an effective strategy for improving classroom behavior, with inattentive and inappropriate behavior decreasing over the course of the study and mean percentages of on-task behavior increasing (about 42%, 51%, 53%, and 65% during baseline, treatment, reversal, and second treatment, respectively).

Horn, W. F., Chatoor, I., & Conners, C. K. (1983). Additive effects of Dexedrine® and self-control training. *Behavior Modification, 7*(3), 383–402.

A 9-year-old boy diagnosed with ADHD and undersocialized conduct disorder was the single participant in this 10-week study to determine the independent and combined effects of medication and self-control training on behavior. A psychiatric inpatient in an intensive diagnostic and treatment program for children, the individual participated in academic classes held at the hospital housing the psychiatric program, during which his behavior was observed three times each week for 20-minute periods (at 15-second intervals). No intervention took place during baseline, which was followed by phases of placebo, medication, placebo plus self-control training, and medication plus self-control training. In addition to the participant's classroom behavior, data were collected using teacher ratings of the child's behavior, academic performance (math and spelling problems, twice weekly), and measures of attention and impulse control. Results showed that medication plus self-control training was the most effective of the interventions at increasing on-task behavior and that none of the interventions improved academic performance for this individual.

Kern, L., Ringdahl, J. E., Hilt, A., & Sterling-Turner, H. E. (2001). Linking self-management procedures to functional analysis results. *Behavioral Disorders, 26*(3), 214–226.

Three boys with varying behavioral issues participated in this two-phase study of how self-management is related to functional analysis results. The functional analysis phase was conducted in a hospital facility where all the participants had been admitted for the treatment of their respective problem behaviors. Descriptive analyses of the events that directly preceded and followed problem behaviors were developed based on observations of each child interacting with his mother. During the self-management phase, the participants learned how to record and manage their own behavior, with rewards earned for appropriate behavior. Data were collected on rates of inappropriate behavior during two baseline and two self-management periods. Results demonstrated that the self-management intervention decreased problem behaviors for all of the participants. Moreover, the 3 students demonstrated the ability to choose appropriate alternative behaviors.

Varni, J. W., & Henker, B. (1979). A self-regulation approach to the treatment of three hyperactive boys. *Child Behavior Therapy, 1*(2), 171–192.

This investigation studied the effects of a self-regulation intervention package (self-instructional training, self-monitoring, and self-reinforcement) on the academic performance and behavior of 3 boys diagnosed with hyperactivity. After baseline, the self-regulation behaviors were taught in succession: first self-instructional, then self-monitoring, followed by self-reinforcement. The children were observed in both clinical and school settings, with data being collected during all phases of the study on math and reading performance (number of problems completed and percentage of accuracy) and rates of off-task behavior (recorded 5 days a week during periods of 15 minutes in the clinic and 20 minutes in the classroom). Results showed that the self-instructional phase had no effect on behavior and the self-monitoring phase had only minimal effect on behavior in both the clinic and school settings. In contrast, all 3 children showed marked academic and behavioral improvement during the self-reinforcement phase; however, the researchers noted that improvement was not consistent over the course of the phase. Rather, the children had high-performance days as well as days during which performance regressed to baseline levels. This variance was attributed to the choice given to the participants throughout the study of whether or not to work on any given day.

Considerations

For Teaching

When teaching children to self-manage, it is important to thoughtfully consider the goal of the intervention. If the objective is to reduce fidgety behaviors, the intervention and outcome will be different than improving a class of behaviors, such as listening or assignment completion. For example, targeting fidgety behaviors may result in solely monitoring and recording the tapping of a foot or pencil, which may not produce the same results that monitoring on-task behavior or task completion might. However, reducing fidgety behaviors may be the primary goal in other situations. For example, if a student's behavior interrupts the other students' class work or creates a negative relationship with the teacher, it may be best to focus on reducing those behaviors, even if the student's overall academic performance is not targeted.

V. Task Modification

Task modification as an intervention for hyperactivity involves modifying aspects of specific instructional tasks or assignments. Teachers can modify tasks by giving the student a choice of activities or assignments (Dyer, Dunlap, & Winterling, 1990; Koegel, Dyer, & Bell, 1987) or modifying intratask stimulation (Zentall, 1989; Zentall & Leib, 1985). Examples of intratask stimulation include adding color to written assignments, decreasing task-overlapping noise, requiring structured response patterns, and adding motor activity to rote tasks (Zentall & Dwyer, 1989; Zentall & Leib, 1985; Zentall & Meyer, 1987; Zentall & Shaw, 1980).

For example, Ian, a 12-year-old with ADHD, becomes highly frustrated when he is unable to complete all five essay questions on a written assignment in history class. His teacher insists that he write the answers to all five questions before moving on to the next lesson. Using task modifications, the teacher can ask Ian to answer three of the five questions before moving on or can allow Ian to type his answers on a computer.

Implementation

Based on information obtained through a functional assessment, alter tasks using antecedent instructional modifications (Ervin et al., 1998; Kern & Clemens, 2007; Raggi & Chronis, 2006). A number of modification strategies have been recommended by researchers (Carbone, 2001; Kern & Clemens, 2007; Montague & Warger, 1997; Salend, Elhoweris, & van Garderen, 2003). Each of these strategies is detailed in this implementation section, including:

- Offering a choice of instructional activities

- Using high-interest activities and hands-on demonstrations

- Providing increased opportunities to respond

- Varying the pace of instruction

Offering a Choice of Instructional Activities

Encouraging students to engage in active decision-making and to exercise control over making choices can help increase their level of attention. Using this approach, students are allowed to choose activities, materials, or a task sequence within a set of instructional materials outlined by the teacher (Dunlap et al., 1994; Kern, Bambara, & Fogt, 2002; Powell & Nelson, 1997). For example, a student might get to choose the order of assignment completion, decide which group of classmates he or she will work with, or select the type of responses (e.g., verbal, typed on a computer). However, this approach is successful only when the choices offered for student selection are relevant to the curriculum or learning objectives, and consideration should be given to ensuring that learning goals are not compromised. For example, choosing between two equally unattractive options will be unpopular with the student, and doing only half of the assignment versus doing all of the assignment will be unacceptable to the teacher. Agree on the conditions for each choice prior to class time to decrease conflicts between student and teacher interests.

Using High-Interest Activities and Hands-on Demonstrations

Activities and tasks that are novel and interesting to students can increase work productivity (Carbone, 2001; Clarke, et al., 1995). Also, providing moderate levels of auditory stimuli (e.g., music) during familiar tasks with structured responses and reducing classroom noise during times when students are engaged in learning new concepts can cue students to the different types of attention each task requires (Scott, 1970; Zentall, 1983). Teachers can begin lessons with high-interest activities that require participation and facilitate attention, such as demonstrating practical applications (especially for math or science topics), playing music or film clips, engaging in role-plays, or using examples related to current community events or student activities.

Providing Increased Opportunities to Respond

In this strategy, students are given increased opportunities to respond to academic material using varied response methods (Montague & Warger, 1997; Sutherland, Alder & Gunter, 2003). This increased opportunity to respond increases engagement and attention, and improves academic performance as a secondary benefit. Counting the number of responses per child per hour is one way to monitor the amount of interaction between the students and the teacher (and consequently how difficult it may be for students to sustain attention). For example, if a class has 20 students and the teacher asks 20 questions during a 20-minute presentation, each student actively participates approximately one time. However, if a teacher instead uses individual student answer cards on which each student writes a response and shows the teacher by holding up the card, every student participates 20 times in 20 minutes. In this case, attention is maintained due to the pace and immediacy of the task.

Varying the Pace of Instruction

Briskly paced instruction increases levels of on-task behavior because rapid pacing requires more attending effort (Kern & Clemens, 2007; Skinner, Johnson, Larkin, Lessley, & Glowacki, 1995). Teachers can increase the pacing of their instruction either by increasing their rate of presenting material or by decreasing the length of instructional pauses (Kern & Clemens, 2007).

Evidence for Use

Task modification for students with hyperactivity has been found to decrease disruptive behavior, impulsive errors, and task-irrelevant noise making, as well as to increase task engagement and activity levels (Dunlap et al., 1994; Zentall & Dwyer, 1989; Zentall & Leib, 1985; Zentall & Meyer, 1987). The following studies summarize some of the key research findings associated with task modification interventions for children and adolescents with hyperactivity.

Dunlap, G., dePerczel, M., Clarke, S., Wilson, D., Wright, S., White, R., et al. (1994). Choice making to promote adaptive behavior for students with emotional and behavioral challenges. *Journal of Applied Behavior Analysis, 27*(3), 505–518.

This investigation consisted of two studies to evaluate the effects of choice making on the classroom behavior of 3 children with emotional and behavioral disorders. Two 11-year-old boys enrolled in a special education classroom for students diagnosed as emotionally handicapped participated in Study 1. Two conditions were employed: no choice, in which assignments were selected by the teacher, and choice, in which the students were allowed to select assignments from a list generated by the teacher. Results demonstrated that disruptive behavior decreased for both students under the choice condition as compared to under the no-choice condition. In Study 2, data were collected during story time on the on-task and disruptive behavior of a 5-year-old boy attending a class for students with severe emotional disturbances. Choice (student-selected books) and no-choice (teacher-selected) conditions were again employed. Results of Study 2 showed that the participant displayed high levels of on-task behavior during the choice condition phases and very low levels during the no-choice condition phases. The results of these two studies demonstrated the effectiveness of choice making in reducing disruptive behavior and increasing on-task behavior of students with emotional and behavioral disorders.

Zentall, S. S., & Dwyer, A. M. (1989). Color effects on the impulsivity and activity of hyperactive children. *Journal of School Psychology, 27,* 165–173.

This study utilized the Matching Familiar Figures Test-20 (MFFT-20), a measure of impulsivity, to examine the impact of color on the behavior of 24 children (12 diagnosed as hyperactive and 12 normally functioning). The MFFT-20 form was divided into two equivalent halves—form A and form B—and each form was produced in a black and white version (low stimulation condition) and a color version (high stimulation condition). The participants were randomly assigned to complete one version of the forms; 1 month later, participants completed the opposite form and version (e.g., color form A followed by black and white form B). Data were collected on performance (latency to the first choice, total errors, and time required) and activity level (via an actometer, a motion recorder). Results showed that participants diagnosed as hyperactive were more active only during the low stimulation condition and that the presence of color slowed these children down, relative to the control group, but did not improve performance.

Zentall, S. S., & Leib, S. L. (1985). Structured tasks: Effects on activity and performance of hyperactive and comparison children. *Journal of Educational Research, 79*(2), 91–95.

Fifteen 8- to 12-year-old boys diagnosed as hyperactive and 16 normally functioning boys participated in this study which examined the effects of structure on behavior and performance levels. The children participated in two separate art projects, one with a high level of structure (replication of a design presented by the instructor) and one with a low level of structure (students created their own design). The children were divided into two groups (each with equal numbers of hyperactive and nonhyperactive boys). Group one first completed the low-structure activity followed by the high-structure activity, and group two reversed the order of activities. Results showed that physical activity diminished during the high-structure assignment for both the hyperactive and nonhyperactive participants, and activity levels were comparable regardless of the structure level ($M = 653.1$ activity units and $M = 657.3$ activity units for hyperactive and control groups, respectively). The authors suggested that, based on the results, the addition of response requirements (i.e., structure) in task-oriented settings can reduce activity levels in hyperactive children and further suggested that differences between hyperactive and nonhyperactive children in structured settings may be more a factor of task difficulty than of an applied structure.

Zentall, S. S., & Meyer, M. J. (1987). Self-regulation of stimulation for ADD-H children during reading and vigilance task performance. *Journal of Abnormal Child Psychology, 15*(4), 519–536.

The effects of self-regulation of stimulation on socially disruptive classroom behavior was the focus of this study involving 47 children (22 with attention-deficit/hyperactivity disorder and 25 control), all between the ages of 6 and 12 years. Two repetitive tasks—an auditory vigilance task and a word decoding task—were given during two different stimulation conditions: low-stimulation passive response (LS-P) and high-stimulation active response (HS-A). Behavior data were collected via observation and actometer (a motion recorder attached to a wrist and ankle of each participant). Results demonstrated that impulsive activity in the children with hyperactivity was comparable to that of their control group peers during the active condition. However, while behavior activity improved for both tasks during the active condition, performance only improved for the vigilance task. The findings suggested that the attraction to novel stimuli and the excessive activity of children with ADHD can be channeled to prompt appropriate behaviors.

Zentall, S. S., & Shaw, J. H. (1980). Effects of classroom noise on performance and activity of second-grade hyperactive and control children. *Journal of Educational Psychology, 72*(6), 830–840.

This study, involving two experiments, investigated the effects of different levels of classroom noise on the behavior and academic performance of 48 second-grade students (24 students with hyperactivity and 24 control students). In Experiment 1, the participants completed a familiar task (i.e., math problems) while being subjected via headphones to high and low levels of classroom noise. The order of noise level experienced by the students was randomly assigned for the two sessions. Results of Experiment 1 showed that students diagnosed with hyperactivity had greater difficulty coping with classroom noise, as evidenced by lower percentages of correct responses and higher levels of activity during the sessions. In Experiment 2, high and low levels of classroom noise were presented via speakers to groups of 8 participants each (4 students with hyperactivity and 4 control students) during new tasks (i.e., reading lessons). The order of presentation (high or low) was randomly assigned to the groups. Results of Experiment 2 showed that while all participants committed more errors under high-level noise conditions as compared to low-level conditions, the children with hyperactivity made more errors than their control group peers under both conditions. Overall data seemed to indicate that high levels of classroom noise have a diminishing effect, especially when the task at hand is new (i.e., more difficult).

Considerations

For Teaching

While modifying tasks can be beneficial to the student, teachers may perceive this approach as adding to their workload, cheating, or providing an advantage, especially in a time of high-stakes testing and competitive academic conditions. First, remind teachers that spending time up front does not require more time but rather different time, and leads to more instructional time in the long run and less time spent managing a child's behavioral problems. In many schools, there are often a few teachers who are very skilled in implementing task modifications. They can be invaluable resources for other teachers learning how to incorporate this strategy into their own teaching programs efficiently and effectively. Second, consider carefully the modifications included in individual education plans for both classroom and annual assessment. Modifications in classroom and assessment conditions are sometimes expected to be parallel, regardless of test validity issues. Be cautious to distinguish between modifications and accommodations.

VI. Multimodal Interventions

Multimodal interventions for hyperactivity consist of various combinations of interventions to reduce problem behavior. Typically, multimodal interventions include stimulant medication plus one of the behavioral interventions described in this chapter. Thus, the use of medication will be discussed in combination with other interventions.

Multimodal interventions teach new skills to reduce hyperactivity and prevent future problems while also remediating the deficits that may exist academically, socially, or in self-regulation due to problem behavior. These combined treatments are more complex to initiate and involve multiple participants. Sometimes it is difficult to review and assess which relative parts were responsible for improvements.

For example, 7-year-old Star was diagnosed with ADHD by a child psychiatrist and takes methylphenidate with breakfast and lunch. However, the effects of her medication begin to wear off in the afternoon while she is still in school. As the medication wears off, Star begins to act out in class, constantly moving around the room, disrupting her classmates' work, and speaking loudly. When she arrives home, her behavior is unmanageable for her parents, who become easily irritated and complain that it takes Star 2 hours to complete what should be about 30 minutes of homework. To address Star's declining behavior at school and uncontrollable behavior at home, the school psychologist could design a multimodal behavior management plan to assist her teacher and parents. The plan could involve a combination of intervention methods to remediate her disruptive behaviors, such as additional or different dosages of medication to extend the effects, task modification in the classroom to limit disruptions and improve her focus, and behavioral parent training to assist her parents in managing her behavior at home.

Implementation

The goals of multimodal interventions are to identify and provide a broad spectrum of approaches that address current performance and behavior problems while remediating deficits in skills across social, behavioral, or academic environments. The objective of this multifaceted intervention program is to create self-regulating individuals that need little or no intervention to maintain functional levels of activity. The essential features in these types of interventions vary dramatically based on their components and the individual being treated. The basic elements of multimodal interventions include the following:

1. Provision of multiple treatments with appropriate personnel simultaneously or in sequence, including:

    a. Functional assessment

    b. Contingency management

    c. Parent training

    d. Self-management

    e. Task modification

2. Determination of responsible parties to implement and monitor treatments in order to identify issues and best solutions

3. Communication with teachers, parents, physicians, and related service providers

The five procedural steps for implementing multimodal interventions for the treatment of a child with hyperactivity are listed in Figure 4.5. First, determine the exact interventions within the multimodal framework based on assessment results that indicate the causal factors associated with the conduct problems. Second, determine the length of treatment based on the severity of the causal factors. With multimodal interventions, treatment may be provided for longer periods of time than with single interventions. Third, based on the prescribed intervention, identify the specific members of the team that will provide services (e.g., psychologist, social worker, case worker). Fourth, implement the interventions simultaneously. Fifth, transfer the learned behaviors and techniques to the natural environment.

> ### Figure 4.5 Procedural steps for the application of multimodal interventions
>
> 1. Determine the intervention approaches to be used.
>
> 2. Determine the length of treatment.
>
> 3. Determine the person most qualified to implement the interventions (this may be an individual or a team of professionals).
>
> 4. Implement the interventions simultaneously, as described in the procedural steps for each intervention.
>
> 5. Generalize treatment effects to natural environments.

Evidence for Use

Evidence-based multimodal intervention packages primarily combine two or more of the following interventions: medication, parent training, individual contingency management with and without response cost, daily behavior report cards (DBRC), group contingency management, timeout from reinforcers and activities, social skills training, self-management, peer-mediated interventions, and teacher consultation. Many of the studies described below were completed using data from manualized treatment programs, such as the Summer Treatment Program (Pelham, Greiner, & Gnagy, 1997) and the National Institute of Mental Health's Multisite Treatment of Attention Deficit Disorders (MTA Cooperative Group, 1999). Only a selected sampling of these studies is presented here. There are two main categories of studies involving multimodal interventions: with medication and without.

Studies of Multimodal Treatment With Medication

Horn et al. (1983) and Hinshaw, Henker, and Whalen (1984) found that the combination of medication and self-management techniques reduced inappropriate social behavior, vocalizations, and noise making. The combination of medication, individual contingency management, DBRCs, response cost, and timeout was found to decrease disruptive behavior and increase on-task behavior (Carlson, Pelham, Milich, & Dixon, 1992; Pelham et al., 1993). By adding parent training, social skills training, and teacher consultation to a medical intervention, the MTA Cooperative Group (1999) found a decrease in inattention, hyperactivity, and impulsivity.

Studies of Multimodal Treatment Without Medication

DuPaul and Hoff (1998) combined individual contingency management with self-management and found decreased disruptive behavior. Horn, Ialongo, Popovich, and Peradotto (1987) combined parent training and self-management, and Owens et al. (2005) combined parent training, DBRCs, and teacher consultation; both studies found decreases in hyperactivity after their respective intervention programs. Davies and Witte (2000) combined individual contingency management, group contingency management, social skills training, and peer mediation, and found it resulted in decreased disruptive behavior (i.e., talking out). Coles et al. (2005) found that the combination of parent training, individual contingency management, DBRCs, response cost, group contingency management, timeout, and social skills training resulted in decreased negative behavior.

The following studies summarize in more detail some of the key research findings associated with multimodal interventions for children and adolescents with hyperactivity.

Carlson, C. L., Pelham, W. E., Jr., Milich, R., & Dixon, J. (1992). Single and combined effects of methylphenidate and behavior therapy on the classroom performance of children with attention-deficit hyperactivity disorder. *Journal of Abnormal Child Psychology, 20*(2), 213–232.

Twenty-four boys, aged between 6 and 12 years, attending a summer treatment program for children with ADHD participated in this study that investigated the effects of a comprehensive behavior management system and medication on the participants' behavior and academic performance. The behavior management system involved token reinforcement; classroom structure, rules, and feedback; timeouts; an honor roll system; and daily reports home. Two behavior conditions were studied: behavior management and regular classroom (removal of behavior management components). In addition, three medication conditions were compared: placebo, low dose, and high dose. The order of the medication conditions was random, with each student receiving each dose once over the course of 3 days. Data were collected during daily 60-minute classroom sessions for 6 days over the course of 2 weeks on occurrence of disruptive behavior, number of behavior points earned, and accuracy and percentage attempted of academic work. Results showed that classroom behavior improved with both the behavioral intervention condition and medication conditions alone, but only the medication conditions affected academic performance. Additionally, the combination of behavioral intervention and medication was found to be most effective for producing behavioral improvement.

Coles, E. K., Pelham, W. E., Gnagy, E. M., Burrows-MacLean, L., Fabiano, G. A., Chacko, A., et al. (2005). A controlled evaluation of behavioral treatment with children with ADHD attending a summer treatment program. *Journal of Emotional and Behavioral Disorders, 13*(2), 99–112.

The Summer Treatment Program (STP), a behavioral treatment intervention implemented across academic and recreational settings, was the focus of this study which sought to document STP's effectiveness on the behavior of 4 children diagnosed with ADHD and attending an 8-week STP. Behavior modification procedures were in effect for 6 of the 8 weeks, split into three treatment phases (weeks 1 and 2, week 4, and weeks 6, 7, and 8), and the remaining 2 weeks were split into two withdrawal phases (week 3 and week 5). During treatment phases, children earned points for appropriate behavior and lost points for inappropriate behavior; points were then exchangeable for reinforcers. Furthermore, the participants continually received behavioral feedback, praise for appropriate behavior, and daily report cards targeting individualized behavioral goals. All aspects of the intervention were removed during withdrawal phases. Data were collected on the frequency of point system behaviors, classroom behavior, and academic productivity throughout all phases of the study. Results showed that appropriate behaviors increased for all participants during the treatment phases despite differences in their medication, gender, and comorbid behaviors. Such results support the previously documented efficacy of behavioral modification in the treatment of children with ADHD.

Davies, S., & Witte, R. (2000). Self-management and peer-monitoring within a group contingency to decrease uncontrolled verbalizations of children with attention-deficit/hyperactivity disorder. *Psychology in the Schools, 37*(2), 135–147.

This study evaluated the effectiveness of a self-management/group contingency intervention in improving classroom behavior (i.e., reducing inappropriate verbalizations) for students diagnosed with ADHD. Four children diagnosed with ADHD and 4 matched-control peers from a third-grade classroom of 30 students were observed during lesson or work time in the classroom. Baseline data on the targeted behavior (frequency counts of inappropriate verbalizations made by all 8 participants during a daily 30-minute period for 4 days) were collected, followed by intervention training in which the class was divided into groups and the students were taught how to define, monitor their groups for, and record the target behavior. Students were also taught how to evaluate and record their own behavior. Reinforcers were selected by the class and were earned for meeting set levels of appropriate behavior. Data were then collected, in the same manner as baseline data, for the intervention phase (12 days), second baseline (4 days), and second intervention phase (10 days). Results showed that rates of inappropriate verbalizations fell dramatically from baseline levels during both phases of the intervention for the students with ADHD and the matched-control students. Moreover, differences in talking-out behavior rates between students with ADHD and matched controls narrowed from the initial baseline (ranging from 2.5 to 22.5 for students with ADHD, and 0 to 15 for matched-control students) to nearly identical for the two sets of students during the second baseline.

DuPaul, G. J., & Hoff, K. E. (1998). Reducing disruptive behavior in general education classrooms: The use of self-management strategies. *School Psychology Review, 27*, 290–303.

This study examined the effects of a self-evaluation procedure on the disruptive and aggressive behavior of three 9-year-old fourth-graders who exhibited behaviors consistent with either ODD or ADHD and who were identified as at risk for later conduct disorder. To collect baseline data, the participants were observed during two academic classes and during recess (15-minute periods at 15-second intervals), as were 3 average students (matched for gender), to determine a typical level of disruptive behavior in the study setting. Data were then collected in the same manner during two additional phases: a teacher-evaluation phase (to teach the rating scale), in which students received verbal feedback and earned tokens for appropriate classroom behavior, and a self-evaluation phase (i.e., intervention phase), in which the participants received self-monitoring training, then self-evaluated with concurrent evaluation by teacher, and later, as teacher evaluation was faded, rated their own behavior. Results showed that self-evaluation effectively reduced the incidence of disruptive behavior in both academic and playground settings for all the participants, suggesting that self-management strategies are useful tools for combating this type of behavior across school settings.

Hinshaw, S. P., Henker, B., & Whalen, C. K. (1984). Cognitive–behavioral and pharmacologic interventions for hyperactive boys: Comparative and combined effects. *Journal of Consulting and Clinical Psychology, 52*(5), 739–749.

This study investigated the effects of reinforcement and reinforced self-evaluation treatment conditions on the playground behavior of 24 boys who had been diagnosed with ADHD and were receiving medication. Hypothesizing that reinforced self-evaluation (RSE) would offer greater benefits (i.e., reduction of negative and an increase in positive social behaviors) than reinforcement alone (RA), the participants first received daily instruction for 3 weeks in self-instruction with regards to academic tasks, anger management with regards to peer pressure, and self-evaluation of behavior. During the fourth week, the participants' playgroup behavior was observed over the course of 2 days. On day one, the children were randomly assigned to one of two cohorts: RSE or RA. Assignments were then reversed on day two. All participants were trying to earn swimming privileges. Observers were unaware of cohort assignments and collected data on appropriate social behavior, negative social behavior, and nonsocial behavior. The collected data revealed that RSE resulted in significantly better behavior than RA when the participants received a placebo in place of medication and that RSE plus medication resulted in the highest levels of appropriate behavior and lowest levels of negative and nonsocial behavior.

Horn, W. F., Chatoor, I., & Conners, C. K. (1983). Additive effects of Dexedrine and self-control training. *Behavior Modification, 7*(3), 383–402.

A 9-year-old boy diagnosed with ADHD and undersocialized conduct disorder was the single participant in this 10-week study to determine the independent and combined effects of medication and self-control training on behavior. A psychiatric inpatient in an intensive diagnostic and treatment program for children, the individual participated in academic classes held at the hospital housing the psychiatric program, during which his behavior was observed three times each week for 20-minute periods (at 15-second intervals). No intervention took place during baseline, which was followed by phases of placebo, medication, placebo plus self-control training, and medication plus self-control training. In addition to the participant's classroom behavior, data were collected using teacher ratings of the child's behavior, academic performance (math and spelling problems, twice weekly), and measures of attention and impulse control. Results showed that medication plus self-control training was the most effective of the interventions at increasing on-task behavior and that none of the interventions improved academic performance for this individual.

Horn, W. F., Ialongo, N., Popovich, S., & Peradotto, D. (1987). Behavioral parent training and cognitive-behavioral self-control therapy with ADD–H children: Comparative and combined effects. *Journal of Clinical Child Psychology, 16*(1), 57–68.

Nineteen elementary school children and their parents participated in this study examining the impact of behavioral parent training and self-control training on the behavior of children with ADD–H. The families were randomly assigned to one of three groups: behavioral parent training ($n = 6$), child self-control training ($n = 6$), or behavioral parent training plus self-control training ($n = 7$). Pretest measures were administered prior to training, including child self-report and laboratory measures, parent report of child behavior, parent self-report, and classroom and academic measures. Trainings then took place over the course of eight 90-minute sessions, after which the effects were assessed via the previously mentioned measures and again at 1-month follow-up. Results indicated that each of the treatment groups resulted in improved behavior at home at posttest and 1-month follow-up; however, combining the two therapies did not offer greater treatment effects than either parent behavioral training or child self-control training alone.

MTA Cooperative Group. (1999). A 14-month randomized clinical trial of treatment strategies for attention-deficit/hyperactivity disorder (ADHD). *Archives of General Psychiatry, 56*, 1073–1086.

Attempting to determine the long-term effectiveness of various treatment strategies on behaviors associated with ADHD, this investigation studied 579 children, aged between 7 and 9 years and diagnosed with ADHD, who were randomly assigned to one of four treatment conditions: behavioral treatment, medication management, combined treatment (behavioral and medication), and community care. While the behavior of participants improved in all four conditions, results showed significant differences between the improvement levels of the groups. The combined treatment group and the medication management group showed the highest levels of improvement in the behavioral symptoms of

ADHD, proving to be both clinically and statistically superior to the behavioral and community care treatments. While combined treatment did not offer significantly better results than medication management, the dosage level utilized to obtain these outcomes was much lower in the combined group than in the medication management group.

Owens, J. S., Richerson, L., Beilstein, E. A., Crane, A., Murphy, C. E., & Vancouver, J. B. (2005). School-based mental health programming for children with inattentive and disruptive behavior problems: First-year treatment outcome. *Journal of Attention Disorders, 9*(1), 261–274.

Participants in this study were 42 children in kindergarten through sixth grade who were referred for inattention, hyperactivity, or related disorders. Thirty children formed the treatment group and participated in the Y.E.S.S. program, a school-based intervention for ADHD; the other 12 served as the control group. In the Y.E.S.S. program, teachers provided daily report cards to parents, clinicians met regularly with teachers, and teachers met with children and parents to discuss progress. Teacher and parent rating scales were completed at three times during the school year. Results showed that the treatment not only improved symptoms of ADHD but also ameliorated related problems, such as opposition, defiance, and aggression, and helped with social functioning, academics, and teacher–student relationships. Teachers and parents gave positive feedback about the program. However, it was a challenge for teachers to make time for this program in their already-busy schedules, and most parents did not make use of many of the meeting times available to them.

Pelham, W. E., Jr., Carlson, C., Sams, S. E., Vallano, G., Dixon, M. J., & Hoza, B. (1993). Separate and combined effects of methylphenidate and behavior modification on boys with attention deficit–hyperactivity disorder in the classroom. *Journal of Consulting and Clinical Psychology, 61*(3), 506–515.

Seeking to clarify the inconsistent results of previous studies on the subject, this 8-week study investigated the effects of behavior modification techniques and medication on the classroom behavior of 31 boys diagnosed with ADHD who were attending a summer treatment program. The study's design allowed for two behavior conditions (behavior modification and no behavior modification) and three medication conditions (placebo, low dose, and high dose). The behavior conditions alternated on a weekly basis. Medication was introduced during week 3, with conditions changing daily and randomly and each condition occurring each week. Data were collected via observation (3 children per observer) on disruptive and on-task behavior during the first 50 minutes (at 15-second intervals) of daily 60-minute academic sessions. In addition, data were gathered on the participants' accuracy and productivity on academic assignments, teacher ratings of the children, and the social validity of the intervention. Results demonstrated that behavior modification alone improved behavior but did not result in academic improvements, while medication alone improved both the behavior and academic performance of the participants. Furthermore, the combination of behavior modification and medication did not offer significant improvement in either area over the levels obtained with medication alone.

Considerations

As with individual approaches, identifying the best treatment options for everyone involved is important. Pharmacology has generally been shown to be an effective intervention. However, the most recent findings from a comprehensive, longitudinal study suggest that while pharmacological approaches have demonstrated effectiveness at 14 and 24 months, follow-up assessments at 36 months showed pharmacological approaches to have no greater effects than behavioral or combined treatment approaches (Swanson et al., 2008). As the authors of this guide have stressed, the decision to use psychopharmacological interventions is a matter for careful consideration among parents, the child, and the physician who would manage such an intervention and is not a decision to be taken lightly. Less intrusive interventions, such as behavior modification, should typically be attempted before trying more complicated approaches. Taking a wait-and-see approach or leaving improvement to chance or future development is ill-advised. There is often little risk in taking some action early, especially using interventions that involve home–school communication, teaching parenting and self-regulation skills, and modifying problem behavior. It is best to keep an open mind regarding proactive approaches that may benefit children (even those who may not warrant a diagnosis of attention problems).

Summary

This chapter presented a review of the characteristics and conditions of hyperactive symptomatology, and summarized the intervention methods that have been shown to be effective in remediating hyperactive behaviors. The discussion of interventions included functional assessment, contingency management, parent training, self-management, task modification, and multimodal interventions. While each intervention method presented differs in its application of one or more behavioral, cognitive–behavioral, or social learning theories, all are shaped by the fundamental goals of treatment: prevention, remediation, and/or management of emotional and behavioral problems related to hyperactivity. The information presented in this chapter forms the basis of the supplemental classroom- and home-based materials that correspond to this book.

References

Abikoff, H., & Hechtman, L. (1994). Multimodal treatment of ADHD: One year treatment outcome data. *Proceedings of the Sixth Annual CHADD Conference, 50–56.*

Abramowitz, A. J., & O'Leary, S. G. (1991). Behavioral interventions for the classroom: Implications for students with ADHD. *School Psychology Review, 20,* 220–234.

American Psychiatric Association. (2000). *Diagnostic and statistical manual of mental disorders* (4th ed., text revision). Washington, DC: Author.

Ayllon, T., Layman, D., & Kandel, H. J. (1975). A behavioral–educational alternative to drug control of hyperactive children. *Journal of Applied Behavior Analysis, 8*(2), 137–146.

Ayllon, T., & Roberts, M. D. (1974). Eliminating discipline problems by strengthening academic performance. *Journal of Applied Behavior Analysis, 7*(1), 71–76.

Barkley, R. A. (2000). Commentary: Issues in training parents to manage children with behavior problems. *Journal of the American Academy of Child and Adolescent Psychiatry, 39,* 1004–1007.

Barkley, R. A. (2006). *Attention-deficit hyperactivity disorder: A handbook for diagnosis and treatment* (3rd ed.). New York: Guilford.

Barkley, R. A., Copeland, A. P., & Sivage, C. (1980). A self-control classroom for hyperactive children. *Journal of Autism and Developmental Disorders, 10,* 75–89.

Blackman, G. J., & Silberman, A. (1980). *Modification of child and adolescent behavior* (3rd ed.). Belmont, CA: Wadsworth.

Bor, W., Sanders, M. R., & Markie-Dadds, C. (2002). The effects of the Triple P—Positive Parenting Program on preschool children with co-occurring disruptive behavior and attentional/hyperactive difficulties. *Journal of Abnormal Child Psychology, 30*(6), 571–587.

Broussard, C. D., & Northup, J. (1995). An approach to functional assessment and analysis of disruptive behavior in regular education classrooms. *School Psychology Quarterly, 10*(2), 151–164.

Brown, R. T., & Sammons, M. T. (2002). Pediatric psychopharmacology: A review of new developments and recent research. *Professional Psychology: Research and Practice, 33*(2), 135–147.

Carbone, E. (2001). Arranging the classroom with an eye (and ear) to students with ADHD. *Teaching Exceptional Children, 34*(2), 72–81.

Carlson, C. L., Pelham, W. E., Jr., Milich, R., & Dixon, J. (1992). Single and combined effects of methylphenidate and behavior therapy on the classroom performance of children with attention-deficit hyperactivity disorder. *Journal of Abnormal Child Psychology, 20*(2), 213–232.

Christie, D. J., Hiss, M., & Lozanoff, B. (1984). Modification of inattentive classroom behavior: Hyperactive children's use of self-recording with teacher guidance. *Behavior Modification, 8*(3), 391–406.

Chronis, A. M., Chacko, A., Fabiano, G. A., Wymbs, B. T., & Pelham, W. E., Jr. (2004). Enhancements to the behavioral parent training paradigm for families of children with ADHD: Review and future directions. *Clinical Child and Family Psychology Review, 7,* 1–27.

Chronis, A. M., Fabiano, G. A., Gnagy, E. M., Wymbs, B. T., Burrows-MacLean, L. & Pelham, W. E., Jr. (2001). Comprehensive, sustained behavioral and pharmacological treatment for attention-deficit/hyperactivity disorder: A case study. *Cognitive and Behavioral Practice, 8,* 346–359.

Chronis, A. M., Jones, H. A., & Raggi, V. L. (2006). Evidence-based psychosocial treatments for children with attention-deficit/hyperactivity disorder. *Clinical Psychology Review, 26,* 486–502.

Clarke, S., Dunlap, G., Foster-Johnson, L., Childs, K. E., Wilson, D., White, R., et al. (1995). Improving the conduct of students with behavioral disorders by incorporating student interests into curricular activities. *Behavioral Disorders, 20*(4), 221–237.

Coles, E. K., Pelham, W. E., Gnagy, E. M., Burrows-MacLean, L., Fabiano, G. A., Chacko, A., et al. (2005). A controlled evaluation of behavioral treatment with children with ADHD attending a summer treatment program. *Journal of Emotional and Behavioral Disorders, 13*(2), 99–112.

Crenshaw, T. M., Kavale, K. A., Forness, S. R., & Reeve, R. E. (1999). Attention deficit hyperactivity disorder and the efficacy of stimulant medication: A meta-analysis. In T. J. Scruggs and M. Mastropieri (Eds.), *Advances in Learning and Behavioral Disabilities* (Vol. 13, pp. 135–165). Greenwich, CT: JAI.

Daly, B. P., Creed, T., Xanthopoulos, M., & Brown, R. T. (2007). Psychosocial treatments for children with attention deficit/hyperactivity disorder. *Neuropsychology Review, 17,* 73–89.

Davies, S., & Witte, R. (2000). Self-management and peer-monitoring within a group contingency to decrease uncontrolled verbalizations of children with attention-deficit/hyperactivity disorder. *Psychology in the Schools, 37*(2), 135–147.

DeNisco, S., Tiago, C., & Kravitz, C. (2005). Evaluation and treatment of pediatric ADHD. *Nurse Practitioner, 30,* 14–23.

Dunlap, G., dePerczel, M., Clarke, S., Wilson, D., Wright, S., White, R., et al. (1994). Choice making to promote adaptive behavior for students with emotional and behavioral challenges. *Journal of Applied Behavior Analysis, 27*(3), 505–518.

DuPaul, G. J., & Eckert, T. L. (1997). The effects of school-based interventions for attention deficit hyperactivity disorder: A meta-analysis. *School Psychology Review, 26,* 5–27.

DuPaul, G. J., & Ervin, R. A. (1996). Functional assessment of behaviors related to attention deficit/hyperactivity disorder: Linking assessment to intervention design. *Behavior Therapy, 27,* 601–622.

DuPaul, G. J., Guevremont, D. C., & Barkley, R. A. (1992). Behavioral treatment of attention-deficit hyperactivity disorder in the classroom: The use of the Attention Training System. *Behavior Modification, 16*(2), 204–225.

DuPaul, G. J., & Hoff, K. E. (1998). Reducing disruptive behavior in general education classrooms: The use of self-management strategies. *School Psychology Review, 27,* 290–303.

DuPaul, G. J., & Weyandt, L. L. (2006). School-based interventions for children and adolescents with attention-deficit/hyperactivity disorder: Enhancing academic and behavioral outcomes. *Education and Treatment of Children, 29*(2), 341–358.

Dyer, K., Dunlap, G., & Winterling, V. (1990). Effects of choice making on the serious problem behaviors of students with severe handicaps. *Journal of Applied Behavior Analysis, 23,* 515–524.

Ervin, R. A., DuPaul, G. J., Kern, L., & Friman, P. C. (1998). Classroom-based functional and adjunctive assessments: Proactive approaches to intervention selection for adolescents with attention deficit/hyperactivity disorder. *Journal of Applied Behavior Analysis, 31*(1), 65–78.

Fabiano, G. A., & Pelham, W. E., Jr. (2003). Improving the effectiveness of behavioral classroom interventions for attention-deficit/hyperactivity disorder: A case study. *Journal of Emotional and Behavioral Disorders, 11,* 124–130.

Frazier, M. R., & Merrell, K. W. (1997). Issues in behavioral treatment of attention deficit/hyperactivity disorder. *Education and Treatment of Children, 20,* 441–461.

Gresham, F. M., Watson, T. S., & Skinner, C. H. (2001). Functional behavioral assessment: Principles, procedures, and future directions. *School Psychology Review, 30,* 156–172.

Harlacher, J. E., Roberts, N. E., & Merrell, K. W. (2006). Classwide interventions for students with ADHD: A summary of teacher options beneficial for the whole class. *Teaching Exceptional Children, 39*(2), 6–12.

Hinshaw, S. P., Henker, B., & Whalen, C. K. (1984). Cognitive–behavioral and pharmacologic interventions for hyperactive boys: Comparative and combined effects. *Journal of Consulting and Clinical Psychology, 52*(5), 739–749.

Hoffmann, H. (1845). *Lustige geschichten und drollige bilder mit 15 schön kolorierten tafeln für kinder von 3–6 jahren (Funny stories and jocose pictures with 15 beautifully coloured panels for children aged 3 to 6).* Frankfurt: Literarische Anstalt Rütten & Loening.

Horn, W. F., Chatoor, I., & Conners, C. K. (1983). Additive effects of Dexedrine and self-control training. *Behavior Modification, 7*(3), 383–402.

Horn, W. F., Ialongo, N., Popovich, S., & Peradotto, D. (1987). Behavioral parent training and cognitive-behavioral self-control therapy with ADD–H children: Comparative and combined effects. *Journal of Clinical Child Psychology, 16*(1), 57–68.

Huang, H.-L., Chao, C.-C., Tu, C.-C., & Yang, P.-C. (2003). Behavioral parent training for Taiwanese parents of children with attention-deficit/hyperactivity disorder. *Psychiatry and Clinical Neurosciences, 57*, 275–281.

Kern, L., Bambara, L., & Fogt, J. (2002). Class-wide curricular modification to improve the behavior of students with emotional or behavioral disorders. *Behavior Disorders, 27*(4), 317–326.

Kern, L., & Clemens, N. H. (2007). Antecedent strategies to promote appropriate classroom behavior. *Psychology in the Schools, 44*(1), 65–75.

Kern, L., Ringdahl, J. E., Hilt, A., & Sterling-Turner, H. E. (2001). Linking self-management procedures to functional analysis results. *Behavioral Disorders, 26*(3), 214–226.

Koegel, R. L., Dyer, K., & Bell, L. K. (1987). The influence of child preferred activities on autistic children's social behavior. *Journal of Applied Behavior Analysis, 20*, 243–252.

Kotchick, B. A., & Forehand, R. (2002). Putting parenting in perspective: A discussion of the contextual factors that shape parenting practices. *Journal of Child and Family Studies, 11*(3), 255–269.

Mace, F. C., Belfiore, P. J., & Hutchinson, J. M. (2001). Operant theory and research on self-regulation. In B. J. Zimmerman & D. H. Schunk (Eds.), *Self-regulated learning and academic achievement: Theoretical perspectives* (2nd ed., pp. 39–65). Mahwah, NJ: Erlbaum.

McCleary, L., & Ridley, T. (1999). Parenting adolescents with ADHD: Evaluation of a psychoeducation group. *Patient Education and Counseling, 38*, 3–10.

McGoey, K. E., & DuPaul, G. J. (2000). Token reinforcement and response cost procedures: Reducing the disruptive behavior of preschool children with attention-deficit/hyperactivity disorder. *School Psychology Quarterly, 15*(3), 330–343.

Montague, M., & Warger, C. (1997). Helping students with attention deficit hyperactivity disorder succeed in the classroom. *Focus on Exceptional Children, 30*(1), 1–16.

MTA Cooperative Group. (1999). A 14-month randomized clinical trial of treatment strategies for attention-deficit/hyperactivity disorder (ADHD). *Archives of General Psychiatry, 56*, 1073–1086.

National Institute of Mental Health. (2006). *Attention deficit hyperactivity disorder.* Bethesda, MD: Author. (NIH Publication Number: NIH 5124)

Owens, J. S., Richerson, L., Beilstein, E. A., Crane, A., Murphy, C. E., & Vancouver, J. B. (2005). School-based mental health programming for children with inattentive and disruptive behavior problems: First-year treatment outcome. *Journal of Attention Disorders, 9*(1), 261–274.

Pelham, W. E., Jr., Carlson, C., Sams, S. E., Vallano, G., Dixon, M. J., & Hoza, B. (1993). Separate and combined effects of methylphenidate and behavior modification on boys with attention deficit–hyperactivity disorder in the classroom. *Journal of Consulting and Clinical Psychology, 61*(3), 506–515.

Pelham, W. E., Jr., & Gnagy, E. M. (1999). Psychosocial and combined treatments for ADHD. *Mental Retardation and Developmental Disabilities Research Reviews, 5*(3), 225–236.

Pelham, W. E., Jr., Greiner, A. R., & Gnagy, E. M. (1997). *Summer treatment program manual.* Buffalo, NY: Comprehensive Treatment of Attention Deficit Disorders.

Pelham, W. E., Jr., Wheeler, T., & Chronis, A. (1998). Empirically supported psychosocial treatments for attention deficit hyperactivity disorder. *Journal of Clinical Child Psychology, 27,* 190–205.

Pfiffner, L. J., & O'Leary, S. G. (1987). The efficacy of all-positive management as a function of the prior use of negative consequences. *Journal of Applied Behavior Analysis, 20,* 265–271.

Pisterman, S., McGrath, P., Firestone, P., Goodman, J. T., Webster, I., & Mallory, R. (1989). Outcome of parent-mediated treatment of preschoolers with attention deficit disorder with hyperactivity. *Journal of Consulting and Clinical Psychology, 57*(5), 628–635.

Powell, S., & Nelson, B. (1997). Effects of choosing academic assignments on a student with attention deficit hyperactivity disorder. *Journal of Applied Behavior Analysis, 30*(1), 181–183.

Raggi, V. L., & Chronis, A. M. (2006). Interventions to address the academic impairment of children and adolescents with ADHD. *Clinical Child and Family Psychology Review, 9*(2), 85–111.

Reid, R., Trout, A. L., Schartz, M. (2005). Self-regulation interventions for children with attention deficit/hyperactivity disorder. *Exceptional Children, 71*(4), 361–377.

Reitman, D., Hupp, S. D. A., O'Callaghan, P. M., Gulley, V., & Northup, J. (2001). The influence of a token economy and methylphenidate on attentive and disruptive behavior during sports with ADHD-diagnosed children. *Behavior Modification, 25*(2), 305–323.

Reynolds, C. R., & Kamphaus, R. W. (2004). *Behavior Assessment System for Children* (2nd ed.). Circle Pines, MN: AGS Publishing.

Salend, S. J., Elhoweris, H., & van Garderen, D. (2003). Educational interventions for students with ADD. *Intervention in School and Clinic, 38*(5), 280–288.

Scott, T. J. (1970). The use of music to reduce hyperactivity in children. *American Journal of Orthopsychiatry, 40*(4), 677–680.

Skinner, C. H., Johnson, C. W., Larkin, M. J., Lessley, D. J., & Glowacki, M. L. (1995). The influence of rate of presentation during taped-words interventions on reading performance. *Journal of Emotional and Behavioral Disorders, 3*(4), 214–223.

Sonuga-Barke, E. J. S., Daley, D., Thompson, M., Laver-Bradbury, C., & Weeks, A. (2001). Parent-based therapies for preschool attention-deficit/hyperactivity disorder: A randomized, controlled trial with a community sample. *Journal of the American Academy of Child and Adolescent Psychiatry, 40*(4), 402–408.

Stein, D. B. (1999). A medication-free parent management program for children diagnosed as ADHD. *Ethical Human Sciences and Services, 1*(1), 61–79.

Spaccarelli, S., Cotler, S., & Penman, D. (1992). Problem-solving skills training as a supplement to behavioral parent training. *Cognitive Therapy and Research, 16*(1), 1–17.

Sutherland, K. S., Alder, N., & Gunter, P. L. (2003). The effect of varying rates of opportunities to respond to academic requests on the classroom behavior of students with EBD. *Journal of Emotional and Behavioral Disorders, 11*(4), 239–248.

Swanson, J., Arnold, L. E., Kraemer, H., Hechtman, L., Molina, B., Hinshaw, S., et al. (2008). Evidence, interpretation, and qualification from multiple reports of long-term outcomes in the multimodal treatment study of children with ADHD (MTA): Part I: Executive summary. *Journal of Attention Disorders, 12*(1), 4–14.

Tamm, L., & Carlson, C. L. (2007). Task demands interact with the single and combined effects of medication and contingencies on children with ADHD. *Journal of Attention Disorders, 10*(4), 372–380.

Umbreit, J. (1995). Functional assessment and intervention in a regular classroom setting for the disruptive behavior of a student with attention deficit hyperactivity disorder. *Behavioral Disorders, 20*(4), 267–278.

Varni, J. W., & Henker, B. (1979). A self-regulation approach to the treatment of three hyperactive boys. *Child Behavior Therapy, 1*(2), 171–192.

Zentall, S. S. (1983). Learning environments: A review of physical and temporal factors. *Exceptional Education Quarterly, 4*(2), 90–115.

Zentall, S. S. (1989). Attentional cuing in spelling tasks for hyperactive and comparison regular classroom children. *The Journal of Special Education, 23*(1), 83–93.

Zentall, S. S., & Dwyer, A. M. (1989). Color effects on the impulsivity and activity of hyperactive children. *Journal of School Psychology, 27,* 165–173.

Zentall, S. S., & Leib, S. L. (1985). Structured tasks: Effects on activity and performance of hyperactive and comparison children. *Journal of Educational Research, 79*(2), 91–95.

Zentall, S. S., & Meyer, M. J. (1987). Self-regulation of stimulation for ADD-H children during reading and vigilance task performance. *Journal of Abnormal Child Psychology, 15*(4), 519–536.

Zentall, S. S., & Shaw, J. H. (1980). Effects of classroom noise on performance and activity of second-grade hyperactive and control children. *Journal of Educational Psychology, 72*(6), 830–840.

Chapter 5

Interventions for Attention Problems

This chapter contains critical information for effective school site-initiated interventions for children and adolescents identified as at risk for or demonstrating difficulties remaining on task or maintaining attention in school settings. In the first section, the characteristics and conditions of attention problems are presented through a brief description of the construct of attention problems, a discussion of the prevalence and etiology of attention problems, and sample items from the BASC–2 Attention Problems scale. The second section describes the theoretical framework for approaching attention problems and provides a basis from which clinicians and practitioners can select evidence-based interventions derived from the specific BASC–2 indicators for attention problems. In the third section, interventions are described that have evidence or show promise for remediation of attention problems in school settings. The presentation of each provides an overview of the intervention and is divided into three subsections: Implementation, Evidence for Use, and Considerations. The chapter's three main sections provide the foundation on which additional BASC–2 intervention components are built, including both classroom-based and home-based strategies.

Characteristics and Conditions of Attention Problems

Attention problems are defined as chronic and severe inconsistencies in the ability to maintain and regulate focus to tasks for more than short periods of time (Barkley, 1997; Douglas, 1983; Hooks, Milich, & Lorch, 1994; Seidel & Joschko, 1990). Attention problems are often characterized by distractibility, an inability to concentrate, an inability to maintain attention to tasks for long periods of time, disorganization, failure to complete tasks, and a lack of study skills (Atkins, Pelham, & Licht, 1985; Evans et al., 2006; Kerns, Eso, & Thomson, 1999; Mash & Barkley, 2003; Reynolds & Kamphaus, 2004). Children and adolescents with attention problems exhibit an inability to control and direct attention to the demands of a task (Loge, Staton, & Beatty, 1990; Semrud-Clikeman et al., 1999) and are frequently distracted by irrelevant stimuli, even in a relatively quiet classroom environment, or by internal distractions. Attention problems are often experienced by children diagnosed with attention-deficit/hyperactivity disorder (ADHD), as well as children with acquired brain injury (Sohlberg, McLaughlin, Pavese, Heidrich, & Posner, 2000), depression (*DSM–IV–TR,* APA, 2000), acute stress (Hancock & Warm, 2003), and anxiety (LaBerge, 2002). However, significant attentional problems, herein defined as those that rise to the level of interfering with academic learning, can exist and require management in the absence of any other clinical or educational disorder.

The BASC–2 Attention Problems scale, in conjunction with the Hyperactivity scale, is useful for identifying problems associated with ADHD. Distinguishing between problems with attention and hyperactivity can be important, as attention problems have been shown to have a stronger relationship with academic problems than does hyperactivity (Hartley, 1998). Items on the BASC–2 Attention Problems scale include, among many others, "Has a short attention span," and "Is easily distracted" (Reynolds & Kamphaus, 2004).

Theoretical Framework for Approaching Attention Problems

To date, research suggests there is no single cause of attention problems. While a variety of causes have been cited (including brain injury, food additives, and genetics; NIMH, 2006), there is strong evidence supporting a neurobiological basis that stems from the irregular and inefficient transmission of information (DuPaul & White, 2006; Solden, 1995). In such cases, children experience extreme difficulty filtering irrelevant information from the environment (Semrud-Clikeman et al., 1999). Riccio, Reynolds, and Lowe (2001) have provided a discussion of the neurobiological basis of attention in the context of performance-based measures of attention and the relationship of attention problems to learning as well as to impulsive response styles. While this chapter focuses on interventions that are primarily behavioral, psychopharmacology can also play a role in the treatment of attention problems. Psychostimulant medications and behavioral interventions are commonly used in combination when treating attention problems and have been shown to be effective in reducing attention problems (American Academy of Pediatrics, 2001; Chronis, Jones, & Raggi, 2006; DuPaul & Eckert, 1998; DuPaul & Weyandt, 2006). Medication interventions are beyond the scope of this intervention guide. However, practitioners will frequently find themselves choosing interventions for students who have been prescribed stimulant medication by a licensed physician; therefore, evidence for the use of behavioral interventions in combination with stimulant medications will be discussed in this chapter within the multimodal intervention section (but only within the context of concurrent treatment per physician recommendation). Note that, in the authors' view, the best practice is to implement behavioral interventions first to determine if they are sufficient.

Interventions

The interventions included in this chapter are behaviorally based, and involve strategies that include learning new behaviors and learning how to monitor existing behavior periodically. These interventions include:

I. Contingency Management

II. Daily Behavior Report Cards

III. Modified Task-Presentation Strategies

IV. Self-Management

V. Classwide Peer Tutoring

VI. Computer-Assisted Instruction

VII. Multimodal Interventions

I. Contingency Management

Contingency management as an intervention for attention problems uses positive or negative consequences for maintaining, or failing to maintain, attention to tasks (Wolery, Bailey, & Sugai, 1988). This approach integrates positive reinforcement and response cost (i.e., negative consequences) into individual behavior intervention plans with the goal of increasing desired behavior and decreasing problem behavior (Harlacher, Roberts, & Merrell, 2006). Contingency management works best when it is used consistently in both home and school environments (DuPaul & White, 2006). Token economy systems are an example of an effective contingency management system. (Details for implementing a token economy are found in chapter 3.)

Implementation

The goal of contingency management is to shape existing behavior or provide an opportunity for new behavior to take root and become a part of a child's daily behavior. Behavioral objectives for children with attention problems may include increasing the duration of attention, decreasing episodes of inattention, decreasing the latency between requests and attending to the task, or decreasing the number of prompts required to gain the child's attention. The basic elements of contingency management include the following:

1. Defining the targets for attention

2. Providing appropriate levels of positive reinforcement

3. Implementing response-cost contingencies when positive reinforcement is unsuccessful

The procedural steps for implementing contingency management are provided in Figure 5.1. When implementing contingency-management strategies, it can be helpful to offer fixed-choice opportunities or to allow a child to select from a list of available, appropriate reinforcers rather than asking the child to generate his or her own list of desired reinforcers that may be unrealistic (e.g., a trip to Disneyland, a cell phone for a 7-year-old). Also, keep in mind that competing reinforcement outside the control of the practitioner can affect the strength of this intervention. Positive reinforcers such as reward tokens or extra computer time might not be able to compete with other available reinforcers. Satiation can also have an effect on the value of a reinforcer; extensive access to the reinforcer may diminish its reinforcement properties.

Special consideration should be given to the amount of reinforcement provided when using contingency management with children who experience attention problems. Attention problems often are associated with a low level of tolerance for frustration. As a result, the use of continuous reinforcement can be particularly effective. While a reliance on continuous reinforcement can sometimes be faded successfully, reinforcement should be reintroduced immediately when behavior levels fall below expectations. Continuous external reinforcement of attention serves as a functional replacement for the child's self-regulation skills, which may or may not be developed.

For example, during independent seatwork in a general education classroom, Clint often talks to the student sitting behind him before completing his assignment. Using contingency management, his teacher can use positive reinforcement (e.g., earning additional free-time options) and negative consequences (e.g., forfeiting his turn to feed the classroom's pet turtle) to motivate Clint to complete his seatwork. Clint can earn reinforcers for increasing the length of time he attends to tasks or for reducing the amount of time it takes him to get back on task.

Figure 5.1 Procedural steps for the implementation of contingency management

1. Define the child's behavior in operational terms, and determine the baseline rating of attention. For example, "Sarah typically attends to math problems consistently for 7 minutes."

2. Use the baseline data to set behavioral goals. Common goals include increasing the amount of time spent on task (keep in mind that modest increases such as 20% are more appropriate than large increases such as 100%) or decreasing the amount of off-task behavior (e.g., decreasing the number of times a child is out of his or her seat during a specific time interval).

3. Consider the child's preference of reinforcers. For example, if the student likes computer games, computer time can be earned or lost. Reinforcement surveys can help to determine reinforcers that are appropriate and meaningful to the child.

4. Review the rules for providing reinforcers and ensure that the child understands them.

5. Provide the reinforcer to the child when he or she meets the goal. Alternatively, do not provide the reinforcer if the goal is not met. Previously earned reinforcers, such as tokens, may be taken away when a goal is not met.

Evidence for Use

Contingency management is an efficient and effective method for improving outcomes of children with attention problems in classroom and home settings. It has been found to increase time on task and level of attention to task, to improve task accuracy, and to improve task completion (Anhalt, McNeil, & Bahl, 1998; Barber, Milich, & Welsh, 1996; Carlson, Mann, & Alexander, 2000; Gordon, Thomason, Cooper, & Ivers, 1991; Robinson, Newby, & Ganzell, 1981). The following studies summarize some of the key research findings associated with the use of contingency management in children and adolescents with attention problems.

Barber, M. A., Milich, R., & Welsh, R. (1996). Effects of reinforcement schedule and task difficulty on the performance of attention deficit hyperactivity disordered and control boys. *Journal of Clinical Child Psychology, 25*(1), 66–76.

Ninety boys aged 7 to 10 participated in this study; 45 had been diagnosed with ADHD and 45 acted as a control group. The students were asked to recall both easy and difficult sets of paired words. Three reinforcement schedules were utilized: continuous (reinforcer earned upon every correct answer), partial (reinforcer earned upon some correct answers), and never (no reinforcers earned). Results showed both groups of boys had lower performance when partially reinforced than when either continuously or never reinforced ($p < .01$). Among the boys with ADHD, those given the easier sets first performed significantly better than those initially given the more difficult sets, suggesting students with ADHD may benefit from being presented with a less-demanding task first.

Carlson, C. L., Mann, M., & Alexander, D. K. (2000). Effects of reward and response cost on the performance and motivation of children with ADHD. *Cognitive Therapy and Research, 24*(1), 87–98.

This experiment investigated the influence of reward and response cost contingencies on the academic performance and motivation of children with ADHD. Two groups of forty 8- to 12-year-old children (one group with ADHD and one control group) were assigned to one of three conditions: reward (tokens received for correctly completing problems), response cost (tokens lost for problems incorrectly completed), or none (no tokens earned or lost). Children completed math problems, before and after which they rated themselves on performance and motivation. Then the children completed a free-choice task as a measure of intrinsic motivation. Results for children with ADHD showed that performance and intrinsic motivation increased with a response-cost contingency as compared to reward, but reward had a positive effect on self-rated motivation.

Gordon, M., Thomason, D., Cooper, S., & Ivers, C. L. (1991). Nonmedical treatment of ADHD/hyperactivity: The attention training system. *Journal of School Psychology, 29*, 151–159.

This study explored changes in attentiveness and task persistence in children with ADHD who participated in a response cost contingency management program. Six children between the ages of 6 and 9 participated in nine classroom sessions in which each child sat in front of an electronic module called "Mr. Attention." The module flashed when the child was off task (a signal generated by an observer watching for time out of seat, etc., via a one-way mirror) and visibly deducted points from a total that could be used to purchase rewards. Five out of 6 children exhibited markedly fewer off-task behaviors during sessions with the module compared to baseline. However, when the modules were removed in later sessions, off-task behavior returned to baseline levels, indicating the need for continuous reinforcement and response cost.

Pfiffner, L. J., O'Leary, S. G., Rosén, L. A., & Sanderson, W. C., Jr. (1985). A comparison of the effects of continuous and intermittent response cost and reprimands in the classroom. *Journal of Clinical Child Psychology, 14*(4), 348–351.

This study examined the efficacy of verbal reprimands and response cost, implemented either continuously or intermittently, to decrease off-task behavior. Participants were 2 females and 3 males enrolled in either second or third grade at a school for children with behavioral problems. After a 5-day baseline condition, students were assigned for 10 days each to four conditions: continuous response cost, intermittent response cost, continuous verbal reprimands, and intermittent verbal reprimands. Response cost consisted of minutes taken off of recess time. All four conditions produced decreases in off-task behavior, with the continuous response-cost condition yielding the most significant decrease.

Rapport, M. D., Murphy, A., & Bailey, J. S. (1980). The effects of a response cost treatment tactic on hyperactive children. *Journal of School Psychology, 18*(2), 98–111.

This study examined the impact of a response cost system on the off-task behavior of children diagnosed with hyperactivity. In Experiment 1, a 7-year-old male was observed for 1 hour daily for 36 days. For every time he was off task, he lost 1 minute of free time. This response-cost method decreased his percentage of off-task behavior from 73% at baseline to 6% during intervention. In Experiment 2, an 8-year-old female was observed for 30 minutes daily for 30 days under four treatment conditions: baseline, medication only, medication plus response cost, and response cost only. Results showed that the medication plus response-cost condition had the greatest effect on off-task behavior, decreasing it from an average of 69% during baseline to 9%.

Robinson, P. W., Newby, T. J., & Ganzell, S. L. (1981). A token system for a class of underachieving hyperactive children. *Journal of Applied Behavior Analysis, 14*(3), 307–315.

This study investigated the efficacy of a token economy reinforcement system on the reading achievement of a large group of children with hyperactivity and low reading ability. Eighteen third-grade males identified as hyperactive and performing below grade reading level participated. Tokens were awarded for learning a reading unit or teaching a unit to another student and were redeemed for time spent playing a video game or pinball. Students completed nine times as many reading assignments during the token-economy condition as during the reversal period, when the tokens were removed ($p < .05$). Students also passed more standardized level tests required by the district during the token-economy condition.

Considerations

For Age and Developmental Level

When asking children to generate a list of desired reinforcers, it is important to remind them to list things that are both realistic and age-appropriate. In order to avoid problems, consider asking a parent to provide some examples of attainable reinforcers and then give the child the option to choose from such a list. When generating a list of reinforcers, consult with teachers or other adults who may be able to provide clues about preferences and high-interest activities. Young children may be more comfortable with a small number of choices, such as a fruit snack, rocking in a chair, or choosing a song for circle time. Older students may prefer access to music on an MP3 player, social time with peers, or one-on-one time with a teacher. As mentioned previously, be sure to consider the effects of satiation; if the child has unlimited or extensive access to the reinforcer, the item will have less reinforcement strength.

II. Daily Behavior Report Cards

Daily behavior report cards (DBRCs; also referred to as home notes, home-based reinforcement, daily report cards, and home–school notes) are used to record a child's behavior each day (Chafouleas, Riley-Tillman, & McDougal, 2002; Riley-Tillman, Chafouleas, & Briesch, 2007). Here, DBRCs are discussed as a specific intervention strategy for students with attention problems. Although they don't require home–school communication, each of the DBRCs discussed here recommend home–school communication.

There are many variations of DBRCs that make this approach easy to customize for a particular child or situation. For example, a DBRC can include either a short list of appropriate behaviors with each behavior receiving a grade or a single behavior that the child is working on. DBRCs can also be used with more than one teacher. These records can be managed and shared in various ways, using either electronic transmission (Burke & Vannest, 2008) or a simple log or notebook kept for parent signatures. DBRCs provide a reliable way to track behavioral goals and objectives that are included in an individualized education program (IEP) (Vannest et al., 2008), and to monitor progress in response to intervention models.

Implementation

The goal of implementing a DBRC strategy is to change behavior by providing systematic feedback on performance and progress to students and parents, followed by appropriate reinforcement. The result is increased attention (or decreased inattention) during specific tasks and conditions. The basic elements of a DBRC intervention include the following:

1. Defining target behaviors

2. Daily monitoring and recording of behaviors

3. Communicating the results to both students and parents

The procedural steps for implementing a DBRC strategy are provided in Figure 5.2. When making the initial behavior rating, it is important to be accurate with the estimate of current performance and to avoid overrating. For example, classifying a child's current attention level as a "B" grade might indicate that his or her current performance level is above average, calling into question why the report card is needed in the first place. In addition, this grade may not allow the student enough room for improvement, leading to increased frustration. Instead, "C" or "D" grades should be anchored as a student's present level of performance. If a student is upset by these initial ratings, provide encouragement so that he or she understands that the current behavior level is less than desirable for success in school. Identify areas for improvement in a way that is not damaging to a child's feelings or self-concept.

It may seem that using letter grades to rate behavioral performance, unlike more typical measures of behavior (e.g., frequency counts, duration measures), will appear subjective or unfair to parents and students. However, the ease of understanding letter grades outweighs the possible benefits of using behavior measures that seem more scientific. Discuss the behavioral anchors (i.e., typical behavior for earning each grade) with parents and students before implementing this strategy, and explain how the grades will be used to minimize differences among multiple raters, lessening any impact on student behavior grades.

When setting performance goals, be sure to set a level that is challenging but attainable. Goals should become more difficult with time, which will encourage shaping of the behavior to the desired level (Chronis, Jones, & Raggi, 2006). Setting unattainable goals only leads to frustration.

For example, Ben is a first-grade student who has difficulty attending to tasks. Each morning, Ben's teacher reads a short book to the class. While she reads, Ben often sprawls out on the floor, picks at the carpet, and fidgets with his shirt. Ben is usually unable to answer questions about the story, indicating he may have been listening but was not truly attending. Using a DBRC, his teacher identifies the target behaviors of sitting, listening, and attending to the morning's story. She then assigns a letter grade to evaluate Ben's performance. A grade higher than a "C" means that he paid attention to the story. This grade is given to Ben, charted in a report, and sent home daily for his parents to sign. After reading time, Ben's teacher allows him to look at a graph of his rate of attention to the story, and she praises each daily increase. When Ben gets home, his mother rewards him with 30 minutes of computer game time for each day that he receives an "A" or "B" grade.

Figure 5.2 Procedural steps for the implementation of daily behavior report cards

1. Identify the target behaviors for improving attention. Include other adults who will help, such as behavioral consultants, teachers, or parents. Decide who will participate in rating.

2. Ask the rater to assign a letter grade (A, B, C, or D) to the child's performance for each day. Each target behavior is rated daily. Letter grades (instead of frequency of behavior, for example) are preferable because they are usually more meaningful to students and families. Explain the behavioral anchors (i.e., typical behavior for earning each grade) to avoid variance among raters or differences in personal tolerance levels. For example, attending during 10 out of 20 minutes of class time may earn a "C," 15 minutes may earn a "B," and 17 minutes or more might earn an "A."

3. Give feedback to the student using a daily check-in/check-out system (where the child checks in to receive the day's goals and checks out to receive his or her grade), a home-note correspondence system, or a teacher conference with graphs and/or charts.

4. Reward the student, either at home or school, for meeting performance goals. This step may or may not be needed for each child.

Evidence for Use

DBRCs have a long history of teacher-reported success and are a common intervention in most schools. Using DBRCs for students with attention problems has been found to improve academic performance, increase attentiveness, decrease disruptive behavior, and decrease the number of times a child switches among activities (Kelley & McCain, 1995; McCain & Kelley, 1993). Although there have only been a limited number of studies to date concerning the effects of DBRCs specifically on improving attention problems, the use of performance feedback on regular and predictable intervals (e.g., daily) is implicitly supported in the literature on behavior change. The following studies summarize some of the key research findings associated with the use of DBRCs for children and adolescents with attention problems.

Drew, B. M., Evans, J. H., Bostow, D. E., Geiger, G., & Drash, P. W. (1982). Increasing assignment completion and accuracy using a daily report card procedure. *Psychology in the Schools, 19*(4), 540–547.

This study assessed the effectiveness of a daily report card procedure in increasing assignment completion and accuracy in 2 elementary school boys who had a history of not completing assignments. Teachers gave daily reports to parents indicating whether or not the students had completed at least 76% of math problems correctly. Performance below this percentage was penalized by withdrawal of a privilege at home that evening. Completion and accuracy both improved dramatically when the intervention began, with baseline completion rates ranging from 0% to 56% and improving to 100% all days except one. Accuracy ranged from a baseline of 0% to 56% and improved to 70% to 100%. This study demonstrated that a report card procedure can significantly improve assignment completion and accuracy.

Fabiano, G. A., & Pelham, W. E., Jr. (2003). Improving the effectiveness of behavioral classroom interventions for attention-deficit/hyperactivity disorder: A case study. *Journal of Emotional and Behavioral Disorders, 11*(2), 124–130.

This case study involved modifying an intervention program that had been ineffective for one 8-year-old student with ADHD and then measuring the effects of the modifications on his behavior. Observation of the student in class led the author to prescribe three modifications: offering small daily rewards for good behavior, providing immediate verbal feedback for unacceptable behavior, and withdrawing rewards when more than two reminders for target behaviors were required. As a result, the student's disruptive behaviors decreased from about 30% of intervals to about 10% of intervals, and on-task behaviors increased from about 62% to 84%. This case illustrated the benefit that minor changes to an existing behavior intervention plan can have for students with ADHD.

Karraker, R. J. (1972). Increasing academic performance through home-managed contingency programs. *Journal of School Psychology, 10*(2), 173–179.

This experiment examined three approaches to instructing parents in employing contingency consequences for improving academic outcomes: a 15-minute conference, two 1-hour conferences, and a letter. Sixteen males in three second-grade classrooms completed daily in-class mathematics assignments for which report cards were sent to parents daily. Parents granted a positive consequence for a good grade and gave no reaction to a poor grade. Students in all conditions improved their mathematics performance, with no significant difference found based on the mode of instruction the parent received. However, parents who received the 2 hours of conference training indicated that they would use this type of contingency management technique on other behaviors.

Kelley, M. L., & McCain, A. P. (1995). Promoting academic performance in inattentive children: The relative efficacy of school-home notes with and without response cost. *Behavior Modification, 19*(3), 357–375.

This study investigated the efficacy of school–home notes with and without response cost as a methodology for improving classroom behavior and academic achievement. Five elementary school-age children referred for disruptive behavior or low academic performance were monitored for on- or off-task or disruptive behavior. Parents delivered rewards or response cost measures based on the day's performance. Results demonstrated that classroom behavior and academic performance improved with use of school–home notes; for many participants, the added measure of response cost resulted in even further improvement. Teacher, parent, and student ratings were obtained pre- and posttreatment; all groups preferred notes plus response cost over notes alone.

McCain, A. P., & Kelley, M. L. (1993). Managing the classroom behavior of an ADHD preschooler: The efficacy of a school-home note intervention. *Child and Family Behavior Therapy, 15*(3), 33–44.

This case study examined the effect of a daily behavior report card on the classroom behavior of a preschooler diagnosed with ADHD. A developmentally appropriate note was constructed, making use of symbols such as sad and happy faces. For each target behavior (e.g., "used class time well"), the student helped to monitor his progress by coloring in the appropriate symbol. Based on predefined criteria, reinforcers were given. Compared to baseline, on-task behavior increased from 57% to 85% when the note was used. Additionally, instances of disruptive behavior decreased from an average of 29% to 7%, and his average number of activity changes during play fell from eight to two.

Considerations

Effectiveness of the contingency is indicative of whether or not the interaction with the adult who does the rating and hands out the praise and reinforcement is a positive or negative (i.e., punitive) one for the child. DBRCs are not meant as a channel for communicating punishment or for reporting daily bad behavior; ideally, they are used to provide objective and frequent feedback to the student and to communicate progress to the family.

For Culture and Language Differences

A DBRC is only as effective as the reinforcement or contingency attached to it, and communication with families can be a component of that reinforcer or contingency. Therefore, effective communication with the family may necessitate use of the home language, or extra consideration may be needed to accurately explain the purpose and process of the DBRC.

For Age and Developmental Level

Age may also be a consideration; younger children often respond quickly and positively to teacher attention and feedback, while adolescents may be embarrassed to receive daily grades on behavior, which would indicate to peers that the child had a problem.

III. Modified Task-Presentation Strategies

Modified task-presentation strategies refer to a collection of specific options that can be used to increase the interest level of an activity, which will increase the amount of time the child attends to learning the task or activity. Based on information obtained through a functional assessment, tasks are altered using antecedent instructional modifications (Ervin, DuPaul, Kern, & Friman, 1998; Kern & Clemens, 2007; Raggi & Chronis, 2006). A number of modification strategies have been recommended by researchers (e.g., Carbone, 2001; Kern & Clemens, 2007; Montague & Warger, 1997; Salend, Elhoweris, & van Gardener, 2003). Each of these strategies is detailed in the following implementation section, including:

1. Offering a choice of instructional activities

2. Providing guided notes and instruction in attending to relevant information

3. Using high-interest activities and hands-on demonstrations

4. Modifying in-class assignments and responses

5. Modifying homework

6. Highlighting relevant material or key information with colors, symbols, or font changes

7. Providing increased opportunities to respond

8. Varying the pace of instruction

Implementation

Offering a Choice of Instructional Activities

Encouraging students to engage in active decision making and to exercise control over making choices can help increase their level of attention. Using this approach, students are allowed to choose activities, materials, or a task sequence within a set of instructional materials outlined by the teacher (Dunlap et al., 1994; Kern, Bambara, & Fogt, 2002; Powell & Nelson, 1997). For example, a student might get to choose the order of assignment completion, decide which group of classmates he or she will work with, or select among types of responses (verbal, written, etc.). However, this approach is successful only when the choices offered for student selection are relevant to the curriculum or learning objectives, so consideration should be given to ensure that learning goals are not compromised. For example, choosing between two equally unattractive options will be unpopular with the student, and doing only half of the assignment versus doing all of the assignment will be unacceptable to the teacher. Agreeing on the conditions for each choice is critical and is best done prior to such conflicts between student and teacher interests.

Providing Guided Notes and Instruction in Attending to Relevant Information

In this strategy, the teacher provides guided notes to help the student follow along during lectures and class presentations. Guided notes contain some information about the lecture or presentation, but spaces are left for students to fill in the most relevant and important ideas. Schematic maps that outline relationships between concepts and require students to fill in relevant details are another useful form of guided notes. Additionally, the teacher can provide direct instruction on note taking, help directly with note taking, or involve a peer who can help (Evans, Pelham, & Grudberg, 1995). These strategies help correctly focus a student's attention and require an active written response, which increases attending behavior.

Using High-Interest Activities and Hands-on Demonstrations

Activities and tasks that are novel and interesting to students can increase work productivity (Carbone, 2001; Clarke, et al., 1995). Also, providing moderate levels of auditory stimuli (e.g., music) during familiar tasks with structured responses, and in turn, reducing classroom noise while students are engaged in learning new concepts, can cue students to the different types of attention each task requires (Scott, 1970; Zentall, 1983). Teachers can begin lessons with high-interest activities that require participation and facilitate attention. Examples include demonstrating practical applications (especially in subjects such as math or science), playing music or film clips, engaging in role-plays, or using examples related to current events (either community or world events, or events related to student activities).

Modifying In-Class Assignments and Responses

There are many ways assignments can be modified to accommodate students who struggle with attention problems. These modifications include allowing students to use a computer or tape recorder when completing written assignments (Council for Exceptional Children [CEC], 1992; Kern, Childs, Dunlap, Clarke, & Falk, 1994; Kern & Clemens, 2007), dividing longer assignments into multiple shorter tasks, reducing the number and types of items (Kern et al., 1994), allowing oral responses, and giving written directions with expectations for completing the assignment (Ervin, DuPaul, Kern, & Friman, 1998). Some students may perform better if they can listen to music while doing work (Abikoff, Courtney, Szeibel, & Koplewicz, 1996). However, modifications are not a permanent solution for many students. While modifications and supports are in place, interventions to increase attention on a long-term basis must also be implemented.

Modifying Homework

Homework requires good attention skills on many levels. Not only must the student complete the assignment, but he or she must also bring the work home, understand the directions for starting the assignment, remember to complete the assignment, and return it to school. While these aspects of homework are taken for granted by many, they can be a source of stress for students with attention problems. Homework can be modified very successfully by decreasing the amount given, allowing extended time for its completion, using routine procedures (e.g., homework planners), providing assistance through one-on-one or group tutoring or via the telephone or Internet (Habboushe et al., 2001; Salend, Elhoweris, & van Garderen, 2003; Stormont-Spurgin, 1997), or allowing it to be completed at school instead of at home.

Highlighting Relevant Material or Key Information With Colors, Symbols, or Font Changes

Provide cues in large or complex tasks and lessons so that students can easily attend to the most relevant material and filter out unnecessary stimuli that prevent them from attending to the correct information. Possible cues include using highlighters or using larger or different fonts or graphics. (These cues can be facilitated with most computer word-processing programs or via student teams that identify these cues prior to presentation of the lesson.) Also, adding novelty through color increases intra-task stimulation, which, in turn, increases the importance of task features (Zentall, 1993). Teachers may also do this with the class as a group by leading students through exercises where main ideas are highlighted in one color, vocabulary words in another color, etc.

Providing Increased Opportunities to Respond

In this strategy, students are given increased opportunities to respond to academic material using varied response methods (e.g., written responses, the class answering in unison, individual student answer cards; Montague & Warger, 1997; Sutherland, Alder, & Gunter, 2003). An increased opportunity to respond increases engagement and attention and, as a secondary benefit, improves academic performance. Counting the number of responses per child per hour is one way to monitor the amount of interaction between the students and the teacher (and consequently how difficult it may be for students to sustain attention). For example, if a class has 20 students, and the teacher asks 20 questions during a 20-minute presentation, each student should actively participate approximately one time. However, a teacher could instead use individual student answer cards and ask each student to write a response on his or her card and then show the teacher his or her response by holding up the card. In this case, every student participates 20 times in 20 minutes and attention is maintained due to the pace and immediacy of the task.

Varying the Pace of Instruction

Briskly paced instruction increases levels of on-task behavior because rapid pacing is thought to require more attending effort (Kern & Clemens, 2007; Skinner, Johnson, Larkin, Lessley, & Glowacki, 1995). Teachers can increase the pacing of their instruction either by increasing their rate of presenting material or by decreasing the length of instructional pauses (Kern & Clemens, 2007).

Evidence for Use

Adjusting specific academic tasks can encourage better performance in students with attention problems. Approaches such as adding color to tasks, allowing for a choice between tasks, and making modifications to curriculum have all been shown to have a positive effect on task performance (Belfiore, Grskovic, Murphy, & Zentall, 1996; Dunlap et al., 1994; Kern, Bambara, & Fogt, 2002; Zentall & Kruczek, 1988). The following studies summarize some of the key research findings associated with the use of various instructional modifications to enhance attention in classroom settings.

Abikoff, H., Courtney, M. E., Szeibel, P. J., & Koplewicz, H. S. (1996). The effects of auditory stimulation on the arithmetic performance of children with ADHD and nondisabled children. *Journal of Learning Disabilities, 29*(3), 238–246.

This study evaluated the impact of stimulating, extraneous factors such as music and speech on the academic task performance of children with ADHD and children without disabilities. Forty children, Grades 2 through 6, half with ADHD and half without, worked math problems while exposed to counterbalanced sequences of speech, silence, and music. Results showed that children with ADHD completed more problems correctly in the music condition than during either the speech or silence conditions. These results demonstrated that speech and music do not impede academic performance and the latter may actually enhance the attention of students with ADHD.

Belfiore, P. J., Grskovic, J. A., Murphy, A. M., & Zentall, S. S. (1996). The effects of antecedent color on reading for students with learning disabilities and co-occurring attention-deficit/hyperactivity disorder. *Journal of Learning Disabilities, 29*(4), 432–438.

This study examined the effect of adding color to reading tasks for boys with ADHD who also had learning disabilities (LD). Three boys with this diagnosis were presented with a sight-word reading task with the words either in black and white or color. There were no significant effects of the color on this task. However, students then read stories in both black and white and color. Results showed they correctly answered more comprehension questions on the stories that were printed in color. These results demonstrated that adding color to more lengthy tasks may help maintain the attention of students with ADHD and LD.

Clarke, S., Dunlap, G., Foster-Johnson, L., Childs, K. E., Wilson, D., White, R., et al. (1995). Improving the conduct of students with behavioral disorders by incorporating student interests into curricular activities. *Behavioral Disorders, 20*(4), 221–237.

This study examined the effect of individualized curricular modifications based on personal preferences for 4 male elementary students with a history of behavior problems. Their diagnoses ranged from autism to severe emotional disturbance to ADHD, and all attended special education classes. After each child identified his or her most disliked academic task, elements from a favorite interest were integrated into the task, such as an alphabet drill being illustrated with cars and motorcycles. The children showed reductions in disruptive behavior, increases in productivity, and increases in desirable behaviors. The results confirmed the value of curriculum adjustments and the importance of designing curriculum with individual behavior goals in mind.

Dunlap, G., dePerczel, M., Clarke, S., Wilson, D., Wright, S., White, R., et al. (1994). Choice making to promote adaptive behavior for students with emotional and behavioral challenges. *Journal of Applied Behavior Analysis, 27*(3), 505–518.

This experiment examined the effects of academic choice-making on elementary school students with emotional and behavioral disorders (EBD). In Study 1, two 11-year-old boys enrolled in a fifth-grade class for students with EBD were given lists of possible academic tasks daily within a consistent subject area. They were allowed to select an activity for the seatwork session. Each student showed higher levels of task engagement and lower levels of disruptive behavior when allowed this choice. In Study 2, a 5-year-old boy enrolled in an EBD classroom showed improved task engagement and fewer incidences of disruptive behavior when allowed daily to choose to have the book read to him, providing further evidence for the benefit of choice-making for students with emotional and behavioral problems.

Ervin, R. A., DuPaul, G. J., Kern, L., & Friman, P. C. (1998). Classroom-based functional and adjunctive assessments: Proactive approaches to intervention selection for adolescents with attention deficit hyperactivity disorder. *Journal of Applied Behavior Analysis, 31*(1), 65–78.

This study measured the effect of interventions chosen as a result of functional assessment on 2 adolescents with both ADHD and oppositional defiant disorder. Results of the functional assessment for Student 1 demonstrated he was often off task during pencil-and-paper writing tasks; during the intervention phase, he was allowed to write on a computer instead. Student 2's off-task behavior was often reinforced by peer attention. In the intervention phase, he was taught to self-manage his attention, and his entire class was put on a point system that penalized them for responding to attention-getting behaviors. During intervention phases, both students improved in time spent on task (Student 1 from about 65% to about 97% on task and Student 2 from about 63% to about 92%).

Evans, S. W., Pelham, W., & Grudberg, M. V. (1995). The efficacy of notetaking to improve behavior and comprehension of adolescents with attention deficit hyperactivity disorder. *Exceptionality, 5*(1), 1–17.

This study examined the effect that taking structured notes and reviewing them has on comprehension and classroom behavior in adolescents with ADHD. After a pilot study demonstrated young adolescents with ADHD could improve their notetaking skills through specific instruction, 14 adolescents received this instruction daily for 3 weeks. Following the instruction period, students were assigned to either take notes or not take notes in class and to review or not review notes during a study hall. Results showed time on task increased significantly in conditions in which the students took notes, and assignment scores were greater in conditions where the students either took or reviewed notes.

Kern, L., Bambara, L., & Fogt, J. (2002). Class-wide curricular modification to improve the behavior of students with emotional or behavioral disorders. *Behavioral Disorders, 27*(4), 317–326.

This study examined the effect of inclusion of high-interest activities and student choice on engagement and classroom behavior of students. Participants were six 13- and 14-year-old students with varied behavioral and emotional diagnoses (4 of the 6 were diagnosed with ADHD) who had difficulty attending to class activities and often displayed destructive behaviors. With the introduction of high-interest activities (such as hands-on experiments) and student voting on choice of activity, materials, or task sequence, engagement rose from a baseline mean of 57% to 87% and 89% during two intervention periods. Destructive behavior fell from a baseline mean of 8% to 1% and 0%. This study demonstrated positive behavior gains can result from fairly simple curricular modifications.

Kern, L., Childs, K. E., Dunlap, G., Clarke, S., & Falk, G. D. (1994). Using assessment-based curricular intervention to improve the classroom behavior of a student with emotional and behavioral challenges. *Journal of Applied Behavior Analysis, 27*(1), 7–19.

This study examined the effects of curricular modifications on the on-task behavior and assignment completion of an 11-year-old boy. Based on the results of a functional assessment, the student received individualized changes in curriculum that included alternatives to pencil-and-paper writing, a higher ratio of problem-solving to rote tasks, multiple short tasks substituted for long tasks, self-monitoring, and completing work in a study carrel away from visual distraction. In response, the student's on-task behavior improved from 62% to 89% and his work completion improved from 14% of assignments to 62%. This study supported the use of curricular modifications based on functional assessment for improving on-task behavior.

Powell, S., & Nelson, B. (1997). Effects of choosing academic assignments on a student with attention deficit hyperactivity disorder. *Journal of Applied Behavior Analysis, 30*(1), 181–183.

This study examined the effect of allowing a second-grade boy with ADHD to make choices about academic assignments. In the choice condition, the student was allowed to choose from three different assignments, all on the same topic and all of approximately equal length and difficulty. When allowed to choose a task to complete, his incidence of off-task behaviors (e.g, being out of seat, staring into space, disturbing others) decreased dramatically, demonstrating that providing students with ADHD with a choice of tasks can improve on-task behavior.

Skinner, C. H., Johnson, C. W., Larkin, M. J., Lessley, D. J., & Glowacki, M. L. (1995). The influence of rate of presentation during taped-words interventions on reading performance. *Journal of Emotional and Behavioral Disorders, 3*(4), 214–223.

This study examined the effects of two modeling interventions: fast-taped words (FTW; one word per second) and slow-taped words (STW; one word every 5 seconds) on word-list reading. Participants were 3 elementary students with ADHD and difficulty learning new words. During daily sessions, students were randomly presented with the lists of FTW, STW, and a control list with no tape. With the taped lists, students read the words along with the corresponding tape; with the control, students read the word list on their own. All students read more words correctly and more words correctly per minute with the tapes, and 1 student did better with the FTW, while the other 2 did better with the STW.

Sutherland, K. S., Alder, N., & Gunter, P. L. (2003). The effect of varying rates of opportunities to respond to academic requests on the classroom behavior of students with EBD. *Journal of Emotional and Behavioral Disorders, 11*(4), 239–248.

This study examined the effect of offering increased opportunities to respond (OTR; e.g., questions directed toward students) during instructional time. In a classroom for students with emotional and behavioral disorders (EBD), 9 elementary school students were observed for correct responses, disruptive behaviors, and on-task behaviors. During intervention phases, the teacher initiated more opportunities for students to respond (an average of 3.52 OTR per minute, as compared to 1.68 during baseline). Results showed when the students received more OTR, they displayed fewer disruptive behaviors, provided more correct responses, and increased their percentage of on-task intervals.

Zentall, S. S. (1985). Stimulus-control factors in search performance of hyperactive children. *Journal of Learning Disabilities, 18*(8), 480–485.

This study examined the effect of color on performance of a computer-based visual search task. Seventy children ages 5 through 13 (35 identified as hyperactive and 35 acting as a control group) pressed a button if a dot appeared in a square of a matrix. Children identified as hyperactive made significantly more errors with a gray matrix than controls; however, they performed as well as controls when a colored matrix was used. This performance level held true until later trials, when children identified as hyperactive made significantly more errors, even with the colored matrix. This study showed that adding color to tasks requiring sustained attention may improve attention performance in children with hyperactivity, but these effects may wear off rapidly, especially in tasks that require a very narrow attention focus.

Zentall, S. S. (1989). Attentional cuing in spelling tasks for hyperactive and comparison regular classroom children. *The Journal of Special Education, 23*(1), 83–93.

This study examined the effect that strategically placed color for task-relevant cues and presentation order—color-enhanced presented earlier vs. later in learning task—had on performance of a spelling recognition task. Twenty boys identified as hyperactive and 26 comparison boys in third through sixth grade were asked to select correctly spelled words from lists that included misspelled versions. Each group was tested with grade-level lists of words with difficult spellings presented in two formats: all black and white or in colored text with difficult or nonphonetic letters. Lists were presented in counterbalanced order (black then color or vice versa). It was found that color added to relevant task cues during the initial exposure to a difficult task resulted in a decrease in activity for hyperactive children. However, when the task was initially practiced in the black and white format first and then in color, the children with hyperactivity outperformed the comparison children. It was concluded that the use of color in a spelling-recognition task increased attention in hyperactive children and that as an applied selective attention task these results could be generalized to other tasks that may require search and selective attention.

Zentall, S. S., Falkenberg, S. D., & Smith, L. B. (1985). Effects of color stimulation and information on the copying performance of attention-problem adolescents. *Journal of Abnormal Child Psychology, 13*(4), 501–511.

This study examined the effect of color stimulation on handwriting performance of boys aged 14 to 18 years. Each of 16 boys with attention problems and 16 controls copied the contents of low-stimulation booklets (letters in black and white) and high-stimulation booklets (both black and white and colored letters). Half of each group received high-stimulation booklets with relevant letter information colored or high-stimulation booklets with letters randomly colored. Boys with attention problems made significantly fewer errors when using colored booklets. The study showed that color-added stimulation reduces errors in adolescent boys with attention problems but makes no difference in controls.

Zentall, S. S., & Kruczek, T. (1988). The attraction of color for active attention-problem children. *Exceptional Children, 54*(4), 357–362.

This study tested the effect of adding color to letters in a copying task. Participants were 17 elementary-aged boys identified as having attention problems by Abbreviated Teacher Rating Scale scores. Seventeen peers who scored within normal ranges served as a control group. The groups were matched on handwriting (as measured by the Test of Written Language). The use of color was both relevant (added to the parts of letters that most often lead to copying errors) and nonrelevant (randomly added to 50% of the total number of letters). Results showed that the attention-problem group benefited more from use of color, particularly relevant color, than the controls, demonstrating that color can successfully highlight relevant task details for children with attention problems.

Considerations

For Teaching

Instructional interventions require compatibility between teacher disposition and skill. A teacher may be less willing to make changes because he or she is committed to a particular style or teaching method based on personal values and beliefs about education. A teacher may also view an attention problem as lack of effort rather than a valid learning problem. He or she may feel threatened, or appear insensitive, when instructional changes are suggested for students who are already demanding, and who represent a fraction of the children the teacher must serve. A well-intentioned teacher, on the other hand, may simply not have enough time or resources to adapt his or her lesson plans. Always keep the complex relationship between teachers and students in mind; teachers and students often have reciprocal behaviors, and the dynamics of this exchange may reinforce or punish the type of teaching being used in the classroom. Rely on the experience of the classroom teacher and his or her appraisal of the situation, and anticipate the level of control and effort teachers will expect when recommending changes in instructional behaviors.

Because there are many different types of instructional modification interventions for attention problems, they have the largest likelihood of success when implemented after a functional assessment. Such an assessment can help to uncover the antecedents and consequences, describe the topography of the attention problems, and reveal the environmental and setting events for the attention problems. For example, using guided notes won't help a student who is out of his or her seat for the majority of the lecture. Likewise, a student who struggles to bring back completed homework will not find high-interest, novel, or engaging classroom activities helpful in learning the specific attention skill needed to improve his or her grades.

IV. Self-Management

Self-management strategies for attention problems are techniques that students can use to become more aware and develop better management of their own behavior. Students are taught to pay attention to their attention through self-observation, self-recording, self-evaluation, self-monitoring, and self-reinforcing (Harris, Friedlander, Saddler, Frizzelle, & Graham, 2005; Mace, Belfiore, & Hutchinson, 2001; Reid, Trout, & Schartz, 2005). Through self-management strategies, students continuously assess their attention behavior, self-cue appropriate behavior, and eventually learn to inhibit automatic responses (Barkley, 1997). This type of meta-cognitive activity is helpful for students across ages and settings.

Implementation

Self-management of attention enables students to monitor and manage their own attention skills. Students who successfully learn this strategy can feel a great sense of self-determination, which can have a positive impact on their opinions of themselves. The basic elements of self-management strategies include the following:

1. Self-observing

2. Self-monitoring or self-recording

3. Self-evaluating

4. Self-reinforcing

An outline of the procedures for implementing self-management of attention is presented in Figure 5.3, and the following examples illustrate instructional situations for which self-management could be implemented. At Wrightway Middle School, Ms. Wilson, an eighth-grade math teacher, instructs her students to turn in the daily assignment at the end of the class period. One student, Linda, turns her paper in with only 6 out of 20 problems completed. When the teacher asks, Linda says she understands the work but was "thinking about something else" during independent work time. Ms. Wilson assumes Linda was daydreaming or writing a note because she was not disruptive, so Ms. Wilson assigns the remainder of the assignment to Linda as homework. The next day, Linda says that she did the work at home but can't find it in her backpack and that she can't remember where she left it. This situation creates frustration for both Linda and her teacher. A self-monitoring system could help Linda recognize when she is and is not paying attention to a task, and why time gets away from her. A self-monitoring system could also be used to help Linda transport her homework from home to school and from her locker or backpack to the teacher's desk.

Joel, another student in Ms. Wilson's class, spends most of the independent work time sitting near the teacher's desk, where he plays with his pencil, invents games with paperclips, and looks around frequently to see what the teacher is doing. Self-monitoring with a cuing system could help Joel pay attention to his assignment and allow him to complete assignments and earn rewards. If he learns to use the system, it could help Joel to start and finish relevant tasks throughout his schooling.

Figure 5.3 Procedural steps for the implementation of self-management

1. Determine the specific area for self-management of attention (e.g., attention to task, completion of assignments, impulsivity, organizational skills).

2. Explain both the rationale for using self-management techniques and the specific benefits the student might expect.

3. Demonstrate the self-monitoring technique, and explain to the student how to use any equipment or forms (e.g., audio cue tape, self-recording form, wrist counter).

4. Discuss current classroom functioning using baseline data, and have the student set a goal for the target behavior (e.g., an amount of focused attention, a number of assignments completed, an organizational skill such as being prepared for class).

5. Determine a reinforcer.

6. Demonstrate how the student will record his or her attention to task when the cue is heard. The cues or prompts can be recorded on a tape or CD or generated by a watch with intermittent beeps; intervals from 15 seconds up to 2 minutes can be used, depending on the student. At the sound of each prompt, the student records if he or she is or is not paying attention by placing a check mark on the self-monitoring sheet.

7. Ensure that the student records his or her state of attention when each cue is heard. Although not required, a teacher's participation provides helpful supplemental information about the child's performance.

8. Ask the student and teacher to compare their recording forms and discuss if the scores are dramatically different. Allowing for some degree of error is acceptable and expected. Perfectly matched scores might be highly praised and encouraged as a goal depending on the number of intervals.

9. Graph the scores and monitor progress toward goals.

10. Encourage the student to self-reinforce the behavior both for attending and for consistently and accurately recording attending behavior. Reinforcement is ultimately faded as naturally occurring reinforcement takes place (e.g., better grades, better skills, less discipline in classrooms).

Evidence for Use

Self-management techniques can increase performance in a number of ways, including increasing attention to a task, productivity, and schoolwork accuracy (Edwards, Salant, Howard, Brougher, & McLaughlin, 1995; Harris et al., 2005; Mathes & Bender, 1997; Shimabukuro, Prater, Jenkins, & Edelen-Smith, 1999). The following studies summarize some of the key research findings associated with using self-management strategies to address attention problems.

Christie, D. J., Hiss, M., & Lozanoff, B. (1984). Modification of inattentive classroom behavior: hyperactive children's use of self-recording with teacher guidance. *Behavior Modification, 8*(3), 391–406.

Three elementary-aged male children, noted by parents and teachers alike as struggling with hyperactivity and inattentiveness, participated in this study, which examined whether self-monitoring of behavior would lead to a decrease in students' inattentiveness. Each student was trained to record his behavior on a sheet when signaled, choosing one of eight behavior categories, such as "inattentive," "aggression," "talking," or "on task." The classroom teachers recorded the students' behaviors at the same times, and at the end of the study, their progress was charted. In general, inattentive behaviors decreased throughout the treatment time when compared with the baseline.

Edwards, L., Salant, V., Howard, V. F., Brougher, J., & McLaughlin, T. F. (1995). Effectiveness of self-management on attentional behavior and reading comprehension for children with attention deficit disorder. *Child and Family Behavior Therapy, 17*(2), 1–17.

In a study that combined self-management with incentives, 3 male elementary students diagnosed with ADHD were asked to write a plus or minus sign indicating whether or not they were on task when cued. Points were earned based on the percentage of times students were on task, and these points could be exchanged for incentives such as computer games or treats. Throughout the study, reading comprehension and behavior were monitored, and regular improvement was shown in both areas during treatment. However, teachers found the point system to be time-consuming. Nevertheless, on-task behavior increased an average of 37.5% between the original baseline and the final stage.

Harris, K. R., Friedlander, B. D., Saddler, B., Frizzelle, R., & Graham, S. (2005). Self-monitoring of attention versus self-monitoring of academic performance: Effects among students with ADHD in the general education classroom. *Journal of Special Education, 39*(3), 145–157.

This study examined whether self-monitoring of attention (SMA) and self-monitoring of performance (SMP) have effects on the spelling study and on-task behavior of 6 elementary students with ADHD in the general education classroom. On-task behavior during baseline averaged 55% for the 6 participants. During the SMA phase, the students' on-task behavior averaged 94%. In the SMP phase, the students' on-task behavior averaged 92%. Results show that self-monitoring interventions using both SMA and SMP had positive effects on each student's on-task behavior.

Mathes, M. Y., & Bender, W. N. (1997). The effects of self-monitoring on children with attention-deficit/hyperactivity disorder who are receiving pharmacological interventions. *Remedial and Special Education, 18*(2), 121–128.

This study, which examined three 8- to 10-year-old male children with ADHD who were already taking regular pharmacological treatments, assessed the effects of a combined intervention of self-monitoring with medication. After tracking behavior during a baseline stage, the general education teachers led these students in recording "yes" or "no" as to whether or not they were paying attention each time they were cued at random intervals of 45 seconds to 20 minutes. Students' attentive behavior increased drastically during treatment—from 37% to 40% on-task behavior to 87% to 97%—showing that a combination of medical and self-monitoring interventions can be successful in increasing on-task behavior of students with ADHD.

Shimabukuro, S. M., Prater, M. A., Jenkins, A., & Edelen-Smith, P. (1999). The effects of self-monitoring of academic performance on students with learning disabilities and ADD/ADHD. *Education and Treatment of Children, 22*(4), 397–414.

Three male students were observed in this study: 1 sixth-grade and 2 seventh-grade students, all who had been diagnosed with a learning disability as well as attention-deficit disorder or attention-deficit/hyperactivity disorder (ADD/ADHD). Students recorded their own academic accuracy (based on the number of items answered correctly) and academic productivity (based on the number of items completed), and their teachers recorded on-task behavior based on observations at 10-second intervals. The study showed gains in all three areas over three subjects (reading comprehension, math, and written expression) for all 3 students. However, the degree of improvement varied greatly among students and subjects.

Considerations

For Teaching

Self-management techniques can be effective even when students are inaccurate in their recording. Accuracy, and thus attention to detail, can be encouraged by matching the student's and teacher's ratings. If teacher ratings aren't available, or aren't a viable option, students can submit self-recorded information to another adult (for a contingent reward). Keep in mind that the most effective rewards using this approach are self-rewards (i.e., those given by the student to himself or herself), not rewards from the adult with whom the student has contact.

Self-management strategies can be effective in improving many aspects of daily life that require a student's attention. Behavior, academic performance, and social interactions, for example, can benefit from this approach. Therefore, thoughtfully consider the goal of the intervention. If the objective is to increase attention for better academic performance, simply monitoring and recording attention to task may not produce the same results that monitoring and recording task accuracy or completion might. However, attention to the task may be the primary goal in other situations. For example, if a student's inattention causes problems working on group assignments or creates a tense student–teacher relationship, but the student's grades aren't suffering, better attention to the task itself may be the best solution. Self-management of attention in social situations (both at home and school) can involve teaching students to paraphrase mentally, to silently count their distracting thoughts as a prompt to refocus attention, or to select only a few things to pay attention to.

For Age and Developmental Level

Sometimes attending to stimuli is a challenge beyond the child or adolescent's abilities. The boredom factor in inattention is a lack of stimulation that many people have experienced at one time or another in long meetings or social activities. Individuals with strong social skills know how to read the environment for social cues and expectations, and are able to effectively present the necessary cues for paying attention, even when not fully attending. As mentioned, some students with attention problems do not experience concurrent academic failure or learning problems but simply have discipline issues related to their attention problems. In some cases, speaking frankly with older students about how to present appropriate social cues, such as making eye contact, nodding, or finding ways to stay engaged so as not to disrupt someone else, can do much to assist a bright student who is struggling to maintain attention when there is not enough stimulation in the environment. It is important to present students with socially acceptable methods of operating in their environment. For example, telling the geometry teacher the lecture is boring has worse consequences than a quick lesson on social skills and how to doodle discretely.

V. Classwide Peer Tutoring

Classwide peer tutoring (CWPT) is a multicomponent and multistrategy treatment program (Greenwood, Delquadri, & Carta, 1997; Greenwood, Maheady, & Delquadri, 2002; Harlacher, Roberts, & Merrell, 2006) that consists of peer tutoring and interdependent, group-oriented, contingency management. CWPT is an instructional intervention characterized by trained and monitored peers supporting, instructing, and providing immediate corrective feedback to each other on academic assignments (Greenwood, Maheady, & Carta, 1991). Interdependent, group-oriented, contingency management is a system of providing positive reinforcement to a group of students for the cumulative behavior of the entire group (Alberto & Troutman, 2002). Combining the instructional characteristics of these two components creates a system to enhance attention and learning for students with attention problems. CWPT is based on the principles of maximizing student-engaged time, providing frequent opportunities for practice, increasing rates of student responding and feedback loops, and minimizing errors in learning and off-task behavior. CWPT also incorporates an element of progress monitoring by recording performance over time.

For example, Mr. Mason's philosophy class has weekly quizzes on names of theoreticians and their major works. Two self-named larger teams (the Piagets and the Montessoris) consist of rotating partners who spend the last 10 minutes of each class quizzing each other from a notebook preprepared with questions, a recording sheet, and a key. Points are awarded to the individual pairings as well as the overall teams, with the larger team scores recorded on the SMART Board™ to monitor as a class who is approaching a preset winning level and who could earn a grand prize at the end of the semester.

Evidence for Use

CWPT has been found to increase academic engagement, decrease off-task behavior, increase on-task behavior, and increase academic performance in students with attention problems across grade levels, socioeconomic status (SES), disability types, and ethnic categories (DuPaul, Ervin, Hook, & McGoey, 1998; DuPaul & Henningson, 1993). The following studies summarize some of the key research findings associated with classwide peer tutoring and attention problems.

DuPaul, G. J., Ervin, R. A., Hook, C. L., & McGoey, K. E. (1998). Peer tutoring for children with attention deficit hyperactivity disorder: Effects on classroom behavior and academic performance. *Journal of Applied Behavior Analysis, 31*(4), 579–592.

This study examined the effect of classwide peer tutoring on the behavior of 18 elementary school students with ADHD and 10 peer-comparison students in two school districts. During the intervention, average on-task behaviors among children with ADHD rose and off-task behaviors fell to almost the same level as peer-comparison students not receiving the intervention. Half of the children with ADHD improved their posttest scores by 10% or more. The study showed that peer tutoring can increase engagement and decrease off-task behavior in children with ADHD without having a negative impact on their peers.

DuPaul, G. J., & Henningson, P. N. (1993). Peer tutoring effects on the classroom performance of children with attention deficit hyperactivity disorder. *School Psychology Review, 22*(1), 134–143.

This study examined the effects of classwide peer tutoring (CWPT) on classroom behavior and academic performance for students diagnosed with ADHD. A case study of 1 student, Don, diagnosed with ADHD, was used to illustrate the effectiveness of a classwide peer tutoring program implemented in a second-grade math classroom. A baseline of Don's behavior during teacher-mediated instruction was measured, followed by similar observations during peer tutoring, then for a second baseline and peer-tutoring condition. For each peer-tutoring condition, Don was paired with another boy (without behavior problems and doing well in math), and the remaining 28 students were all randomly placed in tutoring pairs. The results of the case study indicated that the frequency of Don's attention to instruction improved from the first baseline to second peer tutoring condition (39% to 90%, respectively). Additionally, the consistency of his attention improved (31% vs. 3.8%, respectively). Don's academic performance improved as well (mean for math accuracy, m=5 to m=13.3, respectively). The results indicated that CWPT benefits children with ADHD by offering more opportunities to actively respond, more prompts to attend to tasks, and more immediate feedback on performance.

Plumer, P. J., & Stoner, G. (2005). The relative effects of classwide peer tutoring and peer coaching on the positive social behaviors of children with ADHD. *Journal of Attention Disorders, 9*(1), 290–300.

This study examined 3 third- and fourth-grade students diagnosed with ADHD and social skills deficits to determine whether classwide peer tutoring (CWPT) and peer coaching would positively affect their social interactions. Observers noted the number of positive social interactions each student had during recess and lunch. In the CWPT stage, pairs of students took turns tutoring each other in spelling. In the next stage, the target students were each assigned a peer coach to help them set a social goal each day, remind them of the goal, and give feedback afterward. Results showed that CWPT alone produced increased positive social interactions, but CWPT combined with peer coaching brought each participant near the level of typically functioning students.

Considerations

Time for material development and student training must be taken into consideration before implementing CWPT (Harlacher et al., 2006). It is important that teachers continually monitor tutor–tutee teams, especially in order to systematically assign points as reinforcers for appropriate behavior and good tutoring. Additionally, it may be wise to avoid pairing students with attention problems together initially, in order for the entire class to adapt smoothly to CWPT procedures.

VI. Computer-Assisted Instruction

As an intervention for attention problems, computer-assisted instruction (CAI) presents academic content on a computer, to supplement direct teacher instruction. CAI can be an effective way to heighten a student's attention and interest. Learning software provides opportunity to control and maintain the frequency of feedback and level of engagement.

Constantly on, computers do what teachers cannot—provide a constant source of activity and stimulation. For rote memorization tasks, complex research and synthesis, and the creation of new knowledge, computers are well suited as an intervention for students with attention problems.

For example, Gwynne carries a laptop and uses it to take notes in all her classes. She finds the novelty and constant activity more engaging than paper–pencil tasks, so it keeps her focused and less distracted by peers.

Additionally, Jack enters the room in a daydream fashion each morning when school starts. The teacher uses a computer center in her second-grade room, and Jack knows he is to go to the computers first. This routine has immediate appeal for Jack, and he walks purposely to the computer to start math fact games rather than the seatwork his friends begin.

Implementation

The objectives of CAI include increasing attention, minimizing distractibility, providing an engaging learning environment, and providing a reinforcing, errorless learning opportunity. The basic elements of computer-assisted instruction include the following:

1. Desktop, laptop, handheld (PDA) computer

2. Internet or software that:

    a. Helps define instructional objectives

    b. Highlights essential material (e.g., large print, color)

    c. Provides multiple methods of presentation (e.g., visual, auditory, text/graphic, illustrative)

    d. Divides content into smaller bits of information efficiently

    e. Provides immediate feedback

For example, Karen has difficulty paying attention to a science lecture in which her teacher, Mrs. Yang, lists types of rocks and describes their differences. As she tries to recall names such as sedimentary and igneous, she misses the explanation of the assignment. While the rest of the class is engaged in the activity, Karen wanders the perimeter of the room to look at other students' work and see what to do. Mrs. Yang spends 10 extra minutes with Karen, teaching the lesson and demonstrating the assignment again just for her.

To help students like Karen, Mrs. Yang chooses a program from the Internet (that relates the content covered in the rock unit). During lecture time, Karen can use the computer to listen to descriptions of rock types and watch videos that show the rock formations.

No specific functional steps are given for this intervention as implementation will vary greatly depending on the accessibility of computers and the availability of appropriate software. Many programs are available free or for a nominal fee on the Internet. Such programs may not align perfectly with state instructional objectives and curriculum, but typical units of instruction are generally available. Some schools support computer labs where classes of students, such as math or language arts, go to access programs. On a smaller scale, individual students with attention problems may be able to use trial versions of software or public shareware.

Evidence for Use

Technology-based interventions can promote success in specific academic skills such as reading, math, and science (Clarfield & Stoner, 2005; Ford, Poe, & Cox; 1993; Mautone, DuPaul, & Jitendra, 2005; Ota & DuPaul, 2002; Shaw & Lewis, 2005). Such interventions have also been shown to increase productivity and engagement by offering alternate response formats (Kleiman, Humphrey, & Lindsay, 1981). The following studies summarize some of the key research findings associated with using computer-assisted instruction to address attention problems.

Clarfield, J., & Stoner, G. (2005). The effects of computerized reading instruction on the academic performance of students identified with ADHD. *School Psychology Review, 34*(2), 246–254.

This study evaluated the effectiveness of the Headsprout reading software program on 3 boys with ADHD. The subjects, in kindergarten and first grade, were at risk for reading difficulties. They worked with the program 3 days a week, generally completing one episode per session. Each student demonstrated higher average levels of oral reading fluency and greater rates of reading skill growth during the intervention, while off-task behaviors decreased immediately and dramatically compared to former levels. The study showed computerized instruction in reading can help children with ADHD stay on task and accelerate growth in reading skill.

Ford, M. J., Poe, V., & Cox, J. (1993). Attending behaviors of ADHD children in math and reading using various types of software. *Journal of Computing in Childhood Education, 4*(2), 183–196.

This study examined the effect of different software programs on the attention of elementary school children with frequent nonattending behaviors and/or formal diagnosis of ADHD. Four commercial software packages in reading or math were used by 21 third- and fourth-grade children with ADHD once a week for 4 weeks each. Results showed that programs in a game format without excessive animation received increased attention, and programs with games held attention better than tutorials with animation but no games. Software package characteristics such as difficulty, format, animation, and content appear to influence attention behaviors of children with ADHD.

Kleiman, G., Humphrey, M., & Lindsay, P. H. (1981). Microcomputers and hyperactive children. *Creative Computing, 7*(3), 93–94.

This study compared the performance of 18 children with hyperactivity ages 6 to 14 when using a computer to answer math problems vs. using pencil and paper. The computer program's characteristics included problem difficulty tailored to each child, an easily readable display, an answer format similar to pencil and paper, self-paced problem-solving, motivational features (e.g., praise statements for correct responses), and feedback specialized to children with hyperactivity (e.g., a message "STOP IT" if a child made too many inappropriate button presses). Children chose to do an average of 31.4 problems on the computer compared to 17.6 on pencil and paper, with no significant difference in accuracy or speed. The results suggested that children with hyperactivity will remain on task for longer periods if allowed to work on a computer.

Mautone, J. A., DuPaul, G. J., & Jitendra, A. K. (2005). The effects of computer-assisted instruction on the mathematics performance and classroom behavior of children with ADHD. *Journal of Attention Disorders, 9*(1), 301–312.

This study examined the effect of computer-assisted instruction on the mathematics performance and on-task behavior of 3 male second- through fourth-grade students with ADHD. Public school students used a math program for 10 to 15 minutes, two to three times a week. In response, mathematic performance improved and off-task behavior decreased in all three students. The teachers and two of the students found CAI to be highly acceptable.

Ota, K. R., & DuPaul, G. J. (2002). Task engagement and mathematics performance in children with attention-deficit hyperactivity disorder: Effects of supplemental computer instruction. *School Psychology Quarterly, 17*(3), 242–257.

This study examined the effect of math instruction software (Math Blaster™) with a game format on the attention and academic performance of 3 male private-school students, fourth through sixth grade, with ADHD. Using the software for 20 minutes three to four times per week, each student increased his active engaged time and decreased his off-task behaviors. Although math performance increased only slightly, the study showed that using math software with a game format promotes attention among children with ADHD.

Shaw, R., & Lewis, V. (2005). The impact of computer-mediated and traditional academic task presentation on the performance and behaviour of children with ADHD. *Journal of Research in Special Educational Needs, 5*(2), 47–54.

This study examined the effect of computer-mediated academic tasks on performance and behavior of children with ADHD. Forty students aged 7 to 12 years read information and answered science questions presented in four formats:

a pen-and-paper workbook, a workbook with a colorful cartoon character, a computer-based workbook presenting text in a simple word processing format, and a computer-based workbook with animation. The 20 students with ADHD significantly increased their on-task time and correct responses when using computerized workbooks, and they answered the greatest number of questions correctly when using the computer workbook without animation. The study showed basic-format computerized presentation can help children with ADHD stay on task and better learn science-related content.

Considerations

Consider all the issues involved with CAI. Certain details can derail an otherwise thoughtful program. Examples of questions that should be asked are: Are there sufficient electrical outlets to support a computer and printer, and are these outlets located near the equipment? Do firewalls in the district protect students while allowing them to use computers for research, or will they simply run software? Does the computer have adequate server and memory space to save student work, send attachments with e-mail, or receive large files?

Overlooking these issues can lead to larger ones. For example, one school district received a large grant to purchase computers, only to discover that it had no funds to hire someone to set them up and no teacher with the time or expertise to run a lab. Another district bought computers for a lab, only to discover that its brand-new computer room didn't have adequate power or sufficient network strength to keep the entire lab running at one time.

For Teaching

In order to be effective, interventions must be consistent and persistent (Evans et al., 2006). This is especially true in the use of computer-assisted instruction to remediate attention problems. Sporadic implementation may be frustrating for students, as it often takes several sessions for them to become acquainted with the details of a program.

While a school-supported computer lab can be a wonderful resource, a program of this nature requires substantial investment and maintenance. An individual teacher can implement CAI without such resources, even though it initially may be time-consuming to find and manage good software. Students should not be placed in front of computers if the teacher has not had the time to find and teach an appropriate program. Despite the work involved prior to implementing the intervention, finding good computer software or web content that maintains student interest and generates positive learning outcomes is well worth the effort. School psychologists may offer to help by locating resources or volunteering to supervise during transition times.

VII. Multimodal Interventions

Multimodal interventions for attention problems are based on the view that attention problems likely cause multiple factors that impact a student, and that multiple solutions for previously learned maladaptive behaviors, current performance, and future learning are often needed. Multimodal interventions typically involve both home and school environments for a variety of reasons. For example, consistent application of treatments is most effective, and students improve more quickly when parents and schools work together to set expectations of behavior and implement consequences. In addition, pharmacology has been widely successful in treating attention problems in the majority of studies, although its effects may diminish over time (Swanson et al., 2008). Such use of medication is implemented under the control of the family in careful consultation with the family physician but may be administered in school settings. Feedback on drug effects and side effects may come from school officials more so than at home, where task demands are different. Also, one or both parents may report that their child is "just like I was" in school and that this apparent genetic link may contribute to a lack of compensatory skills. Parents may believe that the student's inattention in school is simply something to be outgrown.

Multimodal interventions employ teaching new skills to improve attention and prevent future problems while also remediating any deficits that exist academically, socially, or in self-regulation. These combination treatments are more complex to initiate and involve multiple participants. Sometimes it is difficult to ascertain which relative parts are responsible for improvements. The effect of the whole treatment is often more beneficial than the sum of its parts.

Implementation

The goal of a multimodal intervention is to identify a full menu of intervention options that can help address current performance problems; remediate deficits in skills across social, behavioral, or academic domains; and build a strong foundation for learning the new skills necessary for success in school and beyond. The synergy from multiple interventions applied at the same time can help shape self-regulating individuals who need little or no intervention to maintain attention in a way that is functional, allowing them to achieve their goals without outside support.

The basic elements of multimodal interventions include the following:

1. Provide multiple treatments with appropriate personnel simultaneously or in sequence, including:

    a. Contingency management

    b. Daily behavior report cards

    c. Modified task-presentation strategies

    d. Self-management of attention

e. Classwide peer tutoring

f. Computer-assisted instruction

2. Determine the responsible parties for implementing and monitoring treatments.

The implementation of multimodal interventions consists of five procedural steps. First, determine the exact interventions within the multimodal framework based on assessment results that indicate the causal factors associated with the attention problems. Second, determine the length of treatment based on the severity of the causal factors. (With multimodal interventions, treatment may be provided for longer periods of time than with single interventions.) Third, based on the prescribed intervention, identify the specific team members that will provide services (e.g., psychologist, social worker, case worker, parents). Fourth, implement the interventions simultaneously. Fifth, transfer the learned behaviors and techniques to the natural environment. An outline of these procedures is presented in Figure 5.4, and the following example illustrates both the complexity and benefits of a multimodal intervention.

Randall is a bright, energetic, 6-year-old who loves to take things apart. His daydreaming makes him difficult to teach in the classroom, and repeating instructions frustrates the teacher. His mom thinks Randall is a typical boy, much like her three brothers who share in the family's small-engine repair business. She thinks Randall simply needs more time to mature and jokes that his future wife will need to organize things like she does for her brothers. Randall's dad, however, disagrees and believes Randall needs more discipline.

Randall's inattention may be at the root of his poor reading performance, which is significantly below his peers. Randall's teacher, Mr. Johnson, is concerned that he is not an immature or indulged 6-year-old, but rather a child who struggles to pay attention. During a parent–teacher conference, Mr. Johnson describes Randall's reading problems and new behavior showing signs of frustration and aggression when he is frequently reprimanded for not paying attention or doing his work. After asking about a family history of attention problems, Mr. Johnson suggests a medical exam to rule out attention problems. The test confirms that Randall is suffering from attention problems and supports Mr. Johnson's theory about Randall's reading performance.

Several weeks later, Randall is evaluated for the effects of a stimulant medication and behavior management plan. Randall receives cookies and milk as an after-school snack when he comes home with a good teacher report. His teacher and parents closely monitor Randall's response to the stimulant, looking for any changes in sleeping, eating, weight, and motor activity. Both the school and his parents communicate weekly via email to see how things are going. Randall seems happier in class and says that the medicine takes away the noise of the cars in the parking lot and the clicking heels in the hallway. Randall's improved ability to attend has lessened Mr. Johnson's frustration, and he now has more time to focus on positive classroom activities instead of Randall's discipline issues.

Figure 5.4 Procedural steps for the implementation of multimodal interventions

1. Determine the intervention approaches to be used.

2. Determine the length of treatment.

3. Determine the person most qualified to implement the interventions (an individual or team of professionals).

4. Implement the interventions simultaneously, as described in the procedural steps for each intervention.

5. Generalize treatment effects to natural environments.

Evidence for Use

The various methodologies within multimodal intervention strategies are designed to promote the most successful behavior outcomes for an individual student's needs. The following studies summarize some of the key research findings associated with using multimodal interventions to address attention problems.

Anhalt, K., McNeil, C. B., & Bahl, A. B. (1998). The ADHD classroom kit: A whole-classroom approach for managing disruptive behavior. *Psychology in the Schools, 35*(1), 67–79.

This discussion of *The ADHD Classroom Kit: An Inclusive Approach to Behavior Management* (Kit) is punctuated by a case study demonstrating the Kit's effectiveness in diminishing disruptive classroom behavior of a 6-year-old girl in first grade with ADHD. Classroom behavior was observed using components of the Classroom Coding System—specifically appropriate vs. oppositional and on-task vs. off-task behavior—during baseline, treatment, and reversal phases. The baseline and reversal phases utilized the school's current discipline program, while the treatment phase utilized the Kit. Results showed that the child's behavior improved when the Kit was in use, with mean frequencies of on-task behavior and appropriate behavior at about 76% and 61% (baseline), 88% and 79% (treatment), and 83% and 71% (reversal).

Chase, S. N., & Clement, P. W. (1985). Effects of self-reinforcement and stimulants on academic performance in children with attention deficit disorder. *Journal of Clinical Child Psychology, 14*(4), 323–333.

Six boys, aged 9 to 12 years, participated in this study comparing the impact of Ritalin®, self-reinforcement, and Ritalin plus self-reinforcement on academic performance. Students attended a 30-minute tutoring session each school-day morning, receiving 80 cents per session. During baseline, students who had been taking medication for ADHD prior to the study stopped medication, and no behaviors were targeted other than attending tutoring sessions and arriving on time. During the Ritalin condition, students were instructed to take their physician-prescribed dose of Ritalin before each session (confirmed by a parent's note). During the self-reinforcement condition, students received instruction on self-reinforcement of their behavior and academic performance. Some students continued to receive Ritalin and others received a placebo. The Ritalin plus self-reinforcement condition was identical to the self-reinforcement condition, except that all students received Ritalin. Results indicated that Ritalin alone does not improve the academic performance of children with ADHD, self-reinforcement alone significantly improves academic performance, and Ritalin plus self-reinforcement greatly improves academic performance.

Coles, E. K., Pelham, W. E., Gnagy, E. M., Burrows-MacLean, L., Fabiano, G. A., Chacko, A., et al. (2005). A controlled evaluation of behavioral treatment with children with ADHD attending a summer treatment program. *Journal of Emotional and Behavioral Disorders, 13*(2), 99–112.

This study alternated the application and removal of behavioral modification on 4 children with ADHD in a summer treatment program (STP). In an 8-week period, the children received constant behavioral feedback via a point system, timeouts, and praise during weeks 1, 2, 4, 6, 7, and 8. Behavior modification was withdrawn during weeks 3 and 5. Behavior during all weeks was monitored in classroom and recreational settings. For all 4 children, behavior generally improved during treatment conditions and deteriorated when treatment was withdrawn. Individual differences, however, were noted in how quickly and to what extent behavior worsened during withdrawal and how quickly it was recovered when behavior modification was reintroduced.

Conners, C. K., Epstein, J. N., March, J. S., Angold, A., Wells, K. C., Klaric, J., et al. (2001). Multimodal treatment of ADHD in the MTA: An alternative outcome analysis. *Journal of the American Academy of Child and Adolescent Psychiatry, 40*(2), 159–167.

This study compared the effects of a behavior therapy program, a medication management strategy, a combination of the two treatments, and community care resources on 579 children aged 7 through 9 years with ADHD, combined type. Reanalysis of data from the NIMH Collaborative Multisite Multimodal Treatment Study of Children with Attention-Deficit/Hyperactivity Disorder revealed combination therapy was significantly better than the other three treatments. In particular, its effects were seen to be better, rather than equivalent to, that of medication management only. The authors concluded ". . . combined multimodal therapy has a clinically meaningful and statistically significant advantage over monotherapies and community treatment."

Evans, S. W., Axelrod, J., & Langberg, J. M. (2004). Efficacy of a school-based treatment program for middle school youth with ADHD. *Behavior Modification, 28*(4), 528–547.

Seven students in sixth through eighth grades who had been diagnosed with ADHD participated in the Challenging Horizons Program (CHP), a behavioral and educational school-based treatment program. The adolescents attended the program for 130 minutes, 3 days each week. During each session, the students met with their primary counselors to identify and prioritize goals and to discuss and implement interventions. Next, the students received Interpersonal Skills Training to learn and role-play social and problem-solving skills. Then the students participated in recreational activities to practice these skills. Finally, the adolescents attended the education group, designed to help improve their academic performance. Additionally, parent training and family counseling were utilized. As assessed by student grades, ADHD Rating Scale–IV (inattention, hyperactivity, and overall) scores, and Children's Impairment Scale scores, the results of this study showed that CHP may be an effective psychosocial treatment program for adolescents with ADHD.

Evans, S. W., Langberg, J., Raggi, V., Allen, J., & Buvinger, E. C. (2005). Development of a school-based treatment program for middle school youth with ADHD. *Journal of Attention Disorders, 9*(1), 343–353.

This study, which focused specifically on young adolescents with ADHD, examined the effects of the Challenging Horizons Program (CHP), a school-based after-school treatment program that incorporated multiple intervention methods. Two stages were reviewed in this study: the first compared students in the CHP to those from schools that did not offer a similar program, and the second tracked the academic and social progress of students in the CHP over 2 years. Results showed that improvements made by students in the CHP, while not dramatic, were greater than those of students not involved in such a program.

Gureasko-Moore, S., DuPaul, G. J., & White, G. P. (2006). The effects of self-management in general education classrooms on the organizational skills of adolescents with ADHD. *Behavior Modification, 30*(2), 159–183.

This study assessed the effect of a self-management program on the classroom preparation behaviors of 3 seventh-grade male students with ADHD. During their homeroom periods, students were trained in self-management and informed of their current performance in classroom preparation tasks. In regular meetings, they used logs and a daily self-monitoring checklist to review their progress and reflect on needed changes. The teachers reported that the 3 students, exhibiting target behaviors 50%, 53%, and 40% of the time during the baseline phase, all improved to 100% during the maintenance phase.

Hoza, B., Pelham, W. E. Jr., Sams, S. E., & Carlson, C. (1992). An examination of the "dosage" effects of both behavior therapy and methylphenidate on the classroom performance of two ADHD children. *Behavior Modification, 16*(2), 164–192.

This study examined individualized interventions when treating the school behavior problems of children with ADHD, including varying levels of drug dosage, behavioral modification, and intensity. Participants were 2 adolescent boys with ADHD who attended the Western Psychiatric Institute and Clinic's Children's Summer Day Treatment Program (STP) for children diagnosed with behavioral problems. Data was gathered over 8 weeks during daily 1-hour classroom sessions involving individualized assignments in each child's areas of academic weakness. While standard STP classroom procedures were in place every week, contingencies varied from week to week. Results showed that for Student 1, behavior therapy was comparable to a low dose of methylphenidate (MPH) and increased medication did not improve behavior or academic performance, suggesting that a low dose of medication in combination with behavior modification worked best for this individual. For Student 2, who had more significant behavior problems, data indicated that behavioral modification did not notably improve behavior or performance, while behavior therapy combined with a relatively high dose of MPH resulted in the greatest degree of positive change.

Owens, J. S., Richerson, L., Beilstein, E. A., Crane, A., Murphy, C. E., & Vancouver, J. B. (2005). School-based mental health programming for children with inattentive and disruptive behavior problems: First-year treatment outcome. *Journal of Attention Disorders, 9*(1), 261–274.

Forty-two male and female students in kindergarten through sixth grade participated in this year-long study of the Youth Experiencing Success in School (Y.E.S.S.) Program, a mental health program utilizing evidence-based treatment in the form of daily report cards, parenting sessions, and teacher consultations. Thirty students received Y.E.S.S. Program services, while the control group of 12 students was allowed to receive any treatment services available. All students had diagnoses involving inattention, hyperactivity and impulsivity, oppositional or defiant behavior, and/or aggression. Treatment outcomes were assessed via rating scales completed by parents and teachers at three points during the year. Results showed that the Y.E.S.S. Program positively affected symptoms of ADHD, oppositional defiant disorder (ODD), and aggression, as well as academic and social functioning.

Pelham, W. E. Jr., Carlson, C., Sams, S. E., Vallano, G., Dixon, M. J., & Hoza, B. (1993). Separate and combined effects of methylphenidate and behavior modification on boys with attention deficit–hyperactivity disorder in the classroom. *Journal of Consulting and Clinical Psychology, 61*(3), 506–515.

This study examined the effects of behavior modification, dosages of methylphenidate (MPH), and a combination of the two on the behavior of 31 boys with ADHD. Children aged 5 to 9 in a summer day-treatment program attended a class in which a highly structured behavior modification program alternated weekly with a normal classroom management approach. In random order, each child received a placebo, a low dose, or a high dose of methylphenidate (MPH) daily. Significant effects were observed for both behavior modification and MPH, with MPH showing twice the effect of behavior modification. Only MPH improved academic performance, and the combined treatment yielded better results than behavior modification alone. The study clarified the effects of these interventions on a range of specific behaviors, supporting a nuanced approach to intervention decisions.

Richardson, E., Kupietz, S., & Maitinsky, S. (1986). What is the role of academic intervention in the treatment of hyperactive children with reading disorders? *Journal of Children in Contemporary Society, 19*(1–2), 153–167.

This 5-year study investigated the interaction between ADHD and developmental reading disorder (DRD) in 42 students, aged 7 to 12 years, diagnosed with both ADHD and DRD. Looking at the effects of methylphenidate and reading intervention and therapy on reading achievement, the students were randomly assigned to one of three methylphenidate dosage levels or the placebo group. Students took several academic/reading achievement tests over the course of the study. The Conners Behavior Rating Scale was administered at pretest (no medication), 2 weeks later (medication, but before weekly Integrated Skills Method [ISM] reading intervention sessions), after 3 months of reading intervention, and after 6 months of reading intervention. Results indicated that a functional relationship exists between ADHD and DRD and that most students with diagnoses of both can effectively be taught to read. However, the success of the ISM intervention was dependent on the effectiveness of methylphenidate in treating ADHD symptoms.

Solanto, M. V., Wender, E. H., & Bartell, S. S. (1997). Effects of methylphenidate and behavioral contingencies on sustained attention in attention-deficit hyperactivity disorder: A test of the reward dysfunction hypothesis. *Journal of Child and Adolescent Psychopharmacology, 7*(2), 123–136.

Twenty-two students, aged 6 to 10 years, participated in this study involving four treatment conditions combining drug and behavioral interventions: methylphenidate (MPH) plus auditory feedback, MPH plus auditory feedback with contingencies, placebo plus auditory feedback, and placebo plus auditory feedback with contingencies. Each student participated in each treatment condition and was tested during each condition using a modified continuous performance test (CPT). Treatment conditions with contingencies involved the students selecting desirable toys, earning pennies for correct answers, and using the pennies to buy a toy at the end of the testing session. Results showed that MPH had varied effects; for example, a positive effect was observed on stimulus evaluation processes and accuracy and reaction time improved, while no effect was seen on response bias or false alarm rates. Contingencies were shown to be less effective than MPH, as they did not increase performance.

Considerations

Like with individual approaches, it is important to identify the best treatment options for everyone involved. Pharmacology has generally been shown to be an effective intervention. However, the most recent findings from a comprehensive, longitudinal study suggest that while pharmacological approaches have demonstrated effectiveness at 14 and 24 months, follow-up assessments at 36 months showed pharmacological approaches to have no greater effects than behavioral or combined treatment approaches (Swanson et al., 2008). As stressed in other sections of this book, the decision to use psychopharmacological interventions is a matter for careful consideration among parents, the child, and the physician who would manage such an intervention. Less intrusive interventions, such as behavior modification, should typically be attempted before trying more complicated ones. Parents, counselors, and teachers should not take a wait-and-see attitude or leave improvement to chance or future development. Instead, early action involves little risk, especially when using interventions that involve home–school communication, teaching skills, and modifying problem behavior. Keeping an open mind toward proactive approaches that benefit students (even those who may not warrant a diagnosis of attention problems) is best.

In some cases, children with attention problems simply lack listening skills and study skills. Strategic listening and study skills can be taught. Instruments such as the *School Motivation and Learning Strategies Inventory* (SMALSI; Stroud & Reynolds, 2006) are specifically designed to assess listening, study skills, and related learning strategies and may be useful in determining whether the observed attention problems are the result of a lack of skills. When skill deficits are determined to be a root cause of attentional problems or a related cause, such skills can be taught effectively using common approaches taken from direct instruction methods.

Summary

This chapter presented a review of the characteristics and conditions for attention problems, along with a summary of interventions that have been shown to be effective in remediating them. These interventions included contingency management, daily behavior report cards, modified task-presentation strategies, self-management of attention, classwide peer tutoring, computer-assisted instruction, and multimodal interventions. While each intervention strategy presented differs in its application of one or more behavioral, cognitive–behavioral, or social learning theories, all are shaped by the fundamental goals of treatment: prevention and remediation of problem behaviors. The information presented in this chapter forms the basis of the supplemental classroom-and home-based materials that correspond to this book.

References

Abikoff, H., Courtney, M. E., Szeibel, P. J., & Koplewicz, H. S. (1996). The effects of auditory stimulation on the arithmetic performance of children with ADHD and nondisabled children. *Journal of Learning Disabilities, 29*(3), 238–246.

Alberto, P. A., & Troutman, A. C. (2002). *Applied behavior analysis for teachers* (6th ed.). Upper Saddle River, NJ: Prentice Hall.

American Academy of Pediatrics. (2001). Clinical practice guideline: Treatment of the school-aged child with attention-deficit/hyperactivity disorder. *Pediatrics, 108*(4), 1033–1044.

American Psychiatric Association. (2000). *Diagnostic and statistical manual of mental disorders* (4th ed., text revision). Washington, DC: Author.

Anhalt, K., McNeil, C. B., & Bahl, A. B. (1998). The ADHD classroom kit: A whole-classroom approach for managing disruptive behavior. *Psychology in the Schools, 35*(1), 67–79.

Atkins, M. S., Pelham, W. E., & Licht, M. H. (1985). A comparison of objective classroom measures and teacher ratings of attention deficit disorder. *Journal of Abnormal Child Psychology, 13*(1), 155–167.

Barber, M. A., Milich, R., & Welsh, R. (1996). Effects of reinforcement schedule and task difficulty on the performance of attention deficit hyperactivity disordered and control boys. *Journal of Clinical Child Psychology, 25*(1), 66–76.

Barkley, R. A. (1997). Behavioral inhibition, sustained attention, and executive functions: Constructing a unifying theory of ADHD. *Psychological Bulletin, 121*(1), 65–94.

Belfiore, P. J., Grskovic, J. A., Murphy, A. M., & Zentall, S. S. (1996). The effects of antecedent color on reading for students with learning disabilities and co-occurring attention-deficit/hyperactivity disorder. *Journal of Learning Disabilities, 29*(4), 432–438.

Burke, M. D., & Vannest, K. J. (2008). Behavioral-progress monitoring using the electronic daily behavioral report card (e-DBRC) system. *Preventing School Failure, 52*(3), 51–60.

Carbone, E. (2001). Arranging the classroom with an eye (and ear) to students with ADHD. *Teaching Exceptional Children, 34*(2), 72–81.

Carlson, C. L., Mann, M., & Alexander, D. K. (2000). Effects of reward and response cost on the performance and motivation of children with ADHD. *Cognitive Therapy and Research, 24*(1), 87–98.

Chafouleas, S. M., Riley-Tillman, T. C., & McDougal, J. L. (2002). Good, bad, or in-between: How does the daily behavior report card rate? *Psychology in the Schools, 39*(2), 157–169.

Chase, S. N., & Clement, P. W. (1985). Effects of self-reinforcement and stimulants on academic performance in children with attention deficit disorder. *Journal of Clinical Child Psychology, 14*(4), 323–333.

Christie, D. J., Hiss, M., & Lozanoff, B. (1984). Modification of inattentive classroom behavior: Hyperactive children's use of self-recording with teacher guidance. *Behavior Modification, 8*(3), 391–406.

Chronis, A. M., Jones, H. A., & Raggi, V. L. (2006). Evidence-based psychosocial treatments for children and adolescents with attention-deficit/hyperactivity disorder. *Clinical Psychology Review, 26*(4), 486–502.

Clarfield, J., & Stoner, G. (2005). The effects of computerized reading instruction on the academic performance of students identified with ADHD. *School Psychology Review, 34*(2), 246–254.

Clarke, S., Dunlap, G., Foster-Johnson, L., Childs, K. E., Wilson, D., White, R., et al. (1995). Improving the conduct of students with behavioral disorders by incorporating student interests into curricular activities. *Behavioral Disorders, 20*(4), 221–237.

Coles, E. K., Pelham, W. E., Gnagy, E. M., Burrows-MacLean, L., Fabiano, G. A., Chacko, A., et al. (2005). A controlled evaluation of behavioral treatment with children with ADHD attending a summer treatment program. *Journal of Emotional and Behavioral Disorders, 13*(2), 99–112.

Conners, C. K., Epstein, J. N., March, J. S., Angold, A., Wells, K. C., Klaric, J., et al. (2001). Multimodal treatment of ADHD in the MTA: An alternative outcome analysis. *Journal of the American Academy of Child and Adolescent Psychiatry, 40*(2), 159–167.

Council for Exceptional Children. (1992). *Children with ADD: A shared responsibility*. Reston, VA: Author.

Douglas, V. I. (1983). Attentional and cognitive problems. In M. Rutter (Ed.), *Developmental neuropsychiatry* (pp. 280–329). New York: Guilford.

Drew, B. M., Evans, J. H., Bostow, D. E., Geiger, G., & Drash, P. W. (1982). Increasing assignment completion and accuracy using a daily report card procedure. *Psychology in the Schools, 19*(4), 540–547.

Dubey, D. R., & O'Leary, S. G. (1975). Increasing reading comprehension of two hyperactive children: Preliminary investigation. *Perceptual and Motor Skills, 41*, 691–694.

Dunlap, G., dePerczel, M., Clarke, S., Wilson, D., Wright, S., White, R., et al. (1994). Choice making to promote adaptive behavior for students with emotional and behavioral challenges. *Journal of Applied Behavior Analysis, 27*(3), 505–518.

DuPaul, G. J., & Eckert, T. L. (1998). Academic interventions for students with attention-deficit/hyperactivity disorder: A review of the literature. *Reading and Writing Quarterly, 14*(1), 59–82.

DuPaul, G. J., Ervin, R. A., Hook, C. L., & McGoey, K. E. (1998). Peer tutoring for children with attention deficit hyperactivity disorder: Effects on classroom behavior and academic performance. *Journal of Applied Behavior Analysis, 31*(4), 579–592.

DuPaul, G. J., & Henningson, P. N. (1993). Peer tutoring effects on the classroom performance of children with attention deficit hyperactivity disorder. *School Psychology Review, 22*(1), 134–143.

DuPaul, G. J., & Weyandt, L. L. (2006). School-based interventions for children and adolescents with attention-deficit/hyperactivity disorder: Enhancing academic and behavioral outcomes. *Education and Treatment of Children, 29*(2), 341–358.

DuPaul, G. J., & White, G. P. (2006). ADHD: Behavioral, educational, and medication interventions. *Education Digest, 71*(7), 57–60.

Edwards, L., Salant, V., Howard, V. F., Brougher, J., & McLaughlin, T. F. (1995). Effectiveness of self-management on attentional behavior and reading comprehension for children with attention deficit disorder. *Child and Family Behavior Therapy, 17*(2), 1–17.

Ervin, R. A., DuPaul, G. J., Kern, L., & Friman, P. C. (1998). Classroom-based functional and adjunctive assessments: Proactive approaches to intervention selection for adolescents with attention deficit hyperactivity disorder. *Journal of Applied Behavior Analysis, 31*(1), 65–78.

Evans, S. W. (1995). Reflections on "The efficacy of notetaking to improve behavior and comprehension of adolescents with attention deficit hyperactivity disorder". *Exceptionality, 5*(1), 45–48.

Evans, S. W., Axelrod, J., & Langberg, J. M. (2004). Efficacy of a school-based treatment program for middle school youth with ADHD. *Behavior Modification, 28*(4), 528–547.

Evans, S. W., Langberg, J., Raggi, V., Allen, J., & Buvinger, E. C. (2005). Development of a school-based treatment program for middle school youth with ADHD. *Journal of Attention Disorders, 9*(1), 343–353.

Evans, S. W., Pelham, W., & Grudberg, M. V. (1995). The efficacy of notetaking to improve behavior and comprehension of adolescents with attention deficit hyperactivity disorder. *Exceptionality, 5*(1), 1–17.

Evans, S. W., Timmins, B., Sibley, M., White, C., Serpell, Z. N., & Schultz, B. (2006). Developing coordinated, multimodal, school based treatment for young adolescents with ADHD. *Education and Treatment of Children, 29*(2), 359–378.

Fabiano, G. A., & Pelham, W. E., Jr. (2003). Improving the effectiveness of behavioral classroom interventions for attention-deficit/hyperactivity disorder: A case study. *Journal of Emotional and Behavioral Disorders, 11*(2), 124–130.

Ford, M. J., Poe, V., & Cox, J. (1993). Attending behaviors of ADHD children in math and reading using various types of software. *Journal of Computing in Childhood Education, 4*(2), 183–196.

Gordon, M., Thomason, D., Cooper, S., & Ivers, C. L. (1991). Nonmedical treatment of ADHD/hyperactivity: The attention training system. *Journal of School Psychology, 29,* 151–159.

Greenewald, M. J., & Walsh, C. (1996). *The effect of environmental accommodations on attending behavior of an ADHD Chapter 1 student: An action research study.* Paper presented at the American Education Research Association, New York. (ERIC Document Reproduction Service No. ED 395254)

Greenwood, C. R., Delquadri, J. C., & Carta, J. J. (1997). *Together we can! Class wide peer tutoring to improve basic academic skills.* Longmont, CO: Sopris West.

Greenwood, C. R., Maheady, L., & Carta, J. J. (1991). Peer tutoring programs in the regular education classroom. In G. Stoner, M. R. Shinn, & H. M. Walker (Eds.), *Interventions for achievement and behavior problems* (pp. 179–200). Washington, D.C.: National Association of School Psychologists.

Greenwood, C. R., Maheady, L., & Delquadri, J. (2002). Class-wide peer tutoring. In G. Stoner, M. R. Shinn, & H. M. Walker (Eds.), *Interventions for achievement and behavior problems: Preventive and remedial approaches* (2nd ed., pp. 611649). Washington, D.C.: National Association of School Psychologists.

Gureasko-Moore, S., DuPaul, G. J., & White, G. P. (2006). The effects of self-management in general education classrooms on the organizational skills of adolescents with ADHD. *Behavior Modification, 30*(2), 159–183.

Habboushe, D. F., Daniel-Crotty, S., Karustis, J. L., Leff, S. S., Costigan, T. E., Goldstein, S. G., et al. (2001). A family-school homework intervention program for children with attention-deficit/hyperactivity disorder. *Cognitive and Behavioral Practice, 8*(2), 123–136.

Hancock, P. A., & Warm, J. S. (2003). A dynamic model of stress and sustained attention. *Human Performance in Extreme Environments, 7*(1), 15–28.

Harlacher, J. E., Roberts, N. E., & Merrell, K. W. (2006). Classwide interventions for students with ADHD: A summary of teacher options beneficial for the whole class. *Teaching Exceptional Children, 39*(2), 6–11.

Harris, K. R., Friedlander, B. D., Saddler, B., Frizzelle, R., & Graham, S. (2005). Self-monitoring of attention versus self-monitoring of academic performance: Effects among students with ADHD in the general education classroom. *Journal of Special Education, 39*(3), 145–157.

Hartley, M. M. M. (1998). The relationships among disruptive behaviors, attention, and academic achievement in a clinic referral sample. Unpublished doctoral dissertation, University of Georgia, Athens.

Hooks, K., Milich, R., & Lorch, E. P. (1994). Sustained and selective attention in boys with attention deficit hyperactivity disorder. *Journal of Clinical Child Psychology, 23*(1), 69–77.

Hoza, B., Pelham, W. E., Jr., Sams, S. E., & Carlson, C. (1992). An examination of the "dosage" effects of both behavior therapy and methylphenidate on the classroom performance of two ADHD children. *Behavior Modification, 16*(2), 164–192.

Karraker, R. J. (1972). Increasing academic performance through home-managed contingency programs. *Journal of School Psychology, 10*(2), 173–179.

Kelley, M. L., & McCain, A. P. (1995). Promoting academic performance in inattentive children: The relative efficacy of school-home notes with and without response cost. *Behavior Modification, 19*(3), 357–375.

Kern, L., Bambara, L., & Fogt, J. (2002). Class-wide curricular modification to improve the behavior of students with emotional or behavioral disorders. *Behavioral Disorders, 27*(4), 317–326.

Kern, L., Childs, K. E., Dunlap, G., Clarke, S., & Falk, G. D. (1994). Using assessment-based curricular intervention to improve the classroom behavior of a student with emotional and behavioral challenges. *Journal of Applied Behavior Analysis, 27*(1), 7–19.

Kern, L., & Clemens, N. H. (2007). Antecedent strategies to promote appropriate classroom behavior. *Psychology in the Schools, 44*(1), 65–75.

Kerns, K. A., Eso, K., & Thomson, J. (1999). Investigation of a direct intervention for improving attention in young children with ADHD. *Developmental Neuropsychology, 16*(2), 273–295.

Kleiman, G., Humphrey, M., & Lindsay, P. H. (1981). Microcomputers and hyperactive children. *Creative Computing, 7*(3), 93–94.

Kos, J. M., Richdale, A. L., & Hay, D. A. (2006). Children with attention deficit hyperactivity disorder and their teachers: A review of the literature. *International Journal of Disability, Development and Education, 53*(2), 147–160.

LaBerge, D. (2002). Attentional control: brief and prolonged. *Psychological Review, 66,* 220–233.

Loge, D. V., Staton, R. D., & Beatty, W. W. (1990). Performance of children with ADHD on tests sensitive to frontal lobe dysfunction. *Journal of the American Academy of Child and Adolescent Psychiatry, 29*(4), 540–545.

Mash, E. J., and Barkley, R. A. (2003). *Child psychopathology* (2nd ed.). New York: Guilford.

Mace, F. C., Belfiore, P. J., & Hutchinson, J. M. (2001). Operant theory and research on self-regulation. In B. J. Zimmerman & D. H. Schunk (Eds.), *Self-regulated learning and academic achievement: Theoretical perspectives* (2nd ed., pp. 39–65). Mahwah, NJ: Erlbaum.

Mathes, M. Y., & Bender, W. N. (1997). The effects of self-monitoring on children with attention-deficit/hyperactivity disorder who are receiving pharmacological interventions. *Remedial and Special Education, 18*(2), 121–128.

Mautone, J. A., DuPaul, G. J., & Jitendra, A. K. (2005). The effects of computer-assisted instruction on the mathematics performance and classroom behavior of children with ADHD. *Journal of Attention Disorders, 9*(1), 301–312.

McCain, A. P., & Kelley, M. L. (1993). Managing the classroom behavior of an ADHD preschooler: The efficacy of a school-home note intervention. *Child and Family Behavior Therapy, 15*(3), 33–44.

Merrell, C., & Tymms, P. B. (2001). Inattention, hyperactivity, and impulsiveness: Their impact on academic achievement and progress. *British Journal of Educational Psychology, 71*(1), 43–56.

Montague, M., & Warger, C. (1997). Helping students with attention deficit hyperactivity disorder succeed in the classroom. *Focus on Exceptional Children, 30*(4), 1–16.

National Institute of Mental Health. (2006). *Attention deficit hyperactivity disorder.* Bethesda, MD: Author. (NIH Publication Number: NIH 5124)

Ota, K. R., & DuPaul, G. J. (2002). Task engagement and mathematics performance in children with attention-deficit hyperactivity disorder: Effects of supplemental computer instruction. *School Psychology Quarterly, 17*(3), 242–257.

Owens, J. S., Richerson, L., Beilstein, E. A., Crane, A., Murphy, C. E., & Vancouver, J. B. (2005). School-based mental health programming for children with inattentive and disruptive behavior problems: First-year treatment outcome. *Journal of Attention Disorders, 9*(1), 261–274.

Pelham, W. E., Jr., Carlson, C., Sams, S. E., Vallano, G., Dixon., M. J., & Hoza, B. (1993). Separate and combined effects of methylphenidate and behavior modification on boys with attention deficit–hyperactivity disorder in the classroom. *Journal of Consulting and Clinical Psychology, 61*(3), 506–515.

Pfiffner, L. J., O'Leary, S. G., Rosén, L. A., & Sanderson, W. C., Jr. (1985). A comparison of the effects of continuous and intermittent response cost and reprimands in the classroom. *Journal of Clinical Child Psychology, 14*(4), 348–351.

Plumer, P. J., & Stoner, G. (2005). The relative effects of classwide peer tutoring and peer coaching on the positive social behaviors of children with ADHD. *Journal of Attention Disorders, 9*(1), 290–300.

Powell, S., & Nelson, B. (1997). Effects of choosing academic assignments on a student with attention deficit hyperactivity disorder. *Journal of Applied Behavior Analysis, 30*(1), 181–183.

Raggi, V. L., & Chronis, A. M. (2006). Interventions to address the academic impairment of children and adolescents with ADHD. *Clinical Child and Family Psychology Review, 9*(2), 85–111.

Rapport, M. D., Murphy, A., & Bailey, J. S. (1980). The effects of a response cost treatment tactic on hyperactive children. *Journal of School Psychology, 18*(2), 98–111.

Reid, R., Trout, A. L., & Schartz, M. (2005). Self-regulation interventions for children with attention deficit/hyperactivity disorder. *Exceptional Children, 71*(4), 361–377.

Reid, R., & Lienemann, T. O. (2006). Self-regulated strategy development for written expression with students with attention deficit/hyperactivity disorder. *Exceptional Children, 73*(1), 53–68.

Reynolds, C. R., & Kamphaus, R. W. (2004). *Behavior Assessment System for Children* (2nd ed.). Circle Pines, MN: AGS Publishing.

Riccio, C. A., Reynolds, C. R., & Lowe, P. A. (2001). *Clinical applications of continuous performance tests: Measuring attention and impulsive responding in children and adults.* New York: Wiley.

Richardson, E., Kupietz, S., & Maitinsky, S. (1986). What is the role of academic intervention in the treatment of hyperactive children with reading disorders? *Journal of Children in Contemporary Society, 19*(1–2), 153–167.

Riley-Tillman, T. C., Chafouleas, S. M., & Briesch, A. M. (2007). A school practitioner's guide to using daily behavior report cards to monitor student behavior. *Psychology in the Schools, 44*(1), 77–89.

Robinson, P. W., Newby, T. J., & Ganzell, S. L. (1981). A token system for a class of underachieving hyperactive children. *Journal of Applied Behavior Analysis, 14*(3), 307–315.

Salend, S. J., Elhoweris, H., & van Garderen, D. (2003). Educational interventions for students with ADD. *Intervention in School and Clinic, 38*(5), 280–288.

Scott, R. (1970). The use of music to reduce hyperactivity in children. *American Journal of Orthopsychiatry, 40*(4), 677–680.

Seidel, W. T., & Joschko, M. (1990). Evidence of difficulties in sustained attention in children with ADDH. *Journal of Abnormal Child Psychology, 18*(2), 217–229.

Semrud-Clikeman, M., Nielsen, K. H., Clinton, A., Sylvester, L., Parle, N., & Connor, R. T. (1999). An intervention approach for children with teacher- and parent-identified attentional difficulties. *Journal of Learning Disabilities, 32*(6), 581–590.

Shaw, R., & Lewis, V. (2005). The impact of computer-mediated and traditional academic task presentation on the performance and behaviour of children with ADHD. *Journal of Research in Special Educational Needs, 5*(2), 47–54.

Shimabukuro, S. M., Prater, M. A., Jenkins, A., & Edelen-Smith, P. (1999). The effects of self-monitoring of academic performance on students with learning disabilities and ADD/ADHD. *Education and Treatment of Children, 22*(4), 397–414.

Skinner, C. H., Johnson, C. W., Larkin, M. J., Lessley, D. J., & Glowacki, M. L. (1995). The influence of rate of presentation during taped-words interventions on reading performance. *Journal of Emotional and Behavioral Disorders, 3*(4), 214–223.

Sohlberg, M. M., McLaughlin, K. A., Pavese, A., Heidrich, A., & Posner, M. I. (2000). Evaluation of attention process training and brain injury education in persons with acquired brain injury. *Journal of Clinical and Experimental Neuropsychology, 22*(5), 656–676.

Solanto, M. V., Wender, E. H., & Bartell, S. S. (1997). Effects of methylphenidate and behavioral contingencies on sustained attention in attention-deficit hyperactivity disorder: A test of the reward dysfunction hypothesis. *Journal of Child and Adolescent Psychopharmacology, 7*(2), 123–136.

Solden, S. (1995). *Women with attention deficit disorder: Embracing disorganization at home and in the workplace.* Nevada City, CA: Underwood Books.

Smith, B. H., Waschbusch, D. A., Willoughby, M. T., & Evans, S. (2000). The efficacy, safety, and practicality of treatments for adolescents with attention-deficit/hyperactivity disorder (ADHD). *Clinical Child and Family Psychology Review, 3*(4), 243–267.

Stormont-Spurgin, M. (1997). I lost my homework: Strategies for improving organization in students with ADHD. *Intervention in School and Clinic, 32*(5), 270–274.

Stroud, K., & Reynolds, C. R. (2006). School Motivation and Learning Strategies Inventory (SMALSI). Los Angeles: Western Psychological Services.

Sutherland, K. S., Alder, N., & Gunter, P. L. (2003). The effect of varying rates of opportunities to respond to academic requests on the classroom behavior of students with EBD. *Journal of Emotional and Behavioral Disorders, 11*(4), 239–248.

Swanson, J., Arnold, L. E., Kraemer, H., Hechtman, L., Molina, B., Hinshaw, S., et al. (2008). Evidence, interpretation, and qualification from multiple reports of long-term outcomes in the multimodal treatment study of children with ADHD (MTA): Part I: Executive Summary. *Journal of Attention Disorders, 12*(1), 4–14.

Vannest, K. J., Burke, M. D., Parker, R. I., Mason, B., Davis, C., Barrios, L., et al. (2008). DBRC: A meta analysis. Manuscript submitted for publication.

Volpe, R. J. Heick., P.F., & Guerasko-Moore, D. (2005). An agile behavioral model for monitoring the effects of stimulant medication in school settings. *Psychology in the Schools, 42*(5), 509–523.

Weinstein, C. (1976, April). *The effect of a change in the physical design of an open classroom on student behavior.* Paper presented at the annual meeting of the American Educational Research Association, San Francisco, CA.

Wolery, M., Bailey, D. B., & Sugai, G. M. (1988). *Effective teaching: Principles and procedures of applied behavior analysis with exceptional students.* Boston: Allyn & Bacon.

Zentall, S. S. (1983). Learning environments: A review of physical and temporal factors. *Exceptional Education Quarterly, 4*(2), 90–115.

Zentall, S. S. (1985). Stimulus-control factors in search performance of hyperactive children. *Journal of Learning Disabilities, 18*(8), 480–485.

Zentall, S. S. (1989). Attentional cuing in spelling tasks for hyperactive and comparison regular classroom children. *Journal of Special Education, 23*(1), 83–93.

Zentall, S. S. (1993). Research on the educational implications of attention deficit hyperactivity disorder. *Exceptional Children, 60*(2), 143–153.

Zentall, S. S., & Kruczek, T. (1988). The attraction of color for active attention-problem children. *Exceptional Children, 54*(4), 357–362.

Zentall, S. S., Falkenberg, S. D., & Smith, L. B. (1985). Effects of color stimulation and information on the copying performance of attention-problem adolescents. *Journal of Abnormal Child Psychology, 13*(4), 501–511.

Zentall, S. S., Grskovic, J. A., Javorsky, J., & Hall, A. M. (2000). Effects of noninformational color on the reading test performance of students with and without attentional deficits. *Diagnostique, 25*(2), 129–146.

Chapter 6

Interventions for Academic Problems

This chapter reviews interventions that have been shown to be effective for children and adolescents identified as having academic problems. It is divided into three sections. First, the characteristics and conditions of academic problems are presented. This initial section gives a brief description of academic problems and includes sample items from the BASC–2 Learning Problems, Study Skills, Attitude to Teachers, and Attitude to School scales. Second, a theoretical framework for addressing academic problems is described, providing a context for the selection of interventions. Third, interventions that have evidence or show promise for remediation of academic problems in school settings are described. These interventions are organized according to who is primarily responsible for the implementation of the intervention—teacher, peer, or student. The presentation of each provides an overview of the intervention and is divided into three subsections: Implementation, Evidence for Use, and Considerations. The chapter's three main sections provide the foundation on which additional BASC–2 intervention components are built, including both classroom-based and home-based strategies.

Characteristics and Conditions of Academic Problems

On the BASC–2 rating scales, learning problems are defined as the presence of academic difficulties, particularly in understanding or completing homework. Learning problems can encompass a variety of academic domains, such as reading, writing, mathematics, and spelling. Both the BASC–2 teacher and student forms identify learning problems. On the teacher form, learning problems are identified via the Learning Problems and Study Skills scales. Items from these scales include: "Has trouble keeping up in class," "Gets failing school grades," "Has reading problems," "Has good study habits," and "Is well organized" (Reynolds & Kamphaus, 2004). On the student self-report form, learning problems are assessed indirectly through the Attitude to School and Attitude to Teachers scales. Items from these scales include: "I don't like thinking about school," "I feel like I want to quit school," and "Teachers make me feel stupid" (Reynolds & Kamphaus, 2004).

Academic failure and learning problems are evidenced across content areas and skill sets. Students with learning problems are typically inefficient information processors (Swanson & Deshler, 2003). These students achieve significantly below grade-level expectations: 61% fall in the bottom quartile in reading; 43% fall in the bottom quartile in math;

85% score below the norm on language measures; and 68% have clinical language deficits and are unsuccessful in written expression, performing more than a grade level below norms (Coutinho, 1986; Cullinan, Epstein, & Lloyd, 1991; Epstein, Kinder, & Bursuck, 1989; Kauffman, Cullinan, & Epstein, 1987; Scruggs & Mastriopieri, 1986; Trout, Nordness, Pierce, & Epstein, 2003; Wagner, Kutash, Duchnowski, Epstein, & Sumi, 2005). The pervasive nature of academic problems—their influence on numerous content areas and academic skills—often makes dealing with academic problems challenging for both teacher and student alike and requires diligence and a long-term approach to intervention strategies to achieve successful remediation.

These challenges can be compounded for students with emotional and behavioral disorders, whose academic failures are also due to problems with acquiring and processing information (Lane, Carter, Pierson, & Glaeser, 2006; Mooney, Epstein, Reid, & Nelson, 2003; Wagner et al., 2005). These learning problems are significant contributors to increased risk of retention, dropping out of school, and earning lower grades (Locke & Fuchs, 1995). Therefore, academic intervention is as important as the typical social and behavioral interventions (Landrum, Tankersley, & Kauffman, 2003; Lane, 2004; Lane, Barton-Arwood, Nelson, & Wehby, 2008; Simpson, 1999; Vannest, Harrison, Ramsey, & Harvey, 2008; Vannest, Harvey & Mason, in press).

Theoretical Framework for Approaching Academic Problems

Learning is defined as a change in behavior. An individual demonstrates learning through successful academic performance such as writing, speaking, or demonstrating knowledge. Learning that is internalized (e.g., a student says, "I understand") is difficult to verify without a corresponding demonstration of the understanding through an observable behavior. Therefore, although learning is certainly a cognitive process, the behaviors associated with it make up the basis for judgment and intervention.

There are different types of learning: cognitive learning, affective learning, and psychomotor learning. The academic problems highlighted in this chapter are primarily related to factors included in the cognitive learning process. Cognitive learning involves knowledge and the development of intellectual skills and abilities, and its process has been conceptualized as a series of levels, progressing from simple to most complex, defined by Bloom (1956) as: Knowledge, Comprehension, Application, Analysis, Synthesis, and Evaluation. Progression from one level to the next requires mastery of the preceding one, and difficulty in any of these areas constitutes an academic problem.

The interventions presented in this chapter fit in a cognitive–behavioral model. Cognitive–behavioral approaches to academic interventions are highlighted in this chapter for two reasons. First, they have been shown to be highly effective; second, biological causes of learning problems (e.g., synaptic plasticity and structure of the cerebral cortex) are unlikely to give rise to educational intervention at the school site. There is a neurological and physiological basis of learning that involves the neural network and accounts for factors such as hormonal influences on memory and performance. However, whatever the causes, be they biological (e.g., attention deficits, head injury) or environmental (e.g., impoverished early childhood experiences, lack of language experience during critical learning periods), academic problems can be addressed by a cognitive–behavioral intervention approach.

Interventions

A variety of interventions have been shown to be effective in remediating academic problems. These interventions are considered research-based practices, as evidenced by peer-reviewed research literature. This discussion of interventions is not exhaustive; rather, it represents the literature on effective instructional practices and interventions for use specifically with students who have emotional and behavioral problems. The interventions in this chapter have been organized into three categories:

I. Teacher-Mediated Interventions

II. Peer-Mediated Interventions

III. Self-Mediated Interventions

Teacher-mediated interventions focus on the teacher as the primary behavioral change agent, while peer-mediated interventions emphasize peers helping peers. Self-mediated interventions are used independently by the student to regulate learning. Within each category, interventions have been classified based on their underlying principles.

I. Teacher-Mediated Interventions

Teacher-mediated interventions involve organizing and structuring learning, presenting information, and selecting independent tasks. These effective teaching behaviors can improve student learning and decrease the effects of academic problems. The teacher-mediated interventions included in this chapter are: advance organizers, presentation strategies, and task-selection strategies.

A. Advance Organizers

Teachers are faced with the challenging task of presenting information in a way that can be understood by a classroom of students representing diverse sets of knowledge, skills, and ability levels. An advance organizer, a common instructional tool used by teachers, can be effective in helping a diverse group of students learn everyday material. The effectiveness of an advance organizer is directly related to how well it links information that has already been learned with the information that is about to be taught.

For example, Ms. Hamilton teaches an 11th-grade general education Texas history class using the required textbook, which is written at a 9th-grade reading level. The reading abilities of the students in her class range from college level to fifth grade. Several of her students have learning problems that are either English as a second language (ESL) or developmentally related. Ms. Hamilton provides her class with an advance organizer at the beginning of each instructional unit, such as the Battle of the Alamo. The advance organizer helps the students relate the current lesson to their previous lesson about the battle of Goliad, showing the similar themes and concepts of both battles. She explains that the purpose of the lesson is to demonstrate the major themes of the Battle of the Alamo and states that each student will be expected to be able to relate verbally the sequence of events and the key players. The following lesson plan advance organizer (see Figure 6.1) and related student-completed example (see Figure 6.2) were adapted from the sample in Boudah, Lenz, Bulgren, Schumaker, & Deshler (2000); they include strictly heuristic information, presenting the key details and conceptual links.

Figure 6.1 Example of lesson plan advance organizer

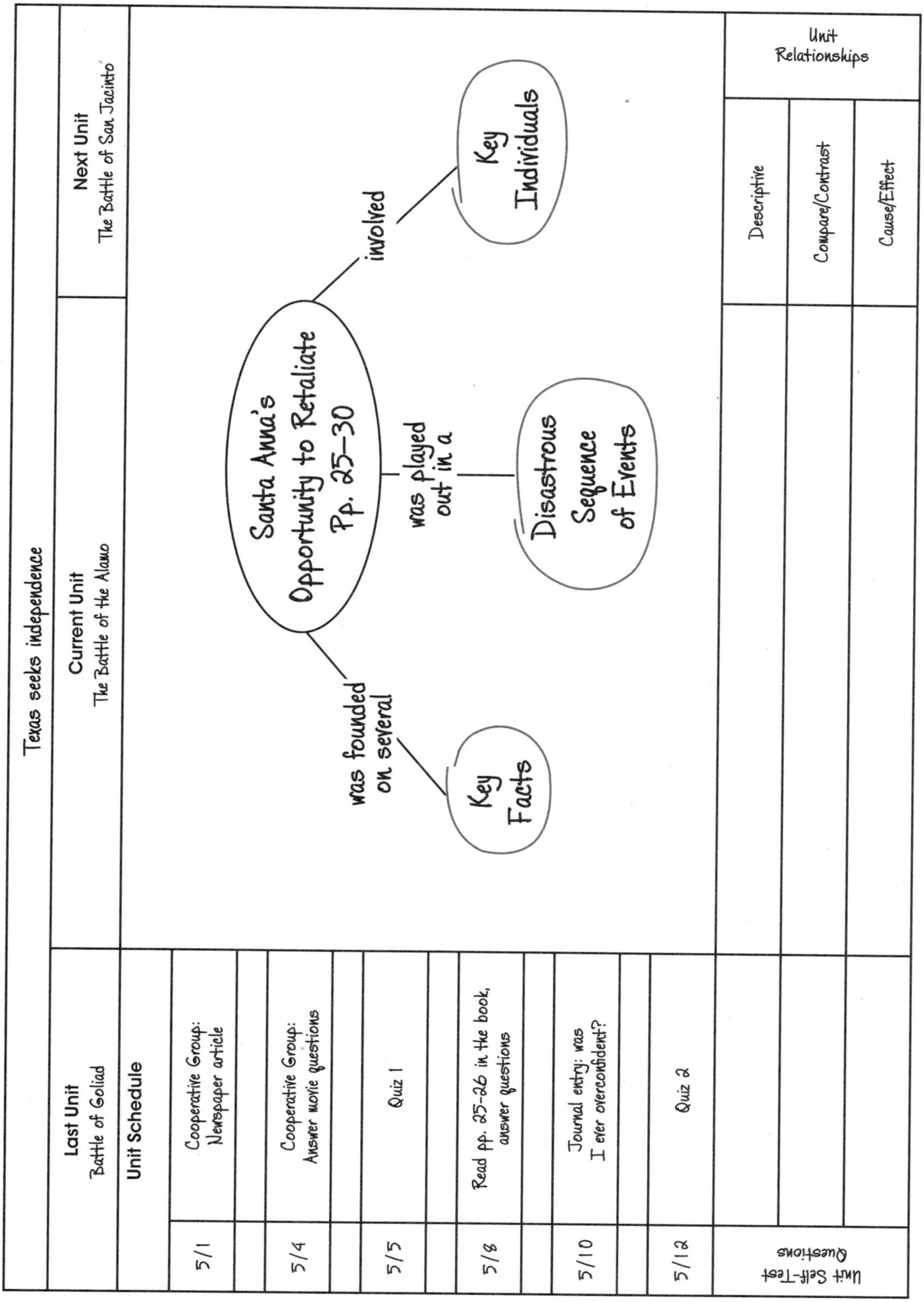

Figure 6.2 Example of student-completed advance organizer

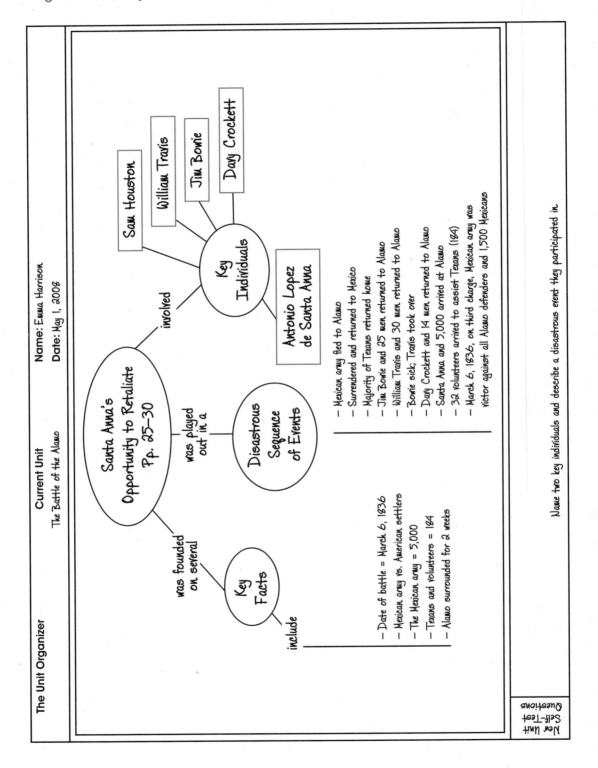

Implementation

The goals of using advance organizers are to retrieve prior knowledge as a foundation for new information, supply an antecedent to the main instructional activity, and provide a structure for the new information (Swanson & Deshler, 2003). Advance organizers may contain the following components:

1. Review of the previous lesson

2. Purpose of the current lesson

3. Rationale for the lesson

4. Statement of expectations

Using advance organizers requires teachers to explicitly outline the structure of the lesson and materials. This outline should reflect the relationships between concepts, describe the information to be learned, and detail how the information will be taught. Therefore, prior to the construction of the advance organizer, an analysis should be done to define the content coverage of the lesson based on previous and future lessons while considering overall expectations for the course. This stage of the process should identify the required learning outcomes for the lesson, articulate the procedures and routines for teaching those concepts, and establish the performance indicators for successful student learning.

In identifying the learning outcomes, aim for a list of three or four items, avoiding general terminology for objectives (e.g., understands, develops). Concentrate on concrete, specific language (e.g., describes, uses, lists). Also, describe these items in terms of necessity (e.g., will describe), not conditionality (e.g., should be able to describe). Next, determine the student learning experiences that will facilitate knowledge or skill acquisition (i.e., how the listed items will be taught). Then, generate the student performance expectations by translating the listed items into measurable learning goals.

After the lesson analysis, construct an advance organizer containing the components previously listed (review, purpose, rationale, and expectations). In the organizer, the review of the previous lesson should emphasize the connections from already-learned material to new information and serve a purpose similar to that of a map. It should provide a way by which students can orient themselves to a lesson and allow them to see where they are, where they were, and where they are going. The purpose statement explains the importance and relevance of the lesson, and the rationale and procedure statements ensure that students understand the pre-established expectations for successful academic performance. Figure 6.3 describes the steps to implementing an advance organizer.

For example, a teacher may distribute an advance organizer for a lesson on comparing themes in a reading unit about Mark Twain and then say, "Last week, we finished *The Adventures of Tom Sawyer* by Mark Twain. We learned about conflict and character development and how both were used throughout the story to represent the struggles people had with themselves and with each other. Today we will begin *The Adventures of Huckleberry Finn,* also by Mark Twain. When I introduce the main characters, be looking for the struggles the characters have with themselves and with others. See if you can find similar themes in this story." During the lesson, students would be shown an overhead with graphics displaying parallels between the stories, and they would complete a blank form in their notebooks that mimicked what the teacher was demonstrating on the overhead.

Figure 6.3 Procedural steps for the application of advance organizers

1. Prepare the information for the advance organizer.

    a. Analyze the overall content of the lesson. What are the major concepts that every student must learn? Aim for a list of three or four concepts.

    b. Analyze and articulate the procedures and routines for teaching those concepts.

    c. Determine the performance expectations for students.

2. Present the information using a graphic or visual representation that will:

    a. Connect and review previously learned information

    b. Convey a purpose statement

    c. Provide a rationale statement to the student

    d. State the expectations

    e. Review the relevant academic strategies for instructional routines and content

3. Teach lessons and create classroom routines that follow the outline of the organizer. Each session, as relevant, reorients the students to where they are, where they were, and where they are going, with particular emphasis on the structure and expectations of the unit or lesson.

Evidence for Use

Advance organizers have been found to help children experiencing academic problems learn new material. The following studies summarize some of the key research findings associated with implementing advance organizers as an intervention for students with academic problems.

Darch, C., & Gersten, R. (1986). Direction-setting activities in reading comprehension: A comparison of two approaches. *Learning Disability Quarterly, 9*(3), 235–243.

This study compared two methods for teaching comprehension to 24 high school students with learning disabilities (LD). The students were randomly assigned to one of two treatment groups: an advance organizer group and a basal discussion group. In the advance organizer group, students were presented with an advance organizer consisting of an outline/overview prior to reading from the text. The basal discussion group listened to a teacher's lecture prior to reading from the text. The advance organizer group received an average of 75% correct on the posttest, compared to 53% for the basal group. The results showed that a structured, organized framework increases the likelihood that LD students will be successful in retaining unit concepts.

Swanson, H. L., & Deshler, D. (2003). Instructing adolescents with learning disabilities: Converting a meta-analysis to practice. *Journal of Learning Disabilities, 36*(2), 124–135.

This study was a meta-analysis of 93 group design studies that focused on the efficacy of various academic interventions for adolescents aged 12 to 18 years with learning disabilities (LD). Of the eight factors used to examine the intervention studies, the Organization/Explicit Practice factor was found to have the greatest impact on learning outcomes. The two instructional components that make up this factor are advance organizers (linking existing student knowledge to what will be learned in a lesson) and explicit practice (providing opportunities to apply newly acquired knowledge). The meta-analysis suggested that students, especially those with learning disabilities, require distributed practice to maximize long-term retention and that an intervention that includes an integrated combination of instructional methods, applied consistently, will significantly improve academic gains.

Considerations

For Teaching

These types of interventions require moderate to significant levels of preparation prior to use in instruction. However, the time spent preparing advance organizers is generally an initial investment; once the materials are created and organized, only minor investments of time are required for updating them. This preparation time pays off in additional benefits to the instruction, such as making repeated coverage of material more prescriptive for students who miss critical components and providing another method to help focus student attention, which saves time in discipline-related activities.

For Culture and Language Differences

Using advance organizers creates visual memory prompts and provides nonverbal context clues that can assist ESL students in learning content. With irrelevant language stimuli removed, the visual connections to prior learning and illustrated relationships between materials are easier to grasp for students learning a second language.

For Age and Developmental Level

Students in very early grades are unlikely to require this level of content knowledge or be exposed to reading materials with abstract concepts and relationships. This type of instructional intervention would be most commonly used from fifth grade and up, with evidence demonstrating effective use across content areas throughout the secondary years.

B. Presentation Strategies

The degree of structure provided within a lesson, the amount and quality of time allocated for teaching the content of the lesson, and the frequency and types of student and teacher responses during that learning process are all components of presentation strategy. As such, each component affects how lessons are delivered. Within the category of structuring are presentation strategies such as scaffolding, procedural prompts, instructional sequencing, and scripted lessons. Strategies that would modify the time aspect of presentations include changes to the rate and pacing of instruction, pauses during instruction, and amounts of allocated and engaged time within a lesson. Responding refers to strategies that alter the inclusion of student responses to instruction and the teacher–student response loop of dialogue and correction or confirmation. Using presentation strategies that alter structure, time, and student responding to assist students with academic problems creates optimal learning environments and provides opportunities for improved student learning.

Presentation strategies rely on an awareness of the match (or mismatch) between a student's skill and ability levels and the requirements of the learning task. Inherent in each strategy is the planning and forethought that goes into preparation of materials and content delivery, with careful attention to maximizing students' learning time.

The ineffective use of structuring, time, and responding can compound the struggles experienced by students with academic problems. Although sometimes challenging to assess, instructional presentation strategies should not be overlooked in remediating academic problems. However, these strategies should be considered a small part of the whole. For example, strong scaffolding will not replace insufficient instructional time nor will large quantities of engaged time accommodate poor matches between instructional delivery and learner ability.

Each presentation component (structuring, time, and responding) has its own unique role in the successful delivery of instruction. As such, each has its own procedure for implementation and integration into lesson planning and classroom instruction. What follows are overviews of these presentation components and common methods employed when developing and implementing each.

Implementation

Structuring

The presentation strategy that refers to the formation or development of the instructional content and the organization of its delivery is structuring. Well-designed curriculum will have an implicit structure, and good instruction will present that structure explicitly to students. Common methods used for structuring include the following:

1. Scaffolding

2. Procedural prompts

3. Instructional sequencing

4. Scripted lessons

Scaffolding is the generic term for the instructional support provided by the teacher until the student is able to transition into independent thinking and learning (Bruner, 1985; Rosenshine & Meister, 1992; Vygotsky, 1978). Teachers sometimes employ scaffolding naturally when they provide hints or clues to guide students who are struggling with an answer (e.g., pointing to a section of a page or starting to sound out a word as the student attempts to decode it). Scaffolds can be aids to developing and applying cognitive strategies (Palincsar & Brown, 1984; Swanson & Deshler, 2003). Scaffolded instruction provides an instructional bridge between existing student knowledge and new content.

Scaffolded instruction has been described as systematic sequencing (Dickson, Chard, & Simmons, 1993; Kame'enui, Carnine, Dixon, Simmons, & Coyne, 2002). One example of scaffolded instruction is providing traceable outlines of letters for students who are learning to write the alphabet. The outlines may start dark and then fade to dotted lines before disappearing altogether. Other examples include: the dotted half-line that appears in beginners' writing composition notebooks to provide spacing and to distinguish between uppercase and lowercase letters, the large dots that appear in touch math to assist students in counting, and worksheets that have hints or page number references for finding answers.

There are three components that typically influence the development of scaffolding applications. The students' present levels of performance and their future goals need to be considered. The curriculum and learning objectives have to be incorporated. And, a concerted effort should be made to provide instructional bridges (visual or verbal) between knowledge gaps based on student needs. For example, a second-grade student who reads at a kindergarten level needs to understand the food chain and water cycle in science. Visual support and scaffolding might include preteaching key vocabulary, providing diagrams with correctly spelled words to match to figures, adding more white space on the page for below-grade-level written responses (i.e., large printing), and using fewer text distracters. Such scaffolding will result in a learning process with fewer student errors and greater focus on the science concepts rather than secondary aspects of spelling or neatness. Using these presentation strategies also may contribute to task completion by making the expectations clear and completion of the assignment more obvious.

Another example to consider is that of a struggling high school junior in a secondary language arts classroom. During composition writing, he benefits from a feedback process for developing paragraphs. The process begins with the student outlining each paragraph by writing topic sentences. He then writes the numerals 1, 2, and 3 to note placement of the subsequent detail sentences of each paragraph and inserts an asterisk (*) to denote where to put each concluding sentence. The teacher first checks the initial outline and then provides suggestions for changes to the topic sentences. The teacher provides one keyword for each of the numbered sentences. The student uses the keywords to begin working through each supporting sentence. After each phase of paragraph development, the teacher provides just enough support for the student to achieve the next step. This scaffolded process limits the frustration the student normally experiences when writing by reducing effort on unrelated sentences and increasing structured thinking about the topic.

Scaffolding is appropriate for all ages, and it can circumvent language and cultural differences. It is unlike differentiated instruction in that it maintains a unique relationship to learning goals. The technique allows teachers to support students who struggle academically, and it can be tailored to regulate the amount of effort students should make to complete tasks. This technique helps students learn independently and reduces the likelihood that they will either act out in class or ignore instruction that is above their skill level. Scaffolding also provides signals for the teacher to determine how to increase student learning, by facilitating teacher awareness of the points at which students become bogged down in new concepts or tasks.

Another common method for structuring are procedural prompts. Procedural prompts/facilitators are visual, verbal, or auditory prompts (Scardamalia & Bereiter, 1985). These prompts help students to organize and remember new material and are important for the storage and retrieval of new information. Organization and retrieval are critical components in understanding (Rosenshine, 1997).

Examples of procedural prompts include the guiding questions that prompt cognitive processes and assist students in storing and retrieving information, such as: "How are____and ____ alike in the story?" or "What other chemical process causes expansion?" or "Do you agree with ____? Why or why not?" These types of questions have embedded cues that prompt thinking.

There are two main steps to follow when applying procedural prompts. First, determine if the challenge to learning is related to organization (memory) or application (thinking). Second, ask questions that create opportunities for chunking (remembering concepts together), linking (connecting items sequentially or by relation to each other), retrieval (accessing the information more efficiently), or schema (connecting newly learned material with previously learned material).

Both memory and thinking are facilitated by prompting strategies. One of the best illustrative examples of memory function is walking through a field of tall grass or deep snow. The first time across is difficult; this is akin to learning something the first time. Subsequent crossings create a pathway that is much easier to access, and memory, like this pathway, becomes more automated. Mental connections are like learning a physical route. The first time you drive a route you need signposts, you frequently check a map to make sure you are on the right track, and you typically find landmarks to help you remember the way the next time you travel the route. Memory's role in learning new material or concepts in education is similar, needing frequent reference points to stay on track. Young children do not have the practical or life skills to effectively harness their memories, and they need both the strategies and signposts to learn how to recall information. Both the ins and the outs of memory benefit from procedural prompting.

Instructional sequencing, another structuring method, refers to the order in which information is presented to a student, as well as how a student structures his or her learning. This sequencing is fundamental to learning (Glynn & DiVesta, 1977; Lorch & Lorch, 1985; Van Patten, Chao, & Reigeluth, 1986). No one specific sequence is required for instruction to be successful; however, applicable literature has shown the following sequencing to be effective for students and instruction. Teachers can select other instructional methods, but students may take longer to learn, may pick up errors in learning, and may begin the cycle of frustration and withdrawal that sometimes accompanies unclear instruction.

Sequencing incorporates the information to be learned into the context of previously learned information. When presenting information, provide clear and explicit expectations for student performance. Information should be presented using examples and nonexamples, and should be explicitly linked or connected to previously learned information. Throughout the lesson, students should be given ample opportunities to respond to questions. They also should receive consistent reinforcement for correct responses and frequent feedback loops to correct and shape incorrect responses. Information that is learned should then be reviewed and practiced. In order to promote retention of the learned information, provide opportunities when possible to demonstrate that information has been learned.

Scripted lessons are a variant of the instructional sequencing concept. Teachers write scripts for lesson plans, including how the information will be presented, the desired responses by students, and the routines that will be used for learning the material. Prompts for teacher and students are included in the scripts. Although scripted lessons can take a variety of forms, they generally follow the same steps as instructional sequencing. Scripted lessons can be beneficial to teachers who want to assess the fidelity of the teaching objectives. Since the lesson plans are written, they know exactly how information was presented. If the students' performance on a particular lesson is not what was desired, the teacher can modify the lesson as needed to obtain the desired performance outcome. The nature of scripted lessons provides a structure for teachers and students, helps eliminate or reduce errors in teaching and learning, and allows for subsequent modifications that would improve the curriculum and instruction.

Time

Time is the component of presentation strategies that refers to how much instruction is presented, how quickly, and how smoothly. These variables often directly impact student learning. For example, time is a central component and salient variable in Carroll's model of school learning (1963, 1989) and the effective instruction literature of the 1970s and 1980s, and current federal education policy seeks to improve educational outcomes through the efficient use of time (U.S. Department of Education, 1994; Individuals With Disabilities Education Improvement Act, 2004).

Learning itself can be viewed as a function of time. How quickly a student acquires new knowledge and becomes fluent with that knowledge is a measure of competency. Students with learning problems are particularly susceptible to processing time issues. Difficulties arise when instructional time is not appropriately matched to student needs, particularly when the student is not engaged during the lesson.

There are three major components of time:

1. Rate and pacing

2. Pausing

3. Allocated and engaged time

Rate and pacing refer to the speed and regularity of the presentation and practicing of new material. The speed of a lesson can determine not only the amount of material that is covered and the amount of practice in which students engage, but also the interest level of the students. Quickly paced lessons are more interesting, and a brisk tempo with frequent opportunities for students to respond and participate provides a sense of excitement and urgency to learning activities. Conversely, a pace that is too fast may lead to an instructor glossing over information without covering content. Therefore, a good fit between the time needed for learner processing and the pace needed for effective instruction is required to optimize learning time.

Pausing is the delay in time between instructional prompts and expected student responses. It can help to maintain a brisk rate of instruction and provide a rhythm in which students intently listen to the instruction and process the information prior to responding. Pausing can also be used to increase exposure to material through repetition. Providing an instructional prompt, such as "The Eiffel tower was nearly dismantled because . . . (pause)" following portions of instruction in a lesson can provide students the opportunity to consider the answer and create memory through active repetition of new knowledge.

Allocated time refers to the time dedicated to instruction and learning. Engaged time is the component of allocated time that reflects the time a student spends learning tasks. Allocated and engaged times vary dramatically across teachers, students, and tasks but both are correlated with successful learning. It is suggested that teachers maximize their instructional time to reflect a minimum of 50% active instruction, 35% active monitoring, and 15% or less organizing and managing (Stallings, 1986). The level of student engagement in learning tasks can be monitored and increased individually through a variety of self-monitoring techniques or the use of reinforcers contingent on levels of on-task behavior.

The amount of both allocated and engaged time should be assessed when students are struggling with learning problems. For example, increasing instruction time by 60 minutes will be ineffective if the student is not already engaged in learning during the current period of time provided for instruction. Conversely, increasing on-task learning by adding after-school or pullout instruction will be equally ineffective if the teacher's administrative responsibilities decrease the amount of time left for instruction.

Once allocated time is maximized and engaged time is evaluated, then the instructional elements of rate, pacing, and pausing can be incorporated into the learning process to further increase a student's motivation, engagement, and success. For example, Jack is a quick learner who rapidly completes his work and then disrupts the class. For Jack, allocated time and engaged time are not well matched because he has time left over to engage in nonproductive behavior. Meanwhile, Katie, another student in the class, is a slow processor with language, learning, and behavior problems. The teacher's quick presentation and questioning strategies are excellent for keeping the whole class on task, but Katie needs additional time before the teacher moves from one learning objective to the next. The teacher could accommodate both the need for classroom management and Katie's processing need by asking questions that have multiple answers and having Katie answer last, providing her the additional processing time she needs while answers are given by other students. Or, the teacher could ask the class to name five causes of the Mexican–American War and then call on Katie first so that no one will have previously given the more obvious answers.

Monitoring both instructional time and engaged time requires an awareness of how much time is spent on a variety of activities. Appropriate planning, self-recording, and self-evaluating of the use of time will allow teachers to more easily set realistic instructional goals and more readily make effective changes to curriculum or instruction. Students' engaged time can be assessed by routinely checking the level of student engagement— individually or in groups—by counting on- and off-task students. Or, for more detailed information on student engagement, the length of time spent on- and off-task can each be recorded.

Responding

Responding includes the part of instruction where teachers provide opportunities for students to participate by answering questions, restating instruction, or asking questions about content. The research on this loop of student response and teacher feedback via correction or confirmation demonstrates clear evidence of effectiveness in the opportunity-to-respond literature (Sutherland, Alder, Gunter, 2003; Sutherland & Wehby, 2001; Sutherland, Wehby, & Yoder, 2002) and also in the literature about feedback (Gunter, Shores, Jack, Denny, & DePaepe, 1994; Maggs, & Morgan, 1986; McLaughlin, 1992; Schloss, Harriman, & Pfefier, 1985).

The types and frequency of student responses and teacher feedback are fairly easy to assess and relatively pliable. With minimal training, a teacher can dramatically increase both the opportunities for student response and the immediacy and frequency of specific praise or corrective feedback provided during a lesson.

Evidence for Use

Effective instruction has been consistently demonstrated to increase student performance across demographic and disability variables. Structuring, time, and responding are all critical components of effective presentation strategies (Gallagher, 1972; Hawkins, 1988; Rieth, Polsgrove, Semmel, & Cohen, 1980; Rosenberg, Sindelar, & Stedt, 1985; Skinner, Johnson, Larkin, Lessley, & Glowacki, 1995; Sutherland et al., 2003; West & Sloane, 1986). The following studies summarize some of the key research findings associated with using presentation strategies as an intervention for students with learning and behavior problems or emotional–behavioral disabilities.

Hawkins, J. (1988). Antecedent pausing as a direct instruction tactic for adolescents with severe behavioral disorders. *Behavioral Disorders, 13*(4), 263–272.

Eight adolescents in a residential hospital learning setting, with severe behavioral disorders, were studied to evaluate the effectiveness of adding instructional pauses in lectures. Students were split into pairs, and teachers alternated between 4 minutes of instruction and 3-minute pauses, during which students practiced in their pairs. Seven of the eight students showed increases in their ability to identify verbs on their worksheets following intervention. Their improvement, as shown by geometric means, increased between 14% and 29%. Even the 1 student who did not want to participate and did not show improvement in the worksheets showed signs of covert learning, as more correct verbs appeared in his writing. Thus, instructional pauses may be an effective way of increasing learning and retention among both motivated students and those with severe behavioral problems.

Structuring

Belfiore, P. J., Lee, D. L., Scheeler, M. C., & Klein, D. (2002). Implications of behavioral momentum and academic achievement for students with behavior disorders: Theory, application, and practice. *Psychology in the Schools, 39*(2), 171–179.

This study examined the efficacy of using interventions derived from the behavioral momentum paradigm to transfer compliance from preferred tasks (i.e., single-digit addition problems) to nonpreferred tasks (i.e., multiple-digit addition problems). Two 10-year-old students—Lance, diagnosed with an emotional disturbance, and Megan, diagnosed with a learning disability—were asked during baseline to solve a series of nonpreferred tasks for which each student experienced a low probability of success that led to frustration, which manifested as disruptive behavior. During intervention, two methods were implemented: a traditional high-probability condition (TRAD-HP) and an escape from demand + high-probability (ESC-HP). For TRAD-HP, the students were asked to solve identical problems to the baseline set, but each nonpreferred task was preceded by three preferred tasks. For ESC-HP, the students were provided with a set of problems similar to the TRAD-HP condition—a series of three preferred tasks followed by one nonpreferred task—except that every other problem was crossed out (i.e., not to be solved), halving the amount of work. Results showed that the TRAD-HP intervention decreased latency to initiate problems in a series by 37% for Lance and 41% for Megan, relative to baseline. Also, the ESC-HP intervention decreased latencies by 46% and 39%, respectively. These findings reinforced the value of using high-probability sequences prior to nonpreferred tasks to reduce latency to initiate tasks, which can increase the rate of task completion and potentially improve learning by increasing the number of learning trials a student experiences.

Belfiore, P. J., Lee, D. L., Vargas, A. U., & Skinner, C. H. (1997). Effects of high-preference single-digit mathematics problem completion on multiple-digit mathematics problem performance. *Journal of Applied Behavior Analysis, 30*(2), 327–330.

This study examined the potential benefits of pairing preferred tasks with nonpreferred tasks. Participants were 2 female adolescent students in an alternative education school. Single-digit multiplication problems (preferred tasks) were completed prior to multiple-digit multiplication problems (nonpreferred tasks). Results showed a decrease in the latency of initiating completion of the low-preference problem when the preferred problems were administered first, supporting the claim that presenting preferred tasks before nonpreferred tasks can promote momentum in problem completion.

Dawson, L., Venn, M. L., & Gunter, P. L. (2000). The effects of teacher versus computer reading models. *Behavioral Disorders, 25*(2), 105–113.

This study examined the relationship between modeling and the reading performance of 4 elementary school students with emotional and behavior disorders (EBD). Reading passages of at least 200 words were divided into three sections, each comprising 33% of the total words, and assigned to one of three conditions (no modeling, teacher modeling, and computer modeling). Students in the no modeling group were simply asked to read aloud each passage, while students in the teacher modeling and computer groups listened to a passage read by either a teacher or computer (respectively) prior to reading the passage aloud into a tape recorder. Students were judged based on the number of words correctly read per minute and the average percentage of words read correctly. Results showed that the students read more fluently and accurately when presented with teacher modeling than with either computer modeling or no modeling, and that computer modeling produced higher fluency and accuracy rates than no modeling.

Time

Cybriwsky, C. A., & Schuster, J. W. (1990). Using constant time delay procedures to teach multiplication facts. *Remedial and Special Education, 11*(1), 54–59.

The purpose of this study was to extend existing research on constant time-delay methods by teaching multiplication facts to William, a 10-year-old student with learning disabilities. Fifteen targeted multiplication facts were separated into three sets with five additional known facts. They were taught during William's normal instructional period (i.e., training condition). The training consisted of presenting the first 10 facts in a set with a 0-second delay between the cue (i.e., student reading the multiplication question) and the controlling prompt (i.e., teacher stating the correct answer). Afterward, a 4-second delay was inserted between the cue and prompt, allowing William an opportunity to respond independently. Once the multiplication sets were learned, generalization was tested by randomly altering visual presentation (e.g., color, orientation on page), time of day, and persons presenting the cues. The results added to the data supporting the numerous advantages of using a constant time-delay method in teaching: minimal prep time, short session time, low percentage of student error in training, more positive teacher–student interactions, and a positive, game-like format for students.

McCurdy, B. L., Cundari, L., & Lentz, F. E. (1990). Enhancing instructional efficiency: An examination of time delay and the opportunity to observe instructions. *Education and Treatment of Children, 13*(3), 226–238.

The effectiveness of instructional presentation strategies for teaching unfamiliar words was examined using 2 elementary school boys diagnosed with serious emotional and behavior problems. Forty words were randomly assigned to either a trial-and-error or time-delay strategy condition. In the trial-and-error condition, the words were presented for 3 seconds; correct responses earned praise and incorrect responses resulted in verbal correction by the examiner. The time-delay strategy consisted of words presented and then verbalized correctly by the examiner at a delay ranging from 0 to 8 seconds. Results showed that performance improved substantially from baseline during both the trial-and-error and time-delay conditions, with a slightly higher improvement level for the time-delay strategy.

Responding

Gunter, P. L., Shores, R. E., Jack, S. L., Denny, R. K., & DePaepe, P. A. (1994). A case study of the effects of altering instructional interactions on the disruptive behavior of a child identified with severe behavior disorders. *Education and Treatment of Children, 17*(4), 435–444.

This case study examined the hypothesis that when student performance (i.e., task-related errors) indicates a lack of academic understanding, academic activities and teacher mands may serve as aversive stimuli. To test this hypothesis, researchers observed the instructional interaction between Tom, a 12-year-old male student with a severe behavior disorder, and his teacher during mathematics lessons. Observations during baseline indicated that a number of variables (e.g., academic level of materials, lack of positive attention) could be considered aversive stimuli and could be the cause of Tom's disruptive behavior, but the procedure for providing feedback indicated that Tom was being manded to correct errors that he did not have sufficient skill to correct. During intervention, all instructional procedures were maintained except the error feedback process; instead, the teacher was asked to provide correct answers prior to the mand. This process, discussed as a "Talk/Mand" procedure, provided an appropriate means of escape and an alternative to undesired escape behaviors. Disruptive behavior decreased from a mean of .28 during baseline to a mean of .09 during intervention. This study provided evidence that the manner in which information is presented by teachers during corrective feedback could prevent or decrease disruptive classroom behavior and increase compliance and overall academic performance.

Maggs, A., & Morgan, G. (1986). Effects of feedback on the academic engaged time of behaviour disordered learners. *Educational Psychology, 6*(4), 335–351.

This study examined the effects of feedback on on-task behavior and academic performance. Two elementary school children with behavior disorders participated in the study and were given three types of feedback: right-wrong, where feedback was provided for both on- and off-task behavior; right-blank, where feedback was provided only for on-task behavior; and wrong-blank, where feedback was provided only for off-task behavior. Feedback, in the form of a check mark for on-task behavior and a cross for off-task behavior, was given at 1-minute intervals over a 30-minute period. Results showed that both the right-wrong and wrong-blank conditions led to increased on-task behavior; however, they had no effect on academic task accuracy.

McLaughlin, T. F. (1992). Effects of written feedback in reading on behaviorally disordered students. *Journal of Educational Research, 85*(5), 312–316.

This study examined the effects of written feedback on five 10- and 11-year-old male students from a classroom for students with behavioral disorders. A multiple baseline design was used to measure the accuracy of reading performance. Teachers provided written feedback to students who read a passage (e.g., "You've really improved."). Results showed that reading accuracy was greater with written feedback than during the baseline condition, and students reported a preference for the feedback. Accuracy ranged from 5% to 80% during baseline and from 72% to 100% with written feedback, and the improvement was maintained for 1 year.

Schloss, P. J., Harriman, N. E., & Pfefier, K. (1985). Application of a sequential prompt reduction technique to the independent composition performance of behaviorally disordered youth. *Behavioral Disorders, 11*(1), 17–23.

This study examined the effects of prompting on the written language production of 3 adolescents in a class for socially and emotionally disturbed students. Two conditions were used: a baseline condition with random prompting and an instructional condition involving a prompt reduction strategy applied systematically. In the random prompting condition, students were given prompts in random order every 20 seconds until they began writing. In the prompt reduction (i.e., instructional) condition, students were given prompts in order from least intrusive (e.g., "You can do it.") to most intrusive (e.g., "Write this sentence verbatim."). Results showed that the students' independent writing skills increased in the instructional condition. A 60-day follow-up showed continued progress, even without teacher prompts.

Sutherland, K. S., & Wehby, J. H. (2001). Exploring the relationship between increased opportunities to respond to academic requests and the academic and behavioral outcomes of students with EBD: A review. *Remedial and Special Education, 22*(2), 113–121.

The purpose of this literature review was to examine the academic and behavior changes seen in students with emotional and behavior disorders (EBD) when the opportunities to respond (OTR) to academic requests were increased. The results of six major studies were analyzed, all single case design studies with 2–5 subjects per study (N=19, total), ranging from 6 to 18 years in age. The results of the studies indicated that increasing OTR will increase student academic performance and task engagement, and decrease inappropriate and disruptive behavior where measured.

Considerations

For Teaching

Effective instruction is a skill that takes practice. The variety of individual backgrounds and skills training that exists in the teaching profession makes the level of difficulty in acquiring such skill wide ranging. Also, effective instruction is not about rigid and inflexible rote memorization. While many teachers may come from a training program where this type of instructional vocabulary is familiar and comfortable, some teacher-training programs operate from a more constructivist approach, where the expectation of structure and a mandate for explicitness may be seen as negative features of instruction. Some teachers are trained to believe that explicit expectations will minimize students' natural creativity and that they will prevent the development of problem-solving abilities, limit students' appreciation for the subject matter, or dampen the joy of learning.

For Culture and Language Differences

Rate and pacing are particularly critical for second-language learners; implementing think time allows more opportunity for accessing information and responding to instruction. The additional time required for processing is facilitated by careful control of time use through rate, pacing, and pausing. Instructional time and time on task are essential matters for all students regardless of culture or language but may be more salient for students with limited in background knowledge or who are accessing the material in a second language. The judicious use of additional time is warranted for these populations.

For Age and Developmental Level

Scaffolding is especially important for the more complex academic tasks encountered in middle and high school, particularly when student reading level may interfere with the comprehension and application of content area instruction (e.g., literary or historical comparisons). Models, examples, figures, and questions that guide students' thinking are all examples of the types of assisted learning that take place when utilizing scaffolding.

C. Task-Selection Strategies

In addition to advance organizers and presentation strategies, teachers can also focus on task-selection strategies to improve student learning. Task-selection strategies, as their name suggests, focus on the tasks that students are asked to engage in. Tasks that (1) are relevant to the lesson at hand; (2) provide opportunities for students to become familiar with new material, practice skills, and apply knowledge; and (3) match students' abilities and goals with performance expectations will facilitate learning (see Center, Deitz, & Kaufman, 1982; Clarke, Dunlap, Foster-Johnson, Childs, Wilson, White, et al., 1995; Cosden, Gannon, & Haring, 1995; Rosenberg et al., 1985).

The range of selectable tasks will vary by grade level and content area. For early grades, these tasks may include art, representations, puzzles, music, dance, and song, in addition to completing worksheets or writing answers on paper. As children age and the curriculum progresses, tasks become more heavily dependent on verbal skills and written expression. As a result, the complexities of the curriculum for later grades seldom allows for representations without accompanying verbal or written descriptions.

Implementation

The goal of improving task selection is to effectively match learner abilities with curriculum requirements. Student interest can be a component in motivation and in increasing learning. Task-selection strategies typically include the following:

1. Relevance to the curriculum or lesson

2. Opportunities to assimilate newly acquired knowledge

3. Appropriateness for the level of student skill and development

4. Interest to the student

The tasks offered for student selection should be relevant to the curriculum or learning objectives, and consideration should be given to ensure that learning goals are not compromised when implementing task-selection strategies. Additionally, tasks that are relevant to life beyond the classroom are also beneficial. Sometimes this linking can be accomplished through time spent explaining the connections between task expectations and contexts other than those of the classroom (e.g., as it appears on tests or in assignments). The tasks should be at the appropriate difficulty level for the student or students involved while still maintaining a level of instructional rigor to meet academic expectations. Tasks below a 60% accuracy rate cause frustration, while those above 80% cause boredom. This narrow band of appropriate matching facilitates interest, acquisition, and stamina for task completion. The tasks should be interesting to foster student participation and attention. It is important to note, however, that while student interest is one component that is helpful in task-selection strategies, it is unlikely that all students will be equally willing to engage in all activities or have the same level of interest in a task. Overall, tasks that are attractive to students, have a reasonable length, and present engaging materials are ideal.

Evidence for Use

Various task-selection strategies have demonstrated a capacity to improve academic performance across a wide range of students and subject areas. Functional assessment–based academic antecedents (i.e., using functional-based assessments to determine successful and unsuccessful academic strategies), such as allowing students choice in task selection, creating or choosing tasks that match a student's interest area, and matching the difficulty of the task to the ability level of a student, have been shown to improve student performance. The following studies summarize some of the key research findings associated with using task-related strategies as intervention for students with academic and behavior problems.

Center, D. B., Deitz, S. M., & Kaufman, M. E. (1982). Student ability, task difficulty, and inappropriate classroom behavior: A study of children with behavior disorders. *Behavior Modification, 6*(3), 355–374.

The focus of this study was to examine the relationship between academic task level and student ability, specifically, how a mismatch between the two may lead to an increase in inappropriate classroom behavior in children with behavior disorders and how employing a reinforcement contingency on task accuracy may affect the mismatched condition. In this study, 15 male students with behavior disorders, aged between 8 and 12 years, were evaluated to determine their current level of math ability and classroom behavioral status. They were then randomized into three groups: two experimental groups and one control. Through a series of five phases, the two experimental groups were given alternating combinations of success- and failure-level assignments, with and without the reinforcement contingency. The control group received success-level assignments, with and without the reinforcement contingency. Results indicated that matching task difficulty to student ability can decrease incidence of inappropriate classroom behavior. Also, while the study results indicated that the reinforcement contingency appeared to have little effect on inappropriate behaviors during mismatched conditions, the authors noted that the data from the match condition suggest that the reinforcing properties of the contingency employed were limited.

Clarke, S., Dunlap, G., Foster-Johnson, L., Childs, K. E., Wilson, D., White, R., et al. (1995). Improving the conduct of students with behavioral disorders by incorporating student interests into curricular activities. *Behavioral Disorders, 20*(4), 221–237.

This study investigated the effects of matching learning tasks with student interests on the behavior of 4 elementary school students with various behavioral and emotional problems. Direct observation was used to monitor behavior while the students completed both standard assignments and assignments of interest to them. Results demonstrated a reduction in problem behavior, an increase in desirable behavior, and an increase in student productivity.

Cosden, M., Gannon, C., & Haring, T. G. (1995). Teacher-control versus student-control over choice of task and reinforcement for students with severe behavior problems. *Journal of Behavioral Education, 5*(1), 11–27.

The effects of task-selection strategies on academic performance were studied in 3 male adolescents with severe behavior problems. The strategies included: student selection of reinforcers, student selection of tasks, student selection of both reinforcers and tasks, and teacher selection of reinforcers and tasks. Results indicated that student selection of reinforcers or tasks increased student completion and accuracy rates of assignments. Moreover, student selection of both reinforcers and tasks produced even greater rates of completion and accuracy of assignments.

Jolivette, K., Lassman, K. A., & Wehby, J. H. (1998). Functional assessment for academic instruction for a student with emotional and behavioral disorders: A case study. *Preventing School Failure, 43*(1), 19–23.

In this case study, a functional assessment was used to determine math intervention strategies for a second-grade student diagnosed with emotional and behavioral disorders. After medical and sensory conditions were ruled out, structured interviews with the teacher, record reviews, error analysis, and A-B-C (antecedent-behavior-consequence) observations were used to generate a hypothesis for the student's difficulty in solving addition and subtraction problems. The assessment indicated that the student was unable to distinguish between addition and subtraction items. Based on this theory, three intervention strategies were developed to determine which would best provide a strategy for discriminating between problem types: a visual advance organizer, a strategy called "counting up," and a manipulative organizer. After implementing each of the interventions, results indicated that the counting up strategy was the most effective (i.e., produced the highest accuracy rate) of the group of strategies. Functional assessment was determined to be a highly compatible (e.g., uses data already collected by teachers) and easily integrated (e.g., uses existing academic strategies) method for identifying and developing the most efficient and effective interventions for students with academic difficulties.

Jolivette, K., Wehby, J. H., & Hirsch, L. (1999). Academic strategy identification for students exhibiting inappropriate classroom behaviors. *Behavioral Disorders, 24*(3), 210–221.

This study examined the use of a functional assessment with a structural analysis to identify effective mathematics strategies for 3 boys, aged 9 and 10 years, who were receiving services for emotional and behavioral problems and academic difficulties. Information about each student was obtained using a combination of teacher reports, direct observation, preference assessment, and error analysis of math problems. From the data collected, three academic strategies were chosen and then implemented for each student. After implementation, the strategy proven most effective (i.e., producing the highest accuracy rate) was chosen as the long-term intervention strategy. Results showed that all 3 students demonstrated a significant increase in math accuracy when completing problems using the strategy identified during the assessment process, indicating the effectiveness of using academic strategy identification to develop targeted interventions for specific academic difficulties.

Kern, L., Delaney, B., Clarke, S., Dunlap, G., & Childs, K. (2001). Improving the classroom behavior of students with emotional and behavioral disorders using individualized curricular modifications. *Journal of Emotional and Behavioral Disorders, 9*(4), 239–247.

This study examined the effects of modifying task requirements for 2 males, aged 11 years, diagnosed with an emotional and behavior disorder. A functional behavioral assessment was conducted to determine the classroom activities commonly associated with the problem behavior. Results from the assessment indicated an increase in problem behaviors during paper and pencil activities. Task engagement and disruptive behavior were monitored during assigned daily writing activities using a traditional medium (pencil and paper) and a preferred medium (computer). The 2 students averaged 27% and 70% engagement during traditional-medium assignments and 97% and 88% during preferred-medium assignments. Modest positive effects were shown for reducing disruptive behavior and increasing academic productivity.

Lee, Y.-Y., Sugai, G., & Horner, R. H. (1999). Using an instructional intervention to reduce problem and off-task behaviors. *Journal of Positive Behavior Interventions, 1*(4), 195–204.

This study investigated the relationship between the rate of problem behavior and classroom instruction tailored to increase task accuracy. Participants were 2 males, aged 9 years, with emotional or behavior disorders. Functional assessment determined that problem and off-task behavior was maintained as an escape from difficult tasks. Using a within-subjects alternating treatment design, the students participated in two conditions: working independently and receiving individualized instruction on skills that matched their ability levels. When no instruction was given, accuracy on difficult tasks was 0% and problem and off-task behavior rates ranged from 15% to 58%. In contrast, when instruction was given, accuracy rates ranged from 84% to 95% and problem and off-task behavior rates ranged from 0% to 11%.

Penno, D. A., Frank, A. R., & Wacker, D. P. (2000). Instructional accommodations for adolescent students with severe emotional or behavioral disorders. *Behavioral Disorders, 25*(4), 325–343.

This study examined the effects of instructional modification on academic performance and classroom behavior for 3 adolescent boys attending a school for students with severe emotional and behavioral disorders. Instructional modifications were hypothesized for each student based on classroom observation and student and teacher interviews. The modifications (e.g., completing assignments on a computer instead of on paper, completing assignments with a peer tutor) were implemented, resulting in an increase in academic performance and a decrease in problem behavior.

Rosenberg, M. S., Sindelar, P. T., & Stedt, J. (1985). The effects of supplemental on-task contingencies on the acquisition of simple and difficult academic tasks. *The Journal of Special Education, 19*(2), 189–203.

This study examined the relationship between reinforcement contingencies and the skill acquisition of 44 students, aged between 8 and 12.5 years, who were identified as having either learning disabilities, emotional disorders, or mild mental retardation and were frequently off task. Students were taught either simple or difficult tasks, with half of the participants receiving reinforcement for on-task behavior and correct answers and half receiving reinforcement for correct answers only. Time on task was measured daily, as was academic performance on seatwork assignments. Results showed no significant difference in academic performance on simple tasks between the two reinforcement contingencies. Academic performance on difficult tasks was greatly influenced, however, with students who received both attention and performance reinforcement earning significantly higher scores than those receiving only performance reinforcement.

Considerations

For Teaching

Teachers sometimes find the issue of student choice in conflict with their authority in the classroom. However, it is important to realize that choice is not about students being in charge. Rather, choice is about providing equally acceptable selections that are educationally appropriate. In doing so, student needs are met through selection based on either interest or difficulty level. Task differentiation, then, can be a way to minimize resistance, prevent failure, eliminate frustration and learned helplessness, and create a culture of responsiveness.

For Culture and Language Differences

Tasks that range in difficulty level or language acquisition requirements facilitate learning by providing students who have learning difficulties with opportunities to complete reasonable assignments, access the material, and demonstrate mastery. Consideration should be given not to label assignments as easy or hard or to shame students based on ability levels.

For Age and Developmental Level

Task choice is most commonly used in early childhood settings where free-time periods provide students an opportunity to engage in preferred activities or to demonstrate skills in ways they find most comfortable. Although less common in secondary settings, the use of choice and variations in difficulty provide the same opportunities for older students and should be encouraged. Teachers of middle and secondary students are typically trained first in subject or content area and second in pedagogy or teaching methods, so teachers of older grade levels may have less exposure to methods that encourage flexibility in how students demonstrate mastery of content knowledge or engage in the curriculum.

II. Peer-Mediated Interventions

In addition to teacher-based strategies, peer-based strategies can be an effective way to help students who are having academic problems. Peer-mediated interventions typically involve training students on how to be tutors and prescribing what is to be taught. After training, these students typically work with other students who have been experiencing difficulty learning a subject or content area. The peer-mediated interventions included in this chapter are peer tutoring and classwide peer tutoring.

A. Peer Tutoring

Peer tutoring is the process of students assisting other students in learning through teaching (Goodlad & Hirst, 1990; Topping, 2001). Peer tutoring is a reciprocal process and has been found to improve learning in both the tutee and the tutor (Franca & Kerr, 1990; Maher, 1982; Scruggs, Mastropieri, & Richter, 1985). Peer tutoring is also known by several other names, including peer-assisted learning, peer monitoring, peer facilitation, and peer-mediated instruction.

Implementation

Peer tutoring has goals that are both academic and social in nature. Goals can be affective, classroom climate-related, or academic. Here we discuss the goals of improved academic performance (both individually and classwide). Peer tutoring also provides an opportunity for students to participate in semi-social activities with structured relationships. Peer tutoring can take many forms. Students can be paired with others who are on different academic levels or the same academic level, or pairings can be made between students of different ages. However, as discussed by Good and Brophy (2003) and Greenwood, Delquadri, and Carta (1988), and for the purposes of this discussion, peer tutoring must contain the seven essential elements listed below. These elements cover both the setup for peer tutoring and the behaviors used by the peer tutors in their pairs. The following elements must be incorporated with the features outlined in the procedures presented in Figure 6.4:

1. Teacher-established pairs

2. Teacher-established procedures via explanation and practice

3. Tutor-to-tutee problem presentation

4. Tutee-to-tutor problem solution

5. Tutor-to-tutee feedback (praise, encouragement, corrections)

6. Teacher monitoring of peer tutoring time by circulating in classroom

7. Teacher reinforcement of appropriate tutor and tutee behavior

The teacher may establish age-based (i.e., same- or different-aged students) as well as ability-based (i.e., same or differing ability levels) pairs. No matter the arrangement method, the procedures for tutoring are taught, modeled, and practiced during the first stage. Once established, the peer-tutoring sessions can be implemented.

During the sessions, the tutor first provides an example of the problem or question. The tutee then attempts the problem solution. Based on the response, the tutor praises the correct answer, records the point or points, and presents the next problem, or, if the tutee made an incorrect response, requests a second attempt by saying "try again." After the second response attempt, the tutor either praises a correct response or provides the correct answer and moves on to the next problem or question. Points for a correct answer on the first attempt would be more than for a correct answer given on a second attempt. For example, a fifth-grade social studies class that is studying U.S. national monuments may have pairs of equal skill level. Using the established procedures for the tutoring session, the exchange may resemble the following:

Teacher/Tutor: "What four presidents are featured on Mount Rushmore?"

Student: "Washington, Adams, Roosevelt, and Lincoln."

Teacher/Tutor: "Good try, but you only named three of the four correctly: Washington, Roosevelt, and Lincoln. Who are the four presidents featured on Mount Rushmore?"

Student: "Washington, Roosevelt, Lincoln. And, Jefferson?"

Tutor: "Correct. Good job. George Washington, Thomas Jefferson, Theodore Roosevelt, and Abraham Lincoln."

In the example, the points system for correct responses could be 2 points for each correct president's name, 1 point for a correct name on the second try, and 0 points if the tutee does not provide a correct answer and the tutor has to move on. In this case, the tutee would get a total of 7 points.

As with most academic interventions, considerable attention should be given to the preparation and planning stages to ensure a well-structured program. For peer tutoring, this process begins by student matching and student training. Scripts and organizational notebooks are important to facilitate smooth working of groups. Practicing procedures and using points for both tutor and tutee engagement and skill are essential for a well-structured program.

Figure 6.4 Procedural steps for the application of peer tutoring

1. Define the tutoring context, such as when tutoring will occur, its duration, and the general rules that will apply to the tutoring sessions.

2. Define the objectives of the tutoring program for the students. Objectives can be written academic or social goals, and can be individual or group based, but should include both tutor and tutee learning.

3. Choose the subject or content area that will be taught during the tutoring program.

4. Notify parents that peer tutoring is going to be implemented in the class. This notice should include information about the purpose of peer tutoring, the role of the students involved, the date tutoring will begin, the skills that will be practiced or taught, and the contact information for further questions.

5. Write a lesson plan for the tutors. This plan should be scripted for reading and following directions, including the examples and the correction procedures.

6. Select and match participants. Assign a tutor to one or two students for a specific period of time. The period of time should be long enough for the tutor and tutee to become comfortable with each other and for the instruction to complete a sequence. All students should rotate through tutor or tutee positions equally.

7. Train the tutors. In the first tutoring session, the teacher models being the tutor. That is, the teacher actually does the tutoring during this lesson. While modeling, the teacher assesses the tutors' understanding of the process.

8. Monitor the tutoring process. During subsequent sessions, the teacher observes peer-tutoring sessions for student focus, understanding of the process, and student progress.

9. Evaluate the program by determining if the initial objectives have been met.

10. Provide feedback to students and other interested persons (e.g., parents, school administrators) about how the program went.

Evidence for Use

Peer tutoring has a lengthy history of success (with origins dating to the mentoring proposals of Plato) and has demonstrated its strength as an intervention in elementary, middle, and high schools in a number of content areas. The entire body of literature on peer mentoring across student populations is quite extensive; therefore, the following studies summarize some of the key research findings associated with using peer tutoring as an intervention for students who have learning and behavior problems.

Franca, V. M., & Kerr, M. M. (1990). Peer tutoring among behaviorally disordered students: Academic and social benefits to tutor and tutee. *Education and Treatment of Children, 13*(2), 109–128.

This study examined the effects of peer tutoring on 8 male students, ranging in age from 13 to 16 years, who were experiencing academic difficulties and a wide range of behavioral problems. The students were divided into four groups of two, and tutors underwent training prior to the intervention. Results showed significant increases in academic success, attitudes toward math, and positive social interactions between tutors and tutees. Academic improvement was also shown for tutors.

Maher, C. A. (1982). Behavioral effects of using conduct problem adolescents as cross-age tutors. *Psychology in the Schools, 19*(3), 360–364.

In this study of cross-age tutoring, 18 high school students (11 males, 7 females), aged 15 to 18 years, were randomly assigned to one of three conditions: participate as a tutor, participate as a tutee, or participate in a group counseling program led by a school psychologist. Outcomes examined in this study included academic performance, frequency of disciplinary referrals, and attendance. Results showed that students who acted as tutors had significantly higher grades in language arts and social studies, fewer days absent, and fewer disciplinary referrals than students receiving peer tutoring or group counseling.

Scruggs, T. E., Mastropieri, M. A., & Richter, L. (1985). Peer tutoring with behaviorally disordered students: Social and academic benefits. *Behavioral Disorders, 10*(4), 283–294.

This study reviewed the efficacy of tutoring programs involving students diagnosed with behavioral disorders by examining the research findings of 17 peer-tutoring intervention research studies. Tutoring subjects included reading, math, spelling, and social skills. The review focused on the academic and social benefits of each study, concluding that both tutees and tutors benefit academically and socially from peer-tutoring interventions, specific to the subject area(s). However, the benefits in these studies did not appear to extend to the student's overall social functioning or self-esteem.

Considerations

For Teaching

Peer tutoring requires a commitment of time in order to pair students, write scripts, prepare materials, and teach procedures, but the outcomes are worth the initial investment. Students receive much larger slices of instructional time and engaged time as well as additional opportunities to respond and receive corrective feedback. Also, the peer-tutoring structure allows the teacher to become the instructional leader or facilitator, monitoring a classroom of students who are teaching and learning in pairs, and permits the teacher to provide more one-on-one instruction. In addition to these advantages, materials can be reused and modifications on pairings or rotation of pairs of students can be made in an ongoing manner.

For Culture and Language Differences

Peer tutoring has a distinct literature on its effectiveness for second-language learners. Use in rural and urban schools shows evidence of effectiveness in a variety of classroom settings, making peer tutoring a strong intervention for classroom use.

For Age and Developmental Level

Peer tutoring and cross-age tutoring both appear to work well with early grades. Naturally, the instructor should consider the developmental level of the students, the types of tasks assigned, and the training elements involved, all of which might make peer-tutoring instruction less feasible for very young children.

B. Classwide Peer Tutoring

Classwide peer tutoring (CWPT) is a form of peer tutoring in which students in the same class help one another during the lesson (Greenwood et al., 1988). Even more narrowly defined than peer tutoring, CWPT has very specific procedural requirements and a definitive body of literature. CWPT is based on the principles of maximizing student engaged time, providing frequent opportunities for practice, increasing rates of student response and feedback loops, and minimizing errors in learning and off-task behavior. CWPT also incorporates an element of progress monitoring by recording performance over time.

Implementation

Like peer-tutoring, CWPT focuses on improving the academic performance of students. However, whereas peer-tutoring can be implemented in a variety of settings, CWPT is designed for classroom settings and can be used to facilitate large-group instruction. The defining characteristics of CWPT include the following (Terry, 2005):

1. Peer teams in any subject matter

2. Competitive partnerships where peer teams are a part of a larger team

3. Tutors and tutees engage in assignments, provide feedback, score and record points

Implementation of CWPT should begin with an assessment of student skill levels so that effective tutor–tutee pairs can be formed and so that skill levels of classroom teams can be equal. Prior to beginning CWPT, create and prepare the tutor–tutee folders with appropriate materials for the lesson. The materials should provide directions for the presentation of practice work (e.g., how to query for spelling words, how to give correct feedback) and contain the rules for points scoring and team play, as well as guidelines for tutor–tutee interaction (e.g., rules for positive, reciprocal relationships).

At the start of CWPT in the classroom, divide the students into the two teams previously determined during skill level assessment and into their first set of tutor–tutee pairs. Tutor–tutee pairs, assigned by the teacher, should rotate frequently so that no one student is paired with another for an extended amount of time. Class teams consist of multiple tutor–tutee pairs, totaling one-half of the larger class, and should rotate on a regular basis as well.

Each CWPT session should last for 15 minutes and occur two to three times a week. During a session, each student in the tutor–tutee pair acts as tutor for 5 minutes, with 5 minutes at the end of the session reserved for tallying the points earned by the pairs and each team (both recorded on a point chart). Individuals can earn points as either tutors or tutees by getting correct answers, giving positive feedback, following directions, and working well within pairs. Like individuals, teams earn points for correct responses, positive feedback from tutor to tutee, and accurate tutoring.

The teams compete against each other to earn the most points, which are compiled after each session and totaled at the end of each week. Neither teams nor individual students are penalized for skill differences because both teams have an equal distribution of student skill levels. One common scoring procedure is to have the tutor provide feedback (i.e., by reading from the materials) for correct or incorrect answers and to assign 2 points for correct answers, 1 point for an answer that was initially incorrect but corrected after feedback from the tutor, and 0 points for incorrect answers left uncorrected after feedback from the tutor. An outline of the procedural steps for implementing classwide peer tutoring is provided in Figure 6.5.

Figure 6.5 Procedural steps for the application of classwide peer tutoring

1. Create and prepare the tutor–tutee folders with appropriate materials for the lesson.

2. Review the tutor–tutee rules with the students.

3. Create two large teams within a class that are equal in terms of the students' skill levels.

4. Assign tutor–tutee pairs (these will rotate within the larger team).

5. Monitor the scoring used by the students.

6. Switch roles after 5 minutes (with the tutor becoming the tutee and vice versa).

7. Record points on a class chart.

Evidence for Use

Classwide peer tutoring has demonstrated success in reading, spelling, math, and writing for students of all ages (preschool to high school) and across settings (both urban and rural schools). CWPT has also demonstrated effectiveness with English-language learners, students with disabilities, and students who are at risk due to socioeconomic disadvantages. CWPT interventions increase the completion and accuracy rates of classwork, provide more opportunities for practice, and increase time spent on task. The following studies summarize some of the key research findings associated with using classwide peer tutoring as an intervention for students with learning problems.

Chun, C. C., & Winter, S. (1999). Classwide peer tutoring with or without reinforcement: Effects on academic responding, content coverage, achievement, intrinsic interest and reported project experiences. *Educational Psychology, 19*(2), 191–205.

The effects of CWPT with reinforcement (CWPT+R) and CWPT without reinforcement (CWPT-R) on the spelling performance of 77 Chinese students were studied. The reinforcement condition consisted of praise after correct responses, points given for proper tutoring behavior (points were posted in the classroom, and teams competed against each other), and certificates for the winning team. The CWPT-R condition did not include any of these measures. Both CWPT approaches led to improvements in spelling performance; however, the CWPT+R group made greater learning gains than did the CWPT-R students. The researchers hypothesized that the increased gains of the CWPT+R group were a result of higher rates of responding.

Fuchs, D., Fuchs, L. S., & Burish, P. (2000). Peer-assisted learning strategies: An evidence-based practice to promote reading achievement. *Learning Disabilities Research and Practice, 15*(2), 85–91.

This article offers support for the efficacy of peer-assisted learning strategies (PALS), an intervention that aims to strengthen the capacity of mainstream education to meet the academic needs of a broader range of students, specifically in the area of reading. PALS was designed for use in Grades 2 through 6 and involves students taking turns as tutor and tutee and providing corrective feedback to each other. Several previous studies have shown that compared to students receiving conventional reading instruction, PALS students demonstrated greater improvement in fluency, accuracy, and comprehension. The authors have also had some success in establishing PALS as a viable intervention for younger children and high school students.

Fuchs, D., Fuchs, L. S., Mathes, P. G., & Simmons, D. C. (1997). Peer-assisted learning strategies: Making classrooms more responsive to diversity. *American Educational Research Journal, 34*(1), 174–206.

Forty classrooms participated in this study examining the effects of CWPT on the reading skills of three types of learners: low achievers with and without disabilities and average learners. Twenty classrooms implemented the peer-tutoring program for 15 weeks (35 minutes, three times per week); the other 20 classrooms did not. The three learner types were represented in each class and were measured pretreatment and posttreatment in reading achievement using the Comprehensive Reading Assessment Battery. Results indicated that reading progress was significantly greater in the peer-tutoring environment, regardless of the type of learner.

Fuchs, L. S., & Fuchs, D. (1995). Acquisition and transfer effects of classwide peer-assisted learning strategies in mathematics for students with varying learning histories. *School Psychology Review, 24*(4), 604–621.

This study examined the effects of peer-assisted learning strategies (PALS), an intervention that involves students taking turns as tutor and tutee and providing corrective feedback to each other, on three types of mathematics students: average-achieving, low-achieving, and low-achieving with an identified learning disability. Forty general educators were randomly assigned to either incorporate PALS into their mathematics instruction (n = 20) or to use regular mathematics-instruction curriculum (n = 20). Students in the PALS treatment outperformed those in the contrast group across types of learning abilities. Additionally, teachers who implemented PALS indicated many advantages, such as increased capacity to respond to unique learning needs and more efficient classroom organization.

Greenwood, C. R., & Delquadri, J. (1995). Classwide peer tutoring and the prevention of school failure. *Preventing School Failure, 39*(4), 21–25.

This article discussed a longitudinal study of at-risk first-graders who received CWPT in Grades 1 through 4 as compared to an equally at-risk control group who did not receive CWPT. Both academic and behavioral outcomes were assessed at various points over 12 years. By sixth grade, fewer students in the CWPT group had received special services (academic or behavioral). By 11th grade, students in the CWPT group had a lower school dropout rate. These results suggested that teaching methods can greatly influence a student's academic success and may be critical in preventing early school failure.

Maheady, L., Harper, G. F., & Sacca, K. (1998). A classwide peer tutoring system in a secondary, resource room program for the mildly handicapped. *Journal of Research and Development in Education, 21*(3), 76–83.

CWPT was implemented in two secondary classrooms for mildly handicapped (MH) students in this study examining CWPT's effect on student performance on weekly social studies tests. Participants were 20 MH students between the ages of 14 and 19. Students were randomly paired to tutor each other during daily 30-minute sessions. Results showed that in Classroom 1 and Classroom 2 mean test scores increased an average of 20 and 8 points, respectively, from the first baseline and an average of 17 and 29 points, respectively, over the second baseline. Additionally, student responses to a study questionnaire indicated that the majority of participants reported both academic and social benefits from the experience.

Considerations

For Teaching

Classwide peer tutoring has many of the same preliminary issues as peer tutoring, such as preparation time and considerations for student abilities, curriculum levels, and pairings. It also has implementation issues, such as the need for close monitoring of student engagement and classroom behavior during tutoring. However, classwide peer tutoring also includes competition among teams. The effects of competition can sometimes include covert behaviors such as cheating or undermining of peer relationships (e.g., "I don't want Joe on my team; he brings our scores down."). The rotation of pairs ensures some degree of equality for all individuals, and team points are awarded. Matching the teams so that each team has a similarly distributed group of student scores ensures greater equality as well. Another possible solution is to concentrate on point levels rather than a win/lose system of reinforcement. Additionally, the use of a raffle for any team members that beat a previous score or achieve above a certain level can be an effective deterrent for the drawbacks to competitiveness. Strong monitoring of the peer-tutoring process is important, as is the distribution of points for appropriate behavior, so that verbal encouragement is worth as much as an accurate answer.

III. Self-Mediated Interventions

Self-mediated interventions are techniques that students can use individually. The learning techniques or strategies included in this chapter help teach students to store, retrieve, and generalize information for academic task completion and to manage their own behavior and learning (Alberto & Troutman, 2003; Coyne, Kame'enui, & Simmons, 2001; Schumaker & Deshler, 1992; Schumaker, Deshler, Alley, Warner, & Denton, 1982). These self-mediated strategies are not instinctive and must be explicitly taught before independent use can be expected (Good & Brophy, 2003).

Strategies discussed in this chapter include cognitive organizers (i.e., concept maps, knowledge maps, concept diagrams), mnemonics, self-monitoring, self-instruction, and reprocessing strategies (i.e., summarization; paraphrasing; cover, copy, and compare [CCC]; and self-questioning).

A. Cognitive Organizers

A variety of curriculum can be supported through the use of cognitive organizers. They aid students by structuring learning, identifying relationships between concepts and facts, presenting the sequence of instruction, and providing a method of self-monitoring and self-questioning (Rosenshine, 1995). Cognitive organizers, also referred to as maps, diagrams, and webs, are used to represent intricate concepts and their relationships in a consistent and concrete manner (Bulgren, Lenz, Schumaker, Deshler, & Marquis, 2002). These organizers come in many different forms with their structures often determined by a range of factors, including the information being presented, the goals of instruction (e.g., recall of dates, recognition of conceptual relationships), and the educational and developmental levels of the student or classroom. However, in order to use cognitive organizers effectively, a student must have the prerequisite skills needed to apply or create organizational structures. These skills can be taught or scaffolded by providing outlines and graphics.

For example, a teacher could use a hierarchical structure to determine prior student knowledge. First, the teacher would draw on the board a large circle with arrows radiating from it to smaller circles. Then, the teacher would write the main topic in the large circle and ask the students to name facts about the topic, writing their answers in the smaller circles. To present information such as dates or times in a sequential manner, teachers might provide directional cognitive organizers composed of several blank information boxes connected by arrows. To aid in the comparison or contrasting of two or more ideas, multiple titled information boxes might be used, providing an organizational structure for easily viewing the comparison of overall concepts, the shared or contrasting characteristics of those concepts, a summary statement of these characteristics, and any concept extensions (Bulgren et al., 2002).

Implementation

The goal of cognitive organizers is to help students learn concepts, identify associations, and understand curriculum content through graphic representations. The structure of the organizer can take several different forms, including structures that are hierarchical, directional, or comparative. The information boxes are often represented by rectangles, ovals, or circles, and are often used to represent concept names, definitions, main ideas, subtopics, or similarities and differences. These boxes are connected by lines or arrows, representing the flow or logical sequence of the various pieces of information. The basic elements of cognitive organizers include the following:

1. Structure

2. Information boxes

3. Connecting lines or arrows

The focus of the initial phase of implementation is the structural design and purpose of the cognitive organizer. The teacher chooses a structure appropriate for the lesson content and provides the students with a blank copy of the organizer prior to instruction, explaining its purpose within the context of the lesson (Crank & Bulgren, 1993). Then, the teacher explains the steps in completing the cognitive organizer. For example, these steps could include listening to the lecture (or skimming the material), writing the name of the main concept in the primary box, writing the name of the subtopics in the boxes connected to the main concept and listing some characteristics or facts about them, and, when appropriate, comparing and contrasting subtopics.

The goal of the second phase of implementation is for the students to master verbalizing the procedures for using or completing a given cognitive organizer. The teacher writes the steps on the board or overhead projector and models each step with verbalization. For instance, the teacher might write "Ocean Life" in the main concept box and then say, "How many kinds of ocean life are there? Let's see, plants and animals should cover it," while simultaneously writing "plants" and "animals" in the subtopic information boxes. The teacher provides feedback as the students complete their own copies, saying the steps aloud. Later, each completed cognitive organizer can be used as a presentation or study guide for self-questioning or writing a prompt/outline. This process is repeated until the students can name the steps for using the given organizer without teacher prompting.

The final phase of implementation focuses on independent use and practice of the strategy. The teacher instructs the students to complete the same type of cognitive organizer for a similar lesson while using silent self-talk. During this time, the teacher monitors and provides feedback as needed.

For generalization of the cognitive organizer learned, the teacher and students can brainstorm different subjects or assignments in which a given concept organizer can be used. After lists are generated, further discussion can help isolate best-practice models for those assignments or learning situations most often experienced by the students. An outline of the procedural steps for implementing cognitive organizers to aid instruction is provided in Figure 6.6.

Figure 6.6 Procedural steps for the application of cognitive organizers

1. Explain to students the purpose and rationale for using cognitive organizers.

2. Give the students a blank cognitive organizer.

3. Guide the students to set individual academic goals.

4. Teach the steps for using the cognitive organizer in a visual manner by writing the steps on the board or an overhead projector.

5. Model the use of the strategy to students by completing a blank organizer.

6. Ask students to practice using the cognitive organizer independently while verbalizing their decision making.

7. Provide feedback as the students practice using the steps, asking students to name and explain each step.

8. Have students present their completed cognitive organizers to a parent, teacher, or the class.

9. Instruct the students to use the cognitive organizer as a study guide (or writing outline, etc.).

10. Brainstorm with the students, identifying different subjects or assignments in which the cognitive organizer can be used.

Evidence for Use

After the necessary skills are taught and practiced repeatedly, cognitive organizers can be generalized and used independently by students in multiple classroom settings or content areas. Teaching students with learning problems to use cognitive organizers has been found to increase reading comprehension, improve independent reading of content area texts, and increase concept understanding (Babyak, Koorland, & Mathes, 2000; Blankenship, Ayres, & Langone, 2005; Bulgren, Schumaker, & Deshler, 1988; Rosenshine, 1995). Cognitive organizers can also be constructed on the computer for students who are motivated by technology. Using computer-based cognitive organizers has been found to increase reading comprehension (Blankenship et al., 2005; Boon, Fore, Ayres, & Spencer, 2005), but it is unclear if the increase is due to the presentation method used for the organizer (i.e., computer administration) or the organizer itself. The following studies summarize some of the key research findings associated with using cognitive organizers as an intervention for students with learning problems.

Alvermann, D. E. (1981). The compensatory effect of graphic organizers on descriptive text. *Journal of Educational Research, 75*(1), 44–48.

This study examined whether graphic organizers aided recall of text for a group of 114 high school students. In two experimental conditions, the same information was presented two different ways. One presented the information in a comparative format and the other a descriptive format. Students using the graphic organizer technique under the descriptive text condition recalled significantly more information than those not using the organizer (i.e., control). However, in the comparative text condition, no significant difference was found between those who used the organizer and those who did not (i.e., control). These results supported the conclusion that organizers aid recall when students are required to reorganize the information but have little impact otherwise.

Babyak, A. E., Koorland, M., & Mathes, P. G. (2000). The effects of story mapping instruction on the reading comprehension of students with behavioral disorders. *Behavioral Disorders, 25*(3), 239–258.

The effect of story-mapping instruction on the reading comprehension of students with behavioral disorders (BD) was examined in this 6-week study. Participants were 4 fourth- and fifth-grade students in a program for children with BD and poor reading scores. The students received story-mapping instruction, which included definition of story elements, assistance in identifying those elements, and guided practice. Following instruction, participants were asked to retell a story, answer comprehension questions, and identify the main idea. During guided and independent practice, participants exhibited higher percentages of correct responses to comprehension questions in comparison to their baseline percentages.

Blankenship, T. L., Ayres, K. M., & Langone, J. (2005). Effects of computer-based cognitive mapping on reading comprehension for students with emotional behavior disorders. *Journal of Special Education Technology, 20*(2), 15–23.

This study evaluated the effect of using cognitive-mapping computer software on reading comprehension in students with behavior disorders. The participants were 3 students, aged 15 years, who were identified as having emotional–behavioral disorders and reading difficulties that hindered their schoolwork. In the experimental phase, the students created concept maps using the software while they read. Scores on daily quizzes and chapter tests showed an upward trend following this intervention, with all students eventually able to obtain passing grades on chapter tests. Students and teachers reported greater autonomy and academic success in general education coursework based on using this cognitive-mapping software.

Boon, R. T., Fore, C., Ayres, K., & Spencer, V. G. (2005). The effects of cognitive organizers to facilitate content-area learning for students with mild disabilities: A pilot study. *Journal of Instructional Psychology, 32*(2), 101–117.

Ten 10th-graders with mild to moderate disabilities participated in this pilot study to examine the effects of using computer-based cognitive organizers on social studies learning. The students were given a pretest and then instructed in using the software to create cognitive organizers. The students then completed a posttest and a delayed posttest 1 week later. The statistically significant differences indicated improved learning of the content using the computer-based cognitive organizer technique. Additionally, a satisfaction survey indicated that a majority of the students liked using the software and thought it helped them to remember important information.

Bos, C. S., & Anders, P. L. (1990). Effects of interactive vocabulary instruction on the vocabulary learning and reading comprehension of junior-high learning disabled students. *Learning Disability Quarterly, 13*(1), 31–42.

Sixty-one junior high students diagnosed with learning disabilities participated in this study of the effects of different types of vocabulary instruction on measures of vocabulary learning and reading comprehension. Participants were divided into four groups: three involving interactive vocabulary instruction (semantic mapping, semantic-feature analysis, and semantic/syntactic-feature analysis) and one involving traditional instruction (definition instruction). Students in the interactive conditions received discussion-oriented instruction designed to help students activate prior knowledge and organize concepts based on their relationships. Both tests of written recall and reading comprehension showed that students who were instructed using interactive techniques demonstrated greater comprehension and learning than students receiving definition instruction.

Bos, C. S., Anders, P. L., Filip, D., & Jaffe, L. E. (1989). The effects of an interactive instructional strategy for enhancing reading comprehension and content area learning for students with learning disabilities. *Journal of Learning Disabilities, 22*(6), 384–390.

Fifty adolescents with learning disabilities participated in this study examining the effectiveness of a learning task strategy called semantic-feature analysis (SFA) on text comprehension. Students in the SFA condition completed a relationship chart (a matrix where important ideas are listed at the top and related vocabulary is listed down the side), and students in the control group used the dictionary to write definitions of and sentences using the vocabulary words. Comprehension was measured on a multiple-choice test, with measurements taken immediately following instruction and again 6 months later. Results indicated that students in the SFA instructional condition had significantly greater comprehension immediately following and 6 months after the initial instruction.

Bulgren, J., Schumaker, J. B., & Deshler, D. D. (1988). Effectiveness of a concept teaching routine in enhancing the performance of LD students in secondary-level mainstream classes. *Learning Disability Quarterly, 11*(1), 3–17.

This study examined the use of concept diagrams to aid in content area learning of students with and without learning disabilities (LD). Participants were 475 students in Grades 9 through 12, 32 of whom had learning disabilities. Teachers were given training on the use of concept diagrams, and student performance was assessed both before and after the concept teaching routine was implemented in the classroom. Results showed that students with and without LD both scored significantly higher after the concept training was implemented. However, instruction outside the mainstream class may be necessary to teach students with LD how to fully benefit from the organizer, as one-third of the students still did not show enough improvement to exhibit concept mastery.

Darch, C., & Carnine, D. (1986). Teaching content area material to learning disabled students. *Exceptional Children, 53*(3), 240–246.

This study analyzed the effects of using graphic organizers to aid in teaching material to students with learning disabilities. Participants were 24 fourth-, fifth-, and sixth-grade students with learning disabilities, randomly assigned to two groups. The experimental group was presented social studies and science material in the visual display of a graphic organizer, while the control group was presented the same material in a text format. The teachers of both groups used scripts to maintain consistency of material presented, and both groups engaged in a structured group study session. Results showed that the graphic organizer group outperformed the text-only group 86% to 56% on a posttest.

Horton, S. V., Lovitt, T. C., & Bergerud, D. (1990). The effectiveness of graphic organizers for three classifications of secondary students in content area classes. *Journal of Learning Disabilities, 23*(1), 12–22, 29.

This study consisted of three experiments exploring the use and effectiveness of graphic organizers (GOs) with students with disabilities, remedial students, and students in regular education classes. Experiment 1 compared a teacher-directed GO (designed by the teacher and filled in as a class) and self-study. Experiment 2 compared student-directed GOs (filled in independently by the students) with references for finding answers in the text to a self-study condition. Experiment 3 studied the impact of a student-directed GO in which lists of clues contained the information needed to complete the diagram. Results of all three experiments demonstrated that each type of GO generated higher academic performance than self-study for all three student groups in both middle school and high school.

Idol, L. (1987). Group story mapping: A comprehension strategy for both skilled and unskilled readers. *Journal of Learning Disabilities, 20*(4), 196–205.

A story-mapping strategy to improve reading comprehension was taught to 22 third- and fourth-graders of varying abilities, including 5 students who were identified as learning disabled (LD) or low-achieving (LA). Results indicated a significant shift in reading comprehension ability from baseline for all students, regardless of initial ability. Additionally, students continued to improve without teacher assistance, and improvement was maintained even after the mapping itself was removed. All of the students identified as LD or LA continued to benefit from the story-mapping instruction, receiving comprehension scores above 75% despite reading materials more difficult than their placement levels.

Vallecorsa, A. L., & deBettencourt, L. U. (1997). Using a mapping procedure to teach reading and writing skills to middle grade students with learning disabilities. *Education and Treatment of Children, 20*(2), 173–188.

This study examined whether teaching the elements of story form to students with learning disabilities (LD) would improve reading comprehension and story writing. Participants were 3 males, aged 13 years, with learning disabilities in reading and writing. They were instructed in the eight important story elements familiar to normal-developing students of this age (e.g., characters, locale, action, etc.). Based on these elements, a story map was used to teach the text structures of the story form. Results showed that students' story comprehension skills were improved by teaching concrete elements of story form and using the corresponding story maps; however, there was no effect on story-writing ability.

Considerations

For Language Differences

Cognitive organizers are especially helpful for students with language differences. Material is presented in a way that reduces the use of language, thereby decreasing the language demands of the task. This strategy is helpful for students whose native language is different from the language being used in the classroom.

B. Mnemonics

Another self-mediated method used to support learning in a variety of academic areas is a mnemonic device, which can be used to enhance student recall of facts or other memorized information. Mnemonic devices facilitate learning by employing visual and auditory clues to aid in retrieval of information (Scruggs & Mastropieri, 1990). There are several variations of mnemonic methods, including first letter, keyword, picture, physical, and musical.

While these mnemonic devices share common pedagogical principles, their structure and instructional applications vary. A first-letter mnemonic device can often represent the steps to an activity with a phrase made up of words corresponding to the first letter of each activity. For instance, the six steps in the process of problem solving could be represented by the phrase "Rascally dogs get extra dirty eventually" (recognize, define, generate, evaluate, design, and evaluate). Keyword mnemonic devices use familiar words that sound similar to the term being learned to trigger past learning and assist in learning new terms. For example, carta means "letter" in Spanish, and the word "cart" could be used as a keyword for remembering this definition by picturing a letter in a cart. Mnemonic pictures reinforce learning of concepts by visualizing the concept being taught in conjunction with a more familiar concept that sounds like the concept being taught. For example, the word "carline" means "old woman," so the mnemonic picture could be of an old woman driving a car with the word "carline" written underneath the car. Examples of musical mnemonics would be the alphabet song and the multiplication rap. Using your knuckles to represent the months of the year to remember if a month has 30 or 31 days is a physical mnemonic.

Implementation

When using mnemonics, it is important to determine which mnemonic device is appropriate for the information being learned. Then, corresponding materials must be developed. For example, in keyword picture mnemonics, the teacher determines keywords for the concepts that will be easily understood by the students. The teacher determines a way that the keyword can interact with the definition or concept being taught and then creates materials used to teach the concept (e.g., flash cards with the picture and keyword on one side of the card and the definition or explanation of the concept on the other). An outline of the procedural steps for implementing mnemonics is provided in Figure 6.7.

Figure 6.7 Procedural steps for the application of mnemonics

1. Determine the type of mnemonic device to be used, depending on the material to be learned.

2. Develop the mnemonic material, sometimes with the help of the students.

3. Present the materials to the students, and rehearse.

Evidence for Use

Using mnemonics as a learning strategy has been found to improve student performance in solving basic division problems, to increase information recall, and to increase overall academic performance (Bulgren, Deshler, & Schumaker, 1997; Bulgren, Hock, Schumaker, & Deshler, 1995; Cade & Gunter, 2002). Poor memory skills, often a characteristic of students with learning problems, can be improved with the use of mnemonics (Cade & Gunter, 2002; Mastropieri & Scruggs, 1989; Miller & Mercer, 1993). The following studies summarize some of the key research findings associated with using mnemonics as an intervention for students with learning problems.

Bulgren, J. A., Deshler, D. D., & Schumaker, J. B. (1997). Use of a recall enhancement routine and strategies in inclusive secondary classes. *Learning Disabilities Research and Practice, 12*(4), 198–208.

This investigation examined the impact of a mnemonic teaching system, the recall enhancement routine (RER), on the teaching practices of secondary general-education teachers. In Study 1, nine teachers were taught the RER and then observed to determine to what extent they utilized it, what mnemonic devices they created, and their satisfaction. Study 2 examined whether students (both with learning disabilities and without) could learn to independently identify and create mnemonic devices after watching their teachers use the RER. Results showed that the teachers incorporated the RER into their teaching, utilizing acronyms, mental images, and keywords most frequently. Moreover, satisfaction levels were relatively high for both teachers and students. However, the student results were mixed, with students able to identify and create appropriate mnemonic devices independently only 24% to 42% of the time.

Bulgren, J. A., Hock, M. F., Schumaker, J. B., & Deshler, D. D. (1995). The effects of instruction in a paired associates strategy on the information mastery performance of students with learning disabilities. *Learning Disabilities Research and Practice, 10*(1), 22–37.

Twelve students with learning disabilities were presented with mnemonic instruction as part of the paired associates strategy, a strategy designed to help students recall factual information. As part of the strategy, students were taught four mnemonic techniques (e.g., creating a mental image, making a code). Students were tested using controlled tests (consisting of fill-in-the-blank recall items) and content tests (consisting of passages of text for which the student was required to identify and memorize main ideas for recall). After instruction with the paired associates strategy, all students eventually reached or exceeded the mastery criterion of 80% correct on controlled tests and 75% on content tests.

Bulgren, J. A., Schumaker, J. B., & Deshler, D. D. (1994). The effects of a recall enhancement routine on the test performance of secondary students with and without learning disabilities. *Learning Disabilities Research and Practice, 9*(1), 2–11.

This study investigated the effects of a recall enhancement routine (RER) that utilized three mnemonic devices (acronyms, visual images, and keywords) on the recall performance of 41 seventh- and eighth-graders. The participants were a mix of students with and without learning disabilities (LD), assigned evenly to the control and experimental groups. Data were collected on student recall via a multiple-choice test. For students both with and without LD, results demonstrated that use of mnemonic devices improved test scores and increased the percentage of passing grades. While the feasibility of incorporating the RER into the curriculum on a daily basis was not studied, it has the potential to benefit students at a variety of ability levels.

Cade, T., & Gunter, P. L. (2002). Teaching students with severe emotional or behavioral disorders to use a musical mnemonic technique to solve basic division calculations. *Behavioral Disorders, 27*(3), 208–214.

Participants in this study, 3 students aged 11 to 14 who were diagnosed with severe emotional or behavioral disorders, were trained using a musical mnemonic technique (a rhyming song containing the factors of 7) and were instructed to use this technique to solve a worksheet containing 24 division-by-7 problems. The technique was taught in one intensive session; at all subsequent sessions, the students were provided with only a short review of the song. Performance of all 3 students improved significantly over baseline when using the mnemonic strategy. They were able to complete 100% of the problems correctly after no more than two intervention sessions.

Greene, G. (1999). Mnemonic multiplication fact instruction for students with learning disabilities. *Learning Disabilities Research and Practice, 14*(3), 141–148.

Twenty-three students identified as learning disabled, ranging in age from 8 to 13 years, participated in this study on the efficacy of using a mnemonic technique to help recall difficult multiplication facts. The students were divided into two groups, with each group receiving both mnemonic and traditional instruction in a counterbalanced order. The mnemonic condition consisted of flash cards containing a multiplication problem along with peg words and a cartoon illustration (e.g., for 6 x 7 = 42, the mnemonic was "sticks in heaven with a warty shoe" plus the illustration of that phrase). The traditional condition consisted of flash cards with numbers only. Results showed that mnemonic training led to greater retention of math facts than traditional methods.

Mastropieri, M. A., Emerick, K., & Scruggs, T. E. (1988). Mnemonic instruction of science concepts. *Behavioral Disorders, 14*(1), 48–56.

This study examined the effectiveness of using a keyword mnemonic technique with behaviorally disordered students. Participants were 8 students, aged 7 to 11 years, who were identified as seriously emotionally disturbed. Students were instructed using two methods: keyword mnemonic (in which science vocabulary concepts were presented together with a keyword and a corresponding picture) and traditional (in which the concepts were presented in words only). Each student received instruction in both conditions for two science chapters. Results showed that students performed better in the mnemonic condition on recalls ranging from immediate to 1-week delay (average of about 95% correct across all delay intervals) compared to the traditional condition (average of about 59% correct).

Mastropieri, M. A., Scruggs, T. E., Levin, J. R., Gaffney, J., & McLoone, B. (1985). Mnemonic vocabulary instruction for learning disabled students. *Learning Disability Quarterly, 8*(1), 57–63.

Two experiments using mnemonic techniques to help students learn vocabulary words were conducted with junior-high school students with learning disabilities. In the first experiment, 16 students were assigned to the mnemonic picture condition, in which target vocabulary words were associated with keywords and presented with a visual stimulus. The control group of 16 students received traditional direct vocabulary instruction. Results showed that the mnemonic picture group scored significantly higher on the posttest than the direct instruction group. The second experiment required the students to create their own mnemonic pictures (instead of having them provided). Results demonstrated that the mnemonic picture group still outperformed the control group about 69% to 47% on the posttest.

Considerations

For Culture and Language Differences

Both culture and language differences have at least the possibility of making mnemonics use more difficult for learning new material. Care should be used to develop mnemonics that make sense for a primary language and cross-culturally, or the necessary steps should be taken to have students create their own.

C. Self-Monitoring

Self-monitoring, also referred to as self-recording or self-observation, requires a person to record information about his or her personal performance on a task (Alberto & Troutman, 2003). Self-monitoring consists of several components, including awareness, observation, monitoring, and documentation (Mace, Belfiore, & Hutchinson, 2001). Self-monitoring places control of behavioral change on the student, deemphasizing external control agents (Carter, 1993).

For example, Ramon, an eleventh-grade student with learning problems, is failing geometry because he doesn't complete his assignments or submit them to his teacher, Mrs. Suez. Mrs. Suez determines that Ramon has not submitted any assignments in two weeks. She notes that he did complete two out of five assignments but didn't submit them. His teacher presents this baseline data and a self-monitoring form to Ramon and instructs him to write the number of problems he has completed each time a timer rings. At the end of the lesson, Ramon records the number of problems completed and submits the assignment to his teacher. Ramon is taught to self-reward by saying to himself, "I finished my work and turned it in to the teacher. I will pass geometry and graduate." His teacher presents him with a no-homework pass if he completes 90% of his work and turns in assignments for three consecutive days.

Implementation

The goal of self-monitoring is to improve skills needed for self-regulation of behavior (Hallahan, Lloyd, & Stoller, 1982). The elements of self-monitoring include the following:

1. Problem identification

2. Replacement behavior identification

3. Behavioral monitoring and recording

4. Self-evaluation

5. Self-rewarding or reinforcing

The teacher (sometimes in conjunction with the student) identifies a behavior for change, either to increase or decrease. Self-monitoring works best with high-frequency behaviors such as off-task behavior (Vanderbilt, 2005). The teacher explains the behavior to the student, articulating a definition to the extent necessary (e.g., explaining what "off task" means, explaining that turning in homework on time means at the beginning of class). Together, the teacher and student construct an appropriate method and appropriate interval for self-monitoring and self-recording. The method for recording can be as simple as making tally marks on a piece of paper at each instance of the behavior or as complex as writing a descriptive account of the behavior. Appropriate intervals for recording can include observing and recording off-task behavior in 1-minute intervals during class or checking for homework completion at the beginning of each class. The student practices the technique with teacher prompting but self-monitors and self-records independently. The teacher and student then compare notes, and reinforcement is provided for accurate self-recording. In some scenarios, positive feedback alone is a sufficient reinforcer; in others, tangible rewards are needed initially. An outline of the procedural steps for implementing self-monitoring is provided in Figure 6.8.

Figure 6.8 Procedural steps for the application of self-monitoring

1. Identify and operationally define the behavior of concern (e.g., being off task, causing classroom disruptions, failing to complete assignments).

2. Collect baseline data (e.g., grades or observations).

3. Meet individually with the student and review the baseline data in a nonthreatening, nonaccusatory way, emphasizing the benefits of changing the behavior and the consequences of continuing the behavior.

4. Identify with the student a replacement behavior, set a behavioral goal, and determine a reinforcer for achieving this goal.

5. Select the type of information that will be recorded, specifying both when and how it will be recorded.

6. Choose an appropriate recording form or method for tracking the selected behavior or charting the academic data. Forms and methods employed may include using a tone or stopwatch, checklist, frequency counts, tally sheets, event recording, time sampling, narrative diary, wrist counters, graphs, charts, or tangible item counters.

7. Gradually fade the use of self-monitoring after goal mastery.

Evidence for Use

Self-monitoring has been found to increase productivity, on-task behavior, spelling study behavior, and task accuracy (Carr & Punzo, 1993; Harris, Friedlander, Saddler, Frizzelle, & Graham, 2005; Levendoski & Cartledge, 2000; Lloyd, Bateman, Landrum, & Hallahan, 1989; McLaughlin & Truhlicka, 1983). The following studies summarize some of the key research findings associated with using self-monitoring as an intervention for students with learning problems.

Carr, S. C., & Punzo, R. P. (1993). The effects of self-monitoring of academic accuracy and productivity on the performance of students with behavioral disorders. *Behavioral Disorders, 18*(4), 241–250.

This study examined the effects of self-monitoring on academic performance using 3 adolescent males with behavioral disorders. The students received instruction in self-monitoring behaviors and were then assessed in reading, mathematics, and spelling. Data were collected on the percentage of problems correctly completed and dictated words correctly written (accuracy), the percentage of problems completed and number of words written (productivity), and the percentage of time spent seated and working (on-task behavior). Results demonstrated that each student made significant gains in all three subject areas in accuracy (increases ranged from 16% to 63%). Gains made in productivity and on-task behavior were more modest, ranging from negligible to 20% and from 11% to 22%, respectively.

Dunlap, G., Clarke, S., Jackson, M., Wright, S., Ramos, E., & Brinson, S. (1995). Self-monitoring of classroom behaviors with students exhibiting emotional and behavioral challenges. *School Psychology Quarterly, 10*(2), 165–177.

This study investigated the impact of a self-monitoring strategy on disruptive and on-task behavior using 2 elementary school students diagnosed with severe emotional disturbance and exhibiting high rates of behavior problems. After receiving training on the strategy, which utilized individualized behavior forms and 1-minute monitoring intervals, observers collected behavior data during class while the students monitored their own behavior via the forms. Results showed that the self-monitoring intervention was effective. For both participants, mean levels of on-task behavior increased (from 59% and 77% to 93% and 99%) and disruptive behavior decreased (from 13% and 48% to 2% and 2%). Additionally, the students' ratings of their own behavior were highly and consistently accurate when compared to the observers' ratings.

Harris, K. R., Friedlander, B. D., Saddler, B., Frizzelle, R., & Graham, S. (2005). Self-monitoring of attention versus self-monitoring of academic performance: Effects among students with ADHD in the general education classroom. *Journal of Special Education, 39*(3), 145–156.

This study investigated the effects of self-monitoring of attention (SMA) and self-monitoring of performance (SMP) on spelling and on-task behavior among students with attention-deficit/hyperactivity disorder (ADHD). Participants were 6 elementary students with ADHD. During the SMA phase, students were taught to ask themselves "Was I paying attention?" upon hearing a tone and record "yes" or "no." During the SMP phase, the students were taught to count and record the number of times spelling words were practiced correctly. Results showed that on-task behavior increased from an average of 55% to an average of 94% after implementation of SMA. SMP increased the average number of correct answers from 38 to 83. These results demonstrated the effectiveness of both types of self-monitoring interventions.

Lazarus, B. D. (1993). Self-management and achievement of students with behavior disorders. *Psychology in the Schools, 30*(1), 67–74.

Eighteen adolescents with behavior disorders participated in this study of self-management strategies and their impact on mathematics achievement. The participants received 6 weeks of self-management skills training. During the intervention phase, the students received prompts to use self-management strategies, scored their math worksheets, and recorded their scores on a graph. Additionally, each student created a reinforcer list to choose from after completing a worksheet. Results showed that self-management strategies greatly impacted the students' achievement and on-task behavior, with performance (weekly mean percentage of correct answers) increasing from a range of 7% to 24% (baseline) to a range of 72% to 93% and maintenance levels ranging from 81% to 91%.

Levendoski, L. S., & Cartledge, G. (2000). Self-monitoring for elementary school children with serious emotional disturbances: Classroom applications for increased academic responding. *Behavioral Disorders, 25*(3), 211–224.

Four male elementary school students with serious emotional disturbances participated in this study investigating the relationship between a self-monitoring strategy and rates of on-task behavior and academic productivity. Each student assessed his own behavior through the use of self-monitoring cards containing the question, "At this exact second am I doing my work?" and the words "yes" and "no." Data were collected at 10-minute intervals (prompted by a bell) during 20-minute sessions in which the students completed math worksheets. During the self-monitoring phases, percentages of on-task time and math worksheet problems correctly completed increased. In addition, increased on-task behavior levels were generally sustained during the fading phase; however, gains made in productivity were not maintained.

Lloyd, J. W., Bateman, D. F., Landrum, T. J., & Hallahan, D. P. (1989). Self-recording of attention versus productivity. *Journal of Applied Behavior Analysis, 22*(3), 315–323.

Five upper-elementary special education students participated in this study to determine the effects of self-recording of attentive behavior and academic productivity. Self-recording of attention involved training students to record whether or not they were attending to their assigned task when a tape-recorded tone sounded. Self-recording of productivity involved training students to record how much work they had completed when the tone sounded. Both interventions significantly increased productivity for each student, although there were no clear differences between the attention and productivity procedures. Results were maintained over a 5-week period, and participants reported preferring the self-recording of attention condition. Students were generally found to record their data accurately.

McLaughlin, T. F., & Truhlicka, M. (1983). Effects on academic performance of self-recording and self-recording and matching with behaviorally disordered students: A replication. *Behavioral Engineering, 8*(2), 69–74.

Twelve students with behavior disorders, aged 9 to 11 years, were randomly assigned to one of three groups: control, self-recording (students performed an assignment and kept track of their on- and off-task behavior), or self-recording plus matching (students performed an assignment and kept track of their own behavior, which was compared to the teacher's record and reinforced based on the degree of agreement). Data were collected on percentage of correct answers and accuracy of self-recording. Results demonstrated that the average percentage of correct answers increased for the two experimental groups. Significant differences were found between the self-recording plus matching and self-recording groups and both experimental groups and the control group. In addition, accuracy of self-recording increased when the matching contingent was included.

Todd, A. W., Horner, R. H., & Sugai, G. (1999). Self-monitoring and self-recruited praise: Effects on problem behavior, academic engagement, and work completion in a typical classroom. *Journal of Positive Behavior Interventions, 1*(2), 66–76, 122.

This study investigated the effectiveness of utilizing self-management techniques to improve problem behavior, task engagement, task completion, perception of student performance, and teacher praise. Nine male students in a fourth-grade classroom participated in the study: 1 target and 8 comparison students. The target student was instructed in the use of a self-monitoring technique that involved self-evaluation every time a signal was heard and self-recruitment of reward from the teacher when certain positive criteria were met. Results showed that the self-management techniques employed were functionally related to decreased problem behaviors and increased on-task behavior, task completion, teacher praise, and perception of student performance.

Considerations

For Teaching

Self-monitoring can be used as a classwide or individual intervention. In addition to this flexibility, self-monitoring is usually very well received by both parents and students. Students and teachers report a preference for monitoring the tasks accomplished (Alberto & Troutman, 2003). Peers see self-monitoring as positive and adult-like behavior, and self-monitoring emphasizes the positive aspects of changing behavior since goals and targets are usually to increase a desirable behavior.

Stringent accuracy of monitoring is unimportant. The most important factor in this intervention is the self-monitoring itself and the cognitive changes that presumably occur. However, if inaccuracy becomes problematic (i.e., the student is unable to correctly record data a majority of the time), target behaviors may need to be re-explained, self-monitoring skills and procedures may need to be retaught, or teacher matching (i.e., student self-scores and simultaneous teacher recordings matched) may need to be employed with reinforcement contingent on accuracy.

For Age and Developmental Level

Self-monitoring is most appropriate for students in third grade or higher, although simplified variations have been effective with younger students (Goldstein, 1995). Self-monitoring is highly applicable and developmentally appropriate for use with adolescents.

D. Self-Instruction

Self-instruction, a form of verbal mediation, is a learning strategy or process in which students use verbal self-prompts (i.e., self-talk) to self-direct or mediate learning behavior (Alberto & Troutman, 2003; Graham, Harris, & Reid, 1992; Harris, 1990). Self-instruction allows students to guide themselves through the steps to solve problems or complete tasks (Alberto & Troutman, 2003). Elements of self-instruction identified by Meichenbaum and Goodman (1971) include cognitive modeling, overt external guidance, overt self-guidance, faded overt self-guidance, and covert self-instruction.

For example, Keon is learning how to plot points on a graph. His teacher instructs him to say, "The first number is 3. I will start at the center and count three squares to the right. The second number is 2. Now, I will count two squares up. I will place a dot there. I have plotted the point (3, 2)." Keon initially repeats this aloud, but over time this self-instruction is repeated silently in his head as he plots points on graphs.

Implementation

Self-instruction for students with learning problems consists of five basic steps, as described in Figure 6.9. In learning the self-instruction technique, the student transitions from watching the teacher model verbal self-instruction to actually using self-instruction silently by himself or herself. Consequently, the foundation for self-instruction is the verbalization of the necessary steps for academic task completion. For this to occur, the teacher first models task completion using verbal self-instruction. Next, the teacher provides the verbal instruction as the student completes the task. Then, the teacher provides feedback and reinforcement as the student completes the task using verbal self-instruction. Finally, verbal cues are slowly faded until the student is able to use self-instruction silently (i.e., thinking the steps in his or her head).

Figure 6.9 Procedural steps for the application of self-instruction

1. Model and verbalize the necessary steps to complete the task.

2. Ask the student to complete the task, and verbalize the steps while the student completes the task.

3. Ask the student to verbalize the steps and complete the task simultaneously.

4. Ask the student to whisper the self-talk script while completing the task.

5. Ask the student to use silent self-talk while completing the task.

Evidence for Use

Self-instruction has been found to increase homework completion and improve academic performance for students with learning problems (Fish & Mendola, 1986; Miller, Miller, Wheeler, & Selinger, 1989; Swanson & Scarpati, 1984). The following studies summarize some of the key research findings associated with using self-instruction as an intervention for students with learning problems.

Burgio, L. D., Whitman, T. L., & Johnson, M. R. (1980). A self-instructional package for increasing attending behavior in educable mentally retarded children. *Journal of Applied Behavior Analysis, 13*(3), 443–459.

The use of self-instructional techniques among students with mental retardation was examined. Three students in special education, ranging in age from 9 to 11 years, were rated for distractibility and performance on arithmetic, printing, and phonics tasks. Two of the students were then trained in self-instruction techniques, namely verbalizing steps to complete in-class work, cope with distraction, and practice self-reinforcement; the third student acted as a control. Results of this study showed that the students who received intervention learned successfully to self-instruct and their off-task behavior decreased. In addition, there was transfer of the use of the self-instructional skills into a nontraining (i.e., regular classroom) situation.

Case, L. P., Harris, K. R., & Graham, S. (1992). Improving the mathematical problem-solving skills of students with learning disabilities: Self-regulated strategy development. *Journal of Special Education, 26*(1), 1–19.

Four fifth- and sixth-grade students with learning disabilities participated in this study to determine the effectiveness of a problem-solving strategy using self-regulation in solving addition and subtraction word problems. The strategy involved five steps: read the problem aloud, circle important words, draw pictures to gain understanding of the problem, write out the equation, and record the answer. These steps were modeled using self-instruction (i.e., thinking aloud), including self-evaluation and self-reinforcement. Results showed that the strategy worked well for students with learning disabilities, with performance gains made in both addition (from an average of 82% correct to 95% correct) and subtraction (from an average of 56% correct to 82% correct).

Cassel, J., & Reid, R. (1996). Use of a self-regulated strategy intervention to improve word problem-solving skills of students with mild disabilities. *Journal of Behavioral Education, 6*(2), 153–172.

This investigation studied the effectiveness of teaching a self-regulated strategy for solving math word problems to students diagnosed with learning disabilities (LD) or mild mental retardation (MMR). Four third- and fourth-grade students participated in the study, two with LD and two with MMR. The problem-solving strategy was taught to the students in 35-minute sessions held three times weekly and involved modeling self-instruction techniques, including self-monitoring, self-evaluation, and self-reinforcement. Results demonstrated that all students were able to master the strategy and each student's performance improved when using the self-instruction method, reaching mastery levels of 80% and above at the end of the study and maintaining gains at 6 and 8 weeks poststudy.

Fish, M. C., & Mendola, L. R. (1986). The effect of self-instruction training on homework completion in an elementary special education class. *School Psychology Review, 15*(2), 268–276.

This study investigated the impact of self-instruction training on homework completion. Participants were 3 students, aged between 8 and 9 years, who were diagnosed as emotionally disturbed. Self-instruction training specifically related to homework completion and staying on task (e.g., "I'm going to do homework. If I get distracted, I will tell myself to keep going.") was presented in eight 30-minute individual training sessions over the course of 2 weeks. Results showed that homework completion rates increased for each of the students, from a range of 29% to 40% during baseline to 75% after self-instruction training. Follow-up data, obtained 13 weeks after the study, showed completion rates of 87% to 96% (data were available for only 2 of the 3 students).

Harris, K. R., & Graham, S. (1985). Improving learning disabled students' composition skills: Self-control strategy training. *Learning Disability Quarterly, 8*(1), 27–36.

In this study, self-control strategy training was given to 2 students, aged 12 years, with learning disabilities in an effort to improve school writing and composition skills. After training on self-instruction aspects specific to writing (such as finding a topic, planning to write, evaluating writing, and providing self-reinforcement), the students' stories increased from 108 and 98 words at baseline to an average of 146 and 138 words per story. Quality of the stories was also rated much higher than during baseline, and these positive results were maintained 14 weeks after training.

Miller, M., Miller, S. R., Wheeler, J., & Selinger, J. (1989). Can a single-classroom treatment approach change academic performance and behavioral characteristics in severely behaviorally disordered adolescents: An experimental inquiry. *Behavioral Disorders, 14*(4), 215–225.

This study consisted of two experiments to assess the effect of self-instruction on learning. Each experiment had a single participant diagnosed with a severe behavior disorder and living in a mental health institution. Each participant was taught self-instruction strategies focusing on improving academic performance in mathematics or reading. Experiment 1 assessed only academics, while Experiment 2 also monitored the rate of on- and off-task behavior. Results showed that both students made significant academic gains when utilizing self-instruction. Experiment 2 results demonstrated that behavior and attention also improved, suggesting that students with behavior disorders may be acting out as a result of a learning problem and may benefit from a self-instructional intervention focusing on academics rather than behavior.

Swanson, H. L., & Scarpati, S. (1984). Self-instruction training to increase academic performance of educationally handicapped children. *Child and Family Behavior Therapy, 6*(4), 23–39.

Two experiments about the effects of self-instruction on academic performance were described in this study. The first experiment involved 2 male students, aged 13 and 14 years, with learning disabilities. After baseline, the students were given training in self-instruction techniques, focusing on error monitoring, self-interrogation, making predictions, and using self-reinforcement. Results from this experiment demonstrated increased reading comprehension and spelling performance in the self-instruction phase as compared to baseline. The second experiment evaluated self-instruction's effectiveness using a different task (math) with a 13-year-old boy. Similar self-instruction training was given in this experiment, and results also showed improvement (from 55% correct to 81% correct) from baseline to training.

Considerations

For Age and Developmental Level

Self-instruction, like self-monitoring, requires the cognitive and verbal ability to understand the steps involved in the process. Successful implementation of self-instruction requires an adult to teach the steps and the students to memorize and internalize them. Difficulty in using self-instruction can typically be resolved through thoughtful modeling, adequate practice, and honest feedback to the student who is struggling. Self-instruction can be useful for children starting at about age 6, when attention can be focused long enough to repeat and remember steps while engaging in an action. For example, when asking a 4- or 5-year-old to repeat steps, it is common to hear a repetition that is quite different from what was initially stated. Similarly, if the 5-year-old child could accurately repeat the steps, he or she would probably forget them once he or she began to engage in the behavior, because the cognitive requirements of both repeating the steps and doing them are too demanding for most 5-year-olds.

For Cultural and Language Differences

Talking to oneself occurs naturally for many students but may seem unusual for some children and families. The concepts of "self-talk" or "internal dialogue" may not be able to be translated literally. Care should be taken when working with children and families of other cultures, languages, and spiritual beliefs so as not to misrepresent self-instruction.

E. Reprocessing Strategies

Reprocessing strategies are those that require a student to review material in a way that is different from the way it was originally presented. Examples of reprocessing strategies include summarization, paraphrasing, CCC (cover, copy, and compare), and self-questioning. These strategies are useful for all stages of learning, from acquisition through fluency and into mastery. They help a student review newly learned information in a way that increases the associations between the new information and pre-existing knowledge.

For example, in learning about the water cycle in their eighth-grade Earth science class, students might be given an assignment to summarize a section of their textbook that covers the topic. After creating their summaries, the next assignment might require them to paraphrase what they have read, reinforcing the key elements in the process as it is explained in each student's own words. Prior to a quiz on the water cycle, students use a graphic organizer supplied in class to review the five stages of the process and the key elements involved in each stage by covering it, copying it onto a blank organizer, and comparing the two. The students then use a self-questioning process while reading the section on water pollution in their textbook. By formulating questions about what they are reading and applying existing knowledge about water cycles, the students begin to develop a fuller understanding of larger environmental relationships.

Implementation

The goal for all reprocessing strategies is to enhance learning by providing opportunities for students to process newly acquired knowledge in alternative contexts through actively restructuring, reorganizing, and re-examining its content. The basic elements of reprocessing strategies include the following:

1. Repeat exposure to the academic task through task completion.

2. Check for comprehension and correct errors.

Summarization is a reprocessing procedure in which important details are identified and less important details are discarded. Summarization involves creating keywords or statements that simplify the most important details. Then, one key idea (sometimes a topic sentence) is created to represent these keywords. This process takes reading from a passive to an active cognitive task for some students.

Paraphrasing is the reprocessing of information that requires reorganization of knowledge using new words. Paraphrasing involves focusing attention and memory on the most important concepts and their relationships, and discarding the details that are secondarily important or reordering them to show their relational importance. This process promotes repetition, sorting, and application of ideas by reconceptualizing them.

CCC is the process of looking at an instructional stimulus, removing it, and responding, followed by an immediate check for accuracy. In the case of an inaccurate response, the student repeats the steps. Variations on CCC include using a verbal response instead of a written response. This process allows for near-errorless learning and immediate corrective feedback loops. It also creates a stress-free environment for learning because no outside evaluator is looking at the work until the student deems it ready.

Self-questioning is the reprocessing of information by the student asking himself or herself questions about the information he or she is reading, predicting the answers to the questions, and then finding and talking about the answers. This process assists students in locating patterns and helps them sort and discard irrelevant information.

Evidence for Use

Reprocessing strategies, such as summarization and cover, copy, and compare (CCC), have been demonstrated to be highly effective across grades, ages, and content areas for students who have minimal reading and comprehension skills. The following studies summarize some of the key research findings associated with using reprocessing strategies as an intervention for students with learning problems.

Summarization

Gajria, M., & Salvia, J. (1992). The effects of summarization instructions on text comprehension of students with learning disabilities. *Exceptional Children, 58*(6), 508–516.

Thirty students with learning disabilities participated in this study to determine the effect of using a summarization strategy on comprehension of expository text. Students in Grades 6 through 9 were randomly assigned to either receive or not receive strategy training. A separate group of 15 students who were average readers served as a comparison group. Individuals in the experimental group participated in 35- to 40-minute summarization training sessions in small groups until they mastered the strategy. Data were collected on the students' reading performance using multiple-choice comprehension tests. The experimental group scored significantly higher than both the other groups on condensation questions. Gains were maintained at the 4-week follow-up, indicating that students were able to generalize their summarization skills to new material.

Jitendra, A. K., Hoppes, M. K., & Xin, Y. P. (2000). Enhancing main idea comprehension for students with learning problems: The role of a summarization strategy and self-monitoring instruction. *Journal of Special Education, 34*(3), 127–139.

This study investigated the effects of instruction in main-idea identification on reading comprehension. Participants were 33 middle school students with high-incidence (e.g., learning and behavioral) disabilities, divided into two groups. The experimental group received training in identifying main ideas, based on summarization strategy steps (Jitendra, Cole, Hoppes, & Wilson, 1998), while the control group received general reading instruction. Students in the experimental group outperformed students in the control group on both posttest and delayed posttest measures of reading comprehension and maintained strategy usage 6 weeks later.

Malone, L. D., & Mastropieri, M. A. (1991). Reading comprehension instruction: Summarization and self-monitoring training for students with learning disabilities. *Exceptional Children, 58*(3), 270–279.

This study followed 45 students with learning disabilities in sixth, seventh, and eighth grade who had weak reading comprehension and decoding skills. Each student was randomly assigned to one of three interventions: summarization training, summarization training with self-monitoring, or traditional reading-comprehension instruction. Instruction was delivered individually, with all students receiving condition-specific training, recall-comprehension practice, a think-aloud strategy, and performance and strategy feedback. Results showed that students in the two summarization training conditions performed significantly better on all measures of reading comprehension performance and strategic knowledge than students who received traditional instruction, indicating support for the use of summarization strategies with individuals with learning disabilities.

Cover, Copy, and Compare (CCC)

Nies, K. A., & Belfiore, P. J. (2006). Enhancing spelling performance in students with learning disabilities. *Journal of Behavioral Education, 15*(3), 162–169.

This study compared two strategies for teaching spelling skills to 2 third-graders with learning disabilities. The students (a boy and a girl) were introduced to 12 new spelling words each week for 3 weeks. Six of the words were given using a cover, copy, and compare (CCC) technique, and the other six were assigned with a copy-only spelling method, which was the strategy in place in the classroom prior to the study. Both students learned more words in the CCC condition (an average of 22 words, compared to 11 in the copy-only condition) and retained them longer. The students also reported enjoying learning more under the CCC condition.

Skinner, C. H., & Belfiore, P. J. (1992). Cover, copy, and compare: Increasing geography accuracy in students with behavior disorders. *School Psychology Review, 21*(1), 73–81.

A cover, copy, and compare (CCC) intervention was evaluated for its efficacy in improving students' accuracy in identifying states on a map of the United States. Participants were 7 students (mean age 10 years, 8 months) with emotional–behavioral disorders (EBD). Students were given two maps of the United States—one labeled correctly and one blank. Students used CCC to test themselves for approximately 5 minutes each day. Results showed that the CCC intervention increased accuracy in labeling states for all students. In addition, students all rated CCC favorably, reporting it to be fun and a good way to learn The results demonstrate that CCC could be successfully applied to other areas of study in classes of students with EBD.

Skinner, C. H., Ford, J. M., & Yunker, B. D. (1991). A comparison of instructional response requirements on the multiplication performance of behaviorally disordered students. *Behavioral Disorders, 17*(1), 56–65.

This study compared two cover, copy, and compare (CCC) strategies—written response (WCCC) and verbal response (VCCC)—on the written multiplication performance of 2 male elementary school students with behavior disorders. Problem sets were randomly assigned to either WCCC (in which students wrote the problem on paper), VCCC (in which students recited the problem aloud), or a no-treatment condition. Data were collected on the number of correct digits per minute and the percentage of correct answers. Results demonstrated that VCCC produced the highest rates of fluency and accuracy. The researchers hypothesized that this was due to increased practice in the VCCC condition because it was more efficient to verbalize than to write, despite the fact that the posttests used a written format.

Skinner, C. H., Turco, T. L., Beatty, K. L., & Rasavage, C. (1989). Cover, copy, and compare: A method for increasing multiplication performance. *School Psychology Review, 18*(3), 412–420.

Three individuals, one 4th-grader and two 10th-graders, participated in this study examining the impact of a cover, copy, and compare (CCC) intervention on the mathematics skills of students with behavior disorders. The students received training in CCC and then completed multiplication worksheets utilizing the CCC technique. Data were collected from daily assessments on the number of seconds needed to complete each test sheet, the number of correct digits, and percentage of correct items. Results showed that all 3 students improved the speed and accuracy of answers after the CCC intervention, demonstrating that it is an effective and efficient approach to improving academic performance.

Considerations

For Teaching

Each of these strategies requires the preparation of practice questions, materials, or task assignments so that students can engage with the content or material in a repetitive method to gain mastery and fluency. Self-checking for errors and error correction ideally should be monitored by a classroom teacher, and answer keys should be created for repeated use and durability to save time and resources in the future. Students respond well to this type of independent work because of the fast pace, the self-direction, and the error-free assignments turned in as a final product, which in turn eliminate frustration and prevent the need for escape.

For Age and Developmental Level

Young children checking their work will need additional supervision and are unlikely to be independent; however, these children can still lead the process, evaluating and correcting as necessary. Students with cognitive challenges and attention problems may need additional scaffolding for the steps required to create a response, check the response, fix errors, and move forward on the assignment.

General Considerations for Academic Problems

There is a variety of types and causes of academic problems; however, they all have enough in common to indicate several general considerations for intervention and remediation. When addressing academic problems, it is important to reflect on not only learning as a function of ability but also a student's age, developmental progression, and the expectations the student has been given. Teacher-, student-, and peer-mediated strategies are affected by each of these issues.

Conceptualization of learning as a function of an individual's ability to acquire new material over time lends itself to the principle of repetition. Intuitively, it is understood that individuals acquire some material at first glance and other material only after extended, repeated exposures, or, in some cases, not at all. This principle of time to acquire new information can sometimes create conditions in which educators overdrill, meaning that they employ constant repetition of concepts and/or information. However, there are occasions where continual, repeated teaching ceases to be useful and alternative approaches should be considered. For example, an adolescent who is still being taught basic math facts after more than 10 years of instruction should have the opportunity to use a calculator or learn other compensatory strategies.

Innate ability, environmental conditions, learning history, injury or illness, and internal states (such as motivation) all contribute to an individual's propensity for learning new material. Based on these factors, learning problems have various degrees of resolution. For example, memory and learning problems resulting from a brain injury or other medical conditions have very specific curves of recovery with general time references for when and to what degree healing occurs. Learning problems that are a result of environmental deprivation may become permanent conditions, especially in cases of language acquisition. Learning problems that are manifestations of poor instruction or lack of opportunity for education may resolve differently, depending on the length of the absence of good instruction. Students with two consecutive years of bad classroom teaching or learning experiences are statistically significantly more likely to drop out of school and have higher probabilities of nonrecovery (Hughes, 2007). Retention is the single most powerful predictor for dropping out (Rumberger, 1995), and a student who is retained two grades has his or her risk of dropping out of high school increased by 90% (Roderick, 1995). Age is also a factor to consider. Early intervention for learning problems, much like interventions for behavior problems, is critical to successful remediation. Consider a young child experiencing problems learning to read. Treating the reading problem right away may prevent learning problems in other content areas. For example, a fourth-grader experiencing reading problems will probably have trouble not just in reading but also in learning history, science, geography, and any other subject matter that uses reading as the primary means to learn new material. Thus, as children age and develop, learning problems become more pronounced. Just as there are negative consequences for a wait-and-see attitude toward behavioral problems, there can be negative consequences with this approach for learning problems as well. False positives in the identification and treatment of learning problems should be more acceptable to school professionals than false negatives. Treatment in these cases involves strategies for more effective instruction, strategies to empower students to help themselves learn, and strategies to create environments using peers as mediators to assist cooperatively in the teaching and learning processes.

The remediation of skill deficits versus performance deficits should also be considered, as each involves different strategies for intervention. In the case of skill deficits, no amount of motivation or punishment can teach a student to exhibit a skill that he or she does not possess. Motivation to earn or avoid something may increase a student's intention or attention to learn the skill, but paying him or her $100 to speak Latin will only work if he or she already knows enough Latin to speak. A skill-deficit learning problem requires effective instruction, strategy training, and creation of a positive learning environment from acquisition through mastery of the new skill. A performance deficit, on the other hand, calls for instructional techniques or strategies and behavior management that will create conditions for optimal performance and reinforce appropriate skill use. It is common to see performance-deficit techniques used inappropriately for students who possess skill deficits and skill-deficit techniques used inappropriately for students who possess performance deficits.

Individual versus small group instruction is another consideration in the remediation of academic problems. Interventions involving participation in pullouts, extended school time, or alternative classrooms, campuses, or districts have their place in the remediation of learning problems. The most efficient instructional model is a one-to-one ratio of teacher to student. In this way, an adult can introduce, practice, and assess new material at the fastest rate. However, this ratio is not a realistic expectation for most public school settings, where classrooms generally have more than 20 students and a reasonable rate of learning is expected. Some states regulate class size by grade level or topic (e.g., kindergarten classes tend to be smaller; an advanced placement class may be smaller than the average class size). Students who struggle with learning disabilities tend to need more individualized time and instruction. Structuring the learning environment with small groups within a large group can be an efficient method for teaching new skills. Large groups can sometimes facilitate modeling or demonstration requirements, with small groups or individual sessions used for practice and queries.

English-language learners experience learning problems not unlike their native English-speaking peers. The challenges of learning in a nonnative language are not fully understood but can involve the complexities of both language and cultural differences as they apply to academic performance. For example, hand raising, volunteering, working alone or in groups, sharing answers, debating peers or teachers, defending responses, or elaborating on thinking may be cultural artifacts that do not translate universally. It is important to consider the general expectations that schools and teachers in the United States have that are not explicitly articulated. Consider how your school context may create an environment that inhibits the identification and remediation of learning problems. Some examples of this include the role of parental involvement, the value of homework, the right or ability to challenge a teacher or school about decision making, or an instructional style that may seek participation and democratic equality between classes or genders.

Expectation for change is a final consideration. In general, individuals rise to expectations, but unrealistic or inappropriate goals can deflate student efforts and leave a student feeling a loss of control and a lack of opportunities to succeed, thereby creating learned helplessness. Thorough assessment of family history, school records, and standardized assessments of academic performance can assist in gauging appropriate goals. When appropriate, students can also be included in the goal-setting process for the purposes of creating an internal locus of control and preparing them to be lifelong learners who can incorporate learning into their daily lives outside the classroom.

Considerations for Assessment

Many students without disabilities experience difficulties or frustrations in the classroom with learning and/or test taking. A variety of constructs associated with academic motivation and learning strategies can be assessed using the *School Motivation and Learning Strategies Inventory* (SMALSI; Stroud & Reynolds, 2006), including study strategies, time management, organizational techniques, attention and concentration, writing and research skills, test-taking strategies, and test anxiety, each of which has an established history in educational psychology and general education literature.

The SMALSI is useful in identifying specific problem areas for students whose academic problems may be remediated prior to a referral for special education. Poor learning strategies, study skills, and test-taking skills are often overlooked due to a lack of appropriate measurement devises that would allow accurate conceptualization and assessment of these problem areas.

The SMALSI is also designed in such a way that group administrations are easy to accomplish. Group administration will allow teachers to screen entire classrooms so they can detect not only individual students with specific motivation and learning strategy problems but trends in the classroom that could be targeted for specific classwide remedial activities.

Summary

This chapter presented a review of the characteristics and conditions for academic problems, along with a summary of interventions that have been shown to be effective in remediation of academic problems. These remediation strategies were categorized under three intervention types: teacher-, peer-, and self-mediated. The teacher-mediated interventions included advance organizers, presentation strategies, and task-selection strategies. The peer-mediated interventions included peer tutoring and classwide peer tutoring. The self-mediated interventions included cognitive organizers, mnemonics, self-monitoring, self-instruction, and reprocessing strategies. While each intervention presented differs in its application of one or more instructional or behavioral theories, all are shaped by the fundamental goals of treatment: prevention and remediation of academic problems. The information presented in this chapter forms the basis of the supplemental classroom- and home-based materials that correspond to this book.

References

Alberto, P. A., & Troutman, A. C. (2003). *Applied behavior analysis for teachers* (6th ed.). Columbus, OH: Merrill Prentice Hall.

Alvermann, D. E. (1981). The compensatory effect of graphic organizers on descriptive text. *Journal of Educational Research, 75*(1), 44–48.

Babyak, A. E., Koorland, M., & Mathes, P. G. (2000). The effects of story mapping instruction on the reading comprehension of students with behavioral disorders. *Behavioral Disorders, 25*(3), 239–258.

Belfiore, P. J., Lee, D. L., Scheeler, M. C., & Klein, D. (2002). Implications of behavioral momentum and academic achievement for students with behavior disorders: Theory, application, and practice. *Psychology in the Schools, 39*(2), 171–179.

Belfiore, P. J., Lee, D. L., Vargas, A. U., & Skinner, C. H. (1997). Effects of high-preference single-digit mathematics problem completion on multiple-digit mathematics problem performance. *Journal of Applied Behavior Analysis, 30*(2), 327–330.

Blankenship, T. L., Ayres, K. M., & Langone, J. (2005). Effects of computer-based cognitive mapping on reading comprehension for students with emotional behavior disorders. *Journal of Special Education Technology, 20*(2), 15–23.

Bloom, B. S. (Ed.). (1956). *Taxonomy of educational objectives. Handbook I: Cognitive domain.* White Plains, NY: Longman.

Boon, R. T., Fore, C., Ayres, K., & Spencer, V. G. (2005). The effects of cognitive organizers to facilitate content-area learning for students with mild disabilities: A pilot study. *Journal of Instructional Psychology, 32*(2), 101–117.

Bos, C. S., & Anders, P. L. (1990). Effects of interactive vocabulary instruction on the vocabulary learning and reading comprehension of junior-high learning disabled students. *Learning Disability Quarterly, 13*(1), 31–42.

Bos, C. S., Anders, P. L., Filip, D., & Jaffe, L. E. (1989). The effects of an interactive instructional strategy for enhancing reading comprehension and content area learning for students with learning disabilities. *Journal of Learning Disabilities, 22*(6), 384–390.

Boudah, D. J., Lenz, B. K., Bulgren, J. A., Schumaker, J. B., & Deshler, D. D. (2000). Don't water down! Enhance content learning through the unit organizer routine. *Teaching Exceptional Children, 32*(3), 48–56.

Bruner, J. (1985). Vygotsky: A historical and conceptual perspective. In J. V. Wertsch (Ed.), *Culture, communication and cognition: Vygotskian perspectives.* Cambridge: Cambridge University Press.

Bulgren, J., Schumaker, J. B., & Deshler, D. D. (1988). Effectiveness of a concept teaching routine in enhancing the performance of LD students in secondary-level mainstream classes. *Learning Disability Quarterly, 11*(1), 3–17.

Bulgren, J. A., Deshler, D. D., & Schumaker, J. B. (1997). Use of a recall enhancement routine and strategies in inclusive secondary classes. *Learning Disabilities Research and Practice, 12*(4), 198–208.

Bulgren, J. A., Hock, M. F., Schumaker, J. B., & Deshler, D. D. (1995). The effects of instruction in a paired associates strategy on the information mastery performance of students with learning disabilities. *Learning Disabilities Research and Practice, 10*(1), 22–37.

Bulgren, J. A., Lenz, B. K., Schumaker, J. B., Deshler, D. D., & Marquis, J. G. (2002). The use and effectiveness of a comparison routine in diverse secondary content classrooms. *Journal of Educational Psychology, 94*(2), 356–371.

Bulgren, J. A., Schumaker, J. B., & Deshler, D. D. (1994). The effects of a recall enhancement routine on the test performance of secondary students with and without learning disabilities. *Learning Disabilities Research and Practice, 9*(1), 2–11.

Burgio, L. D., Whitman, T. L., & Johnson, M. R. (1980). A self-instructional package for increasing attending behavior in educable mentally retarded children. *Journal of Applied Behavior Analysis, 13*(3), 443–459.

Cade, T., & Gunter, P. L. (2002). Teaching students with severe emotional or behavioral disorders to use a musical mnemonic technique to solve basic division calculations. *Behavioral Disorders, 27*(3), 208–214.

Carr, S. C., & Punzo, R. P. (1993). The effects of self-monitoring of academic accuracy and productivity on the performance of students with behavioral disorders. *Behavioral Disorders, 18*(4), 241–250.

Carroll, J. B. (1963). A model of school learning. *Teachers College Record, 64,* 723–733.

Carroll, J. B. (1989). The Carroll model: A 25-year retrospective and prospective view. *Educational Researcher, 18*(1), 26–31.

Carter, J. F. (1993). Self-management: Education's ultimate goal. *Teaching Exceptional Children, 25*(3), 28–32.

Case, L. P., Harris, K. R., & Graham, S. (1992). Improving the mathematical problem-solving skills of students with learning disabilities: Self-regulated strategy development. *Journal of Special Education, 26*(1), 1–19.

Cassel, J., & Reid, R. (1996). Use of a self-regulated strategy intervention to improve word problem-solving skills of students with mild disabilities. *Journal of Behavioral Education, 6*(2), 153–172.

Center, D. B., Deitz, S. M., & Kaufman, M. E. (1982). Student ability, task difficulty, and inappropriate classroom behavior: A study of children with behavior disorders. *Behavior Modification, 6*(3), 355–374.

Chun, C. C., & Winter, S. (1999). Classwide peer tutoring with or without reinforcement: Effects on academic responding, content coverage, achievement, intrinsic interest and reported project experiences. *Educational Psychology, 19*(2), 191–205.

Clarke, S., Dunlap, G., Foster-Johnson, L., Childs, K. E., Wilson, D., White, R., et al. (1995). Improving the conduct of students with behavioral disorders by incorporating student interests into curricular activities. *Behavioral Disorders, 20*(4), 221–237.

Cosden, M., Gannon, C., & Haring, T. G. (1995). Teacher-control versus student-control over choice of task and reinforcement for students with severe behavior problems. *Journal of Behavioral Education, 5*(1), 11–27.

Coutinho, M. J. (1986). Reading achievement of students identified as behaviorally disordered at the secondary level. *Behavioral Disorders, 11,* 200–207.

Coyne, M. D., Kame'enui, E. J., & Simmons, D. C. (2001). Prevention and intervention in beginning reading: Two complex systems. *Learning Disabilities Research and Practice, 16*(2), 62–73.

Crank, J. N., & Bulgren, J. A. (1993). Visual depictions as information organizers for enhancing achievement of students with learning disabilities. *Learning Disabilities Research and Practice, 8*(3), 140–147.

Cullinan, D., Epstein, M. H., & Lloyd, J. W. (1991). Evaluation of conceptual models of behavior disorders. *Behavioral Disorders, 16,* 148–157.

Cybriwsky, C. A., & Schuster, J. W. (1990). Using constant time delay procedures to teach multiplication facts. *Remedial and Special Education, 11*(1), 54–59.

Darch, C., & Carnine, D. (1986). Teaching content area material to learning disabled students. *Exceptional Children, 53*(3), 240–246.

Darch, C., & Gersten, R. (1986). Direction-setting activities in reading comprehension: A comparison of two approaches. *Learning Disability Quarterly, 9*(3), 235–243.

Dawson, L., Venn, M. L., & Gunter, P. L. (2000). The effects of teacher versus computer reading models. *Behavioral Disorders, 25*(2), 105–113.

Dickson, S. V., Chard, D. J., & Simmons, D. C. (1993). An integrated reading/writing curriculum: A focus on scaffolding. *LD Forum, 18*(4), 12–16.

Dunlap, G., Clarke, S., Jackson, M., Wright, S., Ramos, E., & Brinson, S. (1995). Self- monitoring of classroom behaviors with students exhibiting emotional and behavioral challenges. *School Psychology Quarterly, 10*(2), 165–177.

Epstein, M. H., Kinder, D., & Bursuck, B. (1989). The academic status of adolescents with behavioral disorders. *Behavioral Disorders, 14*(3), 157–165.

Fish, M. C., & Mendola, L. R. (1986). The effect of self-instruction training on homework completion in an elementary special education class. *School Psychology Review, 15*(2), 268–276.

Franca, V. M., & Kerr, M. M. (1990). Peer tutoring among behaviorally disordered students: Academic and social benefits to tutor and tutee. *Education and Treatment of Children, 13*(2), 109–128.

Fuchs, D., Fuchs, L. S., & Burish, P. (2000). Peer-assisted learning strategies: An evidence-based practice to promote reading achievement. *Learning Disabilities Research and Practice, 15*(2), 85–91.

Fuchs, D., Fuchs, L. S., Mathes, P. G., & Simmons, D. C. (1997). Peer-assisted learning strategies: Making classrooms more responsive to diversity. *American Educational Research Journal, 34*(1), 174–206.

Fuchs, L. S., & Fuchs, D. (1995). Acquisition and transfer effects of classwide peer-assisted learning strategies in mathematics for students with varying learning histories. *School Psychology Review, 24*(4), 604–620.

Gajria, M., & Salvia, J. (1992). The effects of summarization instructions on text comprehension of students with learning disabilities. *Exceptional Children, 58*(6), 508–516.

Gallagher, J. (1972). The special education contract for mildly handicapped children. *Exceptional Children, 38,* 527–535.

Glynn, S. M., & DiVesta, F. J. (1977). Outline and hierarchical organization as aids for study and retrieval. *Journal of Educational Psychology, 69*(2), 89–95.

Goldstein, S. (1995). *Understanding and managing children's classroom behavior.* New York: Wiley.

Good, T. L., & Brophy, J. E. (2003). *Looking in classrooms* (9th ed.). Boston: Allyn & Bacon.

Goodlad, S., & Hirst, B. (Eds.). (1990). *Explorations in peer tutoring.* Oxford: Blackwell Education.

Graham, S., Harris, K. R., & Reid, R. (1992). Developing self-regulated learners. *Focus on Exceptional Children, 24*(6), 1–16.

Greene, G. (1999). Mnemonic multiplication fact instruction for students with learning disabilities. *Learning Disabilities Research and Practice, 14*(3), 141–148.

Greenwood, C. R., & Delquadri, J. (1995). Classwide peer tutoring and the prevention of school failure. *Preventing School Failure, 39*(4), 21–25.

Greenwood, C. R., Delquadri, J., & Carta, J. J. (1988). *Together we can! Classwide peer tutoring to improve basic academic skills.* Longmont, CO: Sopris West.

Gunter, P. L., Shores, R. E., Jack, S. L., Denny, R. K., & DePaepe, P. A. (1994). A case study of the effects of altering instructional interactions on the disruptive behavior of a child identified with severe behavior disorders. *Education and Treatment of Children, 17*(4), 435–444.

Hallahan, D. P., Lloyd, J. W., & Stoller, L. (1982). *Improving attention with self-monitoring: A manual for teachers.* Charlottesville: University of Virginia, Learning Disabilities Research Institute.

Harris, K. R. (1990). Developing self-regulated learners: The role of private speech and self-instructions. *Educational Psychologist, 25*(1), 35–49.

Harris, K. R., Friedlander, B. D., Saddler, B., Frizzelle, R., & Graham, S. (2005). Self-monitoring of attention versus self-monitoring of academic performance: Effects among students with ADHD in the general education classroom. *Journal of Special Education, 39*(3), 145–156.

Harris, K. R., & Graham, S. (1985). Improving learning disabled students' composition skills: Self-control strategy training. *Learning Disability Quarterly, 8*(1), 27–36.

Hawkins, J. (1988). Antecedent pausing as a direct instruction tactic for adolescents with severe behavioral disorders. *Behavioral Disorders, 13*(4), 263–272.

Horton, S. V., Lovitt, T. C., & Bergerud, D. (1990). The effectiveness of graphic organizers for three classifications of secondary students in content area classes. *Journal of Learning Disabilities, 23*(1), 12–22, 29.

Hughes, J. N. (2007, November). *Emotions are academic: Promoting children's academic and life success through social and emotional learning.* Distinguished Lecture Series. Office of the Provost and Executive Vice President for Academics, Texas A & M University, College Station, Texas.

Idol, L. (1987). Group story mapping: A comprehension strategy for both skilled and unskilled readers. *Journal of Learning Disabilities, 20*(4), 196–205.

Individuals With Disabilities Education Improvement Act of 2004, 20 U.S.C. §1400 (2004).

Jitendra, A. K., Cole, C. L., Hoppes, M. K., & Wilson, B. (1998). Effects of a direct instruction main idea summarization program and self-monitoring on reading comprehension of middle school students with learning disabilities. *Reading and Writing Quarterly, 14,* 379–396.

Jitendra, A. K., Hoppes, M. K., & Xin, Y. P. (2000). Enhancing main idea comprehension for students with learning problems: The role of a summarization strategy and self-monitoring instruction. *Journal of Special Education, 34*(3), 127–139.

Jolivette, K., Lassman, K. A., & Wehby, J. H. (1998). Functional assessment for academic instruction for a student with emotional and behavioral disorders: A case study. *Preventing School Failure, 43*(1), 19–23.

Jolivette, K., Wehby, J. H., & Hirsch, L. (1999). Academic strategy identification for students exhibiting inappropriate classroom behaviors. *Behavioral Disorders, 24*(3), 210–221.

Kame'enui, E. J., Carnine, D. W., Dixon, R. C., Simmons, D. C., & Coyne, M. D. (2002). *Effective teaching strategies that accommodate diverse learners* (2nd ed.). Columbus, OH: Merrill.

Kauffman, J. M., Cullinan, D., & Epstein, M. H. (1987). Characteristics of students placed in special programs for the seriously emotionally disturbed. *Behavioral Disorders, 12*(3), 175–184.

Kern, L., Delaney, B., Clarke, S., Dunlap, G., & Childs, K. (2001). Improving the classroom behavior of students with emotional and behavioral disorders using individualized curricular modifications. *Journal of Emotional and Behavioral Disorders, 9*(4), 239–247.

Landrum, T. J., Tankersley, M., & Kauffman, J. M. (2003). What is special about special education for students with emotional or behavioral disorders? *Journal of Special Education, 37,* 148–156.

Lane, K. L. (2004). Academic instruction and tutoring interventions for students with emotional/behavioral disorders: 1990 to present. In R. B. Rutherford, M. M. Quinn, & Mathur, S. R. (Eds.), *Handbook of research of emotional and behavioral disorders* (pp. 462–486). New York: Guilford Press.

Lane, K. L., Barton-Arwood, S. M., Nelson, J. R., & Wehby, J. (2008). Academic performance of students with emotional and behavioral disorders served in a self-contained setting. *Journal of Behavioral Education, 17*(1), 43–62.

Lane, K. L., Carter, E. W., Pierson, M. R., & Glaeser, B. C. (2006). Academic, social, and behavioral characteristics of high school students with emotional disturbances or learning disabilities. *Journal of Emotional and Behavioral Disorders, 14*(2), 108–117.

Lazarus, B. D. (1993). Self-management and achievement of students with behavior disorders. *Psychology in the Schools, 30*(1), 67–74.

Lee, Y.-Y., Sugai, G., & Horner, R. H. (1999). Using an instructional intervention to reduce problem and off-task behaviors. *Journal of Positive Behavior Interventions, 1*(4), 195–204.

Levendoski, L. S., & Cartledge, G. (2000). Self-monitoring for elementary school children with serious emotional disturbances: Classroom applications for increased academic responding. *Behavioral Disorders, 25*(3), 211–224.

Lloyd, J. W., Bateman, D. F., Landrum, T. J., & Hallahan, D. P. (1989). Self-recording of attention versus productivity. *Journal of Applied Behavior Analysis, 22*(3), 315–323.

Locke, W. R., & Fuchs, L. S. (1995). Effects of peer-mediated reading instruction on the on-task behavior and social interaction of children with behavior disorders. *Journal of Emotional and Behavioral Disorders, 3*(2), 92–99.

Lorch, R. F., Jr., & Lorch, E. P. (1985). Topic structure representation and text recall. *Journal of Educational Psychology, 77*(2), 137–148.

Mace, F. C., Belfiore, P. J., & Hutchinson, J. M. (2001). Operant theory and research on self-regulation. In B. Zimmerman & D. Schunk (Eds.), *Self-regulated learning and academic achievement: Theoretical perspectives* (pp. 39–66). Mahwah, NJ: Erlbaum.

Maggs, A., & Morgan, G. (1986). Effects of feedback on the academic engaged time of behaviour disordered learners. *Educational Psychology, 6*(4), 335–351.

Maheady, L., Harper, G. F., & Sacca, K. (1998). A classwide peer tutoring system in a secondary, resource room program for the mildly handicapped. *Journal of Research and Development in Education, 21*(3), 76–83.

Maher, C. A. (1982). Behavioral effects of using conduct problem adolescents as cross-age tutors. *Psychology in the Schools, 19*(3), 360–364.

Malone, L. D., & Mastropieri, M. A. (1991). Reading comprehension instruction: Summarization and self-monitoring training for students with learning disabilities. *Exceptional Children, 58*(3), 270–279.

Mastropieri, M. A., Emerick, K., & Scruggs, T. E. (1988). Mnemonic instruction of science concepts. *Behavioral Disorders, 14*(1), 48–56.

Mastropieri, M. A., & Scruggs, T. E. (1989). Constructing more meaningful relationships: Mnemonic instruction for special populations. *Educational Psychology Review, 1,* 88–111.

Mastropieri, M. A., Scruggs, T. E., Levin, J. R., Gaffney, J., & McLoone, B. (1985). Mnemonic vocabulary instruction for learning disabled students. *Learning Disability Quarterly, 8*(1), 57–63.

McCurdy, B. L., Cundari, L., & Lentz, F. E. (1990). Enhancing instructional efficiency: An examination of time delay and the opportunity to observe instructions. *Education and Treatment of Children, 13*(3), 226–238.

McLaughlin, T. F. (1992). Effects of written feedback in reading on behaviorally disordered students. *Journal of Educational Research, 85*(5), 312–316.

McLaughlin, T. F., & Truhlicka, M. (1983). Effects on academic performance of self-recording and self-recording and matching with behaviorally disordered students: A replication. *Behavioral Engineering, 8*(2), 69–74.

Meichenbaum, D. H., & Goodman, J. (1971). Training impulsive children to talk to themselves: A means of developing self-control. *Journal of Abnormal Psychology, 77*(2), 115–126.

Miller, M., Miller, S. R., Wheeler, J., & Selinger, J. (1989). Can a single-classroom treatment approach change academic performance and behavioral characteristics in severely behaviorally disordered adolescents: An experimental inquiry. *Behavioral Disorders, 14*(4), 215–225.

Miller, S. P., & Mercer, C. D. (1993). Mnemonics: Enhancing the math performance of students with learning difficulties. *Intervention in School and Clinic, 29*(2), 78–82.

Mooney, P., Epstein, M. H., Reid, R., & Nelson, J. R. (2003). Status and trends of academic intervention research for students with emotional disturbance. *Remedial and Special Education, 24,* 273–287.

Nies, K. A., & Belfiore, P. J. (2006). Enhancing spelling performance in students with learning disabilities. *Journal of Behavioral Education, 15*(3), 162–169.

Palincsar, A. S., & Brown, A. L. (1984). Reciprocal teaching of comprehension-fostering and comprehension-monitoring activities. *Cognition and Instruction, 1*(2), 117–175.

Penno, D. A., Frank, A. R., & Wacker, D. P. (2000). Instructional accommodations for adolescent students with severe emotional or behavioral disorders. *Behavioral Disorders, 25*(4), 325–343.

Reynolds, C. R., & Kamphaus, R. W. (2004). *Behavior Assessment System for Children* (2nd ed.). Circle Pines, MN: AGS Publishing.

Rieth, H. J., Polsgrove, L., Semmel, M., & Cohen, R. (1980). An experimental analysis of the effects of increased instructional time on the academic achievement of a "behaviorally disordered" high school pupil. *Behavioral Disorders, 3,* 134–141.

Roderick, M. (1995). Grade retention and school dropout: Policy debate and research questions. *Phi Delta Kappa Research Bulletin, 15,* 1–6.

Rosenberg, M. S., Sindelar, P. T., & Stedt, J. (1985). The effects of supplemental on-task contingencies on the acquisition of simple and difficult academic tasks. *Journal of Special Education, 19*(2), 189–203.

Rosenshine, B. (1995). Advances in research on instruction. *The Journal of Educational Research, 88*(5), 262–268.

Rosenshine, B. (1997). Advances in research on instruction. In J. W. Lloyd, E. J. Kameenui, & D. Chard (Eds.), *Issues in educating students with disabilities* (pp. 197–220). Mahwah, NJ: Erlbaum.

Rosenshine, B., & Meister, C. (1992). The use of scaffolds for teaching higher-level cognitive strategies. *Educational Leadership, 49*(7), 26–33.

Rumberger, R. W. (1995). Dropping out of middle school: A multilevel analysis of students and schools. *American Educational Research Journal, 32*(3), 583–625.

Scardamalia, M., & Bereiter, C. (1985). Fostering the development of self-regulation in children's knowledge processing. In S. F. Chipman, J. W. Segal, & R. Glaser (Eds.), *Thinking and learning skills: Vol. 2 Research and open questions* (pp. 563–578). Hillsdale, NJ: Erlbaum.

Schloss, P. J., Harriman, N. E., & Pfefier, K. (1985). Application of a sequential prompt reduction technique to the independent composition performance of behaviorally disordered youth. *Behavioral Disorders, 11*(1), 17–23.

Schumaker, J. B., & Deshler, D. D. (1992). Validation of learning strategy interventions for students with LD: Results of a programmatic research effort. In B. Y. L. Wong (Ed.), *Contemporary research with students with learning disabilities: An international perspective* (pp. 22–46). New York: Springer-Verlag.

Schumaker, J. B., Deshler, D. D., Alley, G. R., Warner, M. M., & Denton, P. H. (1982). Multipass: A learning strategy for improving reading comprehension. *Learning Disability Quarterly, 5*(3), 295–304.

Scruggs, T. E., & Mastropieri, M. A. (1986). Academic characteristics of behaviorally disordered and learning disabled students. *Behavioral Disorders, 11*(3), 184–190.

Scruggs, T. E., & Mastropieri, M. A. (1990). The case for mnemonic instruction: From laboratory research to classroom applications. *Journal of Special Education, 24*(1), 7–32.

Scruggs, T. E., Mastropieri, M. A., & Richter, L. (1985). Peer tutoring with behaviorally disordered students: Social and academic benefits. *Behavioral Disorders, 10*(4), 283–294.

Simpson, R. L. (1999). Children and youth with emotional and behavioral disorders: A concerned look at the present and a hopeful eye for the future. *Behavioral Disorders, 24*(4), 284–292.

Skinner, C. H., & Belfiore, P. J. (1992). Cover, copy, and compare: Increasing geography accuracy in students with behavior disorders. *School Psychology Review, 21*(1), 73–81.

Skinner, C. H., Ford, J. M., & Yunker, B. D. (1991). A comparison of instructional response requirements on the multiplication performance of behaviorally disordered students. *Behavioral Disorders, 17*(1), 56–65.

Skinner, C. H., Johnson, C. W., Larkin, M. J., Lessley, D. J., & Glowacki, M. L. (1995). The influence of rate of presentation during taped-words interventions on reading performance. *Journal of Emotional and Behavioral Disorders, 3*(4), 214–223.

Skinner, C. H., Turco, T. L., Beatty, K. L., & Rasavage, C. (1989). Cover, copy, and compare: A method for increasing multiplication performance. *School Psychology Review, 18*(3), 412–420.

Stallings, J. A. (1986). Effective use of time in secondary reading programs. In J. V. Hoffman (Ed.), *Effective teaching of reading: Research and practice* (pp. 85–106). Newark, DE: International Reading Association.

Stroud, K., & Reynolds, C. R. (2006). *School motivation and learning strategies inventory* (SMALSI). Los Angeles: Western Psychological Services.

Sutherland, K. S., Alder, N., & Gunter, P. L. (2003). The effect of varying rates of opportunities to respond to academic requests on the classroom behavior of students with EBD. *Journal of Emotional and Behavioral Disorders, 11*(4), 239–248.

Sutherland, K. S., & Wehby, J. H. (2001). Exploring the relationship between increased opportunities to respond to academic requests and the academic and behavioral outcomes of students with EBD: A review. *Remedial and Special Education, 22*(2), 113–121.

Sutherland, K. S., Wehby, J. H., & Yoder, P. J. (2002). Examination of the relationship between teacher praise and opportunities for students with EBD to respond to academic requests. *Journal of Emotional and Behavioral Disorders, 10*(1), 5–13.

Swanson, H. L., & Deshler, D. (2003). Instructing adolescents with learning disabilities: Converting a meta-analysis to practice. *Journal of Learning Disabilities, 36*(2), 124–135.

Swanson, H. L., & Scarpati, S. (1984). Self-instruction training to increase academic performance of educationally handicapped children. *Child and Family Behavior Therapy, 6*(4), 23–39.

Terry, B. (2005). An introduction to classwide peer tutoring. Retrieved July 22, 2008, from University of Kansas, Special Connections Web site: http://www.specialconnections. ku.edu/cgi-bin/cgiwrap/specconn/index.php

Todd, A. W., Horner, R. H., & Sugai, G. (1999). Self-monitoring and self-recruited praise: Effects on problem behavior, academic engagement, and work completion in a typical classroom. *Journal of Positive Behavior Interventions, 1*(2), 66–76, 122.

Topping, K. (2001). *Peer assisted learning: A practical guide for teachers.* Cambridge, MA: Brookline Books.

Trout, A. L., Nordness, P. D., Pierce, C. D., & Epstein, M. H. (2003). Research on the academic status of children with emotional and behavioral disorders: A review of literature from 1961 to 2000. *Journal of Emotional and Behavioral Disorders, 11*(4), 198–210.

U.S. Department of Education. (1994). *16th annual report to congress on the implementation of P.L.* (pp. 94–142). Washington, DC: U.S. Government Printing Office.

Vallecorsa, A. L., & deBettencourt, L. U. (1997). Using a mapping procedure to teach reading and writing skills to middle grade students with learning disabilities. *Education and Treatment of Children, 20*(2), 173–188.

Van Patten, J., Chao, C. I., & Reigeluth, C. M. (1986). A review of strategies for sequencing and synthesizing instruction. *Review of Educational Research, 56*(4), 437–471.

Vanderbilt, A. A. (2005). Designed for teachers: How to implement self-monitoring in the classroom. *Beyond Behavior, 15*(1), 21–24.

Vannest, K. J., Harrison, J., Ramsey, L., & Harvey, K. (2008). Improvement rate differences of academic interventions for students with emotional and behavioral disorders. Manuscript submitted for publication.

Vannest, K. J., Harvey, K., & Mason, B. (in press). Meeting annual yearly progress through better teaching for students with emotional and behavioral disorders. *Preventing School Failure.*

Vygotsky, L. S. (1978). *Mind in society: The development of higher psychological processes.* Cambridge, MA: Harvard University Press.

Wagner, M., Kutash, K., Duchnowski, A. J., Epstein, M. H., & Sumi, C. (2005). The children and youth we serve: A national picture of the characteristics of students with emotional disturbances receiving special education. *Journal of Emotional and Behavioral Disorders, 13*(2), 79–96.

West, R. P., & Sloane, H. N. (1986). Teacher presentation rate and point delivery rate: Effects on classroom disruption, performance accuracy, and response rate. *Behavior Modification, 10*(3), 267–286.

Chapter 7

Interventions for Anxiety

This chapter focuses on interventions for children and adolescents identified as having problems with anxiety. The first section in this chapter discusses the conditions and characteristics of anxiety, and provides sample items from the BASC–2 Anxiety and Withdrawal scales. (The Withdrawal scale is included due to its modest behavioral overlap with Anxiety.) The second section describes the theoretical framework for understanding anxiety and for the interventions presented in this chapter. In the third section, interventions that have evidence or show promise for alleviating anxiety and related maladaptive behaviors in children and adolescents are described. Each presentation provides an overview of the intervention method and is divided into three subsections: implementation, evidence for use, and considerations. For the discussion of integrated cognitive–behavioral therapy (CBT), several strategies are reviewed, each with its own overview and procedures for implementation. However, these strategies are often used in various combinations with each other; as such, the research studies supporting their use and the considerations for their implementation are presented in single Evidence for Use and Considerations sections. The chapter's three main sections provide the foundation on which additional BASC–2 intervention components are built, including both classroom-based and home-based strategies.

Characteristics and Conditions of Anxiety

Anxiety disorders are characterized by excessive worry, nervousness, specific or general fears or phobias, and self-deprecation (Reynolds & Kamphaus, 2004). Anxiety problems among children are numerous, affecting up to 13% of children between the ages of 9 and 17 years (U.S. Department of Health and Human Services, 1999). Children who have anxiety disorders may feel overwhelmed easily, feel a sense of dread, and suffer from obsessive, intrusive, and bothersome thoughts. As Reynolds and Kamphaus (2004) note, anxiety disorders are often accompanied by somatic complaints, and anxiety may itself be a symptom of depression. A detailed examination of a child's symptoms is needed in order to determine whether the symptoms are caused by an anxiety disorder, somatoform disorder, depressive disorder, or a combination thereof.

Items on the BASC–2 Anxiety scale include "Worries about things that cannot be changed," "Says, 'I am nervous about tests' or 'Tests make me nervous,'" and "Is fearful." The BASC–2 Withdrawal scale also contains items related to anxiety problems, including "Avoids other children (adolescents)," "Refuses to talk," and "Shows fear of strangers." It is important to keep in mind that a child may show symptoms of anxiety that require intervention but may not warrant a formal diagnosis. Children scoring in the At-Risk or Clinically Significant range on the BASC–2 Anxiety or Withdrawal scales will likely benefit from some type of intervention strategy.

Theoretical Framework for Approaching Anxiety

The anxiety interventions in this chapter reflect a behavioral and/or cognitive–behavioral theoretical framework. A behavioral approach to anxiety is based on the idea that anxiety is a classically conditioned response to specific stimuli and is maintained by negative reinforcement (Compton et al., 2004). For example, if a child who feels anxious in social situations experiences relief when he or she withdraws from a group and seeks solitude, the removal of the anxious sensation may reinforce the child's tendency to again withdraw in subsequent social situations. Cognitive–behavioral theory, on the other hand, conceptualizes the behaviors associated with anxiety as being influenced by a combination of cognitive, behavioral, affective, and social factors (Kendall, Kortlander, Chansky, & Brady, 1992). For instance, a child's anxiety about speaking in class may be related to his or her dislike of particular classmates. In such a case, addressing affective and social factors would be key components of an effective intervention.

The success of an intervention rests on a number of factors. The level of anxiety, hereditary factors, and parental characteristics (e.g., depression, hostility, paranoia) can all impact the success of an intervention for a child (Berman, Weems, Silverman, & Kurtines, 2000). In addition, changes in a child's environment (e.g., peer teasing, adult reprimands) can also affect an intervention's success.

Interventions

Interventions for childhood anxiety—in particular, fears and phobias—are among the oldest evidence-based psychological treatments. A variety of interventions have been shown to reduce, or show promise for reducing, feelings of anxiety. Specific phobias (e.g., fear of dogs, school, water) are typically treated with behavioral interventions, while cognitive–behavioral interventions are often used for general anxiety disorders.

This chapter describes a number of interventions aimed at reducing anxiety, including:

    I. Exposure-Based Techniques

    II. Contingency Management

    III. Modeling

IV. Family Therapy

V. Integrated Cognitive–Behavioral Therapy

Most of the research studying the effects of interventions on reducing anxiety in children occurs in clinical or therapeutic settings, rather than school-based settings. The research included in this chapter provides evidence for interventions that would be expected to generalize to anxiety-related problems typically encountered by those persons working in a school setting.

I. Exposure-Based Techniques

Exposure-based techniques are variants of systematic desensitization (Wolpe, 1958), including emotive imagery (Lazarus & Abramovitz, 1962), imaginal desensitization, and *in vivo* desensitization. Such techniques are counter-conditioning strategies that require a child or adolescent to confront a series of anxiety-producing stimuli in a gradual, systematic progression (building slowly from the least to the most anxiety producing) while simultaneously engaging in behaviors that are incompatible with anxiety (Akande et al., 1999; Compton et al., 2004; Wolpe, 1958). The stimuli in the exercise may be either imaginal or real. The use of relaxation techniques such as progressive muscle relaxation or breathing exercises, applied concurrently with gradual exposure to aversive stimuli, enables the eventual elimination of escape and avoidance behaviors (Compton et al., 2004).

For example, Chuck experienced intense anxiety every day when required to attend first grade. When his mother woke him each morning, Chuck cried and refused to get out of bed. It was determined that no specific negative event had led to his anxious feelings (i.e., there was no functional cause). Using exposure-based techniques, a counselor worked with Chuck and his mother to develop Chuck's tolerance for going to school. As a first step, the counselor showed Chuck pictures of the school. After Chuck was able to look at the pictures without crying, the counselor had Chuck and his mother drive up to the school but not get out of the car. When Chuck could handle driving up to the school without feeling anxious, he progressed to walking up to the school without going in, then to going inside the building, and finally to entering his classroom. Throughout the progression, Chuck used a variety of relaxation techniques to calm himself along the way. When driving up to the school, Chuck concentrated on counting to 30 to distract himself from his anxious feelings. When walking to the school doors, Chuck focused on maintaining a steady rate of breathing.

Implementation

The goal of using exposure-based techniques as an intervention for anxiety is to counter-condition the anxiety response and gradually decrease symptoms of situational anxiety. The basic elements of exposure-based techniques include:

1. Relaxation training

2. Recognition of anxiety hierarchies

3. Gradual presentation of anxiety-producing stimuli

4. Desensitization of the student to the stimuli

The procedural steps for implementing exposure-based techniques are provided in Figure 7.1. Beyond teaching a child to become more aware of physical symptoms of anxiety and relaxation techniques, a key component of this strategy is establishing a child's "anxiety hierarchy." While this can be done in a number of ways, a simple technique is to record each anxiety-producing event or stimulus on a note card, and ask the child to rank the cards from least to most anxiety provoking (Akande & Akande, 1994; Morris, 1980).

The anxiety hierarchy that is created can serve as a guide for dealing with anxiety problems, starting with the event or stimulus that is least anxiety provoking and working up toward events or stimuli that are most anxiety provoking. The therapist may start by presenting the stimulus imaginally (i.e., having the child imagine the stimulus), working toward an *in vivo* exposure where the child confronts the real events or stimuli. Prior to the imaginal exposure exercise, the child can spend 3 to 5 minutes focusing on relaxing the body. Then, the therapist describes the events in the child's anxiety hierarchy, and the child uses relaxation techniques to counter-condition the anxiety response. Throughout the exercise, the therapist conveys warmth and acceptance and answers any questions the child may have. This step is repeated for the prescribed number of sessions or until the child is able to approach the final situation, event, or object in his or her anxiety hierarchy. Homework is assigned, including practicing relaxation techniques and approaching the anxiety-provoking agent (Albano & Barlow, 1996).

Alternatively, emotive imagery, a variant of imaginal desensitization, can also be used to treat anxiety problems. Emotive imagery uses themes with positive emotional resonance for the child, such as superheroes or favorite TV characters, to counter-condition the child's anxiety. To begin the emotive imagery session, the therapist instructs the child to close his or her eyes and concentrate on clearly imagining the scene the therapist describes, thinking not only about the sense of sight, but also hearing, smell, and touch. The child is asked to describe the scene back to the therapist in detail, using all senses. The therapist then uses a carefully constructed script to tell a story that incorporates the child's name, heightens the child's positive feelings, and connects the child to his or her hero. Finally, while the child is focused on a positive image of the hero in the story, the therapist introduces an item on the child's anxiety hierarchy into the plot. The positive emotions associated with the hero interfere with the child's usual anxious response to the stimulus. The therapist asks the child if the scene is too frightening; if it is, the therapist stops the script and helps the child refocus on the positive aspects of the scene.

> **Figure 7.1 Procedural steps for the implementation of exposure-based techniques**
>
> 1. Establish a warm, supportive, therapeutic environment.
>
> 2. Teach the child to recognize the physical cues that signal anxiety (e.g., muscle tension, hands shaking).
>
> 3. Teach the child relaxation techniques (e.g., progressive muscle relaxation, breathing exercises).
>
> 4. Work with the child to determine his or her anxiety hierarchy. List items in the hierarchy according to the degree of fear or anxiety produced by each, beginning with the stimulus that produces the least amount of anxiety or fear and then increasing gradually. It may be helpful to include the parent(s) in this step, as well.
>
> 5. Lead the child through the hierarchy of anxiety-provoking events using imaginal and/or *in vivo* desensitization techniques. For example, guide a young child through a series of carefully scripted emotive imagery exercises that incorporate the child's favorite superheroes while gradually introducing items from the child's anxiety hierarchy into the plot of the story.

Evidence for Use

Exposure-based techniques (e.g., *in vivo* and imaginal desensitization, emotive imagery) have been found to decrease behavioral disturbances associated with fear of the dark, fear of loud noises, and fear of water (Cornwall, Spence, & Schotte, 1996; King, Cranstoun, & Josephs, 1989; Mendez & Garcia, 1996; Pomerantz, Peterson, Marholin, & Stern, 1977; Ultee, Griffioen, & Schellekens, 1982). The following studies summarize some of the key research findings associated with the use of exposure-based techniques as an intervention for children and adolescents with anxiety.

Cornwall, E., Spence, S. H., & Schotte, D. (1996). The effectiveness of emotive imagery in the treatment of darkness phobia in children. *Behaviour Change, 13*(4), 223–229.

This study examined the effects of emotive imagery treatment on 24 children aged 7 to 10 years who had darkness phobia that was unrealistic and excessive and that significantly interfered with their daily lives. Half of the children were randomly assigned to the treatment group, half to a waiting-list control group. In the treatment group, children were told to imagine themselves in different scenes involving darkness combined with positive imagery, such as their favorite superhero, and to rate their level of fear. They were also encouraged to practice recalling the emotive imagery stories as they attempted exposure to different degrees of darkness at home. Results of the study, based on assessments by children and parents, as well as observations and fear ratings, demonstrated that the children who had emotive imagery treatment displayed significantly less fear of the dark following treatment than the children in the control group. This result was maintained at 3-month follow-up.

King, N., Cranstoun, F., & Josephs, A. (1989). Emotive imagery and children's night-time fears: A multiple baseline design evaluation. *Journal of Behavior Therapy and Experimental Psychiatry, 20*(2), 125–135.

This study investigated the use of emotive imagery—a systematic desensitization technique utilizing children's hero images within narratives designed to address phobias—when treating 3 children with excessive fears of the dark. After working with each child to select a theme (Inspector Gadget, Care Bears™, and Goonies) and determine anxiety hierarchies, scripts involving each child's theme and anxieties were generated for use during emotive imagery sessions. The children participated in 6 to 13 sessions, each lasting approximately 30 minutes. Data were collected via parent interviews and questionnaires, darkness tolerance tests, night-time behavior documentation, and the Fear Survey Schedule for Children–Revised (FSSC–R). While all 3 participants showed increased tolerance for darkness (from 10–110 seconds at baseline to peaks of 125–180 during treatment), only 2 of the children decreased the number of nights they slept in their parents' beds; the third child slept in his mother's bed every night throughout baseline and treatment.

King, N. J., Molloy, G. N., Heyne, D., Murphy, G. C., & Ollendick, T. H. (1998). Emotive imagery treatment for childhood phobias: A credible and empirically validated intervention? *Behavioural and Cognitive Psychotherapy, 26,* 103–113.

Seeking to evaluate the effectiveness of emotive imagery for treating childhood phobias, this literature review documented the clinical and research support for this intervention. As evidence, the authors cited several published studies whose participants demonstrated improvement in behaviors associated with their phobias (e.g., dogs, darkness), some of whom completely overcame such phobias. Available studies suggested that participants and their parents found emotive imagery to be effective, acceptable, and ethical. However, methodological and theoretical issues remain, as indicated by the literature's overwhelming focus on the fear of darkness. There is also insufficient information on the efficacy and long-term effectiveness of emotive imagery compared to other treatments. In sum, the authors were encouraged by the preliminary support for emotive imagery's effectiveness but caution that more investigation is needed in order to provide further empirical support for this form of treatment.

Mendez, F. J., & Garcia, M. J. (1996). Emotive performances: A treatment package for children's phobias. *Child and Family Behavior Therapy, 18*(3), 19–34.

This study examined the efficacy of the emotive performances (EP) treatment package, an intervention that utilizes desensitization, participant modeling, and reinforcement to treat children younger than 9 years of age who are experiencing phobias. The 15 participants, all children suffering from fear of the dark and loud noises, each underwent the EP intervention during eight biweekly individual sessions, first addressing the fear of darkness and then the fear of loud noises. Story scripts (darkness: the adventures of Superman; loud noises: a birthday party) and anxiety hierarchies (darkness: light intensity and exposure time; loud noises: noise intensity and distance) were created to address each phobia and were utilized during treatment sessions. In addition, a token reinforcement system was employed that rewarded participants when they behaved in an appropriate manner (i.e., without anxiety) in response to stimuli on the hierarchy. Results confirmed the efficacy of the EP treatment package, with all participants demonstrating significant improvement in phobia-related anxiety, gains that were maintained at 3- and 6-month follow-up.

Menzies, R. G., & Clarke, J. C. (1993). A comparison of *in vivo* and vicarious exposure in the treatment of childhood water phobia. *Behaviour Research and Therapy, 31*(1), 9–15.

Seeking to determine the comparative effectiveness of two exposure-based therapies, this study followed 48 children, aged between 3 and 8 years and suffering from water phobia, who were randomly assigned to one of four treatment groups: *in vivo* plus vicarious exposure (IVVE; live modeling of water activities plus child performing water activities), vicarious exposure (VE; live modeling of water activities), *in vivo* exposure (IVE; child performing water activities), or assessment-only control. Each child assigned to a treatment group participated in three individual therapy sessions over the course of 3 weeks. Results indicated that the IVVE and IVE groups made significant gains in fear reduction from pretreatment to posttreatment as compared to the control group. Conversely, the VE group did not make such gains; rather, the posttreatment assessment results did not differ significantly from those of the control group. Because research has shown that peer models are more effective than adult models when treating children, the authors suggest that the use of an adult model in this study may have been the cause of the VE group's inferior outcome and that future investigations should take this into consideration.

Pomerantz, P. B., Peterson, N. T., Marholin, D., II, & Stern, S. (1977). The *in vivo* elimination of a child's water phobia by a paraprofessional at home. *Journal of Behavior Therapy and Experimental Psychiatry, 8,* 417–421.

This case study documented the treatment of a 4-year-old boy suffering from water phobia. The child underwent a behavioral treatment program—conducted in his home by a paraprofessional and the child's mother—that combined *in vivo* desensitization with participant modeling in 30-minute sessions, five times a week. The paraprofessional and the child's mother first created a hierarchy of desensitization behaviors, which formed the basis for treatment sessions. The two initial sessions were conducted by the paraprofessional in the presence of the mother; all subsequent sessions were conducted by the mother while being coached by the paraprofessional. Results showed that the boy overcame his water phobia in 11 treatment sessions, with no regression noted at 1- and 6-month follow-up. These results offer evidence that systematic desensitization is effective at removing or decreasing phobic reactions and that a well-trained paraprofessional can effectively administer sophisticated behavioral intervention programs.

Sheslow, D. V., Bondy, A. S., & Nelson, R. O. (1982). A comparison of graduated exposure, verbal coping skills, and their combination in the treatment of children's fear of the dark. *Child and Family Behavior Therapy, 4*(2/3), 33–45.

Thirty-two children aged 4 to 5 who attended a day care center were chosen for this study because of parent reports of fearfulness of the dark, which were confirmed by pretests. The children were randomly assigned to four groups: graduated exposure, verbal coping skills, combined (exposure + coping skills), and control. In the first group, the children were gradually exposed to greater degrees of darkness while playing with the therapist in a room. There was always an easy way for the child to choose to have more light. In the second group, children were taught to respond to particular fears about the dark (e.g., hearing noises) with specific phrases (e.g., "it's just people talking"). The third group also learned these coping skills, but during the last session, graduated exposure to darkness was included. Results showed that only the groups with graduated exposure to darkness showed any improvement from pretest to posttest, with the first group (those who had the most exposure to darkness) improving most significantly. The verbal skills group showed no improvement compared to the control group.

Ultee, C. A., Griffioen, D., & Schellekens, J. (1982). The reduction of anxiety in children: A comparison of the effects of systematic desensitization *in vitro* and systematic desensitization *in vivo. Behaviour Research and Therapy, 20,* 61–67.

This study compared the effects of *in vitro* and *in vivo* desensitization for 24 children who were experiencing anxiety during swimming lessons and practicing water-avoidance behaviors. The children, aged between 5 and 10 years, were randomly assigned to one of three study groups: *in vitro, in vivo,* or control. The *in vitro* treatment consisted of four sessions of imagery (*in vitro* exposure, in which contact with water was imagined), followed by four sessions of gradual physical contact with water (*in vivo* exposure). The *in vivo* treatment consisted of eight sessions of gradual physical contact with water. The control group participated in data collection testing only. A hierarchy of desensitization behaviors was created, based on child and swimming instructor interviews, for use with both the *in vitro* and *in vivo* treatment groups. Findings demonstrated that while those in the *in vitro* group initially showed greater reductions in fear symptoms (after four sessions), it was the *in vivo* group that ultimately evidenced the greatest gains after the full eight-session protocol. These results suggest that real-life exposure to feared stimuli is superior to imagery-based exposure and that combining the two may not offer any practical treatment benefits.

Considerations

When implementing exposure-based techniques, it is important to distinguish between anxieties that are learned behaviors and those that are triggered by specific antecedents. Also, keep in mind that some anxieties and behaviors are less appropriate for desensitization training (e.g., fear and anxiety experienced by a person who has been bullied, threatened, or abused).

For Age and Developmental Level

Exposure-based techniques may be too stressful for very young children. A very young child placed in such a stressful therapy session would lack the social and verbal skills to request ending the session. In addition, imaginal desensitization exercises may be too abstract for a very young child to understand.

II. Contingency Management

As an intervention for anxiety, contingency management relies on the use of natural consequences and reinforcers for reducing anxieties associated with specific behaviors or events (Flood & Wilder, 2004). Contingency management for anxiety includes shaping, positive reinforcement, and extinction (King, Muris, & Ollendick, 2005).

The goal of contingency management is to alter anxious or fear-based behavior. Desired outcomes can vary across children. For example, a student experiencing severe test anxiety might prefer to receive an external reward for test taking and test completion. Another student experiencing similar problems might prefer to have the option to forgo completing certain aspects of a task, provided that other tasks or assignments are completed.

Implementation

Contingency-management strategies require rewards and consequences that match the needs and preferences of each child. To be effective, reinforcers must be perceived as desirable by the child, and consequences must be focused on changing maladaptive behavior (e.g., truancy, avoidance, lying to escape) rather than punishing the anxiety. Over time, reinforcers (e.g., tangible rewards) are gradually replaced by social reinforcers (e.g., attention, praise) and ultimately by internal management and reinforcement (e.g., feeling good about the situation and accomplishments). The fading out of reinforcers is important, because it increases the likelihood that desired behavior will continue beyond the period of direct intervention and that the child will learn how to handle future anxiety.

The basic elements of contingency management for anxiety include shaping appropriate behaviors, positive reinforcement, and extinction (King, Muris, & Ollendick, 2005). When implementing contingency-management strategies, it can be helpful to offer fixed-choice opportunities or to allow a child to select from a list of available, appropriate reinforcers rather than asking the child to generate his or her own list of desired reinforcers that may be unrealistic (e.g., a trip to Disneyland, a cell phone for a 7-year-old). Also, keep in mind that competing reinforcement outside the control of the practitioner can affect the strength of this intervention. For example, reinforcers such as reward tokens or extra computer time might not be able to compete with other available reinforcers, such as attention from peers or the feeling of relief that the child may get from crying or making up an excuse to avoid taking a test. Finally, consider the effects of satiation; if the child has extensive access to the reinforcer, its reinforcement properties will be weaker. The procedural steps for implementing contingency management are listed in Figure 7.2.

Figure 7.2 Procedural steps for the implementation of contingency management

1. Identify the specific anxiety-related behaviors that need to be addressed.

2. Ask the child to choose from an existing list of preferred reinforcers.

3. Determine a reinforcement schedule, and review it with the child. During the initial stages, use shaping techniques (i.e., reinforce successive approximations to engage in the desired behavior).

4. Determine appropriate consequences for maladaptive behaviors, and review them with the child (i.e., what will happen if the child responds to anxiety by throwing a tantrum, destroying property, or refusing to do something).

5. Replace tangible reinforcers with social reinforcers. This transition should be planned and should happen gradually, at a pace designed to meet the needs of the child while maintaining the effect of the reinforcement for appropriate behavior.

Evidence for Use

Contingency management for anxiety has been found to decrease phobic reactions (e.g., fear of dogs, water, dark rooms) and separation anxiety (Flood & Wilder, 2004; Glasscock & MacLean, 1990; Leitenberg & Callahan, 1973). The following studies summarize some of the key research findings associated with the use of contingency management as an intervention for children and adolescents with anxiety.

Flood, W. A., & Wilder, D. A. (2004). The use of differential reinforcement and fading to increase time away from a caregiver in a child with separation anxiety disorder. *Education and Treatment of Children, 27*(1), 1–8.

This case study examined the effects of contingent access to reinforcers (i.e., video games, candy, and toy store coupons) and graduated exposure to separation on the symptoms of separation anxiety disorder (SAD). The participant, an 11-year-old boy diagnosed with SAD, attended two sessions per week for 23 weeks. In each session, his mother moved out of sight at increasing distances and for increasing periods of time. Access to reinforcers was contingent upon the child refraining from emotional behavior (i.e., crying and/or asking for a parent more than once) for a predetermined and mutually decided upon time and distance goal. Results showed that the participant, who was only able to contain emotional behavior for a mean of 3 seconds during baseline, met the set goals for all but one session during the intervention phase, increasing the time and distance away to 90 minutes and his mother leaving the building. Moreover, the child's mother reported that the results were replicated in the home, demonstrating the potential of differential reinforcement for treating children with SAD.

Glasscock, S. E., & MacLean, W. E., Jr. (1990). Use of contact desensitization and shaping in the treatment of dog phobia and generalized fear of the outdoors. *Journal of Clinical Child Psychology, 19*(2), 169–172.

This investigation focused on the effects of a contact desensitization and shaping intervention using social reinforcers for a 6-year-old girl who suffered from a phobia of dogs and an aversion to the outdoors after a dog attack. Contact desensitization involved creating a hierarchy of 10 behavioral steps designed to slowly expose the child to her feared situations, progressing from a low-level feared situation (walking outside her house) to her most feared situation (petting and talking to a dog). Shaping involved playing outside, with a dog in her vicinity, for progressively longer periods of time (5, 10, 15, and 20 minutes). Praise from the girl's mother and siblings provided social reinforcement for meeting each time goal. While able to be alone outside for less than 1 minute in each of the studied environments during baseline, the girl was able to do so for 20 minutes by the end of treatment. Moreover, she was able to play alone outside for over an hour at 9-month follow-up, often initiating outdoor play on her own.

Leitenberg, H., & Callahan, E. J. (1973). Reinforced practice and reduction of different kinds of fears in adults and children. *Behaviour Research and Therapy, 11,* 19–30.

A series of four experiments examined the effectiveness of repeated practice, reinforcement, feedback, and therapeutic instruction for alleviating the symptoms of a variety of common fears held by adults (e.g., heights, harmless snakes, electric shock) and children (e.g., darkness). Regardless of fear and age, participants who underwent the intervention procedure in each experiment demonstrated marked improvement in fear symptoms as compared to those in the control groups. These results suggest that a single treatment procedure can be effective in treating the escape and/or avoidance behavior associated with phobias of varying origins and occurring at different ages.

Obler, M., & Terwilliger, R. F. (1970). Pilot study on the effectiveness of systematic desensitization with neurologically impaired children with phobic disorders. *Journal of Consulting and Clinical Psychology, 34*(3), 314–318.

This study—the first to investigate the use of reinforced contact desensitization to treat phobias in children with neurological impairments—followed 30 children diagnosed with minimal brain dysfunction and either a fear of dogs or of riding public buses. The children, aged between 7 and 12 years, were randomly assigned to one of two study groups: treatment or control. The treatment group participated in 5-hour weekly individual sessions for 10 weeks. The therapist first exposed the children to pictures or models of the feared situation/object and then slowly exposed them to greater contact with the actual situation/object, with the therapist acting as a buffer between the children and the feared stimulus. Both social reinforcers (e.g., approval, encouragement) and tangible reinforcers (e.g., toys, books, candy) were provided when the children demonstrated tolerance for progressively higher levels on the anxiety hierarchy. Results demonstrated that those in the treatment group significantly reduced their fear symptoms, whereas the control group evidenced no such gains. At posttreatment, 100% of the treatment group participants were able to either ride a bus or touch a dog with another person present, while just 20% of the control group participants were able to do so.

Considerations

For Age and Developmental Level

When asking children to generate a list of desired reinforcers, it is important to remind them to list things that are both realistic and age-appropriate. In order to avoid problems, consider asking a parent to provide some examples of attainable reinforcers and then give the child the option to choose from such a list. When generating a list of reinforcers, consult with teachers or other adults, because they can sometimes provide clues about preferences and high-interest activities. Young children may be more comfortable with small numbers of choices such as a fruit snack, rocking in a chair, or choosing a song for circle time. Older students may prefer access to music on an MP3 player, social time with peers, or one-on-one time with a teacher. Consider also the effects of satiation; if the child has unlimited and extensive access to the reinforcer, the item will have less reinforcement strength.

For Culture and Language Differences

Be aware that what looks like anxiety may be post-traumatic stress for an individual who may have immigrated under stressful conditions. Consider that a new culture, a new language, and the accompanying expectations may create performance anxiety that is difficult to escape at school, where both academic and social expectations are tied to a specific culture. Use careful consideration of all factors that may contribute to anxious behavior.

For Health and Safety

Some case studies indicate that anxiety or phobic reactions to certain events may be rooted in violence, abuse, or neglect. Consider carefully the antecedents to anxiety. For example, fear of showering may be an indication that the child views undressing and showering as risky activities or associates them with something anxiety producing.

III. Modeling

Showing children examples of successful outcomes in anxiety-provoking situations can effectively reduce anxiety-related beliefs and behaviors. Such modeling can be live or shown on film, and is based on the concept of vicarious conditioning (Berger, 1962; Bandura, 1977). One variation of this approach is to use participant modeling, in which a child who has observed a therapist or other person confronting an anxiety-provoking stimulus will mimic the behavior, thus becoming an active participant in the exercise.

For example, Raymond was afraid of dogs and would not walk to school because he had to pass dogs on the street. He watched a video of a boy walking by several dogs through a neighborhood while on his way to school. Raymond watched the boy successfully reach school, without any negative consequences. The video helped him recognize that he, too, could get through a similar situation.

Implementation

The goals of modeling are to reduce the child's anxiety by demonstrating the event and consequences in a nonanxiety-provoking manner and to help the child acquire a new skill to handle the anxiety (Bandura, 1977; Ollendick & King, 1998). The basic elements of modeling include presenting an anxiety-provoking scenario in a way that demonstrates a desirable and successful outcome. The procedural steps for implementing the modeling strategy are listed in Figure 7.3.

1. Identify, describe, and discuss the anxiety problem and the concept of watching a video or modeling. Reassure the child that nothing bad will happen during the demonstration.

2. Show the child an anxiety-provoking situation or event using video or live models.

3. Discuss with the child the events in the demonstration, identifying the antecedents to the event, the event itself, and the consequences of the event.

4. Identify the responses and behaviors used by the models that the child would feel comfortable using. Ask the child to describe how he or she would engage in such responses and behaviors.

5. Practice the desired responses and behaviors with the child.

Evidence for Use

Filmed and participant modeling have been found to be effective in decreasing phobic reactions and reducing preprocedural distress (e.g., dentist visits, injections) and preoperational anxiety (Bandura, Blanchard, & Ritter, 1969; Faust, Olson, & Rodriguez, 1991; Klingman, Melamed, Cuthbert, & Hermecz, 1984; Melamed, Yurcheson, Fleece, Hutcherson, & Hawes, 1978; Murphy & Bootzin, 1973). The following studies summarize some of the key research findings associated with the use of filmed and participant modeling as interventions for children and adolescents with anxiety.

Bandura, A., Blanchard, E. B., & Ritter, B. (1969). Relative efficacy of desensitization and modeling approaches for inducing behavioral, affective, and attitudinal changes. *Journal of Personality and Social Psychology, 13*(3), 173–199.

Forty-eight adults and teens with a debilitating fear of snakes were randomly assigned to one of four groups: systematic desensitization (i.e., being shown increasingly fear-provoking images of snakes, combined with relaxation methods), symbolic modeling (i.e., viewing photographs of models handling snakes), live modeling with guided participation (i.e., watching a live model handle a snake and then being walked through handling it in the same way), and a control group. After the brief study, all treatment groups showed significant decreases in fear levels and significant increases in their ability and willingness to handle snakes; however, live modeling with guided participation resulted in the greatest improvement.

Faust, J., Olson, R., & Rodriguez, H. (1991). Same-day surgery preparation: Reduction of pediatric patient arousal and distress through participant modeling. *Journal of Consulting and Clinical Psychology, 59*(3), 475–478.

This study investigated the impact of participant modeling in teaching coping skills to children undergoing elective ear tube surgery. It sought to determine whether or not the presence of a caregiver during modeling alleviated the children's preoperative and postoperative distress. The participants were 26 children, aged between 4 and 10 years, who were randomly assigned to one of three groups: participant modeling for the child alone, participant modeling with the child's mother present, or standard procedure. Children in both participant modeling groups viewed a 10-minute slide tape showing a child using techniques such as deep breathing and imagery to deal with preoperative anxiety. Those in the standard procedure group received information about the surgery according to the hospital's standard script and were also allowed to see and touch operating room equipment. Results demonstrated that only the children who experienced participant modeling alone had significantly decreased levels in both heart rate and sweating. The greater effectiveness of modeling when the child was alone (rather than with mother present) suggests that the mother's participation might distract the child from learning the coping techniques presented, or that the mother's own preoperative anxiety may serve as a model for the child.

Klingman, A., Melamed, B. G., Cuthbert, M. I., & Hermecz, D. A. (1984). Effects of participant modeling on information acquisition and skill utilization. *Journal of Consulting and Clinical Psychology, 52*(3), 414–422.

This investigation compared the effectiveness of active participant modeling and symbolic modeling of coping techniques when treating children with fears of injections. Participants were 38 children, aged between 8 and 13 years, who were identified as needing a simple restorative dental procedure that required local anesthesia. After random assignment into two groups, Group A (participant modeling) and Group B (symbolic modeling), each child made two visits to the dental clinic: a screening visit and a treatment visit. During the treatment visit, prior to undergoing the dental procedure, all participants viewed videos portraying two children modeling controlled breathing and imagery to cope with the tooth restoration procedure. However, the video viewed by Group A prompted the viewer to actively practice the coping techniques, while the Group B video merely demonstrated the techniques. The effectiveness of each video was assessed by comparing the participants' responses to a fear survey before and after the video, in addition to observers' ratings of the children's self-control in the operating room and direct measurement of physiological changes (i.e., heart rate, breathing). All measures supported the comparative effectiveness of active participant modeling over symbolic modeling.

Melamed, B. G., Yurcheson, R., Fleece, E. L., Hutcherson, S., & Hawes, R. (1978). Effects of film modeling on the reduction of anxiety-related behaviors in individuals varying in level of previous experience in the stress situation. *Journal of Consulting and Clinical Psychology, 46*(6), 1357–1367.

This study investigated the relative effectiveness of filmed peer modeling versus a filmed demonstration of dental procedures (without modeling) for children of different ages and with previous levels of dental experience. The impact of the length of the film was also examined. Eighty children, aged between 4 and 11 years, who needed to undergo dental procedures due to cavity formation, participated in the study. Just prior to undergoing the tooth restoration procedure, participants were randomly assigned to watch one of five videos: 1) long model [a cooperative and fearless child experiencing cavity restoration, 10 minutes in length], 2) long demonstration [a dentist and assistant demonstrating the restoration procedure without a child model, 10 minutes], 3) short model [a cooperative child receiving anesthesia and an oral exam, 4 minutes], 4) short demonstration [a dentist and assistant demonstrating the injection and exam without a child model, 4 minutes], or 5) unrelated control [a child creating a special place for himself in his living room]. Results indicated that peer modeling was more effective than simple demonstration, with children who viewed the long and short model videos reporting less fear and apprehension and exhibiting fewer disruptive behaviors during procedures than those in the other study groups.

Murphy, C. M., & Bootzin, R. R. (1973). Active and passive participation in the contact desensitization of snake fear in children. *Behavior Therapy, 4,* 203–211.

This study examined the impact of active versus passive participation on the effectiveness of a contact desensitization intervention for 67 children suffering from snake phobia. The participants were randomly assigned to one of three treatment groups: active participation, passive participation, or control. A hierarchy of snake-desensitizing behaviors was created and utilized at pretest, treatment, and posttest. Treatment sessions were conducted one-on-one, with a maximum of four 8-minute sessions per child. Treatment for the active participation group had the participants observe the experimenter modeling each behavior in the hierarchy and then attempt to perform it themselves. Treatment for the passive participation group had the child sit in a chair while the therapist carried a snake slowly toward him or her, gradually coming closer until the therapist was able to touch the snake to the child's hand. Results indicated that contact desensitization was a highly effective and efficient intervention for treating childhood snake phobia, regardless of whether participation was passive or active, with 87% of treated children able to successfully complete all items at posttest, compared to just 23% of participants in the control group.

Considerations

The primary concept in modeling—critical to the effectiveness of the intervention—is a successful experience with the anxiety-provoking event. At any time, if the modeling or video becomes stressful for the participant, the session should stop. The idea should be to build resistance by gradual exposure. Videos or models should be sensitive to culture, language, and age appropriateness. Subjects who are similar to the child are more likely to resonate with the child (e.g., an adult male is unlikely to be a good model for a 6-year-old girl).

IV. Family Therapy

Involving family members in anxiety-related intervention strategies can increase the strategies' effectiveness. Research has examined the effects of several strategies for increasing parental involvement or modifying the type of involvement that currently exists, including modifying attachment levels and caregiving practices, decreasing maternal control, and providing communication training (Ginsburg, Silverman, & Kurtines, 1995; Howes, Galinsky, & Kontos, 1998; Kochanska & Aksan, 1995).

For example, Emily experienced anxiety from several sources, including a fear of dogs, speaking out in school, and talking to other children. One parent was very supportive, bordering on enabling, while the other parent believed Emily needed to be forced to pet dogs, speak in class, and make friends. Emily's parents were taught some effective techniques to support their daughter when she felt anxious and were taught to work with Emily in a more positive and productive way to help her overcome her anxieties.

Implementation

While the implementation of various family involvement approaches will vary, most will require several educational sessions to teach the common causes, consequences, and strategies to combat anxiety. Common examples of training topics include anxiety management, discipline management, and communication. Each of these strategies involves distinct procedural steps for implementation, so a listing of these steps is not provided here.

Evidence for Use

Involving family members in interventions for youth with anxiety has been found to reduce clinically significant levels of anxiety to nonclinically significant levels, to decrease symptoms of anxiety, and to increase effective coping skills (Barrett, 1998; Barrett, Dadds, & Rapee, 1996; Cobham, Dadds, & Spence, 1998; Dadds, Heard, & Rapee, 1992; Mendlowitz et al., 1999; Spence, Donovan, & Brechman-Toussaint, 2000; Wood, Piacentini, Southam-Gerow, Chu, & Sigman, 2006). The following studies summarize some of the key research findings associated with family involvement in interventions for children and adolescents with anxiety.

Barrett, P. M. (1998). Evaluation of cognitive-behavioral group treatments for childhood anxiety disorders. *Journal of Clinical Child Psychology, 27*(4), 459–468.

In this study, 60 students with anxiety disorders were randomly assigned to one of three groups: group cognitive–behavioral therapy for the child only (GROUP-CBT), group cognitive–behavioral therapy plus family management training (GROUP-FAM), or a waiting list. The children in GROUP-CBT were taught anxiety management strategies such as recognizing positive and negative thoughts, coping self-talk, relaxation strategies, realistic self-evaluation, and self-rewards. Modeling and role-playing were used in the training. In the GROUP-FAM treatment, these same child trainings were used and, in addition, parents were taught how to reinforce courageous behavior and help minimize anxiety in their children, as well as how to manage their own anxiety, use problem-solving techniques, and communicate better with each other and with their children. Results showed that both treatment groups greatly reduced the number of children who met diagnostic criteria for anxiety disorders after training: about 65% across treatment conditions vs. 25% for the waiting list. At 12-month follow-up, about 65% and 85% of children were diagnosis free for the GROUP-CBT and GROUP-FAM, respectively, suggesting a marginal (though not statistically significant) advantage for family inclusion in treatment. Clinicians' ratings and parents' and children's self-assessments at posttreatment and 12-month follow-up provided further support for both treatment conditions, with the family inclusion condition showing slight superiority to child-only treatment.

Barrett, P. M., Dadds, M. R., & Rapee, R. M. (1996). Family treatment of childhood anxiety: A controlled trial. *Journal of Consulting and Clinical Psychology, 64*(2), 333–342.

In this study, 79 children aged 7–14 years, identified as having anxiety disorders, were randomly assigned to one of three groups: cognitive–behavioral treatment (CBT), cognitive–behavioral treatment plus family anxiety management (CBT + FAM), or a waiting list. In the CBT group, children attended 12 weekly sessions where they were taught anxiety management strategies such as recognizing positive and negative thoughts, coping self-talk, relaxation strategies, realistic self-evaluation, and self-rewards. In the CBT + FAM group, these same child trainings were used and, in addition, parents were taught how to reinforce courageous behavior and help minimize anxiety in their children, as well as how to manage their own anxiety, use problem-solving techniques, and communicate better with each other and with their children. Results showed that both treatment groups were highly effective in reducing anxiety: about 70% across treatment conditions vs. 26% for the waiting list. Parents' and children's self-report measures as well as clinicians' ratings provided limited support for the superiority of the family involvement condition; however, treatment effectiveness varied depending on the age and sex of the child. Having family involved in treatment led to more positive results for girls and younger children, whereas for boys and older children, either treatment was equally effective.

Cobham, V. E., Dadds, M. R., & Spence, S. H. (1998). The role of parental anxiety in the treatment of childhood anxiety. *Journal of Consulting and Clinical Psychology, 66*(6), 893–905.

This study investigated the impact of child-focused cognitive–behavioral therapy (CBT) with or without a parental anxiety management (PAM) component on the behavior of 67 children, aged between 7 and 14 years, diagnosed with anxiety disorders. Initially, all participants and their parents were administered diagnostic assessments to determine pretreatment levels of anxiety. Participants were then assigned to one of two conditions (child + parental anxiety or child anxiety only) based on the results of the parent assessments. Next, the children were randomly assigned to one of two interventions (CBT or CBT + PAM), resulting in the study's four treatment groups. The 10-week CBT program involved training in basic relaxation techniques, cognitive restructuring, coping self-talk, parent-assisted exposure to feared stimuli, and contingency management. The 4-week PAM program involved training in anxiety disorder etiology, cognitive restructuring, relaxation, and contingency management. For children with one or more anxious parents, posttreatment measures indicated that the treatment incorporating parental anxiety management was significantly more effective (77% of such children were free of anxiety diagnosis following CBT + PAM, compared with only 39% of such children following child-only CBT). No difference between CBT and CBT+PAM was found for children with nonanxious parents. These results underscore the importance of taking parental anxiety levels and management into account when treating childhood anxiety disorders.

Dadds, M. R., Heard, P. M., & Rapee, R. M. (1992). The role of family intervention in the treatment of child anxiety disorders: Some preliminary findings. *Behaviour Change, 9*(3), 171–177.

This study examined the effectiveness of family anxiety management as a component of treatment for children's anxiety disorders. Fourteen children with anxiety disorders were randomly assigned either to a cognitive–behavioral plus family anxiety management treatment group or to a waiting-list control group. Children in the treatment group completed a cognitive–behavioral therapy program incorporating exposure-based techniques and cognitive restructuring, while their parents participated in a series of 12 weekly 90-minute sessions that provided training in anxiety management strategies and effective discipline, communication, and problem-solving. At posttreatment, 70% of the children in the treatment group were free of anxiety diagnosis, and the 2 other children in this group also showed notable improvement. In contrast, none of the children in the control group showed improvement. These results suggest that CBT with family involvement can be an effective treatment for childhood anxiety.

Mendlowitz, S. L., Manassis, K., Bradley, S., Scapillato, D., Miezitis, S., & Shaw, B. F. (1999). Cognitive-behavioral group treatments in childhood anxiety disorders: The role of parental involvement. *Journal of the American Academy of Child and Adolescent Psychiatry, 38*(10), 1223–1229.

While previous studies have demonstrated the efficacy of cognitive–behavioral therapy (CBT) for treating children with anxiety disorders, this 2-year study sought to determine the impact of using CBT in a group setting, as well as to examine the role of parental involvement on treatment outcomes. Participants were 62 children, aged between 7 and 12 years and meeting diagnostic criteria for one or more anxiety disorders, and their parents. Each child was randomly assigned to one of three treatment groups: parent and child, child-only, or parent-only. Treatment was conducted in 12 weekly 90-minute sessions during which children were taught coping skills (e.g., physical relaxation exercises and self-talk) and parents were taught how to best understand and help their children. Results supported the efficacy of group CBT, with all treatment groups demonstrating decreases in anxiety and depressive symptoms from pretreatment through posttreatment assessments. Furthermore, the increased parental involvement in the parent and child condition resulted in additional gains, with those parents reporting more frequent use of coping strategies and rating their children more improved at posttreatment compared to the parents in the other two study groups.

Spence, S. H., Donovan, C., & Brechman-Toussaint, M. (2000). The treatment of childhood social phobia: The effectiveness of a social skills training-based, cognitive-behavioural intervention, with and without parental involvement. *Journal of Child Psychology and Psychiatry, 41*(6), 713–716.

In this study, 50 children diagnosed with social phobia were randomly assigned to one of three treatment groups: cognitive–behavioral therapy (CBT) with parent involvement (PI), CBT without parent involvement (PNI), or wait-list control (WLC). The CBT treatment utilized for both the PI and PNI groups involved training in social skills, positive self-instruction, cognitive challenging, graded exposure to feared social situations, reinforcement games, and homework assignments presented over the course of 12 weekly sessions and 2 booster sessions (at 3 and 6 months posttreatment). The parents of the children in the PI group attended weekly 30-minute sessions during which they learned how to support CBT teachings, including how to model, prompt, and reinforce their children's newly learned skills, model socially confident behavior, and ignore socially anxious behaviors in their children. Parent and child self-report results indicated that social and general anxiety levels significantly decreased in both the PI and PNI groups. These decreases were statistically and clinically significant, with about 88% of the PNI group and 58% of the PI group no longer meeting anxiety diagnostic criteria at posttreatment, as compared to just 7% of the WLC group.

Wood, J. J., Piacentini, J. C., Southam-Gerow, M., Chu, B. C., & Sigman, M. (2006). Family cognitive behavioral therapy for child anxiety disorders. *Journal of the American Academy of Child and Adolescent Psychiatry, 45*(3), 314–321.

In this study, 38 children in elementary and middle school who had anxiety disorders were randomly divided into two groups: child-focused cognitive–behavioral therapy (CCBT) and family cognitive–behavioral therapy (FCBT). In addition to the family anxiety management techniques used in many other studies, the FCBT treatment used in this study also emphasized helping parents give their children autonomy, thus increasing their self-confidence. While the results showed that both treatment conditions greatly reduced the children's anxiety levels, FCBT evidenced significantly better outcomes than CCBT on several measures. For example, independent evaluators' ratings of children's anxiety-related impairments affecting their school, social, and family life were lower among those in the FCBT group, and a significantly higher percentage of students were rated as very much better or completely recovered in the FCBT group, compared to the CCBT group.

Considerations

Families deserve respect as autonomous units that may have different values and structures than either those of the school professional or the school normative culture. The important consideration is sharing of education and expectations, and providing training to the extent it is desired. The focus should be on supporting the family members while they support the child, rather than attributing blame or trying to change a family or child. Culture and language can certainly be challenges to working together, but they can also be strengths. It is important to find common ground and seek a platform of understanding so that information is accurately and helpfully translated.

V. Integrated Cognitive–Behavioral Therapy

Integrated cognitive–behavioral therapy (CBT) for anxiety includes training in both cognitive techniques and behavioral techniques within a prescribed number of therapy sessions. CBT is used to produce changes in thought patterns that will lead to changes in behaviors. CBT typically includes between 5 and 16 sessions, focusing on cognitive techniques during the first half of the sessions and practicing exposure-based techniques (e.g., systematic desensitization) during the second half of the sessions.

Like most CBT therapies, the basic elements of those used to treat anxiety problems consist of problem identification (e.g., recognition of anxious feelings), creating a treatment plan, and evaluating how an individual is doing throughout the sessions. As part of the treatment plan, anxiety CBT sessions will typically include combinations of cognitive strategies, behavioral or exposure-based strategies (supplemented with relaxation activities), and relapse prevention strategies (Flannery-Schroeder & Kendall, 2000).

For example, Shay, a 14-year-old female of average height and weight, refused to go into the high school cafeteria or out to eat in public with her family. When asked about the behavior, Shay related that she felt fat and said, "The other kids watch me eat and think I'm a pig. When they're watching me, I can't swallow and I start sweating. Then I feel sick." The school psychologist implemented an integrated cognitive–behavioral therapy with the dual goal of helping Shay use problem-solving techniques to challenge her own negative self-talk (a cognitive technique) and gradually practice eating in the school cafeteria (a behavioral technique).

Several CBT approaches are discussed below, including psychoeducation, self-monitoring, problem-solving skills training, relaxation training, and cognitive restructuring. Family therapy, discussed previously, is often incorporated into many of these CBT approaches. For each, a brief overview and example are provided, along with the basic elements specific to the intervention and a listing of the procedures for implementation.

A. Psychoeducational Approach

The educational component of cognitive intervention for anxiety focuses on teaching children, and sometimes their families, about the causes and symptoms of anxiety, along with teaching how and why certain events or behaviors may lead to an emotional response (Kearney, 2005; March & Ollendick, 2004). By learning about the thoughts and behaviors that bring about anxiety, children can begin to recognize the relationship between these two factors and lay the groundwork for change in their behavior and emotions.

Implementation

The basic elements of psychoeducation focus on teaching children about the nature of anxiety, its symptoms, and the goal(s) of therapy. Anxiety is sometimes generalized and nonspecific, but typically it is tied to an initial negative experience that triggers a fight or flight response. Individual predispositions vary. For example, some children love the feeling of an elevator or roller coaster; others do not. Some children enjoy the completion of a speech or tennis match; others do not. The physiological responses to events are real, not imagined, and can become generalized. A child who once read a frightening story may transfer that feeling to other similar, or even unrelated, events. The procedural steps listed in Figure 7.4 illustrate how these elements are incorporated into the treatment of an individual child.

> **Figure 7.4 Procedural steps for treating anxiety with education**
>
> 1. Review the common causes of anxiety with the child.
>
> 2. Generate a list of anxiety-provoking stimuli.
>
> 3. Discuss the affective responses that are caused by the anxiety-provoking stimuli.

The information gained from the child during anxiety education sessions also provides a useful basis for creating effective behavioral strategies tailored to the child's specific needs.

B. Self-Monitoring Training

In this approach, the student learns to self-monitor aversive physiological reactions, irrational thoughts, and avoidance behavior (Ginsburg & Walkup, 2004). Diaries, charts, or logbooks can be used to self-monitor. Students are taught to recognize the antecedents (or triggers) and consequences of anxiety. Self-talk is incorporated as part of self-monitoring.

Implementation

The elements essential to self-monitoring training include monitoring, recording, and evaluating behaviors and emotions; learning to recognize when and how to implement new behaviors to reduce the effects of anxiety; and learning when to reinforce changes in behavior. The procedural steps of self-monitoring training presented in Figure 7.5 illustrate how these essential elements are used to remediate symptoms of anxiety. Self-monitoring typically involves physical recording of some kind, which can be done with paper and pencil, or using audio or video. Recording sheets can be as simple as a chart or table for the child to fill in or a graph paper tablet. Some children prefer journaling but may need structure to guide them in recording specific behaviors or feelings rather than just private musings. Frequency and type of recording vary depending on the type and degree of symptomatology.

Figure 7.5 **Procedural steps for self-monitoring training**

1. Develop a way for the child to monitor his or her emotions and behavior by generating a form the child can use to track them, along with a tracking procedure for him or her to follow. Forms used for tracking could be a calendar, notebook, or journal. Recordings could be made hourly or daily. Shorter intervals (e.g., every 15 minutes) might be helpful when there are a number of different transitions made during a day (e.g., classroom changes during school).

2. Determine how often you will check in or meet with the child, and establish a time to review his or her recording form.

3. Review the child's recording form. Discuss with the child how distorted thoughts might be affecting his or her everyday behavior.

4. Choose one or two problem emotions or behaviors to modify, and suggest a solution that the child can implement independently.

5. Check in with the child to mark progress and provide feedback. This check-in can be done at the beginning and end of the school day, for example, or more frequently as needed (particularly in the early stages of intervention).

6. Reward positive efforts, including consistent use of the tracking form and any steps made to resolve problem emotions and behaviors, even though the steps might not always be successful.

C. Problem-Solving Skills Training

Problem-solving strategies can be used to help a child identify specific anxiety-provoking events and replace the thoughts and emotions surrounding those events with healthier thoughts and emotions. Generally speaking, the professional teaches the child to objectify situations and create alternatives for anxiety by identifying appropriate methods to either avoid anxiety or to handle it more effectively. Throughout the learning process, the professional tries to maintain a supportive and safe environment where the child can implement the newly learned methods while being insulated from the event or situation that causes the anxiety (Last, Hansen, & Franco, 1998).

For example, a clinician working with a student suffering from anxiety related to interacting with others may start by helping the child identify where the anxiety is coming from (e.g., feelings of inferiority, lack of social skills, fear of rejection). The clinician would then present the source of the anxiety as a problem and would work with the child to develop a way to address the problem. This approach can help to empower the child to gain control over the anxiety and will promote emotional and behavioral improvement.

Implementation

The elements of problem-solving skills training, which include defining the problem, generating alternative solutions, and choosing and implementing the best solution, are modeled after steps used for problem solving in other disciplines of everyday life. The procedural steps presented in Figure 7.6 illustrate how these essential elements are used to remediate symptoms of anxiety.

Figure 7.6 Procedural steps for treating anxiety with problem solving

1. Discuss with the child the likely causes of his or her anxiety and the resulting symptoms. Present these in the context of a problem to be solved.

2. With the child, brainstorm solutions to the problem. If the problem appears to be too large to solve immediately, break the problem into smaller pieces that are more manageable to work with.

3. Together, evaluate the strengths and weaknesses of each solution and choose the best option to try.

4. Work out a plan with the child, much like a homework assignment, outlining the steps needed and setting a target date for completion.

5. Monitor the child's progress. Consider revising the plan, if needed. Provide plenty of reinforcement for attempts to complete steps and for successes.

D. Relaxation Training

Relaxation training teaches children to begin using ways to relax—for instance, by monitoring muscle tension created by stressful situations and events and by controlling irregular breathing (i.e., teaching the child to slowly breathe in through the nose and out through the mouth) (Kearney, 2005; Ollendick & Cerny, 1981). Physical discomfort caused by tension can exacerbate common anxiety symptoms, causing a child to become even more anxious. Other relaxation techniques include counting, breathing exercises, recall, mental imagery, and progressive muscle relaxation (Kahn, Kehle, Jenson, & Clarke, 1990).

For example, Luanna, a 10-year-old girl, experiences extreme anxiety when placed in new surroundings. To help relieve the anxiety, prior to leaving for a new destination, her parents talk to her about what the location will be like and point out similarities between the new place and other places Luanna has been. When going to places unlike those Luanna has been to previously, her parents search for pictures and/or maps of the location and review with her what it will be like and the places they will visit. By focusing on the positive and familiar aspects of the locations, Luanna begins to create positive associations with the new locations. The positive associations help her to relax and minimize the amount of anxiety she experiences when traveling there.

Implementation

Counting and breathing techniques are simple for children of all ages, requiring the child to concentrate on counting or breathing when feeling symptoms of anxiety. The recall technique requires a child to think about a previous successful or pleasant event; pleasant feelings and emotions associated with the event will help reduce negative feelings and emotions. Mental imagery and progressive muscle relaxation techniques require a child to focus on a specific event or part of the body and envision the steps needed to succeed at the event or relax the affected part of the body. The essential elements of all these techniques include the identification of the emotional triggers and their corresponding physical symptoms, engagement in an activity designed to reduce the negative emotions associated with the anxiety symptoms, and recognition of when the negative emotions and feelings start to improve. The procedural steps of CBT relaxation techniques presented in Figure 7.7 illustrate how these essential elements are used to remediate anxiety symptoms.

Figure 7.7 **Procedural steps for relaxation training**

1. Identify a specific symptom of the child's anxiety, along with the effect it has on the child (e.g., increased breathing, sweating).

2. Teach the child how to perform the relaxation technique.

3. Ask the child to imagine a situation that causes the undesired symptoms.

4. Practice the technique with the child until he or she is able to perform the steps by himself or herself. Model the steps for the child, as needed.

5. Check in with the child periodically to determine if the relaxation techniques are being practiced correctly and at the appropriate times. Provide refresher training as necessary.

E. Cognitive Restructuring

Cognitive restructuring teaches students to identify their own negative irrational thoughts and supplant them with healthier, more realistic thoughts. Students are taught to identify and classify the irrational thoughts they have during anxiety-provoking events and to modify their irrational thoughts by making realistic appraisals of the events. Cognitive restructuring techniques include rational analysis (examining evidence for and against thoughts), decatastrophising (reconsidering how bad the worst-case scenario actually is), cognitive self-control, decentering (increasing awareness through perspective shifting of focus from self to other), reattribution training (helping students determine attributes of failure that are not internal, global, or stable in nature), reframing/relabeling, conducting behavioral experiments, using verbal self-instruction, and engaging in cognitive rehearsal. These strategies can be used to reinforce positive thinking and promote more positive and productive behaviors.

For example, a child suffering from anxiety may have a fear of using a public bathroom. Using cognitive restructuring, the clinician would help the child recognize the aspects of the bathroom that worry the child and talk about what true effects these aspects may have on the child. For instance, a child worried about getting germs can be taught that using a paper towel when touching the bathroom faucet and door handle can help to reduce the number of germs he or she is exposed to. The clinician would then challenge the child to rethink using public bathrooms when using the newly learned behaviors and to use self-talk to remind himself or herself about the effects of the newly learned behaviors (e.g., the child is taught to say to himself or herself, "Using a paper towel when touching things in the bathroom will help to keep germs off of me."). In this way, the child begins to reinterpret the experience of using a public bathroom, seeing it in a more positive light.

Implementation

The goal of cognitive restructuring is to modify cognitions associated with anxiety. The basic elements of cognitive restructuring are identifying, challenging, and changing anxious thoughts and beliefs (Hops & Lewinsohn, 1995). For younger children, tools or methods such as songs, rhymes, or video representations may be helpful in identifying negative cognitions and understanding the connections among thoughts, feelings, and behaviors. Self-evaluation and self-reward are key ingredients for social phobia and anxiety treatment (Albano, Detweiler, & Logsdon-Conradsen, 1999). The ability to self-evaluate and self-reward will increase self-confidence in anxiety-provoking situations. The procedural steps described in Figure 7.8 can help a child to engage in a more rational self-analysis of his or her thoughts.

> **Figure 7.8 Procedural steps for cognitive restructuring**
>
> 1. Identify the child's anxiety symptoms.
>
> 2. Teach the child how to recognize thoughts that are negative. Young children may find cartoons to be helpful. For instance, draw a thought bubble over the head of a character and ask the child to write in (or describe) the thoughts. Older students might keep a diary or journal of their thoughts.
>
> 3. Explain how negative thoughts are connected to anxious feelings or exaggerated and unproductive thinking (as described above, the use of a cartoon or journal might be helpful).
>
> 4. Explore specific actions the child can take to think more adaptively. For example:
>
>   a. *Using a stop sign.* Ask the child to imagine a stop sign when negative thinking occurs. This cue can be used to replace a negative thought with a positive one.
>
>   b. *Self-tracking.* Choose one negative thought (e.g., "other kids are laughing at me") and ask the child to record how often it occurs. Then agree on a new thought to replace the negative one (e.g., "I'm okay just how I am.").
>
> 5. Encourage the child to practice consistently. Monitor his or her progress at future sessions.

F. Relapse-Prevention Training

After anxiety interventions have been successfully implemented, it can be effective to hold a refresher session that will help to prevent a relapse of the problematic behaviors or emotions. Typically, the relapse-prevention training occurs during a single session, where the therapist assists the child in identifying future stressors that might trigger anxiety.

Evidence for Use

Integrated CBT as an intervention for youth with anxiety disorders has been found to reduce or eliminate symptoms of anxiety and to decrease behavioral impairment (Albano, Marten, Holt, Heimberg, & Barlow, 1995; Barrett, 1998; Barrett, Dadds, & Rapee, 1996; Beidel, Turner, & Morris, 2000; Kendall, 1994; Masia Warner, Fisher, Shrout, Rathor, & Klein, 2007; Masia-Warner et al., 2005; Silverman et al., 1999). Research in this area often focuses on manualized treatment programs such as the Coping Cat program (Kendall & Ronan, 1990), the Coping Koala prevention program (Barrett, Dadds, & Rapee, 1996), Social Effectiveness Therapy for Children (Beidel et al., 2000), the Facing Your Fears program (Cobham, Dadds, & Spence, 1998), Social Skills Training (Spence, 1995), and the Skills for Academic and Social Success program (Fisher, Masia-Warner, & Klein, 2004). Maintenance of improvement following CBT has been confirmed 2 to 3 years after treatment (Beidel, Turner, Young, & Paulson, 2005; Dadds et al., 1999).

The following studies summarize some of the key research findings associated with the use of integrated CBT as an intervention for children and adolescents with anxiety.

Albano, A. M., Marten, P. A., Holt, C. S., Heimberg, R. G., & Barlow, D. H. (1995). Cognitive-behavioral group treatment for social phobia in adolescents: A preliminary study. *The Journal of Nervous and Mental Disease, 183,* 649–656.

In this study, 5 adolescents with social phobia attended group cognitive–behavioral therapy that included skill building, phobia exposure, and parental involvement. Multiple evaluations were given before therapy, during therapy, and at various follow-up times. Results showed overall decreases in anxiety as well as other specific phobias and emotional disorders. At 3-month follow-up, only 1 of the 5 adolescents was still diagnosed with social phobia; the rest were diagnosed as being in partial remission. At 12-month follow-up, none of the adolescents were still diagnosed with social phobia; only 1 was diagnosed as in partial remission, while the other 4 were diagnosis free. The participants' self-ratings of anxiety levels and frequency of negative thoughts were also significantly lower after therapy.

Barrett, P. M. (1998). Evaluation of cognitive-behavioral group treatments for childhood anxiety disorders. *Journal of Clinical Child Psychology, 27*(4), 459–468.

In this study, 60 students with anxiety disorders were randomly assigned to one of three groups: group cognitive–behavioral therapy for the child only (GROUP-CBT), group cognitive–behavioral therapy plus family management training (GROUP-FAM), or a waiting list. The children in GROUP-CBT were taught anxiety management strategies such as recognizing positive and negative thoughts, coping self-talk, relaxation strategies, realistic self-evaluation, and self-rewards. Modeling and role-playing were used in the training. In the GROUP-FAM treatment, these same child trainings were used and, in addition, parents were taught how to reinforce courageous behavior and help minimize anxiety in their children, as well as how to manage their own anxiety, use problem-solving techniques, and communicate better with each other and with their children. Results showed that both treatment groups greatly reduced the number of children who met diagnostic criteria for anxiety disorders after training: about 65% across treatment conditions vs. 25% for the waiting list. At 12-month follow-up, about 65% and 85% of children were diagnosis free for the GROUP-CBT and GROUP-FAM, respectively, suggesting a marginal (though not statistically significant) advantage for family inclusion in treatment. Clinicians' ratings and parents' and children's self-assessments at posttreatment and 12-month follow-up provided further support for both treatment conditions, with the family inclusion condition showing slight superiority to child-only treatment.

Barrett, P. M., Dadds, M. R., & Rapee, R. M. (1996). Family treatment of childhood anxiety: A controlled trial. *Journal of Consulting and Clinical Psychology, 64*(2), 333–342.

In this study, 79 children aged 7–14 years, identified as having anxiety disorders, were randomly assigned to one of three groups: cognitive–behavioral treatment (CBT), cognitive–behavioral treatment plus family anxiety management (CBT + FAM), or a waiting list. In the CBT group, children attended 12 weekly sessions where they were taught anxiety management strategies such as recognizing positive and negative thoughts, coping self-talk, relaxation strategies, realistic self-evaluation, and self-rewards. In the CBT + FAM group, these same child trainings were used and, in addition, parents were taught how to reinforce courageous behavior and help minimize anxiety in their children, as well as how to manage their own anxiety, use problem-solving techniques, and communicate better with each other and with their children. Results showed that both treatment groups were highly effective in reducing anxiety: about 70% across treatment conditions vs. 26% for the waiting list. Parents' and children's self-report measures as well as clinicians' ratings provided limited support for the superiority of the family involvement condition; however, treatment effectiveness varied depending on the age and sex of the child. Having family involved in treatment led to more positive results for girls and younger children, whereas for boys and older children, either treatment was equally effective.

Barrett, P. M., Duffy, A. L., Dadds, M. R., & Rapee, R. M. (2001). Cognitive–behavioral treatment of anxiety disorders in children: Long-term (6-year) follow-up. *Journal of Consulting and Clinical Psychology, 69*(1), 135–141.

In an effort to bolster the lack of long-term follow-up data available for the efficacy of cognitive–behavioral therapy (CBT) in treating children diagnosed with anxiety disorders, this study reassessed the participants of a 1996 study (Barrett, Dadds, & Rapee) that compared CBT with CBT plus family anxiety management training (CBT + FAM). Fifty-two of the original 79 subjects agreed to participate in this follow-up assessment, including 31 individuals from the CBT group and 21 from the CBT + FAM group (average time posttreatment = about 6 years). Results of the reassessment measures confirmed the authors' hypothesis that treatment gains would be maintained from the original study's follow-up to this study's long-term follow-up, with about 80% and 86% of the participants no longer meeting diagnostic criteria for any anxiety disorder at 12-month and long-term follow-up, respectively. Contrary to the investigators' expectations, however, the CBT + FAM intervention did not prove to be more effective than CBT alone.

Barrett, P. M., Farrell, L. J., Ollendick, T. H., & Dadds, M. (2006). Long-term outcomes of an Australian universal prevention trial of anxiety and depression symptoms in children and youth: An evaluation of the Friends program. *Journal of Clinical Child and Adolescent Psychology, 35*(3), 403–411.

This follow-up study evaluated 669 children and youth who had earlier participated in a cognitive–behavioral intervention using the FRIENDS program (designed for the prevention of anxiety and depression) to see if treatment gains continued at 24- and 36-month follow-up. (Participants had earlier completed a 12-month follow-up assessment.) All students took a total of three assessments at each follow-up time to determine their levels of anxiety and depression. Results showed that the intervention group, overall, continued to show fewer symptoms of anxiety and depression than did the control group; however, the differences in depression scores were not significant. Age at treatment appeared to have an effect on treatment outcomes at 12-, 24-, and 36-month follow-up. Students who had participated in the program in sixth grade had significantly lower anxiety ratings than the control group at all follow-up points, while those who had completed the program in ninth grade did not. These results suggest that sixth grade may be an ideal age for preventative treatment. Girls, although they were at a higher risk for anxiety, tended to experience more benefits from the program than did boys. However, improvements in anxiety ratings for sixth-grade girls continued only until 24-month follow-up, suggesting the importance of providing booster sessions or ongoing life-skills training to maximize the long-term benefits of cognitive–behavioral interventions.

Beidel, D. C., Turner, S. M., & Morris, T. L. (2000). Behavioral treatment of childhood social phobia. *Journal of Consulting and Clinical Psychology, 68*(6), 1072–1080.

Sixty-seven children, aged between 8 and 12 years, with a primary diagnosis of social phobia participated in this study and were randomly assigned to one of two treatment groups: Social Effectiveness Therapy for Children (SET-C) or a nonspecific treatment control group (Testbusters). Over the course of 12 weeks, children in the SET-C treatment group participated in two weekly sessions (one group, one individual) that focused on providing social phobia information, social skills training, peer generalization training, and *in vivo* exposure. Participants assigned to the control group underwent the Testbusters curriculum, a study-skills and test-taking program, attending two sessions per week (one group, one individual) for 12 weeks. Data were collected via several means, including four self-report inventories, one parent report measure, one clinician rating scale, a behavioral assessment, and a daily diary. Results showed that 67% of the SET-C group no longer met diagnostic criteria for social phobia at posttreatment, compared to just 5% of the Testbusters group. Moreover, 85% of the 22 SET-C group children who completed 6-month follow-up no longer met diagnostic criteria, with only one child who had achieved this status at posttreatment suffering a relapse. Six-month follow-up data were not collected for the Testbusters group.

Beidel, D. C., Turner, S. M., Young, B., & Paulson, A. (2005). Social effectiveness therapy for children: Three-year follow-up. *Journal of Consulting and Clinical Psychology, 73*(4), 721–725.

This study reports the results of a 3-year follow-up assessment of 29 children who earlier completed the Social Effectiveness Therapy for Children (SET-C) program, a cognitive–behavioral intervention for social phobia (Beidel, Turner, & Morris, 2000). Anxiety measurements at follow-up were based on self-reports and parent reports, clinicians' ratings, and independent observers' ratings of the children's anxiety and social effectiveness as they performed two behavioral tasks (role-play and reading out loud). Results indicated that the treatment gains that had been found at posttreatment were still present at 3-year follow-up, with 72% of the children free of social phobia diagnosis at follow-up, compared with 62% at posttreatment. Three children (18%) were found to have relapsed between posttreatment and follow-up. Overall, the follow-up findings supported the long-term effectiveness of SET-C as a treatment for childhood and adolescent anxiety.

Cobham, V. E. (2003). Evaluation of a brief child-focused group-based intervention for anxiety-disordered children. *Behaviour Change, 20*(2), 109–116.

For this pilot study, it was hypothesized that children with anxiety disorders who had nonanxious parents could be treated just as effectively with child-only cognitive–behavioral therapy as with therapy that involved parents. Thus, this study did not include parent anxiety management but focused solely on the children, teaching them ways to think and act in order to reduce their anxiety. The investigator also evaluated a more brief intervention than in past studies: While the interventions in previous, similar studies generally required 10 to 12 sessions, this intervention used only 6, plus 1 booster session. While all 5 children retained their anxiety diagnosis at posttreatment, 12 months later they were all diagnosis-free. These results provided tentative support for the use of a relatively brief, child-only cognitive–behavioral intervention in treating anxious children who have nonanxious parents.

Dadds, M. R., Holland, D. E., Laurens, K. R., Mullins, M., Barrett, P. M., & Spence, S. H. (1999). Early intervention and prevention of anxiety disorders in children: Results at 2-year follow-up. *Journal of Consulting and Clinical Psychology, 67*(1), 145–150.

This article summarizes the 12- and 24-month follow-up conducted with the participants of the Queensland Early Intervention and Prevention of Anxiety Project (QEIPAP). In the QEIPAP study, 128 children either at risk for or currently suffering from mild-to-moderate anxiety disorders participated in one of two study groups: cognitive–behavioral therapy (intervention) or monitoring (control). Results from that study showed that the intervention effectively prevented development of anxiety disorders in children who were deemed at risk and reduced the prevalence in children diagnosed with anxiety disorders. Results of the assessments conducted at 12- and 24-month follow-up demonstrated that the positive effects of the intervention continued, with the percentage of intervention group children who had an anxiety disorder diagnosis falling from 37% at 12-month follow-up to 20% at 24-month follow-up. In contrast, the monitoring group's rate of anxiety disorders remained essentially flat (42% and 39% at 12 and 24 months, respectively). The difference in diagnosis rates between the intervention and monitoring groups was statistically significant at 24-month follow-up.

Dadds, M. R., Spence, S. H., Holland, D. E., Barrett, P. M., & Laurens, K. R. (1997). Prevention and early intervention for anxiety disorders: A controlled trial. *Journal of Consulting and Clinical Psychology, 65*(4), 627–635.

One hundred twenty-eight children with mild-to-moderate-level anxiety disorders or at risk for anxiety disorders participated in this study—the Queensland Early Intervention and Prevention of Anxiety Project (QEIPAP)—examining the posttreatment and 6-month follow-up effects of the Coping Koala anxiety program, a group-based cognitive–behavioral therapy (CBT) intervention for children. Participants were randomly assigned to one of two groups: intervention or monitoring (control). The 10-week Coping Koala program taught participants how to cope with their anxiety through relaxation, positive self-talk, proactive behavior, and self-rewards. Parent sessions were conducted in weeks 3, 6, and 9 that involved training in child management skills, modeling, and coping skills. Results showed that for children who had an anxiety diagnosis at preintervention, both the intervention and control groups considerably decreased their diagnosis rates at posttreatment; however, at 6-month follow-up, the diagnosis rate for those in the intervention group was significantly lower. For those participants who were classified as at risk for anxiety disorders at preintervention (i.e., they had features of anxiety but did not meet diagnostic criteria for a disorder), 54% assigned to the monitoring group met diagnostic criteria at 6-month follow-up, compared to just 16% of those assigned to the intervention group. These findings emphasized the importance of effective early intervention programs in preventing and managing anxiety disorders in childhood.

Eisen, A. R., & Silverman, W. K. (1993). Should I relax or change my thoughts? A preliminary examination of cognitive therapy, relaxation training, and their combination with overanxious children. *Journal of Cognitive Psychotherapy, 7*(4), 265–279.

In this investigation, 4 children and adolescents aged 6 to 15 with anxiety disorders were studied as they underwent three treatments: cognitive therapy (CT), relaxation training (RT), and the combination of both (CT + RT). Each child received all three types of treatment, although the order in which CT and RT were introduced varied so that each treatment came first in half of the cases.

According to child, parent, and clinician ratings, as well as daily diaries, all 4 children improved dramatically. Due to the small number of participants and other limitations in the design of the study, solid conclusions about the relative effectiveness of the treatments could not be drawn; however, the results suggested that CT may be more effective than RT for treating overanxious children. Further, the findings supported the idea that each child's specific anxiety symptoms may influence which type of treatment is most effective. For example, 1 oversensitive participant who was a chronic worrier (a symptom related to cognitive distortions) benefited much more from CT, while another participant with more somatic complaints experienced greater benefits from RT.

Eisen, A. R., & Silverman, W. K. (1998). Prescriptive treatment for generalized anxiety disorder in children. *Behavior Therapy, 29*, 105–121.

For this study, 4 children aged 8 to 12 with generalized anxiety disorder were examined prior to treatment to determine if their primary symptoms were anxiousness or somatization. Two of the children were immediately assigned to the treatment prescribed for their type of anxiety symptoms (cognitive treatment for anxiousness; relaxation therapy for somatization). The other 2 were assigned to the opposite therapy for the first 5-week treatment period and subsequently completed an additional 5-week treatment period using the prescribed intervention. As hypothesized, some improvements were seen in all 4 children, but those who received the prescribed intervention during the first 5 weeks of treatment showed greater decreases in anxiety levels over that period, as measured by multiple child and parent rating scales, a daily diary, and a heart rate change measurement. After completing the prescriptive treatment corresponding to their symptoms, 3 of the 4 participants met the criteria for high end-state functioning.

Flannery-Schroeder, E., Choudhury, M. S., & Kendall, P. C. (2005). Group and individual cognitive-behavioral treatments for youth with anxiety disorders: 1-year follow-up. *Cognitive Therapy and Research, 29*(2), 253–259.

This study evaluated 30 of 37 children aged 8 to 14 who originally participated in either individual cognitive–behavioral therapy (ICBT) or group cognitive–behavioral therapy (GCBT) at 1-year follow-up in order to see if treatment gains were maintained. In the original study, both treatment groups showed comparable improvement in contrast with the waiting list group. In this follow-up study, results were maintained or improved at 1-year follow-up as compared with posttreatment. The ICBT group showed a slightly higher percentage of children free of their original primary diagnosis, but the GCBT group showed a slightly higher percentage of children who were free from any of the three anxiety diagnoses studied. However, these differences were not statistically significant.

Flannery-Schroeder, E. C., & Kendall, P. C. (2000). Group and individual cognitive-behavioral treatments for youth with anxiety disorders: A randomized clinical trial. *Cognitive Therapy and Research, 24*(3), 251–278.

Seeking to expand the literature regarding the efficacy of group cognitive–behavioral interventions for treating childhood anxiety disorders, this preliminary study followed 37 youths, aged between 8 and 14 years, who had been previously diagnosed with an anxiety disorder such as separation anxiety disorder or social phobia. The participants were randomly assigned to one of three conditions: group cognitive–behavioral treatment (GCBT), individual cognitive–behavioral treatment (ICBT), or wait-list control (WL). Those in the GCBT and ICBT groups participated in an 18-week intervention that involved training in coping skills and strategies designed to manage anxiety symptoms. Data were collected using children's self-reports, parent and teacher measures, and diagnostic interviews at pretreatment, posttreatment, and 3-month follow-up. Results showed participants in both GCBT and ICBT improved from pretreatment to posttreatment, with 50% and 73%, respectively, failing to meet criteria for their previously diagnosed anxiety disorders. The difference in improvement between the GCBT and ICBT groups was not statistically significant; however, the authors suggested that further research is warranted to detect possible small to moderate differences between the treatments.

Heyne, D., King, N. J., Tonge, B. J., Rollings, S., Young, D., Pritchard, M., et al. (2002). Evaluation of child therapy and caregiver training in the treatment of school refusal. *Journal of the American Academy of Child and Adolescent Psychiatry, 41*(6), 687–695.

Sixty-one students, aged between 7 and 14 years and each diagnosed with an anxiety disorder, participated in this study exploring the efficacy of three types of interventions in treating the participants' school refusal: child therapy (CH), parent/teacher training (PTT), and child therapy plus parent/teacher training (CH+PTT). CH consisted of eight 50-minute sessions utilizing cognitive therapy, relaxation training, desensitization, and social skills training. PTT involved eight 50-minute sessions teaching behavior-management strategies and offering cognitive therapy to parents. Data were collected on school attendance and a variety of self-, parent-, and teacher-report measures. Results showed that all three treatments were effective in improving school attendance, with nonclinical levels (minimum of 90% attendance) reached at posttreatment for about 54% of students across all groups. At posttreatment, there was a greater chance of children in both of the conditions that included parent/teacher training achieving 90% school attendance compared with those in the child-only treatment group; however, there were no significant differences in school attendance among the three groups at 4.5-month follow-up.

Kendall, P. C. (1994). Treating anxiety disorders in children: Results of a randomized clinical trial. *Journal of Consulting and Clinical Psychology, 62*(1), 100–110.

This study examined the effects of a cognitive–behavioral intervention on the symptoms of 47 children, aged between 9 and 13 years, diagnosed with childhood anxiety disorders. Twenty-seven children were randomly assigned to receive the intervention, and the remaining 20 children were placed in the wait-list control group. Participants in the treatment group received between 16 and 20 individual therapy sessions over 16 weeks that were designed to develop their skills in recognizing anxious feelings, coping with anxiety-producing situations, and evaluating performances. Those in the wait-list group were evaluated at the beginning and end of an 8-week waiting period, after which they commenced treatment. Data were collected on all children via several measures, including parent, teacher, and self-reports; behavioral observations; and cognitive assessments. Results demonstrated the effectiveness of a cognitive–behavioral approach to treating childhood anxiety disorders, with 64% of participants no longer meeting diagnostic criteria for their respective anxiety disorders at the end of treatment, compared to just 5% of the control group at the end of the 8-week waiting period.

Lumpkin, P. W., Silverman, W. K., Weems, C. F., Markham, M. R., & Kurtines, W. M. (2002). Treating a heterogeneous set of anxiety disorders in youths with group cognitive behavioral therapy: A partially nonconcurrent multiple-baseline evaluation. *Behavior Therapy, 33,* 163–177.

This study investigated the effectiveness of group cognitive–behavioral therapy for children with various anxiety diagnoses who were treated in heterogeneous groups rather than being grouped by diagnosis. Twelve students and their mothers participated in the study, with children and parents receiving separate training for 50 minutes each week, followed by 20 minutes of joint child–parent therapy. Therapy sessions included exposure to anxiety-provoking stimuli (for children) and training in cognitive and behavioral techniques (for both children and parents). Children also received some training related to their specific diagnoses, such as social skills training to address social phobia. After the 12 weekly therapy sessions, 50% of the children no longer met criteria for their primary diagnoses. At 12-month follow-up, this increased to 75%. All but 1 of the children (who had also been diagnosed with obsessive compulsive disorder) showed improvements. Although preliminary, this study showed evidence for the effectiveness and efficiency of treating childhood anxiety through group therapy that does not divide children according to their anxiety diagnoses.

Masia Warner, C., Fisher, P. H., Shrout, P. E., Rathor, S., & Klein, R. G. (2007). Treating adolescents with social anxiety disorder in school: An attention control trial. *Journal of Child Psychology and Psychiatry 48*(7), 676–686.

For this study, 32 New York City high school students with social anxiety disorder were randomly assigned to two groups: the Skills for Academic and Social Success (SASS) treatment group and the Educational-Supportive Group Function (ESGF) control group. The SASS treatment, which met weekly in the school setting, included social skills training, realistic thinking training, psychoeducation, and exposure. The ESGF control group participated in sessions that had a comparable format and provided the same amount of professional attention as the SASS group's sessions, but with content focusing on general relaxation strategies. After 12 weekly sessions, 59% of the SASS group members were free of social anxiety diagnosis, compared to 0% of those in the control group. Treatment gains were maintained at 6-month follow-up. Results suggest that school-based cognitive–behavioral interventions for social anxiety in adolescents can be effective.

Masia-Warner, C., Klein, R. G., Dent, H. C., Fisher, P. H., Alvir, J., Albano, A. M., et al. (2005). School-based intervention for adolescents with social anxiety disorder: Results of a controlled study. *Journal of Abnormal Child Psychology, 33*(6), 707–722.

Thirty-five high school students participated in this study of the efficacy of the Skills for Academic and Social Success (SASS) program, an intervention designed to treat adolescent social anxiety disorder by adapting clinical procedures for use in the school setting. Participants were randomly assigned to one of two groups: SASS treatment or wait-list control. The SASS intervention involved social skills and realistic thinking training and consisted of 12 group sessions at school, two individual sessions, four social events, two parent meetings, two teacher meetings, and two booster sessions. Data were collected at pretreatment and posttreatment via several self-report, parent report, and independent evaluator rating measures. No significant differences between the two groups were found at pretreatment. At posttreatment, 67% of the SASS group no longer met diagnostic criteria for social phobia, compared with a mere 6% of the control group—an outcome both statistically and clinically significant. Data collected for the intervention group at 9-month follow-up suggested that treatment effects had been maintained.

Silverman, W. K., Kurtines, W. M., Ginsburg, G. S., Weems, C. F., Lumpkin, P. W., & Carmichael, D. H. (1999). Treating anxiety disorders in children with group cognitive-behavioral therapy: A randomized clinical trial. *Journal of Consulting and Clinical Psychology, 67*(6), 995–1003.

Seeking to confirm and add to the literature supporting the efficacy of group cognitive–behavioral therapy (GCBT) for treating children and youths with anxiety disorders, this study followed the progress of 56 children (aged 6 to 16) randomly assigned to one of two conditions: GCBT or wait-list control. Those assigned to the GCBT condition participated in 40-minute therapy sessions with a group of other children; the parents of these participants met simultaneously with a different therapist. Each session also included a 15-minute joint meeting of both parents and children. Skills addressed included the use of contingency management, modification of self-talk, and gradual exposure to anxiety-provoking stimuli. Data were collected at pretreatment, posttreatment, and 3-, 6-, and 12-month follow-up via multiple measures, including self-report, parent report, and clinician ratings. Results supported the efficacy of using GCBT to treat children with anxiety disorders. At posttreatment, 64% of the GCBT group no longer met diagnostic criteria for their respective diagnoses, compared to just 13% of the control group. Moreover, treatment gains were maintained at 3-, 6-, and 12-month follow-up.

Considerations

Success levels will be different for each child based on factors beyond the strength of the intervention. Research demonstrates poorer treatment responses for children with higher levels of anxiety, trait anxiety, and parental characteristics of depression, hostility, and paranoia (Berman, Weems, Silverman, & Kurtines, 2000). Successful treatment of anxiety will also need to reduce any perceived threats to the child, such as peer teasing or adult reprimands. Other stressors may be apparent in the environment and should be addressed (e.g., multiple exposures to unnecessary stressors).

For Age and Developmental Level

Interventions that have moderate cognitive demands (e.g., cognitive restructuring) should be used primarily with children or adolescents who have the emotional development and executive functioning to perform the tasks they are asked to do (e.g., verbalize fears and phobias and conceptualize them as a cognitive trait). Such interventions will likely be inappropriate with young or nonverbal children.

Summary

This chapter presented a review of the characteristics and conditions of anxiety in children and adolescents, together with a summary of interventions that have been demonstrated to be effective in treating anxiety. The interventions discussed included exposure-based techniques, contingency management, modeling, family therapy, and integrated cognitive–behavioral therapy. The CBT discussion presented several approaches, including psychoeducation, self-monitoring, problem-solving skills training, relaxation training, and cognitive restructuring. While the interventions vary in their theoretical approaches to the treatment of anxiety (cognitive, behavioral, or integrated), they all share the underlying fundamental goal of helping to alleviate children's feelings of anxiety and related maladaptive behaviors. The information presented in this chapter forms the basis for the supplemental classroom- and home-based materials that correspond to this book.

References

Akande, A., & Akande, B. E. (1994). On becoming a person: Activities to help children with their anger. *Early Child Development and Care, 102,* 31–62.

Akande, A., Osagie, J. E., Mwaiteleke, P. B., Botha, K. F. H., Ababio, E. P., Selepe, T. J., et al. (1999). Managing children's fears and anxieties in classroom settings. *Early Childhood Development and Care, 158,* 51–69.

Albano, A. M., & Barlow, D. H. (1996). Breaking the vicious cycle: Cognitive–behavioral group treatment for socially anxious youth. In E. D. Hibbs & P. S. Jensen (Eds.), *Psychosocial treatments of child and adolescent disorders: Empirically based strategies for clinical practice* (pp. 43–62). Washington, DC: American Psychological Association.

Albano, A. M., Detweiler, M. F., & Logsdon-Conradsen, S. (1999). Cognitive–behavioral interventions with socially phobic children. In S. W. Russ & T. H. Ollendick (Eds.), *Handbook of psychotherapies with children and families* (pp. 255–280). New York: Kluwer Academic/Plenum Publishers.

Albano, A. M., Marten, P. A., Holt, C. S., Heimberg, R. G., & Barlow, D. H. (1995). Cognitive-behavioral group treatment for social phobia in adolescents: A preliminary study. *The Journal of Nervous and Mental Diseases, 183,* 649–656.

Bandura, A. (1977). *Social learning theory.* Englewood Cliffs, NJ: Prentice Hall.

Bandura, A., Blanchard, E. B., & Ritter, B. (1969). Relative efficacy of desensitization and modeling approaches for inducing behavioral, affective, and attitudinal changes. *Journal of Personality and Social Psychology, 13*(3), 173–199.

Barrett, P. M. (1998). Evaluation of cognitive-behavioral group treatments for childhood anxiety disorders. *Journal of Clinical Child Psychology, 27*(4), 459–468.

Barrett, P. M., Dadds, M. R., & Rapee, R. M. (1996). Family treatment of childhood anxiety: A controlled trial. *Journal of Consulting and Clinical Psychology, 64*(2), 333–342.

Barrett, P. M., Duffy, A. L., Dadds, M. R., & Rapee, R. M. (2001). Cognitive-behavioral treatment of anxiety disorders in children: Long-term (6-year) follow-up. *Journal of Consulting and Clinical Psychology, 69*(1), 135–141.

Barrett, P. M., Farrell, L. J., Ollendick, T. H., & Dadds, M. (2006). Long-term outcomes of an Australian universal prevention trial of anxiety and depression symptoms in children and youth: An evaluation of the Friends program. *Journal of Clinical Child and Adolescent Psychology, 35*(3), 403–411.

Beidel, D. C., Turner, S. M., & Morris, T. L. (2000). Behavioral treatment of childhood social phobia. *Journal of Consulting and Clinical Psychology, 68*(6), 1072–1080.

Beidel, D. C., Turner, S. M., Young, B., & Paulson, A. (2005). Social effectiveness therapy for children: Three-year follow-up. *Journal of Consulting and Clinical Psychology, 73*(4), 721–725.

Berger, S. M. (1962). Conditioning through vicarious instigation. *Psychological Review, 69*(5), 450–466.

Berman, S. L., Weems, C. F., Silverman, W. K., & Kurtines, W. M. (2000). Predictors of outcome in exposure-based cognitive and behavioral treatments for phobic and anxiety disorders in children. *Behavior Therapy, 31*, 713–731.

Cobham, V. E. (2003). Evaluation of a brief child-focused group-based intervention for anxiety-disordered children. *Behaviour Change, 20*(2), 109–116.

Cobham, V. E., Dadds, M. R., & Spence, S. H. (1998). The role of parental anxiety in the treatment of childhood anxiety. *Journal of Consulting and Clinical Psychology, 66*(6), 893–905.

Compton, S. N., March, J. S., Brent, D., Albano, A. M., Weersing, V. R., & Curry, J. (2004). Cognitive-behavioral psychotherapy for anxiety and depressive disorders in children and adolescents: An evidence-based medicine review. *Journal of the American Academy of Child and Adolescent Psychiatry, 43*(8), 930–959.

Cornwall, E., Spence, S. H., & Schotte, D. (1996). The effectiveness of emotive imagery in the treatment of darkness phobia in children. *Behaviour Change, 13*(4), 223–229.

Dadds, M. R., Heard, P. M., & Rapee, R. M. (1992). The role of family intervention in the treatment of child anxiety disorders: Some preliminary findings. *Behaviour Change, 9*(3), 171–177.

Dadds, M. R., Holland, D. E., Laurens, K. R., Mullins, M., Barrett, P. M., & Spence, S. H. (1999). Early intervention and prevention of anxiety disorders in children: Results at 2-year follow-up. *Journal of Consulting and Clinical Psychology, 67*(1), 145–150.

Dadds, M. R., Spence, S. H., Holland, D. E., Barrett, P. M., & Laurens, K. R. (1997). Prevention and early intervention for anxiety disorders: A controlled trial. *Journal of Consulting and Clinical Psychology, 65*(4), 627–635.

Eisen, A. R., & Silverman, W. K. (1993). Should I relax or change my thoughts? A preliminary examination of cognitive therapy, relaxation training, and their combination with overanxious children. *Journal of Cognitive Psychotherapy, 7*(4), 265–279.

Eisen, A. R., & Silverman, W. K. (1998). Prescriptive treatment for generalized anxiety disorder in children. *Behavior Therapy, 29*, 105–121.

Faust, J., Olson, R., & Rodriguez, H. (1991). Same-day surgery preparation: Reduction of pediatric patient arousal and distress through participant modeling. *Journal of Consulting and Clinical Psychology, 59*(3), 475–478.

Fisher, P. H., Masia-Warner, C., & Klein, R. G. (2004). Skills for social and academic success: A school-based intervention for social anxiety disorder in adolescents. *Clinical Child and Family Psychology Review, 7*(4), 241–249.

Flannery-Schroeder, E., Choudhury, M. S., & Kendall, P. C. (2005). Group and individual cognitive-behavioral treatments for youth with anxiety disorders: 1-year follow-up. *Cognitive Therapy and Research, 29*(2), 253–259.

Flannery-Schroeder, E. C., & Kendall, P. C. (2000). Group and individual cognitive-behavioral treatments for youth with anxiety disorders: A randomized clinical trial. *Cognitive Therapy and Research, 24*(3), 251–278.

Flood, W. A., & Wilder, D. A. (2004). The use of differential reinforcement and fading to increase time away from a caregiver in a child with separation anxiety disorder. *Education and Treatment of Children, 27*(1), 1–8.

Ginsburg, G. S., Silverman, W. K., & Kurtines, W. K. (1995). Family involvement in treating children with phobic and anxiety disorders: A look ahead. *Clinical Psychology Review, 15*(5), 457–473.

Ginsburg, G. S., & Walkup, J. T. (2004). Specific Phobia. In T. H. Ollendick & J. S. March (Eds.), *Phobic and anxiety disorders in children and adolescents: A clinician's guide to effective psychosocial and pharmacological interventions* (pp. 175–197). New York: Oxford Press.

Glasscock, S. E., & MacLean, W. E., Jr. (1990). Use of contact desensitization and shaping in the treatment of dog phobia and generalized fear of the outdoors. *Journal of Clinical Child Psychology, 19*(2), 169–172.

Heyne, D., King, N. J., Tonge, B. J., Rollings, S., Young, D., Pritchard, M., et al. (2002). Evaluation of child therapy and caregiver training in the treatment of school refusal. *Journal of the American Academy of Child and Adolescent Psychiatry, 41*(6), 687–695.

Hops, H., & Lewinsohn, P. M. (1995). A course for the treatment of depression among adolescents. In K. D. Craig & K. S. Dobson (Eds.), *Anxiety and depression in adults and children* (pp. 230–245). Thousand Oaks, CA: Sage.

Howes, C., Galinsky, E., & Kontos, S. (1998). Child care caregiver sensitivity and attachment. *Social Development, 7*(1), 25–36.

Kahn, J. S., Kehle, T. J., Jenson, W. R., & Clark, E. (1990). Comparison of cognitive-behavioral, relaxation, and self-modeling interventions for depression among middle-school students. *School Psychology Review, 19*(2), 196–211.

Kearney, C. A. (2005). Social anxiety and social phobia in youth: Characteristics, assessment, and psychological treatment. New York: Springer.

Kendall, P. C. (1994). Treating anxiety disorders in children: Results of a randomized clinical trial. *Journal of Consulting and Clinical Psychology, 62*(1), 100–110.

Kendall, P. C., Kortlander, E., Chansky, T. E., & Brady, E. U. (1992). Comorbidity of anxiety and depression in youth: Treatment implications. *Journal of Consulting and Clinical Psychology, 60*(6), 869–880.

Kendall, P. C., & Ronan, K. R. (1990). Assessment of children's anxieties, fears, and phobias: Cognitive-behavioral models and methods. In C. R. Reynolds & R. W. Kamphaus (Eds.), *Handbook of psychological and educational assessment of children: Intelligence and achievement.* New York: Guilford.

King, N., Cranstoun, F., & Josephs, A. (1989). Emotive imagery and children's night-time fears: A multiple baseline design evaluation. *Journal of Behavior Therapy and Experimental Psychiatry, 20*(2), 125–135.

King, N. J., Molloy, G. N., Heyne, D., Murphy, G. C., & Ollendick, T. H. (1998). Emotive imagery treatment for childhood phobias: A credible and empirically validated intervention? *Behavioural and Cognitive Psychotherapy, 26,* 103–113.

King, N. J., Muris, P., & Ollendick, T. H. (2005). Childhood fears and phobias: Assessment and treatment. *Child and Adolescent Mental Health, 10*(2), 50–56.

Klingman, A., Melamed, B. G., Cuthbert, M. I., & Hermecz, D. A. (1984). Effects of participant modeling on information acquisition and skill utilization. *Journal of Consulting and Clinical Psychology, 52*(3), 414–422.

Kochanska, G. & Aksan, N. (1995). Mother-child mutually positive affect, the quality of child compliance to requests and prohibitions, and maternal control as correlates of early internalization. *Child Development, 66*(1), 236–254.

Last, C. G., Hansen, C., & Franco, N. (1998). Cognitive-behavioral treatment of school phobia. *Journal of the American Academy of Child and Adolescent Psychiatry, 37*(4), 404–411.

Lazarus, A. A., & Abramovitz, A. (1962). The use of "emotive imagery" in the treatment of children's phobias. *Journal of Mental Science, 108,* 191–195.

Leitenberg, H., & Callahan, E. J. (1973). Reinforced practice and reduction of different kinds of fears in adults and children. *Behaviour Research and Therapy, 11,* 19–30.

Lumpkin, P. W., Silverman, W. K., Weems, C. F., Markham, M. R., & Kurtines, W. M. (2002). Treating a heterogeneous set of anxiety disorders in youths with group cognitive behavioral therapy: A partially nonconcurrent multiple-baseline evaluation. *Behavior Therapy, 33,* 163–177.

March, J. S., & Ollendick, T. H. (2004). Integrated psychosocial and pharmacological treatment. In T. H. Ollendick & J. S. March (Eds.), *Phobic and anxiety disorders in children and adolescents: A clinician's guide to effective psychosocial and pharmacological interventions* (pp. 141–174). New York: Oxford Press.

Masia Warner, C., Fisher, P. H., Shrout, P. E., Rathor, S., & Klein, R. G. (2007). Treating adolescents with social anxiety disorder in school: An attention control trial. *Journal of Child Psychology and Psychiatry, 48*(7), 676–686.

Masia-Warner, C., Klein, R. G., Dent, H. C., Fisher, P. H., Alvir, J., Albano, A. M., et al. (2005). School-based intervention for adolescents with social anxiety disorder: Results of a controlled study. *Journal of Abnormal Child Psychology, 33*(6), 707–722.

Melamed, B. G., Yurcheson, R., Fleece, E. L., Hutcherson, S., & Hawes, R. (1978). Effects of film modeling on the reduction of anxiety-related behaviors in individuals varying in level of previous experience in the stress situation. *Journal of Consulting and Clinical Psychology, 46*(6), 1357–1367.

Mendez, F. J., & Garcia, M. J. (1996). Emotive performances: A treatment package for children's phobias. *Child and Family Behavior Therapy, 18*(3), 19–34.

Mendlowitz, S. L., Manassis, K., Bradley, S., Scapillato, D., Miezitis, S., & Shaw, B. F. (1999). Cognitive-behavioral group treatments in childhood anxiety disorders: The role of parental involvement. *Journal of the American Academy of Child and Adolescent Psychiatry, 38*(10), 1223–1229.

Menzies, R. G., & Clarke, J. C. (1993). A comparison of *in vivo* and vicarious exposure in the treatment of childhood water phobia. *Behaviour Research and Therapy, 31*(1), 9–15.

Morris, D. (1980). Infant attachment and problem solving in the toddler: Relations to mother's family history. Unpublished doctoral dissertation, University of Minnesota.

Murphy, C. M., & Bootzin, R. R. (1973). Active and passive participation in the contact desensitization of snake fear in children. *Behavior Therapy, 4,* 203–211.

Obler, M., & Terwilliger, R. F. (1970). Pilot study on the effectiveness of systematic desensitization with neurologically impaired children with phobic disorders. *Journal of Consulting and Clinical Psychology, 34*(3), 314–318.

Ollendick, T. H., & Cerny, J. A. (1981). *Clinical behavior therapy with children.* New York: Plenum Press.

Ollendick, T. H., & King, N. J. (1998). Empirically supported treatments for children with phobic and anxiety disorders: Current status. *Journal of Clinical Child Psychology, 27*(2), 156–167.

Pomerantz, P. B., Peterson, N. T., Marholin, D., II, & Stern, S. (1977). The *in vivo* elimination of a child's water phobia by a paraprofessional at home. *Journal of Behavior Therapy and Experimental Psychiatry, 8,* 417–421.

Reynolds, C. R., & Kamphaus, R. W. (2004). *Behavior assessment system for children* (2nd ed.). Circle Pines, MN: AGS Publishing.

Sheslow, D. V., Bondy, A. S., & Nelson, R. O. (1982). A comparison of graduated exposure, verbal coping skills, and their combination in the treatment of children's fear of the dark. *Child and Family Behavior Therapy, 4*(2/3), 33–45.

Silverman, W. K., Kurtines, W. M., Ginsburg, G. S., Weems, C. F., Lumpkin, P. W., Carmichael, D. H. (1999). Treating anxiety disorders in children with group cognitive-behavioral therapy: A randomized clinical trial. *Journal of Consulting and Clinical Psychology, 67*(6), 995–1003.

Spence, S. H. (1995). Social skills training: Enhancing social competence with children and adolescents. Windsor, UK: Nelson.

Spence, S. H., Donovan, C., & Brechman-Toussaint, M. (2000). The treatment of childhood social phobia: The effectiveness of a social skills training-based, cognitive-behavioural intervention, with and without parental involvement. *Journal of Child Psychology and Psychiatry, 41*(6), 713–726.

Ultee, C. A., Griffioen, D., & Schellekens, J. (1982). The reduction of anxiety in children: A comparison of the effects of systematic desensitization *in vitro* and systematic desensitization *in vivo. Behaviour Research and Therapy, 20,* 61–67.

U.S. Department of Health and Human Services. (1999). *Mental health: A report of the Surgeon General—Executive summary.* Washington, DC: Author.

Wolpe, J. (1958). *Psychotherapy by reciprocal inhibition.* Stanford, CA: Stanford University Press.

Wood, J. J., Piacentini, J. C., Southam-Gerow, M., Chu, B. C., & Sigman, M. (2006). Family cognitive behavioral therapy for child anxiety disorders. *Journal of the American Academy of Child and Adolescent Psychiatry, 45*(3), 314–321.

Chapter **8**

Interventions for Depression

This chapter focuses on two intervention methods that are effective in the remediation of depression symptoms in children and adolescents: cognitive–behavioral therapy (CBT) and interpersonal therapy (also called interpersonal psychotherapy) (IPT). The discussion of these methods is presented in three sections. The first section provides a brief description of the characteristics and conditions of depression, along with sample items from the BASC–2 Depression scale. The second section describes the theoretical framework for understanding depression and for the interventions presented in this chapter. In the third section, the two intervention methods are described. Each presentation provides an overview of the intervention method and is divided into three subsections: Implementation, Evidence for Use, and Considerations. For CBT, several strategies are reviewed, each with their own overview and procedures for implementation. These strategies are often used in various combinations with each other; as such, the research studies supporting their use and the considerations for their implementation are presented together in single Evidence for Use and Considerations sections. The chapter's three main sections provide the foundation on which additional BASC–2 intervention components are built, including both classroom-based and home-based strategies.

Characteristics and Conditions of Depression

Depression is a common condition in childhood and adolescence, with estimates of 8% to 10% prevalence among school-aged children, and it is the leading cause for suicide in adolescents. Depression is also increasingly being reported in younger children, with up to 1% of preschool children showing signs and symptoms.

While level of severity and duration of the depressive symptoms can vary, depression is generally characterized by a persistent sad or irritable mood, along with decreased pleasure from activities that were previously enjoyable. Other signs and symptoms include sleeping too much or too little, changes in appetite or weight, difficulty concentrating, feelings of worthlessness and guilt, and recurrent thoughts of death or suicide (American Psychological Association [APA], 2000).

On the BASC–2 rating scales, depression is defined as feelings of unhappiness, sadness, and stress that may result in an inability to carry out everyday activities or may bring on thoughts of suicide (Reynolds & Kamphaus, 2004). Items on the Depression scale include many symptoms noted in the *Diagnostic and Statistical Manual of Mental Disorders*, Fourth Edition, Text Revision (*DSM–IV–TR;* APA, 2000) criteria for a major depressive episode, such as "Nothing is fun anymore" (anhedonia), "Says, 'I want to die'" (suicidal ideation), and "I don't seem to do anything right" (feelings of worthlessness). It is important to keep in mind that a child may show symptoms of depression that, while requiring intervention, may not warrant a formal diagnosis. Children scoring in the At-Risk or Clinically Significant range on the BASC–2 Depression scale will likely benefit from some type of intervention strategy.

Theoretical Framework for Approaching Depression

Depression is a mood disorder resulting from a combination of distorted cognitions, a lack of positive reinforcement for rational cognitions and behaviors, and an abundance of negative reinforcement for dysfunctional emotions, thinking, and behaviors (Lewinsohn, Hoberman, Teri, & Hautzinger, 1985). Biological, behavioral, and cognitive factors each play a role in depression. This chapter will focus primarily on the behavioral and cognitive aspects of depression and the corresponding effective interventions.

Behavioral theory considers depression to be a result of stressful events that lead to a disruption of adaptive behavior or stem from a lack of positive reinforcement and an excess of negative consequences (Weersing & Brent, 2006). For example, Isaac, a 9-year-old boy who was always considered normal, experienced a series of negative events over the course of a year (e.g., moved into a new school district and was unable to make new friends, parents were pursuing a divorce) that led to symptoms of depression. Isaac started to perform poorly in school and began to be frequently reprimanded by his parents and teachers for poor academic performance and an inability to socialize with others. Isaac's performance continued to worsen, as did his depressive symptoms. In this case, Isaac experienced several significant, stressful events that resulted in negative consequences.

Cognitive theory, on the other hand, attributes depression to negative or depression-producing thoughts or schemas. Negative events experienced by a person are attributed to internal attributes, resulting in negative thinking that is used to interpret new events, which can ultimately lead to depression (Beck, 1976). For example, Krystal, an 11-year-old girl, has rarely had success in school and has little interest in hobbies or interacting with other children. Her inability to get good grades and make friends has led her to feel a sense of worthlessness about herself and her abilities. Even when Krystal received an invitation to a party from a classmate, she refused to go, saying things like "I won't fit in" and "Nobody really wants me there anyway."

Interventions

A variety of interventions are effective in reducing depressive symptomatology. In this chapter, school- and community-based cognitive–behavioral interventions are presented. As the name implies, cognitive–behavioral interventions are a combination of both cognitive interventions (that consider distorted cognitions about one's self and circumstances to be at the center of the depressive symptomatology) and behavioral interventions (that consider depression to result from stressful events causing a disruption in adaptive behaviors) (Beck, Rush, Shaw, & Emery, 1979; Lewinsohn, Clarke, Rohde, Hops, & Seeley, 1996; Meichenbaum, 1977). The main reason cognitive–behavioral interventions can be effective is that they treat both problems with cognitions and problems with behavior.

Cognitive–behavioral interventions for depression are presented here in the context of two types of therapy:

I. Cognitive–Behavioral Therapy

II. Interpersonal Therapy (or Psychotherapy) for Adolescents

I. Cognitive–Behavioral Therapy

Cognitive–behavioral therapy (CBT) as an intervention for depression integrates cognitive, behavioral, affective, and social strategies to change thought patterns. Changes to these thought patterns result in a change in behavior (Corey, 1991; Kendall et al., 1992). The emphasis during treatment is placed on changing unhealthy thoughts and emotions over the course of a relatively brief period of time (between 5 and 16 sessions, depending on the specific needs of the child) (Lewinsohn & Clarke, 1999; Roberts, Lazicki-Puddy, Puddy, & Johnson, 2003). The total number of sessions is typically determined within the first few sessions and is made explicit to both the child and parent. If the goals for behavioral change are not reached by the end of the prescribed treatment period, booster sessions are sometimes added to increase the effectiveness of the treatment (Lewinsohn & Clarke, 1999).

Most CBT interventions consist of the same basic elements. There is a general planning stage that defines what will be covered over the prescribed number of sessions. Between sessions, individuals are often given homework assignments, which are reviewed during the next session. Throughout the treatment program, participants track their progress, and modifications to the treatment are made as needed.

While most often used on an individual basis, CBT can be implemented with groups as well. Group implementation has an advantage of being perceived as a form of general education, rather than the typical perception of one-on-one sessions as being therapy (Lewinsohn & Clarke, 1999). For example, in group CBT, a number of students might meet to listen to a 30-minute session on a commonly shared topic such as self-image (depression related) or family relationships, with the leader providing instruction on the elements of problem solving based on a general scenario. The instructional presentation and group dynamics would make participation much like a typical classroom session in a school setting. For the same topic, individual CBT might include a one-on-one session that leads the child through the same elements. This structure lacks the classlike feel of a group session but offers the advantage of individualization, allowing for greater focus on specific issues that are troubling the child.

Several CBT approaches are discussed below, including psychoeducation, problem-solving skills training, cognitive restructuring, pleasant-activity planning, relaxation training, and self-management training. Family involvement is also discussed as a separate approach, although it is often incorporated into many of the other CBT approaches. For each, a brief overview and example are provided, along with the basic elements specific to the intervention and a listing of the procedures for implementation.

A. Psychoeducation

The psychoeducational component of CBT focuses on informing children and their parents about depression's causes and symptoms and presenting them as factors that can be changed (Kaslow & Racusin, 1994). This approach can remove some of the mystery around mental health issues and may allow for a comparison to something a family already understands, such as a chronic illness. Additionally, children are provided with some of the understanding necessary for managing their depression. By learning about the thoughts and behaviors that cause and maintain depressive symptomatology and about the possible cognitive–behavioral intervention techniques that can be used to address depression, children can begin to recognize the relationship between these two factors and lay the groundwork for change in their behavior and emotions.

For example, in order to make clear the connection between behavior and outcome for a child in an individualized treatment program, the clinician determines that it may be helpful to illustrate this cause and effect using another child's behavior as an example. The child receiving treatment might be presented with a scenario, such as in a storybook or video, in which a child experiences depressive symptoms such as anger and feelings of poor self-worth. The example would relate how these emotions affect relationships with family and friends, as well as convey the possible effects on school performance (e.g., acting out in class and feeling bad about being sent out of the classroom). The clinician may use the example to describe how the child begins to learn that his or her emotions and behavior are unhealthy and that they may be caused by learning difficulties in school. The example provides a vehicle for initially understanding the connection between emotional stress and the child's behavioral reaction, as well as the negative effects of these two components. As a result, the child begins to develop greater emotional understanding. From that basic insight, the child can attempt to make behavioral changes.

Implementation

Naturally, the basic elements of psychoeducation focus on education—understanding the nature of depression, its symptoms, and the goal(s) of therapy. The procedural steps listed in Figure 8.1 illustrate how these elements are incorporated into the treatment of an individual child.

Figure 8.1 **Procedural steps for the application of psychoeducation**

1. Review the common causes of depression with the child and family.

2. Brainstorm with the child about the possible causes for his or her depressed feelings.

3. Discuss how these causes might be related to his or her depression symptoms.

4. Explain the treatment options, including specific therapeutic activities, and why they might be effective in this situation.

5. Create a treatment plan together with the child and family. State the goals of treatment and describe what is required for success. This plan may include what specific activities will be used; the length of each component of treatment; the expectations of the therapist, family, and child; and what behavioral change is expected.

B. Problem-Solving Skills Training

The goal of problem-solving skills training is to help a child to view situational depression (caused by a lack of positive reinforcement) as a dilemma to be resolved, rather than as a hopeless situation or an incurable disease (Nicolson & Ayers, 2004). To help relieve the emotional symptoms of depression, problem solving enables a child to identify the negative thinking that occurs in a specific situation, to recognize how those thoughts can lead to depression, and to replace those thoughts and subsequent feelings with healthier ones. Generally speaking, the professional teaches the child to objectify situations in order to view and solve them as problems.

For example, a clinician working with a student suffering from depressive feelings about his or her relationships with family and friends may teach the student how to reframe his or her negative thoughts. During clinical sessions, the student might express feelings or thoughts such as "My family doesn't love me" or "I have no friends." The clinician would help the student to interpret these thoughts differently. Through reframing, the student would learn to state these feelings or thoughts more realistically (e.g., "My family shows love by. . ."; "I can make friends by asking one person to go to a movie"), therefore making them more manageable. By reframing the negative feelings and emotions into a more positive light and into actionable behaviors, the student gains more control over the specific situation and can use the reframing technique to further promote emotional and behavioral improvement.

Implementation

The elements of problem-solving skills training, including learning how to define the problem, generating alternative solutions, evaluating solutions, choosing and implementing the best solution, and evaluating outcomes, are basic to any model of problem solving. The procedural steps presented in Figure 8.2 illustrate how these essential elements are used to remediate symptoms of depression.

Figure 8.2 Procedural steps for problem solving

1. Discuss with the child the likely causes of his or her depression and the resulting symptoms. Present these in the context of a problem to be solved rather than an illness to be treated.

2. Brainstorm with the child to generate solutions to the problem. For example, feelings of loneliness may have begun after quitting the swim team. Solutions to this problem might include rejoining the team or joining a similar or more interesting social group.

3. Together, evaluate the strengths and weaknesses of each solution and choose the best option to try.

4. Work out a gradual approach with the child, like you would for a homework assignment, outlining the steps needed and setting a target date for completion.

5. Monitor the child's progress. Consider revising the plan, if needed. Provide plenty of encouragement both for attempts and for successes.

C. Cognitive Restructuring

Cognitive restructuring teaches students to identify their own negative irrational thoughts and to supplant them with healthier, more rational ones. Children are taught to identify thoughts that are negative and are shown how these thoughts can lead to negative beliefs, emotions, and behaviors. Once awareness is obtained, children are then taught strategies that can be used to reinforce positive thinking and promote more positive and productive behaviors.

For example, a child suffering from depression has irrational thoughts about his self-worth, thinking, "This proves that I am useless" whenever he makes a mistake while completing a task. Using cognitive restructuring, the clinician would help the child recognize these negative thoughts and understand their effects. The clinician would then challenge the child to view his mistakes as lessons learned. The child is taught to use self-talk and to think, "It is okay to make mistakes; it's how we learn." In this way, the child begins to reinterpret his response to the negative event of making a mistake, seeing it as a more positive event and changing his response into a healthier one.

Implementation

The goal of cognitive restructuring is to modify depressive cognitions. The basic elements of cognitive restructuring are identifying, challenging, and changing depressive thoughts (Hops & Lewinsohn, 1995). For younger children, tools or methods such as songs, rhymes, or video representations may be helpful in identifying negative cognitions and understanding the connections among thoughts, feelings, and behaviors. The functional steps described in Figure 8.3 can help a child to engage in a more rational self-analysis of his or her thoughts.

Figure 8.3 **Functional steps for cognitive restructuring**

1. Identify the child's negative cognitions.

2. Teach the child how to recognize thoughts that are negative. Young children may find cartoons to be helpful illustrations. For instance, draw a thought bubble over the head of a character and ask the child to write in (or describe) the thoughts. Older students might keep diaries or journals of their thoughts.

3. Explain how negative thoughts are connected to unpleasant feelings or exaggerated and unproductive thinking (as described above, the use of a cartoon or journal might be helpful).

4. Explore specific actions the child can take to think more adaptively. For example:
   a. *Using a stop sign.* Ask the child to imagine a stop sign when negative thinking occurs. This cue can be used to replace a negative thought with a positive one.

   b. *Self-tracking.* Choose one negative thought and ask the child to record how often it occurs (e.g., "Other kids are laughing at me."). Then agree on a new thought to replace the negative one (e.g., "I'm okay just how I am.").

5. Encourage the child to practice consistently. Monitor progress at future sessions.

D. Pleasant-Activity Planning

Pleasant-activity planning encourages children to plan activities and social interactions that they consider pleasurable. When struggling with depression, children may lose interest in the activities that once made them feel happy and may lack the motivation to join them again. Participating in fun activities can promote a more positive outlook and a greater sense of self-worth. The goal of pleasant-activity planning is to make the scheduling process a fun experience. Getting a depressed child to participate in an activity provides reinforcement that is eventually replaced by natural environmental and social reinforcers, resulting in positive feelings within a child that serve to encourage continued participation in the activity.

For example, a child suffering from depression stops participating in French club after school. When asked why, she responds by saying, "I just don't feel like going." Using pleasant-activity planning, a practitioner works with the child to try to select a different after-school activity to get involved in. While they talk, the child discusses her interest in the drama club that is having its first meeting the following week. Together they decide that the child will plan on attending the drama club meeting and will make a list of questions she has about the club. As an added incentive for following through on her plan to attend, the child's parents will take her to dinner afterward, and they will talk about the meeting.

Implementation

The basic elements of pleasant-activity planning for depression are goal setting, developing a plan to engage in an activity, behavioral contracting, and self-reward (Hops & Lewinsohn, 1995). The functional steps for this method, outlined in Figure 8.4, begin with teaching a child that participating in fun activities can reduce the number of depressive feelings and thoughts the child will have. The remaining steps include organizing and planning the event or activity and participating in it.

Figure 8.4 Procedural steps for pleasant-activity planning

1. Teach the child about the benefits of planning for fun activities. Describe how planning and participating in an activity can improve the child's specific depressive symptoms.

2. Create a list of five or so activities the child finds enjoyable that are feasible for the child to participate in. Ask the child to choose two or three favorites from the list.

3. Work with the child to develop a detailed plan for participating in each activity. Help the child discover all the considerations and steps for participating in the activities, such as costs, transportation needs, etc. Try to let the child lead the organization and planning of the activities as much as possible.

4. Choose a reward for participating in each activity. Rewards could be given during the event (e.g., purchasing popcorn while at a movie) or after the event (e.g., getting more computer time for a day or week).

5. Track the number of activities or events the child participates in. Show the child the improvements he or she has made in participation, and discuss how the child's emotions and behavior may have changed during that time.

E. Relaxation Training

Relaxation training teaches children to begin to relax by monitoring muscle tension created by stressful situations and events (Ollendick & Cerny, 1981). Physical discomfort caused by tension can exacerbate common depressive symptoms, causing a child to feel even worse about himself or herself and the situation. Like the pleasant-activity planning intervention, improvements made to an aspect of a child's life (in this case, physical well-being) can spill over into his or her thoughts and emotions, and can lead to a reduction in depression symptomatology.

For example, one of the symptoms of Lauren's depression is her anxiety about going to preschool at the start of every week. To help relieve some of her emotional distress, each Sunday night her parents calmly sit with her and help her recall an enjoyable experience from the previous week at school. Together, they talk about the positive aspects of the experience (e.g., how much fun a game was, how good she felt completing a project). As they talk, the positive thoughts and emotions recalled by Lauren replace the negative ones she has about school, allowing her to relax.

Implementation

There are a number of relaxation techniques available, including counting, breathing exercises, recall, mental imagery, and progressive muscle relaxation (Kahn, Kehle, Jenson, & Clark, 1990). Counting and breathing techniques are easy for children of all ages to learn, as they simply require the child to concentrate on counting or breathing when feeling symptoms of depression. The recall technique requires a child to think about a previous successful or pleasant event; pleasant feelings and emotions associated with the event will help reduce negative feelings and emotions. Mental imagery requires a child to focus on a specific event and envision the steps needed to succeed at the event. Similarly, progressive muscle relaxation techniques require the child to mentally focus on a specific part of the body and concentrate on relaxing it. The essential elements of all these techniques include identifying emotional triggers and their corresponding physical symptoms, engaging in an activity designed to reduce the negative emotions associated with the depressive symptoms, and recognizing when emotions and feelings start to improve. The procedural steps for relaxation training presented in Figure 8.5 illustrate how these essential elements are used to remediate symptoms of depression.

> **Figure 8.5 Procedural steps for relaxation training**
>
> 1. Identify a specific symptom of the child's depression, along with the effect it has on the child (e.g., crying, headaches).
>
> 2. Teach the child how to perform a relaxation technique.
>
> 3. Ask the child to imagine a situation that causes the undesired symptoms.
>
> 4. Practice the technique with the child until he or she is able to perform the steps by himself or herself. Discuss how the technique can help the child feel calmer in the imagined situation. Model the steps for the child, as needed.
>
> 5. Check in with the child periodically to determine if the relaxation technique is being practiced correctly and at the appropriate times. Provide refresher training as necessary.

F. Self-Management Training

Self-management techniques (sometimes called affect regulation) require a child to use information obtained while monitoring his or her behavior to modify and control negative feelings and emotions. Each day, over the course of an extended period of time (e.g., 2 weeks), the child records his or her feelings and behaviors. These records are then reviewed by the child and therapist. Particular attention is given to actions and events that led to changes in emotions or behaviors. The child is taught which actions led (or can lead) to a positive change and learns to implement these solutions by himself or herself during the course of each day. He or she then learns to regulate and self-reward positive moods or thoughts through recognizing, labeling, communicating, monitoring, recording, and finally modifying and controlling them (Braswell & Kendall, 2001; Friedberg et al., 2003; Nicolson & Ayers, 2004).

As an example, Beth reported feeling sad for no reason every day for 6 months before entering therapy, and the sadness was something she wanted to change. Beth was taught to record her mood on a daily basis, using a small notebook. Beth and her therapist decided that Beth could and would carry the notebook with her throughout the day. Beth recorded her mood when she woke up, wrote down any time she had a sad thought, and noted the event that preceded it. During therapy sessions, Beth and the therapist reviewed the notebook together and used it as a tool to develop interventions and discuss the impact of the interventions. Beth identified to the therapist that walking her dog and going to movies were favorite activities, so she self-recorded these also. Beth set two goals: to manage her sadness through increasing her favorite activities, and to find two new positive activities.

Implementation

The elements essential to self-management training include goal setting; monitoring, recording, and evaluating behaviors and emotions; using self-reinforcement; and charting progress over time. The procedural steps of self-management training presented in Figure 8.6 illustrate how these essential elements are used to remediate symptoms of depression. Self-management typically involves physical recording of some kind. This recording can be done with paper and pencil, or using audio or video tools. Recording sheets can be as simple as a chart or table for the child to fill in or a graph paper tablet. Some children prefer journaling but may need some structure to guide them in recording specific behaviors or feelings rather than just private musings. Frequency and type of recording vary depending on the type and degree of depressive symptomatology.

Figure 8.6 Procedural steps for self-management

1. Discuss or coach in the identification of personal goals for the student; keep these as student-directed as possible.

2. Develop a way for the child to monitor his or her emotions and behavior by generating a form the child can use for tracking, along with a tracking procedure for him or her to follow. Forms used for tracking could be a calendar, notebook, or journal. Recordings could be made hourly or daily. Shorter intervals (e.g., every 15 minutes) might be helpful when there are a number of different transitions made during a day (e.g., classroom changes during school).

3. Determine how often you will check in or meet with the child, and set a time to review the student's recording form.

4. Review the student's recording form. Discuss with the child how distorted thoughts might be affecting his or her everyday behavior.

5. Choose one or two problem emotions or behaviors to modify, and suggest a solution that the child can implement independently.

6. Check in with the child to mark progress and provide feedback at the beginning and end of the school day, for example, or more frequently as needed (particularly in the early stages of intervention).

7. Encourage self-rewarding and praise positive efforts, including consistent use of the tracking form and any steps made to resolve problem emotions and behaviors. Provide rewards whether the steps are successful or not.

G. Family Involvement

Family involvement in CBT can be minimal or extensive. For some families, parents or siblings may be included in teaching sessions that provide an overview of what a child with depression may be experiencing, the course of treatment for the child, and how the family members can help. For other families, some members may be asked to join a more extensive program, either to learn specific skills (e.g., negotiation, conflict resolution, communication skills) that will help a family member deal with the child's depression symptoms, or to participate in therapy aimed at resolving extended family issues.

Implementation

Involving family members can be a helpful strategy for any of the CBT interventions. Family members can often provide the support and mentoring needed to help a child deal with his or her depression symptoms. In many cases, family members will be educated on depression-related symptoms and will learn some of the common causes and consequences. Family members are often taught new strategies for interacting with a child through communication skills training, negotiation skills training, and problem-solving training (Beardslee et al., 1997; Hops & Lewinsohn, 1995; Lewinsohn & Clarke, 1999; Stark & Kendall, 1996). Each of these strategies offers its own functional steps for implementation, so a listing of functional steps specific to family involvement is not provided here.

Evidence for Use

The effectiveness of CBT has been established through a variety of research studies spanning more than 2 decades. Different combinations of CBT components have shown effectiveness for decreasing depressive symptoms, symptom severity, and dysfunctional negative thoughts, and have demonstrated clinical significance with total remittance of depressive symptomatology (Ackerson, Scogin, McKendree-Smith, & Lyman, 1998; Asarnow, Scott, & Mintz, 2002; Clarke, Rohde, Lewinsohn, Hops, & Seeley, 1999; Friedberg et al., 2003; Jaycox, Reivich, Gillham, & Seligman, 1994; Kahn et al., 1990; Lewinsohn et al., 1990; Reynolds & Coats, 1986; Stark, Humphrey, Crook, & Lewis, 1990; Stark, Reynolds, & Kaslow, 1987; Weisz, Thurber, Sweeney, Proffitt, & LeGagnoux, 1997). Research has also established the efficacy of several specific manualized treatment programs for children and adolescents with depression—such as Adolescent Coping With Depression Course (CWD-A; Clarke, Lewinsohn, & Hops, 1990) and Stress Busters (Friedberg et al., 2003)— that include the CBT components described in this chapter.

The following studies summarize some of the key research findings associated with the use of CBT in children and adolescents with depression.

Ackerson, J., Scogin, F., McKendree-Smith, N., & Lyman, R. D. (1998). Cognitive bibliotherapy for mild and moderate adolescent depressive symptomatology. *Journal of Consulting and Clinical Psychology, 66*(4), 685–690.

This study examined the effectiveness of a self-administered cognitive therapy for adolescents with mild to moderate depression. The self-administered cognitive therapy—cognitive bibliotherapy—required participants to read *Feeling Good* (Burns, 1980) and receive weekly phone calls monitoring their progress. No counseling was given during telephone conversations. The participants—22 adolescents in Grades 7 through 12—were randomly assigned to one of two treatment conditions: immediate or delayed treatment (i.e., a 4-week waiting period prior to treatment). Data were collected through several independent measures: participants in the immediate-treatment group were assessed at pretreatment, posttreatment, and 1-month follow-up, while those in the delayed-treatment group were assessed prior to the waiting period, at pretreatment (approximately 1 month later), and at posttreatment. Additional data were collected on participation and compliance via participant reports of book exercises completed and number of pages read, respectively. Results supported the potential effectiveness of cognitive bibliotherapy with depressed adolescents, with more than half of the participants scoring in the nondepressed range on two measures at posttreatment (59% on the Hamilton Rating Scale for Depression and 64% on the Child Depression Inventory).

Asarnow, J. R., Scott, C. V., & Mintz, J. (2002). A combined cognitive–behavioral family education intervention for depression in children: A treatment development study. *Cognitive Therapy and Research, 26*(2), 221–229.

Twenty-three students with depression in fourth through sixth grades participated in this study of a 10-session cognitive–behavioral and family education intervention that focused on: 1) improving problem solving and social skills, 2) increasing self-direction of skill acquisition and mastery, 3) generalizing skills across environments, and 4) encouraging parents to support and have positive attitudes about treatment. Participants were randomly assigned to either the intervention group or the wait-list control group. The treatment group met twice each week for nine 90-minute sessions that utilized games, homework, and role-playing to teach treatment skills and objectives to the students. The family education component took place during the tenth treatment session, utilizing the presentation of achievement awards and student-taught games to emphasize the childrens' progress and the parents' role in facilitating continued improvement. Results supported the effectiveness of the combined therapy, with students in the treatment group more likely to exhibit diminished symptoms of depression, negative thoughts, and negative responses to stress as compared with the control group. In addition, satisfaction levels were high for both parents and students, with parents indicating that the brevity of the family education component was both desirable and sufficient.

Brent, D. A., Holder, D., Kolko, D., Birhamer, B., Baugher, M., Roth, C. et al. (1997). A clinical psychotherapy trial for adolescent depression comparing cognitive, family, and supportive therapy. *Archives of General Psychiatry, 54*(9), 877–885.

In this study, 107 adolescents with clinical depression were randomized into three treatment groups: cognitive–behavioral therapy (CBT), systemic behavior family therapy (SBFT), and nondirective supportive treatment (NST). CBT focused on the individual, although it involved the whole family, and dealt with thoughts, assumptions, and beliefs. SBFT focused more on identifying dysfunctional habits and teaching family skill building. NST served as a control group, while accounting for the nonspecific elements of treatment, such as therapist attention, empathy, and the passage of time. Results showed that CBT was more effective than either SBFT or NST in remission rate (60% for CBT compared to 38% and 39% for SBFT and NST, respectively). However, there were no differences in the effects on suicidality and functional impairment.

Butler, L., Miezitis, S., Friedman, R., & Cole, E. (1980). The effect of two school-based intervention programs on depressive symptoms in preadolescents. *American Educational Research Journal, 17*(1), 111–119.

The efficacy of role-playing (R-P) and cognitive restructuring (C-R) for treating children with depression was the focus of this study involving 56 fifth- and sixth-grade students. The participants were randomly assigned to one of four study conditions: R-P, C-R, attention-placebo (Placebo), or classroom control (Control). Students in the R-P group participated in 10 weekly, one-hour, group role-playing sessions that focused on how to solve problems relevant to children with depression. The C-R group received instruction in 10 one-hour sessions on how to recognize and replace irrational and self-defeating thoughts, improve listening skills, and solve problems more effectively. Those in the Placebo group were taught cooperative problem-solving skills through research sharing and information pooling. Data were collected via teacher interviews and four self-report questionnaires administered at pretreatment and posttreatment. The findings showed statistically significant changes in depression scores and locus of control measures for both groups. Role-playing was found to be most effective, with 9 of 14 students demonstrating improved classroom behavior, all 9 with assessment results falling below the depressed range, compared to only 4 of 14 in the C-R group with improved classroom behavior, and 3 of the 4 having considerably improved depression scores.

Clarke, G., DeBar, L., Lynch, F., Powell, J., Gale, J., & O'Connor, E. et al. (2005). A randomized effectiveness trial of brief cognitive-behavioral therapy for depressed adolescents receiving antidepressant medication. *Journal of the American Academy of Child and Adolescent Psychiatry, 44*(9), 888–898.

This study followed 152 adolescents, aged 12 to 18 years, who had been previously diagnosed with depression and prescribed selective serotonergic reuptake inhibitors (SSRIs). Participants were randomly assigned to receive either the treatment-as-usual care (TAU group) of SSRIs alone or the collaborative care of cognitive–behavioral therapy (CBT) plus SSRIs (CBT + TAU group). CBT was delivered in five to nine 60-minute sessions (average attendance = 5.3 sessions) followed by monthly telephone calls to check in with the participants. Data were collected at baseline and 6-, 12-, 26-, and 52-week follow-ups. Results showed that, of those found to be moderately depressed at baseline, fewer participants in the CBT + TAU group (25%) than in the TAU group (44%) remained moderately depressed at the 52-week follow-up. However, this and other study findings offered only minor indications supporting the effectiveness of combining CBT with SSRIs, suggesting that TAU (i.e., SSRIs alone) is a powerful treatment option for adolescents with depression.

Clarke, G. N., Hawkins, W., Murphy, M., Sheeber, L. B., Lewinsohn, P. M., & Seeley, J. R. (1995). Targeted prevention of unipolar depressive disorder in an at-risk sample of high school adolescents: A randomized trial of a group cognitive intervention. *Journal of the American Academy of Child and Adolescent Psychiatry, 34*(3), 312–321.

One hundred fifty adolescents with subdiagnostic levels of self-reported symptoms of depression participated in this study examining the preventative efficacy of a group cognitive intervention, the Coping With Stress Course, for adolescent unipolar affective disorder. Participants (mean age = 15.3 years) were randomly assigned to one of the two study conditions: treatment (*n* = 76) or usual care (*n* = 74). The cognitive intervention course's 15 group sessions (three weekly 45-minute sessions) utilized role-playing, group discussions, and cartoons to teach participants how to identify and confront negative and irrational thoughts. Individuals in the usual care group continued to receive any care they were currently involved in and/or any new treatment they chose to seek on their own. Data were collected via several measures at intake, posttreatment, and 6- and 12-month follow-up. Findings demonstrated that, compared to the control group, fewer participants in the treatment group had developed unipolar depressive disorder at the 12-month follow-up. However, the intervention failed to completely prevent the disorder, with the treatment group's incidence rate at nearly twice that of unselected community samples.

Clarke, G. N., Rohde, P., Lewinsohn, P. M., Hops, H., & Seeley, J. R. (1999). Cognitive-behavioral treatment of adolescent depression: Efficacy of acute group treatment and booster sessions. *Journal of the American Academy of Child and Adolescent Psychiatry, 38*(3), 272–279.

This study followed 123 adolescents, aged between 14 and 18 years, with diagnoses of major depressive disorder or dysthymia, who were randomly assigned to one of three conditions: cognitive–behavioral therapy (CBT), CBT plus parent sessions, or wait-list control. The CBT group utilized the Adolescent Coping With Depression Course, which includes instruction in improving social skills, resolving conflicts, monitoring moods, and improving communication. Individuals in the CBT group participated in 16 two-hour group-treatment sessions over 8 weeks. In the CBT plus parent group, in addition to the participants receiving the same training as the CBT group, their parents attended nine separate sessions. After follow-up assessments, participants in the two treatment groups were randomly assigned to one of two follow-up conditions: boosters or frequent assessments. Individuals in the frequent assessments group were assessed every 4 months, whereas those in the boosters group received one to two booster sessions in addition to being assessed every 4 months. Results showed recovery rates—defined as no longer meeting clinical criteria for major depression or dysthymia—of about 65% for the CBT group and 69% for the CBT plus parent group, compared with about 48% for the wait-list group. In addition, rather than minimizing recurrence, the booster sessions most benefited those who had not responded to initial treatment, regardless of treatment group.

Friedberg, R. D., McClure, J. M., Wilding, L., Goldman, M. L., Long, M. P., Anderson, L., et al. (2003). A cognitive-behavioral skills training group for children experiencing anxious and depressive symptoms: A clinical report with accompanying descriptive data. *Journal of Contemporary Psychotherapy, 33*(3), 157–175.

This study involved eight children who were referred to the program because of anxious or depressive symptoms, although they were not necessarily clinically diagnosed. The children attended 10 group therapy sessions using the new program PANDY (Preventing Anxiety and Depression in Youth), which involved creative and fun ways of helping them learn to evaluate their thoughts, feelings, actions, and physiological responses and learn more ways of coping. The group setting also gave children a chance to address fears such as performance and peer disapproval. Data collected from parent reports on child behavior changes indicated that 57% of the participants worried less about school, 29% worried less about criticism, and 29% worried less about embarrassment.

Jaycox, L. H., Reivich, K. J., Gillham, J., & Seligman, M. E. P. (1994). Prevention of depressive symptoms in school children. *Behaviour Research and Therapy, 32*(8), 801–816.

The effectiveness of the Penn Prevention Program (PPP), a depression prevention program for adolescents that utilizes cognitive–behavioral techniques, was the focus of this study involving 143 individuals, aged 10 to 13 years. The participants were placed into either the PPP treatment group (69 individuals) or one of two control groups (wait-list = 24, no-participation = 50). The groups' levels of distress were not significantly different based on the measures taken at pretest. Students in the PPP treatment group received training in social problem solving, coping with family conflict, thinking flexibly, and evaluating accuracy of beliefs over 12 sessions. Results demonstrated that participants in the PPP group experienced significant reductions in depressive symptoms and demonstrated improved classroom behavior as compared to those in the control groups at both posttreatment and at 6-month follow-up. However, findings showed the PPP treatment did not reduce the occurrence of conduct problems in the home setting.

Kahn, J. S., Kehle, T. J., Jenson, W. R., & Clark, E. (1990). Comparison of cognitive-behavioral, relaxation, and self-modeling interventions for depression among middle-school students. *School Psychology Review, 19*(2), 196–211.

School psychologists provided treatment in the school setting to 68 middle school students with moderate and severe depression in this study comparing three interventions: Adolescent Coping With Depression (CWD-A), a cognitive–behavioral course emphasizing skills and strategies to cope with depression-related problems; relaxation training, which focuses on understanding and managing the relationship between stress and depression; and self-modeling training, in which positive behavioral and cognitive changes are promoted through repeated viewing of oneself role-playing targeted desirable behaviors. The participants were randomized and placed evenly (17 each) into one of the three treatment groups or the wait-list control group. Students in the CWD-A and relaxation groups received their assigned treatment in twelve 60-minute, small-group (two to six students) sessions over the course of 6 to 8 weeks. The participants in the self-modeling group received individual treatment in 12 sessions over 6 to 8 weeks. Results demonstrated the efficacy of each of the three interventions for use with adolescents with depression, with participants in all treatment groups achieving notable positive gains as compared with the wait-list control group.

Kolko, D. J., Brent, D. A., Baugher, M., Bridge, J., & Birmaher, B. (2000). Cognitive and family therapies for adolescent depression: Treatment specificity, mediation, and moderation. *Journal of Consulting and Clinical Psychology, 68*(4), 603–614.

A study comparing the efficacy of cognitive–behavioral therapy (CBT), systemic behavioral family therapy (SBFT), and nondirective supportive therapy (NST) for treating adolescent depression was the focus of this investigation to determine the impact of therapist background, mediators, and moderators on treatment outcomes. Participants—103 adolescents with depression, aged 13–18—were randomly assigned to receive one of the three therapies in two phases. In the active phase, participants in each group received treatment in 12 to 16 sessions over the course of 12 to 16 weeks. In the booster phase, participants received treatment in 2 to 4 sessions over 2 to 4 weeks. Data were collected using measures of psychiatric symptomatology, cognitive functioning, and family environment at intake, after the sixth intervention session, at posttreatment, and at five follow-up points (3, 6, 9, 12, and 24 months). In terms of long-term impact, results showed that therapist variables impacted few outcomes and that assessing cognitive distortion and family dysfunction neither mediated nor moderated outcomes.

Lewinsohn, P. M., Clarke, G. N., Hops, H., & Andrews, J. (1990). Cognitive-behavioral treatment for depressed adolescents. *Behavior Therapy, 21*(4), 385–401.

This 7-week study examined the short- and long-term effectiveness of parent involvement and the Adolescent Coping with Depression (CWD-A) course, a cognitive–behavioral intervention focusing on relaxation techniques, conflict resolution, social skills, and management of negative and irrational thoughts. After the initial assessment and inclusion process, 59 adolescents, aged 14 to 18 years, were randomly assigned to one of three groups: adolescent only (21), adolescent and parent (19), or wait-list control (19). The participants in the adolescent-only group received CWD-A training during bi-weekly two-hour sessions. The participants in the adolescent-and-parent group received the same training, and their parents attended weekly two-hour sessions in which they learned the skills and methods of CWD-A and how to support and reinforce their children's new skills and positive behavior changes. Data were collected via several measures at intake, posttreatment, and at 1-, 6-, 12-, and 24-month follow-ups. From intake to posttreatment, results showed marked declines in the number of participants meeting diagnostic criteria for depression in the two treatment groups (57% in adolescent-only and 52% in adolescent-and-parent), whereas about 95% of the wait-list group continued to meet the criteria. Moreover, targeted behaviors significantly improved in both treatment groups, and these gains were maintained through the 24-month follow-up. The findings support the efficacy of CWD-A and suggest roughly equal results can be achieved with and without parental involvement.

Reynolds, W. M., & Coats, K. I. (1986). A comparison of cognitive–behavioral therapy and relaxation training for the treatment of depression in adolescents. *Journal of Consulting and Clinical Psychology, 54*(5), 653–660.

In this 5-week study, 30 high school students with depression, selected from a group of 800 after a two-stage screening process, were randomly assigned to one of three conditions: cognitive–behavioral therapy, relaxation training, or wait-list control. The cognitive–behavioral therapy focused on self-control skills training and the basic methods for generating a self-change plan. The relaxation training centered on understanding the relationship between stress and depression and learning self-relaxation skills. Each treatment group met for ten 50-minute, small-group sessions over the course of the study. Data were collected using measures of depression, self-concept, and anxiety during the initial screening process and at pretreatment, posttreatment, and 5-week follow-up. Results showed that, based on scores on the Beck Depression Inventory, 83% of the cognitive–behavior group, 75% of the relaxation training group, and 0% of the wait-list group had moved from the moderately depressed range at pretreatment into the nondepressed range at posttreatment. This finding, along with the additional information gathered from all the measures, supports the efficacy of both cognitive–behavioral therapy and relaxation training for treating adolescent depression.

Rosselló, J., & Bernal, G. (1999). The efficacy of cognitive–behavioral and interpersonal treatments for depression in Puerto Rican adolescents. *Journal of Consulting and Clinical Psychology, 67*(5), 734–745.

Seventy-one Puerto Rican adolescents with depression, aged 13 to 17 years, participated in this study comparing the effects of cognitive–behavioral treatment (CBT) and interpersonal treatment (IPT) with a wait-list control group. The students were randomly assigned to one of the conditions, with individuals in the CBT and IPT groups receiving 12 weekly, one-hour, individual therapy sessions and the wait-list group receiving no treatment. Participants in the CBT group learned to identify the thoughts, feelings, and actions that influence feelings of depression in order to diminish depressive symptoms and increase their sense of control. Participants in the IPT group evaluated current problems in their interpersonal relationships and addressed problematic areas as a means to reduce symptoms of depression. Data were collected via five measures, with results demonstrating that both CBT and IPT groups showed striking reductions in depressive symptoms as compared with the wait-list group and that 59% of the CBT group and 82% of the IPT group showed clinically significant improvement (moving from nonfunctional to functional) from pretreatment to posttreatment. The outcomes suggest that both CBT and IPT can be effective for treating depression in adolescents.

Stark, K. D., Humphrey, L. L., Crook, K., & Lewis, K. (1990). Perceived family environments of depressed and anxious children: Child's and maternal figure's perspectives. *Journal of Abnormal Child Psychology, 18*(5), 527–547.

This study assessed and examined the characteristics of families of children with depression and/or anxiety, as well as the children's and mothers' perceptions of their families, using the Self-Report Measure of Family Functioning (SRMFF). The 51 participants, aged 9 to 14 years, were initially assessed via several behavioral measures to determine diagnoses, resulting in the following diagnostic groups: depressed ($n = 11$), depressed and anxious ($n = 15$), anxious ($n = 10$), control (i.e., no psychopathology; $n = 15$). Each participant then completed the child version of the SRMFF (SRMFF-C) in small group settings, and 41 mothers and 3 stepmothers completed the SRMFF. Results demonstrated that a majority of the time the children's perceptions of their family environment accurately predicted each child's diagnosis, with the exception of the control group (71% accuracy in diagnosis of depression, 64% depressed and anxious, 78% anxious, and 23% control). Moreover, in terms of the children's perceptions, families with depressed or anxious children appeared to be less supportive, democratic, and involved in recreational activities; these families also appeared to have more conflict.

Stark, K. D., Reynolds, W. M., & Kaslow, N. J. (1987). A comparison of the relative efficacy of self-control therapy and a behavioral problem-solving therapy for depression in children. *Journal of Abnormal Child Psychology, 15*(1), 91–113.

Rehm's coping skills training program and a behavioral problem-solving approach to treating childhood depression were the focus of this 5-week study to determine each therapy's efficacy in terms of impact across behaviors, across environments, and over time. Twenty-nine children in Grades 4 through 6 were randomly assigned to one of three conditions: self-control therapy (S-C), behavioral problem-solving therapy (BPS), or waiting list (WL). Over the course of 12 sessions, participants in the S-C group learned skills in self-monitoring, self-reinforcement, self-evaluating performance, attributing causes, and determining consequences. The BPS group, in addition to learning improved problem-solving skills, learned to self-monitor behavior and engage in pleasant activities. Data were collected at pretreatment, posttreatment, and an 8-week follow-up. Results showed that symptoms of depression at posttreatment, as well as at the 8-week follow-up, significantly decreased in both the S-C and BPS treatment groups, indicating that both therapies are effective options for treating children with depression.

Treatment for Adolescents With Depression Study (TADS) Team. (2004). Fluoxetine, cognitive–behavioral therapy, and their combination for adolescents with depression: Treatment for Adolescents With Depression Study (TADS) randomized controlled trial. *Journal of the American Medical Association, 292*(7), 807–820.

In this 12-week study of the efficacy of medication and cognitive–behavioral therapy (CBT), separately and in combination, 439 adolescent participants diagnosed with major depressive disorder (MDD), aged 12 to 17 years, were randomly assigned to one of four conditions: fluoxetine alone ($n = 109$), CBT alone ($n = 111$), fluoxetine with CBT ($n = 107$), or placebo ($n = 112$). Students receiving fluoxetine alone were monitored via six 20- to 30-minute medication sessions over the course of the study. Dosages started at 10 mg/d, increased to 20 mg/d, and were capped at 40 mg/d. The CBT alone group received individual and family skills-oriented treatment in goal setting, mood monitoring, increasing positive activities, and social problem solving. The fluoxetine with CBT group received all treatment aspects of both fluoxetine alone and CBT alone. Results showed that fluoxetine with CBT was the most effective (71%) in alleviating symptoms of MDD when compared with the three other study conditions. Fluoxetine alone also proved to be effective (60%), although not as much so when combined with CBT. Additionally, results showed that response rates in the CBT alone group were only slightly better than those in the placebo group (43% vs. 34%, respectively).

Weisz, J. R., Thurber, C. A., Sweeney, L., Proffitt, V. D., & LeGagnoux, G. L. (1997). Brief treatment of mild-to-moderate child depression using primary and secondary control enhancement training. *Journal of Consulting and Clinical Psychology, 65*(4), 703–707.

Forty-eight elementary school–aged students (mean = 9.1 years) participated in this first investigation of the effectiveness of the Primary and Secondary Control Enhancement Training (PASCET) program, an eight-session cognitive–behavioral intervention developed specifically for children with mild-to-moderate depression. Participants were randomly assigned to either the treatment group (16 students) or the no-treatment control group (32 students). For the treatment group, the first six of the 50-minute sessions involved education in five control skills: two primary (identifying and participating in mood-enhancing activities and building skills through goal setting and practice) and three secondary (identifying depressive thoughts, practicing mood-enhancing cognitive techniques, and utilizing relaxation and positive imagery). In the two remaining sessions, each treatment group student met individually with a therapist to discuss the skills learned in relation to his or her specific situation (Session 7) and participated in a "quiz show" designed to review and reinforce the skills (Session 8). Results indicated that children in the treatment group evidenced significantly greater decreases in symptoms of depression as compared to those in the control group—differences that remained at the 9-month follow-up, offering tentative support for the efficacy of short-term treatment programs for children with depression.

Wood, A., Harrington, R., & Moore, A. (1996). Controlled trial of a brief cognitive-behavioural intervention in adolescent patients with depressive disorders. *Journal of Child Psychology and Psychiatry, 37*(6), 737–746.

This study evaluated 53 (48 completers) older children and adolescents with major depressive disorder. The students were randomized into two groups: a brief (five- to eight-session) depression treatment programme (DTP) and a control group using relaxation training (RT). The DTP had three main components: cognitive, social problem solving, and physical symptoms of depression. At posttreatment, the DTP group had significantly lower levels of depression than the RT group. Interestingly, the differences lessened at 3-month follow-up and were negligible at 6-month follow-up, partly because the RT group slowly improved and partly because of relapses in some members of the DTP group. However, in the short-term, this brief DTP programme provided an effective (50% response rate) treatment. Further research is needed for ways to prevent relapse.

Considerations

For Teaching

Cognitive–behavioral therapy approaches blend well with classroom-based approaches because of their inherent teaching nature. The identification of problems, causes, triggers, replacements, and solutions are all facilitated and easily adopted by classroom teachers as topics for teaching if given the opportunity and resources. Problem-solving and self-management skills generalize to a variety of behavioral and academic concerns. Posters can be used to illustrate the steps for a particular technique, classwide instruction can be conducted by a counselor or school psychologist, and teachers can provide time for students with depression or depressive symptoms to engage in recording or writing.

Students can self-record in an inconspicuous manner, such as by making a check mark on a page in a notebook, or they may write sentences about their feelings in a journal-like format. The self-monitoring and self-recording should be accompanied by checking in with an adult to review the recordings, track progress, and provide feedback. This check-in can be done in the morning or afternoon of each school day or more frequently if needed initially. Such check-ins can be done by a teacher.

For Family and Language Differences

Depending on the origins and trajectory of the depression, parent involvement may be limited. Expectations for parent involvement should be clearly communicated in person to the parent(s) with a healthy respect for family perceptions of depression and treatment. Some parents may not be interested in learning about depression and may see it as a weakness in the child; others may reinforce the depression with protection, attention, and caretaking that enables the depressive behavior. Culture, language, and personal experience with depression symptomatology and treatment will all have an impact on parent involvement and interest in training or treatment.

For Age and Developmental Level

For many of the CBT approaches, age and/or developmental level should be primary considerations when selecting an intervention. Many CBT strategies require a child to articulate and document feelings, emotions, and behaviors. As such, the effectiveness may be limited for children with poor verbal, language, or writing skills. It is unlikely that young children or children with developmental delays can truly examine their thought patterns or the origin of those thoughts until they have reached Piaget's stage of formal operations, typically at adolescence (Lewinsohn & Clarke, 1999).

Use of educational strategies will require a match between the information provided to children and their ability to understand and act on it. For example, young children may not understand the purpose of relaxation training at first; they must be given adequate, age-appropriate information in order to understand the nature and use of the technique.

Problem-solving skills training, cognitive restructuring, and self-management training may also be difficult to implement for young children (e.g., aged 7 years or younger) or for children who have minimal verbal skills. In contrast, pleasant-activity planning can be easily understood and effective for children of most ages.

The type of monitoring and recording used for self-management depends on the age and ability level of the student and the level of independence and desire for self-helping strategies. Very young children are more likely to be successful if taught a simple recording strategy, such as making a check mark in the sad or happy face column on a recording sheet; older children may prefer to write about their feelings in narrative form.

For Child Safety

Depression is a very serious condition that can lead to physical harm to a child. Know the warning signs for self-injury and suicide. Take all suicidal threats seriously, and keep parents and other caregivers informed. Provide 24-hour support information when appropriate, such as suicide prevention hotline numbers and emergency room numbers. Request permission to inform physicians and make clear to the child that suicide attempts and self-injury are not options, and that such actions do not result in increased peer or adult attention or revenge. For more information on suicide prevention, see one of the many online resources from the U.S. Department of Human Health Services or the National Institute of Health.

II. Interpersonal Therapy (or Psychotherapy) for Adolescents

Interpersonal psychotherapy for adolescents (IPT or IPT-A) with depression is based on the premise that depression occurs because of limitations in an individual's ability to adapt to changes in interpersonal relationships. Depression is believed to begin with cognitions and feelings associated with interpersonal relationships across several situations, including grief, role transitions, role disputes, and interpersonal deficits (Klerman, Weissman, Rounsaville, & Chevron, 1984; Mufson & Sills, 2006; Rosselló & Bernal, 1999). IPT is generally considered a cognitive–behavioral approach, even though it originated in psychodynamic theories, because its primary effects include increases in communication ability, self-efficacy, autonomy, and adaptability. In addition to focusing on improving interpersonal relationships, IPT also centers on cognitive aspects of depression. The specific treatment goals, interventions, and strategies are chosen based on the issues identified by the student and clinician together. IPT is typically a short-duration treatment used to understand the child's personality, relationships to others, and relationships to the environment; it is also often a manualized treatment program (Mufson, Dorta, Moreau, & Weissman, 2004; Weissman, Markowitz, & Klerman, 2000).

For example, Brittany, a 15-year-old female, was very close to her grandmother, who had lived with the family since Brittany's birth. After her grandmother's death, Brittany does not seem to be able to adjust to life without her grandmother's presence. The use of IPT in grief recovery can help Brittany understand and manage her grief while adjusting to the change. Specifically, IPT will help Brittany understand the transition she is going through and identify the changes that the loss of her grandmother may cause in her life: whom she will talk with and how to help with tasks that her grandmother often did for the family, such as laundry and meal preparation. Brittany may also feel out of control due to her loss, particularly because it is her first experience with death, and she may wonder when and how the grief will end. The education and interpersonal skill building in IPT should help with each of these issues once they are identified.

Implementation

The primary goal of IPT is to decrease depressive symptoms by improving interpersonal functioning. Successful outcomes of IPT therapy include the establishment of autonomy and an individual's sense of self, development of appropriate and responsible romantic relationships, acceptable management of peer pressure, and when applicable, successful coping with initial experiences of death and loss (Mufson & Sills, 2006). These outcomes are achieved through application of the essential elements of IPT, which include education, development of interpersonal skills, and prevention of relapse (Mufson & Sills, 2006). The procedural steps for IPT presented in Figure 8.7 illustrate how these essential elements are used to remediate symptoms of depression (Mufson & Sills, 2006; Rosselló & Bernal, 1999).

Figure 8.7 Procedural steps for using interpersonal therapy

1. Review the common causes and facts about depression with the child (e.g., depression is normal, depressive experiences are common in life).

2. Present to the child ways that depression symptoms can be reduced and how full recovery can be achieved.

3. Conduct an interview or interpersonal inventory with the child, and discuss his or her feelings or behaviors related to the depression. Identify any interpersonal skills that need work.

4. Create a treatment contract with the child that includes a clear statement of the problem, the expectations of both the child and therapist, and the specific course of treatment (including parameters of the treatment and articulation of desired behaviors). Be sure to clarify any areas that are not well understood.

5. Analyze the communication and decision-making skills of the child by discussing a painful or difficult event.

6. Teach behavior change techniques, including identifying activities that trigger more pleasurable mood responses.

7. Identify and review the behavioral and emotional signs of relapse. Ask the child to practice identifying these signs between sessions.

8. Phase out treatment gradually, over the course of about three sessions.

Evidence for Use

IPT and IPT-A for children with depressive symptomatology improve social functioning, overall functioning, and problem-solving skills, while decreasing symptoms of depression (Mufson, Dorta, Wickramaratne, et al., 2004; Mufson, Weissman, Moreau, & Garfinkel, 1999; Robbins, Alessi, & Colfer, 1989). IPT-A has also been found to result in complete remittance of depressive symptomatology or to reach clinical significance in which the student no longer meets the diagnostic criteria for depression (Mufson et al., 1994; Mufson, Weissman, Moreau, & Garfinkel, 1999; Rosselló & Bernal, 1999).

The following studies summarize some of the key research findings associated with the use of interpersonal psychotherapy in adolescents with depression.

Mufson, L., Dorta, K. P., Wickramaratne, P., Nomura, Y., Olfson, M., & Weissman, M. M. (2004). A randomized effectiveness trial of interpersonal psychotherapy for depressed adolescents. *Archives of General Psychiatry, 61,* 577–584.

This study investigated the suitability and efficacy of interpersonal psychotherapy for adolescents (IPT-A) in comparison with treatment as usual (TAU) in a school-based mental health clinic setting. Sixty-three students, aged between 12 and 18 years and referred for mental health services, were randomly assigned to one of the two treatment conditions. The IPT-A treatment, consisting of psychotherapy focusing on current problems and aiming to reduce the symptoms of depression and improve interpersonal functioning, was delivered during twelve 35-minute sessions over the course of 16 weeks (eight consecutive sessions, four at any time during the subsequent 8 weeks). The TAU condition consisted of the treatment protocols in place at the clinics at the time of the study. Data were collected via three clinician-rated and two self-report measures at baseline and at weeks 4, 8, 12, and 16. Results indicated that students receiving IPT-A had significantly reduced symptoms of depression and significantly improved social functioning as compared with the TAU group. Moreover, students in the IPT-A group improved more quickly than their TAU peers, suggesting there is great potential in IPT-A's use in a school setting.

Mufson, L., Moreau, D., Weissman, M. M., Wickramaratne, P., Martin, J., & Samoilov, A. (1994). Modification of interpersonal psychotherapy with depressed adolescents (IPT-A): Phase I and II studies. *Journal of the American Academy of Child and Adolescent Psychiatry, 33*(5), 695–705.

Seeking to adapt interpersonal psychotherapy (IPT) for use with depressed adolescents (IPT-A), this article documented the first two of a three-phase study (still ongoing at the time of publication) that attempted to define therapeutic practices that had potential to affect individual patients and to refine and test these practices, ultimately seeking to establish the efficacy of IPT-A. Phase I involved exploring modifications that would help to tailor IPT to adolescents, developing an IPT-A manual, and treating five depressed adolescents with IPT-A. The five cases were analyzed based on the frequency and number of sessions, length of treatment, and patient outlook posttreatment. While continuing to refine the treatment, Phase II utilized a 12-week clinical trial of 14 depressed adolescents receiving IPT-A. Participants were assessed via seven measures (a combination of parent- and self-reported) at baseline and at weeks 2, 4, 8, and 12. Results of this Phase II study demonstrated the potential effectiveness of IPT-A as evidenced by the adolescents' significant reduction in the symptoms of depression and increase in overall functioning.

Mufson, L., Weissman, M. M., Moreau, D., & Garfinkel, R. (1999). Efficacy of interpersonal psychotherapy for depressed adolescents. *Archives of General Psychiatry, 56,* 573–579.

Forty-eight adolescents with depression, aged 12 to 18 years, participated in this 12-week study comparing interpersonal psychotherapy for adolescents (IPT-A) with clinical monitoring. Randomly assigned to one of the two treatment groups, individuals in the IPT-A group attended 12 weekly 45-minute sessions and 4 weekly telephone contacts (over the first 4 weeks of the study), and individuals in the clinical monitoring group attended 3 monthly 30-minute sessions, with the option of one additional session each month. Data were collected on diagnoses, symptoms, global and social functioning, and problem-solving skills via multiple independent measures. Thirty-two of the participants completed the study (21 receiving IPT-A and 11 receiving clinical monitoring). With results showing marked reductions in symptoms of depression and improvements in social functioning in the adolescents receiving IPT-A (75%) as compared with those in the clinical monitoring group (46%), this study offered further support for the effectiveness of IPT-A for use with depressed adolescents.

Robbins, D. R., Alessi, N. E., & Colfer, M. V. (1989). Treatment of adolescents with major depression: Implications of the DST and the melancholic clinical subtype. *Journal of Affective Disorders, 17,* 99–104.

This article recounts an uncontrolled clinical experience of the treatment of 38 adolescents (aged 13 to 17 years) hospitalized with major depression. All participants received intensive psychosocial treatment for a minimum of 6 weeks, involving individual psychotherapy (three weekly sessions), group therapy (twice weekly), and family therapy (once weekly). Those participants determined to have persisting symptoms of depression (i.e., did not respond to therapy alone) then received tricyclic antidepressants (TCA) while continuing with the therapy program. Twenty-three participants (47%) responded to psychosocial treatment alone; of the remaining 15 participants, 92% responded to a combination of psychosocial treatment and TCA. In terms of the dexamethasone suppression test (DST) and melancholic subtype in relation to response to therapy alone, 31 participants were DST suppressors (18 responded) while 7 were DST nonsuppressors (zero responded) and 19 participants were melancholic (5 responded) while 19 were nonmelancholic (13 responded).

Rosselló, J., & Bernal, G. (1999). The efficacy of cognitive–behavioral and interpersonal treatments for depression in Puerto Rican adolescents. *Journal of Consulting and Clinical Psychology, 67*(5), 734–745.

Seventy-one Puerto Rican adolescents with depression, aged 13 to 17 years, participated in this study comparing the effects of cognitive–behavioral treatment (CBT) and interpersonal treatment (IPT) with a wait-list control group. The students were randomly assigned to one of the conditions, with individuals in the CBT and IPT groups receiving 12 weekly, 1-hour, individual therapy sessions and the wait-list group receiving no treatment. Participants in the CBT group learned to identify the thoughts, feelings, and actions that influence feelings of depression in order to diminish depressive symptoms and increase their sense of control. Participants in the IPT group evaluated current problems in their interpersonal relationships and addressed problematic areas as a means to reduce symptoms of depression. Data were collected via five measures, with results demonstrating that both CBT and IPT groups showed striking reductions in depressive symptoms as compared with the wait-list group and that 59% of the CBT group and 82% of the IPT group showed clinically significant improvement (moving from nonfunctional to functional) from pretreatment to posttreatment. The outcomes suggest that both CBT and IPT can be effective for treating depression in adolescents.

Considerations

For Culture, Religious, and Language Differences

Some children may have different coping skills and belief sets that accompany religious or cultural values. These beliefs should be respected while teaching skills to create more adaptive behaviors. For example, a child who is experiencing depression due to the death of a parent may be hearing from other adults that the parent is in heaven, which is a better place, and that there should be no sadness. But the child's feelings may differ from these beliefs, resulting in cognitive distortions. This disconnect (adults say, "You should be happy that your mother is in heaven," while the child feels sadness that his or her mother is gone) may be contributing to the depression, and both issues may need to be addressed.

For Age and Developmental Level

Due to the relatively high cognitive demands of this approach, IPT strategies are generally used with adolescent-aged children. Younger children may have difficulty articulating feelings or attributing them to an event. Depression symptoms can occur during times of developmental change, such as the transition into adolescence. Malaise and other depression symptoms may be the result of uncertainty about the future of adolescence or adulthood.

Summary

This chapter presented a review of the characteristics and conditions of depressive symptomatology, along with a summary of the two intervention methods that have been shown to be effective in remediation of child and adolescent depression: cognitive–behavioral therapy (CBT) and interpersonal psychotherapy for adolescents (IPT-A). The discussion of interventions included the CBT techniques of psychoeducation, problem-solving skills training, cognitive restructuring, pleasant-activity planning, relaxation training, self-management skills training, and family involvement, as well as a discussion of the use of IPT-A for depression. While each intervention method presented differs in its application of cognitive–behavioral theory, both are shaped by the fundamental goals of treatment: prevention and remediation of emotional and behavioral problems related to depression. The information presented in this chapter forms the basis of the supplemental classroom- and home-based materials that correspond to this book.

References

Ackerson, J., Scogin, F., McKendree-Smith, N., & Lyman, R. D. (1998). Cognitive bibliotherapy for mild and moderate adolescent depressive symptomatology. *Journal of Consulting and Clinical Psychology, 66*(4), 685–690.

American Psychiatric Association. (2000). *Diagnostic and statistical manual of mental disorders* (4th ed., text revision). Washington, DC: Author.

Asarnow, J. R., Scott, C. V., & Mintz, J. (2002). A combined cognitive–behavioral family education intervention for depression in children: A treatment development study. *Cognitive Therapy and Research, 26*(2), 221–229.

Beardslee, W. R., Versage, E. M., Wright, E. J., Salt, P., Rothberg, P. C., Drezner, K., et al. (1997). Examination of preventive interventions for families with depression: Evidence of change. *Development and Psychopathology, 9,* 109–130.

Beck, A. T. (1976). *Cognitive therapy and the emotional disorders.* New York: International Universities Press.

Beck, A. T., Rush, A. J., Shaw, B. F., & Emery G. (1979). *Cognitive therapy of depression.* New York: Guilford Press.

Braswell, L., & Kendall, P. C. (2001). Cognitive-behavioral therapy with youth. In K. S. Dobson (Ed.), *Handbook of cognitive-behavioral therapies* (2nd ed., pp. 167–213). New York: Guilford Press.

Brent, D. A., Holder, D., Kolko, D., Birhamer, B., Baugher, M., Roth, C., et al. (1997). A clinical psychotherapy trial for adolescent depression comparing cognitive, family, and supportive therapy. *Archives of General Psychiatry, 54*(9), 877–885.

Burns, D. D. (1980). *Feeling good: The new mood therapy.* New York: William Morrow and Co.

Butler, L., Miezitis, S., Friedman, R., & Cole, E. (1980). The effect of two school-based intervention programs on depressive symptoms in preadolescents. *American Educational Research Journal, 17*(1), 111–119.

Clarke, G., DeBar, L., Lynch, F., Powell, J., Gale, J., O'Connor, E., et al. (2005). A randomized effectiveness trial of brief cognitive-behavioral therapy for depressed adolescents receiving antidepressant medication. *Journal of the American Academy of Child and Adolescent Psychiatry, 44*(9), 888–898.

Clarke, G. N., Hawkins, W., Murphy, M., Sheeber, L. B., Lewinsohn, P. M., & Seeley, J. R. (1995). Targeted prevention of unipolar depressive disorder in an at-risk sample of high school adolescents: A randomized trial of a group cognitive intervention. *Journal of the American Academy of Child and Adolescent Psychiatry, 34*(3), 312–321.

Clarke, G. N., Lewinsohn, P., & Hops, H. (1990). *Leader's manual for adolescents groups: Adolescent Coping with Depression Course.* Portland, OR: The Center for Health Research.

Clarke, G. N., Rohde, P., Lewinsohn, P. M., Hops, H., & Seeley, J. R. (1999). Cognitive-behavioral treatment of adolescent depression: Efficacy of acute group treatment and booster sessions. *Journal of the American Academy of Child and Adolescent Psychiatry, 38*(3), 272–279.

Corey, G. (1991). *Theory and practice of counseling and psychotherapy* (4th ed.). Pacific Grove, CA: Brooks/Cole Publishing.

Friedberg, R. D., McClure, J. M., Wilding, L., Goldman, M. L., Long, M. P., Anderson, L., et al. (2003). A cognitive-behavioral skills training group for children experiencing anxious and depressive symptoms: A clinical report with accompanying descriptive data. *Journal of Contemporary Psychotherapy, 33*(3), 157–175.

Hops, H., & Lewinsohn, P. M. (1995). A course for the treatment of depression among adolescents. In K. D. Craig, & K. S. Dobson (Eds.), *Anxiety and depression in adults and children* (pp. 230–245). Thousand Oaks, CA: Sage Publications.

Jaycox, L. H., Reivich, K. J., Gillham, J., & Seligman, M. E. P. (1994). Prevention of depressive symptoms in school children. *Behaviour Research and Therapy, 32*(8), 801–816.

Kahn, J. S., Kehle, T. J., Jenson, W. R., & Clark, E. (1990). Comparison of cognitive-behavioral, relaxation, and self-modeling interventions for depression among middle-school students. *School Psychology Review, 19*(2), 196–211.

Kaslow, N. J., & Racusin, G. R. (1994). Family therapy for depression in young people. In W. M. Reynolds & H. F. Johnston (Eds.), *Handbook of depression in children and adolescents* (pp. 345–364). New York: Plenum Press.

Kendall, P. C., Chansky, T. E., Kane, M. T., Kim, R. S., Kortlander, E., Ronan, K. R., et al. (1992). *Anxiety disorders in youth: Cognitive-behavioral interventions.* Needham Heights, MA: Allyn & Bacon.

Klerman, G. L., Weissman, M. M., Rounsaville, B. J., & Chevron, E. S. (1984). *Interpersonal psychotherapy of depression.* New York: Basic Books.

Kolko, D. J., Brent, D. A., Baugher, M., Bridge, J., & Birmaher, B. (2000). Cognitive and family therapies for adolescent depression: Treatment specificity, mediation, and moderation. *Journal of Consulting and Clinical Psychology, 68*(4), 603–614.

Lewinsohn, P. M., & Clarke, G. N. (1999). Psychosocial treatments for adolescent depression. *Clinical Psychology Review, 19*(3), 329–342.

Lewinsohn, P. M., Clarke, G. N., Hops, H., & Andrews, J. (1990). Cognitive-behavioral treatment for depressed adolescents. *Behavior Therapy, 21*(4), 385–401.

Lewinsohn, P. M., Clarke, G. N., Rohde, P., Hops, H., & Seeley, J. R. (1996). A course in coping: A cognitive–behavioral approach to the treatment of adolescent depression. In E. D. Hibbs & P. S. Jensen (Eds.), *Psychosocial treatments for child and adolescent disorders: Empirically based strategies for clinical practice* (pp. 109–136). Washington, DC: American Psychological Association.

Lewinsohn, P. M., Hoberman, H. M., Teri, L., & Hautzinger, M. (1985). An integrated theory of depression. In S. Reiss & R. R. Bootzin (Eds.), *Theoretical issues in behavior therapy* (pp. 331–359). New York: Academic Press.

Meichenbaum, D. (1977). *Cognitive-behavior modification: An integrative approach.* New York: Plenum Press.

Mufson, L., Dorta, K. P., Moreau, D., & Weissman, M. M. (2004). *Interpersonal psychotherapy for depressed adolescents* (2nd ed.). New York: Guilford Press.

Mufson, L., Dorta, K. P., Wickramaratne, P., Nomura, Y., Olfson, M., & Weissman, M. M. (2004). A randomized effectiveness trial of interpersonal psychotherapy for depressed adolescents. *Archives of General Psychiatry, 61,* 577–584.

Mufson, L., Moreau, D., Weissman, M. M., Wickramaratne, P., Martin, J., & Samoilov, A. (1994). Modification of interpersonal psychotherapy with depressed adolescents (IPT-A): Phase I and II studies. *Journal of the American Academy of Child and Adolescent Psychiatry, 33*(5), 695–705.

Mufson, L., & Sills, R. (2006). Interpersonal psychotherapy for depressed adolescents (IPT-A): An overview. *Nordic Journal of Psychiatry, 60*(6), 431–437.

Mufson, L., Weissman, M. M., Moreau, D., & Garfinkel, R. (1999). Efficacy of interpersonal psychotherapy for depressed adolescents. *Archives of General Psychiatry, 56,* 573–579.

Nicolson, D., & Ayers, H. (2004). *Adolescent problems: A practical guide for parents, teachers, and counsellors* (2nd ed.). London: David Fulton Publishers.

Ollendick, T. H., & Cerny, J. A. (1981). *Clinical behavior therapy with children.* New York: Plenum Press.

Reynolds, C. R., & Kamphaus, R. W. (2004). *Behavior Assessment System for Children* (2nd ed.). Circle Pines, MN: AGS Publishing.

Reynolds, W. M., & Coats, K. I. (1986). A comparison of cognitive–behavioral therapy and relaxation training for the treatment of depression in adolescents. *Journal of Consulting and Clinical Psychology, 54*(5), 653–660.

Robbins, D. R., Alessi, N. E., & Colfer, M. V. (1989). Treatment of adolescents with major depression: Implications of the DST and the melancholic clinical subtype. *Journal of Affective Disorders, 17,* 99–104.

Roberts, M. C., Lazicki-Puddy, T. A., Puddy, R. W., & Johnson, R. J. (2003). The outcomes of psychotherapy with adolescents: A practitioner-friendly research review. *Journal of Clinical Psychology, 59*(11), 1177–1191.

Rosselló, J., & Bernal, G. (1999). The efficacy of cognitive–behavioral and interpersonal treatments for depression in Puerto Rican adolescents. *Journal of Consulting and Clinical Psychology, 67*(5), 734–745.

Stark, K. D., Humphrey, L. L., Crook, K., & Lewis, K. (1990). Perceived family environments of depressed and anxious children: Child's and maternal figure's perspectives. *Journal of Abnormal Child Psychology, 18*(5), 527–547.

Stark, K. D., & Kendall, P. C. (1996). *Treating depressed children: Therapist manual for "taking action."* Ardmore, PA: Workbook Publishing.

Stark, K. D., Reynolds, W. M., & Kaslow, N. J. (1987). A comparison of the relative efficacy of self-control therapy and a behavioral problem-solving therapy for depression in children. *Journal of Abnormal Child Psychology, 15*(1), 91–113.

Treatment for Adolescents With Depression Study (TADS) Team. (2004). Fluoxetine, cognitive–behavioral therapy, and their combination for adolescents with depression: Treatment for Adolescents With Depression Study (TADS) randomized controlled trial. *Journal of the American Medical Association, 292*(7), 807–820.

Weersing, V. R., & Brent, D. A. (2006). Cognitive behavioral therapy for depression in youth. *Child and Adolescent Psychiatric Clinics of North America, 15*(4), 939–957.

Weissman, M. M., Markowitz, J. C., & Klerman, G. L. (2000). *Comprehensive guide to interpersonal psychotherapy.* New York: Basic Books.

Weisz, J. R., Thurber, C. A., Sweeney, L., Proffitt, V. D., & LeGagnoux, G. L. (1997). Brief treatment of mild-to-moderate child depression using primary and secondary control enhancement training. *Journal of Consulting and Clinical Psychology, 65*(4), 703–707.

Wood, A., Harrington, R., & Moore, A. (1996). Controlled trial of a brief cognitive-behavioural intervention in adolescent patients with depressive disorders. *Journal of Child Psychology and Psychiatry, 37*(6), 737–746.

Chapter 9

Interventions for Somatization

This chapter, which focuses on interventions for children and adolescents identified as having problems with somatization (also called "somatoform disorder"), has three major sections. First, the characteristics and conditions of somatization are briefly presented, together with sample items from the BASC–2 Somatization scale. Second, the theoretical framework for approaching behaviors associated with somatization is described. Third, interventions that have evidence or show promise for reducing somatization behaviors in school settings are described. Each presentation provides an overview of the intervention method and is divided into three subsections: Implementation, Evidence for Use, and Considerations.

Characteristics and Conditions of Somatization

Somatization is identified by medically unexplained physical symptoms or by complaints of physical symptoms and pain with no physiological basis (American Psychiatric Association [APA], 2000; Essau, 2006; Kellner, 1991; Lipowski, 1988). Somatoform disorders are characterized by a pattern of somatic complaints involving multiple body parts and continuing over a period of several years. The overall prevalence of somatization has been estimated to be anywhere from 0.2% to 2% among women and less than 0.2% in men (APA, 2000). There have been few studies that have examined the prevalence rates of somatization in children. In one study, of the 10% to 15% of children who were found to complain of recurrent abdominal pain or other somatic symptoms, only 10% were shown to have an underlying medical condition (Apley, 1975). When somatization occurs in youth, professionals often consider these types of complaints as an attempt by the child or adolescent to communicate emotional or social difficulties (Taylor & Garralda, 2003). Somatization has been found to co-occur with anxiety and mood disorders (Reynolds & Kamphaus, 2004).

The BASC–2 Somatization scale is designed to identify "the tendency to be overly sensitive and complain about relatively minor physical problems or ailments and to over report the occurrence of various physical complaints" (Reynolds & Kamphaus, 2004, p. 63).

Children's verbal complaints are the primary behaviors identified as problematic; such complaints typically are not associated with an actual physical origin (APA, 2000; Reynolds & Kamphaus, 2004). Items on the BASC–2 Somatization scale include "Complains of pain," "Has stomach problems," "Has a headache," "Visits the school nurse," and "Says, 'I think I'm sick.'"

Specific somatoform disorder diagnoses include undifferentiated somatoform disorder, conversion disorder, pain disorder, hypochondriasis, body dysmorphic disorder, and somatoform disorder not otherwise specified (APA, 2000). It is important to note that these disorders are not synonymous with factitious disorders or malingering. While the latter two disorders are both associated with fabricated or intentionally caused physical symptoms (APA, 2000; Campo & Fritz, 2001; Oyama, Paltoo, & Greengold, 2007), somatization behaviors do not reflect a conscious effort to invent symptoms.

Some conditions may mirror somatization but have different underlying causes. Bullying, abuse, neglect, or exposure to drugs may result in somatic complaints among children, but the key to resolving the complaints in such cases lies not in treating the child for somatization, but rather in changing some aspect of the child's interpersonal relationships or environment. For example, Tanya, a seventh grader, complains regularly of headaches, leg cramps, and other physical symptoms, which her teachers perceive as an attempt to avoid the locker room. When the teachers begin watching more closely, they discover that Tanya is being harassed in the locker room. As soon as the root problem (harassment) is eliminated, Tanya's physical complaints go away.

For this reason, it is important to assess fully the child's situation to determine that there are no other medical or nonmedical causes for the physical complaints. The child's case history should also be examined to determine if the complaints have been long-standing or are recent. Children who have been abused are more likely to express somatic complaints and, if a recent, acute onset of these complaints is noted, an interview about this possibility is reasonable. Somatic complaints can also accompany the onset of a more generalized anxiety disorder, and additional assessment with instruments such as the Revised Children's Manifest Anxiety Scale: Second Edition (RCMAS-2; Reynolds & Richmond, 2008) may assist in clarifying the diagnostic issue. School personnel should consider that a sudden increase in physical complaints from multiple children could indicate there is a specific individual (e.g., a new student, a new staff member) contributing to these complaints. Additional support on the playground or in the lunchroom where a larger student population is less supervised may also prove helpful.

Theoretical Framework for Approaching Somatization

In this chapter, the theoretical framework for approaching somatization with youth is a wellness model—a multidisciplinary rehabilitative approach with both a behavioral and cognitive–behavioral conceptualization. The term "multidisciplinary" is included to stress the necessity for school personnel to work closely in a collaborative effort with medical providers (Haugaard & Hazan, 2004). The rehabilitative framework encompasses both behavioral and cognitive–behavioral approaches, and indicates that physical symptoms and wellness behavior should be framed as a challenge for the child (i.e., a challenge to be managed internally by the child with outside support) as opposed to an illness that must be controlled via external measures (Campo & Fritz, 2001).

Interventions

Few experimental studies of interventions for childhood and adolescent somatization have been completed (Campo & Fritsch, 1994; Campo & Fritz, 2001; Campo & Negrini, 2000; Eminson, 2007); thus, only two categories of interventions appear in this chapter:

I. Behavioral Interventions

II. Multimodal Cognitive–Behavioral Therapy

Behavioral interventions for somatization include the use of reinforcement (both positive and negative) and punishment, such as a timeout from preferred activities. Each of these intervention methods is discussed in detail below.

I. Behavioral Interventions

Reinforcement applied to somatization is the systematic presentation or removal of stimuli to increase coping ability and healthy behavior (Campo & Fritz, 2001). Positive reinforcement includes the immediate, contingent presentation of a reward for healthy behaviors that have been identified jointly by the child and adult. Negative reinforcement is the removal of an aversive stimulus contingent on the child engaging in an appropriate healthy behavior or coping behavior that has been jointly identified. In the literature, punishment for somatic symptoms is frequently reported as a form of timeout (removal) from preferred activities. When used appropriately, this method of punishment leads the child to see removal from enjoyable activities as a natural, automatic consequence of any sick episode. If timeouts do not result in a decrease in somatic complaints, it is possible the child desires to escape from the given activity, in which case the timeout is actually functioning as a reinforcer rather than as a punishment.

For example, Holly, a 16-year-old, complains daily of a stomachache, which often causes her to be absent from school. When she does attend school, she complains to the school nurse and requests to be allowed to return home. When Holly returns home, she remains in bed. Typically, her mother entertains her with books and games, or they watch television. Holly's mother has repeatedly taken her to several doctors, none of whom found any physiological reason for her stomachaches. Holly's mother, doctor, psychiatrist, and psychologist identify three factors that are serving to reinforce Holly's behavior: 1) being home, 2) attention from her mother, and 3) attention from doctors. Therefore, they identify reading time with Mom as an appropriate reinforcer for Holly's staying at school without complaints of a stomachache. Holly's adherence to a no-complaints policy is to be communicated using a school–home note filled out by the school nurse; healthy behavior at school will result in Holly being able to exchange the school–home note for immediate reading time with Mom. In contrast, if Holly complains of a stomachache and goes home from school, she will be subject to a no-reading, no-TV, no-play-date condition for 24 hours or until the next time she receives a note from the nurse for healthy behavior.

Implementation

The goal of using behavioral interventions to address somatoform disorders is to reduce somatization behaviors that are interfering with functional activities and to increase healthy behavior, allowing the child to return to pre-illness functioning (e.g., attending school, demonstrating responsible behavior). The basic elements of behavioral interventions for somatization include the following:

1. Consulting with the child's physician to rule out real medical conditions

2. Identifying the specific somatization behavior(s) to change

3. Determining appropriate reinforcers and punishments

4. Identifying the timeline and conditions under which reinforcement and punishment will be applied

5. Determining who will apply reinforcement and punishment

6. Using and evaluating the plan

The procedural steps for implementing contingent reinforcement and timeout from preferred activities as an intervention for somatization are summarized in Figure 9.1. First, and most importantly, the school psychologist consults with the child's medical doctor (physician and/or psychiatrist) to ensure that no medical conditions exist that explain the physical complaints being made by the child. The school psychologist should discuss the use of contingent reinforcement and punishment with the family and the child's physician, and obtain their agreement that behavioral interventions are appropriate. Without the complete agreement of parents and doctors, this intervention should be reconsidered. The psychologist should consider the following questions: Is this the least intrusive intervention? Have other methods been tried unsuccessfully? Is the health of the child within normal limits?

If the child's parents and physician do agree with the use of behavioral interventions, the school psychologist, in conjunction with the child's parents or caregivers, then identifies the specific somatization behaviors to be changed and determines replacement behaviors that are functionally equivalent or that belong to the same response class. Any existing reinforcrs for the behavior (e.g., getting out of challenging classroom tasks by going to the nurse's office) should also be identified at this point. Next, the psychologist and parents together identify potential reinforcers and punishments that are appropriate and naturally occurring in the child's daily life. (Note that for the purpose of reinforcer selection, consulting with the child is appropriate, as it will eliminate time spent on trial and error.)

The parents, school psychologists, and any teachers or other school staff (e.g., nurses, classroom aides) who interact with the child regularly must all be fully informed and should agree to work cooperatively if contingent reinforcers and punishments are to be effective. The child's specific somatization behaviors should be listed in writing, with healthy coping strategies also listed. The team should be clear and in agreement that certain behaviors (e.g., using coping strategies, having a complaint-free day) will be reinforced and that other behaviors (e.g., requests to go to the nurse) will be punished. The school psychologist should also monitor and communicate with the child's parents or caregivers when home–school contingencies are in operation to ensure that timeout from preferred activities occurs if the child misses school. For example, if the child stays home sick, he or she should not be allowed to play computer games, watch television, or go outside to play.

Prior to implementing the intervention plan, the school psychologist or another team member conducts a psychoeducational session with the child's parents. During this session, somatization is explained to the parents, emphasizing that the symptoms are real, not faked by the child. The plan of action is described to the parents, including the goals of behavioral treatment and the specific techniques to be implemented. The psychologist reassures the parents that contact with the primary care physician will be maintained and then addresses any concerns the parents may have regarding the interventions. Next, the school psychologist meets with the child to explain the interventions that will be used. Through this process, the child is encouraged to return to normal functioning, while the parents are taught to support the child's efforts. The school psychologist continues to coordinate services and training with the parents, as needed, throughout treatment.

After providing thorough explanations of the intervention to the parents and the child, the schedule for contingent reinforcement and timeout from preferred activities is implemented. The multidisciplinary team monitors the child's progress until the stated goals and objectives have been achieved. Finally, the school psychologist coordinates a plan for fading and eventually withdrawing the intervention as healthy, prosocial behaviors increase and somatization behaviors decrease.

Figure 9.1 **Procedural steps for implementing behavioral interventions (reinforcement and punishment)**

1. Consult with the child's physician (and psychiatrist, if applicable) to ensure that no medical cause exists for the child's complaints. Continue communication throughout the intervention.

2. Work with the multidisciplinary team to establish agreement between all key stakeholders (e.g., physician, parents, teachers, school administrators, counselor, school psychologist) that the use of contingent reinforcers and timeout from preferred activities is the intervention of choice.

3. Complete a functional behavioral assessment to clearly define and document the specific somatization behavior(s) to be changed. In addition, identify any activities or personal interactions (e.g., being able to watch movies while home sick, getting one-on-one attention from a parent) that are reinforcing the somatization behavior.

4. Work with the child and parent(s) to identify appropriate reinforcers and punishments for use in the intervention.

5. In collaboration with other members of the multidisciplinary team (e.g., physician, psychologist, counselor, teacher, parent), design an intervention plan to address the underlying cause of the somatization behavior, and communicate the plan to all stakeholders. The intervention should include these components:

   a. Psychoeducation

   b. Contingent reinforcement for engagement in alternative (i.e., healthy) behavior and reductions in illness-related behavior

   c. Contingent punishment (e.g., timeout from preferred activities) for engaging in illness-related behavior

   d. Parent training

6. Working with the multidisciplinary team, implement the intervention components. Keep in mind the following:

   a. In psychoeducational sessions, clearly explain somatization to the child and family, clarify the goals of behavioral treatment, and discuss the intervention methods to be implemented.

   b. Implement family training (or refer the family to an outside agency for training) on how to ignore somatic symptoms and reinforce healthy behaviors.

   c. Along with other team members, encourage the child to return to pre-illness functioning (e.g., attending school, completing homework and chores).

Continued on next page

d. Assist teacher(s) and parent(s) in implementing the program of contingent reinforcement and punishment with the child.

e. Maintain communication with the family throughout treatment, including monitoring or surveying home practices to ensure compliance with the behavioral intervention.

7. Coordinate a plan for fading (gradual withdrawal) positive reinforcement and timeout from preferred activities as the child attains specified goals for reducing somatization behavior and increasing healthy behavior.

Evidence for Use

Evidence for the use of behavioral interventions (reinforcement and punishment) with somatization is emergent. Most studies to date that have investigated the effectiveness of such interventions have been case studies; a review of the literature found no randomized control trials of behavioral interventions with somatization. However, behavioral interventions are repeatedly referenced in the literature as evidence-based practice or practical approaches for somatization (Campo & Fritz, 2001; Fritz, Fritsch, & Hagino, 1997); therefore, they are included in this chapter. Specifically, contingent reinforcement and timeout from preferred activities have been shown in case studies to eliminate a lack of functioning or limited physical mobility with no known physical cause, to decrease symptoms of somatization, and to decrease complaints of pain (Campo & Negrini, 2000; Gooch, Wolcott, & Speed, 1997; Maisami & Freeman, 1987; Miller & Kratochwill, 1979; Mizes, 1985; Sank & Biglan, 1974; Warzak, Kewman, Stefans, & Johnson, 1987).

The following studies summarize some of the key research findings associated with the use of contingent reinforcement and punishment as an intervention for children and adolescents with somatization.

> Campo, J. V., & Negrini, B. J. (2000). Case study: Negative reinforcement and behavioral management of conversion disorder. *Journal of the American Academy of Child and Adolescent Psychiatry, 39*(6), 787–790.

A 12-year-old boy with a 3-month history of chronic pain and immobility of his right arm was the subject of this case study that investigated the efficacy of treating conversion disorder with negative reinforcement techniques. After consultations with pediatrics, orthopedics, rheumatology, and neurology suggested no physical cause of the boy's symptoms, he was referred for a psychiatric evaluation. The evaluation resulted in a preliminary diagnosis of conversion disorder based on the persistence of symptoms, inconsistencies in the boy's apparent ability to use his right arm during a physical exam, the presence of family stressors, and his learning difficulties at school. Conversion disorder and behavioral intervention were discussed with mother and child, and, with the support of the parents, complete bed rest was prescribed until the symptoms resolved. Within 24 hours of the start of bed rest, the boy regained full use of his arm and experienced no residual pain; he returned to his normal activities and remains symptom-free. Results of this case study indicate that negative reinforcement, when supported by the parents, can be an effective treatment option for children diagnosed with conversion disorder, suggesting the need for further controlled trials of such interventions.

Gooch, J. L., Wolcott, R., & Speed, J. (1997). Behavioral management of conversion disorder in children. *Archives of Physical Medicine and Rehabilitation, 78,* 264–268.

Three case studies of 8 patients involved in the study are presented in detail in this article discussing the efficacy of using traditional behavior management strategies when treating children with conversion disorder. The participants, aged 9 to 12 years, were all inpatients in a rehabilitation unit for various symptoms, including abdominal pain, nausea, rash, headaches, joint pain, leg pain, and inability to walk. In all cases, it was determined that inadvertent reinforcement of illness behavior was occurring. In case one, a 10-year-old girl and her family received counseling to address communication strategies and conflict issues; in case two, a 9-year-old boy was taught distraction, pain control switches, and imagery techniques to cope with pain; and in case three, a 12-year-old girl received daily therapy sessions to learn coping strategies for stress and self-hypnosis for pain management and relaxation. Reward systems were established for each patient for good attainment; some patients (e.g., case three) had a level system instituted, with increasing privileges for goal achievement. In addition, all patients and their families received psychological assessment and instruction in pain and stress management strategies. While the authors acknowledge that the results are preliminary, the case studies presented offer tentative support for the use of behavior management techniques for treating children with conversion disorder and suggest the need for further study of the short- and long-term efficacy of the treatment.

Maisami, M., & Freeman, J. M. (1987). Conversion reactions in children as body language: A combined child psychiatry/neurology team approach to the management of functional neurologic disorders in children. *Pediatrics, 80,* 46–52.

This article documents four illustrative case studies from a 7-year program that utilized a neurologic and psychiatric team approach to treating 41 children with conversion reactions. The participants all received parallel evaluations from a neurologist and a psychiatrist while inpatients at a hospital for their respective symptoms. After discussing the results of the evaluations, the two professionals determined individual treatment plans that they presented to the children and their parents. These treatment plans involved first explaining that the children's physical symptoms were real and worthy of serious consideration, and second explaining that no medical causes had been uncovered and it was suspected that the children's symptoms were caused by stresses and anxieties (i.e., the children's bodies used physical symptoms to express the inability to cope with stress and anxiety). Treatment plans were individualized for each participant, always incorporating ongoing psychiatric care along with objectives relating to the reduction and elimination of symptoms (e.g., increasing mobility or decreasing medication use). Attainment of goals was reinforced through encouragement from medical staff and other contingent rewards (e.g., being allowed to go home once a certain goal was reached). In all, 31 patients were classified as having positive results (full or partial recovery), 8 were classified as uncertain (lost to follow-up or left program), and 2 had organic diseases. Overall, results supported the use of combined psychiatry/neurology treatment for children with conversion reactions to maximize the gains of health over the sick role that generates attention and sympathy.

Miller, A. J., & Kratochwill, T. R. (1979). Reduction of frequent stomachache complaints by time out. *Behavior Therapy, 10,* 211–218.

This study assessed the effectiveness of timeouts from social attention and focused on a 10-year-old girl experiencing chronic stomach pain with no organic cause for more than a year. The girl's mother typically responded to the child's complaints by offering medication (Donnatal®) and having her rest until she felt better. The mother offered constant attention and comfort measures throughout the child's rest periods. During the timeout intervention, researchers maintained the girl's Donnatal dosage but required her to rest in bed for the remainder of the day without toys, television, snacks, or social attention. Results showed the number of stomachache episodes, occurring approximately 1.5 times per day before treatment, decreased from nine episodes during the first 30 days of treatment to three during the subsequent 56 days of treatment. In addition, no reoccurrences were reported at 4, 6, and 8 weeks or at 1-year follow-up, indicating timeouts from preferred activities may be an effective intervention strategy for children demonstrating somatic behaviors.

Mizes, J. S. (1985). The use of contingent reinforcement in the treatment of a conversion disorder: A multiple baseline study. *Journal of Behavior Therapy and Experimental Psychiatry, 16*(4), 341–345.

This study examined the effects of a contingent reinforcement intervention on the conversion symptoms of a 13-year-old girl experiencing chronic lower-back pain and an inability to bend at the waist for 5 months. Target behaviors were identified (stomach contractions and leg lifts), as were discharge behaviors (e.g., bending of the back, walking unassisted down a hallway). The first phase of treatment, Contingent Reinforcement I, tied the stomach exercises to predetermined strength and frequency goals; if the child met the goals, she earned television and telephone privileges for the day. During the second phase, Contingent Reinforcement II, the stomach contraction goals initially remained the same but the reinforcement was modified to parent visits. Then, leg lift exercises were added to the goal requirements. Finally, a series of discharge behaviors were identified as goals, and discharge from the hospital became the reinforcement. Results showed that Contingent Reinforcement I had little effect on the girl's symptoms, whereas each component of Contingent Reinforcement II, which included more powerful rewards, had substantial effects that culminated in her discharge from the hospital. However, the girl's behavior regressed somewhat at 5-month and 1-year follow-up, as evidenced by an inpatient stay at a pain clinic 8 months after the study. In sum, this study provides tentative support for the effectiveness of contingent reinforcement in the short term, but indicates that further research is needed concerning how best to maintain treatment gains.

Sank, L. I., & Biglan, A. (1974). Operant treatment of a case of recurrent abdominal pain in a 10-year-old boy. *Behavior Therapy, 5,* 677–681.

This case study focused on one 10-year-old boy who complained of daily abdominal pain, sometimes severe, which was thought to be the result of somatization. Researchers tracked occurrences of the boy's major pain attacks and daily pain levels on a scale of 0–10. The boy received positive reinforcement in the form of points (that he could apply toward rewards) for days without attacks where his pain levels were below his baseline average. He also received points for days he attended school. Researchers gradually raised standards to require lower levels of pain and longer periods of time in school for a reward. Immediately upon beginning treatment, the child's average pain levels went below the target point, and he had very few occurrences of major pain attacks (none in the last 15 weeks). The boy, who had missed about half of the school days in the first quarter, attended 86% of the time after treatment began.

Warzak, W. J., Kewman, D. G., Stefans, V., & Johnson, E. (1987). Behavioral rehabilitation of functional alexia. *Journal of Behavior Therapy and Experimental Psychiatry, 18*(2), 171–177.

A 10-year-old boy suffering from alexia with no apparent organic cause was the focus of this investigation of behavioral treatment approaches for children with functional visual problems. After determining that positive reinforcement had little impact on the boy's symptoms and motivation, a negative reinforcement approach utilizing escape/avoidance procedures was instituted. The treatment involved informing the child that his visual problems were due to eye weakness resulting from a previous illness and that eye exercises would help to improve his vision. The boy participated in daily treatment sessions, ranging in length from 45 minutes to 2 hours, that utilized reading and focusing exercises. Results demonstrated that the patient's performance improved from correctly reading 0% of the targeted words during baseline to 100% after 3 weeks of treatment. Furthermore, 100% accuracy was maintained at 2-week, 4-week, and 3-month follow-up, and no relapse, no visual difficulties, and above-average academic performance at school were reported at 1-year follow-up. The swift and successful outcome of the intervention supports its potential effectiveness for use with functional visual disorders.

Considerations

In order for behavioral interventions for somatization to be successful, it is crucial for practitioners to recognize that effective reinforcers and punishments differ from person to person. Some individuals may be strongly reinforced by chocolate ice cream while others could easily forgo it. Likewise, attention may function as a reinforcer for some children but not for others. Indeed, some adolescents may find teacher attention punishing rather than reinforcing, just as some children may find increased social time to be aversive—something to be avoided at all costs. It is important to examine the function of the somatization; otherwise, inadvertent reinforcement of the maladaptive behavior may occur. Discussing the likes and dislikes of the child and conducting a reinforcement survey may be useful in identifying appropriate reinforcers.

For Communicating With Parents

The terms "reinforcement" and "punishment" are very loaded in the lay population. Some parents and practitioners may have a misconception that reinforcement is a form of bribery or mind control, or that it discounts feelings. Likewise, the word "punishment" can elicit frightening images of corporal punishment (such as spanking) or other harsh disciplinary measures. Therefore, accurate definitions of reinforcement and punishment, as they relate to the goals of the intervention, should be presented: Reinforcement is something that results in an increase in the target behavior, while punishment results in a decrease in the behavior. Parents should also understand that reinforcement may be accomplished either through providing something pleasant (positive reinforcement) or through removing something unpleasant (negative reinforcement). Clarifying these terms helps with team communication when implementing interventions or measuring the integrity of an intervention.

Ongoing communication between school, family, and medical staff is critical to detect and effectively treat children's somatization. Nothing could be more damaging to the trust relationship between the child and the adults involved than if the child's accounts of somatization were ignored, minimized, or discounted as existing merely in the child's head. In addition, practitioners should keep in mind that young children may use physical descriptions (such as "a tummy ache") to talk about completely unrelated feelings or issues (such as fear) or to respond to a traumatic event. A young child may not be able to articulate an episode of sexual abuse but may describe "not feeling well" or "feeling funny." Open communication is important to maintain trust and to accommodate the development of appropriate interventions as symptoms occur.

For Culture, Gender, Age, and Developmental Level

When planning for somatization intervention, consider the age and developmental level of the child and the culture of the child's family. To what degree is the observed behavior to be expected or deemed within normal limits, based on the child's age, development, gender, and culture? Are there other disabling conditions, such as cognitive impairment, that could interfere with the child's ability to articulate physical complaints accurately enough to ensure a correct medical diagnosis? Some studies indicate that hormonal cycles in adolescents may mirror somatic complaints, although no specific physical cause can be identified. In addition, normal physical changes may account for some behavior and should not be completely discounted. Replacement or coping strategies, rather than elimination of the behavior, may be called for in such cases.

II. Multimodal Cognitive–Behavioral Therapy

Multimodal cognitive–behavioral therapy as an intervention for somatization is an approach that incorporates self-evaluation and one or more other methods of intervention based on the individual needs of the child. The approach emphasizes coping, which encourages children to continue functional activities with minimal complaints of illness (Schulman, 1988). Cognitive–behavioral components are selected based on individual assessment data as well as the age and development of the child.

For example, Ben, who is 6 years old, frequently reports minor daily injuries, such as scrapes, bumps, and bruises from the playground, calling them "broken" arms and legs. He then elects to sit out of the remainder of recess, requests bandages or wraps from the school nurse, and sometimes wants to call home to report his injuries. Denise, a junior high student, greets her teacher each morning with a complaint about how heavy her backpack is and how much her shoulders hurt, requesting time to lie down before starting to work. Denise also lets the teacher know that she might not be able to use a pencil, displaying her arm hanging limply at her side. Sometimes, Denise complains about the bumpy bus ride that "jars her spine," resulting in a need to stand for a while in the classroom. At other times, she expresses a belief that the air conditioner filter is dusty and reports having difficulty breathing. In both Ben's and Denise's cases, their somatization behaviors are enabling them to receive additional adult, one-on-one attention; sometimes, perceived special treatment; and possibly, an escape from a nonpreferred activity.

Both children are old enough to engage in conversations about their behavior, including how it differs from their peers' behavior in similar situations and how it may be interfering with their relationships with other children. They are also old enough to self-monitor and to learn cognitive coping strategies that can help them handle their perceived pain. To encourage Ben to remain active at recess, the playground monitor arranges for him to play with a different group of children who like to look for rocks and plants and who avoid the soccer field. If Ben gets through recess without complaining of injuries, he is rewarded with one-on-one time with his teacher after school to show her the rocks he collected. Denise acknowledges that although her back and arms do hurt, she might be able to wait until lunch time to discuss them with her teacher, and she begins to use a self-monitoring chart to keep a list of her physical complaints. Denise's teacher consistently reinforces Denise with praise and encouragement when she successfully limits her complaints to the number agreed upon (two per day). When Denise and Ben begin engaging in more prosocial behaviors, they naturally receive more social reinforcement, which in turn reduces their feelings of needing to engage in attention-getting behavior; consequently, their reports of injury decrease.

Implementation

The goal of multimodal cognitive–behavioral therapy as an intervention for somatization is to decrease exaggeration of physical symptomatology and increase functional behavior (Gutsch, 1988). The basic elements of cognitive–behavioral therapy with somatization include the following:

1. Assessment/information gathering
2. Problem conceptualization
3. Relationship/rapport building
4. Psychoeducation
5. Implementation of therapeutic strategies
6. Generalization of strategies and coping skills to other contexts

The procedural steps for the six phases of multimodal cognitive–behavioral therapy for somatization (incorporating the basic elements listed above) are described in Figure 9.2.

First, establish the team that will verify a nonmedical diagnosis based on information collected from the child's primary care physician and/or psychiatrist, as well as from the child's parents or caregivers, and that will perform a functional behavior analysis to identify the maintaining conditions for the behavior. Any interviews needed for the analysis can be used to build relationships that will facilitate effective intervention. During educational sessions for the child and family on the nature of somatic illness, emphasize the importance of education and school attendance, and stress that the child is required to follow school district attendance policies. Once behavioral guidelines are established, the team can then select the therapeutic strategies to be implemented and develop the schedule for implementation. Effective treatment of a selected behavior is a signal to begin generalization by practicing in new settings or, when there is more than one targeted behavior, to begin intervention for additional behaviors. For all treatment scenarios, ongoing support is generally required but is systematically faded over time.

Figure 9.2 Procedural steps for implementing multimodal cognitive-behavioral therapy

Phase 1: Assessment/Information Gathering

1. In collaboration with the multidisciplinary team, coordinate and consult with the child's primary care physician and/or psychiatrist, as well as with the child's parents or caregivers, to ensure that the child's symptoms have been thoroughly investigated for a possible medical diagnosis.

2. Conduct a functional behavioral assessment to clearly define and document the specific somatization behavior(s) to be changed. In addition, identify any factors that are currently reinforcing the somatization behavior.

3. Interview the child and parents, gathering a broad base of information about the child's background. During the interviews, explore the following issues:

   - child and family attitudes about the child's illness

   - possible anxieties and stressors in the child's life or prior experiences

   - any treatments that have been tried in the past and how effective they were

   - family complaints about the child's behavior

   - the extent to which the child has stopped normal activities

   - possible underlying emotional causes for the child's behavior

   - child and family fears

Phase 2: Problem Conceptualization

1. Assist the child in reconceptualizing the problem as less threatening, shifting attention from illness to treatment.

2. Reframe the problem for the parents and the child, from finding a cure to coping.

3. Assist the parents in evaluating and articulating the impact of the illness on the child and family, and in determining the steps necessary for the child to return to normal functioning.

4. Stress that the child's role in treatment is that of an active agent coping with a difficult but manageable problem, and that improvement is a personal success.

5. Stress that since doctors can't relieve symptomatology and the likely duration of the symptoms cannot be determined, the child must return to normal functioning.

6. Provide examples of others with severe illnesses who continue normal activities.

Continued on next page

7. While emphasizing the need for improvement and normalization, assure the child and parents that the child's physical complaints are not being ignored.

Phase 3: Relationship/Rapport Building

1. Acknowledge the child's suffering, address any parental concerns, and provide reassurance to the family regarding the treatment plan.

2. Ensure that the parents, child, and physician all agree to the coping and behavioral techniques that will be implemented.

3. Provide information to the parents and the child in an honest and direct manner in order to build a trusting relationship.

4. Reassure the parents and the child that symptoms can be reduced.

Phase 4: Psychoeducation

1. Help the parents understand the somatization diagnosis, stressing the fact that the child's physical symptoms are not based on any known illness. Reassure the parents and child that coordination with the primary physician will be ongoing.

2. Educate the child and parents about the connection between distress and symptoms.

3. Help the child and parents to determine sources of stress and anxiety and to identify alternative coping strategies.

4. Educate the family members about how their habitual reactions to the child's sick role may, in fact, be reinforcing the maladaptive behavior. Help them develop a plan to remove such reinforcements.

5. Emphasize the importance of education and school attendance, and stress that the child is required to follow school district attendance policies.

6. Educate the child about the benefits and importance of participating in routine activities.

Phase 5: Implementation of Therapeutic Strategies

1. In collaboration with the multidisciplinary team, choose the therapeutic strategies to be implemented. Strategies may include:

   a. Coping skills training, including self-instruction and self-monitoring training

   b. Teaching the child to identify certain situations as antecedents (i.e., triggers for somatic complaints)

Continued on next page

    c. Training in problem-solving techniques

    d. Removing reinforcement for illness-related behavior

    e. Differential reinforcement of competing (healthy) behavior

    f. Relaxation training

    g. Parent training to teach contingency management, how to prompt and reinforce coping behaviors, how to use negative reinforcement to encourage healthy behavior, and the importance of withdrawing attention to sickness-related behavior

2. Work with the child and parents to establish a set daily or weekly time for the child to explain his or her pain to the parents.

3. Encourage the child to return to his or her usual activities and responsibilities.

4. Help the child develop and implement a plan for reducing or effectively coping with stressors.

5. In collaboration with the multidisciplinary team and the child's parents, implement strategies to support the child's return to previous activities and to encourage the child to increase social activities and exercise.

6. Enlist all members of the multidisciplinary team in actively discouraging the child's illness-related behaviors and providing positive reinforcement for healthy behaviors.

7. Decrease possible gains from illness-related behavior by insisting on school attendance.

8. Ensure that the parents do not allow attention and pleasant activities at home during sickness-related episodes.

Phase 6: Generalization

1. When effects of treatment appear to be evident independent of intervention, begin programming for generalization.

2. Integrate scenarios where the newly learned behaviors are transferred to other problem behaviors or other problem settings.

3. Provide support for successful generalization but fade as quickly as possible. Any relapse is addressed with a reinstitution of the intervention.

Evidence for Use

Multimodal cognitive–behavioral therapy (CBT) has been found to decrease complaints of pain, decrease school absenteeism, and decrease health care utilization in children and adolescents with somatization, as well as to result in a return to pre-illness functioning (Finney, Lemanek, Cataldo, Katz, & Fuqua, 1989; Linton, 1986; Sanders et al., 1989; Sanders, Shepherd, Cleghorn, & Woolford, 1994; Schulman, 1988).

The following studies summarize some of the key research findings associated with the use of multimodal cognitive–behavioral therapy as an intervention for children and adolescents with somatization.

Finney, J. W., Lemanek, K. L., Cataldo, M. F., Katz, H. P., & Fuqua, R. W. (1989). Pediatric psychology in primary health care: Brief targeted therapy for recurrent abdominal pain. *Behavior Therapy, 20,* 283–291.

This study followed 16 children with recurrent abdominal pain (RAP) who had been referred for psychological consultations due to the absence of physical causes of their symptoms. The children all received targeted cognitive–behavioral therapy at a suburban pediatric clinic with onsite psychiatric services and learned one or more of the following techniques: how to monitor the frequency and intensity of their RAP, cope using relaxation, determine the situations in which pain occurs most often, reduce the need for parental attention to their RAP, increase fiber intake, and increase functional activities. Sixteen children with similar symptoms to those in the treatment group, but who had not been referred for psychological consultation, were randomly selected from the same clinic and served as the comparison group. After treatment, data were collected on outcome ratings of pain (as assessed by parents and therapists). Both prior to and after treatment, data were collected on absences from school (average days missed per month), visits to the school nurse (average visits per month), and visits to the clinic (average visits per month, general and RAP-specific). Results demonstrated that 81% of parents reported their children's symptoms as improved or resolved after treatment. Mean numbers of general clinic visits, RAP-specific clinic visits, and school absences all showed a statistically significant decrease from pretreatment to posttreatment (1.41 to 0.67, 0.41 to 0.06, and 1.69 to 0.68, respectively).

Linton, S. J. (1986). A case study of the behavioural treatment of chronic stomach pain in a child. *Behaviour Change, 3*(1), 70–73.

This case study tracked the pain of one 17-year-old girl who complained of chronic, unexplainable stomach pain, as well as headaches, insomnia, nausea, and problems at school. A multimodal CBT intervention with strategies chosen based on functional assessment data was implemented when it was determined that the chronic pain was caused by stress, anxiety, and cognitive misperceptions, and that the condition was being maintained through negative reinforcement (escape and avoidance of difficult circumstances at home and school). With the implementation of the multimodal intervention, downtime, depression, and nausea decreased while activity level, mood, and health were enhanced. Results were maintained at 9-month follow-up.

Sanders, M. R., Rebgetz, M., Morrison, M., Bor, W., Gordon, A., Dadds, M., et al. (1989). Cognitive–behavioral treatment of recurrent nonspecific abdominal pain in children: An analysis of generalization, maintenance, and side effects. *Journal of Consulting and Clinical Psychology, 57*(2), 294–300.

Operating on the assumption that the pain symptoms/behaviors associated with recurrent abdominal pain (RAP) with no organic basis can trigger responses (e.g., sympathy or attention) that reinforce the behavior, this study documented the effects of a cognitive–behavioral intervention on the symptoms of 16 children suffering from RAP. The participants were randomly assigned to either a treatment group or a wait-list group. Those in the treatment group attended eight counseling sessions during which they learned symptom-reduction techniques such as self-monitoring of pain, self-instruction, relaxation, and imagery. Data were collected at pretreatment and posttreatment and at 3-month follow-up via four observational measures (parent, teacher, trained observer, and self-report). Results showed that the percentage of children experiencing pain dropped from 100% at baseline to 25% at posttreatment and 12.5% at follow-up. While children in both groups demonstrated improvement in pain behaviors, the treatment group's behaviors improved more quickly, more dramatically, and across environments.

Sanders, M. R., Shepherd, R. W., Cleghorn, G., & Woolford, H. (1994). The treatment of recurrent abdominal pain in children: A controlled comparison of cognitive–behavioral family intervention and standard pediatric care. *Journal of Consulting and Clinical Psychology, 62*(2), 306–314.

Forty-four children, aged between 7 and 14 years, with recurrent abdominal pain (RAP) participated in this study of the impact of a cognitive–behavioral family intervention, as compared with standard pediatric care, on the pain level, incidence of relapse, and extent of activity interference caused by RAP. The children were randomly divided into two groups: cognitive–behavioral family intervention (CBFI) and standard pediatric care (SPC). The CBFI group participated in six 50-minute sessions devoted to self-management training for the children and contingency management training for their parents. Those in the SPC group had four to six visits with a gastroenterologist. Data were collected using several measures assessing pain intensity, pain behavior, maternal caregiving, self-coping skills, child adjustment, treatment expectations, relapse, and parent satisfaction. Results showed that while both treatment groups attained clinically significant improvements in daily functioning, the CBFI treatment proved to be superior based on several of the assessed outcomes, including a higher percentage of pain-free ratings by the children, lower incidence of relapse, and lower rates of pain interference with daily activities.

Schulman, J. L. (1988). Case study: Use of a coping approach in the management of children with conversion reactions. *Journal of the American Academy of Child and Adolescent Psychiatry, 27*(6), 785–788.

Treating children with conversion reactions is more challenging when physicians and parents cannot agree on a diagnosis or when an organically based problem is confounded by a secondary conversion reaction in the same part of the body. This article documents four case studies involving a coping approach designed to deal with these types of difficult cases. Components of the coping approach included continuing medical care due to the possibility of a hard-to-find organic cause, discussing a return to normal activities despite the pain, comparing the child's situation with the situations of others in much graver circumstances (e.g., a child coping with cancer pain who continues to attend school), explaining the possibility of the pain continuing indefinitely due to the inability of doctors to find a cause or relieve symptoms, and encouraging the child to cope with the pain without complaint due to the stress and burden that such behavior places on family and friends. All case study participants were able to regain functioning and return to normal activities relatively quickly after the coping intervention was instituted.

Considerations

For Teaching

School personnel should remain in contact with the child's primary care physician and proceed with school-based interventions only with the approval of both the physician and the child's parent(s). Physical illness, neglect, and abuse must be ruled out before intervention for somatization proceeds; therefore, collaboration and communication with the child's primary care physician and family are essential (Campo & Fritz, 2001). Intervention by a pediatrician made early and explained clearly and with certainty to the child and parent(s) makes parental acceptance of the diagnosis, as well as the child's recovery, easier and faster (Zeharia et al., 1999).

For Culture, Gender, and Home Environment

The child's culture and home environment should be evaluated both to determine how they may have contributed to the maladaptive behavior and to identify ways in which they may affect the child's response to the intervention. When prosocial repertoires are limited, avoidant behavior may be a function of limited skills or a culturally appropriate response to conflict. Gender and cultural differences may also account for familial belief systems about how illness (mental or physical) is viewed and handled. For example, some individuals and families may view occasionally calling in sick as an adaptive behavior (e.g., by considering the sick day a "mental health day" and dedicating the time off to activities that reduce stress and enhance coping), whereas in other families, the same behavior may be maladaptive (e.g., avoiding specific problems at work or at school).

Practitioners should recognize that parental acceptance of the concept of somatization and parents' beliefs about which types of treatments are acceptable will vary. A preference for self-reliance versus community responsibility will vary by family, by culture, and by gender of the dominant parent. Consideration should also be given to cultural expectations about physical appearance and self-presentation (APA, 2000), which may lead to behaviors that appear somatic.

For Age and Developmental Level

Attention should be given to developmental characteristics of youth, particularly since diagnosis of youth and adults with somatoform disorders is not differentiated (Eminson, 2007). Age and development are key factors in creating and implementing any kind of self-evaluation or self-monitoring component of an intervention. For instance, considerations should be made for language development and cognitive development. If the verbal or cognitive abilities of the individual are not well suited to the task of comprehending and using self-awareness and self-regulatory strategies, these components will be less successful. Under conditions where age or developmental readiness is a factor, more direct environmental approaches such as reinforcement and timeout from preferred activities would have a greater likelihood of success.

Summary

This chapter presented a review of the characteristics and conditions of somatization, together with a summary of interventions that have been shown to be effective in remediating somatization behaviors. The types of interventions outlined were grouped into two categories: behavioral interventions (reinforcement and punishment) and multimodal cognitive–behavioral therapy. While these two methods of treatment differ in their theoretical approach to treating somatization (purely behavioral versus cognitive–behavioral), they share the same fundamental goal of reducing children's somatic symptoms and increasing their healthy, prosocial behavior. The information in this chapter provides the foundation for the supplemental classroom- and home-based materials that correspond to this book.

References

American Psychiatric Association. (2000). *Diagnostic and statistical manual of mental disorders* (4th ed., text revision). Washington, DC: Author.

Apley, J. (1975). *The child with abdominal pains.* London: Blackwell.

Campo, J. V., & Fritsch, S. L. (1994). Somatization in children and adolescents. *Journal of the American Academy of Child and Adolescent Psychiatry, 33*(9), 1223–1235.

Campo, J. V., & Fritz, G. (2001). A management model for pediatric somatization. *Psychosomatics, 42,* 467–576.

Campo, J. V., & Negrini, B. J. (2000). Case study: Negative reinforcement and behavioral management of conversion disorder. *Journal of the American Academy of Child and Adolescent Psychiatry, 39*(6), 787–790.

Eminson, D. M. (2007). Medically unexplained symptoms in children and adolescents. *Clinical Psychology Review, 27*(7), 855–871.

Essau, C. A. (2006). Somatoform disorders. In C. A. Essau (Ed.), *Child and adolescent phsychopathology: Theoretical and clinical implications* (pp. 221–245). New York: Routledge.

Finney, J. W., Lemanek, K. L., Cataldo, M. F., Katz, H. P., & Fuqua, R. W. (1989). Pediatric psychology in primary health care: Brief targeted therapy for recurrent abdominal pain. *Behavior Therapy, 20,* 283–291.

Fritz, G. K., Fritsch, S. L., & Hagino, O. (1997). Somatoform disorders in children and adolescents: A review of the past 10 years. *Journal of the American Academy of Child and Adolescent Psychiatry, 36*(10), 1329–1338.

Gooch, J. L., Wolcott, R., & Speed, J. (1997). Behavioral management of conversion disorder in children. *Archives of Physical Medicine and Rehabilitation, 78,* 264–268.

Gutsch, K. U. (1988). *Psychotherapeutic approaches to specific DSM-III-R categories: A resource book for treatment planning.* Springfield, IL: Charles C. Thomas Publisher.

Haugaard, J. J., & Hazan, C. (2004). Recognizing and treating uncommon behavioral and emotional disorders in children and adolescents who have been severely maltreated: Somatization and other somatoform disorders. *Child Maltreatment, 9*(2), 169–176.

Kellner, R. (1991). *Psychosomatic syndromes and somatic symptoms.* Arlington, VA: American Psychiatric Publishing.

Linton, S. J. (1986). A case study of the behavioural treatment of chronic stomach pain in a child. *Behaviour Change, 3*(1), 70–73.

Lipowski, Z. J. (1988). Somatization: The concept and its clinical application. *American Journal of Psychiatry, 145*(11), 1358–1368.

Maisami, M., & Freeman, J. M. (1987). Conversion reactions in children as body language: A combined child psychiatry/neurology team approach to the management of functional neurologic disorders in children. *Pediatrics, 80,* 46–52.

Miller, A. J., & Kratochwill, T. R. (1979). Reduction of frequent stomachache complaints by time out. *Behavior Therapy, 10,* 211–218.

Mizes, J. S. (1985). The use of contingent reinforcement in the treatment of a conversion disorder: A multiple baseline study. *Journal of Behavior Therapy and Experimental Psychiatry, 16*(4), 341–345.

Oyama, O., Paltoo, C., & Greengold, J. (2007). Somatoform disorders. *American Family Physician, 76*(9), 1333–1338.

Reynolds, C. R., & Kamphaus, R. W. (2004). *Behavior Assessment System for Children* (2nd ed.). Circle Pines, MN: AGS Publishing.

Reynolds, C. R., & Richmond, B. O. (2008). *Revised Children's Manifest Anxiety Scale:* Second Edition (RCMAS-2). Los Angeles: Western Psychological Services.

Sanders, M. R., Rebgetz, M., Morrison, M., Bor, W., Gordon, A., Dadds, M., et al. (1989). Cognitive–behavioral treatment of recurrent nonspecific abdominal pain in children: An analysis of generalization, maintenance, and side effects. *Journal of Consulting and Clinical Psychology, 57*(2), 294–300.

Sanders, M. R., Shepherd, R. W., Cleghorn, G., & Woolford, H. (1994). The treatment of recurrent abdominal pain in children: A controlled comparison of cognitive–behavioral family intervention and standard pediatric care. *Journal of Consulting and Clinical Psychology, 62*(2), 306–314.

Sank, L. I., & Biglan, A. (1974). Operant treatment of a case of recurrent abdominal pain in a 10-year-old boy. *Behavior Therapy, 5,* 677–681.

Schulman, J. L. (1988). Case study: Use of a coping approach in the management of children with conversion reactions. *Journal of the American Academy of Child and Adolescent Psychiatry, 27*(6), 785–788.

Taylor, S., & Garralda, E. (2003). The management of somatoform disorder in childhood. *Current Opinion in Psychiatry, 16*(2), 227–231.

Warzak, W. J., Kewman, D. G., Stefans, V., & Johnson, E. (1987). Behavioral rehabilitation of functional alexia. *Journal of Behavior Therapy and Experimental Psychiatry, 18*(2), 171–177.

Zeharia, A., Mukamel, M., Carel, C., Weitz, R., Danziger, Y., & Mimouni, M. (1999). Conversion reaction: Management by the paediatrician. *European Journal of Pediatrics, 158*(2), 160–164.

Chapter 10

Interventions for Problems With Adaptability

This chapter, which focuses on interventions for children and adolescents identified as at risk for problems with adaptability, has three major sections. First, the characteristics and behaviors associated with adaptability deficits are briefly presented, together with selected items from the BASC–2 Adaptability scale. Second, the theoretical framework for approaching interventions to enhance adaptability is described. Third, interventions that have evidence or show promise for increasing adaptability in school settings are described, with the presentation of each intervention divided into three subsections: Implementation, Evidence for Use, and Considerations. The chapter's three main sections provide the foundation on which additional BASC–2 intervention components are built, including both classroom-based and home-based strategies.

Characteristics and Conditions of Problems With Adaptability

Adaptability is described as "the ability to adjust to changes in routine and teacher assignments, to shift from one task to another, and to share toys or possessions with other children" (Reynolds & Kamphaus, 2004, p. 64). Deficits in adaptability are demonstrated in a variety of behaviors. For some children with adaptability problems, a change in a routine may result in defiance or resistance. For others, this may result in crying, throwing tantrums, abandoning the original task, or other problem behaviors. Children with deficits in adaptability skills are often those who depend on predictability, order, and consistency and who appear to be rigid or inflexible.

Deficits in adaptability are characteristic of children with pervasive developmental disorders (PDD; *DSM–IV–TR*), such as autism spectrum disorder (ASD) and Asperger's disorder (AD; *DSM–IV–TR*), children with attention-deficit/hyperactivity disorder (ADHD; Reynolds & Fletcher-Janzen, 2007), as well as those with issues common to obsessive compulsive disorders (Reynolds & Livingston, in press). In addition, decreases in adaptability in children who have previously adapted to change might be associated with high levels of anxiety, as is often observed in children with social phobia and/or anxiety-based school refusal. If assessment indicates that the decrease in adaptability is a manifestation of anxiety experienced in the school setting, the practitioner should also reference the interventions in the Anxiety chapter in this book.

The Adaptability scale of the BASC–2 (Reynolds & Kamphaus, 2004) is an adaptive (positive) scale, and includes items such as "Seems to take setbacks in stride," "Recovers quickly after a setback," "Adjusts well to changes in routine," "Complains when asked to do things differently," and "Shares toys or possessions with other children."

Theoretical Framework for Approaching Adaptability Deficits

The theoretical orientation of this chapter is a behavioral and cognitive–behavioral approach. The behavioral aspect addresses the distinctive observable problems associated with adaptability deficits, and the cognitive–behavioral aspect addresses the potential causes and origins of these issues. Behavioral approaches presume that problems are learned and expressed as physical or verbal behaviors. Cognitive–behavioral approaches rely on the combination of metacognitive processes with antecedent and consequent changes to modify the mental and physical aspects that sustain the problem behavior.

Interventions

The interventions for increasing or enhancing adaptability presented in this chapter aim to help children develop the skills to adapt to planned and unplanned changes without exhibiting aberrant or inappropriate behavior. When selecting interventions to treat adaptability deficits, the practitioner should first consider the child's specific characteristics and the function served by the child's negative behavioral response to changes in routines or activities. This information may be gathered systematically by conducting a functional behavioral assessment (FBA). While FBA is not necessarily an intervention, research indicates that conducting a functional assessment is necessary with some children who experience adaptability problems—particularly children with ASD and other developmental disorders—in order to select effective interventions (Flannery, O'Neill, & Horner, 1995; Sterling-Turner & Jordan, 2007). Research evidence also suggests that interventions selected based on FBA are three times as likely to be successful as those selected without FBA (Newcomer & Lewis, 2004). Thus, a discussion of functional assessment is included here.

Intervention strategies for enhancing adaptability fall into two broad categories: those that focus on changing some aspect of the antecedent events (i.e., trigger situations) that tend to bring about the maladaptive behavior, and those that seek to improve the child's ability to self-regulate through cognitive and behavioral training. Evidence-based interventions that primarily manipulate antecedent events include (1) precorrection, in which the practitioner gives the child advance warning of any activity or schedule change and teaches expected transition behaviors ahead of time, and (2) procedural prompts—visual, verbal, or auditory signals that cue appropriate behavior during transitions (Schmit, Alper, Raschke, & Ryndak, 2000). The use of behavioral momentum (e.g., issuing several "easy" requests to build momentum in favor of compliance before issuing a "difficult" request) is also included in the discussion of procedural prompts. Finally, two cognitive–behavioral interventions for adaptability deficits are presented: self-management training and cognitive behavior management (CBM).

In sum, this chapter discusses each of the following interventions:

I. Functional Behavioral Assessment

II. Precorrection

III. Procedural Prompts and Behavioral Momentum

IV. Self-Management Training

V. Cognitive Behavior Management

Children who have deficits in adaptability are often mistakenly described as "strong-willed," "stubborn," or "challenging." Due to these misconceptions, there can be a tendency to use punishment or harsh verbal redirections, ultimatums, or even shaming with children who are resistant compared with their compliant peers. Punishment should not be used for treating adaptability deficits. Antecedent interventions and reinforcement for alternative, healthy behaviors and/or lower rates of the maladaptive behavior are the most effective and least intrusive interventions. Also, note that parents, teachers, peers, and other well-meaning individuals may have unintentionally reinforced the child's fear, anxiety, and troubling behaviors associated with lack of adaptability if they have responded to the maladaptive behavior by giving the child attention or an opportunity to escape the situation. Teachers, parents, and other caregivers may need additional training and assistance to cease reinforcing the maladaptive behavior and to provide effective intervention in classroom or home settings.

I. Functional Behavioral Assessment

Conducting a functional assessment of behaviors associated with adaptability problems allows practitioners to determine the function of particular maladaptive behaviors—in other words, what the child hopes to achieve through the behavior (e.g., to gain attention; to gain access to objects, events, or people; or to escape certain events, situations, or people). Knowing the behavior's function helps the practitioner address the two primary goals of adaptability intervention much more efficaciously: (1) eliminating problem behaviors by modifying the antecedents and/or consequences of the behavior, and (2) teaching appropriate replacement behaviors. Through functional behavioral assessment (FBA), practitioners assess the effect of antecedents and consequences on the observed behavior. Antecedents to behaviors associated with adaptability deficits (e.g., aberrant, rigid, and/or inflexible behavior) may be identified as unscheduled changes in routine or environment, and the function of the subsequent aberrant behavior may be stimulation such as self-soothing or escape from the change. The results of a child's FBA are used to select evidence-based interventions to increase acceptable behaviors that are functionally equivalent (i.e., accomplish the same purpose) to the problem behaviors. For example, if Boris exhibits aberrant behavior that is determined through FBA to serve a self-soothing purpose, he may be given access to a rocking chair when he is agitated, thus replacing the maladaptive behavior with an acceptable alternative behavior that accomplishes the same purpose.

In another example, whenever Tabori arrives in class and sees a substitute teacher, he cries and complains of a stomachache, and consequently is allowed to go lie down in the nurse's office. Ms. Harris, the school psychologist, completes an FBA and determines that the function of Tabori's behavior is escape from unexpected situations or changes in routine. Interventions are planned that identify substitute teachers ahead of time for Tabori and prohibit him from escaping to the nurse's office. To provide Tabori with a sense of familiarity and continuity during the regular teacher's absence, a preferred peer, Susan, is allowed to sit next to Tabori as long as he does not cry and remains in the classroom.

FBA could reveal that another child with behavior like Tabori's may use the same behavior to achieve a different purpose—for instance, to escape not from the substitute teacher, but rather from peers who often engage in teasing when the regular classroom teacher is not present. Intervention in this case might include teaching and reassuring the child that substitute teachers will not allow teasing, either. The child could also be granted a new place to sit that is a safe distance away from the children doing the teasing, thus allowing a more limited form of escape without reducing the child's time in the classroom. In addition, self-management techniques, precorrection, or procedural prompts could be used to increase appropriate behavior and decrease problem behavior (e.g., verbalizing when upset rather than crying or complaining, or using a "seating pass" to move farther away from teasing children rather than escaping to the nurse's office).

In sum, the findings from a functional assessment of behavior are critical in helping the practitioner determine effective interventions and appropriate replacement behaviors for a particular child.

Implementation

The goals of conducting an FBA of adaptability problems are 1) to determine the function of a specific behavior the child exhibits related to a deficit in adaptability, and 2) to identify one or more interventions that will effectively enable the child to increase adaptive behavior while still accomplishing the desired effect (e.g., self-soothing) or eliciting the same environmental response (e.g., getting the attention of the teacher).

The basic elements of functional behavioral assessment include the following:

1. Conducting a functional assessment (including interviews and direct observation)

2. Developing hypotheses for why the behavior occurs

3. Evaluating or testing the hypotheses

4. Selecting an evidence-based intervention strategy

The practitioner begins the process by gathering information through interviews with the child's teacher(s) and parent(s). By asking carefully phrased questions that focus on the child's transition problems, the practitioner tries to determine the specific situations (e.g., expected and/or unexpected changes in routine) in which the child tends to exhibit problem behaviors reflecting a deficit in adaptability. The practitioner then tries to determine if the problem is related to a change in the sequence in which events occur; the time at which a particular event occurs; changes in the content of the situation (e.g., different people, location, or materials than the usual); or the introduction of something new (e.g., doing a new activity, meeting a new teacher).

Next, the practitioner observes the child during problematic transitions or changes. For instance, if the parent indicated that the child has problems with schedule changes, the practitioner would observe the child during transitions on days when schedule changes occur. Based on these initial observations, the practitioner or another member of the multidisciplinary team writes a testable hypothesis regarding the function of the behavior. For instance, the hypothesis about Tabori's behavior might be, "When Tabori has a substitute teacher, he cries, complains of a stomachache, and requests to go to the nurse's office in order to escape an unfamiliar situation that he perceives as frightening. He is upset by the disruption of the regular classroom routine, and escaping to the nurse's office calms him down."

To test the hypothesis, the practitioner observes the child in the classroom again, targeting the identified problem situations (e.g., transitions on days with schedule changes, or days with substitute teachers). The initial hypothesis about the function of the problem behavior is either confirmed or revised based on these observations. Finally, using the results of the FBA, the practitioner chooses an appropriate, evidence-based intervention to help the child develop the skills to accomplish the same function through socially acceptable behaviors.

The procedural steps for conducting an FBA listed in Figure 10.1 are modifications of the steps provided by Flannery et al. (1995) and Kern and Vorndran (2000).

Figure 10.1 **Procedural steps for using functional behavioral assessment (FBA) to select interventions for adaptability deficits**

1. Interview parent(s) and teacher(s) to gather information about the problematic elements of transitions. Use carefully phrased questions to determine the key variables that predict problem behavior.

   a. Sequence: Is the problem behavior brought on by a change in the order of events/activities?

   b. Content: Is the problem behavior associated with a change in materials, location, procedure for an activity, or the people present?

   c. Novelty: Is the problem behavior associated with the addition of new items, activities, or people?

   d. Time: Is the problem behavior associated with a change in the time at which expected events/activities occur?

2. Observe the child during transitions. Focus on the aspect(s) of change (sequence, content, novelty, and/or time) that, according to the parent and teacher interviews, appear to be creating the problem behavior.

3. Write a testable hypothesis regarding the function of the child's behavior.

4. Observe the child again to test the hypothesis and revise it, if necessary.

5. Select an appropriate intervention based on the findings of the FBA.

Evidence for Use

FBA has been found to assist practitioners in selecting interventions that remediate behaviors associated with a lack of adaptability and that increase compliance during transitions, decrease problem behavior, reduce self-injury, and decrease disruptive behaviors and tantrums (Dooley, Wilczenski, & Torem, 2001; Kern & Vorndran, 2000; Mace, Shapiro, & Mace, 1998; Repp & Karsh, 1994; VanDerHeyden, Witt, & Gatti, 2001).

There is a large body of literature on the use and application of FBA. Here, we examine selected studies that demonstrate the use of FBA specifically related to behaviors associated with or characterized by problems with adaptability. This is not intended to represent the entirety of the FBA literature.

Dooley, P., Wilczenski, F. L., & Torem, C. (2001). Using an activity schedule to smooth school transitions. *Journal of Positive Behavior Interventions, 3*(1), 57–61.

Chris, a 3-year-old boy with pervasive developmental disorder (PDD), regularly exhibited dangerous and disruptive behaviors at school and at home. Based on an FBA that included 17 days of classroom observation as well as consultations with Chris's parents, it was hypothesized that transitions or changes in routine were unsettling for Chris and that his problem behaviors functioned as communication of distress and confusion. Intervention for him involved using the Picture Exchange Communication System (PECS™) to create an activity schedule board, where pictures of each school activity were placed in order. Chris was taught to take the first picture, match it to the activity, and engage in that activity until the lights were turned off to signal that it was time to return to the activity board and transition to the second activity. This intervention caused a marked decrease in disruptive behaviors during transitions, and Chris's parents were able to implement a similar system at home as well.

Flannery, K. B., & Horner, R. H. (1994). The relationship between predictability and problem behavior for students with severe disabilities. *Journal of Behavioral Education, 4*(2), 157–176.

Two single-case studies were conducted to determine the effect of predictability on levels of problem behaviors in students with disabilities. In the first study, a functional assessment of the behavior of a 14-year-old boy with autism indicated that he found novel tasks aversive, and that his maladaptive responses to such tasks were reinforced by opportunities to escape from the tasks. Based on this assessment, a predictability strategy was chosen in which unfamiliar tasks were modeled and clearly explained before they were assigned. This led to a reduction in problem behavior. For the second study, a functional assessment was conducted for a 17-year-old boy with autism and cerebral palsy. Interview and observation data suggested that the boy's problem behaviors (destruction of property and aggression) served the function of enabling escape from classes where the duration and sequence of activities were not clearly communicated. Intervention strategies for the remainder of the study were designed based on these findings, and problem behaviors were reduced. The results of these two case studies indicate that consistency may not be needed for students with severe disability, provided the tasks are in some way predictable. Moreover, the findings support the idea that predictability could replace rigid consistency, which is often difficult to implement in school and real-life settings, for controlling problem behaviors.

Kern, L., & Vorndran, C. M. (2000). Functional assessment and intervention for transition difficulties. *Journal of the Association for Persons With Severe Handicaps, 25*(4), 212–216.

One 11-year-old girl with mental retardation and ADHD was examined for this study. She was observed engaging in challenging behaviors multiple times a day—most predominantly "flopping," which involved lying on the ground and refusing to move, sometimes accompanied by aggression. During the first phase of assessment, she was observed during multiple transitions to different activities, and it was discovered that flopping occurred only when transitioning to school. Two hypotheses emerged: 1) that she flopped as a result of leaving preferred tasks, and 2) that she did so when losing staff interaction. To evaluate these hypotheses, the girl was told during transitions to school that she would be allowed to play for 5 minutes upon arrival at school, talk with someone for 5 minutes, or a combination of the two. Each of these options reduced the problem behavior, but interaction eliminated it, showing that this one simple adjustment was effective in restraining her problem behavior.

Mace, A. B., Shapiro, E. S., & Mace, F. C. (1998). Effects of warning stimuli for reinforcer withdrawal and task onset on self-injury. *Journal of Applied Behavior Analysis, 31*(4), 679–682.

This study examined one 7-year-old girl with autism who had problems with self-injurious behavior (SIB). Baseline functional analysis of her behavior suggested that her SIB functioned to provide access to preferred objects or escape from task demands. During treatment, the girl was observed when she received preferred objects or escaped from demands noncontingently (i.e., not as a result of SIB), as well as when she received multiple warnings before a negative occurrence (e.g., removing a desired object or beginning a demanding task). It was shown that providing multiple warnings before the negative occurrence, as well as removing the reinforcement, were effective in greatly reducing her use of SIB.

Repp, A. C., & Karsh, K. G. (1994). Hypothesis-based interventions for tantrum behaviors of persons with developmental disabilities in school settings. *Journal of Applied Behavior Analysis, 27*(1), 21–31.

Two girls, Alicia (age 9) and Sarah (age 7), both diagnosed with mental disabilities and significant behavioral problems, were observed in this study. A functional analysis examining both antecedent conditions and consequences was used, leading to a hypothesis that, even though the problem behavior usually occurred during demand settings, its purpose was to gain attention. During baseline, problem behavior was consistently followed by teacher attention but rarely brought removal of demands. During treatment, teachers were instructed to ignore problem behaviors but to consistently pay attention when the girls were on task. This instruction style was largely effective with both girls. Alicia's tantrums decreased from 41% of the day to 4% of the day, and this level was maintained at follow-up a year later. Sarah's tantrums were reduced from 22 to 4 times per day and were reported at follow-up to no longer occur.

VanDerHeyden, A. M., Witt, J. C., & Gatti, S. (2001). Research into practice: Descriptive assessment method to reduce overall disruptive behavior in a preschool classroom. *School Psychology Review, 30*(4), 548–567.

Two classrooms were analyzed during this study in which two alternating treatments were used to reduce disruptive behavior: differential reinforcement of alternative behavior (DRA), where attention was given to appropriate behavior and problem behavior was ignored; and reprimand, where all problem behavior was dealt with using reprimands. Classroom 1 consisted of 8 children (ages 2 to 4) in a nursery school program, all diagnosed with mild to moderate speech delays. Classroom 2 consisted of 22 4-year-old students in a Head Start program from which 6 students were randomly selected. Based on functional assessment of both classrooms, it was hypothesized that most disruptive behavior was aimed at receiving teacher attention. For each classroom, both the indicated treatment (i.e., DRA) and the contraindicated treatment (i.e., reprimand) were employed. While both treatments served to stabilize levels of disruptive behavior somewhat, the DRA intervention was more effective. In Classroom 1, disruptive behaviors decreased from 39% during baseline to 23% using DRA, compared to 32% using reprimands. In Classroom 2, disruptive behavior decreased from 31% at baseline to 16% and 27% for DRA and reprimands, respectively.

Considerations

FBA is a technically sound approach to intervention planning; however, an assessment is only as reliable as the data that are collected. In some situations, the function of a child's behavior may be nearly self-evident and minimal effort may be required to collect high-quality data that are both valid and reliable. For example, in the case of a child who throws tantrums whenever a stranger enters the classroom, parent and teacher interviews are likely to yield an accurate hypothesis about the function of the child's tantrum behavior. In this case, data collection to confirm the hypothesis would simply involve observing the child on several different occasions when a stranger enters the classroom and documenting the child's response. However, some other behaviors related to adaptability deficits may belong to behavior classes that are more difficult to operationally define and whose antecedents are more difficult to determine. In these situations, collecting good data and finding clear patterns in the child's behavior will be much more challenging. In instances where the behavior is topographically complicated or not readily observed (e.g., occurs with high intensity but low frequency or occurs at times or in locations not accessible to school personnel), the use of a team of professionals is highly encouraged until sufficient data are gathered to produce a solid hypothesis about the behavior's function.

If practitioners already have extensive professional experience working with a certain child, they may be tempted to draw conclusions about the function of a particular behavior without going through formal data collection procedures; however, the authors strongly advise against this practice. It is crucial to view preliminary ideas about the behavior's possible function as a hypothesis only and to enter the observation/hypothesis-testing step with an open mind, since data tends to become a self-fulfilling prophecy when the observer feels strongly invested in an *a priori* hypothesis. This is not to suggest that professional knowledge of and history with the child should not influence what kind of data are collected and what data collection methods are used (e.g., identifying the conditions or behaviors of interest and choosing the time periods for observation). However, there is a marked difference between drawing on one's experience to conduct informed data collection and undertaking data collection to support a biased or predetermined attribution of cause.

Some teachers and/or administrators may be hesitant to participate in formal data collection due to the time-consuming nature of the process, particularly if the problem behavior interferes with classroom or campus life or if parents are demanding immediate, effective intervention. In some cases, a "best match" approach is warranted, in which intervention is based on professional judgment and informal assessment of the conditions surrounding the problem behavior.

II. Precorrection

Precorrection involves the provision of prompts for desired behaviors in certain circumstances that are determined to be antecedents to problem behavior (De Pry & Sugai, 2002). Precorrection may also familiarize children with behavior that is acceptable during expected or unexpected changes in routine or schedule by explaining, teaching, and/or practicing the desired behavior prior to the event or task (VanDerHeyden et al., 2001). Precorrection can take the form of verbal directions, visual schedules (i.e., schedules that use a picture or photo to represent each task), or both. Combining symbols with written schedules is helpful in establishing expectations for all stages of transitions (Olive, 2004). The terms previewing, systematic preparation, and priming all refer to similar precorrection techniques in which the child is prepared for an upcoming event through modeling (either filmed or *in vivo*), practice, and/or verbal instruction (Schreibman, Whalen, & Stahmer, 2000). Often, precorrection activities are conceptualized as "readiness signals" for changes that will occur in the near future.

For example, Harrison, a sixth-grade student with Asperger's disorder, becomes highly agitated on days when the school schedule is changed for pep rallies or other assemblies. Using precorrection, on the day before an expected schedule change, Harrison's teacher explains to him that the schedule the next day will be different, explains to him how to follow the new schedule, and shows him a visual schedule that lists the new class times. She sends Harrison home that day with a note asking his mother to remind him about the schedule change in the morning. The next day, when Harrison arrives at school, his teacher greets him with a familiar visual cue representing a pep assembly day, as well as a class schedule for the day that Harrison can carry with him.

In another case, Mike, an adolescent with obsessive-compulsive disorder, often becomes angry and starts fights when his gym teacher changes the arrangement of the physical fitness weight equipment. To help Mike deal effectively with the change, the teacher gives Mike a map of the new arrangement the day before moving the equipment, with arrows and numbers showing the correct order in which to use the machines and the number of reps to do at each station. The advance knowledge of the change and having a map to refer to alleviates Mike's anxiety and allows him to function as part of the class the next day without starting any fights.

Implementation

The goal of precorrection is to increase predictability by using prompts and explaining expectations for behavior when there are expected or unexpected changes in schedules, tasks, and activities. Precorrection can be verbal or can take the form of a visual schedule.

The basic elements of precorrection include the following:

1. Identifying transitions that might lead to problems

2. Teaching expected transition behavior

3. Using visual schedules

The procedural steps for implementing precorrection as an intervention for adaptability deficits are listed in Figure 10.2. First, the practitioner identifies problematic changes or transitions (e.g., by reviewing the results of the child's FBA), as well as determining if the child will respond to verbal or visual precorrection. Next, the child's current schedule and transitions are identified and modified as needed to be as structured as possible. An emphasis on routine and predictability are part of the scheduling. At the same time, prospects for unscheduled changes or scheduled but infrequent changes to daily routines are identified as sources of threat for the child. Precorrection should be implemented before these changes (representing antecedents or setting changes) in order to minimize the child's potential transitioning problems.

For verbal precorrection, the practitioner first describes the problematic transition or schedule change and the expected behavior to the child. The practitioner models the behavior and then practices it with the child, reinforcing correct responses and effort. If the practitioner has evidence that the child does not understand the transition or schedule change or has not mastered the appropriate behavior, the practitioner repeats the steps until the child demonstrates mastery.

With visual precorrection, the practitioner establishes a visual schedule for the child and uses it to alert and prepare the child both for expected transitions (e.g., transitioning from classtime to recess every day) and for unexpected schedule changes (e.g., altering the order and length of the next day's classes to accommodate an afternoon field trip). A special change symbol may be used to call the child's attention to parts of the schedule that differ from the norm.

For example, Jillian becomes agitated when the teacher changes the sequence of activities during the class's morning meeting. Typically, the teacher discusses the day of the month first and the weather second, but on days when the weather is unusually cold or hot, the teacher begins with the weather. On these days, Jillian screams and points at the calendar, demanding that the teacher begin with the day of the month. The teacher decides to use precorrection to mitigate the problem behavior. On days when the morning meeting sequence will be different, she explains to Jillian before the lesson begins that weather will be first and states why (e.g., because it is very hot today). She asks Jillian to sit quietly during the weather and tells her that if she does, she will be allowed to attach the sticky-back number to the calendar during calendar time. The teacher models sitting quietly and practices this skill with Jillian.

In another example, Candy is disturbed when she is not first in line for the bathroom or when the school sirens go off during thunderstorms. Candy's teacher precorrects her by using a picture schedule to represent the bathroom line, with children's photos and names arranged in order on a felt board by the door. Candy is reminded to check the board for the line order and told that "lucky lineups" (i.e., those in which Candy stands quietly in the appropriate spot in line) will be rewarded with time in the beanbag chair during reading. Thunderstorms are another unplanned change that causes difficulty for Candy. If the sky clouds over or the adults in the classroom know about a probability of rain, they precorrect Candy by verbally reminding her that today there might be a thunderstorm and showing her how to use her hands to cover her ears if it gets loud. They also remind her that she is allowed to quietly approach and stand next to a teacher if the sirens go off rather than crying and crawling under a table. Candy's new skills—covering her ears and standing next to an adult during a storm—are both age-appropriate and socially appropriate behaviors that help reduce the age-inappropriate and socially stigmatizing behaviors (such as crying and crawling under tables) that often prevented her inclusion in general education settings.

Figure 10.2 **Procedural steps for implementing precorrection**

1. Identify situations that tend to trigger problem behaviors. Triggers may include regular transitions and/or unexpected changes in the child's schedule.

2. Determine if the child responds better to verbal or visual precorrection (or a combination of both).

3. Review the daily schedule and transitions with the child. If necessary and feasible, make modifications to the schedule to ensure a high degree of structure and predictability.

4. Provide verbal and/or visual precorrection to help make problematic situations more predictable for the child.

   a. Verbal precorrection: Name, describe, and discuss the problem situation with the child.

   b. Visual precorrection: Point to, show, or refer to the photo, drawing, or symbol that represents the problem situation.

5. Introduce the expected transition behavior verbally and/or visually.

   a. Verbal precorrection: Name, describe, and discuss the behavior with the child.

   b. Visual precorrection: Point to, show, or refer to the photo, drawing, or symbol that represents the expected behavior.

6. Model the expected behavior and engage the child in practicing it (e.g., through role play).

7. Communicate to the child, prior to a potentially problematic situation, a reward (contingent reinforcement) that he or she will receive for engaging in appropriate behavior.

8. Reinforce appropriate behavior.

9. Teach (or reteach) and practice the skill as necessary in a separate lesson if the child demonstrates a lack of understanding or a deficit in performing the target behavior.

Evidence for Use

Precorrection has been found to increase compliance and decrease behavioral incidents during transitions, decrease transition times, and decrease overall student problem behavior (Colvin, Sugai, Good, & Lee, 1997; De Pry & Sugai, 2002; Dettmer, Simpson, Myles, & Ganz, 2000; Dooley et al., 2001; Flannery & Horner, 1994; Stormont, Smith, & Lewis, 2007). In combination with prompts and reinforcement, priming has been found to improve verbal and physical sharing (Sawyer, Luiselli, Ricciardi, & Gower, 2005). The following studies summarize some of the key research findings associated with the use of precorrection in children and adolescents with adaptability deficits.

Colvin, G., Sugai, G., Good, R. H., & Lee, Y. Y. (1997). Using active supervision and precorrection to improve transition behaviors in an elementary school. *School Psychology Quarterly, 12*(4), 344–363.

A schoolwide treatment plan was implemented in this study to see if using active supervision and precorrection would reduce the problem behaviors (e.g., running, hitting, yelling) of elementary children during three key transitions: Transition 1, when entering the school building; Transition 2, when moving to the cafeteria for lunch; and Transition 3, when exiting the school building. Teachers were taught to remind students of proper behavior just before entering the transition period, and teachers responsible for supervision of the transitions were taught to move around the area, scan to observe all the children, and interact with the children as much as possible. Both of the interventions had positive effects: problem behaviors decreased at the implementation of precorrection and tended to be lower when interaction of supervisors was higher. Average incidents dropped from 40 to 8 in Transition 1, from 25 to 12 in Transition 2, and from 23 to 11 in Transition 3. Interestingly, the amount of supervisor interaction with the children was significantly more effective for incident reduction than the number of supervisors per transition period.

De Pry, R. L., & Sugai, G. (2002). The effect of active supervision and pre-correction on minor behavioral incidents in a sixth grade general education classroom. *Journal of Behavioral Education, 11*(4), 255–267.

This study measured the effects of proactive (versus reactive) correction of minor behavioral incidents (e.g., eating, talking out, getting out of one's seat) in a sixth-grade classroom of 26 students in two intervention phases. The classroom teacher was taught two proactive strategies: active supervision (e.g., circulating in the classroom, reinforcing positive student behaviors) and precorrection (e.g., giving reminders of proper behavior before instances in which problem behavior regularly occurred). For both intervention phases, the researcher met with the teacher each morning before class to discuss progress and encourage use of the interventions. Immediately upon implementation of the interventions in the first phase, the average occurrence of minor behavioral problems in the classroom went down from 95% at baseline to 62%. During the second intervention phase, the average occurrence dropped from the second baseline of 72% to 34%. The results demonstrate a relationship between proactive instruction and decreases in minor behavioral incidents. Moreover, the study suggests that even low levels of proactive instruction result in moderate decreases of minor behavioral incidents.

Dettmer, S., Simpson, R. L., Myles, B. S., & Ganz, J. B. (2000). The use of visual supports to facilitate transitions of students with autism. *Focus on Autism and Other Developmental Disabilities, 15*(3), 163–169.

In this study, visual prompts were used to help two young boys with autism transition between activities. Seven-year-old Jeff was given two visual schedules, one kept in the car and a portable one carried by his caretaker, and he was shown a picture of each activity before it happened. Five-year-old Josh, in addition to a visual schedule, was given a box in which he could place index cards of tasks as he completed them, and a visual timer, where he could see the time "run out" as his time for a particular task ended. For both boys, these interventions produced marked improvements in transition time. Transitions that used to take Jeff a mean of over 6 minutes took less than 2. Josh went from 2.5 minutes to 0.7 minutes on average. Upon return to baseline conditions, both boys reverted to long transitions and repeatedly asked for the visual interventions, showing that it was not only effective but also preferred by the boys.

Dooley, P., Wilczenski, F. L., & Torem, C. (2001). Using an activity schedule to smooth school transitions. *Journal of Positive Behavior Interventions, 3*(1), 57–61.

Chris, a 3-year-old boy with pervasive developmental disorder (PDD), regularly exhibited dangerous and disruptive behaviors at school and at home. After classroom observation and parent interviews, it was hypothesized that transitions or changes in routine were unsettling for Chris and that his problem behaviors functioned as a means of communicating distress and confusion. Intervention for him involved using the Picture Exchange Communication System (PECS) to create an activity schedule board, where pictures of each school activity were placed in order. Chris was taught to take the first picture, match it to the activity, and engage in that activity until the lights were turned off to signal that it was time to return to the activity board and transition to the second activity. This intervention caused a marked decrease in disruptive behaviors during transitions, and Chris's parents were able to implement a similar system at home as well.

Flannery, K. B., & Horner, R. H. (1994). The relationship between predictability and problem behavior for students with severe disabilities. *Journal of Behavioral Education, 4*(2), 157–176.

Two single-case studies were conducted to determine the effect of predictability on levels of problem behaviors in students with disabilities. In the first study, a functional assessment of the behavior of a 14-year-old boy with autism indicated that he found novel tasks aversive, and that his maladaptive responses to such tasks were reinforced by opportunities to escape from the tasks. Based on this assessment, a predictability strategy was chosen in which unfamiliar tasks were modeled and clearly explained before they were assigned. This led to a reduction in problem behavior. For the second study, a functional assessment was conducted for a 17-year-old boy with autism and cerebral palsy. Interview and observation data suggested that the boy's problem behaviors (destruction of property and aggression) served the function of enabling escape from classes where the duration and sequence of activities were not clearly communicated. Intervention strategies for the remainder of the study were designed based on these findings, and problem behaviors were reduced. The results of these two case studies indicate that consistency may not be needed for students with severe disability, provided the tasks are in some way predictable. Moreover, the findings support the idea that predictability could replace rigid consistency, which is often difficult to implement in school and real-life settings, for controlling problem behaviors.

Mace, A. B., Shapiro, E. S., & Mace, F. C. (1998). Effects of warning stimuli for reinforcer withdrawal and task onset on self-injury. *Journal of Applied Behavior Analysis, 31*(4), 679–682.

This study examined one 7-year-old girl with autism who had problems with self-injurious behavior (SIB). Through observation, it was determined that her SIB was used to access preferred objects or to escape from demands. She was further observed when she received preferred objects or escaped from demands regularly (not as a result of SIB), as well as when she received multiple warnings before a negative occurrence (e.g., removing a desired object, beginning a demanding task). It was shown that multiple warnings before the negative occurrence, as well as removing the reinforcement, were effective in greatly reducing her use of SIB.

Sawyer, L. M., Luiselli, J. K., Ricciardi, J. N., & Gower, J. L. (2005). Teaching a child with autism to share among peers in an integrated preschool classroom: Acquisition, maintenance, and social validation. *Education and Treatment of Children, 28*(1), 1–10.

This study focused on 1 preschool-age boy with autism and interventions aimed at helping him share. Regular care providers implemented both phases of intervention and recorded data. Phase 1 involved priming, prompting, and praise. At the beginning of a play session, the boy and a playmate were instructed on the importance of sharing and how to share. During playtime, the boy was regularly prompted to share if a minute went by when he was not doing so, and he was praised every time he shared. During Phase 2, only prompting and praise were used. Data show that the interventions did have a significant effect on the frequency of his sharing, both verbally and physically, but Phase 1 was more effective in raising and maintaining his frequency of physical sharing. The results indicate that priming before a classroom play session, combined with reinforcement during play, resulted in higher levels of sharing behavior.

Stormont, M. A., Smith, S. C., & Lewis, T. J. (2007). Teacher implementation of precorrection and praise statements in Head Start classrooms as a component of a program-wide system of positive behavior support. *Journal of Behavior Education, 16,* 280–290.

Based on observations and low use rates for specific praise statements taught during a program-wide training given at the beginning of the school year, 3 teachers of preschool Head Start classrooms were chosen for this study. All 3 teachers were given individual instruction on the use of precorrective statements to orient students at the beginning of a lesson and on the use of specific praise statements when student behavior matched expectations. The teachers were given feedback on their use of the interventions throughout the study. Data were collected on child problem behavior as well as the rate of teacher use of precorrective and specific praise statements. Two of the 3 teachers increased their use of precorrection (1 teacher already used that intervention regularly and maintained use during the study), and each of the teachers increased his or her rate of use of specific praise statements. Overall, these combined interventions reduced the rate of student problem behavior across all 3 groups; the results also indicate that the increased use of precorrective statements prior to a lesson perhaps sets the stage for more appropriate interactions between teachers and students.

Considerations

For Teaching

Precorrection is an effective and efficient technique for school professionals. Once practitioners become skilled at using precorrection strategies, they can begin to incorporate them into their regular interactions with students, anticipate the potential for problems in certain situations, and teach behavioral expectations before the problematic scenarios present themselves. For example, a fifth-grade teacher initially used precorrection to help her class of children with autism deal with a few specific, problematic transitions. Later, she began to generalize her use of precorrection strategies by implementing them multiple times a day while watching for any changes in the classroom and school environment that had the potential to cause problems for students with adaptability deficits.

This type of behavioral coaching is also easily generalized to other types of problem behaviors as a general principle of effective behavior management and intervention. Extensive use of precorrection, however, may cause some children to become dependent on outside prompting in order to engage in appropriate behavior. Care should be taken to precorrect only when needed; this practice will prevent children from beginning to rely on this external source of information processing. To help children with adaptability deficits develop their ability to independently engage in appropriate transition behavior, precorrection can gradually be transferred from an adult's voice to children's own voices as they learn to signal themselves, cognitively process scenarios, and effectively prepare for transitions.

Larger but less-frequent transitions (e.g., moving from one grade to the next or from one campus to another, or seasonal changes in routine) are also good candidates for precorrection. Children can be prepared for these types of transitions using video or pictures of new staff and environments. Ideally, children should spend time in the new classroom or on the new campus to practice the transition, decrease uncertainty, and become familiar with the skills and expectations that accompany the new place. Precorrection is especially helpful when it focuses on the positive aspects of what is coming next.

III. Procedural Prompts and Behavioral Momentum

Procedural prompts (often referred to as visual or auditory cuing or signaling) help to increase adaptability by (1) providing information that cues the student to transition from one activity or event to another, or (2) informing the student about changes in schedules and/or events (Dalrymple, 1995). Procedural prompts are similar to precorrection activities. However, procedural prompts are used as a stimulus to prompt the child to transition at the time of the new event or activity, while precorrections are used as an antecedent for appropriate behavior and are implemented before the transition or change in activity.

There are three main categories of procedural prompts: visual, verbal, and auditory. Visual prompts can be pictures, gestures, or written directions. Verbal prompts are language cues, such as words, songs, or spoken directions. Auditory prompts include music, beeps, chimes, bells, whistles, buzzers, or the ringing of a timer or alarm clock. For children who respond better to kinesthetic prompting, objects may be used as an alternative to visual or auditory cues (e.g., the teacher may hand the child a basketball to signal that it is time to go to gym class). Other examples of commonly used prompts are dimming the lights, visual timers (e.g., timers that represent the amount of time left in an activity with a colored wedge that grows smaller as the end time approaches), stop lights, transition songs like "Clean Up," or call-and-response clapping routines such as the teacher clapping twice and the students clapping once in response. These signals all serve to communicate that a particular type of behavior or transition will occur.

For example, Jerrod has difficulty disengaging from one activity and beginning the next. His teacher uses an auditory prompt (a doorbell chime) to signal Jerrod that it is time to put away his reading books and begin math. Jerrod's teacher also uses a toy chirping bird (a combination of a visual and an auditory prompt) to signal Jerrod and other students that it is time to listen.

Behavioral momentum has not traditionally been considered a type of procedural prompt, but its similar means of implementation and ultimate goal—namely, providing a specific stimulus at the beginning of a transition for the purpose of increasing children's appropriate behavior and compliance with change—warrants its inclusion here. Behavioral momentum as an intervention is based on the idea that issuing several behavioral requests with a high probability of compliance creates positive momentum that, in turn, increases the likelihood of a child fulfilling a request that would ordinarily have a low probability of compliance (Nevin, 1996). Verbal reinforcement is incorporated as frequently as is feasible with comments such as "Right," "Thanks," or "You bet."

For example, Barb, a high school senior with mild cognitive impairment, frequently says "no" to teacher requests and is known for her stubborn characteristics toward faculty members; however, she readily engages with teachers socially. One of her teachers, Mrs. Wayne, instructs Barb to move from working on the history mural to the computer, but Barb continues to paint. In the past, if Mrs. Wayne confronted Barb about not following directions, Barb's noncompliant behavior would quickly escalate to shouting or running out of the classroom. Mrs. Wayne finds she is more successful with Barb's transitions when she approaches her with a series of easy questions or high-compliance requests in rapid succession. For instance, Mrs. Wayne stands next to Barb, smiles, and says, "Tell me your name." Barb smiles back and says, "Barb." Mrs. Wayne then asks, "Barb, what color is this paint?" Barb answers that it is blue. Mrs. Wayne says, "Barb, please keep painting," and Barb does. Mrs. Wayne then asks, "Barb, do you like painting the Statue of Liberty?" and Barb says yes. Finally Mrs. Wayne says, "Barb, let's move to the computer," and Barb complies with the transition request.

Implementation

The goal of procedural prompting is to increase adaptation to changes in routine or schedule by providing the child with a prompt for the activity or event transition, or, in the case of behavioral momentum, to ease the transition by incorporating small instances of rule-governed behavior. The basic elements of procedural prompting and behavioral momentum include the following:

1. Identifying an appropriate form of prompting

2. Teaching the child to associate the prompt with the target behavior

In the case of behavioral momentum, basic elements include (1) identifying a selection of easy questions or high-compliance requests; (2) reinforcing compliance with each request; and (3) delivering several easy requests shortly before a difficult request.

An appropriate, minimally intrusive form of prompting is determined by an individual practitioner or an intervention team. Use the simplest type of prompt that will be effective. If a hand signal is sufficient, avoid use of bells, gestures, and picture cues. However, if a simple hand signal or auditory cue is insufficient, increase the dominance of the prompt or combination of prompts until the child is alerted sufficiently to avoid the maladaptive behavior.

When identifying the type of prompt to use with a particular child, consider any stigma that might be associated with the prompt and whether this can be avoided. One method for avoiding stigmatizing or calling attention to one child is to implement a classwide prompt. When this approach is used, the prompts often improve performance for various children, even if they are truly required for just one. Classwide prompting may take the form of a single cue that all children see or hear at the same time (e.g., songs, chimes, lights), or individual cues (e.g., providing a separate, portable picture schedule for each child).

Next, the practitioner explicitly teaches, models, and leads the child(ren) in practicing the use of the prompt in conjunction with the expected transition behavior. It is recommended that while new behaviors are being taught, a reinforcement be provided for every effort. As the child becomes more comfortable with and skilled at performing the new behavior, reinforcement can fade to an interval or ratio schedule (e.g., praise offered every five minutes or after every five good efforts).

To ease a difficult transition through behavioral momentum, the practitioner predetermines three to five directives or requests that the child is known to follow quickly and consistently. Then, at the time of the transition, the practitioner first gives the child the preidentified directives/requests in rapid succession, verbally reinforcing the child after he or she fulfills each one. Immediately after fulfilling the final easy request, the practitioner delivers the potentially problematic request to transition or change activities. Finally, the practitioner provides verbal reinforcement for compliance with the transition request.

The procedural steps for implementing procedural prompts and behavioral momentum as interventions for adaptability deficits are presented in Figures 10.3 (procedural prompts) and 10.4 (behavioral momentum).

Figure 10.3 Procedural steps for implementing procedural prompts

1. Determine the minimum level of prompting that is effective for the child, as well as the most effective type(s) of prompts (visual, verbal, auditory, or an object). Avoid prompting techniques that could be stigmatizing.

2. Teach the child to associate each prompt with its meaning. As necessary, model the appropriate response to the prompt or guide the child to demonstrate the expected action. Practice routines with the child as necessary to ensure mastery.

3. Consistently provide reinforcement (e.g., praise, encouragement) while teaching the prompt associations. Gradually discontinue this use of reinforcement in cases where the change in behavior leads to natural social reinforcement.

Figure 10.4 Procedural steps for using behavioral momentum

1. Identify simple questions or verbal requests that will very likely result in compliance. For example, "Pat your head," "Jump up and down," "Stick out your tongue," "Turn around," and "Do you like chocolate?"

2. When the potentially problematic transition is about to occur, have the child respond in quick succession to several of the easy questions or requests identified in Step 1. Provide verbal reinforcement immediately after compliance with each request.

3. After the student has complied with all of the easy requests, make the request related to the desired transition behavior (e.g., "Let's line up to go to lunch now."). Verbally reinforce compliance.

Evidence for Use

Most forms of procedural prompts have been found to be useful in limiting problem behaviors and/or increasing the success of transitions. Visual prompts have been found to decrease transition times, auditory prompts have been found to decrease problem behavior and to be superior to peer-mediated transitions, cuing has been found to decrease tantrums during activity change, and behavioral momentum has been found to increase successful transitioning (Dettmer et al., 2000; Ferguson, Ashbaugh, O'Reilly, & McLaughlin, 2004; Flannery & Horner, 1994; Sainato, Strain, Lefebvre, & Rapp, 1987; Schmit, et al., 2000; Singer, Singer, & Horner, 1987).

The following selected studies demonstrate the use of various types of procedural prompts and behavioral momentum as interventions to improve adaptability.

Dettmer, S., Simpson, R. L., Myles, B. S., & Ganz, J. B. (2000). The use of visual supports to facilitate transitions of students with autism. *Focus on Autism and Other Developmental Disabilities, 15*(3), 163–169.

In this study, visual prompts were used to help two young boys with autism transition between activities. Seven-year-old Jeff was given two visual schedules, one kept in the car and a portable one carried by his caretaker, and he was shown a picture of each activity before it happened. Five-year-old Josh, in addition to a visual schedule, was given a box in which he could place index cards of tasks as he completed them, and a visual timer, where he could see the time "run out" as his time for a particular task ended. For both boys, these interventions produced marked improvements in transition time. Transitions that used to take Jeff a mean of over 6 minutes took less than 2. Josh went from 2.5 minutes to 0.7 minutes on average. Upon return to baseline, both boys reverted to long transitions and repeatedly asked for the visual interventions, showing that it was not only effective but also preferred by the boys.

Ferguson, A., Ashbaugh, R., O'Reilly, S., & McLaughlin, T. F. (2004). Using prompt training and reinforcement to reduce transition times in a transitional kindergarten program for students with severe behavior disorders. *Child & Family Behavior Therapy, 26*(1), 17–24.

In this study, 14 boys in a self-contained special education kindergarten class (aged 5 to 6 years), with behavioral disorders that included aggression, destruction, noncompliance, and running away, were taught to "freeze" at the sound of a bell while the teacher gave them instructions about transitioning to their next activity. Then, the children quickly cleaned up their current activity and went to the new area; the children who properly froze were given a small piece of candy as reinforcement. This process was applied during two transitions each to both the morning class (6 boys) and afternoon class (8 boys). This intervention, while very simple to implement, had immediate and significant results. For all transitions, the intervention decreased transition time significantly; in three of the four transitions, time was halved.

Flannery, K. B., & Horner, R. H. (1994). The relationship between predictability and problem behavior for students with severe disabilities. *Journal of Behavioral Education, 4*(2), 157–176.

Two single-case studies were conducted to determine the effect of predictability on levels of problem behaviors in students with disabilities. In the first study, a functional assessment of the behavior of a 14-year-old boy with autism indicated that he found novel tasks aversive, and that his maladaptive responses to such tasks were reinforced by opportunities to escape from the tasks. Based on this assessment, a predictability strategy was chosen in which unfamiliar tasks were modeled and clearly explained before they were assigned. This led to a reduction in problem behavior. For the second study, a functional assessment was conducted for a 17-year-old boy with autism and cerebral palsy. Interview and observation data suggested that the boy's problem behaviors (destruction of property and aggression) served the function of enabling escape from classes where the duration and sequence of activities were not clearly communicated. Intervention strategies for the remainder of the study were designed based on these findings, and problem behaviors were reduced. The results of these two case studies indicate that consistency may not be needed for students with severe disability, provided the tasks are in some way predictable. Moreover, the findings support the idea that predictability could replace rigid consistency, which is often difficult to implement in school and real-life settings, for controlling problem behaviors.

Sainato, D. M., Strain, P. S., Lefebvre, D., & Rapp, N. (1987). Facilitating transition times with handicapped preschool children: A comparison between peer-mediated and antecedent prompt procedures. *Journal of Applied Behavior Analysis, 20*(3), 285–291.

This research was conducted in an integrated preschool classroom in which 3 students with mental handicaps had a difficult time making transitions quickly between locations and activities and required much teacher assistance. The target students (males, aged 3 to 4 years) were rated as severely autistic and exhibited stereotypical behaviors (e.g., perseverative speech and object preoccupation); 2 of the children had little functional communication and avoided or ignored peer contact. All were selected based on direct observation during transitions and on teacher rankings of transitional ability. After two baseline studies, with and without teacher assistance, two interventions were implemented: a bell and a buddy system. For the bell intervention, when it was time for a transition, students were shown a card with a picture of a bell and given verbal directions to go to a specified location and ring a bell. For the buddy system, nonhandicapped students were paired with the target students and were taught to help them get to the target location. While both treatments were effective in increasing transition speed, the bell was more effective, cutting transition time in half for the target students and greatly reducing the amount of teacher assistance needed.

Schmit, J., Alper, S., Raschke, D., & Ryndak, D. (2000). Effects of using a photographic cueing package during routine school transitions with a child who has autism. *Mental Retardation, 38*(2), 131–137.

Alex, a 6-year-old boy with autism, was observed in this study during school transitions (e.g., to another part of the classroom or from the playground to the classroom) to determine the efficacy of a photographic cuing system with a verbal cue as an intervention package for his tantrum behavior. During baseline, when simply told, "It's time to go to _____," Alex regularly responded to transitions with tantrums. During intervention, in addition to being told of the transition, he was shown a photograph with the next setting and one word (e.g., "library") printed on it. Although it did not eliminate tantrums completely, this intervention helped to reduce the number of tantrums and increase the number of transitions Alex made appropriately. In addition, his parents were able to implement the same intervention at home.

Singer, G. H. S., Singer, J., & Horner, R. H. (1987). Using pretask requests to increase the probability of compliance for students with severe disabilities. *The Journal of the Association for Persons With Severe Handicaps, 12*(4), 287–291.

This study examined the effect of pretask requests on transition times for 4 children with disabilities (aged 7 to 10). Previously, these children all had trouble in some school transitions, particularly from preferred activities to nonpreferred activities. Pretask requesting involved having the teacher give the child a series of quick, easily performed commands (e.g., "give me five") before the transition command (e.g., "go inside to the classroom"). Compliance rose significantly during treatment and declined again with a return to baseline, showing that pretask requesting does have a significant effect. Further research is needed to determine if pretask requesting can be faded while maintaining high levels of compliance.

Considerations

For Teaching

Using the same sequence of directives repeatedly during a behavioral momentum procedure has been found to increase problem behavior; thus, directives should be selected at random and changed often (Davis & Reichle, 1996; Zarcone, Iwata, Mazaleski, & Smith, 1994).

For Age and Developmental Level

Be sure to select signals that are age appropriate. Singing about "clean-up time" is appropriate for 4-year-olds, but high school juniors should have different, age-appropriate transition signals that are typical in a high school setting (e.g., a bell). Also, it is important to consider any potential for stigma or an inability to transfer to post-school settings. Picture schedules, for example, might easily transfer to a personal calendar as the child becomes an adult. Complex sequences of bells or chimes would not be typical of a household or work environment; however, some use of alarms and timers is certainly a common adaptive behavior for most adults.

IV. Self-Management Training

Self-management training to increase adaptability aims to help students independently monitor and self-reinforce behaviors associated with adaptability, such as following schedules and sharing. Children are taught to monitor their own behavior when transitioning to new locations or activities, responding to expected or unexpected changes in routine, and sharing toys.

For example, Mrs. Bruhl has successfully used precorrection and prompting to teach Harrison to transition from one activity to the next without exhibiting tantrum behavior. However, her ultimate goal is for Harrison to adapt to changes in activities without adult or teacher intervention. To achieve this, Mrs. Bruhl teaches Harrison self-management skills that gradually enable him to independently monitor and reinforce his own transition behavior.

Implementation

The goal of self-management training to enhance adaptability is to increase the child's ability to independently adapt or transition to new routines or activities.

The basic elements of self-management training include the following:

1. Self-monitoring training

2. Self-reinforcement training

The procedural steps for implementing self-management training as an intervention for adaptability deficits are listed in Figure 10.5. When implementing this intervention, the practitioner first reviews the functional behavioral assessment data for relevant information regarding problematic transitions and the function of the child's maladaptive behavior. Using this information, the practitioner prepares a self-monitoring form for the child with the appropriate readability level and general comprehension (e.g., a brief checklist or a simple table with pictures representing each activity or behavior) focusing on the target behaviors. Next, the practitioner reviews the daily class schedule with the child and talks with him or her about the transitions that have led to problem behaviors in the past. Third, the practitioner teaches the child the expected behavior during transitions by verbally explaining the behavior, modeling it, and practicing it with the child. After the child has demonstrated the ability to perform the desired transition behavior, the practitioner introduces the self-monitoring form and trains the child on how and when to use it to track the target behavior. Initially, reinforcement for engaging in the desired behavior may be provided by the practitioner, but it should be gradually transitioned to the control of the child when possible.

For example, Lydia frequently refused to stop working on tasks before she was finished with them, even if the class period was over. This led to many verbal conflicts with her teachers and caused her to be routinely late to the next class. The desired transition behavior for Lydia was defined as "Putting my work in my 'To Finish Later' box quickly when the class period is over," and was represented by a stop sign on her self-monitoring checklist. At the end of each activity, Lydia wrote a *Y* next to the stop sign if she had stopped working quickly, and an *N* if she had not. Her teachers initially prompted her to fill out the checklist following each activity, but lessened the prompts as Lydia learned to remember the checklist on her own. At the end of each day, Lydia gave the checklist to the school psychologist, who added up the total number of *Y*'s and *N*'s. Initially, the psychologist provided reinforcement in the form of a sticker or a token on any day when Lydia achieved more *Y*'s than *N*'s. However, each week, the performance required for reinforcement became more challenging until Lydia needed to limit her *N*'s to a certain number to receive a reward. In addition, the responsibility for tallying up the day's *Y*'s and *N*'s and choosing a reinforcer (if she had earned one) gradually transitioned to Lydia.

Figure 10.5 Procedural steps for implementing self-management training

1. Review the findings of the functional behavioral assessment for relevant information about specific transitions that have led to problem behaviors and the function of the child's behavior.

2. Discuss the class schedule and discuss the problematic transitions with the child.

3. Define the target behavior to be used during transitions, model it, and practice it with the child.

4. Prepare a self-management form, such as a simple table or checklist, with an appropriate level of sophistication (e.g., reading level, layout, use of pictures) for the child.

5. Introduce the form to the child and model how to fill it out. Also, discuss how often the form should be used (e.g., for the first 10 minutes of each class, at the end of each activity, once every 5 minutes, etc.).

6. Cue or prompt the child when it is time to fill out the self-monitoring form. Gradually discontinue prompting as the child adjusts to the task.

7. Reinforce successful performance and monitoring of the target behavior. Increase the requirements for reinforcement over time.

8. Teach the child to independently select reinforcers and gradually transition the responsibility for reinforcing the target behavior to the child.

Evidence for Use

Self-management has been found to increase independent identification of transitions and increase sharing behavior (Newman et al., 1995; Reinecke, Newman, & Meinberg, 1999). Evidence for the effectiveness of self-management alone to increase adaptability is minimal; however, self-management is often used as a component of integrated cognitive–behavioral therapy, an intervention well supported by research evidence discussed later in this chapter. Independence in adapting to transitions, changing activities, and sharing is the ultimate goal of all the intervention strategies outlined in this chapter; self-management is a necessary step between interventions mediated by professionals and child independence, and thus is included here.

The following studies summarize some of the key research findings associated with the use of self-management training in children and adolescents with adaptability problems.

Newman, B., Buffington, D. M., O'Grady, M. A., McDonald, M. E., Poulson, C. L., & Hemmes, N. S. (1995). Self-management of schedule following in three teenagers with autism. *Behavioral Disorders, 20*(3), 190–196.

Three teenage boys in an after-school program (Scott, age 14; Peter, age 16; and Alex, age 17), all diagnosed with autism, were studied to see if self-management techniques could be used to teach them to follow set schedules independently. The schedule, listing the day's activities and times, was posted in front of the classroom, and a digital clock was in view. The boys were taught to quietly tell their teacher when it was time for them to move on to the next activity. If a transition passed without the student indicating the next activity, the teacher would verbally prompt the end of the current activity. When the teacher was notified correctly, the boy could take one of seven tokens from his back pocket and move it to his front pocket. At the end of the day, tokens could be exchanged for preferred gym activities. Marked increases in the accurate identification of transitions were seen in all 3 boys, even though only 1 of them consistently remembered to transfer tokens.

Reinecke, D. R., Newman, B., & Meinberg, D. L. (1999). Self-management of sharing in three pre-schoolers with autism. *Education and Training in Mental Retardation and Developmental Disabilities, 34*(3), 312–317.

In this study, three 4-year-old boys with autism were taught to share using a self-management technique involving tokens. During all sessions, the boys were given opportunities to share. Sessions ended once each student had received five tokens, which could then be exchanged for an edible reinforcer. If 30 seconds went by while a child was holding a toy and not sharing, he was given the verbal prompt, "Share." If he still did not share, he was physically prompted to do so. During baseline, tokens were given out noncontingently (i.e., regardless of whether the child demonstrated sharing behavior). During treatment, the boys were allowed to take tokens for themselves after each instance of sharing. For all 3 boys, instances of sharing rose from a small amount to close to 100% during treatment. Although these levels were not maintained during a return to baseline, they were quickly regained when self-management treatment was implemented for a second time.

Considerations

For Teaching

Self-management is readily adopted by classroom teachers and philosophically fits with most professionals' view of teaching children to learn self-responsibilities. Intervals for monitoring and recording need to be appropriate both for the behavior in question and for the nature of the classroom. A child is probably unable to monitor him- or herself in 45-second intervals and will need cuing from a teacher or other source (e.g., a watch or other auditory or visual prompt). Keep in mind that frequent cuing can be distracting to the child and to the other students. Tailor cues and cue sheets to fit the environment. For example, if all students keep a calendar or planner on their desks, using these can be an effective cuing device. Additionally, paper comes in a variety of shapes, sizes, and colors and can be used as an inexpensive form for students who are frequency counting. Print shops can also reproduce custom forms with a sticky back and/or can print forms with a tear-off gummy binding; both can be convenient ways to attach forms to a student's desk.

For Age and Developmental Level

This approach is generally considered most appropriate for children aged 4 and above (note that children aged 4 through 6 will probably need adult coaching to determine if they are engaged in the targeted behavior). Teachers can help coach by talking about why a child did or did not successfully monitor the behavior. For young children, a simple yes/no or green/red face may work well. For older children, a simple rating scale can be used for monitoring behavior like completing an assignment or handling a transition, or for evaluating the amount and quality of effort given to a task. For a child who struggles with adaptability, introducing a new routine or procedure requires time, discussion, modeling, and close connection to reinforcement.

V. Cognitive Behavior Management

Using cognitive behavior management (CBM; or cognitive–behavioral therapy) to increase adaptability involves the use of exercises that focus on thinking about behavior paired with reinforcement procedures. Some components of the exercises may include cognitive restructuring and systematic desensitization.

For example, Elizabeth, a 10-year-old girl with ADHD, demonstrates problems with adaptability and hides in the cafeteria rather than attend a new reading class. CBM addresses how Elizabeth thinks about the reading class and provides reinforcement for increasing appropriate behavior (attending class) and decreasing problem behavior (hiding).

Implementation

The goals of CBM for adaptability problems are to increase the child's adaptive or compensatory strategies to deal with change, to mitigate any negative effects of change on the child, and to decrease any maladaptive or aberrant behaviors that the child employs to achieve a particular desire.

The basic elements of CBM include the following:

1. Recognition of antecedents (settings or events that tend to trigger the problem behavior)

2. Recognition and modification of any maladaptive or catastrophic self-talk

3. Identification of maladaptive behaviors and appropriate replacement behaviors

4. Opportunities to practice recognizing problem events and associated feelings

5. Opportunities to practice thinking through options and making good choices about replacement thinking and behavior

6. Evaluation of and reward for performance

The procedural steps for the application of CBM as an intervention for adaptability deficits are listed in Figure 10.6, and the following example illustrates how this approach can be implemented. Buck is a bright, high school senior who appreciates structure and is fairly rigid in his daily routine. Any changes to plans or events that impact his daily routine upset him, resulting in agitation that can lead to aggression. Rather than try to send Buck to the principal or punish him (more change that causes agitation), the school counselor talks to Buck about the consequences of his lack of adaptability: fewer friends, teachers who shy away from trying to help him, problems with his job, and problems with his girlfriend. The counselor identifies several positive things that could happen if Buck learns to become more adaptable, and together they agree to try some ways to become more adaptable. First, Buck lists the types of things that really agitate him: when too many people stand in front of his locker so he can't get the door open, when his Social Studies teacher schedules a particular activity for class and then changes it, or when he has to attend a pep assembly (that is crowed, noisy, and interrupts his daily routine). Although there are more examples, the counselor and Buck agree to work on the school-related issues first and tackle the relationship and job-related problems later.

Buck and the counselor meet again to discuss the things Buck thinks about when these events occur. Buck thinks his classmates are rude when they crowd his locker, and that they may step on his toes or get fingerprints on his locker. Buck also believes the teacher is disorganized and that his daily activities are more important than interruptions such as pep rallies. He worries that these interruptions will cause him to miss out on important information that he will need for writing his essay for his college application.

Buck and the counselor identify the irrational or catastrophic thinking in both of these scenarios and talk through the realities (e.g., his toes might get stepped on but it won't kill him). Replacement thinking is identified as "it is cool to have others by my locker," and "my teacher cares about me and what I need, and is looking out for me." Buck begins to practice the new thinking and reports his progress and feelings back to his counselor. Buck and the counselor keep track of the number of setbacks Buck has, and talk about how Buck is beginning to believe that his new strategies are working.

Figure 10.6 Procedural steps for implementing cognitive behavior management

1. Identify the triggers for problem behaviors associated with the child's adaptability deficits.

2. Work with the child to identify the antecedents, behaviors, and consequences involved, as well as the associated thoughts and feelings.

3. Create a list of alternative "thinking scripts" and behaviors that are good replacements for the problem thinking and behavior.

4. Role-play or model the problem scenarios to allow the child to practice the alternative thinking and behavior.

5. Have the child try using alternative thinking and behavior independently and report back on the results. Repeat modeling and role-play of the new skills, if necessary.

6. Use a predetermined reinforcement schedule to reward the child for successfully implementing cognitive and behavioral strategies.

Evidence for Use

Approaches using CBM have resulted in improvements in adaptability and other closely related areas such as social skills, school attendance, and reduction of anxiety and school phobia (Albano, Marten, Holt, Heimberg, & Barlow, 1995; Heyne et al., 2002; King et al., 1998; Lopata, Thomeer, Volker, & Nida, 2006; Masia-Warner et al., 2005; Shortt, Barrett, & Fox, 2001).

The following studies summarize some of the key research findings associated with the use of CBM in children and adolescents with adaptability deficits. Since decreases in adaptability are often associated with high levels of anxiety, as in the case of some children with social phobia or anxiety-based school refusal, several CBM studies addressing these related issues are included here as well.

Albano, A. M., Marten, P. A., Holt, C. S., Heimberg, R. G., & Barlow, D. H. (1995). Cognitive-behavioral group treatment for social phobia in adolescents: A preliminary study. *The Journal of Nervous and Mental Disease, 183*, 649–656.

In this study, 2 female and 3 male adolescents (aged 13 to 17) with social phobia attended 16 sessions of group therapy that included skill building, phobia exposure, and parental involvement. Multiple evaluations were given before therapy, during therapy, and at various follow-up times. Results showed overall decreases in anxiety and in other specific phobias and emotional disorders. Specifically, at the 3-month follow-up, only 1 of the 5 adolescents was still diagnosed with social phobia; the rest were in remission. At the 12-month follow-up, 4 of the adolescents were still in full remission, and 1 was in partial remission. Overall, the individuals rated their anxiety levels and frequency of negative thoughts significantly lower after therapy.

Heyne, D., King, N. J., Tonge, B. J., Rollings, S., Young, D., Pritchard, M., et al. (2002). Evaluation of child therapy and caregiver training in the treatment of school refusal. *Journal of the American Academy of Child and Adolescent Psychiatry, 41*(6), 687–695.

For this study, 58 children aged 7 to 14 who exhibited school refusal and had been diagnosed with anxiety disorders were assigned to one of three groups: child therapy (CH), parent/teacher training (PTT), or a combination of the two (CH + PTT). It was hypothesized that the combination would be the most effective. After treatment, 69% of the children were no longer diagnosed as having anxiety disorders, and 60% showed no clinical disorders at all. School attendance increased for all groups. At post-treatment, the PTT and CH + PTT groups had significantly higher rates of school attendance, but, interestingly, at follow-up the rates leveled, showing that combination therapy is not always necessary or desired. Parent therapy, alone or in combination with child therapy, produced immediate results, but in the end, all three forms of therapy increased school attendance and lowered levels of anxiety.

King, N. J., Tonge, B. J., Heyne, D., Pritchard, M., Rollings, S., Young, D., et al. (1998). Cognitive-behavioral treatment of school-refusing children: A controlled evaluation. *Journal of the American Academy of Child and Adolescent Psychiatry, 37*(4), 395–403.

To determine the efficacy of a cognitive–behavioral treatment (CBT) program, this study divided 34 children (aged 5 to 15 years) who had problems with school refusal into two groups, one of which received CBT, and one of which was placed on a waiting list and served as the control group (WLC). The children in the CBT group received six therapy sessions over a period of 4 weeks, and their parents received the same. Teachers were also contacted and involved in the process. Results showed that the percentage of days present at school for the CBT group went from 62% to 94% at post-treatment, and the gains were maintained at follow-up. In contrast, for the waiting list group, percentage of days present at school increased only modestly, from 40% to 56% at post-treatment. In addition, significant differences were seen between CBT and WLC on various pretreatment and post-treatment self-report measures of emotional distress, with the CBT group showing more favorable ratings than the control group.

Lopata, C., Thomeer, M. L., Volker, M. A., & Nida, R. E. (2006). Effectiveness of cognitive-behavioral treatment on the social behaviors of children with Asperger disorder. *Focus on Autism and Other Developmental Disabilities, 21*(4), 237–244.

Twenty-one male children aged 6 to 13 years were observed in this preliminary study to determine the overall effectiveness of a 6-week, summer treatment program for children with Asperger's disorder (AD). Additionally, two treatment regimens were compared to determine if data supported one over the other. Two groups were formed, with one group receiving social skills training and one group receiving both social skills training and CBT in the form of a token system. Over the course of the 6 weeks, parents and teachers reported an overall increase in social skills in the children from both groups. Parents also reported an increase in adaptability and a decrease in atypical behaviors. While further study is needed, this preliminary examination supports using a combination of CBT and social skills education for children with AD.

Masia-Warner, C., Klein, R. G., Dent, H. C., Fisher, P. H., Alvir, J., Albano, A. M., et al. (2005). School-based intervention for adolescents with social anxiety disorder: Results of a controlled study. *Journal of Abnormal Child Psychology, 33*(6), 707–722.

This study examined the efficacy of a social skills intervention program for adolescents with social phobia. The program was conducted in school during regular school hours. Of the 35 students (26 female) who met diagnosis criteria, 18 students (14 female) were randomly assigned to the intervention and the other 17 (12 female) to the wait-list control group. Students in the intervention program were taught social skills, put in role-play situations, and provided with real-life social events to practice their skills around peers. Sessions were also offered to educate teachers and parents about social anxiety and to teach them techniques for managing children's anxiety. At the end of the study, 67% of the intervention group no longer met diagnostic criteria for social phobia, compared to only 6% of the control group. In addition, 94% of the intervention group showed moderate to marked improvement, contrasted with only 12% of the control group. These results indicate that a school intervention consisting of social skills training, exposure, and realistic thinking can significantly improve the functioning of adolescents with social anxiety disorder and, therefore, is encouraging for those considering social anxiety intervention in the schools.

Shortt, A. L., Barrett, P. M., & Fox, T. L. (2001). Evaluating the FRIENDS program: A cognitive–behavioral group treatment for anxious children and their parents. *Journal of Clinical Child Psychology, 30*(4), 525–535.

This study evaluated the efficacy of the FRIENDS program, a family-oriented group cognitive–behavioral program for children with clinical anxiety. Seventy-one children aged 6:6 to 10:0 years were observed in this study; 54 were randomly assigned to treatment groups and 17 to a waiting list. All of the children had clinical diagnoses of anxiety. Throughout the 10 weeks of the FRIENDS program, children and parents attended separate weekly behavioral training sessions. At the end of the program, 69% of the children in the treatment group were diagnosis-free, compared to only 6% of the wait-list group. At 12-month follow-up, 68% of those who completed treatment were still diagnosis-free, indicating that group cognitive–behavioral training sessions for children and parents can be effective in helping children develop and maintain successful coping strategies.

Considerations

For Teaching

CBM may also be implemented in small group settings. However, carefully consider sex, age, and sensitivity of topics prior to leading group discussions or group therapy for issues that are potentially embarrassing or that involve personally identifiable attributes. For example, children may not be embarrassed by some adaptability issues related to food consumption (e.g., a child's refusal to try any food in the school cafeteria); however, an issue related to personal hygiene routines is more likely to cause embarrassment.

For Age and Developmental Level

To successfully learn and use CBM techniques, it is imperative that students possess the cognitive and verbal abilities necessary to articulate problem behaviors, feelings, and thoughts. If the child cannot initially articulate feelings, at minimum, he or she should have the ability to respond when a skilled professional names or describes different feelings to choose from.

Self-awareness is also a critical requirement for the successful use of CBM techniques; therefore, very young children or those with developmental delays may not be a good fit for this intervention strategy. In such cases, a strictly behavioral approach will probably be sufficient. Most adolescents in upper elementary school or older grades possess the cognitive skills and self-awareness needed to benefit from CBM techniques.

Summary

This chapter presented a review of the characteristics and conditions of adaptability deficits, along with a discussion of interventions that have been shown to be effective in enhancing adaptability. These interventions included precorrection, procedural prompts, behavioral momentum, self-management training, and cognitive–behavioral management (CBM). One recommended preintervention assessment procedure, functional behavioral assessment (FBA), was also presented. While these interventions differ in the timing of their use relative to the transition (e.g., well before versus immediately prior to the transition) as well as in their theoretical approach, all share the underlying goal of increasing children's ability to adapt effectively to expected or unexpected changes in situations or routines. The information presented in this chapter forms the basis of the supplemental classroom- and home-based materials that correspond to this book.

References

Albano, A. M., Marten, P. A., Holt, C. S., Heimberg, R. G., & Barlow, D. H. (1995). Cognitive-behavioral group treatment for social phobia in adolescents: A preliminary study. *The Journal of Nervous and Mental Disease, 183,* 649–656.

Colvin, G., Sugai, G., Good, R. H., & Lee, Y. Y. (1997). Using active supervision and precorrection to improve transition behaviors in an elementary school. *School Psychology Quarterly, 12*(4), 344–363.

Dalrymple, J. (1995). It's not as easy as you think! Dilemmas and advocacy. In J. Dalrymple & J. Hough (Eds.), *Having a voice: An exploration of children's rights and advocacy.* Birmingham, England: Venture Press.

Davis, C. A., & Reichle, J. (1996). Variant and invariant high-probability requests: Increasing appropriate behaviors in children with emotional-behavioral disorders. *Journal of Applied Behavior Analysis, 29*(4), 471–482.

De Pry, R. L., & Sugai, G. (2002). The effect of active supervision and pre-correction on minor behavioral incidents in a sixth grade general education classroom. *Journal of Behavioral Education, 11*(4), 255–267.

Dettmer, S., Simpson, R. L., Myles, B. S., & Ganz, J. B., et al. (2000). The use of visual supports to facilitate transitions of students with autism. *Focus on Autism and Other Developmental Disabilities, 15*(3), 163–169.

Dooley, P., Wilczenski, F. L., & Torem, C. et al. (2001). Using an activity schedule to smooth school transitions. *Journal of Positive Behavior Interventions, 3*(1), 57–61.

Ferguson, A., Ashbaugh, R., O'Reilly, S., & McLaughlin, T. F. (2004). Using prompt training and reinforcement to reduce transition times in a transitional kindergarten program for students with severe behavior disorders. *Child and Family Behavior Therapy, 26*(1), 17–24.

Flannery, K. B., & Horner, R. H. (1994). The relationship between predictability and problem behavior for students with severe disabilities. *Journal of Behavioral Education, 4*(2), 157–176.

Flannery, K. B., O'Neill, R. E., & Horner, R. H., et al. (1995). Including predictability in functional assessment and individual program development. *Education and Treatment of Children, 18*(4), 499–509.

Heyne, D., King, N. J., Tonge, B. J., Rollings, S., Young, D., Pritchard, M., et al. (2002). Evaluation of child therapy and caregiver training in the treatment of school refusal. *Journal of the American Academy of Child and Adolescent Psychiatry, 41*(6), 687–695.

Kern, L., & Vorndran, C. M. (2000). Functional assessment and intervention for transition difficulties. *Journal of the Association for Persons With Severe Handicaps, 25*(4), 212–216.

King, N. J., Tonge, B. J., Heyne, D., Pritchard, M., Rollings, S., Young. D., et al. (1998). Cogitive-behavioral treatment of school-refusing children: A controlled evaluation. *Journal of the American Academy of Child and Adolescent Psychiatry, 37*(4), 395–403.

Lopata, C., Thomeer, M. L., Volker, M. A., & Nida, R. E. (2006). Effectiveness of cognitive-behavioral treatment on the social behaviors of children with Asperger disorder. *Focus on Autism and Other Developmental Disabilities, 21*(4), 237–244.

Mace, A. B., Shapiro, E. S., & Mace, F. C. (1998). Effects of warning stimuli for reinforcer withdrawal and task onset on self-injury. *Journal of Applied Behavior Analysis, 31*(4), 679–682.

Masia-Warner, C., Klein, R. G., Dent, H. C., Fisher, P. H., Alvir, J., Albano, A. M., et al. (2005). School-based intervention for adolescents with social anxiety disorder: Results of a controlled study. *Journal of Abnormal Child Psychology, 33*(6), 707–722.

Nevin, J. A. (1996). The momentum of compliance. *Journal of Applied Behavior Analysis, 29*(4), 535–547.

Newcomer, L. L., & Lewis, T. J. (2004). Functional behavioral assessment: An investigation of assessment reliability and effectiveness of function-based interventions. *Journal of Emotional and Behavioral Disorders, 12*(3), 168–181.

Newman, B., Buffington, D. M., O'Grady, M. A., McDonald, M. E., Poulson, C. L., & Hemmes, N. S., et al. (1995). Self-management of schedule following in three teenagers with autism. *Behavioral Disorders, 20*(3), 190–196.

Olive, M. L. (2004). Assessment and intervention for young children with nonphysiological feeding concerns. *Young Exceptional Children, 7*, 10–19.

Reinecke, D. R., Newman, B., & Meinberg, D. L. (1999). Self-management of sharing in three pre-schoolers with autism. *Education and Training in Mental Retardation and Developmental Disabilities, 34*(3), 312–317.

Repp, A. C., & Karsh, K. G. (1994). Hypothesis-based interventions for tantrum behaviors of persons with developmental disabilities in school settings. *Journal of Applied Behavior Analysis, 27*(1), 21–31.

Reynolds, C. R., & Fletcher-Janzen, E. (Eds.). (2007). *Encyclopedia of special education: A reference for the education of children, adolescents, and adults with disabilities and other exceptional individuals* (3rd ed., Vol. 1). New York: John Wiley & Sons.

Reynolds, C. R., & Kamphaus, R. W. (2004). *Behavior Assessment System for Children* (2nd ed.). Circle Pines, MN: AGS Publishing.

Reynolds, C. R., & Livingston, R. A. (in press). *Children's measure of obsessive compulsive symptoms*. Los Angeles: Western Psychological Services.

Sainato, D. M., Strain, P. S., Lefebvre, D., & Rapp, N. (1987). Facilitating transition times with handicapped preschool children: A comparison between peer-mediated and antecedent prompt procedures. *Journal of Applied Behavior Analysis, 20*(3), 285–291.

Sawyer, L. M., Luiselli, J. K., Ricciardi, J. N., & Gower, J. L. (2005). Teaching a child with autism to share among peers in an integrated preschool classroom: Acquisition, maintenance, and social validation. *Education and Treatment of Children, 28*(1), 1–10.

Schmit, J., Alper, S., Raschke, D., & Ryndak, D., et al. (2000). Effects of using a photographic cueing package during routine school transitions with a child who has autism. *Mental Retardation, 38*(2), 131–137.

Schreibman, L., Whalen, C., & Stahmer, A. C. (2000). The use of video priming to reduce disruptive transition behavior in children with autism. *Journal of Positive Behavior Interventions, 2*(1), 3–11.

Shortt, A. L., Barrett, P. M., & Fox, T. L. (2001). Evaluating the FRIENDS program: A cognitive–behavioral group treatment for anxious children and their parents. *Journal of Clinical Child Psychology, 30*(4), 525–535.

Singer, G. H. S., Singer, J., & Horner, R. H. (1987). Using pretask requests to increase the probability of compliance for students with severe disabilities. *Journal of the Association for Persons With Severe Handicaps, 12*(4), 287–291.

Sterling-Turner, H. E., & Jordan, S. S. (2007). Interventions addressing transition difficulties for individuals with autism. *Psychology in the Schools, 44*(7), 681–690.

Stormont, M. A., Smith, S. C., & Lewis, T. J. (2007). Teacher implementation of precorrection and praise statements in Head Start classrooms as a component of a program-wide system of positive behavior support. *Journal of Behavior Education, 16*, 280–290.

VanDerHeyden, A. M., Witt, J. C., & Gatti, S., et al. (2001). Research into practice: Descriptive assessment method to reduce overall disruptive behavior in a preschool classroom. *School Psychology Review, 30*(4), 548–567.

Zarcone, J. R., Iwata, B. A., Mazaleski, J. L., & Smith, R. G. (1994). Momentum and extinction effects on self-injurious escape behavior and noncompliance. *Journal of Applied Behavior Analysis, 27*(4), 649–658.

Chapter 11

Interventions to Enhance Functional Communication

This chapter focuses on interventions for children, adolescents, and young adults with challenges in functional communication. It is divided into three sections. The first section discusses the characteristics and conditions for the behaviors commonly presented by children experiencing functional communication issues. This section offers a brief description of the construct of functional communication and also includes sample items from the BASC–2 Functional Communication scale. In the second section, the theoretical framework used to approach problem behaviors associated with functional communication is described, providing contexts for the selection of interventions. This third section describes interventions that have evidence or show promise for enhancing functional communication in school settings. Each presentation provides an overview of the intervention method and is divided into three subsections: Implementation, Evidence for Use, and Considerations.

Characteristics and Conditions of Functional Communication Deficits

Students with severe disabilities often experience deficits in communication that interfere with independence and functioning. Communication in social environments is an essential skill for students: "Functional communication skills are communication forms that work to inform listeners of students' needs, wants, interests, and feelings" (Kaiser, 2000, p. 453). Put another way, functional communication refers to skills and behaviors that enable a successful interaction between a person delivering a message and those persons who are receiving it (Charlop & Trasowech, 1991; Kaiser, 2000).

On the BASC–2 rating scales, functional communication measures a child's "ability to express ideas and communicate in ways that others can easily understand" (Reynolds & Kamphaus, 2004, p. 64). The Functional Communication scale of the BASC–2 is one of the six adaptive scales that measure positive behaviors, in which low scores (standard scores of 40 or lower) indicate possible problem areas. Sample items on this scale include: "Responds appropriately when asked a question," "Communicates clearly," and "Is clear when telling about personal experiences."

Theoretical Framework for Approaching Functional Communication Problems

The theoretical framework emphasizes social interaction theory and includes both behavioral and functional components. Each intervention is influenced by the individual needs of the child. For example, whereas some students have little or no spontaneous speech, others need assistance only in conversational speech and social interactions.

Typically, functional communication research examines the effects of interventions for children who are diagnosed with pervasive developmental disorders (e.g., autism, Asperger's disorder) and intellectual disabilities. A common characteristic of children with these problems is limited or severely limited speech-language ability that causes social or communication problems. The interventions presented in this chapter are typically designed for children with these types of speech-language issues. However, with respect to the BASC–2 teacher and parent rating scales, the Functional Communication scale provides a more general view of one's ability to effectively communicate with others. As such, a child who receives a score in the At-Risk or Clinically Significant range may have adequate speech but have difficulty being understood by those who interact with him or her. Interventions discussed in this chapter cover a range of functional and social communication skills but are less appropriate for children with adequate speech skills. For these children, the video modeling intervention strategy will be most applicable.

Interventions

The interventions included in this chapter should be carried out by all key stakeholders (e.g., parents, teachers, siblings) in all of the child's relevant environments (e.g., home, school, daycare, church), and not just in conjunction with clinical practitioners. The success of skill acquisition dramatically improves when all adults can be "teachers" and are trained to use the communication methods being taught to the student.

As mentioned earlier, the selected interventions should be applied to meet the specific behavioral or functional needs of the child. This chapter describes five interventions that have demonstrated effectiveness for enhancing functional communication in children:

I. Functional Communication Training

II. Picture Exchange Communication System

III. Video Modeling

IV. Milieu Language Teaching

V. Pivotal Response Training

I. Functional Communication Training

Functional communication training (FCT) is the process of teaching a student to communicate effectively (i.e., without the use of aberrant behavior) to satisfy his or her needs and wants. It can be applied in social situations or in any routine that requires good communication. FCT is used to determine the function of aberrant behavior and then to teach a communicative replacement behavior with an equivalent functional response (Mancil, 2006).

For example, Gary, an 11-year-old student with autism, shrieks loudly and points at the computer when he wants to play a game. When Gary wants to play a game, he can be taught to say, "Game, please," or to give a picture of the computer to his teacher, in order to be given contingent access to the game.

Implementation

The goal of functional communication training is not only to increase functional communication but also to decrease aberrant behavior. The two basic elements of FCT are:

1. Completing a functional analysis of behavior

2. Teaching functionally equivalent replacement behavior(s)

By using replacement behaviors, the child learns that the aberrant behavior will no longer be effective and that appropriate communication will be successful. The replacement behaviors in this case are communication skills that may be verbal or nonverbal. For example, some students can learn to verbalize questions or preferences while others might learn to use gestures (e.g., pointing, signing). Other communication options include assistive technology and picture card systems (discussed later in this chapter).

The six procedural steps that incorporate the basic elements of FCT (see Figure 11.1) are described in detail for successful application of this method (Brady & Halle, 1997; Lalli, Casey, & Kates, 1995). A functional analysis of behavior is critical for identifying replacement behaviors.

For example, Kay, an 8-year-old student, frequently has trouble during lunchtime. She often throws food and cries, and it's hard for the other students or lunchroom attendants to know how to help her. Her counselor, after talking with her parents and lunchroom staff, suspects that Kay's outbursts are expressions of frustration about her food choices. Instead of asking, she throws her chocolate milk because she wants plain milk. He tests this hypothesis by giving Kay plain milk instead of chocolate milk and observing her response. The counselor chooses a communicative replacement for the aberrant behavior of throwing and crying. Although the cafeteria staff does not use American Sign Language and Kay is still learning to sign, the staff is taught to recognize the letter "C" for chocolate milk and "P" for plain milk. Kay's teacher also provides her with training to wait for attention and hold her place in line until she receives the milk she wants. Both Kay and the cafeteria staff practice before the lunch rush. The lunchroom staff can encourage Kay by providing her milk choice immediately and also by praising her for using her signs.

Figure 11.1 Procedural steps for using functional communication training

1. Complete a functional analysis of the aberrant behavior. Possible causes might include wanting something tangible (e.g., a toy), intangible (e.g., attention), or sensory (e.g., rocking in the teacher's chair, using special school supplies), or might include escaping something unpleasant (e.g., a chore, a social situation, a sensory experience).

   a. Interview the parents, teachers, and other caregivers about the aberrant behavior that is being used for communication.

   b. Observe the student's behavior in all relevant environments.

   c. Form a hypothesis regarding the function of the behavior. Use the interview and observation data to support any hypotheses.

   d. Manipulate or change the consequences of the behavior to validate the hypothesis.

2. Choose a replacement communicative response with the stakeholders. Optimal replacement communication behaviors should be:

   a. Within the student's ability level

   b. Applicable to other situations and in other environments

   c. Clearly resulting in the same outcome as the undesirable behavior

   d. As equal as possible to the degree of effort expended for the undesirable behavior

   e. As efficient as the undesirable behavior

3. Teach the child the replacement response. Either the clinician or teacher can present this new behavior. The replacement behavior is taught by modeling, providing verbal mands, and, when appropriate, including hand-over-hand prompting (i.e., putting the student's hand where it belongs, with your hand on top guiding it).

4. Implement the replacement response. Prompt the new behavior and consistently ignore the aberrant behavior (in order to extinguish it).

5. Reinforce the replacement response. It's important that the communication partner respond immediately. Acknowledge the use of the replacement communicative behavior with praise or other reinforcers, such as smiles or preferred or requested objects.

Evidence for Use

FCT has been found to reduce a number of problem behaviors, including self-injury, aggression, inappropriate verbalizations, tantrums, hand biting, body rocking, slapping, and biting (Carr & Durand, 1985; Durand & Carr, 1992; Lalli et al., 1995; Mancil, Conroy, Nakao, & Alter, 2006; Wacker et al., 1990). It has also been shown to increase preferred communication responses (Durand & Carr, 1992; Mancil et al., 2006).

The following studies summarize some of the key research findings associated with the use of functional communication training in children and adolescents with impeded or delayed communication abilities.

Carr, E. G., & Durand, V. M. (1985). Reducing behavior problems through functional communication training. *Journal of Applied Behavior Analysis, 18*(2), 111–126.

This study consisted of two phases. In the first phase, four developmentally disabled students were taught a set of both easy and hard tasks. As expected, hard tasks resulted in the students engaging in more problem behaviors than when they undertook easy tasks. In the second phase, each student was taught how to ask an adult for praise or assistance when he or she felt the task was becoming too difficult. This action led to a significant decrease in problem behavior, demonstrating that helping students to express their desires verbally can lead to positive outcomes.

Durand, V. M., & Carr, E. G. (1992). An analysis of maintenance following functional communication training. *Journal of Applied Behavior Analysis, 25*(4), 777–794.

Three studies were conducted to evaluate the effectiveness of functional communication training (FCT) in reducing problem behaviors. Specifically, FCT was compared to time-out strategies. Twelve children, who were displaying a number of problem behaviors stemming from a strong need for attention from others, were split into two groups (six children in each: one female, five males) based on chronological age, mental age, and language age. One group was taught how to seek attention using newly learned communication strategies (e.g., asking, "Am I doing good work?"). The second group was taught how to use a time-out strategy. The children's subsequent behavior was recorded during specified intervals. A reduction in the average number of intervals that included problem behaviors was found (about 60% to 5%) even when the experience level (i.e., naïve vs. experienced) of the trainer varied. Children who were taught only the time-out strategy also saw a reduction in the average number of intervals that included problem behaviors (from 49% to 8%), but such effects were not found with less experienced (i.e., naïve) trainers.

Lalli, J. S., Casey, S., & Kates, K. (1995). Reducing escape behavior and increasing task completion with functional communication training, extinction, and response chaining. *Journal of Applied Behavior Analysis, 28*(3), 261–268.

When functional communication is taught as a way to escape an undesired task, it is often effective in reducing problem behaviors. In the case of homework assignments, however, it can negatively impact learning because the student is allowed to miss the assignment. This study addressed this problem by adding response chaining to the functional communication training and extinction. After the three participants learned to verbalize "no" to request a break, they were gradually required to complete more of the task before being allowed to request the break, until eventually the whole task was completed. All three students showed continued low occurrences of problem behaviors and increased compliance in completing the tasks before requesting a break.

Mancil, G. R., Conroy, M. A., Nakao, T., & Alter, P. J. (2006). Functional communication training in the natural environment: A pilot investigation with a young child with autism spectrum disorder. *Education and Treatment of Children, 29*(4), 615–633.

This study observed one 4-year-old boy who was diagnosed with a pervasive developmental disorder and exhibited frequent tantrums. Through a series of trials, clinicians determined that his tantrums were mechanisms used to get a preferred tangible object. Following this discovery, a functional communication training was implemented to teach the child to obtain a desired object through presenting a picture card rather than throwing a tantrum. The child's communication increased and the problem behavior decreased. This behavior was generalized across objects and people, even when the child had to distinguish between picture cards.

Wacker, D. P., Steege, M. W., Northup, J., Sasso, G., Berg, W., Reimers, T., et al. (1990). A component analysis of functional communication training across three topographies of severe behavior problems. *Journal of Applied Behavior Analysis, 23*(4), 417–429.

Three people with mental disabilities, a lack of speech or communicative gestures, and regular inappropriate behavior participated in this study: a 30-year-old woman and two boys (aged 7 and 9 years). Functional behavioral analysis was used to determine the antecedents of the problem behavior, and then the participants were taught a nonverbal response to use to indicate a preferred object, task, or escape. Trials were conducted with and without negative consequences for the inappropriate behavior. Results indicated that only combined treatment with reinforcement of appropriate behavior and consequences for inappropriate behavior was effective in eliminating inappropriate behavior and increasing appropriate behavior.

Considerations

For Teaching

The success of this approach will depend on finding the best possible replacement behavior. Using a child's preferences increases the likelihood of success for FCT. It is also important that the replacement communicative responses are recognizable to individuals besides those who trained the response. For example, Voice Output Communication Aids (VOCAs) can be used as the replacement communicative response, as can picture cards or some gesticulation, as long as these responses are reasonably universal and thus functional in the community beyond the classroom.

As hypotheses are formed, keep in mind that there are some behavioral influences that should not be (or cannot be) manipulated during functional analysis (Durand & Merges, 2001). For instance, if the student cries for attention only when he or she is ill, the illness condition cannot be manipulated to determine if it truly is influencing the student's behavior. In this case, the aberrant behavior should be redirected. For example, self-injury cannot be ignored, but the potential sensory reinforcement could be redirected to another sensory activity (e.g., dragging fingers through rice, wearing wrist bands, stretching yoga bands) while the replacement behavior is being taught and learned.

Two important parts of implementing FCT are to make the challenging behavior as nonfunctional as possible (Durand & Merges, 2001) and to create scenarios for using the replacement behavior. For example, a child who yells out in class may receive attention; ideally a group of classmates could support the use of verbal or other communication and ignore the yelling. It is also possible that attention and/or escape may not be the function of the behavior; instead, it may be sensory or it may be used to receive access to something tangible. It is critical to identify the function of the behavior in any case.

II. Picture Exchange Communication System

The Picture Exchange Communication System (PECS; Bondy & Frost, 1994) can be used to teach communication skills to primarily nonverbal children with developmental delays (Bondy & Frost, 1994). PECS is an alternative communication system that involves exchanging a picture or symbol for a desired event or item (Carr & Felce, 2007; Charlop-Christy, Carpenter, Le, LeBlanc, & Kellet, 2002). Its conceptual simplicity and positive results make it an appealing intervention choice when working with nonverbal children.

For example, Shandalynn, a 6-year-old girl with autism, wants to watch her favorite movie, *Bambi*. She takes her mom's hand, sits in front of the television, and begins to cry when she realizes the movie is not the one she wanted to watch. Using PECS, Shandalynn can get her communication book and select a picture of the specific movie, eventually working up to using a sentence strip with pictures representing, "I want *Bambi*," and showing it to her mother.

Implementation

The goal of PECS is to increase spontaneous functional communication that will foster meaningful interactions between the child, his or her environment, and a communication partner (Bondy & Frost, 1994; Charlop-Christy et al., 2002; Howlin, Gordon, Pasco, Wade, & Charman, 2007; Magiati & Howlin, 2003). The basic elements of PECS are:

1. Creating picture symbols

2. Providing positive reinforcement

3. Backward chaining

Picture symbols can be made from digital photographs or reproduced from commercially distributed computer programs. Images can be compiled into books or placed on flip pages. Sentence strips, or note cards with complete sentences, can be included under the pictures. Positive reinforcement is maintained by granting access to the object or activity involved in the communication, such as food, entertainment, or access to people. Backward chaining consists of identifying first the final outcome and then creating small links to prompt verbal behavior that will result in that final outcome. This process is similar to an if-then statement, starting with the "then" portion and working backward to the "if" portion of the statement. It can be visualized as a reversed, linear pattern in that the step that is closest to the goal is taught first, and steps that precede it are taught next. For example, a child who wants to be picked up by his or her parent learns to first point at the parents, then to say "da," then "daddy." That language evolves into more complex language that involves "daddy" and an activity or time frame.

This intervention requires careful planning and execution. Therefore, the steps for using picture communication to develop and increase functional communication are organized here in two stages: assessment/preparation and implementation. The procedural steps for these stages and their phases are outlined in Figure 11.2.

The first stage, assessment/preparation, begins with assessing a child's preferences. One way to do this is for someone who knows the child to create lists of desired food, entertainment, and activities. Another method involves placing an assortment of things (e.g., food, toys, games, movies) within the child's reach and watching to see which items the child selects first.

After a child's preferences are determined, individuals who will be communication partners must be trained. Several communication partners may be selected from each of the child's environments. At home, different family members or friends can serve as the communication partner. At school, different professionals (e.g., teacher, paraprofessional, principal, custodian) can fill the role.

The implementation stage is broken into six phases (Bondy & Frost, 1994, 2001). The first phase involves teaching a child how to communicate a basic need by exchanging a picture for a desired object. This task can be taught by placing the desired object within the child's view. As the child reaches for the object, the practitioner physically blocks access to the object and places a picture of the object in the child's hand. Next, the practitioner physically guides the child to give the picture to the communication partner. The communication partner accepts the picture, states the name of the picture, and immediately gives the object to the child. For instance, if the child reaches for a yo-yo, the child is instead given a picture of the yo-yo and is then assisted in approaching the communication partner and placing the picture in the communication partner's hand. The communication partner says, "yo-yo," and gives the yo-yo to the child. The child plays with the yo-yo for a few seconds and then the process is repeated. Physical prompts are slowly faded. This phase is continued until the child reaches for the picture and places it in the communication partner's hand without prompting.

The second phase is designed to expand the child's spontaneity when requesting desired objects. This is accomplished by adjusting the distance of the object from the child. The communication partner and the picture of the desired object are moved away from the child, and the communication partner avoids making eye contact with the child. If the child does not initiate eye contact with the communication partner, the practitioner touches the communication partner (modeling) or prompts the child to touch the communication partner to draw attention and initiate eye contact. When the child touches the communication partner, immediate eye contact is made and the communication partner opens his or her hand to receive the picture from the child. This gesture is faded during the intervention. When the child places the picture in the communication partner's hand, the reinforcing object is immediately given to the child. No verbal interactions occur until the picture is placed in the communication partner's hand. At this point, the communication partner might say something like, "You want the yo-yo."

In the third phase, the practitioner teaches the child to discriminate between pictures or symbols. Different pictures are added to the communication board or book in an ongoing manner. First, one preferred and one nonpreferred object (to be used as a distracter) are placed within the child's reach, and two corresponding pictures are presented to the student: a picture of the preferred object used in phases 1 and 2 and a picture of a nonpreferred object. If the child places the picture of the preferred object in the communication partner's hand, the communication partner gives the object to the child, provides reinforcement, and allows the child to play with the object for a few seconds. If the child gives the picture of the nonpreferred object to the communication partner, the communication partner gives the child the nonpreferred object. When the child indicates that the wrong object was selected, the practitioner completes an error correction sequence by modeling the selection of the appropriate picture to receive the preferred object. Next, the child is prompted to select the correct picture and is praised when the correct selection is made; however, the object is not given to the child. The practitioner removes the picture of the nonpreferred object and repeats the process, this time allowing the student to receive the object. Next, the practitioner replaces both pictures and repeats the process. Once this skill is mastered, the communication partner replaces handing the child the object with the words "take it." If the child chooses the picture of the nonpreferred object but reaches for the preferred object, the practitioner blocks the preferred object from the child's reach and repeats the error correction sequence. When the child masters the skill of selecting the picture of the preferred object, more items are added to the communication book or board and the process is repeated.

In the fourth phase, the practitioner begins to teach the child to differentiate between requesting and commenting phrases. First, a sentence strip is added to the communication board or book with icons representing the words "I want." Next, the practitioner models placing the picture of the preferred object on the communication board or book and receiving the desired object. For instance, if the child's preferred item is a pretzel, the practitioner places a picture of a pretzel next to "I want" and eats the pretzel. The picture is then removed, and when the child places the picture next to icons representing the words "I want," the child is given the desired object and the practitioner says, "I want a pretzel."

The delineation between phrase types continues in the fifth phase, as the child is taught to answer the question "What do you want?" First, the practitioner says, "What do you want?" while placing the "I want" sentence strip on the communication book or board. The child receives the desired object after placing the picture on the communication book or board. Gradually, after asking the question, the practitioner delays placing the sentence strip on the board until enough time has passed for the child to place the sentence strip on the board without prompting.

In the sixth phase, the child is taught how to comment. A new sentence strip is introduced that includes icons representing comment phrases such as "I hear" or "I see." Interesting items are arranged for the child to hear or see. The practitioner asks the child, "What do you see?" while pointing to the symbol representation of "I see." The practitioner then provides a social response, such as "I see a horse, too!" More commenting phrases are added, such as "I hear" in response to "What do you hear?" or "I have," in response to "What do you have?" Gradually, the practitioner fades the use of the question and waits for the child to request or comment by independently approaching multiple communication partners in multiple environments without prompting (Carr & Felce, 2007).

Figure 11.2 Procedural steps for using the Picture Exchange Communication System

Stage 1: Assessing Preferences, Preparing Materials, and Training

1. Assessing the Child's Preference for Objects and/or Activities

    a. Interview the key stakeholders to compile a list of the child's preferred objects. Be sure to include activities the child especially enjoys, as these activities may not be observed directly.

    b. Place the objects within the child's reach (e.g., food items, toys, movies).

    c. Monitor and document the child's most frequently chosen object(s).

    d. Make a list of the objects from most preferred to least preferred.

2. Preparing the Materials

    a. Select picture icons (or symbols) for the student's preferred objects. It can be helpful to mount the pictures on card stock and place reusable adhesive strips on the back of each one.

    b. Create a communication board or book. Depending on the child's physical ability or developmental level, choose either a laminated piece of cardboard on which the student can place his or her picture cards, or create flip pages or a portable flip-type book. Place the reusable adhesive strips on the board or in the book, making it the place to keep all the cards a child may want to use.

    c. Create sentence strips with picture representations of phrases (i.e., a two-picture sentence), such as "I want," "I see," "I have," or "I hear." Eventually, these can be added to enhance communication and help further develop word and object recognition in a variety of settings (e.g., classroom, home, grocery store, park).

3. Training the Communication Partners

    a. Compile a list of communication settings (e.g., classroom, home, cafeteria, playground, bus, grocery store, park). Be creative and consider the widest range of relevant environments.

    b. Identify communication partners for the child (e.g., parents, other family members, other caregivers, teachers, principals). Choosing a variety of communication partners among a number of environments will help the student begin to apply new skills to different situations.

    c. Teach each communication partner how to respond to requests and comments made by the child using the communication board or book.

Continued on next page

Stage 2: Implementation

Phase 1: Communicating a Basic Need or Want

1. Choose a preferred object and place it within the child's view. The communication partner should be present when this happens.

2. Block the child if he or she reaches for the object and physically guide the child to pick up the picture of the object (i.e., the picture card) instead. If the child doesn't reach for the object, place the picture card in his or her hand.

3. Physically guide the child's hand with the picture card to the hand of the communication partner.

4. Direct the communication partner to accept the picture card, state the object's name, and give it to the child.

5. Allow the child to engage with the object for a few seconds.

6. Repeat the steps as needed for additional objects. Continue the process with multiple communication partners in various settings, until the child reaches for the card and places it in the communication partner's hand without prompting.

Phase 2: Increasing Spontaneity of Communication

1. Move the picture card of a preferred object (or the entire communication book/board) and the communication partner away from the student.

2. Place the preferred object within the child's reach.

3. Model how to approach the communication partner with the picture card in hand and how to gain the attention of the communication partner with a gentle touch.

4. Prompt the child to pick up the picture card. If he or she does not initiate eye contact with the communication partner, model touching the communication partner or prompt the child to touch him or her. The communication partner should not make eye contact until it is initiated by the child.

5. When the child touches the communication partner, immediate eye contact is made and the communication partner opens his or her hand to receive the picture card from the child. If necessary, guide the child to place the picture card in the communication partner's hand.

6. Direct the communication partner to say, "You want the (name of the desired object)."

7. Direct the communication partner to give the object to the child.

8. Allow the child to engage with the desired object for a few seconds.

9. Repeat the steps until the child can successfully communicate without prompting.

10. Repeat the steps with multiple communication partners in multiple settings.

Continued on next page

Phase 3: Discriminating Among Pictures or Symbols

1. Add a picture card of a nonpreferred object to the communication book/board.

2. Place a preferred and a nonpreferred object picture card within the child's reach.

3. Wait for the child to select a picture card and place it in the communication partner's hand.

4. Give the child the object represented by the selected picture card, and allow the child to engage with it for a few seconds.

5. If the child selects the nonpreferred object and shows displeasure, follow these steps for error correction:

   a. Model choosing the correct picture card to receive the preferred object.

   b. Prompt the child to select the correct picture card.

   c. Provide social reinforcement through verbal praise or gesture (e.g., "good job," thumbs up).

   d. Repeat the steps of phase 1 for selecting one picture card and the corresponding object.

   e. Allow the child to engage with the object for several seconds.

6. Once the child has mastered selecting the picture card of the preferred object, repeat the process but substitute handing the object to the child with saying, "Take it."

7. If the child takes the preferred object, then he or she is discriminating between the images. If the child chooses the picture of the nonpreferred object but reaches for the preferred object, block the preferred object from the child's reach. Use the error correction process in step 5 as needed; however, do not give the object to the child. Remove the picture of the nonpreferred object and repeat the steps, this time allowing the student to receive the object. Then replace both pictures and repeat the steps again.

8. Gradually add more picture cards to the communication book/board, repeating these steps with multiple communication partners in multiple settings.

Phase 4: Using Phrases

1. Add a two-picture sentence card (often called a "sentence strip") representing the words "I want" to the communication book/board.

2. Model placing a picture card of the preferred object (or activity) after "I want" and receiving the object.

Continued on next page

3. When the child places a picture card of a desired object after the picture representations of "I want," direct the communication partner to say, "I want (name of the desired object)."

4. Direct the communication partner to give the desired object to the child.

5. Allow the child to engage with the object.

6. Repeat these steps with multiple desired objects and communication partners in different settings.

Phase 5: Answering a Direct Question

1. Ask the child, "What do you want?"

2. Place a sentence strip for the words "I want" on the communication book/board.

3. When the child places the picture card of a desired object (or activity) in the sentence, allow the child to have it.

4. Gradually delay placing the sentence strip on the communication book/board after asking the question until the child begins to independently place the strip and picture card of the desired item/activity on the communication book/board, making a statement about his or her preference in response to a question.

Phase 6: Commenting Words

1. Place a new sentence strip representing commenting words on the communication book/board (e.g., "I see," "I hear," "I have").

2. Place pictures cards of interesting objects that can be seen or heard in that setting, or choose a picture of something the child is holding.

3. Ask the corresponding question, "What do you see?" (or "What do you hear?" or "What do you have?") and point to the appropriate sentence strip.

4. Model placing the corresponding picture card after the sentence strip and saying the complete phrase or sentence. For example, place a picture card of a dog and say, "I hear a dog."

5. Ask the question again, point to the sentence strip, and wait for the child to place a picture card to complete the sentence.

6. Provide social praise with comments such as, "I hear a dog, too!"

7. Increase the amount of time between asking the question and placing the sentence strip on the communication book/board until the child does it independently.

Evidence for Use

PECS has been used with children who have developmental disabilities and has been found to increase the frequency of child-to-adult communication initiations, linguistic communication, spontaneous speech, and social communication, as well as to decrease problem behaviors (Carr & Felce, 2007; Charlop-Christy et al., 2002).

The following studies summarize some of the key research findings associated with the use of PECS training in children and adolescents with impeded or delayed communication abilities.

Bock, S. J., Stoner, J. B., Beck, A. R., Hanley, L., & Prochnow, J. (2005). Increasing functional communication in non-speaking preschool children: Comparison of PECS and VOCA. *Education and Training in Developmental Disabilities, 40*(3), 264–278.

This study compared two methods of augmentative and alternative communication (AAC): the Picture Exchange Communication System (PECS) and Voice Output Communication Aids (VOCAs). Six 4-year-old boys who did not speak and who had been diagnosed with developmental delays were chosen to go through both rounds of interventions simultaneously. The PECS involved choosing a picture to communicate a desire for an object; VOCA involved pressing a button near a picture that would activate a recorded word, which would communicate their desire for an object. Both were fairly effective in helping these nonverbal children to communicate their desires, and the children were able to generalize these behaviors to the classroom after interventions. Some children had a stronger preference for either PECS or VOCA, showing that deciding on an intervention tool depends on the individual.

Bondy, A., & Frost, L. (1994). The Picture Exchange Communication System. *Focus on Autistic Behavior, 9*(3), 1–19.

This article explains how the Picture Exchange Communication System (PECS) works, including the rationale behind the processes of each phase. In general, a trainer who uses PECS determines what a child consistently wants through observation. Then the trainer will introduce a small picture of the object the child most consistently wants and help the child understand that by giving the trainer the picture, the child will receive the desired object. As the training progresses, the child is required to distinguish between pictures, be more intentional in seeking out the trainer, make full picture sentences, and eventually use speech. This process has been shown to be very effective with young children. In the Delaware Autistic Program, where PECS is used, 80% of students develop effective communication through speech, vs. 50% nationwide.

Carr, D., & Felce, J. (2007). The effects of PECS teaching to phase III on the communicative interactions between children with autism and their teachers. *Journal of Autism and Developmental Disorders, 37*(4), 724–737.

This study compared 17 children diagnosed with autism, aged 3 to 7 years, who participated in 15 hours of Picture Exchange Communication System (PECS) instruction through Phase III with a control group who did not. Both groups were made up of students from multiple classrooms (9 for the intervention group, 11 for the control group). It was confirmed that use of the PECS teaching significantly increased the number of times children initiated communication with an adult as well as responded to an adult's initiation. The control group did not show these same improvements.

Charlop-Christy, M. H., Carpenter, M., Le, L., LeBlanc, L. A., & Kellet, K. (2002). Using the Picture Exchange Communication System (PECS) with children with autism: Assessment of PECS acquisition, speech, social-communicative behavior, and problem behavior. *Journal of Applied Behavior Analysis, 35*(3), 213–231.

This study observed three boys with autism who rarely communicated verbally in both academic and play settings. The three areas primarily observed were vocal communication, social-communicative behaviors, and problem behaviors. These areas were observed during a baseline study, while the children were being taught the Picture Exchange Communication System (PECS), and during post-study. All three boys learned the PECS system quickly and also were able to generalize these new communication skills to incorporating speech. In addition, social-communicative skills (e.g., eye contact, attention, playing together) increased throughout the course of this study, and problem behaviors (e.g., tantrums, grabbing, out-of-seat behaviors) decreased. The marked increase in verbal communication in all three boys is further evidence of the effectiveness of the PECS.

Ganz, J. B., & Simpson, R. L. (2004). Effects on communicative requesting and speech development of the Picture Exchange Communication System in children with characteristics of autism. *Journal of Autism and Developmental Disorders, 34*(4), 395–409.

This study examined three children with autism who were trained in the Picture Exchange Communication System (PECS) in order to see if this system increased their use of spoken language. All three participants mastered the PECS system and increased the number of intelligible words spoken per session. They also showed an increase in the complexity of their sentences. All three started with only one-word verbalizations (if any at all) and by the end were saying three- or four-word phrases. Contrary to expectations, there was no decrease in nonword verbalizations.

Howlin, P., Gordon, R. K., Pasco, G., Wade, A., & Charman, T. (2007). The effectiveness of Picture Exchange Communication System (PECS) training for teachers of children with autism: A pragmatic, group randomised controlled trial. *Journal of Child Psychology and Psychiatry, 48*(5), 473–481.

This study—one of the few randomized controlled trials to look at the effectiveness of the Picture Exchange Communication System (PECS)—examined 17 classrooms of children aged 4 to 11 years, each of which contained at least three children with autism or autism spectrum disorders. These classrooms were randomly divided into three groups: immediate treatment, delayed treatment, and no treatment. Children in the treatment classroooms attended a two-day PECS training session and had consultants come to the classroom to follow up. Children in the treatment groups showed an increase in communication initiations and in PECS use compared to the control group, although a 10-month follow-up study with the first group showed that the results were not maintained. More research is needed to determine how maintenance might be improved and whether the ages of children affected the results.

Magiati, I., & Howlin, P. (2003). A pilot evaluation study of the Picture Exchange Communication System (PECS) for children with autistic spectrum disorders. *Autism, 7*(3), 297–320.

This pilot study examined the effects of PECS training on 34 children aged 5 to 12 years from multiple schools across the U.K. Although initial language skills varied among the children, none were fluent communicators at the beginning and all showed significant improvements in their communication, particularly in their use of PECS. Interestingly, those with the lower initial communication levels gained the most (and the most consistently), while those who began with higher communication levels had a quick gain at the beginning but then tended to plateau. Weaknesses of this study were the lack of a control group and a reliance on teacher and parent ratings without outside evaluation. However, the study still seemed to show clear improvement in communication due to PECS training.

Schwartz, I. S., Garfinkle, A. N., & Bauer, J. (1998). The Picture Exchange Communication System: Communicative outcomes for young children with disabilities. *Topics in Early Childhood Special Education, 18*(3), 144–159.

This study examined 31 children from a special education preschool. Some of the children had been diagnosed with autism; others had Down syndrome, severe mental retardation, or other diagnoses. All children began the study as nontalkers. In the classroom, the children were trained in the Picture Exchange Communication System (PECS), including creating sentences and generalizing to peers as well as adults. All of the students successfully completed the PECS training, requiring an average of 14 months. In a second experiment, 18 of these 31 children were observed to see if their verbal communication skills were affected by the PECS training. Of the 18, 44% gained spontaneous speech to the point that they ceased to use the PECS system. The other 56% gained very little, if any, speech, but they continued to use the PECS system effectively.

Yoder, P., & Stone, W. L. (2006). Randomized comparison of two communication interventions for preschoolers with autism spectrum disorders. *Journal of Consulting and Clinical Psychology, 74*(3), 426–435.

This study examined 36 preschoolers with autism spectrum disorders randomly assigned to two treatment groups: either responsive education and prelinguistic milieu teaching (RPMT) or the Picture Exchange Communication System (PECS). The children attended three 20-minute training sessions per week for 6 months and were studied for the effect of these training sessions on requesting, turn taking, and initiating joint attention. It was found that RPMT was significantly more effective in increasing turn taking and initiating joint attention for children who already exhibited some initiating of joint attention before beginning training. The PECS, on the other hand, was more effective in increasing spontaneous requesting in children with very little communication before beginning training.

Considerations

For Teaching

PECS is heavily classroom based, as the functional nature of communication and access to people and things are emphasized in the teaching. School psychologists, counselors, and/or speech-language pathologists are encouraged to train and assist teachers in using PECS procedures, developing places for practicing generalization, and creating materials. Some suggest that modifications to the classroom and teacher training are needed (Howlin et al., 2007); teacher assistance teams can provide this type of support.

PECS, like all communication systems or strategies, is most effective when used across settings, such as home or nonschool environments. Language differences would imply that families would need to be involved in either dual-language applications for sentence strips or in developing pictures that reflect activities that are important to the family and the family's culture.

III. Video Modeling

Video modeling is the use of video technology to help students see the accurate performance of a target behavior (Charlop-Christy, Le, & Freeman, 2000). Video modeling is founded on the observational learning principles of Bandura (1977), who said that observational learning "refers to cognitive and behavioral change that results from observation of others engaged in similar actions" (p. 39). For this discussion, the targeted or observed behaviors are functional communication skills.

For example, Ivan, a 14-year-old student with autism spectrum disorder (ASD), constantly attempts to talk to his peers about a black hole in outer space that can be utilized to create energy for earth. His peers typically are not interested and walk away. However, Ivan does not notice and continues to engage in this topic of discussion. Using video modeling, the practitioner can help Ivan identify external cues that signal how well a message is being received by others.

Implementation

The goal of video modeling with functional communication is to increase sustained functional and social communication with peers and other communication partners (Apple, Billingsley, & Schwartz, 2005; Bellini & Akullian, 2007). Video modeling has two basic elements: observation and imitation of functional communication skills. These two elements are incorporated into the three stages for implementation: (a) planning, video preparation, and production; (b) video observation; and (c) generalization. Following are illustrative examples of key components of these stages, and Figure 11.3 provides the procedural steps needed to implement video modeling to enhance functional communication.

Determining the Communicative Needs of the Child

Beth, a 5-year-old child with autism, sits in front of the toy shelf and makes different sounds for each of her favorite toys when she wants to play with them. Beth's mother understands what each sound means, but other caregivers might not. From talking with her mother and through other assessments, the practitioner believes that communicative behaviors that model requesting items would be good content for Beth's video.

In another instance, Andre, a 10-year-old student with autism spectrum disorder, requests items by using two- or three-word phrases, but he pushes other children when he wants to play with them. The practitioner might select communication skills related to initiating play with other students as the video content for Andre.

Similarly, Wayne, a 10-year-old with autism spectrum disorder, can request items he wants to play with by using two- or three-word phrases, but he pushes other children when he wants to play with their toys. The practitioner, Mrs. Hudson, interviews Wayne's teachers and observes his behavior on the playground and in the classroom. She then decides that communication skills related to initiating play with other students would be good content for Wayne's video.

Writing and Recording the Script

Mrs. Hudson plans to use video modeling to teach Wayne how to initiate conversations with peers. The video script begins with either Wayne or Wayne's best friend, Peter, acting as a peer model, approaching a peer playing with a toy car (i.e., Wayne's favorite toy). Reading from the script, Wayne (or Peter) says, "Cool car," and the peer responds with, "Thanks. Do you want to play together with it?" Both boys then play with the car, passing it back and forth. In some instances, the practitioner narrates the appropriate use of the communication skill, for example, saying, "Wayne (Peter) likes the toy car, so he says that it is cool." Next, the practitioner records the video segment(s). After videotaping, the practitioner edits the tape, removing nontargeted or inappropriate behaviors and adult prompts that are not included in the script, leaving only the correct models of the functional communication skills being presented. Each video segment typically lasts from 1 to 4 minutes.

Watching the Video

When Wayne watches the video, Mrs. Hudson reminds him to sit and watch quietly. (If needed, the practitioner can model the correct way to pay attention to the video, and the child can practice this behavior prior to viewing.) Mrs. Hudson sits next to Wayne during the video and prompts Wayne along the way, saying things like, "See what a good time you (they) are having." Mrs. Hudson and Wayne watch the video a second time and then role-play the communication skills learned in the video to reinforce the newly acquired behaviors.

Generalizing the Learned Behavior

To reinforce the application of the newly learned behavior in common settings, Mrs. Hudson asks Peter to show Wayne a toy car in the classroom and on the playground. Peter responds to Wayne's communication attempt, "Cool car," with, "Thanks. Do you want to play together?" Later, another friend with the same toy car approaches Wayne and follows the same steps. The teacher shows Wayne other preferred toys and responds to Wayne when he says, "Cool (name of toy)." Slowly, peers and adults fade the prompt. (Optionally, the practitioner can include a self-management phase in which the student self-monitors and self-reinforces the use of the communication skill.)

Figure 11.3 Procedural steps for using video modeling

Stage 1: Planning, Video Preparation, and Production

1. Decide the most appropriate video models (e.g., the child, a preferred peer, familiar adults and peers).

2. Select the individual video models if someone other than the child will be included.

3. Determine the content of the video. This content should include specific communicative needs of the student discovered in prior assessments (e.g., making a request, initiating a conversation).

4. Find a natural setting (e.g., classroom, hallway, home, cafeteria) for the video. Multiple natural settings can be used and may be helpful.

5. Determine how many segments or scenarios to include.

6. Use a preference assessment, observation, and interviews with others (e.g., parents, teachers) to select child-preferred activities or objects.

Continued on next page

---

7. Write a script for each video segment. The scripts should be brief, typically between 1 and 4 minutes long.

8. Record the models performing the targeted communication behavior.

9. Edit the video to include only competent performance of the targeted skill and remove any adult prompts or questions that are not part of the script.

Stage 2: Video Observation

1. Tell and model for the child appropriate video-watching behavior (i.e., ask the child to sit and watch quietly).

2. Sit beside the child and prompt him or her to maintain attention (e.g., say, "Good watching.").

3. Play the video for the child on two separate occasions.

4. If the child does not master the content after two separate viewings, repeat the video-watching session. If the child does not begin to use the learned communication skill, the video-watching session can be repeated.

5. Role-play the video content with the child.

Stage 3: Generalization

1. Train peers and/or significant adults (e.g., parents, teachers, siblings, caregivers) to prompt the child to use the skill modeled in the video, in different environments (e.g., classroom, playground, home).

2. Guide the significant adults to fade prompts and allow the child to use the skill in common instances.

3. Optional: Include a self-management phase.

   a. Contract with the child to perform the skill with reinforcement (activity or tangible).

   b. Create a self-management data collection instrument with the child.

   c. Model the use of the self-management instrument.

   d. Practice the use of the self-management instrument with the child.

   e. Ask the child to self-monitor use of the communication skill, and provide reinforcement with a visual schedule, such as a progress chart.

   f. Fade and withdraw tangible or activity reinforcement.

Evidence for Use

Video modeling has been found to increase compliment-giving, requesting, socially initiated play, and conversational skills, and it has been proven more effective than *in vivo* (i.e., live) modeling in students with autism spectrum disorder (Apple et al., 2005; Charlop & Milstein, 1989; Charlop-Christy et al., 2000; Hepting & Goldstein, 1996; Nikopoulos & Keenan, 2003; and Wert & Neisworth, 2003).

The following studies summarize some of the key research findings associated with the use of video modeling in children and adolescents with impeded or delayed communication abilities.

Apple, A. L., Billingsley, F., & Schwartz, I. S. (2005). Effects of video modeling alone and with self-management on compliment-giving behaviors of children with high-functioning ASD. Journal of Positive Behavior Interventions, 7(1), 33–46.

Two experiments were conducted in this study to show the effect of video modeling on how often children with high-functioning autism spectrum disorder (ASD) gave compliments. Two 5-year-old boys were studied in the first experiment, during which they were shown short videos instructing them in giving compliments. They were then monitored during play time to see how many compliments they initiated or gave as a response. One phase included receiving a prize from the teacher if a certain number of compliments were given. During the second experiment, 3 preschoolers were also shown the videos, but this time they monitored their own behavior (with a wrist counter or checklist) in order to receive their prize. In both experiments, compliment-giving increased significantly, but the self-monitoring phase was most effective in helping the children initiate compliments.

Charlop, M. H., & Milstein, J. P. (1989). Teaching autistic children conversational speech using video modeling. Journal of Applied Behavior Analysis, 22(3), 275–285.

Therapists in this study examined the use of video modeling in 3 boys with autism ages 6 to 7. After a baseline study, each of the boys was shown videos of model conversations, where the child and adult would take turns answering a question and asking another. The boys were then asked by the therapists to have the same conversation, mimicking the video clip. Once each boy could do this, he was given prompts to start similar but distinct conversations. After the video modeling and during follow-up studies, each of the 3 boys showed a significant increase in his ability to hold a conversation and to generate novel responses and questions.

Charlop-Christy, M. H., Le, L., & Freeman, K. A. (2000). A comparison of video modeling with *in vivo* modeling for teaching children with autism. *Journal of Autism and Developmental Disorders, 30*(6), 537–552.

This study was undertaken to determine whether video modeling or *in vivo* (i.e., live) modeling was more effective in teaching target behaviors to children with autism. Each of the 5 children used in the study was given one or two target behaviors, and each target behavior had two unique but similar tasks: one that was taught through video modeling and one that was taught through *in vivo* modeling. For all but 1 of the children, video modeling resulted in faster acquisition of the target behaviors. (For the fifth child, acquisition took only two models for either medium.) Most notably, none of the behaviors taught via *in vivo* modeling were generalized, whereas all of the behaviors taught through video modeling were generalized across settings. In addition, it was determined that in all but one case, video modeling was less expensive and less time-consuming than *in vivo* modeling.

Hepting, N. H., & Goldstein, H. (1996). Requesting by preschoolers with developmental disabilities: Videotaped self-modeling and learning of new linguistic structures. Topics in Early Childhood Special Education, 16(3), 407–427.

For this study, 3 preschoolers with developmental disabilities were videotaped saying target-requested phrases unique to each child. Following baseline, the children were individually taken into a separate room and shown their self-modeling video before being returned to the classroom, where each child was given eight opportunities per session to request items. Although each of the children did show an increase in his or her targeted requests over the course of the 4-month study, the request structure was not as quickly generalized to the classroom setting as anticipated. Three branching steps—increased time delay, questions or mands (i.e., requests), and viewing the video in the classroom—were added, with limited success, to help facilitate generalization to the classroom.

Nikopoulos, C. K., & Keenan, M. (2003). Promoting social initiation in children with autism using video modeling. *Behavioral Interventions, 18*(2), 87–108.

Seven children, aged 9 to 15, with severe problems related to autism were used in this study to identify whether video modeling could help them develop appropriate initiation and play skills. After watching a brief video modeling initiation of play with a certain toy and another person, each child was taken to the room shown in the video, where the same toy was present (sometimes by itself, sometimes among others). Each child was then observed to see if he or she would initiate play. For 4 of the 7 children, both initiation and social play were enhanced, and learning was generalized across setting, people, and toys. Three of the 7 children, however, showed no social initiation throughout any of the trials and did not display any play skills. It was suggested that these children may have needed to learn imitation skills and attention skills (for watching the video) before beginning this type of training. Nevertheless, for certain children, video modeling does seem to have beneficial effects.

Wert, B. Y., & Neisworth, J. T. (2003). Effects of video self-modeling on spontaneous requesting in children with autism. *Journal of Positive Behavior Interventions, 5*(1), 30–34.

Four preschoolers with autism were chosen for this study. They had all previously been taught to verbally request items, but they did so at a very low frequency. For this study, each child was individually videotaped in his or her home with preferred play items. The child was prompted to request items so that a significant number of requests showed up in the video for self-modeling. After taping, most adult prompts and all negative child behavior was edited out of the video. Then the video was played in front of the child once a day for 5 days, right before school. Data on the frequency of spontaneous requesting were collected at school. All 4 children had large increases in the frequency of spontaneous requests. Three of the 4 children were studied 2 to 6 weeks later as follow-up, and each of the 3 children maintained high levels of spontaneous requesting.

Considerations

For Teachers

Teaching specific linguistic rules prior to the use of video modeling or embedded within the video model increases the effectiveness of the intervention (Apple et al., 2005; Hepting & Goldstein, 1996). Make videos as realistic as possible by using peers as models or the student as a lead actor when possible, as well as by filming in natural settings such as classrooms. For some students, using adults to model behavior may not be as effective.

For Safety

Talk with the student's family about protecting his or her privacy; everyone should understand that the video content is confidential material. Students and their families must be reassured that use of any video imagery or photos will be strictly controlled to prevent misuse (e.g., by getting posted on social networking websites).

IV. Milieu Language Teaching

Milieu language teaching is a "naturalistic, conversation-based teaching procedure in which the child's interest in the environment is used as a basis for eliciting elaborated child communicative responses" (Kaiser, 1993, p. 77). Milieu teaching is the combination of behavioral principles, incidental teaching, time delay, and the mand-model procedure (Alpert & Kaiser, 1992). Milieu language teaching allows the practitioner to optimize generalization of communicative initiations and responses throughout the day by observing naturally occurring teachable moments in child activity.

This application of the word "milieu" means the physical or social setting where something commonly takes place; therefore, milieu language teaching can include such everyday situations as parents at a park asking a child to name objects and then asking for the child to describe the object by having the child name the color. For example, the parent might ask, "What is this?" while pointing to the slide, and the child would respond, "Slide." The parent would then ask, "What color is the slide?" to further engage the child, and the child would respond, "Red." This exchange could be followed with, "What do we do on a slide?" The child might say, "Go down."

In a classroom setting, a teacher could ask one student, "What is Nancy doing?" while pointing to another student in the room, and the student might say, "Drawing." The teacher might then affirm the response and ask, "What is she drawing a picture of?" The dialog would continue with prompting, pausing, and natural events.

Implementation

The goal of milieu teaching is to increase appropriate spontaneous speech in natural settings. Through the use of spontaneous speech, children have more social interactions and can solicit information, objects, and attention (Charlop & Trasowech, 1991). Milieu teaching includes the following basic elements (elements 3 through 6 are not necessary when using the least obtrusive process):

1. Assessment

2. Environmental arrangement

3. Time-delay procedure

4. Incidental teaching procedure

5. Modeling

6. Mand-model procedure

The procedural steps for using milieu language teaching are outlined further in Figure 11.4. To begin, the practitioner selects an appropriate natural-environment setting based on the child's typical daily routines. Then, as natural opportunities arise, the four components of milieu language teaching (time delay, incidental teaching, modeling, and mand modeling) are used as needed, providing an unconstrained system for learning new communication skills.

Time Delay

Using the time-delay procedure, the target item or activity (e.g., cookie, mom walking into the bedroom in the morning) is presented and the expected response is modeled for the child. The amount of time between the presentation of the target item and a prompt is gradually increased. For instance, Jimmy wants an apple from the refrigerator. When the door is open, he points at the apple. His mother says, "Do you want one green apple?" His mom waits for him to respond with "one green apple" and then gives it to him. Each day, Jimmy's mother increases the time between Jimmy seeing or pointing to the apple and the time that she prompts him to ask for the apple. The response can later be generalized to other environments. Jimmy's mother can integrate a new skill by prompting Jimmy with the question, "Do you want two green apples?" Jimmy's mother intermittently asks Jimmy if he wants one green apple or two green apples, thus associating a new skill (in this case, assigning a quantity of one or two) with an old skill (naming a green apple).

Incidental Teaching

Using incidental teaching, the child is observed in a natural setting for the purpose of finding teachable moments. The four levels identified by Hart & Risley (1974) include: 1) a 30-second delay; 2) a prompt to request an object; 3) a prompt that is a more elaborate request; and 4) a response that is modeled and the child is encouraged to mimic. The practitioner implements the lowest of the four prompt levels necessary to enhance the communicative response of the student. First, the practitioner notes items or activities that the student seems to like. When the student indicates a desire for an item, activity, or to engage with peers, the practitioner first waits 30 seconds for the child to initiate communication without prompting. After 30 seconds, the second step is a verbal prompt provided to request the object (e.g., "Eat?" or "What do you want?"). The third level of prompting is a more elaborate question, such as, "Do you want to eat now?" or "Would you like a green apple to eat?" The final, or fourth prompt, is a phrase to be repeated, such as, "I want apple," or, "I want to eat green apple." This most intensive prompt requires the practitioner to model the correct response, and the child imitates the adult or peer behavior.

Modeling and Mand Modeling

These techniques are similar. Using modeling, the practitioner observes the student showing interest in an item and models the correct communicative response for the item (e.g., "That's a toy car."). Mand modeling, however, involves the practitioner observing the student's natural interest in an item or activity and manding (i.e., requesting) a communicative response from him or her (e.g., "Tell me what you want."). If the child provides the correct response, the child is immediately given the item or activity. If the child provides an incorrect response, the practitioner models the correct response (e.g., "Say 'toy car'.").

Figure 11.4 Procedural steps for using milieu language teaching

1. Assessment

    a. Assess the child's level of spontaneous speech, including interviews with key stakeholders, or review a prior assessment.

    b. Determine the communication skill(s) to be learned.

    c. Observe the child's daily routine and note typical settings and activities.

    d. Select the best setting for milieu language teaching in the child's natural environment.

2. Environmental Arrangement

    a. Include materials that are of interest to the child.

    b. Place interesting objects in view but out of reach so that the child needs help to obtain them.

    c. Offer choices of activities.

    d. Create situations that are unexpected by the child.

3. Implement one of the four components using the listed steps:

    a. Time-Delay Procedure

        i. Notice or present a preferred object or activity (e.g., cookie, mom walking in the bedroom in the morning).

        ii. Model the correct response (e.g., say, "I want the cookie.").

        iii. Maintain a time delay (i.e., wait time) between presenting the target object and modeling the response.

        iv. Provide verbal praise for the child's correct response, and present the object as a reinforcer.

        v. Gradually increase the time delay between the presentation of the stimulus and the prompt.

        vi. Continue increasing the length of the time delay until the child spontaneously initiates communication (with no prompt or modeling).

        vii. Show how the response works in other environments and with other people.

    b. Incidental Teaching

        i. Select activities or objects the child prefers in naturally occurring situations.

Continued on next page

ii. Implement the lowest of the four levels of graduated prompts necessary for student response (Hart & Risley, 1974) as described below.

> **Level 1:** When the child indicates an interest in an activity or object, implement a 30-second prompt.

> **Level 2:** Prompt the child to ask for the object or activity.

> **Level 3:** Approach the child with a question requiring a communicative response (e.g., "What is this?").

> **Level 4:** Model the correct response, prompting the child to imitate it.

c. Modeling

> **i.** Observe the child showing interest in an object or activity.

> **ii.** Model the correct communicative response (e.g., "That's a toy car.").

d. Mand Modeling Procedure

> **i.** Observe the child's interest in an object or activity.

> **ii.** Mand (i.e., request) a communicative response from the child (e.g., "Tell me what you want.").

> **iii.** If a correct response is given, provide the object or activity immediately.

> **iv.** If an incorrect response is given, model a correct response (e.g., "Say, 'toy car'.").

Evidence for Use

Milieu teaching has been found to increase the mean length of utterances, the number of words produced, the generalization of target phrases, target language use, spontaneous communication, positive and balanced communication between siblings, item requesting, and receptive language and expressive communication (Alpert & Kaiser, 1992; Charlop-Christy & Carpenter, 2000; Hancock & Kaiser, 1996; Hancock & Kaiser, 2002; Hemmeter & Kaiser, 1994; Olive et al., 2007; Yoder et al., 1995). In addition, the time-delay procedure used with milieu teaching has been found to increase both spontaneous speech and use of target phrases (Charlop & Trasowech, 1991; Charlop & Walsh, 1986).

The following studies summarize some of the key research findings associated with the use of milieu language teaching in children and adolescents with impeded or delayed communication abilities.

Alpert, C. L., & Kaiser, A. P. (1992). Training parents as milieu language teachers. *Journal of Early Intervention, 16*(1), 31–52.

In this study, trainers taught 6 mothers of young children with language disabilities to use milieu language training with their children. The mothers were instructed in four types of milieu training, one at a time, and were given as many training sessions as needed to master one type of training before moving on to the next. Each mother was observed with her child at home during play sessions, and generalization studies were conducted during household chores and when the television was on. In general, the mothers mastered three of the four types but implemented the incidental teaching procedure (the final type) inconsistently. However, growth was seen in the language of the children, and mothers gave the intervention fairly positive ratings.

Charlop, M. H., & Trasowech, J. E. (1991). Increasing autistic children's daily spontaneous speech. *Journal of Applied Behavior Analysis, 24*(4), 747–761.

The 3 children in this study were taught a series of target greetings and sentences to be used at appropriate times and settings throughout the day through their parents' use of the time-delay method. At first, the parent would instruct the child to say a particular sentence (such as "Good morning, Mom.") in a particular setting (such as in the child's bedroom in the morning). Gradually, the parent would increase the amount of time delay before giving the prompt, allowing the child to speak spontaneously. The children, for the most part, learned spontaneous speech in a few weeks and maintained it over a period of up to 30 months. In general, the target speech was also generalized within settings across locations and persons. In addition, time delay was an easy method for parents to learn and implement in everyday family settings.

Charlop, M. H., & Walsh, M. E. (1986). Increasing autistic children's spontaneous verbalizations of affection: An assessment of time delay and peer modeling procedures. *Journal of Applied Behavior Analysis, 19*(3), 307–314.

Two methods of teaching autistic children to spontaneously say "I like (love) you" were studied in this experiment. First, 2 of the 4 children were taught using a time-delay method across three different settings. The experimenter (or their mother) would say, "Give me a hug," wait 2 seconds, and then say, "I like (love) you." The children were given reinforcements when they responded (or initiated) with the same phrase. Afterward, those 2 children were used as peer models for the other 2 children. However, possibly due to the unstructured setting of these peer models, the other children did not learn from this method. All 4 children were successful in generalizing the spontaneous verbalizations of affection when taught using the time-delay method.

Charlop-Christy, M. H., & Carpenter, M. H. (2000). Modified incidental teaching sessions: A procedure for parents to increase spontaneous speech in their children with autism. *Journal of Positive Behavior Interventions, 2*(2), 98–112.

Experimenters in this study taught parents to use three different methods to teach their autistic children to spontaneously use a specific phrase. Three autistic boys were chosen for this study, which used discrete trial (focusing on mass repetition), incidental teaching (focusing on a natural environment), and the authors' idea of combining these two principles to make modified incidental teaching sessions (MITS). The study found that while 1 of the boys acquired the target phrase during incidental teaching and 2 acquired their phrases during discrete trial, only MITS helped the boys to generalize their learning to other situations. All 3 boys successfully acquired the target phrases and generalized that learning through MITS.

Hancock, T. B., & Kaiser, A. P. (1996). Siblings' use of milieu teaching at home. *Topics in Early Childhood Special Education, 16*(2), 168–190.

The researchers focused this study on the effectiveness of teaching older siblings of children with autism to use milieu teaching during their playtime to help improve the language skills of their younger brothers. Three pairs of siblings were used in this study, and all 3 older siblings learned to use training techniques. Language increases were seen in all 3 target children, and both the language increases and the siblings' teaching patterns were maintained during follow-up. Two of the 3 sibling pairs generalized their behavior from a play setting to a snack setting. Parents reported more positive interactions between the siblings as a result of this intervention.

Hancock, T. B., & Kaiser, A. P. (2002). The effects of trainer-implemented enhanced milieu teaching on the social communication of children with autism. *Topics in Early Childhood Special Education, 22*(1), 39–54.

Unique because of its focus on how language training with children with autism affects their communication with their parents at home, this study used the enhanced milieu teaching (EMT) method in simple 15-minute sessions with 4 young children and gauged progress in the children's language abilities both in the clinic and in their homes. The parents were not aware of the training method, but they were asked to give feedback on their children's improvement over the course of the intervention and during follow-up. All 4 children saw marked increases in their speech—both in mean length of utterance and in diversity of words—between pretreatment and follow-up studies, although there was variance in the extent of improvement, and all of them generalized at least somewhat to the home. All of the parents ranked the intervention very highly.

Hemmeter, M. L., & Kaiser, A. P. (1994). Enhanced milieu teaching: Effects of parent-implemented language intervention. *Journal of Early Intervention, 18*(3), 269–289.

In this study, 4 parents (3 mothers and 1 father) of children with language disabilities were trained to use enhanced milieu teaching with their children. Overall, the parents learned the training method quickly and accurately, and they seemed to enjoy it. Language skills improved for all 4 children, although there was a greater improvement for younger children whose delays were not as significant. Three of the 4 children generalized their newly learned language skills to a new communication partner, and all 4 generalized the skills to the home setting. The parents all rated the intervention highly and were pleased with the results in their children's development.

Olive, M. L., de la Cruz, B., Davis, T. N., Chan, J. M., Lang, R. B., O'Reilly, M. F., et al. (2007). The effects of enhanced milieu training and a voice output communication aid on the requesting of three children with autism. *Journal of Autism and Developmental Disorders, 37*(8), 1505–1513.

This study was the first to combine enhanced milieu training (EMT), which includes natural reinforcers, prompting, and adults following the children's lead, with Voice Output Communication Aids (VOCAs). In an EMT setting, 3 preschool children with autism were taught to use the VOCAs, and 2 of the 3 did not initiate any type of communication (gesturing, vocalizing, etc.). After intervention, all 3 used both VOCAs and gestures independently, and 1 child included vocalizations.

Yoder, P., Kaiser, A. P., Goldstein, H., Alpert, C., Mousetis, L., Kaczmarek, L. et al. (1995). An exploratory comparison of milieu teaching and responsive interaction in classroom applications. *Journal of Early Intervention, 19*(3), 218–242.

In this study, 36 preschoolers from six classrooms across two states were assigned by classroom to either milieu teaching or responsive interaction treatments. Students were matched across treatments according to pretest levels in multiple language areas in order to best compare the two treatments, and individual language goals were set for each student, according to his or her abilities. Both of the treatments were implemented by trained teachers in the classroom. Overall, all students saw improvements in their language, but it was discovered that milieu teaching was more effective for children with language levels of less than 22–26 months who had vocabulary goals, and responsive interaction treatment was more effective for children with higher pretest language levels who had syntactic language goals. Possible reasons for this finding are discussed in the article.

Considerations

For Teaching

Teaching children with speech and language delays involves a curricular focus on adaptive or functional skills that depend on the age of the child. Academic goals and behavioral goals will co-vary and overlap; as verbal skills improve, maladaptive behavior should decrease. Generalization and transfer of skills to other educational and home settings are important considerations that are also based, at least in part, on age and developmental level. Community issues, transportation needs, workplace transitions, and social needs will all vary according to the environmental demands associated with both school and home.

V. Pivotal Response Training

Pivotal response training (PRT) is an intervention that targets specific central response areas in natural environments that, if modified, will generalize to other behaviors and result in widespread behavioral change (Koegel & Koegel, 1995; Koegel, Koegel, Harrower, & Carter, 1999). Examples of central response areas that are often targeted include initiation, motivation, responsiveness to multiple cues, and self-direction (Koegel & Koegel, 1995). Motivation is assessed by observable characteristics, such as responding to the environment or rate of responding. If children are taught pivotal skills, such as initiation or the behaviors that look like motivation, these skill sets will affect a variety of behaviors in a multitude of settings rather than a discrete response to a discrete cue.

For example, Elmer is taught to ask "wh" questions, such as "What is that?" or "Where is X?" These questions are socially appropriate in a variety of settings, provide social interactions, and initiate communication with others. Leon, age 8, is taught to carry a small yo-yo, a pen, and a small notebook in his pocket. When he is bored (self-assessment, self-management), he knows that he can yo-yo if there is room, or he can practice his signature rather than rocking or wandering about the room.

Implementation

The goal of pivotal response training with functional communication problems or strengths is to enhance spontaneous interaction. The basic elements of pivotal response training are:

1. Identifying pivotal responses that will affect multiple conditions and behaviors

2. Teaching these behaviors and reinforcing clear communication

3. Introducing the use of descriptive responses using multiple examples

This approach can be implemented by parents, teachers, caregivers, and other professionals. Peers and/or siblings of typical development can also learn to use PRT. Successful PRT will lead to better communication in environments where multiple variables exist and more specific language is required.

First, the practitioner or communication partner structures the environment to provide an opportunity for the child to respond. For instance, John's favorite toy is a red basketball. John's mother places the ball within eyesight but out of John's reach. Next, the practitioner or communication partner allows the child to select an activity by structuring the environment to prompt a communicative response. The practitioner can turn the child's attention to a task by stating the child's name, touching the child, or making eye contact. The practitioner asks questions only when needed to provide clear and simple instructions for the opportunity to respond. For instance, Joey grabs the bike from his brother when he wants to ride. His brother holds Joey's hands, makes eye contact, and says, "Do you want to ride the bike?"

Next, the practitioner or communication partner allows time for the student to respond, models the targeted behavior, and reinforces each attempt by the child to respond. Then, tasks that have been mastered by the child are combined with new tasks, and the practitioner or communication partner provides reinforcers that are logical and naturally related to the targeted communicative response for all communicative attempts.

The 10 procedural steps to implement pivotal response training presented in Figure 11.5 are derived from the PRT manual developed by Koegel, Schreffirnan, Good, Cerniglia, Murphy, and Koegel (1989).

Figure 11.5 Procedural steps for using pivotal response training

1. Structure the environment to provide an opportunity to respond. For example, place a desired object within the child's sight but out of reach.

2. Allow the child to choose an activity by structuring the environment to prompt communicative responses.

3. Prompt the child to attend to the task (e.g., state the child's name, touch the child, make eye contact).

4. Ask questions, only when needed, to provide clear and simple instructions for the opportunity to respond.

5. Allow time for the child to respond.

6. Model the targeted behavior.

7. Reinforce each attempt by the child to respond.

8. Combine mastered tasks with new tasks.

9. Provide logical and natural reinforcers related to the targeted communicative response for all communicative attempts.

10. Teach peers and/or siblings to use PRT to further help the child interact with others.

Evidence for Use

Pivotal response training has been found to improve adaptive functioning and social interaction, as well as increase acquisition and generalization of student communicative initiations, conversational functional communication, frequency of child verbalization, positive peer interactions, initiated play and interactions, and positive social behavior (Baker-Ericzén, Stahmer, & Burns, 2007; Koegel, Camarata, Koegel, Ben-Tall, & Smith, 1998; Koegel, Carter, & Koegel, 2003; Laski, Charlop, & Schreibman, 1988; Pierce & Schreibman, 1995; Pierce & Schreibman, 1997).

The following studies summarize some of the key research findings associated with the use of pivotal response training in children and adolescents with functional communication problems.

Baker-Ericzén, M. J., Stahmer, A. C., & Burns, A. (2007). Child demographics associated with outcomes in community-based pivotal response training. *Journal of Positive Behavior Interventions, 9*(1), 52–60.

The purpose of this study was to examine the effects of home-based pivotal response training (PRT) in a large-scale, community setting. In one community clinic, 158 families of children with autism disorder or pervasive developmental disorder not otherwise specified (PDDNOS) were chosen. The parents participated in a 12-week parent-education program learning PRT. The *Vineland*™ *Adaptive Behavior Scales* was administered after both the first and last session to assess the students' progress. Significant improvement was seen in all areas for the total sample of children, with little variance in the amount of improvement seen across sex and race/ethnicity (between white and Hispanic families). The study found that this intervention, while somewhat effective for all ages, was most effective for younger children. The older the children were, the more impaired they were at the beginning of the study and the less they improved; these results emphasized the importance of early intervention.

Koegel, L. K., Carter, C. M., & Koegel, R. L. (2003). Teaching children with autism self-initiations as a pivotal response. *Topics in Language Disorders, 23*(2), 134–145.

In this study, 2 children with autism were taught to ask a simple question in order to self-initiate learning of a specific verb tense. For example, 1 child was taught to manipulate a pop-up book page and then ask, "What happened?" When the clinician answered with a simple, regular past-tense verb, such as, "He pinched," the child would repeat it. The children were observed during interventions as well as during generalization periods at the clinic and in their homes. At the end of the study, both children were regularly using the verb forms that had previously been absent from their vocabularies. In addition, their rate of question-asking in general, as well as the number of verbs they used and their mean length of utterance, increased greatly.

Koegel, R. L., Camarata, S., Koegel, L. K., Ben-Tall, A., & Smith, A. E. (1998). Increasing speech intelligibility in children with autism. *Journal of Autism and Developmental Disorders, 28*(3), 241–251.

Five children with autism, aged 3 to 5 years, whose speech was mostly intelligible, were studied during two types of intervention: analog and naturalistic. During analog intervention, clinicians taught the target sounds through rote drills and then incorporated the sounds into words, phrases, and sentences, reinforcing with verbal praise and treats. During naturalistic intervention, the clinicians selected objects for which each particular child had a preference and included the target sounds and natural reinforcement (receipt of the desired object when its name was pronounced). While both showed overall gains in the pronunciation of target sounds during training sessions, only the naturalistic training showed widespread generalization of the target sounds in other settings, such as during playtime and at home. All 5 children learned the sounds taught through naturalistic training, and their overall intelligibility rose throughout the course of the study.

Laski, K. E;, Charlop, M. H., & Schreibman, L. (1988). Training parents to use the natural language paradigm to increase their autistic children's speech. *Journal of Applied Behavior Analysis, 21*(4), 391–400.

In this study, parents of 8 autistic children were trained to use the natural language paradigm (NLP) with their children in order to increase speech. Parents were observed interacting with their children in a clinic setting and at home; results were compared with observations of parents with normally developing children as well as with 3 siblings of the autistic children. All of the parents trained in the NLP showed increases in their own verbalizations, providing more naturally occurring opportunities for their children to use speech. In addition, all of the children showed increases in speech, although the children with the least speech in the beginning showed the most dramatic increases. Improvements were generalized to the home setting.

Pierce, K., & Schreibman, L. (1995). Increasing complex social behaviors in children with autism: Effects of peer-implemented pivotal response training. *Journal of Applied Behavior Analysis, 28*(3), 285–295.

For this study, two 10-year-old boys with autism were paired with 2 peers, who were taught to use pivotal response training (PRT) with their playmates. Each pair was individually brought to a room with toys and was told to play together. The peer used techniques such as initiating, modeling conversations and play, and taking turns in order to engage the playmate. Both target children, during baseline, showed little to no initiation, little maintenance of interaction, and poor attention. Following the training, maintenance levels rose to nearly 100%, and initiation and joint attention rose significantly. Both boys generalized these behaviors across settings and toys, and one of them generalized to a non-PRT-trained peer.

Pierce, K., & Schreibman, L. (1997). Multiple peer use of pivotal response training to increase social behaviors of classmates with autism: Results from trained and untrained peers. *Journal of Applied Behavior Analysis, 30*(1), 157–160.

In this study, the authors examined 10 boys aged 7 to 9 years, including 2 boys with autism. Six of the other children (3 for each autistic child) were taught, one at a time, to use peer pivotal response training (PRT) in a naturalistic training with their autistic peer in order to help him initiate and maintain interactions with other children. Both boys, during baseline, showed few initiations (4% and 7%), but by the post-study they had both increased to 16% and 19%, respectively. Maintaining interactions rose from inconsistent to 100% for both boys, and these interactions were generalized across settings, toys, and people, including untrained peers.

Thorp, D. M., Stahmer, A. C., & Schreibman, L. (1995). Effects of sociodramatic play training on children with autism. *Journal of Autism and Developmental Disorders, 25*(3), 265–282.

Three young boys with autism were observed in this study, in which they were taught sociodramatic play by an experimenter in a natural play environment to see if this would improve their play and language skills. Sociodramatic play involves role-playing, persistence (continuing a storyline), make-believe transformations (using imaginary objects), social behavior, and verbal communication; many of these skills, which are natural for normally developing children, are rare or difficult for children with autism. However, all 3 boys, who initially demonstrated very few of these skills, engaged in sociodramatic play consistently after training. Improvements were also seen in their social behavior and language skills. These skills were generalized to new settings and to their parents, although the effects were more limited.

Considerations

Individuals appear to respond uniquely to pivotal response training, and no one protocol suits all situations. This is a naturalistic, culturally sensitive process with no known risk.

Summary

This chapter presented a review of the characteristics and conditions related to functional communication problems, along with a summary of the intervention methods that have been shown to be effective for enhancing functional communication in school settings. The discussion of interventions included functional communication training, the Picture Exchange Communication System, video modeling, milieu teaching, and pivotal response training. While each intervention method presented differs in its application of one or more behavioral, cognitive–behavioral, or social learning theories, all are shaped by the fundamental goals of treatment: prevention and remediation of emotional and behavioral problems related to delayed or limited functional communication abilities. The information presented in this chapter forms the basis of the supplemental classroom- and home-based materials that correspond to this book.

References

Alpert, C. L., & Kaiser, A. P. (1992). Training parents as milieu language teachers. *Journal of Early Intervention, 16*(1), 31–52.

Apple, A. L., Billingsley, F., & Schwartz, I. S. (2005). Effects of video modeling alone and with self-management on compliment-giving behaviors of children with high-functioning ASD. *Journal of Positive Behavior Interventions, 7*(1), 33–46.

Baker-Ericzén, M. J., Stahmer, A. C., & Burns, A. (2007). Child demographics associated with outcomes in community-based pivotal response training. *Journal of Positive Behavior Interventions, 9*(1), 52–60.

Bandura, A. (1977). *Social learning theory.* Englewood Cliffs, NJ: Prentice Hall.

Bellini, S., & Akullian, J. (2007). A meta-analysis of video modeling and video self-modeling interventions for children and adolescents with autism spectrum disorders. *Exceptional Children, 73*(3), 264–287.

Bock, S. J., Stoner, J. B., Beck, A. R., Hanley, L., & Prochnow, J. (2005). Increasing functional communication in non-speaking preschool children: Comparison of PECS and VOCA. *Education and Training in Developmental Disabilities, 40*(3), 264–278.

Bondy, A., & Frost, L. (1994). The Picture Exchange Communication System. *Focus on Autistic Behavior, 9*(3), 1–19.

Bondy, A., & Frost, L. (2001). The picture exchange communication system. *Behavior Modification, 25*(5), 725–744.

Brady, N. C., & Halle, J. W. (1997). Functional analysis of communicative behaviors. *Focus on Autism and Other Developmental Disabilities, 12*(2), 95–104.

Carr, D., & Felce, J. (2007). The effects of PECS teaching to phase III on the communicative interactions between children with autism and their teachers. *Journal of Autism and Developmental Disorders, 37*(4), 724–737.

Carr, E. G., & Durand, V. M. (1985). Reducing behavior problems through functional communication training. *Journal of Applied Behavior Analysis, 18*(2), 111–126.

Charlop, M. H., & Milstein, J. P. (1989). Teaching autistic children conversational speech using video modeling. *Journal of Applied Behavior Analysis, 22*(3), 275–285.

Charlop, M. H., & Trasowech, J. E. (1991). Increasing autistic children's daily spontaneous speech. *Journal of Applied Behavior Analysis, 24*(4), 747–761.

Charlop, M. H., & Walsh, M. E. (1986). Increasing autistic children's spontaneous verbalizations of affection: An assessment of time delay and peer modeling procedures. *Journal of Applied Behavior Analysis, 19*(3), 307–314.

Charlop-Christy, M. H., & Carpenter, M. H. (2000). Modified incidental teaching sessions: A procedure for parents to increase spontaneous speech in their children with autism. *Journal of Positive Behavior Interventions, 2*(2), 98–112.

Charlop-Christy, M. H., Carpenter, M., Le, L., LeBlanc, L. A., & Kellet, K. (2002). Using the Picture Exchange Communication System (PECS) with children with autism: Assessment of PECS acquisition, speech, social-communicative behavior, and problem behavior. *Journal of Applied Behavior Analysis, 35*(3), 213–231.

Charlop-Christy, M. H., Le, L., & Freeman, K. A. (2000). A comparison of video modeling with *in vivo* modeling for teaching children with autism. *Journal of Autism and Developmental Disorders, 30*(6), 537–552.

Durand, V. M., & Carr, E. G. (1992). An analysis of maintenance following functional communication training. *Journal of Applied Behavior Analysis, 25*(4), 777–794.

Durand, V. M., & Merges, E. (2001). Functional communication training: A contemporary behavior analytic intervention for problem behaviors. *Focus on Autism and Other Developmental Disabilities, 16*(2), 110–119.

Ganz, J. B., & Simpson, R. L. (2004). Effects on communicative requesting and speech development of the Picture Exchange Communication System in children with characteristics of autism. *Journal of Autism and Developmental Disorders, 34*(4), 395–409.

Hancock, T. B., & Kaiser, A. P. (1996). Siblings' use of milieu teaching at home. *Topics in Early Childhood Special Education, 16*(2), 168–190.

Hancock, T. B., & Kaiser, A. P. (2002). The effects of trainer-implemented enhanced milieu teaching on the social communication of children with autism. *Topics in Early Childhood Special Education, 22*(1), 39–54.

Hart, B., & Risley, T. R. (1974). Using preschool materials to modify the language of disadvantaged children. *Journal of Applied Behavior Analysis, 7*(2), 243–256.

Hemmeter, M. L., & Kaiser, A. P. (1994). Enhancing milieu teaching: Effects of parent-implemented language intervention. *Journal of Early Intervention, 18*(3), 269–289.

Hepting, N. H., & Goldstein, H. (1996). Requesting by preschoolers with developmental disabilities: Videotaped self-modeling and learning of new linguistic structures. *Topics in Early Childhood Special Education, 16*(3), 407–427.

Howlin, P., Gordon, R. K., Pasco, G., Wade, A., & Charman, T. (2007). The effectiveness of Picture Exchange Communication System (PECS) training for teachers of children with autism: A pragmatic, group randomised controlled trial. *Journal of Child Psychology and Psychiatry, 48*(5), 473–481.

Kaiser, A. P. (1993). Parent implemented language intervention: An environmental system perspective. In A. P. Kaiser & D. B. Gray (Eds.), *Enhancing children's communication: Research foundations for interventions* (pp. 63–84). Baltimore: Brookes.

Kaiser, A. P. (2000). Teaching functional communication skills. In M. E. Snell & F. Brown (Eds.), *Instruction of students with severe disabilities* (5th ed., pp. 453–492). Upper Saddle River, NJ: Prentice Hall.

Koegel, L. K., Carter, C. M., & Koegel, R. L. (2003). Teaching children with autism self-initiations as a pivotal response. *Topics in Language Disorders, 23*(2), 134–145.

Koegel, L. K., Koegel, R. L., Harrower, J. K., & Carter, C. M. (1999). Pivotal response intervention I: Overview of approach. *The Journal of the Association for Persons with Severe Handicaps, 24*(3), 174–185.

Koegel, R. L., Camarata, S., Koegel, L. K., Ben-Tall, A., & Smith, A. E. (1998). Increasing speech intelligibility in children with autism. *Journal of Autism and Developmental Disorders, 28*(3), 241–251.

Koegel, R. L., and Koegel, L. K. (Eds.). (1995). *Teaching children with autism: Strategies for initiating positive interactions and improving learning opportunities.* Baltimore: Brookes.

Koegel, R. L., Schreffirnan, L., Good, A., Cerniglia, L., Murphy, C., & Koegel, L. K. (1989) *How to teach pivotal behaviors to children with autism: A training manual.* Retrieved March 4, 2008, from http://www.users.qwest.net/~tbharris/prt.htm

Lalli, J. S., Casey, S., & Kates, K. (1995). Reducing escape behavior and increasing task completion with functional communication training, extinction, and response chaining. *Journal of Applied Behavior Analysis, 28*(3), 261–268.

Laski, K. E., Charlop, M. H., & Schreibman, L. (1988). Training parents to use the natural language paradigm to increase their autistic children's speech. *Journal of Applied Behavior Analysis, 21*(4), 391–400.

Magiati, I., & Howlin, P. (2003). A pilot evaluation study of the Picture Exchange Communication System (PECS) for children with autistic spectrum disorders. *Autism, 7*(3), 297–320.

Mancil, G. R. (2006). Functional communication training: A review of the literature related to children with autism. *Education and Training in Developmental Disabilities, 41*(3), 213–224.

Mancil, G. R., Conroy, M. A., Nakao, T., & Alter, P. J. (2006). Functional communication training in the natural environment: A pilot investigation with a young child with autism spectrum disorder. *Education and Treatment of Children, 29*(4), 615–633.

Nikopoulos, C. K., & Keenan, M. (2003). Promoting social initiation in children with autism using video modeling. *Behavioral Interventions, 18*(2), 87–108.

Olive, M. L., de la Cruz, B., Davis, T. N., Chan, J. M., Lang, R. B., O'Reilly, M. F., et al. (2007). The effects of enhanced milieu training and a voice output communication aid on the requesting of three children with autism. *Journal of Autism and Developmental Disorders, 37*(8), 1505–1513.

Pierce, K., & Schreibman, L. (1995). Increasing complex social behaviors in children with autism: Effects of peer-implemented pivotal response training. *Journal of Applied Behavior Analysis, 28*(3), 285–295.

Pierce, K., & Schreibman, L. (1997). Multiple peer use of pivotal response training to increase social behaviors of classmates with autism: Results from trained and untrained peers. *Journal of Applied Behavior Analysis, 30*(1), 157–160.

Reynolds, C. R., & Kamphaus, R. W. (2004). *Behavior Assessment System for Children* (2nd ed.). Circle Pines, MN: AGS Publishing.

Schwartz, I. S., Garfinkle, A. N., & Bauer, J. (1998). The Picture Exchange Communication System: Communicative outcomes for young children with disabilities. *Topics in Early Childhood Special Education, 18*(3), 144–159.

Thorp, D. M., Stahmer, A. C., & Schreibman, L. (1995). Effects of sociodramatic play training on children with autism. *Journal of Autism and Developmental Disorders, 25*(3), 265–282.

Wacker, D. P., Steege, M. W., Northup, J., Sasso, G., Berg, W., Reimers, T., et al. (1990). A component analysis of functional communication training across three topographies of severe behavior problems. *Journal of Applied Behavior Analysis, 23*(4), 417–429.

Wert, B. Y., & Neisworth, J. T. (2003). Effects of video self-modeling on spontaneous requesting in children with autism. *Journal of Positive Behavior Interventions, 5*(1), 30–34.

Yoder, P., & Stone, W. L. (2006). Randomized comparison of two communication interventions for preschoolers with autism spectrum disorders. *Journal of Consulting and Clinical Psychology, 74*(3), 426–435.

Yoder, P., Kaiser, A. P., Goldstein, H., Alpert, C., Mousetis, L., Kaczmarek, L., et al. (1995). An exploratory comparison of milieu teaching and responsive interaction in classroom applications. *Journal of Early Intervention, 19*(3), 218–242.

Chapter 12

Intervention to Enhance Social Skills

This chapter provides evidence-based interventions to address problems identified primarily on the BASC–2 Social Skills and Interpersonal Relations scales. These interventions are presented in the three main sections of this chapter. The first section discusses the characteristics and conditions of deficits in social skills and interpersonal relations and presents sample items from each BASC–2 scale. The second section presents the theoretical framework for approaching behaviors identified on these scales. The third section addresses the primary approach intervention that has evidence for enhancing social skills and interpersonal relations, and is divided into three subsections: Implementation, Evidence for Use, and Considerations. The chapter's three main sections provide the foundation on which additional BASC–2 intervention components are built, including both classroom-based and home-based strategies.

Characteristics and Conditions of Social Skills Problems

Social Skills (found on the BASC–2 Teacher Rating Scales and Parent Rating Scales) and Interpersonal Relations (found on the BASC–2 Self-Report of Personality) are closely related scales on the BASC–2; both reflect the skills necessary for developing and maintaining social relationships. A child with strong social and interpersonal skills is considered to have achieved social competence. Social competence includes the absence of significant maladaptive behaviors, the presence of positive relationships with others, accurate and age-appropriate social cognition, and effective social behaviors needed for children to be accepted by peers (Bierman, Miller, & Stabb, 1987). Social and interpersonal skills are adaptive, or positive, scales on the BASC–2 and represent skills that are important to a child's behavioral and emotional functioning in a number of ways. The skills develop resiliency, increase desirable behaviors, and mediate behaviors associated with externalizing and internalizing problems such as aggression, conduct problems, anxiety, somatization, depression, hyperactivity, and inattention.

Social skills are learned, situation-specific behaviors (both verbal and nonverbal) that are demonstrated in particular social contexts (Spitzberg & Dillard, 2002; Van Hasselt, Hersen, Whitehill, & Bellack, 1979). Interpersonal relations skills are needed to interact effectively with people; as such, they form the foundation for social relationships. Deficits in social or interpersonal relations skills interfere with social, emotional, and academic functioning

(Bellini, Peters, Benner, & Hopf, 2007; Welsh, Parke, Widaman, & O'Neil, 2001) and are frequently characteristic of children with emotional and behavioral disorders, especially autism spectrum disorders, attention-deficit/hyperactivity disorder (ADHD), conduct problems, social anxiety, and children with learning disabilities (Bellini et al., 2007; Forness & Knitzer, 1992; Foster & Bussman, 2008; Kavale & Forness, 1996; Sullivan & Mastropieri, 1994; Walker, Colvin, & Ramsey, 1995). Example items from the BASC–2 Social Skills scale include "Compliments others," "Shows interests in others' ideas," and "Makes suggestions without offending others." Example items from the Interpersonal Relations scale include "My classmates don't like me," "I feel that nobody likes me," "Other children don't like to be with me," and "Other people make fun of me."

Social skills deficits can be classified into three categories: (1) skill or acquisition deficits, (2) performance deficits, and (3) self-control deficits (Gresham, 1981, 1998; Gresham, Sugai, & Horner, 2001). Children with skill or acquisition deficits lack the knowledge necessary to perform a social skill. In contrast, children with performance deficits know how to perform a social skill but do not perform it or do so in an awkward fashion. In some cases, children who have social skills knowledge will not exhibit appropriate social skills due to the presence of social maladjustment, such as in conduct disorder. Children with self-control deficits exhibit maladaptive behaviors that impede or compete with performing the appropriate skill (Kavale & Forness, 1996). For example, verbal aggression might compete with the social skill of expressing understanding for the feelings of others. Or, a child with the knowledge of how to respond positively may not do so due to issues associated with other developmental disorders, such as ADHD, where impulsive responding may overpower the individual's knowledge of how to respond appropriately. In such instances, the underlying disorder should be targeted for intervention in addition to methods that are specific to treating knowledge and performance deficits.

Theoretical Framework for Approaching Social Skills Problems

Childhood behavioral problems involving social and interpersonal relationships often are linked to the absence of particular social skills. This lack of social skills indicates a deficiency in the child's social competency. While social skills and social competency may seem synonymous, the two are not. Social competency encompasses social skills and other important factors, such as positive relationships with others, accurate and age-appropriate social cognition, absence of maladaptive behaviors, and effective social behaviors (Vaughn & Hogan, 1990). Social competency, therefore, is the necessary construct for successful treatment and remediation of problem behaviors of a social and interpersonal nature.

Social competency is made up of discrete skills that must be taught separately but integrated seamlessly into the individual's life and actions. Typically, when a child lacks social competency, his or her behavioral deficiency is remediated through a training program based on a series of related skills. For example, it is insufficient to teach a child to be nice, behave, or play fair, because the skill sets that make up being nice and playing fair (such as taking turns and sharing) have to be taught individually before being incorporated into the child's repertoire of generalized social skills.

Social skills, as a part of social competency, consist of the interpersonal behaviors that allow individuals to work cooperatively with others, form groups and bonds, communicate, and develop relationships. These behaviors may be demonstrated when an individual exhibits interpersonal skills such as empathy and sympathy, which motivate or predispose a person to relate to others and want to work cooperatively with them.

Social skills and interpersonal behaviors are learned, although innate abilities or predispositions for certain behaviors may enhance the rate and degree of mastery in acquiring social skill sets. The intervention strategy for increasing or enhancing competence in the areas of social skills presented in this chapter is considered cognitive–behavioral in its approach because it addresses both the mental factors involved (e.g., self-awareness) and the tendency for certain behaviors to be reinforced by the environment.

Intervention

The intervention strategy presented in this chapter can be implemented to build or strengthen social and interpersonal skills. The discussion follows the same format as that used in previous chapters; however, because of the vast amount of research literature related to social skills training, the evidence for that intervention is reported in the form of summaries of a number of published meta-analyses. Recommendations for how to maximize the effectiveness of social skills training are presented in the Considerations section.

Ratings from multiple informants are useful in focusing interventions on the most appropriate settings. It is possible for a child to exhibit better social skills in one setting than another; for example, a child may behave better with parents somewhere in the community than without parents at school (Kamphaus, 1987). Thus, intervention implementation may focus on either the home or school setting for some children, or both settings for others. Or, the implementation may focus on the development of interpersonal social skills for a child who primarily displays skill deficits in interacting with peers.

When selecting interventions for any behavioral or emotional disorder, practitioners should take into account whether social or interpersonal skills have been identified as strengths or weaknesses. Practitioners can use an identified strength to address co-morbid deficits by selecting interventions from other chapters in this book that will allow the child to draw on his or her stronger social skills to mediate the identified behavioral deficits. In contrast, for children with scores that fall within the at risk or clinically significant range on the Social Skills or Interpersonal Relations scales, the practitioner should consider the child's specific externalizing or internalizing behavior problems and use this information to help select the skills to be taught within social skills training. This approach is consistent with Reynolds and Kamphaus's (2004) conceptualization that "inclusion of social skills as an adaptive domain allows the examiner to take account of behavioral deficits when making differential diagnoses" (p. 65). Volkmar et al. (1987) provide an example of using social skills assessment as a tool for differentiating between a diagnosis of autism and mental retardation, with children with autism exhibiting significantly more impaired socialization than those with mental retardation.

For example, if Campbell was identified by the BASC–2 rating scales as being at risk for problems with aggression, but he scored high on the Social Skills scale, the practitioner should consider Campbell's social skills strength when selecting from evidence-based interventions identified in the Aggression chapter of this book (chapter 2). Knowing of Campbell's strength, the practitioner might select peer-mediated conflict resolution as the intervention, teaching Campbell to use his social skills to take on the role of peer mediator. Conversely, if instead Campbell had a clinically significant score on both the Social Skills and Aggression scales, and the practitioner noted that he tended to respond to others' anger by using physical aggression, the practitioner might choose to focus on the skill of responding to others' anger in Campbell's social skills training.

Social Skills Training

Social skills training is a cognitive–behavioral approach to teaching prosocial concepts needed for children and adolescents to function successfully in multiple social environments. Social skills training includes teaching interpersonal skills, which enable children to function cooperatively and effectively with other individuals.

The term "social skills" generally refers to skills that enable effective functioning when interacting with others. Social skills have been noted by Gresham (1986) to include dimensions of peer acceptance, behavioral skills, and social validity. Social validity refers to the social importance of the targeted skills and to teacher acceptance of the intervention. Social skills training or similar intervention programs generally present a child with a series of lessons, each targeting a specific social skill, so that the newly learned skills can be applied by the child when opportunities arise.

For example, Barry, a 6-year-old with social skills deficits, takes toys out of his peers' hands when he wants to play. Barry's teacher helps him to learn to share, a developmentally appropriate interpersonal skill that involves asking politely, taking turns, and remaining calm when playing with others.

Implementation

The goal of social skills training is to develop skills that will enable children to engage in appropriate interactions with others by remediating the behavioral challenges associated with their social skills deficits. The basic elements of many social skills training programs follow a model of direct instruction and typically include the following:

1. Teaching the skill and talking about the problem or area of weakness

2. Modeling the skill through active demonstration

3. Practicing the skill in a controlled environment while receiving feedback

4. Generalizing the skill by practicing it in new environments

Social skills training is grounded in a behaviorist framework and places a strong emphasis on behavior replacement training and the differential reinforcement of behaviors that exhibit strong social validity. These training programs often require a child to generate multiple strategies for engaging in appropriate social behavior. These strategies may include the expression of empathy, an awareness of the consequences of one's own and others' behavior, and the identification of appropriate paths to reach desired goals.

The procedural steps for implementing social skills training, listed in three phases in Figure 12.1, are adapted from current literature on the topic (Foster & Bussman, 2008; Quinn, Kavale, Mathur, Rutherford, & Forness, 1999; Rutherford, Quinn, & Mathur, 1996; Spitzberg & Dillard, 2002).

In the pre-intervention phase, the practitioner first assesses the child's social skills and determines the specific skill(s) the child needs to master. For instance, if the child throws tantrums to get desired objects, the practitioner will teach the skill of asking for objects. Target social skills should not be selected based on a set list or a fixed curriculum but rather the child's specific needs.

Second, the practitioner determines the format of instruction. The target social skills can be taught in a group or individually, and they can be taught in either a more clinical or a more natural environment. While conducting training in a natural environment is the ideal scenario for generalization, training sessions are not always possible in school settings due to environmental constraints (e.g., lack of personnel, lack of adequate training, competing demands of classroom settings). Groups can be composed of children with similar social skills deficits (homogeneous grouping) or children with different deficits (heterogeneous grouping). When working with a homogeneous group, particularly one composed of children who exhibit antisocial behavior, be sure to provide enough supervision and structure to prevent modeling of inappropriate behaviors (i.e., behaviors that contradict the skills being taught). For instance, if some children in a social skills training program group frequently mimic wrestling moves or use inappropriate language, others in the group may adopt these behaviors. The selection of members for group-based social skills training should be made based on information about the specific behavioral challenges and social skills deficits of the individual children.

Next, the practitioner schedules consistent times for social skills training, keeping in mind that high training intensity (both frequency of meetings and overall program duration) is desirable (Taylor, Eddy, & Biglan, 1999). If the practitioner determines that the skill will be taught to an individual child in his or her natural environment, then the choice of time will be based on the child's current schedule (e.g., getting along with others might be taught during recess). If the skill will be taught in a pull-out group session, then the practitioner selects a specific time during the day that will not interfere with academic instruction. The practitioner determines the behavioral expectations for the group and posts them in a highly visible area.

The second phase of social skills training is the intervention phase. During this phase, the practitioner first explains the purpose of the training and defines the concept of social skills for the participants. Then the children are directly taught the steps to master the selected skills, focusing on one skill per lesson. At the beginning of each lesson, the steps for the previously taught skill are reviewed.

One approach for the direct instruction of a given social skill begins with a visual representation (either written or pictorial) of the steps for performing the skill; the practitioner then asks the children to write down the steps on note cards or paper. Pictorial representations of the steps should be provided to children who either don't have the ability to read the steps or who perform better with visual depictions. If desired, the practitioner has the children verbalize the steps of the social skill using choral responding (i.e., reciting them aloud and in unison) and verbally reinforces children as they recite the steps. At this point in instruction, the practitioner may choose to provide video representation of other children of a similar age demonstrating appropriate use of the skill.

Next, the practitioner can demonstrate the appropriate use of the skill by modeling it with another adult or other children. For instance, the practitioner might demonstrate joining in by approaching two children playing a game and asking, "Can I play?" The practitioner asks the children to provide examples of appropriate times to use this skill and situations in the recent past when this skill could have been useful. For instance, 9-year-old Randy described the following situation: "Yesterday, I wanted to play dominoes with my friends. I sat down at the table and told them, 'Give me some dominoes!' Clint told me that I couldn't play because they were in the middle of the game, and so I just reached out and took seven dominoes. Clint yelled at me, and the teacher made both of us quit playing."

Once a situation has been identified, the practitioner selects several children to role-play use of the skill in the given situation. The practitioner instructs the rest of the children to review the steps for performing the social skill and to encourage Randy and Clint to follow the steps. During the role-play, the practitioner provides feedback and reinforcement to the actors, and to the children who are monitoring the use of the steps. After the role-play, all children provide feedback on how effectively the skill was used.

The practitioner ends the lesson by having the participants identify and describe social situations they might encounter in which they could use the newly learned skill. In addition, the practitioner provides the relevant adults (e.g., teachers, parents, tutors, classroom volunteers) with a copy of the steps of the skill. The practitioner asks the adults to model the skill, encourage the child to apply the new skill, and reinforce all efforts.

The third phase in social skills training—maintenance and generalization—is a vital component of all skills training programs. During this phase, the practitioner provides reinforcement to the children for situational use of the skill. The practitioner may ask children to record in a journal all social situations in which they used the skill. The practitioner continually monitors, collects data, and assesses group participants' use of the skill (either through direct observation or by reviewing participants' journals) to identify any skills that need to be re-taught or reinforced.

Figure 12.1 Procedural steps for social skills training

Pre-Intervention Phase

1. Assess the child's social skills and determine the specific skill(s) the child needs to master.

2. Determine the format of instruction (individual or group).

3. If applicable, select members for groups. Groups can be homogeneous (with all children sharing similar social skills deficits) or heterogeneous (with children exhibiting a variety of deficits).

4. Schedule consistent times for social skills training sessions.

5. Establish group norms in the form of well-defined behavioral expectations and boundaries, and post them in a highly visible area.

Intervention Phase

1. Explain the purpose of the training to the participants, and discuss the meaning of social skills.

2. Teach one social skill per session.

3. Visually represent and explain the target skill, as well as its component steps.

4. Ask the children to write the steps on note cards or paper.

5. Demonstrate appropriate use of the skill to the children.

6. Instruct the children to recite the steps verbally. Provide reinforcement for accurate verbalization.

7. If desired, provide video models of peers performing the skill in simulated situations.

Continued on next page

---

8. Assist participants in brainstorming recent events that called for the use of the skill.

9. Choose a scenario from the brainstorming session to use as the foundation for a role-play scenario. Have several children simulate the situation and practice using the target social skill. Instruct the remaining group participants to verbally coach the actors during the role-play to help them appropriately use the target skill. Assist with and guide the coaching as needed. Provide feedback and reinforcement for effective use of social skills during role-plays.

10. Send a written copy of the steps for using the target skill to each child's teachers, parents, and other relevant adults, and ask them to practice and reinforce appropriate use of the skill with the child.

11. Help the children identify social situations in which to apply the new skill.

12. At the beginning of each session, review the skill taught during the previous session.

Generalization and Maintenance

1. Encourage generalization of new social skills by practicing with and coaching the children in natural settings and situations.

2. Have each child write in a journal about his or her use of the target skills in natural settings when practitioner coaching is not available.

3. Continually collect data and assess the outcomes of social skills training with specific children to determine the effectiveness of the training and to identify social skills that need to be re-taught.

4. Re-teach any skills that are not maintained over time.

5. Hold periodic refresher courses on the skills taught in order to maintain skill acquisition.

Evidence for Use

Due to the importance of social skills for both school and life success, social skills training has become a common and widely accepted intervention in the field. The extensive research that has been conducted to assess the effectiveness of such training programs has produced mixed results. Several meta-analyses of individual studies have found social skills training to have small to moderate positive effects, both in overall measures and for students with learning disabilities, autism spectrum disorder, and emotional and behavioral disorders (Beelmann, Pfingsten, & Lösel, 1994; Foster & Bussman, 2008; Kavale & Mostert, 2004; Mathur, Kavale, Quinn, Forness, & Rutherford, 1998; McConnell, 2002; Quinn et al., 1999; Zaragoza, Vaughn, & McIntosh, 1991). However, the meta-analysis provided in Bellini et al. (2007) found social skills training to have only minimal effects, particularly for students with autism spectrum disorders.

Gresham et al. (2001) noted that the effectiveness of different social skills training interventions varied widely depending on the characteristics of the children being treated and whether the skills targeted were matched to the children's specific needs. Similarly, in a review of reviews, Maag (2006) identified a number of problems with the design, implementation, and evaluation of social skills training programs that may have resulted in previous meta-analyses underestimating the potential for effectiveness of well-designed social skills interventions. Maag and other authors suggest that if these problems are addressed, future social skills training programs could demonstrate greater treatment effects and higher rates of skill maintenance and generalization.

The following studies summarize some of the key research findings associated with the use of social skills training as an intervention for children and adolescents with social skills deficits.

Beelmann, A., Pfingsten, U., & Lösel, F. (1994). Effects of training social competence in children: A meta-analysis of recent evaluation studies. *Journal of Clinical Child Psychology, 23*(3), 260–271.

The results of 49 evaluative studies of the effects of social competence training (SCT) in children aged 3 to 15 years were examined in this meta-analysis, with a focus on the variability of effects for different participant characteristics and program types. Program types were coded according to their complexity (monomodal or multimodal) and content focus (e.g., social problem solving, behavioral). The participants in the studies were classified into five diagnostic groups: externalizing syndromes, internalizing syndromes, intellectual problems, at risk (e.g., due to stressful life events), and normal. The analysis showed that, overall, most SCT interventions, regardless of the style or focus of the training, are effective at bringing about the targeted changes in the short term. The effects were greatest for at-risk children and lowest for normal children, while those with externalizing and internalizing syndromes showed moderate treatment effects. In addition, while monomodal training was somewhat more effective for the youngest children, multimodal training proved most effective for older children. The analysis also revealed that social problem-solving training was the only multimodal training that showed clear, long-term effects and indicated that self-control training exhibited the greatest short-term gains. The authors noted that more research is needed in specific areas: generalization, maintenance, and matching training to individual student needs.

Bellini, S., Peters, J. K., Benner, L., & Hopf, A. (2007). A meta-analysis of school-based social skills interventions for children with autism spectrum disorders. *Remedial and Special Education, 28*(3), 153–162.

The authors analyzed 157 children with autism spectrum disorder (ASD) from 55 previous studies to examine the results of social skills training on the social competency of the children. Overall, results showed that social skills training is only minimally effective in improving the social skills of children with ASD. However, most of the gains that were made during intervention were maintained at follow-up. In addition, training that took place in the children's normal classrooms, as opposed to pull-out sessions, was found to be more effective. Only one of the studies specifically matched the training to the type of deficit shown by individual children; such a matching approach may be an important focus of future research. The authors also note that only 14 of the 55 studies measured the fidelity of implementation, and only 12 studies collected data on the social validity of the targeted interventions. The authors stressed the importance of monitoring and measuring implementation fidelity in order to draw sound conclusions about the effectiveness of any given type of treatment.

Foster, S. L., & Bussman, J. R. (2008). Evidence-based approaches to social skills training with children and adolescents. In R. G. Steele, T. D. Elkin, & M. C. Roberts (Eds.), *Handbook of evidence-based therapies for children and adolescents: Bridging science and practice* (pp. 409–427). New York: Springer.

In this evaluation, researchers reviewed three specific social skills interventions for at-risk children and adolescents, and gave broader comments concerning previous meta-analyses of social skills interventions. The three main studies discussed here examined the intervention programs Dinosaur School, a 24-session intervention for children aged 4 to 7 years; Coping Power, studied as an intervention for fourth- and fifth-grade boys, their parents, and combined; and Fast Track, which had an in-school program for entire classrooms as well as an after-school program for at-risk students in Grades 1 through 6. These three programs were selected for review because they had been shown to be effective in at least two randomized controlled trials or in a multisite evaluation. The review authors offered a series of suggestions for improving next-generation social skills interventions, including developing effective strategies for dealing with disruptive behavior and missed sessions; involving peers, parents, and teachers in order to enhance generalization; and using other interventions to treat children's behavior problems (e.g., aggression) in tandem with social skills training.

Gresham, F. M., Sugai, G., & Horner, R. H. (2001). Interpreting outcomes of social skills training for students with high-incidence disabilities. *Exceptional Children, 67*(3), 331–344.

Researchers in this meta-analysis examined six narrative reviews on the effects of social skills training (SST). The results varied widely, from very little effect to large effect. Several reasons were suggested for this variance. Population variance was one reason: Children with learning disorders and emotional–behavioral disorders seemed to show resistance to intervention. Also, most studies failed to consider students' specific social skills deficits when determining which skills would be included in training. Very few of the studies assessed treatment integrity, which made it difficult to determine the effectiveness of the intervention. In addition, not all of the assessments used to determine intervention effectiveness were equally valid, and some had very little social validity. Finally, newly learned social skills often failed to be generalized and maintained because they were taught out of context or because there were competing behaviors that produced more efficient or reliable results. The authors recommended that these pitfalls be addressed in future social skills training research and practice in order to achieve greater treatment effects.

Kavale, K. A., & Mostert, M. P. (2004). Social skills interventions for individuals with learning disabilities. *Learning Disability Quarterly, 27*(1), 31–43.

A total of 53 studies composed of 2,113 subjects were studied in this meta-analysis to determine the effectiveness of social skills intervention on children with learning disabilities. Overall, the studies showed only small improvements; the average effect size was .211, meaning that the average student with learning disabilities who participated in social skills intervention advanced from the 50th percentile to the 58th percentile. It was suggested that this low level of intervention efficacy could be due to ineffective training programs, insufficient training time, poor measurements, controversial vocabulary, or a lack of construct validity. However, the authors encouraged the continued use of social skills training as an experimental intervention. The training does often produce gains, even if small, and it has also been shown to increase self-esteem and self-perceived improvement among the children with learning disabilities who participate.

Maag, J. W. (2006). Social skills training for students with emotional and behavioral disorders: A review of reviews. *Behavioral Disorders, 32*(1), 4–17.

This article examined 13 reviews of studies evaluating social skills training for students with emotional and behavioral disorders (EBD). All of the reviews revealed only little to moderate improvement; however, the author hypothesized that the modest treatment gains could be due to flaws in the design and implementation of the interventions. In particular, the following three problems were consistently cited in reviews: a lack of emphasis on generalization, ineffective assessments used to monitor improvement, and a failure to monitor treatment fidelity. Improvements in these areas could lead to larger gains in future social skills training interventions. In addition, the authors suggested several other directions for future study, such as evaluating only those students diagnosed with EBD by state or federal eligibility criteria, conducting pretreatment assessments to determine target skill areas, and extending the length of interventions.

Mathur, S. R., Kavale, K. A., Quinn, M. M., Forness, S. R., & Rutherford, R. B., Jr. (1998). Social skills interventions with students with emotional behavioral problems: A quantitative synthesis of single-subject research. *Behavioral Disorders, 23*(3), 193–201.

Sixty-three single-subject studies including 283 participants with emotional or behavioral problems from preschool to secondary school were analyzed in this meta-analysis for the purpose of determining the effectiveness of social skills training for this population. Participants included those with emotional/behavioral disorders, autism, and delinquency. Results were analyzed by looking at the percentage of nonoverlapping data (PND) between the baseline and intervention phases. They showed delinquent students to be the most responsive to social skills training (mean PND of 76%) and students with autism to be the least responsive (mean PND of 54%). The mean PND across studies was 62%, with a standard deviation of 33%, suggesting that treatments were mildly effective. In addition, preschoolers were not as responsive as older students, perhaps showing that training needs to be further tailored to the needs of very young students. Training was also shown to be more effective in some skill areas than others; more improvements were seen in social interaction than in social communication or other social skills. While overall results showed only mild improvement, that improvement was significant.

McConnell, S. R. (2002). Interventions to facilitate social interaction for young children with autism: Review of available research and recommendations for educational intervention and future research. *Journal of Autism and Developmental Disorders, 32*(5), 351–372.

An in-depth evaluation of approximately 55 studies on social skills interventions for children with autism under the age of 9 years was conducted for this review, with the goal of determining how effective such interventions were on this population and which types or components of interventions were most efficacious. The majority of studies pointed to child-specific and peer-mediated interventions as most successful. The review also emphasized the importance of assessing individual children's social skills in naturalistic settings, arranging the environment to allow for frequent interactions with normally developing children, teaching specific social skills to both children with autism and their peers, fading direct intervention to natural reinforcement, incorporating treatment into other activities throughout the day, and monitoring effects over time.

Quinn, M. M., Kavale, K. A., Mathur, S. R., Rutherford, S. R., Jr., & Forness, S. R. (1999). A meta-analysis of social skill interventions for students with emotional or behavioral disorders. *Journal of Emotional and Behavioral Disorders, 7*(1), 54–64.

This meta-analysis examined 35 group studies on the effects of social skills interventions on children with behavioral and emotional disorders. The studies included 1,123 participants and yielded a total of 328 effect size measurements, including measurements of the effects on prosocial behaviors (e.g., social competence, social problem solving), problem behaviors (e.g., disruptive behavior, family relations problems), and specific behavior traits (e.g., anxiety, cooperation, and aggression). These studies were analyzed according to types of interventions, child demographics, and other criteria to see if there were any discernable patterns in what made interventions effective. The overall effect size (ES) was .199, indicating modest improvement. Using established social skills programs versus experimental programs did not seem to make a difference, nor did high internal validity rankings, length of programs, or age of students. The only significant improvement (ES above .4) noted was in anxiety, which had an ES of .422; however, this ES was based on a small number of cases. Overall, improvement due to social skills interventions alone was minimal; regardless, because mastery of social skills is necessary for children's long-term mental health and social development nonetheless, further research to determine effective intervention practices is crucial.

Spitzberg, B. H., & Dillard, J. P. (2002). Social skills and communication. In M. Allen, R. W. Preiss, B. M. Gayle, & N. Burrell (Eds.), *Interpersonal communication research: Advances through meta-analysis* (pp. 89–107). Mahwah, NJ: Erlbaum.

In this book chapter, the authors provide commentary on the definition and the importance of social skills, as well as ways of measuring such skills. In addition, they report on a meta-analysis conducted on 18 studies of adults' and adolescents' social skills that involved analyzing specific, discrete social behaviors (e.g., talk time, eye contact, gestures) and their effects on perceived social competence. Twelve such behaviors (nine nonverbal and three verbal) were examined, and each of these alone had an effect on perceived social competence. Talk time was the most significant measure; this single indicator accounted for 46% of the variance in social competence ratings. These results are encouraging because they suggest that training people to use simple social skills, such as head movements, questions, and talk time, can greatly increase others' perception of their social competence.

Taylor, T. K., Eddy, J. M., & Biglan, A. (1999). Interpersonal skills training to reduce aggressive and delinquent behavior: Limited evidence and the need for an evidence-based system of care. *Clinical Child and Family Psychology Review, 2*(3), 169–182.

This article examined results from 19 studies that met the following criteria: 1) examined the effect of interpersonal skills training on aggressive or antisocial behavior; 2) used a randomized, controlled design; and 3) published results in a peer-reviewed journal. Overall, the results from these studies provided some evidence for modest, short-term effects of interpersonal skills training on behavior; however, they provided limited evidence for maintenance of treatment effects over time. The authors noted that even using the most promising skills training program delivered under optimal conditions, the majority of children treated remained in the clinical range for measured behavior problems after treatment. They concluded, based on these results, that while interpersonal skills training is not effective on its own for remediating conduct problems, it may be useful as one component of a multifaceted intervention program.

Vaughn, S., Kim, A., Sloan, C. V. M., Hughes, M. T., Elbaum, B., & Dheepa, S. (2003). Social skills interventions for young children with disabilities: A synthesis of group design studies. *Remedial and Special Education, 24*(1), 2–15.

This article synthesized the findings of 23 group-design studies focusing on preschool children (aged 3 to 5 years) with any sort of disability, with the goal of determining whether social skills training was effective for this population and, if so, which methods were most effective. Results showed that social skills training is effective when a variety of methods are used. Particularly beneficial were interventions that included modeling, play-related activities, rehearsal, and/or prompting. These trainings took place in natural settings in the regular classroom environment and produced significant improvements in the social skills of the preschoolers with disabilities. Encouragingly, the most significant improvements were seen in children with behavioral and emotional disorders (i.e., the children who most needed social skills training).

Zaragoza, N., Vaughn, S., & McIntosh, R. (1991). Social skills interventions and children with behavior problems: A review. *Behavioral Disorders, 16*(4), 260–275.

Twenty-seven studies, involving 574 school-aged participants (aged 7 to 18 years) with behavior problems, were examined in this review of the effects of social skills interventions. Almost all of the studies reported significant positive changes on one or more of the outcome measures, including peer ratings, specific social behaviors, problem-solving skills, and teacher and parent ratings of behavior problems and aggression. Parents and teachers almost always perceived positive change in the students; peers seemed resistant to changing their views of the students. These findings suggest a need for the development, testing, and evaluation of programs that include peers in treatment to help them see and support the improvements in students with behavioral problems.

Considerations

Social skills training programs have been found to be more effective for children at risk of developing internalizing or externalizing disorders than for children diagnosed with such disorders (Beelmann et al., 1994; Quinn et al., 1999). In addition, social skills training has been found to be more effective for children with internalizing disorders than for children with externalizing disorders (Erwin, 1994). Therefore, early identification of potential deficits increases the likelihood of successful intervention.

For Teaching

Social skills training is implemented easily within the classroom because it can be presented as a lesson. In fact, many social skills curricula are structured and formatted to be taught campus-wide as a lesson within a content area, such as social studies or health.

Prior to teaching social skills, practitioners should consider which specific social skills should be taught and, if desired, which social skills program should be used. A social skills program with established social validity (Bullis, Walker, & Sprague, 2001; Foster & Bussman, 2008; Gresham et al., 2001) should be chosen based on the needs of the individual child (Quinn et al., 1999). Interventions should be systematically matched to the type of skill deficit (acquisition, performance, or self-control) the child exhibits (Gresham et al., 2001; Quinn et al., 1999). There are a number of commercially available social skills programs; a quick Internet search will provide many options. One of the most recent programs comes from the *Social Skills Improvement System* (SSIS) and includes both a social skills classroom curriculum (SSIS Classwide Intervention Program, Elliott & Gresham, 2007) and a resource book for small-group social skills training (SSIS Intervention Guide, Elliott & Gresham, 2008).

For maximum effectiveness, social skills training should be implemented in an intense and frequent manner (Bierman, 2004; Bullis et al., 2001; Gresham et al., 2001), with more than 30 hours of instruction over a 10- to 12-week period. This schedule may be difficult to achieve in school environments that focus on academics only. Social skills training can be incorporated as one component of a multiple-stage or -tier approach to preventing or remediating behavior disorders (Quinn et al., 1999). Strong consideration should be given to the possible negative impact of conducting social skills training with homogenous groups of students (Bierman, 2004; Dishion, McCord, & Poulin, 1999). Finally, if social skills training is adopted as a schoolwide program, administrators should plan for certain potentially problematic aspects of implementation. Specifically, administrators should plan strategies for preventing and dealing with missed sessions, engaging students actively in the curriculum, managing disruptions and attention problems, and enhancing generalization and maintenance by involving all relevant adults. Further, administrators should 1) consider the educational goals of the school and of those practitioners implementing the social skills interventions; 2) identify methods for monitoring the fidelity of implementation; 3) develop appropriate training for the implementers of the social skills program; and 4) assess the needs for community, administrative, and technical support.

Failure to consider methods for maintaining and generalizing the skills learned by the participants is common and often compromises the effectiveness of social skills training interventions (Bierman, 2004; Gresham et al., 2001). In situations where the skills are taught in pull-out programs, rather than in the children's natural environments, practitioners can increase maintenance and generalization by practicing and reinforcing skills in more natural settings. Further, all relevant adults should have knowledge of the procedural steps for the skill being taught and should be encouraged to model, reinforce, and practice the skill with the children (Taylor et al., 1999).

For Culture and Language Differences

Careful consideration must be given to the acceptance of specific social skills within different cultures. For instance, the procedural steps for socially engaging in conversation might be different across families. When uncertain, asking is the best practice, because social norms such as gender expectations and making eye contact may vary by culture. By the same token, children can and should be taught to differentiate appropriate social skills for various environments. For instance, Jake's father use phrases such as, "Only dummies use calculators" and "Laundry is women's work" when his son attempts to help with household chores. Although neither statement is generally considered socially acceptable and would result in unusual looks from other adults, the social norms of a family can be greatly shaped by region and economics, and such norms can be rigid.

Parent involvement in social skills training is the optimal solution, but it may not always be practical. It may be helpful to involve parents in understanding the social norms of the school culture and to identify familial vernacular. In cases of second-language families, providing the social skills steps in their native language is the first step to overcoming any additional barriers.

For Age and Developmental Level

Social skills training can be implemented across a wide variety of ages and developmental levels. However, the curriculum, structure of the lessons, and materials used must be appropriate for each participant's age and developmental level. For instance, for a student who is a nonreader, present the steps to social skills with pictures instead of written language.

Summary

This chapter presented a review of the characteristics and conditions for problems associated with social skills deficits, along with a discussion of how social skills training has been shown to be effective in remediation of problem behaviors related to social skills deficits. The information presented in this chapter forms the basis of the supplemental classroom- and home-based materials that correspond to this book.

References

Beelmann, A., Pfingsten, U., & Lösel, F. (1994). Effects of training social competence in children: A meta-analysis of recent evaluation studies. *Journal of Clinical Child Psychology, 23*(3), 260–271.

Bellini, S., Peters, J. K., Benner, L., & Hopf, A. (2007). A meta-analysis of school-based social skills interventions for children with autism spectrum disorders. *Remedial and Special Education, 28*(3), 153–162.

Bierman, K. L. (2004). *Peer rejection: Developmental processes and intervention strategies.* New York: Guilford.

Bierman, K. L., Miller, C. L., & Stabb, S. D. (1987). Improving the social behavior and peer acceptance of rejected boys: Effects of social skill training with instruction and prohibitions. *Journal of Consulting and Clinical Psychology, 55*(2), 194–200.

Bullis, M., Walker, H. M., & Sprague, J. R. (2001). A promise unfulfilled: Social skills training with at-risk and antisocial children and youth. *Exceptionality, 9*(1/2), 67–90.

Dishion, T. J., McCord, J., & Poulin, F. (1999). When interventions harm: Peer groups and problem behavior. *American Psychologist, 54*(9), 755–764.

Elliott, S. N., & Gresham, F. M. (2007). *SSIS classwide intervention program teacher's guide.* Minneapolis, MN: NCS Pearson.

Elliott, S. N., & Gresham, F. M. (2008). *SSIS intervention guide.* Minneapolis, MN: NCS Pearson.

Erwin, P. G. (1994). Social problem solving, social behavior, and children's peer popularity. *Journal of Psychology, 128*(3), 299–307.

Forness, S. R., & Knitzer, J. (1992). A new proposed definition and terminology to replace "serious emotional disturbance" in Individuals with Disabilities Education Act. *School Psychology Review, 21*(1), 12–20.

Foster, S. L., & Bussman, J. R. (2008). Evidence-based approaches to social skills training with children and adolescents. In R. G. Steele, T. D. Elkin, & M. C. Roberts (Eds.), *Handbook of evidence-based therapies for children and adolescents: Bridging science and practice* (pp. 409–427). New York: Springer.

Gresham, F. M. (1981). Social skills training with handicapped children: A review. *Review of Educational Research, 51*(1), 139–176.

Gresham, F. M. (1986). Conceptual and definitional issues in the assessment of children's social skills: Implications for classification and training. Social Skills Training [Special issue]. *Journal of Clinical Child Psychology, 15*(1), 3–15.

Gresham, F. (1998). Social skills training: Should we raze, remodel, or rebuild? *Behavioral Disorders, 24*(1), 19–25.

Gresham, F. M., Sugai, G., & Horner, R. H. (2001). Interpreting outcomes of social skills training for students with high-incidence disabilities. *Exceptional Children, 67*(3), 331–344.

Kamphaus, R. W. (1987). Conceptual and psychometric issues in the assessment of adaptive behavior. *Journal of Special Education, 21*(1), 27–35.

Kavale, K. A., & Forness, S. R. (1996). Social skill deficits and learning disabilities: A meta-analysis. *Journal of Learning Disabilities, 29*(3), 226–237.

Kavale, K. A., & Mostert, M. P. (2004). Social skills interventions for individuals with learning disabilities. *Learning Disability Quarterly, 27*(1), 31–43.

Maag, J. W. (2006). Social skills training for students with emotional and behavioral disorders: A review of reviews. *Behavioral Disorders, 32*(1), 4–17.

Mathur, S. R., Kavale, K. A., Quinn, M. M., Forness, S. R., & Rutherford, R. B., Jr. (1998). Social skills interventions with students with emotional behavioral problems: A quantitative synthesis of single-subject research. *Behavioral Disorders, 23*(3), 193–201.

McConnell, S. R. (2002). Interventions to facilitate social interaction for young children with autism: Review of available research and recommendations for educational intervention and future research. *Journal of Autism and Developmental Disorders, 32*(5), 351–372.

Quinn, M. M., Kavale, K. A., Mathur, S. R., Rutherford, S. R., Jr., & Forness, S. R. (1999). A meta-analysis of social skill interventions for students with emotional or behavioral disorders. *Journal of Emotional and Behavioral Disorders, 7*(1), 54–64.

Reynolds, C. R., & Kamphaus, R. W. (2004). *Behavior assessment system for children* (2nd ed.). Circle Pines, MN: AGS Publishing.

Rutherford, R. B., Jr., Quinn, M. M., & Mathur, S. R. (1996). *Effective strategies for teaching appropriate behaviors to children with emotional/behavioral disorders.* Reston, VA: Council for Children with Behavior Disorders.

Spitzberg, B. H., & Dillard, J. P. (2002). Social skills and communication. In M. Allen, R. W. Preiss, B. M. Gayle, & N. Burrell (Eds.), *Interpersonal communication research: Advances through meta-analysis* (pp. 89–107). Mahwah, NJ: Erlbaum.

Sullivan, G. S., & Mastropieri, M. A. (1994). Social competence of individuals with learning disabilities. In T. E. Scruggs & M. A. Mastropieri (Eds.), *Advances in learning and behavioral disabilities* (Vol. 8, pp. 171–213). Greenwich, CT: JAI Press.

Taylor, T. K., Eddy, J. M., & Biglan, A. (1999). Interpersonal skills training to reduce aggressive and delinquent behavior: Limited evidence and the need for an evidence-based system of care. *Clinical Child and Family Psychology Review, 2*(3), 169–182.

Van Hasselt, V. B., Hersen, M., Whitehill, M. B., & Bellack, A. S. (1979). Social skill assessment and training for children: An evaluative review. *Behaviour Research and Therapy, 17*(5), 413–437.

Vaughn, S., & Hogan, A. (1990). Social competence and learning disabilities: A prospective study. In H. L. Swanson & B. K. Keogh (Eds.), *Learning disabilities: Theoretical and research issues* (pp. 175–191). Hillsdale, NJ: Erlbaum.

Vaughn, S., Kim, A., Sloan, C. V. M., Hughes, M. T., Elbaum, B., & Dheepa, S. (2003). Social skills interventions for young children with disabilities: A synthesis of group design studies. *Remedial and Special Education, 24*(1), 2–15.

Volkmar, F. R., Sparrow, S. S., Goudreau, D., Cicchetti, D. V., Paul, R., & Cohen, D. J. (1987). Social deficits in autism: An operational approach using the Vineland Adaptive Behavior Scales. *Journal of the American Academy of Child and Adolescent Psychiatry, 26*(2), 156–161.

Walker, H. M., Colvin, G., & Ramsey, E. (1995). *Antisocial behavior in school: Strategies and best practices.* Pacific Grove, CA: Brooks/Cole.

Welsh, M., Parke, R. D., Widaman, K., & O'Neil, R. (2001). Linkages between children's social and academic competence: A longitudinal analysis. *Journal of School Psychology, 39*(6), 463–481.

Zaragoza, N., Vaughn, S., & McIntosh, R. (1991). Social skills interventions and children with behavior problems: A review. *Behavioral Disorders, 16*(4), 260–275.

Conduct problems,
    interventions for, 57–59, 62–64, 66–68, 70–72, 75, 76, 79, 80, 83–86, 89–91, 95–97, 100
    risk factors, 56
    types, 55, 56
Conflict resolution. *See* Peer-mediated conflict resolution and negotiation.
Contingency management, 57, 63, 64, 66, 67, 100, 110, 114–116, 119, 120, 136, 143, 152–154, 157, 175, 182, 190, 276, 283, 284, 286, 287, 312
Conversation skills, 34
Coping, 353, 355, 362, 363, 369
Counter-conditioning strategies, 277
Cover, copy, and compare (CCC), 236, 256
Cuing, 171, 390, 400

D

Daily behavior report card, 16, 152, 157–159, 161, 162, 182, 190. *See also* Home–school note.
Depression,
    causes, 319, 320
    interventions for, 321–330, 340–342, 346
    symptoms, 319, 320
Desensitization training, 283

E

Emotional–behavioral disorder, 71, 452, 453
Emotive imagery, 277, 278
Engaged time, 210, 214, 215, 231
Evaluation,
    frequency, 16, 17
    method, 1, 15, 16
Evidence for use,
    selection of research studies, 10, 12, 13
Exposure-based techniques, 276–278, 283, 295, 312
Extinction, 283, 284

F

Family involvement, 322, 330, 346
Family systems approach. *See* Multisystemic therapy.
Family therapy, 277, 291, 295, 296, 312
Functional behavioral assessment (FBA), 44, 114, 162, 170, 363, 374–377, 381, 383, 397, 406
Functional communication deficits,
    causes, 411, 412
    interventions for, 412, 413, 417–420, 428–430, 434–436, 442, 443, 446
Functional communication training, 412, 413, 417, 446

G

General anxiety disorder, 276
Goal setting, 119, 158, 175, 326, 329

H

Home-based interventions. *See* In-home interventions.
Home–school note, 16, 157, 354. *See also* Daily behavior report card.
Hyperactivity,
    causes, 109, 110
    interventions for, 110–112, 114–116, 119–121, 126, 127, 130–132, 135, 136, 143
    pharmacological treatment of, 110, 111, 135, 143

I

Imaginal desensitization, 277, 278, 283
In vivo desensitization, 277
Incidental teaching, 434–436
Individualized education program (IEP), 158
In-home interventions, considerations for, 100
Instructional sequencing, 210, 211, 213, 214
Intake assessment, 85, 121
Intellectual disabilities, 412
Interdependent group-oriented contingency management, 57, 63, 64, 66, 67, 100, 175
Interpersonal skills, 451, 453, 454
Interpersonal therapy (or psychotherapy) for adolescents, 319, 321, 341, 342, 346
Interventions,
    selection of, 1, 12, 13, 14, 15
    repetition across chapters, 3
Irrational thoughts. *See* Cognitive restructuring.

J

Journals, use of, 67, 68, 329, 340

L

Learning, types of, 202
Lesson presentation. *See* Presentation strategies.

M

Mand modeling, 435, 436
Medication. *See* Pharmacological treatment.
Memory, 203, 209, 212, 213, 215, 256, 260. *See also* Mnemonics.
Mental imagery. *See* Relaxation training.
Milieu language teaching, 412, 434–436, 442, 446
Mnemonics, 236, 242, 243, 246, 263
Modeling, 58, 59, 71, 76, 84, 85, 120, 121, 276, 287, 291, 312, 419, 435, 436, 446, 455, 456
    participant modeling, 287
    video modeling, 287, 291, 412, 428–430, 434
Modified task-presentation strategies. *See* Task modification.
Monitoring progress, 7, 10, 15, 16
Moral development, Kohlberg's theory of, 79, 80
Moral motivation training, 57, 79, 80, 83, 90, 91, 100
Multimodal interventions, 55–57, 70, 90, 91, 95, 100, 110, 111, 135, 136, 143, 153, 182, 183, 189, 190
Multisystemic therapy, 55–57, 70, 96, 97, 100

T

T scores, 14

Task modification, 110, 130–132, 135, 136, 143, 153, 162–165, 170, 190

Task-selection strategies, 203, 221, 222, 226, 263

Time-delay procedure, 435

Time variables in instruction,
    allocated time, 214, 215
    engaged time, 210, 214, 215, 231
    pausing, 214, 215, 221
    rate and pacing, 210, 214, 215, 221

Token economy systems, 57–59, 62, 63, 85, 100, 119, 121, 153

Transitions, problems with, 374, 377, 382–384, 389–391, 397

Treatment fidelity, 7, 10, 12

Treatment plan, writing and modifying, 96, 97

V

Verbal mediation, 20, 30, 31, 34, 48.
    See also Self-instruction.

Verbal prompts, 390

Video modeling. *See* Modeling.

Visual prompts, 390, 400

W

Withdrawal, 275, 276